foundation of
and its evolut
worldview -
dismantle ALI
NATURE & SOCIETY UNDER CAP

alienated metabolism

metabolic rift

THE RETURN OF NATURE

The Return *of* Nature

Socialism and Ecology

JOHN BELLAMY FOSTER

MONTHLY REVIEW PRESS
New York

Library of Congress Cataloging-in-Publication Data available from the publisher.

ISBN 978-158367-836-7 cloth

Typeset in Bulmer Monotype

MONTHLY REVIEW PRESS, NEW YORK
monthlyreview.org

5 4 3 2 1

Contents

To John Mage

Preface

Climate change, the Sixth Extinction, and the COVID-19 pandemic arising from a novel coronavirus, all testify to abrupt changes in humanity's relation to the earth in the twenty-first century. The old notion of the "conquest of nature" is being replaced by a radical conception of the need to restore the human social metabolism with nature while promoting genuine human equality. Although revolutionary in its challenge to capitalism, this conception is not new, rather it is traceable to the long struggle for socialism and ecology beginning in the nineteenth century.

The present work begins where another left off. *Marx's Ecology*, which I completed in 2000, ended with the deaths of Darwin and Marx in 1882 and 1883. *The Return of Nature* starts with their funerals. Its title refers to the reemergence of the natural-material or ecological realm within critical social analysis, where the complex, reflexive relation of nature to human production and reproduction has all too often been downplayed. To be sure, the dialectical interplay of society and nature has never been altogether absent from historical materialism, where it was present at the outset in the foundational works of Karl Marx, Frederick Engels, and William Morris. Nevertheless, for socialist theory as for liberal analysis—and for Western science and culture in general—the notion of the conquest of nature and of human exemption from natural laws has for centuries been a major trope, reflecting the systematic alienation of nature. Society and nature were often treated dualistically as two entirely distinct realms, justifying the expropriation of nature, and with it the exploitation of the larger human population. However, various left thinkers, many of them within the natural sciences, constituting a kind of second foundation of critical thought, and others in the arts rebelled against this narrow conception of human progress, and in the process generated a wider dialectic of ecology and a deeper materialism that questioned the environmental as well as social depredations of capitalist society.

The thinkers who are the focal point in this book are quite varied, stretching from the left Darwinian E. Ray Lankester and the Romantic-Marxist Morris in Part One, to the classical historical materialist Frederick Engels in Part Two, to the Fabian-style socialist ecologist Arthur Tansley, the red scientists J. D. Bernal, J. B. S. Haldane, Joseph Needham, Hyman Levy, and Lancelot Hogben, and the cultural materialist Christopher Caudwell in Part Three. Others are taken up in the Epilogue. But despite their diversity as thinkers all fell into the broad category of socialist materialists concerned with the dialectical interpenetration of nature and society, and the complex relations of evolution and emergence. Central to each of them was a dialectical naturalism that foreshadowed today's systems ecology and Earth System analysis.

This is a story that concerns art as well as science—the two principal means of ascertaining our sensuous relation to the world as a whole. It is the synthesis of the scientific and aesthetic critiques of capitalism that constitutes the basis of the modern ecological critique, leading to the pivotal notion of sustainable human development. As Epicurus said in antiquity, "The justice of nature is a pledge of reciprocal usefulness, neither to harm one another nor be harmed."[1]

The present book has been nearly two decades in gestation and has involved research in numerous archives. In this respect, I would like to acknowledge the following collections of papers upon which I relied to varying degrees for much of the analysis that follows: (1) the E. Ray Lankester Scientific Papers Collection, Marine Biological Association Library, Marine Biological Association, Plymouth, England; (2) the Hyman Levy Collection, 1935–1968, Charles Deering McCormick Library of Special Collections, Northwestern University Library, Evanston, Illinois; (3) the H. G. Wells Papers, 1855–1946, University of Illinois, Urbana; (4) the J. B. S. Haldane Papers, Wellcome Library, University of London; (5) the Joseph Needham Papers and Correspondence, Cambridge University Library; (6) the J. D. Bernal Scientific and Personal Papers, Cambridge University Library; (7) the Christopher St. John Sprigg (Christopher Caudwell) Collection, Harry Ransom Center, University of Texas, Austin; and (8) the Linus Pauling Collection, Special Collections and Archives, Oregon State University, Corvallis, Oregon. I would like to thank Liz Stanley, principal investigator of the online Olive Schreiner Letters Project, for answering my questions with respect to the Schreiner-Lankester correspondence. The bulk of the research was conducted through the University of Oregon library, with the help of the excellent regional Summit library system, and Interlibrary Loan. I owe a debt to the University of Oregon librarians and staff for putting up with my incessant demands. The importance of such backstage work by librarians is often invisible and yet constitutes an invaluable social contribution without which serious scholarship would be rendered much more difficult.

A large part of chapter 4 was published in 2017 as "William Morris's Romantic Revolutionary Ideal: Nature, Labour and Gender in *News from Nowhere*" in a special issue on revolution for the *Journal of William Morris Studies*. In the process, Owen Holland, the gifted editor of JWMS, improved it in both style and content.

In one of my visits to London I received a warm welcome from members of the William Morris Society at Kelmscott House, Morris's home in Hammersmith, the coach house and basement of which are now a museum.

I have greatly benefited in the research and editing of this book from my association over the years with a number of extremely talented *Monthly Review* research assistants, all of whom have gone on to carry out important scholarly research and build careers of their own, including Brett Clark, Hannah Holleman, Ryan Wishart, Jordan Besek, and Intan Suwandi. All of them assisted me at various stages in the long process of producing this book, helping with gathering materials, copyediting, fact checking, and through the critical feedback they often provided. I am grateful especially to Intan for assisting me with the big task of editing at the end. Brett and Hannah both co-authored a number of writings with me at various times in the years in which I was working on this book, which deeply affected my thinking here.

Paul Burkett and I have collaborated on issues of Marxian ecology since the mid-1990s, feeding into his book *Marx and Nature* in 1999 and my *Marx's Ecology* in 2000, and finally our co-authored *Marx and the Earth* in 2016. Although Paul was not directly involved in the research here, the shared understanding of ecological materialism that we have developed over the years is, I believe, inscribed on every page of this book.

Fred Magdoff's presence too is to be found throughout this book. Fred and I co-authored and co-edited three books and numerous articles while I was working on this project, including our 2011 *What Every Environmentalist Needs to Know About Capitalism.* I frequently turn to Fred with questions related to his vast knowledge of ecological science. He and Amy Demarest have provided a mountain of support.

In the early stages of this research, Robert W. (Bob) McChesney and Inger Stole graciously offered their home in Urbana, Illinois, as a base while I explored the Levy archives at Northwestern University. At my request, Bob also obtained copies of some key letters between Lankester and H. G. Wells from the Wells Papers housed at the University of Illinois, Urbana. Since our days as students and roommates at Evergreen State College in Olympia, Washington, in the early 1970s, Bob has been my intellectual and political touchstone, and the very closest of friends. At the very beginning of this book project, he insisted that I should rely on extensive archival documentation in carrying out the historical research. This meant additional years of investigation, given the need to travel long distances to archives and the additional constraints this imposed. Yet, following his advice on this proved essential, resulting in important discoveries. In this respect his own historical works, especially *Telecommunications, Mass Media, and Democracy* (1993), represent a model of committed scholarship, and a reminder of how much can be achieved through historical research.

Others have also helped me in major ways. Richard York and Theresa Koford have patiently and persistently inquired for years, whenever we met, about the progress on my "big book," providing continual encouragement. Richard's own research into ecology and society—extending at times to our own direct collaboration (together with Brett), notably in our 2010 book *The Ecological Rift*—has inspired and informed me in countless ways. Joseph Fracchia and I have shared many discussions on materialism and dialectics, from which I have benefited from his enormous conceptual and philological knowledge of German Idealism, Marx, and contemporary critical philosophy. Ian Angus and I have had a rich correspondence on ecological issues, often related to questions dealt with in this book. My good friend Desmond A. Crooks helped with cover design. My cousins Sandy and Dave Ashton provided me with a rare book at a critical juncture and made possible my visit to the Marine Biological Association Library (housing the E. Ray Lankester Scientific Papers Collection) in Plymouth. The late István Mészáros was at all times unstinting in his support.

Michael Yates, Martin Paddio, John Simon, Susie Day, and R. Jamil Jonna at Monthly Review Press not only helped me immeasurably in various points in this task, but have also offered their full confidence in what amounted to a very extensive and seemingly unending project—a gift for which I am immensely grateful. Michael Yates and Erin Clermont brought their prodigious copyediting skills to bear on every page of the book.

Two people above all provided the insight and support without which this book could not possibly have been written. I have dedicated the book to my close friend John Mage at *Monthly Review*, who has been my primary interlocutor, both for *Marx's Ecology* and the present work. His extraordinary erudition, stretching from the classics to the history of science and society, to Marxian theory, and to contemporary historical conditions have meant that his judgments and advice were at all times indispensable, and often decisive. When over the years I showed signs of leaving this project unfinished he invariably encouraged me to return to it. Whatever value there is in this work owes much to him. The book's demerits are undividedly and insistently my own.

Carrie Ann Naumoff is part of the fabric of my life. She has given me every kind of support: intellectual, political, and emotional. Most of the ideas in this book we have discussed at length, but often transposed within the context of our everyday struggles in relation to humanity and the earth, and the people and the environment we love. She has reaffirmed my belief that not only is imagination ultimately more important than knowledge, but that history is never merely history, it is the witness of our collective struggles and the proof that change is always possible.

—EUGENE, OREGON
MARCH 2020

Introduction

The whole of [Hegel's] *Logic* is proof of the fact that abstract thought is nothing for itself... and that only *nature* is something.

—KARL MARX

The subject of this book is the history and genealogy of the relations between socialism and ecology, primarily in Britain, in the period from the deaths of Charles Darwin and Karl Marx in 1882 and 1883 up to the 1960s.[1] *The Return of Nature* was originally conceived in a fairly linear fashion as a historical sequel to my earlier *Marx's Ecology*.[2] But the profusion of unexpected discoveries encountered along the way, the wide cast of characters over several generations, and the innumerable paths that needed to be pursued, sometimes appearing to extend in all directions at once, ensured that it would emerge as a very different kind of study from its predecessor. This was a story where the main lines of development were not known in advance and had to be unearthed, as key sources were buried in obscure archives—seldom, if ever, penetrated.

Even as a chronological history, *The Return of Nature* broke with my original expectations, as it was necessary to cover the early lives of such figures as Frederick Engels, E. Ray Lankester, and William Morris, all of whom were Marx's contemporaries, before it was possible to go forward. Hence, the organization of this work can be viewed as more genealogical than chronological, tracing out lines of influence. Lankester and Morris, who take up the first four chapters, making up Part One, are related to Marx. Only in Part Two does Engels enter centrally into the story. This establishes another line in Part Three that runs through J. D. Bernal, J. B. S. Haldane, Joseph Needham, Lancelot Hogben, and Hyman Levy, all of whom drew principally on Engels rather than Marx, while Arthur G. Tansley and H. G. Wells, also considered in Part Three, are best understood in relation to their connections to Lankester. Christopher Caudwell, treated in the penultimate chapter of Part Three, is the culmination of a line of inheritance reaching back to both Morris and Engels. The closing chapter in Part Three, on the fall of the British Marxist scientists and their ultimate moral triumph, sets up a logic that points to the present, taken up briefly in the Epilogue.

If *Marx's Ecology* was a compact story of the development of Marx's ecological views in the mid-nineteenth century, when many of the foundations of an ecological critique of capitalist society were being laid, *The Return of Nature* is an odyssey encompassing a considerably longer period when the modern ecological worldview, as we know it today, was first emerging tentatively into the light of day for all to see. It is about the role of numerous socialists and radical materialists, who played key roles in that critical enterprise. I chose to focus almost entirely on Britain, the country in which Marx and Engels had long resided, for five reasons: (1) my own family background and cultural heritage; (2) in Britain one can see the development of an intellectual heritage drawing directly on both Marx and Darwin; (3) the links between the Romantic movement, Marxism, and ecology were strongest in Britain, most notably in the life and work of Morris, but reappearing in a quite different way in Caudwell; (4) among the British Marxists, in particular, there was a strong strain of "emergentist Marxism," its roots going back to ancient Epicurean materialism, inspired in part by knowledge of Marx's own studies of Epicureanism; and lastly (5) a focus on Britain allows for coherence of historical narrative.[3]

The earliest, and in many ways most revolutionary development of Marxian ecology arose in the USSR in the 1920s and early 1930s. But the demise of the most creative period of Soviet ecology followed quickly upon the famous Second International Conference on the History of Science and Technology held in London in 1931. Nikolai Bukharin, N. I. Vavilov, Boris Hessen, and B. Zavadovsky—the four most influential figures in the Russian contingent at the 1931 conference—all fell prey within a few years to Joseph Stalin's purges. It was in Britain, therefore, where the very same conference marked a beginning point rather than an end point for Marxian natural science, that continuity in the emerging dialectic of socialism and ecology was mainly expressed.

The main advantage that socialist thinkers have always had in embracing an ecological worldview, when compared to their liberal counterparts, goes beyond their willingness to contemplate a different, more collective, and egalitarian form of society. Rather, it rests fundamentally on a *materialist and dialectical* critique, originating above all with Marx, that pointed to the alienated metabolism of nature and society under capitalism. It is this *method of ecological critique* arising out of the socialist critique of capitalist society that is seen here as most important, since it provides the indispensable means for a revolutionary dialectical ecology. Hence, the intent in this book is *not simply* to provide a history and genealogy of the interaction of socialism and ecology, though that is the outward form it takes. Rather, as Raymond Williams stated in *Culture and Society*, the hope is that by reaching into the past we can discover how to "understand and act."[4]

It is due to this focus on the emergence of ecological critique, and on the complex and necessarily contradictory search by materialists and socialists for a meaningful ecological praxis, that this work is able to escape many of the methodological traps that have plagued studies in the history of ideas, namely, adoption of one-sidedly internalist or externalist approaches; employment of rigid ideal types; reliance on a few isolated texts; and, above all, succumbing to the hegemony of the present, or what E. P. Thompson called "the enormous condescension of posterity."[5] As Quentin Skinner famously stated—claiming "we are all Marxists to this extent"—the only justifiable reason for carrying out studies in the history of ideas is not to demonstrate the inevitability or superiority of the present in relation to the past, but rather to demonstrate how "our own society places unrecognized constraints on our imaginations."[6]

The chief protagonists in these pages exhibit a certain monotony of masculine gender, reflecting an age when women were largely shut out of intellectual life, as powerfully expressed at the time in Virginia Woolf's *A Room of One's Own.*[7] It seemed all the more important therefore to make a conscious attempt to take note of gender questions, where they arose in the course of the argument, as well as to be cognizant of the women who entered, however tangentially, into the story, including such important historical figures as Phebe Lankester, Olive Schreiner, Eleanor Marx, Mary and Lizzie Burns, Jane Morris, Philippa Fawcett, Florence Kelley, Enid Charles, Lu Gwei-djen, Dorothy Moyle Needham, Charlotte Haldane, Jane Ellen Harrison, Virginia Brodine, Edna Gellhorn, Rachel Carson, and Hilary Rose. Issues of social reproduction and ecological reproduction are necessarily closely intertwined. Here too, as in ecology, the goal is to search for the emergence of radical views, all too often repressed, that hold the promise of a sustainable society rooted in substantive equality. Some attention to these areas is thus given in nearly every chapter. However, the book can claim no thoroughness in this respect, pointing rather to research that still needs to be done.

AN EMERGENTIST ECOLOGICAL MARXISM

Socialism and *ecology* originated as separate but closely related and often converging forms of critique in response to the industrial capitalism of the late eighteenth and nineteenth centuries. The term "socialism" first appeared in England and France in the 1820s and was directly associated with working-class struggles.[8] The word "ecology" was first introduced by Ernst Haeckel in 1866 (the year before the publication of Karl Marx's *Capital*), as a way of referring to Darwin's notion of the "economy of nature." It entered the English language (as œcology) a decade later, in the 1876 translation of Haeckel's *History of Creation*, which was supervised and revised by Darwin's and Thomas Huxley's protégé as well as Marx's friend, Lankester.[9] It was not until the early twentieth century that the term was used with any frequency in science, and it was not until the mid-twentieth century that it entered popular discourse, associated with a broad social and political movement.[10] In the nineteenth century, other ecological concepts were frequently used, such as Darwin's "economy of nature," Lankester's "bionomics," and Justus von Liebig's broad application of metabolism to environmental relations, which helped to inspire Marx's notion of *social metabolism*.

From his earliest writings, Marx adopted what can only be described as a broad ecological worldview through his deep, radical conception of materialism in accord with dialectics. Marx found in what he called the "immanent dialectic" of Epicurus's ancient, emergentist materialism—the subject of his doctoral thesis—the means with which to begin to question the Hegelian system.[11] Together with his studies of Ludwig Feuerbach's philosophy, this enabled him to develop a full-fledged critique of Hegelian idealism. This new materialist dialectic began with human corporeal being, and the need to satisfy human sensuous needs through appropriation from external nature. This was a process in which the distinctly human species, as *homo faber*, could be seen as playing an active role through labor and production, both as agents of their own development and through the transformation of nature.

Human beings, in Marx's conception, related to nature practically through their labor (but also through their conceptions of beauty), involving the human-sensuous interaction with nature via production. This formed what he called the "the dialectic of sensuous certitude," requiring the training of the intellect—"the relation of sensuous knowledge to the sensuous."[12] "*Human sensuousness*," he argued in his dissertation on Epicurus, introducing a philosophical viewpoint that was to be fundamental to his own materialist dialectic throughout his life, "*is . . . embodied time, the existing reflection of the sensuous world in itself*." Mere perception through the senses is only possible because it expresses an active and therefore changing relation to nature and, indeed, a changing relation of nature to itself, since human beings are a part of nature. "In hearing," Marx wrote, "nature hears itself, in smelling it smells itself, in seeing it sees itself."[13] The materialist dialectic, in this view, was based on the corporeal organization of human beings, who as objective, sensuous beings constituted a "part of nature," able to know natural conditions and processes through their interactions with them, as well as through their specifically human productive role, as conscious embodiments of nature engaged in transforming the world around them.[14]

Hence, for Marx, the materialist conception of history was inextricably bound to the materialist conception of nature, requiring constant studies of natural science and the natural conditions of production as a crucial part of his critique of political economy. The labor process itself, he argued in the 1850s, was to be defined as the metabolism of humanity and nature. It was only in the 1860s, however, that this was to emerge, in his conception, as a central contradiction of the system associated with the growing concern over the robbing of the soil and the loss of soil nutrients; the resulting pollution in the cities and nutritive shortages in the diets of the population; the squandering of raw materials; deforestation and desertification; and the exigencies of the world food trade. It was in response to such issues that he developed his theory of metabolic rift, focusing initially on the destruction of the soil metabolism associated with industrialized capitalist agriculture, inspired by the 1862 edition of Liebig's *Agricultural Chemistry* with its critique of the ecological "robbery system."[15]

Engels's ecology complemented Marx's ecology in all of these respects, while extending the analysis in new directions. The young Engels provided an urban-environmental critique, focusing on "social murder," in his 1845 *Condition of the Working Class in England.*[16] Decades later, he was to provide the outlines of a dialectical approach to nature/ecology in his 1878 *Anti-Dühring* and his unfinished *Dialectics of Nature*, written in the late 1870s and early 1880s.[17] Engels was concerned especially with combatting mechanical materialism and providing an analysis that focused on evolutionary change, coevolution, emergence, and the unity of opposites. As a result, he pushed the analysis at every point in the direction of an interconnected, ecological analysis, employing in the process the full array of dialectical categories (including totality, mediation, contradiction, negation, transformative change, qualitative transcendence, the unity of opposites, etc.). His critique of the folly of a social system that treated nature as a "foreign people" to be conquered, leading to the "revenge" of nature, represents one of the most searing indictments of the destructive environmental logic of capitalism ever penned, right down to the present day.[18] As ecosocialist Ted Benton put it, "Engels's position can be seen as a first approximation to a view of emergent properties consequent upon successive levels of organization of matter in motion."[19]

Conceiving the dialectics of nature in this way, Engels, in tune with Marx—and embodying a perspective that went back to ancient Epicurean materialism, which he, like Marx, was able to quote extensively by heart—emphasized that nature, or the material world, was complex, changing, contingent, contradictory, and coevolutionary.[20] As historian of science Thomas S. Hall wrote of Epicurus, in ways that were later applicable to Marx and Engels, natural phenomena are seen as an emergent consequence of organization: "The increasingly complex organization of higher life-forms permits the appearance (the emergence) in them of new modes of life, new functions or behaviors, impossible in less organized forms."[21] Such a "dialectical conception of nature," particularly if given the fluid form with which Marx and Engels approached dialectical evolution, was antithetical at one and the same time to mechanism, idealism, and dualism.[22] For Engels, the natural world was in a process of constant transformation, and therefore so were our ideas of the physical world, which could never achieve completeness or take final form because that would mean that evolutionary change itself would have ceased. "Dialectics," he wrote, "comprehends things and their representations, ideas, in their essential connection, concatenation, motion, origin, and ending. Such [natural] processes as those mentioned above are, therefore, so many corroborations of its own method of procedure. Nature is the proof of dialectics."[23] When united with a rock-bottom materialism, such a perspective necessarily led toward an interconnected, ecological worldview.

For Engels, the relation between "freedom and necessity" had first been correctly understood by G. W. F. Hegel. As Engels was to express it, "Freedom does not consist in any dreamt-of independence from natural laws," and hence the conquest of nature, "but in the knowledge of these laws, and the possibility this gives of systematically making them work towards definite ends," which, however, must remain within nature's laws as a whole. It was this that fed into Engels's critique of capitalism's transgression of nature's laws and the resulting ecological destruction.[24]

But if Engels's powerful analysis of the dialectic of society and nature is little known today and needs to be recovered, even less attention has been given to the pioneering work of an array of thinkers whose conceptions were built directly or indirectly on the materialism of Darwin, Marx, and Engels: figures like Lankester, Tansley, Wells, Bernal, Haldane, Needham, Levy, and Benjamin Farrington—all of whom contributed in various ways to the development of an ecological worldview in relation to science.[25] Moreover, art as well as science was necessarily involved in this struggle of late nineteenth- and early twentieth-century socialism to generate a genuinely egalitarian and ecological worldview. This was shown by Morris's extraordinary merging of Marx's ecological critique with the Romantic-aesthetic critique, and by Caudwell's synthesis of the Marxian ecological dialectic with a revolutionary Romantic aesthetic.

WESTERN MARXISM AND THE DIALECTIC OF NATURE

In the dialectic of nature we encounter a possible roadblock. For those versed in the philosophical debates surrounding Marxism, no question has been more contentious than the dialectics of nature, the adamant rejection of which has separated the philosophical tradition known as "Western Marxism" from the Marxism of the Second and Third Internationals, while also driving a wedge between Marx and Engels.[26] The result was an almost total abandonment of any connection to natural science (seen as inherently positivistic) within Western

Marxism, although, as we shall see, some thinkers within the natural sciences have continued to be influenced by, and even to rely on, the classical Marxist ontology up to the present day.

The birth of Western Marxism as a distinct philosophical tradition is commonly traced to Georg Lukács's 1923 masterpiece *History and Class Consciousness,* particularly to his famous footnote 6 in chapter 1, in which he appeared to reject any extension of the dialectical method from society to nature. As he stated:

> It is of the first importance to realise that the [dialectical] method is limited here to the realms of history and society. The misunderstandings that arise from Engels' account of dialectics can in the main be put down to the fact that Engels—following Hegel's mistaken lead—extended the method to apply also to nature. However, the crucial determinants of dialectics—the interaction of subject and object, the unity of theory and practice, the historical changes in the reality underlying the categories as the root cause of changes in thought, etc.—are absent from our knowledge of nature.[27]

Lukács suggests here that the dialectical method in its full sense (the dialectic as knowledge) necessarily involves reflexivity, the identical subject-object of history. Here the subject (the human being) recognizes in the object of his/her activity the results of humanity's own historical self-creation. We can understand history, as Giambattista Vico said, because we have "made" it.[28] The dialectic thus becomes a powerful theoretical means of discovery rooted in the reality of human praxis itself, which allows us to uncover the totality of social mediations. Yet, such inner, reflexive knowledge arising from human practice, Lukács indicates, is not available where external nature is concerned; there, one is faced with the inescapable Kantian "thing-in-itself." Hence the "crucial determinants of dialectics" are inapplicable to the natural realm; there can be no dialectics of nature—as a method—equivalent to the dialectics of history and society.

The seriousness of the division that arose in Marxian theory between Western Marxism and Marxism more broadly on this basis can hardly be overstated. As Lucio Colletti observed in *Marxism and Hegel*, a vast literature "has always agreed" that differences over (1) the existence of an objective world independent of consciousness (philosophical materialism or realism); and (2) the existence of a dialectic of matter (or of nature) constituted "the two main distinguishing features between 'Western Marxism' and 'dialectical materialism.'"[29] Philosophical Western Marxists, including the Frankfurt School and the entire critical theory tradition, were adamant in following what they viewed to be the position of Lukács in *History and Class Consciousness* and in imposing an interdiction on the dialectics of nature as a method. For Hebert Marcuse in *Reason and Revolution*, "The dialectical totality . . . includes nature, but only in so far as the latter enters and conditions the historical process of social reproduction."[30] Jean-Paul Sartre in the *Critique of Dialectical Reason* wrote: "In the historical and social world . . . there *really* is dialectical reason; by transferring it into the 'natural' world, and forcibly inscribing it there, Engels stripped it of its rationality."[31]

Yet, major problems were to arise from the rejection of the dialectics of nature within Western Marxism, since it relied on the dominant neo-Kantian dualism that separated those *phenomena* that could be experienced from *noumena*, or things-in-themselves. This was then transposed in Western Marxism into the notion that social/historical sciences were reflexive, with an identical subject-object (the Vician principle), whereas natural science relied on a naive positivism, failing to recognize the inherent limitations of our knowledge of the physical world, and the impossibility of a dialectical reasoning where reflexivity did not apply. Thus, one of the criticisms leveled against Engels by Lukács in *History and Class Consciousness*, and by the subsequent Western Marxist philosophical tradition, was that he had gone too far in adopting, following Hegel, a concept of "so-called *objective* dialectics," the reality of which Lukács himself did not expressly deny.[32]

Among the first to raise the alarm with respect to the neo-Kantian character of Lukács's criticism, later embodied in so-called Western Marxism, was Antonio Gramsci, who wrote in his *Prison Notebooks*:

> It would appear that Lukács maintains that one can speak of the dialectic only for the history of men and not for nature. He might be right and he might be wrong. If his assertion presupposes a dualism between nature and man he is wrong because he is falling into a conception of nature proper to religion and to Graeco-Christian philosophy and also to idealism which does not in reality succeed in unifying and relating man and nature to each other except verbally. But if human history should be conceived also as the history of nature (also by means of the history of science) how can the dialectic be separated from nature? Perhaps Lukács, in reaction to the baroque theories of the *Popular Manual* [Bukharin's *Historical Materialism*], has fallen into the opposite error, into a form of idealism.[33]

Ironically, it was Lukács himself who was to emerge as the most powerful critic of Western Marxism's wholesale interdiction of the dialectics of nature as a concept. Lukács, as he was later to insist, had not categorically rejected the notion of the dialectics of nature in *History and Class Consciousness*. He had written there of the "merely objective dialectics of nature," as perceived by the "detached observer," as having a partial validity.[34] For Lukács, what was lacking in "merely objective dialectics" was the full "reciprocal relation in which theory and practice become dialectical with reference to one another." But rather than restricting the dialectic to this form, Lukács insisted that dialectics could be seen in terms of a structured hierarchy in which one could speak of a "typology of . . . dialectical forms," including the objective dialectic of nature as well as the dialectic of human history.[35]

In *Tailism and the Dialectic*, written several years after *History and Class Consciousness* (and rediscovered only recently), Lukács remarked that even his famous footnote in *History and Class Consciousness* was far more nuanced than generally thought and was consistent with the view that "objective dialectics are in reality independent of humans and were there [that is, existed] before the emergence of people."[36]

But how is knowledge of *objective dialectics*, the dialectics of nature, to be obtained, when the subject-object reflexivity (the identical subject-object) does not pertain? In his later writings, Lukács emphasized that this occurs mainly in two ways, drawing on both Marx's theory of social metabolism and Engels's argument on the basis of experimentation. With respect to social metabolism, Lukács, following Marx, contended that "since human life [labor] is based on a metabolism with nature, it goes without saying that certain truths which we acquire in the process of carrying out this metabolism have a general validity—for example the truths of mathematics, geometry, physics and so on."[37] Thus, as Farrington argued, the ancient Greek materialists had used the various forms of production that they were familiar with, representing the human-natural role, as guides to physical properties and laws, extending beyond human action.[38] All of science had arguably originated on this basis, moving from the transitive to the intransitive, as Roy Bhaskar explained in his dialectical critical realism.[39] In Lukács's own terms, we can get closer to a comprehension of the ontology of nature only to the extent that we understand it historically and genetically, which means transcending the mechanistic views that have predominated in natural science.[40] With respect to experimentation Lukács argued, in line with Engels, that scientific experimentation, which involves interaction with nature under controlled conditions, can provide insights into nature's own objective dialectic and its ever-changing laws, though knowledge derived from such experiments and from industrial practice had to be critically assessed as ideologically mediated.[41]

In his later attempts to understand this hierarchy of dialectical forms, Lukács addressed what he called—following the young Hegel—the dialectic of identity and non-identity, superseding the conception of the unity of opposites. Here changing material forms introduced emergent *novel* entities, such as the historical invention of the wheel, in ways that expressed the *unity* with nature and impossibility of entirely superseding natural processes. Thus the historicity of nature, along with the historicity of society, became an essential proposition.[42] Beginning with *The Young Hegel* and to a greater extent in *The Ontology of Social Being*, Lukács explored the role of "reflection determinations" in Hegel's Doctrine of Essence as the key to a dialectical-realist ontology of reciprocal interaction and change. The overriding concern throughout this analysis was the relation between a "merely objective dialectics of nature" and a wider dialectics of social ontology.[43]

Hence, for the later Lukács, the metabolism between humanity and nature was conditioned by nature's dialectic, and at the same time was the source of the human comprehension of that "objective dialectic." Insofar as humanity actively engages in the transformation of nature that "process takes place in the field of social being, as the metabolism between society and nature, the indispensable precondition which is of course the correct comprehension of the dialectic of nature."[44]

In various ways, the major socialist thinkers addressed in this book, all of whom were concerned with the social relation to nature, as mediated by science and art via labor and production, came to similar conclusions with respect to the dialectic in history, seeing this as the realm of "freedom as necessity," in Engels's sense.[45] They all sought to connect the materialist conception of nature and the materialist conception of history through an examination of the complex, changing material interconnections between nature and human history. In this they invariably adopted the materialist principle of *mors immortalis*, perceiving the alienated character of capitalist production (social metabolism) and its destructive effects on nature's metabolism, as the basis of a negative, critical dialectic.[46] All of the Marxian scientists examined here embraced an emergentist, evolutionary view, extending back to ancient Epicurean materialism. Central to the outlook of most of these thinkers was the need for a synthesis of materialist views stemming from Darwin and Marx. Others, such as Morris, arrived at a similar perspective via the relation of art and labor, or through a theory of mimesis, drawing on Aristotle's *Poetics*, as in Caudwell.

Ultimately, these interconnected socialist and ecological analyses pointed to a notion of dialectics, as the necessary intellectual expression of the reciprocal human relation to a complex, changing, and emergent natural-and-social ontology, of which the human species was itself a part. Dialectics, in this sense, superseded rationalism, mechanism, and teleology, since it took as its fundamental reality the ever-changing character—as well as resulting contradictions, negations, and qualitative transformations—of both the material world at large and the human condition within it. As Needham cogently wrote:

> Marx and Engels were bold enough to assert that it [the dialectical process] happens actually in evolving nature itself, and that the undoubted fact that

> it happens in our thought about nature is because we and our thought are a part of nature. We cannot consider nature otherwise than as a series of levels of organisation, a series of dialectical syntheses. From the ultimate physical particle to atom, from atom to molecule, from molecule to colloidal aggregate, from aggregate to living cell, from cell to organ, from organ to body, from animal body to social association, the series of organisational levels is complete. Nothing but energy (as we now call matter and motion) and the levels of organisation (or the stabilised dialectical syntheses) at different levels have been required for the building of our world.[47]

Likewise, for Caudwell, "thought is naturally dialectical," since human beings "live and experience reality dialectically," that is, live in a complex state of contradiction, change, and emergence.[48] Dialectics thus served a heuristic purpose superior to rationalism, mechanism, or teleology in helping us comprehend the material world of nature, of which human production was a part. What made dialectics so crucial in Caudwell's view was not the unity of humanity with the world, but its separation—life in an alienated society. "Either the Devil has come amongst us having great power, or there is a causal explanation for a disease common to economics, science, and art," which only a dialectical criticism could reveal.[49] It was such an uncompromising radical standpoint that drove Caudwell in just a few years, still in his twenties, to an integrative-ecological critique.

THE MOVEMENT TOWARD ECOLOGY

The major socialist (and social-democratic) thinkers who constitute the focus of this book were all politically and socially active in developing a critical-materialist view rooted in ecology and dialectics that extended to science and/or art. Lankester stood as the foremost ecological critic within British science in the late nineteenth and early twentieth centuries. Morris, in his years in the Socialist League and as a leader of the Hammersmith Socialist Society, provided an epic synthesis of the Romantic and Marxian critiques of capitalism's dark satanic mills. Engels sought a dialectics of nature and society aimed at a truly scientific socialism. Tansley and Wells introduced the concepts of ecosystem and human ecology. Hogben launched the first full-fledged materialist-ecological critique of "scientific racism" or eugenics. Bernal, Needham, Haldane, and Levy brought dialectics to twentieth-century natural science and dialectical natural science to the social history of science. Needham developed a Marxian approach to emergence through his theory of integrative levels and played the leading role in linking Western and Eastern ecological philosophies. Caudwell gave a powerful ecological cast to the final works in his *Studies and Further Studies in a Dying*

Culture.[50] Farrington worked at theoretically restoring Epicureanism within the philosophy of praxis. Bernal was a central figure in the first great ecological movement of the post–Second World War period, the movement against above-ground nuclear testing.

Hence, the premise underlying this work is that socialist thinkers provided systematic if uneven and sometimes contradictory ecological critiques of our present society that were crucial both in their day and ours—a legacy that we can no longer afford to do without in our age of combined ecological and social crisis. If ecology has often been seen as arising in a liberal universe, divorced from socialism, the analysis here shows that this received ideology is far from the truth and that ecology was at its inception deeply intertwined with struggles for human equality and the revolt against capitalist society.

Today, *The Return of Nature*—the rediscovery of the ecological roots of human society—is a crucial step in the necessary task of building an organic system of social metabolic reproduction based on substantive equality and ecological sustainability. Above all, this is what defines today's global movement toward ecosocialism. If the thinkers addressed in this book developed their ideas long before ecosocialism emerged as a historically specific form of resistance in the 1980s, they nonetheless prepared the way for all that would follow, often in far more sophisticated ways, by drawing on socialist conceptions to develop the ecological critique and the ecological critique to develop socialism.

Here we need to draw on the past, not simply in a historical sense but because the results that were obtained but now forgotten are crucial to our struggles in the present. The tragedy in Homer's *Iliad* was that the better hero, Hector, was defeated. Yet this came to symbolize a past that would not die and would return again and again.

The story told in this book is replete with its own historical contradictions. For example, in a number of instances and for short periods of time, some of the thinkers in this broad tradition of socialism and ecology seemed to fall prey to a Promethean ecological modernism and a regressive conception of progress, which in the 1940s and early 1950s had become a dominant force on the left as well as the right. Nevertheless, the overall direction of the various socialist thinkers treated in this book was toward an ecological socialism, recognizing the pressing need for a new socioecological metabolism in the "closing circle" of the world environment.[51] In the end, there was no doubt about the ecological as well as social challenges posed by what we now call the Anthropocene. As Bernal declared in 1967: "If life is not to die, we have to see to it that we stop now the forces threatening its existence."[52]

PART ONE

Beyond Marx and Darwin

CHAPTER ONE

Ecological Materialism

The interment of Charles Darwin's mortal remains at Westminster Abbey in London at noon on April 26, 1882, a week after his death, was a magnificent state occasion. Attendees included numerous representatives of the British aristocracy, the speaker of the House of Commons, the chancellor of the University of Oxford, ambassadors of foreign countries, and the cream of British science. Fellows of the Royal Society present on the occasion included such famous figures as Francis Galton, Joseph Hooker, Henry Maine, Thomas Huxley, E. Ray Lankester, John Lubbock, and Alfred Russel Wallace. As the white unpolished oak coffin, covered with a black velvet pall edged with white silk, on which were laid wreaths of white flowers, was moved to the grave, "Beethoven's Funeral March" (now attributed to Johann Heinrich Walch) was played, followed by the more plaintive March in B-Minor by Schubert. The anthem by Handel, "His Body Is Buried in Peace, but His Name Liveth Evermore," was sung. The inscription on the coffin, laid in the northeast corner of the nave next to that of Sir John Herschel, read: "Charles Robert Darwin. Born February 12, 1809. Died April 19, 1882."

In an article that day in *Nature*, Thomas Huxley wrote:

> In France, in Germany, in Austro-Hungary, in Italy, in the United States, writers of all shades of opinion, for once unanimous, have paid a willing tribute to the worth of our great countryman, ignored in life by the official representatives of the kingdom, but laid in death among his peers in Westminster Abbey by the will of the intelligence of the nation. One could not converse with Darwin without being reminded of Socrates. There was the same . . . belief in the sovereignty of reason; the same ready humour; the same sympathetic interest in all the ways and works of men. But instead of turning away from the problems of nature as hopelessly insoluble, our modern philosopher devoted his whole life to attacking them in the spirit of Heraclitus and Democritus. . . . There is a time for all things—a time for glorying in our ever-extended

> conquests over the realm of nature, and a time [for] mourning over the heroes who have led us to victory. None have fought better, and none have been more fortunate than Charles Darwin.[1]

The funeral of Darwin's great contemporary, Karl Marx, in London less than a year later was a far more modest, but no less notable occasion. Marx's body lay in state for a couple of days after his death on Wednesday March 14, 1883, and numerous people came to view him.[2] At noon on a windy, cold, cloudy, rainy Saturday, a small private group of more than a dozen mourners, consisting largely of close family friends and political comrades, followed the horse-driven hearse up to Highgate Cemetery east of Swain Lane where Marx was to be buried in a corner of the cemetery alongside the grave of his wife, Jenny.[3] Among them were Marx's daughter, Eleanor Marx; the Marx family's housekeeper and family friend Helene Demuth; Marx's longtime friend and collaborator Frederick Engels; Friedrich Lessner and George Lochner, both comrades from the days of the Communist League; Marx's sons-in-law Paul Lafargue and Charles Longuet from France; Wilhelm Liebknecht, from the German Social Democratic Party; and Professor Carl Schorlemmer (chemistry) and Professor E. Ray Lankester (zoology), Fellows of the Royal Society of London. Three others known to be at the funeral were the London barrister and socialist poet Ernest Radford, part of Eleanor Marx's circle and a frequent visitor to the Marx home; Edward Aveling, Radford's co-editor at *Progress*, a popular lecturer on biology, and later the partner of Eleanor Marx; and H. B. Donkin, Marx's doctor and Lankester's close friend. Gottlieb Lemke laid two wreaths with red ribbons on behalf of the staff of *Der Sozialdemokrat* (Zurich) and the London Communist Workers Education Association. Engels then delivered in English his now famous "Speech at the Graveside of Karl Marx," followed by the reading in French by Longuet of three telegrams: one from the Russian socialists, one from the Paris Brotherhood of the French Workers' Party, and one from the Spanish Workers' Party. Liebknecht concluded with a memorial speech in German on behalf of the German Social Democratic Party.[4]

Engels spoke of Marx as a scientist and a revolutionary, comparing him to Darwin:

> Just as Darwin discovered the law of evolution in organic nature, so Marx discovered the law of evolution in human history; he discovered the simple fact, hitherto concealed by an overgrowth of ideology, that mankind must first of all eat and drink, have shelter and clothing, before it can pursue politics, science, religion, art, etc. . . .
>
> But that is not all. Marx also discovered the special law of motion governing the present-day capitalist method of production and the bourgeois society that this method of production has created. The discovery of surplus value

> suddenly threw light on the problem in trying to solve which all previous investigators, both bourgeois economists and socialist critics, had been groping in the dark.
>
> Two such discoveries would be enough for one lifetime. Happy the man to whom it is granted to make even one such discovery. But in every single field which Marx investigated—and he investigated very many fields, none of them superficially—in every field, even in that of mathematics, he made independent discoveries.
>
> This was the man of science. But this was not even half the man. Science was for Marx a historically dynamic, revolutionary force. However great the joy with which he welcomed a new discovery in some theoretical science whose practical application perhaps it was as yet quite impossible to envisage, he experienced a quite other kind of joy when the discovery involved immediate revolutionary changes in industry and in the general course of history. For example, he followed closely the discoveries made in the field of electricity and recently those of Marcel Deprez.
>
> For Marx was before all else a revolutionary. His real mission in life was to contribute in one way or another to the overthrow of capitalist society and of the forms of government which it had brought into being, to contribute to the liberation of the present-day proletariat, which he was the first to make conscious of its own position and its needs, of the conditions under which it could win its freedom. Fighting was his element.[5]

In reporting on Marx's death in a letter to Adolf Sorge on March 15, 1883, Engels referred to Marx's wont to quote Epicurus on mortality: "'Death is not a misfortune for him who dies, but for him who survives,' he used to say, quoting Epicurus."[6]

Despite the sharp contrast in their funerals, reflecting the widely different places they occupied in British society—Darwin, rich, famous, and celebrated; Marx, a German revolutionary exile—their deaths, like their lives, suggest a strong historical connection as materialist-scientific thinkers, revolutionizing their times, a connection that has attracted numerous commentators over the past century or more.

Huxley's memorial to Darwin stressed the materialist basis of his thinking, going back to the ancient Greek philosophers, Heraclitus and Democritus, even if Socrates was invoked in more personal and idealist terms. He drew attention to the long struggle that Darwin was consequently forced to fight in order to get his theory of "natural selection" accepted in British society and the world at large. For Huxley, Darwin's burial at Westminster Abbey was a sign of his triumph, even in death: "ignored in life by the official representatives of the kingdom, but laid in death among his peers in Westminster Abbey by the will of the intelligence of the nation." Darwin's great achievement in evolutionary theory was a "victory" for which he had "fought" valiantly. He could thus be seen as a revolutionary scientific figure, who had nonetheless contributed to the strengthening of bourgeois society.

Engels began his memorial statement by comparing Marx's chief discovery in social science to Darwin's achievement in natural science. This fit with the idea that the materialist conception of history, of which Marx was the leading analyst, had its counterpart in the materialist conception of nature, in which Darwin was the greatest contemporary figure. But Marx, Engels argued, had not only uncovered the logic of historical development, he had also disclosed the secret of surplus value as constituting the basis of capital accumulation, the "special law of motion governing the present-day capitalist method of production." Just as Huxley invoked Heraclitus and Democritus as ancient Greek materialist philosophers who had inspired the development of science, of which Darwin's theory of natural selection was the supreme achievement, so Engels in his letter to Sorge called to mind Marx's debt to the ancient Greek philosopher Epicurus, whose notion of "death the immortal" constituted a fundamental materialist principle.[7] Nevertheless, Marx's "real mission in life" was not simply the advancement of science in and of itself, but the revolutionary "overthrow of capitalist society. . . . Fighting was his element." If Darwin's revolutionary materialist science was meant, according to Huxley, to strengthen the existing order by expanding the "conquest" of nature, Marx's revolutionary science and praxis, Engels explained, had to do with promoting "revolutionary changes . . . in the general course of history," ultimately questioning capitalism's so-called conquest of nature.

It is significant that one individual, E. Ray Lankester (1847–1929), then in his mid-thirties, was present at both Darwin's and Marx's funerals. Lankester was well over six feet tall and built to proportion, towering physically over others on both occasions. Combined with his strong intellect, Lankester was thus an extremely imposing figure. The novelist Olive Schreiner, who met him at a dinner party in 1881, wrote that Lankester was "the most powerful human being I ever came into contact with; he is like those winged beasts from Nineveh at the British Museum. What you feel is just immense force."[8]

Lankester was a protégé of Huxley and Darwin, and the son of a fellow of the Royal Society. His father, Edwin Lankester, was a radical in politics and one of the most eminent scientific men of his day. Ray's mother, Phebe Lankester, née Pope, was the daughter of a former mill owner. As a boy, Ray had ridden on Huxley's back, while Darwin had told him stories of great tortoises. At the age of sixteen he published his first scientific article, and while still in his twenties was elected to the Royal Society. Ray Lankester was to emerge as the greatest evolutionary biologist in Britain in the generation after Darwin and Huxley.[9] He was also a good friend of Marx and his youngest daughter, Eleanor, and was a frequent visitor at the Marx family home in the last three years of Marx's life. He read Marx's *Capital* and, though not a Marxist, remained throughout his life a radical freethinker and a Fabian-style socialist.

Both directly and through his students such as Arthur Tansley, H. G. Wells, and Julian Huxley, Lankester was to play a crucial founding role in the development of the ecological critique in the late nineteenth and early twentieth century. In his own person and intellect, he symbolized a continuing, complex critical-historical relation between socialist and Darwinian thought, and between the materialist conception of history and the materialist conception of nature that was to play a major role in British science for half a century or more, and which marked the emergence of modern ecological materialism.

LANKESTER AND DEGENERATION

E. Ray Lankester was born in London in 1847, the year that Marx and Engels wrote *The Communist Manifesto* (published in 1848). He died in 1929 at age eighty-two, two months before the New York stock market crash that marked the beginning of the Great Depression.

Edwin Lankester (1814–1874), Ray's father, was the son of a builder who died of tuberculosis at age twenty-seven, leaving Edwin's mother with no property to speak of and four children to raise. At age twelve, Edwin was apprenticed to a country surgeon. In 1839, by then already a distinguished medical professional, he received his M.D. in Heidelberg, having first mastered German. He became a Fellow of the Royal Society; president of the Royal Microscopical Society; secretary of section D (biology and botany) of the British Association for the Advancement of Science; and president of the Public Health Section of the British Social Science Association. In 1850 he gained the chair in natural science at New College, London.

Edwin Lankester stood out among leading scientists of his day in that he was an English radical, though retaining strong, dissenting, religious beliefs for most of his life. Brought up as a Congregationalist, in his later years he would convert to the Church of England.[10] The elder Lankester knew and admired Robert Owen. He made a diary entry on January 1839 that read: "Should things come to blows, the grand question is for each individual to choose his side. I am no Chartist, but there lies the interest of the masses, and the interest of mankind, should things come to a rupture, the side of the people will be my choice, however injudicious some of their movements may appear." He was a strong supporter of the North in the U.S. Civil War, backed the extension of the franchise to the poor, and supported Irish liberation. In the last decades of his life he devoted himself to public health and the conditions of the working class.

The elder Lankester was also an important scholar and writer, the author of numerous books and professional journal articles. Noted for his contributions to natural history, he was one of the leading early promoters of the modern aquarium. His 1856 book, *The Aquavivarium: An Account of the Principles and Objects Involved in the Domestic Culture of Water Plants and Animals*, was enormously influential. His 1857 work, *Half Hours with the Microscope*, was very popular and continued to be reprinted unaltered for more than fifty years.[11]

In June 1849, Dr. Lankester was elected to the Vestry of the parish of St. James, Westminster. Although "civil parishes" were not formally separated from "ecclesiastical parishes" in England until 1866, by the 1850s the English parish, especially in the large cities, was fulfilling a major civil role, comparable to local government units in the United States and England. By this time, vestries were in specific charge of issues related to local public health. The Vestry of St. James, in particular, was nominally now a lay body, not directly connected to the church, which met at a separate Vestry Hall to the west of St. James Church. Dr. Lankester was active in the Vestry and was reelected in 1851 and in 1854, the year of the great cholera outbreak.[12]

It was in his strategic capacity as chairman of the Vestry's Cholera Inquiry Committee that Edwin Lankester, together with Dr. John Snow and Reverend Henry Whitehead, played a key role in determining that cholera was a water-borne illness. It was partly through his offices that London's worst cholera epidemic—centered in the Berwick Street-Golden Square district of Soho in the City of Westminster in West London, falling within St. James parish—was traced to the water pump on Broad Street fed by a 25-foot-deep well. Thus arose what was to be one of the most famous episodes in the history of epidemiology.[13]

In the last few days of August 1854, a major cholera epidemic broke out in Soho. By September 2, hundreds of residents, and sometimes whole families, were falling prey to the disease within hours of one another. Snow believed, contrary to the general medical opinion, that cholera was a water-borne disease resulting from an external agent in the form of a living organism. This was a time when the role of bacteria as a disease agent had not yet been established, and the only recognized case of a living organism causing a disease had to do with a fungus, affecting silkworms. Although Filippo Pacini in Italy isolated the cholera bacillus in 1854, the same year as the London epidemic, his work remained unknown to the larger scientific community. It was not until Robert Koch, working in India, reported his separate discovery of *Vibrio cholerae* thirty years later, in 1884, that the actual cause of cholera was fully recognized by scientists.[14]

Nevertheless, Snow, believing that an external agent was involved, concluded from investigations into the homes affected that the epicenter of the epidemic was a popular water pump on Broad Street. On September 7, he managed to convince the Board of Governors of St. James Parish to remove the handle to the pump, which was carried out the next morning.[15] On September 13, Marx, who lived with his family in Soho, noted in a letter to Engels that deaths on Broad Street from cholera were averaging three per residence. But within a few days, the death toll was subsiding. Nearly seven hundred people living within 250 yards of the Broad Street pump had died, while on Broad Street itself the death toll was more than 10 percent of the population.[16]

The end of the epidemic was followed by a careful investigation of its cause by the Vestry of St. James Parish under the direction of Edwin Lankester, and through the efforts of Snow and Whitehead. On November 2, Dr. Lankester issued a motion that a Vestry Committee be set up to investigate the causes of the epidemic. The motion passed later that month, and Lankester was made chairman of the committee. The Vestry Committee would hold fourteen meetings between November 1854 and July 1855. Its report, presented at length by Edwin Lankester to the Vestry on August 9, 1855, as Steven Johnson observes in *The Ghost Map: The Story of London's Most Terrifying Epidemic—and How It Changed Science, Cities, and the Modern World,* was "the first time an official committee investigation had endorsed the waterborne theory" of the etiology of cholera. "In the years and decades that followed," Johnson writes, "the Vestry Committee report grew in influence as the story of the Broad Street epidemic was retold."

Two years before the 1854 cholera epidemic, Dr. Lankester had carried out microscopical investigations into the water of the Thames, which supplied the poorer parts of the city, and into which flowed 209 public sewers, the refuse of slaughterhouses, and industrial waste. Like Snow, his neighbor and fellow medical professional, he argued that disease could spread other than through infection (known as the anti-contagion theory). In October 1854, soon after the epidemic ended, he conducted an examination of all the wells in the parish and was able to determine that only the well feeding the Broad Street pump contained detectable organic matter. He reported on the presence of organic matter in the well feeding the Broad Street pump in November, at about the time he was to issue his motion on the establishment by the Vestry of a Cholera Inquiry Committee.[17]

It thus was Edwin Lankester, as chairman of the Vestry Committee on the epidemic, who (1) conducted the investigations into the well water in St. James Parish; (2) brought Snow and Whitehead onto the committee, leading to Whitehead's discovery of the index (first) case of the epidemic associated with a cesspool at number 40 Broad Street that was flowing into the well feeding the Broad Street pump; (3) arranged the financing of a full epidemiological study; (4) contributed massively to the resulting 178-page report, which he presented to the Vestry; and (5) eventually took the lead in publishing the Vestry Committee report, which was to play an important role in the rise of modern epidemiology. Two years later, he published in the *Quarterly Journal of Microscopical Science* the result of his investigations into the well waters of St. James Parish (Soho), showing the fungus (thought then to be the culprit) that had clouded the well water for the Broad Street pump. In 1860, he delivered a lecture on "Sanitary Defects and Medical Shortcomings," in which he referred to his experience with the Cholera epidemic "in Westminster, in 1854, when the pump in Broad Street killed 500 persons in three nights" due to "organic impurities" in the water. In 1866, after another smaller outbreak of cholera in England, he issued a 92-page book, *Cholera: What It Is and How to Prevent It.*[18]

Edwin Lankester's leading role as chairman of the Cholera Inquiry Committee led to his being appointed Medical Officer of Health for the St. James, Westminster, parish in 1856. From the first, in that role and then, beginning in 1862, as coroner for Central Middlesex, he led the battle against overcrowding, overwork, and poor sanitary conditions in workshops. He engaged in the struggle against the social-environmental conditions associated with high infant mortality, a very large portion, as he was to demonstrate, arising from infanticide, but which had deeper social causes.[19] A very larger part of the blame, he argued, could be attributed to the oppression of women.

The 1855 report of St. James's Vestry on the cholera outbreak, written by Edwin Lankester, strongly influenced John Simon, then the Medical Officer of London, and soon the Medical Health Officer for the General Board of Health (and when that was dissolved, for the Privy Council) and therefore the leading public health figure in Britain. Lankester was a close colleague of Simon in a number of scientific and medical capacities, including being appointed vice president of the Society of Medical Health Officers when Simon was president in 1857–59. Edwin Lankester's investigations played a crucial role in getting Simon to conclude in his *Report on the Last Two Cholera-Epidemics of London, as Affected by the Consumption of Impure Water* (1856) that cholera was a waterborne disease and that the commercial companies that supplied London with its water had primary responsibility. Under the influence of these events, Simon gradually abandoned the miasma theory of disease and became a leading proponent of the contagion or germ theory. Marx and Engels had a deep admiration for Simon, whom Marx frequently quoted in *Capital,* for his battles on behalf of the working class.[20]

Edwin Lankester's concern with environmental conditions went beyond epidemiology and took into consideration the urban-rural divide. Like Marx later on, he was a strong proponent of Justus von Liebig's notions of sustaining soil nutrients as a key to maintaining agricultural productivity and an adequate diet for the population.[21]

If Ray Lankester's father, Edwin, was a remarkable figure in his day, his mother, Phebe, was no less so. Unusual in the Victorian Age, she too was a scientist, with a background in biology and microscopy. Quite likely she was involved along with her husband—but, in those days, as a woman behind the scenes—in the microscopical examination of the water coming from the well on Broad Street. She was the daughter of Samuel Pope, a former mill owner and brother to the distinguished barrister (also named Samuel Pope). She was educated at the ladies' academy in Mill Hill, followed by private instruction. Among her numerous writings were works on botany, natural history, and public health, including *Wild Flowers Worth Notice* (1861), illustrated by J. E. Sowerby. Well versed in technical botany, she contributed substantially to J. T. Boswell Syme's *English Botany* (1861–63), writing around four hundred entries, and was a competent microscopist. Phebe was on friendly terms with George Eliot, whom Ray Lankester was afterward to remember as one of the most impressive women he had ever met. The Lankesters were also close friends of Charles Dickens, who often dined with them. They attended the Dickens's picnics and theatrical events until Dickens separated from his wife, Catherine, in 1858.[22]

Darwin, soon to release *The Origin of Species* to the world, was a frequent guest at the Lankester home, as was Huxley. In his early teens, Ray attended John Tyndall's lectures on glaciers at the Royal Institution, along with as many of Huxley's lectures as possible. At the age of fifteen, in 1861, he published his first scientific writing in the form of a letter to *The Geologist*, and the next year his first full scientific paper appeared.[23] At nineteen, he was aiding his father in his cholera investigations, writing an appendix on microscopical investigations related to cholera for *Cholera: What It Is and How to Prevent It*.[24]

Ray Lankester received his university education at Cambridge and Oxford. He rounded out this schooling with years of study in Vienna, Leipzig, Jena, and Naples. In Jena, he worked with Ernst Haeckel, and in 1876 supervised the translation of Haeckel's *History of Creation*, published in English.[25] In the early 1870s, his fame was rising so rapidly that Darwin wrote to him "I can clearly see that you will some day become our first star in Natural History."[26] In 1873, he began writing at Huxley's suggestion for the ninth edition of the *Encyclopedia Britannica*.[27] Two years later, at age twenty-eight, he was appointed to the chair of zoology at University College, London (later endowed as the Jodrell Chair). The same year he was made a Fellow of the Royal Society. Lankester remained at University College and at the Royal Institution, where he served as Fullerian Professor of Physiology, until 1890, when he took up the position of Linacre Professor of Comparative Anatomy at Oxford from 1891 to 1898, after which he became director of the Natural History Museum from 1898 to 1907, called by Stephen Jay Gould "the most powerful and prestigious post in his field."[28]

The course of Lankester's career, however, was far from smooth, despite his obvious abilities, and the direct backing he received from Darwin and Huxley. This was due to his constant, controversial criticisms of Cambridge and Oxford for the dominance exercised by theological doctrines and the emphasis placed on classical (Greek and Latin language) study. Throughout his career, he sought to reform British education. He was at all times a dedicated scientific materialist and a no less dedicated opponent of spiritualism, including that of Alfred Russell Wallace (the co-discoverer with Darwin of the theory of evolution by natural selection). In 1876, together with his close friend Dr. Horatio Bryan Donkin, then an assistant physician at Westminster Hospital, he created a storm in London society by publicly unmasking an American medium, Henry Slade. Lankester carted him off to the police to be prosecuted as a "common rogue," then writing about it in the *Times* and elsewhere. Darwin contributed £10 to the prosecution of Slade, while Wallace, in contrast, spoke in the trial for the defense. (Slade was convicted and sentenced to three months in prison, but he was released on appeal and fled to the United States.)[29] So uncompromising and outspoken was Lankester on the subject of materialism that he constantly made enemies, including many within the upper-class British establishment.

In 1880, Lankester published what would be one of his most important contributions, *Degeneration: A Chapter in Darwinism*, first presented in 1879 as a lecture to the British Association for Science.[30] Here he rejected the popular notion of evolution as a unilinear process of progress from simpler to more complex forms, a rejection that can be considered the necessary starting point for any ecological critique. Instead, he explained that there were three possibilities in the evolution of species: balance, elaboration, or degeneration. For example, "with regard to parasites, naturalists have long recognized what is called *retrogressive metamorphosis*; and parasitic animals are as a rule admitted to be instances of Degeneration." He defined degeneration as

> a gradual change of the structure in which the organism becomes adapted to *less* varied and *less* complex conditions of life.... In Degeneration there is a *suppression* of form, corresponding to the cessation of work.... It is only when the total result of the Elaboration of some organs, and the Degeneration of others, is such as to leave the whole animal in a *lower* condition, that is, fitted to less complex action and reaction in regard to its surroundings, than was the ancestral form with which we are comparing it (either actually or in imagination) that we speak of that animal as an instance of Degeneration.[31]

Lankester argued that forms of adaptation that led to parasitism or immobility could facilitate degeneration, and this could equally apply to human systems. He thus raised the question whether "the white races of Europe" might be prone at some point to degeneration. But he tended to deemphasize race distinctions within the human species, stressing that degeneration in a human context applied to civilization itself (since natural selection had long ceased to operate directly), whereas the educability of human beings and the progress of science constituted their main protection. Nevertheless, civilizational degeneration was a genuine concern:

> In accordance with a tacit assumption of universal progress—an unreasoning optimism—we are accustomed to regard ourselves as necessarily progressing, as necessarily having arrived at a higher and more elaborated condition than that which our ancestors reached, and as destined to progress still further. On the other hand, it is well to remember that we are subject to the general laws of evolution and are as likely to degenerate as to progress. As compared with the immediate forefathers of our civilization—the ancient Greeks—we do not appear to have improved so far as our bodily structure is concerned, nor assuredly so far as some of our mental capacities are concerned. Our powers of perceiving and expressing beauty of form have certainly *not* increased since the days of the Parthenon and Aphrodite of Melos. In matters of reason, in the development of the intellect, we may seriously inquire how the case stands. Does the reason of the average man of civilized Europe stand out clearly as an evidence of progress when compared with that of the men of bygone ages? Are all the inventions and figments of human superstition and folly, the self-inflicted torturing of mind, the reiterated substitution of wrong for right, and of falsehood for truth, which disfigure our modern civilization—are these evidences of progress? In such respects we have at least reason to fear that we may be degenerate.[32]

There were numerous instances of degeneration and fall of civilizations as in Rome and with the Maya of Central America. Moving from natural examples to human (civilization) analogues, he wrote: "Any new set of conditions occurring to an animal which renders its food and safety very easily attained seem to lead as a rule to Degeneration; just as an active healthy man sometimes degenerates when he becomes suddenly possessed of a fortune; or as Rome degenerated when possessed of the riches of the ancient world. The habit of parasitism clearly acts upon animal organization in this way."[33]

For Lankester, the threat to civilization was worth considering. It was possible, he wrote fancifully, that "we are all drifting, tending to the condition of intellectual Barnacles or Ascidians." It was conceivable for a prosperous civilization "to reject the good gift of reason with which every child is borne, and to degenerate into a contented life of material enjoyment accompanied by ignorance and superstition." The issues of the complex nature of the coevolution of humanity and external nature, along with specific threats to civilization that arose from destructive and degenerative forms of human ecology, were to be constant themes in Lankester's writing throughout his life.[34]

There was, however, a more ominous set of concerns with respect to the degeneration of civilization that Lankester did not express in *Degeneration* and which exists in unpublished notes from the same period. "Certainly, in the case of human societies," he wrote, "it is to be supposed that ultimately a degenerate society would be beaten, repressed, and eventually annihilated by other societies. . . . The struggle is so close among civilized men that the possibility of a degeneration and permanent rest does not suggest itself. It is exceedingly probable that a community which aimed at degeneration would end in annihilation."[35] Lankester's *Degeneration* was later to have a direct impact on H. G. Wells, inspiring his 1891 article on "Zoological Retrogression" and his novel *The Time Machine* (1895).[36]

LANKESTER AND MARX

Around 1879–80, when E. Ray Lankester was developing his influential ideas on degeneration in species and civilization, he became close friends with Karl Marx and his daughter Eleanor.[37] When and where the Lankesters and the Marxes first met is unclear. Sociologist Lewis S. Feuer suggested that it may have been through the offices of their common friend Charles Waldstein (from 1918 on, Charles Walston), a lecturer in archaeology and later a professor of fine arts at the University of Cambridge, and a close friend of Karl Marx. Waldstein is mentioned in the first extant letter from Lankester to Marx, dated September 19, 1880.[38] However, other possibilities suggest themselves. Lankester could have just as easily been introduced to Marx by Lankester's colleague at University College, Edward Spencer Beesly, a professor of history and friend of the Marx family, who sympathized with the working class and the International Working Men's Association.[39]

It is even conceivable that the Marx and Lankester families were previously acquainted socially, as they lived in close proximity in Hampstead. It was a mere twenty-one minutes' walk from the Lankester family home at 68 Belsize Park to the Marx family home at 41 Maitland Park Road. (Engels lived at 122 Regent's Park Road, fourteen minutes' walk from the Marx home.)[40]

Both Edwin Lankester and Marx were members of the reform-oriented Society for the Emancipation of the Arts, Manufacture, and Commerce (usually shortened to Society of Arts), which also included in its membership the sanitary reformer, Edwin Chadwick, and the authority on industrial waste, P. L. Simmonds (a close associate of Edwin Lankester), who had nominated Marx for membership. In the 1860s the Society of Arts met at the Adelphi Building on the Thames, and it is possible that Marx and the elder Lankester became acquainted there.[41]

What is clear is that in the last three to four years of Marx's life, Ray Lankester was a frequent visitor at Marx's home and came, as he later recalled to H. G.

Wells, to know Marx "intimately." Karl and Eleanor Marx visited Lankester at his home, and Eleanor Marx by herself visited the Lankester family.[42] Lankester recommended his good friend H. B. Donkin as the doctor to attend Jenny Marx in her final illness. Donkin went on to treat Marx in his final years and later treated Eleanor Marx, after her father's death.[43]

Horatio Bryan Donkin, himself an important figure in British science, had been elected a Fellow of the Royal College of Physicians in 1880 and was much liked and esteemed by Marx. He became a leading neurologist, famous for his work on the inheritance of mental traits and on hysteria, directly influencing Sigmund Freud. Along with Lankester, he was to become a major critic of eugenics. In 1880, around the time he became the doctor to the Marx family, Donkin delivered a lecture, "Thoughts on Ignorance and Quackery," to the Westminster Hospital Medical School, published the same year in the *British Medical Journal*. He insisted that medicine could not consist simply of anatomical and physiological knowledge with various drugs offered up as medicinal remedies; rather, it needed to address the individual as an individual in his/her environment in order to understand the nature of the patient's maladies. This meant learning the patient's entire history and "social surroundings." Mental as well as physical conditions needed to be evaluated. Donkin criticized the growing tendency to overspecialization, with each ailment having its own medical specialist.[44]

Also in 1880, Donkin published "Suggestions as to the Aetiology of Some of the So-Called System-Diseases of the Spinal Cord" in the British medical journal *Brain*. In the midst of this learned discussion of the diseases of the nervous system, he referred to the material basis of language, emphasizing that "impressions made on our individual brains" act on the "heredity capacity for articulate speech," giving children the capacity to learn with ease each and every language if exposed early enough and "placed in similar native surroundings." Here Donkin, a materialist and a radical, drew on Henry George's political-economic study *Progress and Poverty*, which had discussed human speech capacity in these terms in "The Law of Human Progress." Donkin referred to this language capacity as "one of the most important *differentia* of our species."[45]

The intellectual friendship between Marx and Ray Lankester, who visited the Marxes on numerous occasions, both with Donkin and by himself, was undoubtedly a formidable one. Although Lankester was the much younger man, he was by the early 1880s a confident figure, and as Darwin had said, the emerging "first star" in biological science. One of Lankester's former students drew a vivid portrait of him as a lecturer (during the time he knew Marx):

> He looked round the room, surveyed us (as we felt somewhat as if we were cockroaches), and gave for an hour a clear constructive account of forms and

> conceptions wholly new to us, with such skill that we were unconscious of the marvelous scope and concentration of his lecture, and unconscious of the difficulty in the subject. At the same time, apparently without effort, he drew on his many blackboards with firm sweeps of wide lines clear diagrams which were left untouched during the day for those who were unable to copy as quickly as he drew. I have no recollection of seeing him refer to notes, except to dictate the definition of groups, or rarely for some drawing. For us, in 1881, he was infallible.[46]

Marx no doubt found Lankester's thoroughgoing materialism and radicalism attractive. Indeed, as Joseph Lester writes: "It cannot be doubted that Lankester himself had radical political views that would have appealed to Marx."[47] Remarkably, Marx's description of the conditions of overwork and overcrowding in his chapter on "The Working Day" in volume 1 of *Capital* had drawn on descriptions of the conditions in workhouses published in several London papers in June 1863—based on the *Report of the Medical Officer of Health to the Parish Vestry of St. James* by Edwin Lankester. The newspaper reports dwelt on the elder Lankester's account of the death of twenty-year-old Mary Ann Walkley, employed in a dressmaking establishment run by Madame Elise, one of London's better-known millineries. Walkley, along with sixty other young women, had been forced to work 26 1/2 hours straight without a break, confined thirty to a room.

In addition to alluding to the details on Walkley's death, Marx in *Capital* also referred to Lankester's statement, quoted by the Children's Employment Commission (though attributed in a footnote in *Capital* to Dr. Letheby, the Consulting Physician of the Board of Health), that "the minimum air for each adult ought to be in a sleeping room 300, and in a dwelling room 500 cubic feet." Edwin Lankester had followed up inquiries into Walkley's death with repeated inspections of the sanitary conditions of the workrooms/sweatshops.[48] In the conclusion to his "President's Address in the Public Health Department of the Social Science Association" in 1865, he had strongly condemned "the sacrifice of holocausts of victims" among the working classes "every year"—though attributing this largely to lack of education in the principles of public health.[49]

The young Lankester had no doubt learned of these horrendous workplace conditions from his father, and would have shared the latter's outrage.[50] In 1873 Ray declared in a letter to his mother: "I really believe that common property and free love, subject to certain regulations for the common good, will one day have a great development, perhaps not in these old lands, but in new ones, which will increase in population and prosperity as Europe dies of old age. I don't say that I should like to try the experiment in the midst of another kind of life, but it cannot be that men will go on, some deprived of proper food, education, and all that makes life endurable." In 1880, at the time of his friendship with Marx, Ray Lankester declared that the "Liberals are a sham" and "the conservatives genuine unpretending swindlers."[51]

Marx and Ray Lankester's friendship clearly extended to their respective intellectual endeavors. Marx, who had recently taught himself Russian, informed Lankester that *Degeneration* had been translated into that language, asking Nikolai Danielson in Russia with regard to its publication status on Lankester's behalf. These actions suggest Marx was impressed by the intellectual importance of Lankester's theory of degeneration, although his own opinion on it is not known. Marx gave Lankester, who read German, a copy of his great work *Das Kapital,* which would not be translated into English until after Marx's death, and Lankester reported in May 1880 he was "reading it with the greatest pleasure and profit."[52]

Marx and Lankester certainly did not lack subjects in common to discuss, such as materialism, Darwin's evolutionary theory (which fascinated Marx), the state of English and German science, and capitalism.[53] It was quite possible that Lankester introduced Marx to the work of his friend the Canadian naturalist Grant Allen, since Marx took detailed notes on Allen's 1880 article on the role of coal deposits on urban development in Britain.[54]

Marx was enthusiastic about the aquarium at Brighton, which he visited more than once and strongly recommended to Engels. Completed in 1872, it had the largest display tank in the world, holding 100,000 gallons. The main aquarium corridor was 224 feet long. One of the earliest attractions was a large octopus.[55] He thus may have known of Edwin Lankester's book *The Aquavivarium*. The younger Lankester followed in his father's footsteps in his devotion to aquariums as a way of understanding species within whole environments. In 1883, only months after Marx's death, he was to propose the establishment of a Marine Biological Association and a Marine Biological Laboratory in Plymouth, of which he was to emerge as the principal founder.

It is noteworthy that Marx, in the years he knew Lankester, was also deeply involved in writing his *Ethnological Notebooks* in which he was exploring issues related to the discovery of ethnological time. He was also investigating the history of earth's geology and its effects on species, including extinction related to (non-anthropogenic) climate change. In reflecting on Darwin's *Origin of the Species* in the first volume of *Capital* Marx had written:

> Darwin has directed attention to the history of natural technology, i.e. the formation of the organs of plants and animals, which serve as the instruments of production for sustaining their life. Does not the history of the productive organs of man in society, of organs that are the material basis of every particular organization of society, deserve equal attention?... Technology reveals the

> active relation of man to nature, the direct process of the production of his life, and thereby it also lays bare the process of the production of the social relations of his life, and of the mental conceptions that flow from those relations.[56]

Lankester, who had a fascination with, and later became involved in, archaeological controversies over prehistoric tools (the famous eolith dispute) would have been quick to engage in such discussions. He coined many of the terms used to describe stone tools within archaeology.[57] Both thinkers were broad-based system theorists with regard to society/nature who crossed disciplinary boundaries and developed ecological critiques.[58] Lankester's years of friendship with Marx were followed by a clear anti-capitalist sentiment that continually appeared on the margins of his work, as well as in pronounced socialist sympathies of a more Fabian kind.

Lankester left behind no reminiscences on his relation to Marx, upon which he was generally silent. In his article on "The Friendship of Edwin Ray Lankester and Karl Marx," published in in 1979, Feuer went to lengths to develop an argument, based on little more than speculation, that Wells's vague critical portrayal of Marx in his 1926 novel *The World of William Clissold* had its source in information provided by Lankester. As Feuer put it:

> From another source, however, we might possibly infer Lankester's view of Marx. Lankester indeed was probably the principal informant for the brilliant section entitled "Psycho-Analysis of Karl Marx" in H. G. Wells's novel *The World of William Clissold*. . . . Wells believed that he was the first to have applied the psychoanalytical method to Marx and his doctrines. Probably he had often discussed Marx's personality with Lankester, for Lankester was the only man alive to have known Marx's medical and personal problems at first hand.[59]

Feuer then quotes at length from Wells's long calumny against Marx in his novel. Feuer's thesis that Wells built his portrayal of Marx based on information from Lankester is demolished, however, by two letters from Lankester to Wells in September 1926, in response to Wells sending him the newly published novel. On September 3, 1926, Lankester wrote thanking Wells for the portrayal of himself (as "Rupert York") in the novel. In a subsequent letter on September 9, 1926, Lankester added in a postscript, in relation to Wells's portrait of Marx: "Did I tell you that I used to know Karl Marx and his wife and daughters intimately, and with him Engels—a rather rough specimen? Also Herzen—a son of Alex. Herzen"—Lankester is referring to Alexander A. Herzen (1839-1906), the physiologist and son of the Russian revolutionary populist Alexander Ivanovich Herzen (1812–1870).[60] It is clear from this letter that Lankester did not talk to Wells about Marx (certainly not in any detail) until *after* he received a published copy of *The World of William Clissold*. He could not therefore have supplied Wells with information for the harsh portrayal of Marx in the novel.

Lankester, who was anti-Bolshevik (although he had welcomed the first stages of the Russian Revolution), is reported to have responded to an inquiry from David Riazanov, director of the Marx-Engels Institute in Moscow, that he had no letters from Marx and declined to provide any reminiscences. His planned memoir was never written.[61]

LANKESTER AND "THE WOMAN QUESTION"

In late nineteenth-century Britain, the socialist and women's movements arose in tandem, along with developments in science. There was in fact a general revolt against the complacency and narrow-mindedness of the Victorian Age and against the cultural and environmental destruction of capitalist industry. Yet, this same period saw the rise of overlapping, reactionary trends in the form of social Darwinism, biological determinism, and eugenics. In the early twentieth century, the British Eugenics Society was to include in its membership not only the founder of eugenics, Francis Galton, but also such noted, and generally seen as progressive, figures as H. B. Donkin, Havelock Ellis, Patrick Geddes, Julian Huxley, John Maynard Keynes, Harold Laski, Karl Pearson, and Margaret Sanger.[62]

A failure to perceive the sheer complexity of this period of political, social, and scientific transition can lead to serious errors of interpretation. In "The Darwinian Gentleman at Marx's Funeral," Gould played up the seeming anomaly of Lankester's close friendship with Marx, suggesting that Lankester was far from politically progressive. Nevertheless, almost the only evidence that Gould could provide for his claim that Lankester leaned toward political conservatism, was the latter's opposition, when in his sixties, to the extension of suffrage to women. Extrapolating from this, Gould argued that Lankester's "elitist attitudes and fealty to a romanticized vision of a more gracious past" governed his political outlook, not only in his elderly years but when he was in his thirties as well.[63]

Gould's sketch of Lankester's character conflicts sharply with his own main source, Joseph Lester's biography of Lankester, which had uncovered Lankester's history of political radicalism.[64] Indeed, Gould's political portrayal of Lankester as a conservative and conformist "Darwinian gentleman" goes against all that we know of Lankester's anti-capitalist, socialist, materialist, and overall unconventional social outlook. As Peter J. Bowler, who edited Lester's biography, has stated, Lankester was a "radical . . . on social issues."[65] Gould's interpretation also flies in the face of the well-known public scandals that Lankester was periodically caught up in due to his outright defiance of authority, including his scandalous arrest and public trial for accosting police in the streets who were abusing prostitutes.[66] Although Lankester was to revert in his later years to patriarchal views of women (albeit views that were hardly extreme in his time), he was among the most virulent critics of eugenics and of biological determinism, and for most of his life, at least, a promoter of the extension of women's rights.

It is important to guard against simplistic judgments and ahistorical views in relation to the complex, contradictory reality of patriarchy that continued to affect the thinking of many otherwise radical thinkers in Victorian-Edwardian Britain, penetrating even into the socialist movement and Darwinian evolutionary theory. Patriarchal ideology obviously ran deep in the consciousness of the time, and the overturning of it was not the work of a day. Issues of the status of women overlapped in complex ways with questions of biological determinism, social Darwinism, racism, and eugenics.

British male progressive thinkers outside the socialist movement, and occasionally even socialists themselves, tended to be at best only mildly forward-looking where questions of men and women were concerned, however radical and unconventional they may have been in other respects. Darwinian science, while challenging some of the dominant sexual mores, also served in this period to reinforce aspects of the core patriarchal view.

In the years immediately following Marx's death, Lankester was linked through his friends and associates (including Eleanor Marx, Olive Schreiner, Donkin, and Karl Pearson) to various socialist and feminist circles, particularly the famous Men and Women's Club. In 1879, this "heterosocial" discussion group, known simply as "The Club," was formed in London. Engaged in a wide array of social problems, it originally consisted of some twenty individuals, mainly middle-class socialists and feminists geared to changing the conditions of workers and women. Such notable figures as Clementina Black (and her sisters Constance, Emma, and Grace), Ernest Radford, Caroline "Dollie" Maitland, Eleanor Marx, Amy Levy, Emily Ford, Isabella Ford, George Bernard Shaw, and Pearson participated in The Club's discussions. A considerable number of these participants, including Black, Radford, Maitland, and Shaw were close friends with Eleanor Marx. Black, Radford, and Maitland were visitors to the Marx home while her father was alive. Maitland, later Radford, having married Ernest Radford in 1883, served as the final president of The Club, and Black as the final secretary. The Club had a strong socialist orientation and a wide intellectual agenda, which included literary and cultural topics. It operated on the basis of the intrinsic equality of women and men, recognizing the need for women's emancipation.

In 1884, Black wrote to Pearson, who was a member of The Club but intermittent in his attendance, that, due to the changing commitments of current members, it had to be reorganized if it were to continue. Pearson, recently appointed professor of applied mathematics at University College, London, and the future founder of biometrics, took it upon himself to direct the dissolving of the original Club and its formal reorganization as "The Men and Women's Club." All members of its executive committee, aside from Dollie Radford and Black, seceded along with Pearson in 1885, setting up the new Men and Women's Club that year. However, only one woman among the original members of The Club continued to participate regularly in the new club. Though inspired by its predecessor, it was an altogether different group with a changed membership and a different purpose, that of discussing "the mutual position and relation of men and women."

Eleanor Marx (beginning in 1884 known as Eleanor Marx-Aveling due to her common-law marriage with Edward Aveling) was asked by Donkin to join the new Men and Women's Club early in 1886 but declined on the grounds that "probably, many of the good ladies in the Club would be much shocked at the idea of my becoming a member of it" (referring to her relationship with Aveling), and due to the growing demands on her in terms of socialist analysis and activism. She indicated that she was willing to participate on occasion as a guest.

It was at this time that the Socialist League, led by William Morris, was formed as a breakaway from H. M. Hyndman's Social Democratic Federation. The Avelings and the Radfords threw themselves into the work of the Socialist League, while Clementina Black devoted herself to trade union organization. Eleanor Marx-Aveling's supposition that her admission to the new Men and Women's Club would be opposed by many of the "good ladies" in the club turned out to be correct. Strong opposition to her membership was voiced by Maria Sharpe (who was later to become Pearson's wife) and presumably others as well.

Crucial to Pearson's new Men and Women's Club was the involvement of Olive Schreiner, already a well-known South African novelist as a result of her book, *The Story of a South African Farm*, which had taken London literary circles by storm. Schreiner joined the new club from its birth in 1885 and was to become one of its central movers. Eleanor Marx became Schreiner's closest female friend when she arrived in London in the early 1880s, and they remained good friends after that. Donkin, Lankester's longtime friend, and physician to the Marx family, was a member and active participant in the Men and Women's Club during its first two years. Donkin fell in love in those years with Schreiner, proposing to her several times.[67]

Lankester was himself a close friend of Schreiner's and seems to have participated in some of the discussions around the Men and Women's Club in its first two years (1885–86). He was invited to present a paper on the evolution of sexuality. In an 1886 letter to Pearson, Schreiner described how on one occasion Lankester, his sister, and she were driving home, when Lankester had spoken of his admiration for Pearson, as a younger colleague at University College, and of his future intellectual prospects.[68] There is no doubt that Lankester initially thought highly of Pearson, his junior within the academy, and would probably have been familiar with his general approach to "The Woman Question," which for all its many weaknesses recognized that it was a sociological and not a biological question.[69]

Pearson dominated the new Men and Women's Club. Four men, including Donkin, and six women attended the first meeting in 1885. The men were drawn from the professions (university professors, lawyers, and physicians were all represented), while the women were mostly without higher education and were older on average than the women who had been the force behind what was originally The Club. The Men and Women's Club, in particular, lacked the younger socialist-feminist activists like Clementina Black, Dollie Radford, and Eleanor Marx-Aveling—which appears to have led Lankester and even Donkin to poke malicious fun at Pearson while at the Savile Club (to which they all belonged) for starting a club that mainly consisted of "a lot of old maids and manhaters," as Schreiner, who obviously obtained her information secondhand, related it in a letter to Pearson.

Schreiner described herself "as probably the youngest woman there" and was concerned about the composition of the club. The majority of the women in it placed a strong emphasis on social respectability, rejecting the proposed name of "Wollstonecraft" for the Men and Women's Club on the grounds that this would be disreputable in that it would suggest that the club had to do with feminist activism. Nevertheless, a number of younger, more dynamic socialist women remained connected to the Men and Women's Club "through correspondence and papers, and as visitors," sometimes delivering talks, including figures like Annie Besant and Eleanor Marx-Aveling.[70]

In the first meeting Pearson presented his paper "The Woman's Question," which was printed for private circulation, and generated much discussion at the time.[71] This was followed by another essay, "Socialism and Sex," which he presented to the Men and Women's Club in 1886 and published the following year. Pearson, who had been lecturing for a few years on the ideas of Lassalle and Marx, projected in these and other essays of the time a peculiar form of Darwinian "moral socialism" in which some signs of his future support of eugenics could be detected as well as his statist views, which demanded "veneration of the state." He argued in "The Woman's Question" that the emancipation of women would "ultimately involve a revolution in all our social institutions," but where all of this was leading had to be determined scientifically and with respect to various "sexualogical problems." Before women's rights could be meaningfully addressed, it was necessary "to settle what is the physical capacity of woman, what would be the effect of her emancipation on her function of race-reproduction."

There was a general presumption in Pearson's analysis that the emancipation of women should take second place to "the conditions needed for race-permanence." Thus, depending on how it affected "race permanence," he suggested, "the higher education of women may connote a general intellectual progress for the community, or, on the other hand, a physical degradation of the race." The reason a highly intelligent woman like George Eliot was not allowed to vote while the "dullest yokel" among men could needed to be rationally explained, he claimed, in terms of some other function than either intelligence or physical capability, namely childbearing, which made the full entry of women into public life potentially dangerous to the community. One thing that Pearson, who generally took a Malthusian view on the need to restrict population, was clear about was the need for sexual restraint for the good of the state: "If the growing sex-equality connotes sex freedom—a return to general promiscuity—then it connotes a decay of the state, and it will require a second Pauline Christianity and a second subjection of one sex to restore stability."[72]

Pearson promoted the social Darwinian notion of "the survival of the fittest" combined with a statist "socialism." Sex relations and questions of sexual reproduction needed to be subject to the needs of the state, including limitations on population. The economic independence of women, within limits, was seen as a means to that end. Although suggesting that women were "at present" physically and intellectually inferior to men, he drew on the work of the Swiss jurist, historian, and archaeologist Johann Bachofen to suggest that this was a social condition that did not pertain to all periods of history, and could be remedied in large part through opening up education and employment to women, thereby allowing women to have the "economic independence" that was necessary for all human beings. He pointed to a certain plasticity in the social relations of men and women and even in their sexual (or what we now call gender) roles. Women, he went so far as to say, were the first to practice agriculture and to discover medicine. Technology could alleviate the unnecessary "home duties" of women, apart from childbearing. The "sex-relationship" would increasingly be regarded as "the closest form of friendship between man and woman" and no longer "in the first place [as] a union for the birth of children."[73]

Some of the women in the Men and Women's Club, including Schreiner, were critical of Pearson's tendency to reduce women to the status of a problem and to see their reproductive "function" as primary, while not examining the patriarchal role of men, and therefore excluding many of the questions raised by the emerging feminism. Pearson's Darwinian functionalism led him to look at women's advancement as subject to the larger needs of "the race" (implicitly identified with the needs of men. Novelist Emma Brooke dared to argue in the Men and Women's Club that Pearson's elitist approach to women was "in general unsocialistic."[74]

Hence, there is reason to believe the more famous article, "The Woman Question," by Edward Aveling and Eleanor Marx-Aveling was a response in part to Pearson's earlier "The Woman Question," which they had undoubtedly seen. Published in the *Westminster Review* in 1886, their article was an expanded version of Eleanor's earlier review of the 1885 English translation of August Bebel's *Woman in the Past, Present, and Future* (first published in German in 1879 and better known as *Woman and Socialism*). Bebel had made a strong case for the equality of women as intrinsic to the socialist project, countering all arguments that women were inferior to men and that their role in society necessarily centered on childbearing. With this, along with Engels's more powerful 1884 *Origin of the Family, Private Property and the State* as their basis, the Avelings went on to argue that the problems were rooted in economic relations, that is, relations of labor, production, and exploitation, which they saw as encompassing both class relations between capitalists and workers, and patriarchal relations between men and women. As a result, society as a whole had to be changed. There were "excellent and hard-working folk who agitate for that perfectly just aim, woman suffrage; for the repeal of the Contagious Diseases Act, a monstrosity begotten of male cowardice and brutality; for the higher education of women; for the opening to them of universities, the learned professions, and all callings." Yet, three things, they argued, were found wanting. First, all of these issues were primarily deigned to benefit the well-to-do classes. Second, all were "based either on property, or sentimental or professional questions. Not one of them gets down through to the bedrock of the economic basis." Third, none of this agitation sought to promote any object "outside the limits of the society today." Connecting the forms of oppression and the necessary responses, they wrote:

> The truth, not fully recognized even by those anxious to do good to woman, is that she, like the labour-classes, is in an oppressed condition; that her position, like theirs, is one of merciless degradation. Women are the creatures of an organised tyranny of men, as the workers are the creatures of an organized tyranny of idlers. . . . Both the oppressed classes, women and the immediate producers, must understand that their emancipation will come from themselves. Women will find allies in the better sort of men, as the labourers are finding allies among the philosophers, artists, and poets. But the one has nothing to hope from man as a whole, and the other has nothing to hope from the middle class as a whole.[75]

In this view, the term "The Woman Question" drew its validity not, as in Pearson's analysis, from the notion that the problem of women and reproduction in modern society needed to be "perfected" for the betterment of "the race," but from its connection to the class struggle, and from the belief that women's "emancipation will [necessarily] come from [women] themselves" as an end it itself. Looking toward a future beyond capitalism and patriarchy, Aveling and Marx-Aveling stated:

> And now comes the question as to how the future position of women, and therefore of the race, will be affected by all of this. Of one or two things we may be very sure. . . . Clearly, there will be equality for all, without distinction of sex. Thus, woman will be independent: her education and all other opportunities as those of man. . . . Personally, we believe that monogamy will gain the day. There are approximately equal numbers of men and women, and the highest ideal seems to be the complete, harmonious, lasting blending of two human lives. . . . The contract between man and woman will be of a purely private nature. . . . The woman will no longer be the man's slave, but his equal.[76]

Lankester, in the general context of this sometimes heated discussion and debate arising out of the Men and Women's Club, to which he had strong connections through Donkin, Schreiner, Pearson, and Marx-Aveling, and where he had been invited to speak, wrote Schreiner a long letter on "the woman question" in late 1885 or early 1886. There is no extant copy of Lankester's letter, but it was quoted extensively by Schreiner, in a letter she wrote in response, which has come down to us as one of her most open, spontaneous, and passionate discussions of marriage and the condition of women.[77]

Schreiner quotes Lankester as arguing, against Victorian mores, that marriage was "*not* the natural tendency of man, or rather not a necessary characteristic of the race." In this, he appears to have suggested also that monogamy too had no definite natural basis. Lankester saw a permanent and perfect marriage, from a Victorian standpoint, as one in which the "man should obtain the very sweetest kind of service & attention viz. that which is bound up with genuine sexual love. It may not be of very intelligent help or it may be itself of a very high intelligence—that does not much matter—the great point being that it is happily & gladly rendered & that there is a feeling that what is given by the woman in her care to the man is returned by him in his larger but not less genuine care of the woman." Such a marriage, however, he clearly recognized, and Schreiner admitted, was hard to obtain under present social conditions, precisely because women were not free agents. Since it was a question of the bourgeois family, this raised the dual questions of socialism and feminism. The woman, Schreiner wrote back to him, "has to sell herself, whether into the bitter loveless childless deformed untender state of prostitution or into loveless marriage."

Nevertheless, Schreiner argued for monogamy and marriage as natural, countering Lankester's views. "There are some factors," she wrote, "you seem entirely to lose sight of in this man & woman question." Schreiner argued that human beings naturally sought to be of service to others and women especially to men, offering them love, devotion, and worship—these were things that could not be bought in the market.[78]

In Schreiner's perspective, as she told Pearson, Lankester was best viewed as "a vast engine without a driver." She was particularly intent on finding a "woman friend" for him, who would fill all his needs.[79] These needs were demanding. Coming from a family in which both parents were scientists and shared radical political views, collaborating intellectually, as well as raising a large family, Lankester seemed to have expectations with regard to life relationships that went against the whole tenor of Victorian society. He indicated that what he wanted was a life partner who combined love and companionship with shared intelligence. In 1875, he had written to his mother: "If I could only find some woman who had a soul, a belief in things not believed in by society, and who could take a pleasure in existence apart from gossiping and empty distraction, and who would help me to do the same, I should be happy wherever I might be."[80]

Unable to meet his needs in a conventional way, Lankester was to remain single throughout his life; two engagements fell through. In 1876, he became engaged to Ethel Brodie, the daughter of Sir Benjamin Brodie, the Oxford Professor of Biology. However, he soon became disenchanted with her because of what he saw as her excessive piety, Victorian propriety, and "young-lady-ism." Breaking off the engagement at the risk of scandal at Oxford, he wrote, "I don't care if I never marry, if I can't have what I want. I daresay I am very wrong, that is to say, my nature is perhaps a bad one. . . but there it is, and I will not do violence to it." Eighteen years later, in 1894, he became engaged to Mary Eleanor Corbett, an American actress. Though the marriage date was set, it did not come off and Lankester later referred to it as "the fiasco." The two had a quarrel and his fiancée apparently broke off the engagement not long before the marriage.[81]

The broken engagements and the fact that Lankester never married led Gould to speculate he may have been gay (although there is no definitive evidence one way or the other). As Gould put it:

> One additional, and more conjectural, matter must be aired as we try to grasp the extent of Lankester's personal unconventionalities . . . for potential insight into his willingness to ignore the social norms of his time. The existing literature maintains a wall of total silence on this issue, but the pattern seems

unmistakable. Lankester remained a bachelor, although he often wrote about his loneliness and his desires of family life. He was twice slated for marriage, but both fiancées broke their engagements for mysterious and unstated reasons. He took long European vacations nearly every year, and nearly always to Paris, where he maintained clear distance from his professional colleagues. Late in life, Lankester became an intimate platonic friend and admirer of the great ballerina Anna Pavlova. I can offer no proof, but if these behaviors don't point toward the love that may now be freely discussed, but then dared not speak its name (to paraphrase the great line written by Oscar Wilde's paramour, Lord Alfred Douglas), well, then, Professor Lankester was far more mysterious and secretive than even I can imagine.[82]

GENDER, SOCIAL DARWINISM, AND EUGENICS

When it came to gender, a kind of conservative "social Darwinism" penetrated into Darwin's thought and was carried forward in the subsequent development of Darwinian ideas. Hence, Darwinian evolutionary theory, rather than playing a consistently progressive role with respect to gender offered new support to conventional prejudices in relation to patriarchy, giving rise to social Darwinism and eugenics. In *The Descent of Man*, Darwin agreed with Galton (his cousin) in claiming that "if men are capable of decided eminence over women in many subjects, the average standard of mental power in man must be above that of woman"—which he attributed to the process of sexual selection. "Man," Darwin added, "is more powerful in body and mind than woman." He thus adamantly rejected the outlook that John Stuart Mill had expressed in *The Subjection of Women*, which represented the strongest argument then circulating within Victorian circles with respect to the natural equality of women with men in their mental powers.[83]

Still, Darwinian evolutionary theory was somewhat tenuous in actually accounting for the difference in average intelligence between men and women. The emphasis, emanating from Darwin himself, was placed primarily on the perceived fact that men were more biologically variable in nearly every respect than women, and that the woman was the normal type, man, the abnormal. The male line was characterized by a greater share of geniuses, and by more mentally disadvantaged individuals. This argument was put forward influentially by American zoologist W. K. Brooks in "The Condition of Women from a Zoological Point of View," appearing in *Popular Science Monthly* in June 1879, a copy of which Lankester retained in his scientific papers. Brooks later followed this up with his *Law of Heredity* (1883), which presented the same arguments. "If there is this fundamental difference in the sociological influence of the sexes," Brooks argued in a biologically determinist way, "its origin must be sought in the physiological differences between them." For Brooks, "The female organism is the conservative organism, to which is intrusted the keeping of all that has been gained during the past history of the race." Therefore, it followed that "the female mind is a storehouse filled with the instincts, habits, intuitions, and laws of conduct which have been gained by past experience. The male organism being the variable organism, the originating element in the process of evolution, the male mind must have the power of extending experience over new fields." This "progressive power of the male mind" was evident in its great capacity for "abstract thought," giving it its dominant role in science, poetry, and art. Ignoring sociological variables, Brooks declared simply, as if it constituted biological proof, that "it is as impossible to find a female Raphael or a female Händel as a female Shakespeare or a female Newton."[84] It was this view that Virginia Woolf was later to decry in her *A Room of One's Own*, in which she presented the fictional story of Shakespeare's sister in order to explain the barriers that stood in the way of women.[85]

Havelock Ellis (who was an intimate friend/lover of Schreiner and a more distant admirer of Marx-Aveling) was to present almost identical views to those of Brooks in his extremely influential *Man and Woman* (1894).[86] Ellis was an active participant with Schreiner, Shaw, and William Carpenter in the small bohemian club, the Fellowship of the New Life, devoted to pacifism, vegetarianism, and simple living.[87] Ellis trained as a physician (although he never practiced) and was to become best known for his research on sexuality. *Man and Woman* was regarded as expressing the scientific consensus on sexual matters in his day.[88] Not surprisingly, it also reflected Victorian patriarchal prejudices. "There can be little doubt," he proclaimed, "that the smaller size of women as compared to men is connected with the preservation of a primitive character."[89] He promoted the notion of greater male variability—invoking the precedence of Darwin—up through the sixth edition of *Man and Woman* in 1926. Ironically, it was Pearson, Ellis's rival for the heart of Schreiner, who was to be Ellis's chief opponent with respect to male versus female variability, resulting in an intense debate between the two at the turn of the century.

Ellis argued that with the exception of literature, where figures like Jane Austen, George Eliot, and Charlotte Brontë had excelled, women generally lacked genius at the higher level of the arts. Although women were purported to be capable of reaching the highest level in the writing of novels, this did not apply to poetry. He claimed to have done empirical research on English men and women of genius (based on *The Dictionary of National Biography*), through which he had determined that women represented only 5.3 percent of geniuses. (The first and dominating editor of the *Dictionary of National Biography* was Leslie Stephen, father of Virginia Woolf, whose *Science of Ethics* [1882] attempted to wed evolutionary theory to ethics.) Women were said to be good at all practical tasks, including politics and business, but lacking in those intellectual realms relying on high levels of abstraction. Women, according to Ellis's *Man and Woman*, were "nearer to the child-type." He insisted that it was their conservatism, rather than their radicalism, that ostensibly drew them to socialism to a greater degree than men.[90] Known for his unconventional beliefs and a defender of women's rights, Ellis nonetheless came perhaps closer than any other reputed scientific thinker of his time in defending the subjection of women as a necessary part of the subjection of nature. This reflected the merging of gender and nature prejudice within the dominant Western culture, so strongly criticized by Carolyn Merchant in *The Death of Nature*.[91] As Ellis wrote in *Man and Woman*:

> Men have had their revenge on Nature and on her *protégée* [women]. While women have been largely absorbed in that sphere of sexuality which is Nature's, men have roamed the earth, sharpening their aptitudes and energies in perpetual conflict with Nature. It has thus come about that the subjugation of Nature by Man has often practically involved the subjugation, physical and mental, of women by men. The periods of society most favourable for women appear, judging from the experiences of the past, to be somewhat primitive periods in which the militant tendency is not strongly marked. Very militant periods, and those so-called advanced periods in which the complicated and artificial products of the variational tendency of men are held in chief honour, are not favourable to the freedom and expansion of women. Greece and Rome, the favourite types of civilization, bring before us emphatically masculine states of culture.[92]

Such strong patriarchal views go against Rachel Holmes's characterization of Ellis, in her biography of Eleanor Marx, as one of the men who made "major contributions to feminism" in the Victorian age, and who were "genuinely interested in challenging universal patriarchy."[93] It also points to the complexity of these issues. Although Ellis was clearly sympathetic to a degree with the women's struggles and sexual liberation, he retained deep reservations about the equality of women. In the 1929 edition of *Man and Woman*, he was to intone: "When women enter the same fields as men, on the same level and to the same degree, their organic constitution usually unfits them to achieve the same success, or they only achieve it at greater cost. Woman's special sphere is the bearing and the rearing of children, with the care of human life in the home."[94] As Cynthia Eagle Russett was to declare in her *Sexual Science: The Victorian Construction of Womanhood*, "If Pearson and Ellis were friends of woman, she hardly needed enemies."[95]

Scarcely less influential than Ellis's *Man and Nature* was *The Evolution of Sex* (1889) by Scottish biologists Patrick Geddes and J. Arthur Thomson, both of whom were to contribute notably to the development of ecological theory. Geddes and Thomson downplayed Darwin's sexual selection and attempted to develop a chemical essentialism, using the concept of metabolism, to differentiate between men and women, introducing the terms "anabolic" (in this case meaning passive) and "katabolic" (active and variable) for the differing metabolisms of women and men, respectively. In this view, as opposed to the Darwinian one, what distinguished the sexes was quite fixed. Men were more active and variable, women less active and more constant. "What was decided among the prehistoric *Protozoa*," they opined, "can not be annulled by Act of Parliament," that is, women's suffrage.[96]

Lankester, in contrast, seems to have been relatively free for most of his life, particularly in his youth, of such Victorian era prejudices, present even in free-thinking and scientific circles in his day. He clearly despised the extremely narrow-minded, oppressive sexual morality of the day, among them the views: "That copulation is especially a wrong thing. . . . That women are inferior creatures, used by the devil to bring men to misery."[97] He was involved in his thirties in the promotion of women's rights. In 1884, he fought hard to force the medical faculty at the University College, London to open Lectures on the Course of General Biology to women. Although he eventually succeeded, the medical faculty fought back and formally excluded Lankester from their faculty in retaliation. Lankester argued, unusually for the time, that not only "sons" but "daughters too" should be provided with a "reasonable instruction in science" from primary education through college. He had great admiration for his student Philippa Fawcett, who studied at University College and later went on to Cambridge University, where she astounded the university and the nation with her mathematical abilities, scoring first—far outreaching all others—in the 1890 Mathematical Tripos exams.[98]

In a famous 1895 case, leading to a public trial that shocked and amused London society, Lankester, coming out of the Savile Club, had openly challenged police on the street for the abuse of a prostitute. He was arrested and charged with disorder. He enlisted in his defense the famous barrister Sir George Lewis who had helped him in the prosecution of Slade. The dramatic event once again brought the issue of police brutality in the treatment of prostitutes to public attention. Rudyard Kipling, on the occasion of Lankester's fiftieth birthday party at the Savile Club in 1897, was to make light of Lankester's relations with the police, giving the whole event a kind of legendary character.[99]

Nevertheless, Lankester retreated into a conservative, patriarchal view in the opening decade of the twentieth century, writing in response to the 1908 attempt of suffragettes to storm Parliament a column titled "Votes for Women," in which he strongly opposed the extension of the vote to women. Then in his sixties, he sought to justify his resistance by referring to the scientific consensus of his day. He declared it was a settled fact that the intellectual capacity of the average woman was naturally somewhat less than that of the average man, and sought to back this up by fallaciously pointing to women's smaller brain size, while neglecting to relate this to overall body size (a common error in the craniology of this era). Lankester coupled this with the notion of women's physical inferiority. He went so far as to invoke the age-old principle of "paterfamilias" in which the man was the head of the household and the role of women was "to serve him and crown his life." Women, he declared, "should be prepared to accept their natural duties as wives and mothers."[100] A few years later, in a letter to H. G. Wells's wife, he indicated that he opposed the suffragette cause on the grounds that women, as long as they were uneducated and "ignorant," should be denied the vote—a principle he thought should ideally be applied to men as well. However, here at least he appeared to be referring to educability rather than innate ability.[101]

Lankester fell prey here to what Gould, in the title of his famous book, called *The Mismeasure of Man* (or, in this case, mismeasure of woman). In this, of course, he was not alone. Such perspectives could be found among some British socialist men in the late nineteenth and early twentieth centuries. Prominent figures in the Social Democratic Federation, like Ernest Belfort Bax, though unrepresentative of the movement as a whole, exhibited strong patriarchal—in Bax's case even misogynist—views.[102]

Though opposing the extension of the suffrage to women in his later years, and even invoking strong patriarchal justifications in this context, Lankester nonetheless continued to oppose Victorian strictures on women's actual freedom and to defend the rights of women in economic and sexual liberation. Thus, around the same time as he was questioning the extension of the vote to women, he also came out strongly in support of his friend H. G. Wells who was under attack for his novel *Ann Veronica* (1909). Wells portrays the eponymous Ann Veronica as a twenty-one-year-old feminist who not only took part in the storming of Parliament on behalf of women's suffrage but also brazenly initiated a sexual relationship with a married man. The book was roundly condemned in British society, with the *Spectator* (London) stigmatizing it as "capable of poisoning the minds of those who read it."[103] Lankester, along with others, stood by Wells, helping protect him from social ostracism.

Moreover, at the same time he seemed to be backtracking in some respects, adopting conservative views with respect to "the woman question," Lankester, in his usual fiery way, was engaged in a virulent struggle against eugenics, which had become prominent among British professional elites in the period. For Lankester, who was a sharp critic of naive notions of progress, and a proponent of what we would now call an ecological worldview, a line had to be drawn with respect to the often racist understandings of eugenicists, like those presented by Darwin's cousin, Francis Galton, and by Pearson, who all too frequently pointed to a physically degenerating humanity as a justification for "purifying" the human race. Such thinkers advocated restrictions on the breeding of those seen as feebleminded or embodying unfavorable physical characteristics (often based on racial characteristics).

Pearson in later years was to abandon his early mechanistic-socialistic views, becoming an idealist, a follower of Galton and a strident advocate of eugenics, to which he gave a pseudo-scientific basis through his biometrics.[104] It was this idealist and social Darwinist Pearson of whom V. I. Lenin declared in 1908 (somewhat mistakenly, given Pearson's earlier cursory studies of Marx and Engels): "Pearson fights materialism with great determination (although he does not know Feuerbach, Marx, or Engels)."[105]

Much of Pearson's authority derived from the fact that he occupied the Galton Professorship of Eugenics at University College, established by Galton himself.[106] In this capacity he argued strongly in favor of limiting the breeding of the "feeble minded," with Lankester becoming his fiercest opponent in this respect. For Lankester, in advancing eugenics, Pearson was confusing the biological conditions with the "special form of political organization" that dominates modern life, failing to recognize that it was not biological evolution that was now the crucial factor in human progress but the degree of social change and intellectual development. Hence, Lankester vehemently opposed Pearson's claim in the latter's *National Life from the Standpoint of Science* (1905), that warfare was a way of advancing biological evolution, arguing rather that there was "no warrant . . . coming from the standpoint of science" for such claims. Pearson, he scornfully stated, "should tell us more clearly what he means by 'human progress' before he asks us to accept it as the end which justifies human warfare." Sharply differentiating himself from Pearson and eugenics, Lankester proclaimed: "I, for one, do not despair of humanity."[107]

Lankester was particularly incensed when such eugenicist ideas penetrated the general socialist movement. On January 24, 1908, leading social democrat Henry Hyndman (who claimed to be a follower of Marx, but whom Marx disdained) wrote an article for the *Times* titled "The Socialist Victory" in which he referred, as part of his argument for social democracy, to "the physical degeneration of large masses of our population." Lankester had an antipathy for Hyndman, and had no doubt identified to some extent with his friends Morris and Eleanor Marx in the development of the Socialist League, when they broke with Hyndman's Social Democratic Federation. On January 27, he wrote a pointed letter to the *Times,* run under the title "Physical Degeneration and Socialism," asking what Hyndman meant by "physical degeneration," and whether he was contending that there was a definite deterioration of the human "stock" in the manner of Galton. Two days later, Hyndman replied, indicating that "slum dwellers beget slum dwellers, and physical degeneration, under similar conditions, hands on physical degeneration together with accompanying mental and moral enfeeblement to the next generation in a still worse form." Diseases like syphilis and tuberculosis had the effect, he suggested, of deteriorating the human racial "stock" for at least "one generation" and perhaps more. Lankester rebutted that Hyndman was confusing "injurious conditions" that had a negative effect on the population with the deterioration of the physical "stock" of humanity across generations, something for which there was no evidence and that contradicted known scientific knowledge. Lankester ended by saying that there were "many so-called 'Socialists' in these days [referring to figures like Hyndman and Pearson], but that socialism which is to prevail must be founded on a widespread and scientific knowledge of the facts as to human population and the physical laws of heredity, mixture and survival in human societies, and not upon erroneous assumptions and wild rhetoric."[108]

Indeed, turning the arguments of the eugenicists upside down on Darwinian selectionist grounds, Lankester suggested in other writings that, if the physical degeneration of humanity could be said to apply at all to civilized humanity, it was a product of the cessation of natural selection, and thus would apply mainly to the parasitic ruling classes in which the struggle for existence no longer applied, and not to the working class or the poor. As he put it, such physical degeneration was "more probable in the higher propertied classes than in the bare-footed toilers, whose ranks are thinned by starvation and early death."[109]

In contrast to Lankester, his good friend Donkin (the former Marx family doctor and a member of the Men and Women's Club in the mid-1880s) was to join the British Eugenics Society, which included many of the major thinkers of the time. As a physician interested in mental disturbances, he later became Commissioner of Prisons. Nevertheless, Donkin was far from being a reactionary in the context of his times, and publicly argued in the *Times* against Pearson (and others such as Ellis), who insisted that criminality was hereditary.[110] In his 1910 Harveian Oration *On Inheritance of Mental Characters*, he took a strong Darwinian view, rejecting entirely the Lamarckian inheritance of acquired characteristics, and adamantly opposing what he called "the so-called 'criminology'" school of Cesare Limbroso, whose adherents argued for the inheritance of criminal traits. (An illustration from Lombroso's *Criminal Man* was sharply criticized in Gould's *The Mismeasure of Man*.) Donkin also objected to the views of Galton and Pearson, with their "positive eugenics," or selective breeding. For Donkin, "the most important advance in psychology in recent years" had been made by Lankester in his argument that "the mind of the human *adult* is mainly a social product, and can be understood only in relation to the special environment in which it develops." Human beings, Lankester adamantly claimed, did not transmit specific, acquired human mental characteristics by heredity but rather passed on a capacity that he termed "educability," which was affected by their natural and social environments. On this basis, Donkin concluded that the mind of the adult was much more *made* than it was *born*.[111]

Donkin was even more scathing that same year (1910) with respect to Winston Churchill's legislative plan for segregation, confinement, and sterilization of the feebleminded for the good of the British "race." Speaking then in his role as chief medical adviser of prisons, he called Churchill's plan "the outcome of an arrogation of scientific knowledge by those who have no claim to it. . . . It is a monument of ignorance and hopeless medical confusion."[112]

No doubt Lankester, given his utter contempt for "positive" eugenics, would have been, if anything, more harshly critical of Churchill. At all times, Lankester, with the exception of his 1908 article on "Votes for Women," criticized biologically determinist notions of later human evolution, emphasizing educability and the social factor. It was failure to understand the role of educability, he contended, that led some mistakenly to adopt Lamarckian notions of the ability of human beings (and other organisms) to pass on acquired traits, using such erroneous views as the basis for claiming that the mass of the human population was physically degenerating. Changes in social organization by means of science and not eugenics constituted the only feasible path to diminishing and putting "an end to human suffering."[113]

As Lester writes of Lankester's struggle against eugenics, which he carried over into the *Daily Telegraph*:

> He took the Eugenics movements to task. . . . What do we mean by "racial quality" and "improvement"? he asked. The supporters of Eugenics had not defined their terms, while the biometrical studies of Pearson and others confused inborn characters with those due to education. They had based conclusions as to the existence of a law of hereditary transmission on statistics concerning the frequency of characters reproduced by imitation and education. If the cessation of selection led to racial degeneration, then it was in the richer sections of the community where the effects would be most obvious, not in the "half-starved, struggling poor."[114]

The real problem was the threat of *social degeneration* under the present social system and characterizing all class societies.[115] As Lankester wrote in this vein in his preparatory notes for his 1905 "Nature and Man" talk:

> The capitalist wants cheap labour, and he would rather see the English people poor and ready to do his work for him, than better off.
>
> The country is bloodsucked and absolutely ruled; first by the Church, then by the King, then by the "governing class," and now by this new terror the capitalist.

> . . . Asses like the King and his ministers, whether Conservative or Liberal, must hate science, because it inevitably will abolish them and their likes.[116]

BIONOMICS/ECOLOGY

E. Ray Lankester was a zoologist, evolutionary biologist, and pioneer in ecology. At University College, and subsequently at Oxford University, he set up departments focusing on Darwinian selectionism. He followed Huxley in specializing in the comparative morphology of invertebrates. His signal contribution as a comparative morphologist was to demonstrate, in Gould's words, that "the ecologically diverse spiders, scorpions, and horseshoe crabs form a coherent evolutionary group, now called Chelicerata, within the anthropod phylum." This discovery had been presented in his article "Limulus an Arachnid," in the *Journal of Microscopical Science* in 1881. In confirming that Limulus, the horseshoe crab, despite all appearances, was not a crustacean, but more closely related to arachnids, such spiders and scorpions, Lankester had a big effect on the understanding of the origin, evolution, and the interrelationships among various animal types. But Lankester was an exceptionally broad scientist, whose work "ranged widely from protozoans to mammals" and dealt with such varied issues as degeneration, comparative longevity, and ecological relationships. His work on comparative longevity influenced Darwin in writing *The Descent of Man*. Lankester was in Leipzig when the book came out in 1871 and Darwin sent him a copy.[117]

In contrast to his mentor Huxley, whose comparative morphology was directed at dead material, leading some critics subsequently to refer to him as a "necrologist," Lankester insisted that to the extent possible animals be studied in their living environments among other species.[118] The term *ecology* or "œcology" first appeared in English in 1876 in the Lankester-supervised and revised translation of Haeckel's *History of Creation*.[119] Haeckel referred in this work to

> *the* œcology of organisms, the knowledge of the sum of the *relations of organisms to the surrounding outer world*, to organic and inorganic conditions of existence; the so-called *"economy of nature,"* the correlations between all organisms living together in one and the same locality, their adaptation to their surroundings, their modification in the struggle for existence, especially the circumstances of parasitism, etc. It is just these phenomena in "the economy of nature" which the unscientific, on a superficial consideration, are wont to regard as the wise arrangements of a Creator acting for a definite purpose, but which on a more attentive examination show themselves to be the necessary result of mechanical causes.[120]

Lankester did not follow Haeckel in the use of the term "œcology," however. Instead, he introduced, in his landmark 1888 article on "Zoology" for the ninth edition of the *Encyclopedia Britannica*, his own term: "bionomics," which is still seen as synonymous with "ecology" as a field of study. The notion of bionomics was key to the development of Lankester's wide-ranging ecological analysis, and it was to be influential in British science up until the first decade of the twentieth century.[121]

In June 1883, Lankester delivered a talk on science and fisheries at the International Fisheries Exhibition in South Kensington. The exhibition was designed to look at both the commercial and scientific aspects of the fishing industry. Huxley, who had years of experience as a scientific adviser helping to maintain the herring trawling on the coast of Scotland and in evaluating salmon fisheries, opened the exhibition with an inaugural address.[122] But he made the mistake of claiming that

> it may be affirmed with confidence that, in relation to our present modes of fishing, a number of the most important sea fisheries, such as the cod fishery, the herring fishery, and the mackerel fishery, are inexhaustible. And I base this conviction on two grounds, first, that the multitude of these fishes is so inconceivably great that the number we catch is relatively insignificant; and, secondly, that the magnitude of the destructive agencies at work upon them is so prodigious, that the destruction effected by the fisherman cannot sensibly increase the death rate.[123]

Despite Huxley's careful qualification with respect to "our present modes of fishing," the shortsightedness of his view was apparent, and this was to go down afterward as one of the great blunders with regard to ocean conservation. In contrast, Lankester's approach, no doubt influenced in part by his father's aquarium studies, was altogether different. He emphasized in great detail the ecological complexity of fisheries and "interaction of the various organisms." Indeed, so complex were the relationships that it required detailed knowledge of "the habits and life-histories of the animals concerned," including their interactions with all other related species. In Lankester's assessment, fisheries, due to the lack of scientific knowledge of environmental relationships, were far more destructive to species and entire life systems than was usually supposed. He demonstrated that all the stages of the development of fish were crucial to the other animals and plants in the marine environment; fish eggs were food for some small animals, which were the part of the food chain of larger animals. The fishing industry, in removing so many fish, also removed many young fish, not only affecting fish populations, but also other marine animal populations, that were interdependent with them. The complexity of the marine environmental systems made them vulnerable.

Following in his father's footsteps, Lankester argued that what was needed was the establishment on the seacoast of England a major marine laboratory including aquariums for research in the environmental interactions of aquatic species. Three months later, in his presidential lecture on "Biology and the State" to the Biology Section of the British Association for the Advancement of Science in Southport, he carried the argument forward, calling again for the establishment of a national aquarium funded by the state. This led to the establishment of the Marine Biological Association in 1884, and the granting of funds from Parliament for the establishment of a marine biological laboratory in Plymouth that same year. The new marine laboratory came into operation in 1888. Huxley was the first president of the Marine Biological Association, with Lankester taking the position of honorary secretary. Huxley was to play a relatively minor role, however, and Lankester became in effect the acting president. Lankester is thus considered to be the "founding father" of the Marine Biological Association. He supervised the building of the Marine Biological Laboratory on Citadel Hill in Plymouth. Huxley stepped down as president in 1890 and was replaced by Lankester, who remained president until his death in 1929. Today, the Marine Biological Association has over 1,400 members worldwide. It has facilitated the research of twelve Nobel Prize winners and over 170 Fellows of the Royal Society. It is particularly famous worldwide for work on the ecology of plankton.

Writing in *Nature* in 1885, Lankester was severely critical of British industry for its failures in marine conservation: "Our fishery industries are still barbaric; we recklessly seize the produce of the seas, regardless of the consequences of the method, the time, or the extent of our depredations. . . . With the increase of population, and the introduction of steam fishing boats and more effective instruments of capture, there is reason to believe that some at least of our coast fisheries are being destroyed, and that others may follow in the same direction."[124]

Lankester argued that the virtue of botanical gardens, such as Kew Gardens, was that it gave botanists an opportunity to view living things in their total environment, within a kind of laboratory setting, allowing for more complex forms of biological research. Zoological gardens, however, were much harder to establish and maintain and had not been an important part of zoological research since animals are difficult to keep under observation. The establishment of marine biological laboratories and aquariums offered chances for the "bionomist" to study the interrelationship of species and their environment in a more holistic context.[125] In the memoranda and letters he wrote as honorary secretary and then president of the Marine Biological Association, he insisted that it could only serve its function by focusing on the total evolutionary environment of species, by prioritizing "a complete knowledge of the Fauna and Flora and of the exact conditions under which the various species therein included exist."[126]

It was with these considerations partly in mind that Lankester introduced the concept of bionomics. The *Oxford English Dictionary* defines "bionomics" in its current usage somewhat restrictively as "the ecology of a particular species or organism." However, its original meaning, as noted, was equivalent to that of ecology itself, that is, "the branch of biology that deals with the relationships between living organisms and their environment. Also: the relationships themselves, esp. those *of* a specified organism." In a long review essay of Alfred Wallace's *Darwinism* in 1889, Lankester saw bionomics as fulfilling the need that Wallace had raised in his book for "the study of 'the external and vital relations of species to species in a state of nature,' or in one word 'bionomics.'" Lankester noted in his review that the greatest deficiency in biology was that "there are not such facilities for the study of bionomics as are provided in our laboratories for the study of histology, embryology, morphography, and the physics and chemistry of living bodies."[127]

Lankester saw bionomics as a practical and theoretical discipline emerging, on the one hand, out of "thrematology" (meaning "the thing bred"), related to the lore, with respect to heredity and variation, "of the farmer, gardener, sportsman, and field naturalist," and, on the other hand, the science of organic adaptations or evolution (exemplified by Wallace and Darwin). Darwin had opened *The Origin of Species* with a discussion of breeding and had gone on to connect this to the larger conditions of natural evolution. It was Darwin, Lankester contended, who "founded the science of bionomics" in the full sense, which hardly existed prior to him, except in the case of Buffon in the eighteenth century. For Lankester, Buffon represented the bionomic or ecological point of view in that he "deliberately opposed himself to the mere exposition of structural resemblances and differences of animals, and, disregarding classification, devoted his treatise on natural history to a consideration of the habits of animals and their adaptations to their surroundings, whilst a special volume was devoted by him to the subject of reproduction."[128]

In terms of Darwin's (and Wallace's) contemporaries and followers in the period after the publication of *The Origin of Species*, Lankester singled out Fritz Müller, called by Darwin "the prince of observers," as a leading representative of bionomics. Müller had been a medical student in Germany, a member of a radical reading and discussion group in Greifswald in Prussia known as the "Circlet," in which they studied and debated the writings of left Hegelians Ludwig Feuerbach, David Strauss, Max Stirner, and Karl Marx. Müller renounced the Church and became a "radical rationalist." In the 1848 Revolution in Germany, Müller was secretary of the People's Union, consisting mostly of students and workers. In 1852, following the defeat of the revolution, he emigrated with his wife to the German settlement in Blumenau and Santa Catarina in Brazil. There he became a world-famous naturalist, a correspondent of Darwin's, and one of Darwin's chief defenders in his remarkable work *Facts and Arguments for Darwin* (1864; the 1869 English translation was sponsored by Darwin). He later attributed his development into a Darwinian thinker to the radical debates in the left Hegelian circle of his student days, which generated a materialist perspective (and no doubt an awareness of dialectics). In the 1860s, he was to name a genus of orchids that he discovered in Brazil after Feuerbach.

In a detailed treatment of bionomics, the Scottish naturalist Thomson, who had co-authored *The Evolution of Sex* with Geddes, declared that Müller "was preeminently an observer of the web of life, of the interrelations of living creatures," encompassing "the mutual adaptations of plants and animals." According to Thomson, Müller adhered to the principle that "to abstract the plant or animal from the particular *milieu* in which it lives is like trying to understand man apart from society."[129]

Others built on this same legacy. Geddes, as Thomson recognized, was one of the most prominent proponents of Lankester's concept of bionomics. In his 1893 *Chapters in Modern Botany*, Geddes argued that bionomics constituted "the study of natural history in its widest aspects." It meant recognizing within the botanical sphere that "each plant, in fact, like man himself, has many relations to the world around, and the botanist thus becomes a biographer of each; yet though materials abound, the full life-history even of the commonest plants has still to be written." It was this bionomic or ecological sense of things, Geddes explained, that caused Darwin to write *The Various Contrivances by which Orchids Are Fertilised by Insects* (1877). As Mark Largent indicated in his 1999 article "Bionomics": "Geddes wrote *Chapters in Modern Botany* to encourage readers to see nature scene by scene, as it appeared to Darwin's eyes."[130]

This bionomic way of thinking, Thomson explained, had its roots not just in Darwin but was in some ways preceded in chemistry and physiology by the great work of Justus Liebig in 1840 in his *Organic Chemistry in Application to Agriculture and Physiology* (1840; seventh edition, 1862). It was Liebig's work, Thomson noted, that marked "the first concrete realization of the 'circulation of matter'" and the basis for the analysis of "nutritive chains"—to be discovered, for example, in the way in which freshwater fish in a pond depend upon the supply of small crustaceans in the pond, and these in turn "on the bacteria which cause the putrefaction of the dead organic matter," so that "there is circulation of matter from one level of life to another." The environmental changes had to be seen in relation to evolutionary changes in the "metabolism of the organism."[131]

Indeed, what distinguished the work of Darwin, Lankester, Müller, Geddes, and other leading representatives of bionomics from that of the general run of biologists, according to Thomson, was the extent to which they dialectically encompassed both "the organism's action upon its environment" (illustrated by Darwin's 1881 work on earthworms) and "the action of the environment upon organisms." Following Liebig, they stressed the relation between inorganic and organic nature. It was this that constituted the promise of the new science of the "infinite web of life"—or bionomics. "So far as we know," Thomson wrote, "the only other expressive term [for these relations other than bionomics] is that of Œcology, which Haeckel proposed in 1869," defining it as "'the relations of the animal to its organic as well as to its inorganic environment, particularly its friendly or hostile relations to those animals or plants with which it comes into direct contact . . . those complicated mutual relations which Darwin designates as conditions of the struggle of existence.'"[132]

Although Lankester's bionomics and Haeckel's ecology were concerned with the same set of problems in describing the evolution of the web of life, it was the latter term that was to triumph in the early twentieth century. Thus, in his survey of "The Rise and Progress of Ecology" for *Science* in 1903, V. M. Spalding was to write: "The word ecology has come to stay. Personally, I should have preferred bionomics, which has the advantage of indicating in its composition that living things are its subject-matter. This latter term is at all events an acceptable synonym, and as such may properly be used as occasion requires. The question of a name, therefore, is settled and may be dismissed."[133] Nevertheless, though the term ecology largely supplanted bionomics by the early twentieth century, it remains true, as Bowler wrote in his *Science for All*, that Lankester, together with others in his generation of academic biologists, "combined technical evolutionary morphology with an interest in wild nature through topics such as animal behavior and what came to be known as ecology."[134]

NATURE'S REVENGE

More than any other thinker of his time, Lankester emphasized in his writings that humanity was walking an ecological knife's edge. This is most obvious in his 1911 book *The Kingdom of Man*, consisting of his Romanes lecture at Oxford in 1905 titled "Nature's Insurgent Son," his 1906 presidential address to the British Association of the Advancement of Science, and his article "Nature's Revenges: The Sleeping Sickness," reprinted from the *Quarterly Review*—all of which present a kind of radical Baconian view toward nature.

Lankester's lecture "Nature and Man," later better known in its printed version as "Nature's Insurgent Son," was delivered in the Sheldonian Theatre in Oxford to a very distinguished and fashionable gathering. It started off by emphasizing that human beings, while priding themselves on their increasing dominance over nature, were themselves a part of nature. Nature was to be viewed as the entire cosmos of which humanity is nothing more than an "insurgent son." Evoking his general theme, he wrote: "If we may, for the purpose of analysis . . . extract Man from the rest of Nature of which he is truly a product and part, then we may say that Man is Nature's rebel."[135]

In attempting to exert more and more control over nature in the pursuit of human ends, humanity as nature's rebel does not free itself of nature, but, in the process of changing it, creates ever more colossal ecological contradictions threatening humanity's own survival. As Lankester put it: "Man whilst emancipating himself from the destructive methods of natural selection, has accumulated a new series of dangers and difficulties with which he must incessantly contend." The biggest indication was the spread of disease. "In the extra-human system of Nature," he contended, "there is no disease and there is no conjunction of incompatible forms of life, such as Man has brought about on the surface of the globe. . . . It seems to be a legitimate view that every disease to which animals (and probably plants also) are liable, excepting as a transient and very exceptional occurrence, is due to Man's interference." For Lankester, this had to do in part with the growth of human population, but even more important to social organization in a system dominated by "markets" and "cosmopolitan dealers in finance" with all the irrational consequences that ensued, including the opposition to the genuine progress of science.[136]

Lankester argued in "Nature's Revenges" that "before the arrival of man—the would-be controller, the disturber of Nature—the adjustment of living things to their surrounding conditions and to one another has a certain appearance of perfection. . . . Anything like the epidemic diseases of parasitic origin with which civilized man is unhappily familiar seems to be due either to his own restless and ignorant activity, or, in his absence, to great and probably somewhat sudden geological changes—changes of the connexions, and therefore communications, of great land areas." He provided a wealth of examples, related to contacts between human beings and species from various continents, including the intermingling of species that this generated. All this, he explained, was related to the spread of epidemic diseases, both with respect to humanity and other species, in which the disease vectors were able to exploit various vulnerabilities resulting from previous lack of contact.

What especially worried Lankester was the growth of mass epidemics, such as trypanosomiasis, the sleeping sickness that killed hundreds of thousands in Uganda and along the lower Congo River between 1901 and 1906. Although scientific research on the spread of epidemics had rapidly progressed (Lankester was a friend of Louis Pasteur and a frequent visitor at the Pasteur Institute), epidemics seemed to be spreading even faster, particularly in Africa. "We are justified," he wrote,

> in believing that until man introduced his artificially selected and transported breeds of cattle and horses into Africa there was no nagana disease. The *Trypanosoma brucei* lived in the blood of the big game in perfect harmony with the host. So, too, it is probable that the sleeping-sickness parasite flourished innocently in a state of adjustment due to tolerance on the part of aboriginal men and animals of West Africa. It was not until the Arab slave raiders, European explorers, and India-rubber thieves stirred up the quiet populations of Central Africa, and mixed by their violence the susceptible with the tolerant races, that the sleeping-sickness parasite became a deadly scourge.[137]

This was a "disharmony" in nature (and in the relation between human beings and external nature) that was blindly "accumulated" by society in the very process of its commercial accumulation, generating what Lankester called "nature's revenges." Through "his greedy efforts to produce large quantities of animals and plants . . . man has accumulated unnatural swarms of one species in field and ranch and unnatural crowds of his own kind in towns and fortresses." Monocultures and urban congestion associated with capitalist development created grounds for the spread of epidemics.

Humanity, in breaking with original natural selection, had created a situation in which human evolution proceeded mainly through the evolution of human society rather than biological species. There was therefore no option of a return to nature. Nor was there any possibility of proceeding on the basis of the blind, capitalistic exploitation of nature. This simply invited ecological catastrophe. "The world, the earth's surface," he wrote, "is practically full, that is to say, fully occupied."[138] Society is more and more undermining preexisting natural conditions. Under these circumstances, humanity

> must either go on and acquire firmer control of the conditions or perish miserably by the vengeance certain to fall on the half-hearted meddler in great affairs. We may indeed compare civilized man to a successful rebel against Nature who by every step forward renders himself liable to greater and greater penalties, and so cannot afford to pause or fail in one single step. Or again we may think of him as the heir to a vast and magnificent kingdom who has been finally educated so as to fit him to take possession of his property, and is at length left alone to do his best. . . . No retreat is possible—his only hope is to control, as he knows he can, these dangers and disasters.[139]

The penalty for society failing to create a more sustainable relation to nature, "controlling" it, as Francis Bacon said, by learning to follow nature's laws, would be to perish in the struggle. Hence, the only recourse lay in the promotion of social and environmental relations in accordance with knowledge and science. Indeed, science, not commodity relations, would be the essence of civilization. In order to achieve this, as Lankester emphasized in his presidential address to the British Association, science would have to have state support and the state would need to be responsive to science. There was a distinct threat that if present social-environmental relations persisted, the result would be the emergence (over centuries) of "a desperate humanity, brutalized by over-crowding, and the struggle for food." To prevent this, it was necessary that science and education—the latter no longer to be devoted at the higher levels primarily to the ancient classics—should be allowed to do their job and usher in a true "Kingdom of Man" (*Regnum Hominis*).[140] "Science," he wrote in his notes for his Romanes lecture, "is not the golden key by which treasure and luxury are opened to capitalists, and ease and plenty rendered widespread among the masses. . . . Science is the increase of understanding, the essential condition for rational philosophy and the conduct of the community."[141] He strongly believed that "nature's revenges" resulted from the failure of society, organized around commercial interests, to follow the path of education and reason, as laid out in the great public health triumphs of the past, in which he listed John Simon first, ahead of Edwin Chadwick.[142]

The peculiar evolutionary heritage of human beings as the result of increased brain size was greater plasticity of behavior. Inherited instincts were less important than what Lankester called "educability" or "the power of being educated," and evolution was at this stage in human development more social than biological. Human beings were distinguished by their extra-corporeal and economic activity. "Man," Lankester wrote, "is the one highly 'educable' animal." Humanity, then, could choose to develop socially in accordance with knowledge and science rather than as the result of any fundamental biological determinism. As a result, a more sustainable human relation to nature was possible. Humanity, he explained many years later, commenting on his Romanes lecture, may be regarded not so much as "nature's rebel" as "nature's pupil."[143]

Lankester's *Kingdom of Man* was enormously influential among socialists. In *The Profits of Religion: An Economic Interpretation* (1918), Upton Sinclair referred extensively to Lankester's analysis, using it to argue that science pointed to the need for human self-emancipation and self-determination, "the regime of man the creator."[144]

THE EFFACEMENT OF NATURE BY MAN

Lankester's *Kingdom of* Man, though raising radical ecological views, did so primarily in a form that was tempered by a Baconian, anthropocentric framework, no doubt in an effort to exercise influence as a leading representative of British science. Added to this was that the public face Lankester presented at the time he prepared the manuscripts that made up *The Kingdom of Man* was necessarily constrained by his position as director of the Natural History Museum. Not only did he leave his critical notes on capitalism out of his Romanes lecture on "Nature's Insurgent Son," but he also held back on some of his more critical views on the human relation to external nature. However, in 1907 he was dismissed as director of the Natural History Museum—over the objections of many of his scientific colleagues—apparently due to his unrestrained attacks on the museum establishment, including the governors of the museum, and his continual (if muffled) espousal of incendiary views. Seeking a new source of income, Lankester immediately took up the offer to write a regular, weekly nature column for the *Daily Telegraph*, which was to result in nearly four hundred articles for the *Telegraph* alone between 1907 and 1914 (and for a few months in 1919), as well as other articles in *Field*, *Country Life*, and the *Illustrated London News*. Selections of Lankester's essays were collected in a whole series of popular science books. In these essays, he not infrequently espoused controversial views. It is here that he emerged as possibly the strongest critic of the ecological depredations of humanity in the opening decades of the twentieth century.

Several years before he began writing these popular essays, Lankester had delivered the Royal Institution Christmas Lectures of 1902–1904 on the subject of "Extinct Animals." This was turned into an illustrated book in 1905 aimed at young people, with lantern slides reprographically converted into half-tone or "process blocks." *Extinct Animals* was extremely popular and became the basis for Arthur Conan Doyle's 1912 book *Lost World*, in which Lankester was referred to by name along with the title of his book, with the irascible "Professor Challenger" modeled after Lankester himself.[145] In this way, Lankester brought to public attention the problem of extinction, not simply as a phenomenon of the remote past, but also as an increasingly frequent occurrence in the present resulting from the actions of human beings. "It is obvious, in many cases," he wrote, "that another animal, Man, interferes. He either kills and eats animals or takes their food from them, or occupies their ground, or cuts down the forests in which they live, and so on."[146]

"It is only too true," Lankester wrote in *Nature* in 1914, "that man is slowly but surely destroying the beautiful wild animals and plants of the world, and is substituting for them queer domesticated races which suit his convenience and his greed, or else is blasting whole territories with the dirt and deadly refuse of his industries, and converting well-watered forest lands into lifeless deserts by the ravages of his axe."[147]

Lankester's position on ecological depredations introduced by humanity was put most eloquently in his powerful article "The Effacement of Nature by Man." "Very few people," he observed, "have any idea of the extent to which man . . . has actively modified the face of Nature, the vast herds of animals he has destroyed, the forests he has burnt up, the deserts he has produced, and the rivers he has polluted." It was true, he pointed out, that nature (independent of humanity) generated extinctions in its process of "slow, irresistible changes," including such forces as climate change and geological shifts. But above these forces of extinction, especially in the modern world, was "a vast destruction and defacement of the living world by . . . both savage and civilized man which is little short of appalling." Today, the "reckless greed and the mere-insect like increase of humanity" was endangering life throughout the earth. In North America the bison had been nearly exterminated; while Europe had long since decimated its larger animals. "Progressive money-making man" through mining and manufacturing had destroyed trout streams. At its foulest, "the Thames mud was blood-red (really 'blood-red,' since the colour was due to the same blood-crystals which colour our own blood) with the swarms of a delicate little worms like the earth-worm, which has an exceptional power of living in foul water and nourishing itself upon putrid mud."[148]

Like Darwin (and like Engels), Lankester pointed to the decimation of the ecology of St. Helena through the clearing of woods and the introduction of invasive species.[149] Similar, carefully documented examples of ecological destruction in islands could be seen in Christmas Island, two hundred miles South of Java, where Chinese laborers were imported to dig up 15 million tons of phosphate for a profit of a guinea a ton in order to fertilize the despoiled soil of Europe. In New Zealand too the introduction of invasive species had destroyed the greater part of the native species.

Lankester depicted the desertification resulting from the cutting and burning of forests—"wherever man has been sufficiently civilised and enterprising to commit" this "folly"—as a leading example of ecological depredation. It was through the elimination of forests, he observed, that

> man has done the most harm to himself and the other living occupants of many regions of the earth's surface. . . . Forests have an immense effect on climate, causing humidity of both the air and the soil, and give rise to moderate and persistent instead of torrential streams. . . . Sand deserts are not, as used to be supposed, sea-bottoms from which the water has retreated, but areas of destruction of vegetation—often (though not always), both in Central Asia and North Africa (Egypt, etc.), started by the deliberate destruction of forest by man, who has either by artificial drainage starved the forest, or by the simple use of the axe and fire cleared it away.[150]

Lankester here was echoing similar observations made by the German botanist Matthias Schleiden (1804–1881) and the German agronomist Carl Nikolas Fraas (1810–1875), who had explored these issues in depth. Marx too, who was familiar with the work of Schleiden and Fraas, had noted that civilization "leaves deserts behind it," pointing to ancient Mesopotamia and Persia, but also suggesting the connection to the modern period.[151]

In these ecological writings, Lankester referred bitterly to the "pecuniary profits to the capitalists" that governed all such processes of nature's destruction and modification. The corporations or "enterprises of combined capital" that dominated modern economic life were "mere impersonal mechanisms 'driven by the laws of supply and demand.'"[152] One could point to the mass killing and in some case extinction of whales, sea turtles, bison, and other species. In Norway, he wrote, they had built factories around the killing and processing of whales. Wherever possible he recorded the profits that were made through such "revolting butchery . . . carried on solely for the satisfaction of human greed." The Norwegian shot harpoon, "the most deadly and extraordinary weapon ever devised by man for the pursuit of helpless animals," was, he explained, "a commercial, not a scientific discovery!"[153]

Given that the full force of bourgeois civilization was behind the rapid degradation of the environment, there were only two possibilities that offered hope of arresting this deadly process: an "overwhelming catastrophe" of environmental origins, such as a new glacial age or a force of "cosmic origin," that would check human progress, or else "an unforeseen awakening of the human race to the inevitable results of its present recklessness" due to the closing circle of environmental pressures. Still, "whatever may be the ultimate fate of the life of the earth under man's operations," Lankester argued, "we should at this moment endeavour to delay, as far as possible, the hateful consummation looming ahead of us."[154]

Lankester was a strong advocate of nature reserves to protect the fast disappearing "wilderness," but understood their limitations in face of the relentless expansion of commercialism and colonialism. Like Morris, with whom Lankester was on friendly terms, he tried to defend Epping Forest outside of London. He backed the creation of reserves in what remained of Britain's "ancient nature" and commended the creation of Yellowstone in the United States. Yet there were, he insisted, no "absolute nature reserves" in the face of encroaching civilization. This was evident by the mere fact that such reserves themselves needed to be artificially preserved, controlled in terms of the spread of disease, protected from poachers, etc. "In reality a true 'nature-reserve' is not compatible," he wrote, "with the occupation of the land, within some hundreds of miles of it, by civilized, or even semi-civilized, man." Nothing but isolation from society by oceans or high mountain ranges would make that possible. Lankester had been appointed to an international committee on the creation of reserves to protect large game animals in Africa. Hitherto, he argued, malaria had kept Europeans largely out of the African interior. But with the increasing means of fighting malaria, the penetration of Africa was occurring under European colonialism, dooming African wildlife. "If Africa," he indicated, "is to be the seat of a modern human population and supply food to other parts of the world, the whole 'balance of Nature' there must be upset and the big wild animals destroyed. There is no alternative. The practical question is, 'How far is it possible to mitigate this process?' Can a great African 'reserve' of 100,000 square miles be established in a position so isolated that it shall not be a source of disease and danger to the herdsmen and agriculturalists of adjacent territory?"[155]

This deep ecological understanding extended to other areas as well. Lankester wrote of the vast pollution generated by coal, and that oil supplies would peak sooner. He discussed human brutality toward animals (writing a fanciful piece on bullfighting from the standpoint of the bull, who was gifted with intelligence and human speech). He influenced Darwin through his work on earthworms.[156]

Lankester's dialectical and ecological view of both humanity and the earth system was revealed in his general conception of the evolution of life. In the 1870s, in "The Part Played by Labour in the Transition from Ape to Man" (a work not published until the early twentieth century), Engels had put forward the materialist argument that erect posture had allowed the early hominins to develop the hand for tool-making, which led, along with language, to the development of the human brain. Hence, contrary to the dominant idealist conceptions of the time, the brain had not evolved first, but developed only in the context of labor, that is, human efforts to transform their environment, marked by tool-making. Lankester developed a similar argument in his *Daily Telegraph* articles, emphasizing, however, not so much the role of the hand in tool-making as its role in "delicate exploring operations" in the coevolution of human beings with their environment.[157]

THE RADICAL CRITIQUE OF PROGRESS

Ecology only arises as a social concern once the naive conception of progress that has generally characterized bourgeois society is dispensed with. Although socialists have sometimes adopted many of the same teleological notions of progress, their critique of the existing society, and awareness of its contradictions, have again and again—as exemplified by thinkers such as Marx, Morris, and Rosa Luxemburg—led them to an awareness of the threats of social regression and ecological destruction.

As shown in Lankester's early pioneering study on *Degeneration*—which he doubtless discussed with Marx, and in which the latter was interested—he had from the beginning a complex, critical view of the relation of evolution to human "progress," distinguishing him from most scientists in his time. As he was to suggest in his later writings, history offered no simple, unilinear story of unending progress; nor could evolution be viewed in teleological terms. If one were to look back at the evolution of human ancestral (hominin) species, one would, of course, see the gradual elaboration of more complex forms—until the point at which modern humans appeared. This could be seen as a kind of "progress" in natural evolution from a human-centered standpoint. Yet the path was the result of chance and not the fulfillment of final ends. The story of evolutionary descent could not without distortion be turned into a simple story of the steady ascent of humanity.

Moreover, once modern humans arose with a fully developed brain, the dialectic of human evolution assumed a different form. It was no longer dependent principally on *natural* evolution of the human corporeal structure, but rather on *social* evolution, rooted in the transmission through the human brain of the quality of educability and the cumulative products of culture. It therefore rested principally on development of science and knowledge and the accompanying changes in social organization. Aside from the Epicureans, Lankester noted, most ancient philosophers had seen human civilization as cyclical, associated with the rise and fall of civilizations. A consistent materialism, however, pointed to the *possibility* of continuing social advance, precisely because humanity now made its own history, though under biological and social conditions inherited from the past. What distinguished today's human beings, he emphasized again and again, was above all their higher educability.[158]

Given his overall ecological and socialist view, it is not surprising that Lankester remained throughout his life a strong advocate of social and (what we would now call) environmental justice (including the conservation of species), and an opponent of capitalism. He lost his position as director of the Natural History Museum due to his unwillingness to kowtow to moneyed interests. Although it is doubtful that he was ever associated directly with any socialist party, his socialist orientation (albeit of a more Fabian than Marxian variety) was clear. Hyndman spoke of Lankester's strong socialist sympathies. He "knew and admired William Morris" and was on good terms with the socialist parliamentarian John Burns, giving a copy of *Extinct Animals* to Burns's son. He sent a copy of his *Easy Chair* book to the well-known socialist and environmental thinker Robert Blatchford, author of *Merrie England* and editor of the *Clarion* (a follower of Morris). Blatchford in turn wrote a very favorable and extended review of Lankester's book.

In his contribution to "The Making of New Knowledge" in Wells's collection *The Great State*, Lankester argued against the control of universities and sciences by the upper classes and commercial interests, objecting to the institutions of knowledge being made into handmaids "of commerce, industry, and the arts of war."[159] He followed in his father's footsteps in this respect, retaining a sympathetic view of the working class, including their intellectual powers. He considered workers to be more attuned to materialism and more immune to superstition than the English upper classes.[160] In terms of education, Lankester declared: "There is no reason to suppose that the quality of mind we look for is not as abundantly distributed among the poorer classes as the well-to-do. The State must cast its net widely so as to include the whole population without distinction of class or sex."[161]

Lankester was a strident critic not only of anti-materialist spiritualism and idealism, but of all teleological notions of progress. He emphasized the dangers of class-based social degeneration and human-generated ecological destruction. There were signs, he insisted, that human civilization was imperiling itself in relation to its environment.[162] At all times he questioned what he had called in *Degeneration* "the tacit assumption of universal progress."[163]

None of this, however, kept him from insisting on the possibility of general social advance through the unity of science and socialism (in the broad generic sense). Authentic historical progress was not a natural occurrence arising from bourgeois society as in the Whig view of history. Nor was it to be created artificially by means of eugenics. Instead, to the extent that it had any meaning at all, it was a result not of biological factors but of intellectual advance and of changing social relations—a product of the collective *social development* of human beings. What intervened decisively, forever separating the history of humanity from mere biological destiny, was the "new and strangely significant factor of oral and written tradition operative in civilized communities," and the exponential development of knowledge that this entailed.[164]

In aesthetics, Lankester was attracted to the work of Dante Gabriel Rossetti and the Pre-Raphaelites, with whom he was personally acquainted. He clearly admired their emphasis on restoring sensual expression. His views of art thus appear to have overlapped in this respect with those of figures like Heinrich Heine, Marx, Rossetti, Morris, and the Romantic-revolutionary aesthetic tradition, which rejected the then dominant notions of modernity and progress. For Lankester, there was clearly reason to resist "this new terror the capitalist," in art as well as science.[165]

Hope lay in a transformation of class relations and a shift toward a more rational society, rational not only in terms of human interactions but also interactions between human beings and the environment. "We retain in Britain," Lankester wrote in a draft of one of his "Easy Chair" articles, "in spite of all our revolutions and reforms, the structure of a conquered country ruled by the members of a privileged class."[166] This, he believed, had to change if society was to advance. He did not, however, put much hope simply in democracy itself, as long as the "masses," due to the deficiencies of the educational system, were "ignorant of the meaning and the need for making new science, new knowledge."[167]

Given his early friendships with Marx and the younger Herzen, it is not at all surprising that Lankester welcomed the revolution in Russia in 1917, though he was later to develop a negative view of Bolshevism—as it was graphically portrayed to him by his friend Wells.[168]

An organization in which Lankester was actively involved was the Rationalist Press Association, founded in 1899. Its annual gatherings and publications represented the views of Secularists, Radicals, and Socialists, bringing together such figures as Lankester, Donkin, Julian Huxley, Arthur Keith, J. B. S. Haldane, Bertrand Russell, J. A. Hobson, Geddes, H. J. Laski, and Wells. Lankester was made an Honorary Associate in 1914. For a number of years, the *Rational Press Annual* included as an epigraph at the top of each issue a statement by Lankester from May 1921: "There is no Association in this country which has done so much for intellectual progress in the past twenty years as has the R.P.A." He wrote an article titled "Is There a Revival of Superstition" for the 1922 issue of the *Annual*.[169]

In October 1925, Lankester indicated in a letter to Wells that he was particularly impressed by a presentation by J. B. S. Haldane (then emerging as one of Britain's leading scientists and socialist thinkers), whom he considered as perhaps the most promising young Darwinian biologist of his generation, due to Haldane's thorough trouncing of Lamarckian views and his radical materialism. Lankester had just read Haldane's "The Causes of Evolution," which appeared in the *R.P.A. Annual, 1926*. He wrote to Wells that Haldane was a "well-trained biologist and mathematician," and characterized his article as "a model of clear outlook and critical method."[170]

Haldane's "The Causes of Evolution," singled out by Lankester at the end of his life, represented a remarkable explanation and defense of Darwinian natural selection as the basis of evolution. It relied heavily on the concept of "degeneration," as developed by Lankester and others, in order to counter simplistic conceptions of evolution as invariably taking the form of "progress." There Haldane wrote: "We are . . . inclined to regard progress as the rule in Evolution. Actually, it is the exception, and for every case of it there are ten of degeneration." Darwinian evolutionary thinking, according to Haldane, was able to consider an enormous variety of changes, including the numerous extinctions, as well as varying paths in the paleontological record, mutations, coevolution between hosts and parasites, and ecological complexity. For Haldane, Darwinian natural selection made it possible to understand how climate change could lead to the decline of all ecological habitats. "A small change of climate," he wrote, "will lead to the disappearance of forests over a wide area, and with them of most of the animals highly adapted to life in them, such as squirrels, woodpeckers, wood-eating beetles, and so forth." All such species were tied together in a complex ecological web. Darwin remained the key to understanding these processes, and "no facts definitely irreconcilable with Darwinism have been discovered in the sixty years and more that have elapsed since the formulation of Darwin's views."[171]

These critical perspectives on evolution and ecology were closely akin to those that Lankester had long professed. According to Gould, "Lankester never told the young communist J. B. S. Haldane, whom he befriended late in life and admired greatly, that he had known Karl Marx." Yet Haldane was strongly influenced by Lankester's example as a materialist scientist, critic, and popularizer. He was to take Lankester as his model in writing popular science articles—though in Haldane's case, for the *Daily Worker* rather than the *Daily Telegraph*.[172]

CHAPTER TWO

The Art of Labor

A crowd of more than a thousand gathered at around noon on Sunday, March 16, 1884, at Tottenham Court Road in London. Led by banners and a loud band, the procession set out on a march to Highgate Cemetery to commemorate the first anniversary of the death of Karl Marx and the end of the Paris Commune thirteen years before. Among them strode a short, sturdy, mature man with a robust bearing. He was dressed in a rather shabby dark blue suit, carried an oak walking stick in his hand, and wore a soft-crowned felt hat. A closer look revealed "quick, penetrating eyes set in a handsome face, and a fair beard, with grave and abstracted look." Like the others in the march he wore a red ribbon in his buttonhole. Numerous Londoners would have recognized in this distinctive individual the famous artist, craftsman, and poet William Morris, who had joined H. M. Hyndman's Democratic Federation (later the Social Democratic Federation), publicly avowing his support for the socialist cause, in early 1883, only months before the death of Marx.[1]

Others in the march that day included Hyndman, Marx's daughter Eleanor, and her soon-to-be partner Edward Aveling, who had been chosen to give the speech at Marx's grave. When the marchers finally reached Highgate, they were joined by two or three thousand others (some estimates of the crowd were as high as five or six thousand). They found that the authorities had closed the cemetery gates and inside five hundred policemen, six of them mounted, were drawn up barring their way. All the marchers were refused admittance, including Eleanor Marx and other women bearing flower crowns to put on Marx's grave. The procession therefore adjourned to the top of the street near the reservoir. Speeches were made and songs sung. After which the procession "marched off the grounds triumphant with policemen on each side of us like a royal procession."[2]

ARTIST AND DESIGNER

In January 1883, when he joined Hyndman's Socialist Democratic Federation, Morris, age forty-nine, was one of the most renowned artists and poets in England.

Born to affluence, he was the son of a well-to-do London broker who had grown rich, shortly before his death in 1847, from his shares in the Devonshire Great Consolidated Copper Mining Co., later known as the Devon Great Consols, which invested in copper and tin mining in the Southwest of England, primarily Devon and Cornwall. The Devon Great Consols consisted chiefly of a consolidated group of five adjacent mines in Tavistock, and was reputed in the 1850s to be the richest copper mining operation in Europe. One of the five mines, Wheal Emma, which opened in 1848, was named after Morris's mother.[3]

As a result of the Devon Great Consols, Morris entered life with considerable wealth and the freedom to choose his own way. Upon coming of age in March 1855, he received an income of £900 a year (at a time when some poor vicars lived on £40 to £50 a year).[4] Attending Exeter College-Oxford, he early on chose a career as an artist, and his success was to prove dazzling. Morris soon became associated with the aesthetic movement of the Pre-Raphaelites along with the painters Dante Gabriel Rossetti and Edward Burne-Jones. As part of the Romantic movement, the Pre-Raphaelites sought to return to earlier medieval-inspired art and mythology. Their artwork consisted of complex colors and schemes, focusing on mimesis, or the aesthetic imitation of nature.[5]

It was Rossetti and Burne-Jones who first spotted the young working-class Jane Burden at a performance of the Drury Lane Theatre Company in Oxford. Seeing her as a stunning beauty, they asked her to model for them. She was frequently to model for Rossetti, who early on painted her as *Queen Guinevere*. Later she was the model for William Morris in the easel painting *La Belle Iseult*. Morris fell in love with her and they were married in 1859. The marriage had its difficulties, and Jane Morris and Rossetti had an on-again, off-again affair, climaxing in 1870–71, but with a lasting attachment, which Morris seemed to accept, albeit with great difficulty.[6]

Yet here Morris's radical Romantic convictions can be said to have held true. The author of *The Defence of Guenevere and Other Poems,* submitted for publication in in late October 1857, less than two months after meeting Jane Burden, Morris sought in his poetry to break with Victorian sexual mores and the rigid confinement of women associated with bourgeois marriage. In the title poem of his volume, he gave the doomed Guenevere an eloquent, passionate voice, breaking the silence imposed on her by Thomas Malory and others.

> But, knowing now that they would have her speak,
> She threw her wet hair backward from her brow,
> Her hand close to her mouth, touching her cheek.[7]

Guenevere spoke of her own sensual needs. As Anna Marie Attwell writes, "Morris's rejection of Victorian sexual politics was as radical as his critique of capitalism." Confronted afterward with a continuing love affair between his wife and his closest friend, he bore it as a radical dialectic embedded within his own life, a romantic acceptance of nature unbound, not as a mere betrayal.[8]

Much of Morris's work as an artist and designer was to take place in the context of what was colloquially known as "the Firm"—originally Morris, Marshall, Faulkner and Co., and later, after Morris bought out his partners, simply as Morris and Co. The Firm was founded in 1861 by Morris and six other noted artists, including Rossetti and Burne-Jones. Morris and his associates began making useful and beautiful goods, which they designed and produced with the help of worker-artists, including stained glass, furniture, carving, metal work, printed fabrics, tapestries, carpets, and wallpaper. Among its many innovations, the Firm revived the art of weaving, regenerated high-warp tapestry, incorporating extraordinary new designs, and reintroduced the use of vegetable dyes, providing brighter colors. Morris excelled as a wallpaper designer, introducing interconnected flat images. At the end of his life, he revolutionized the art of printing fine books with his Kelmscott Press.[9] These activities were to inspire what was known as the Arts and Crafts movement.[10]

Morris was perhaps even more renowned in his time as a poet. At his death, the *Times* of London accounted him "one of our half dozen best poets, even when Tennyson and Browning were alive."[11] His work of twenty-four narrative poems, *The Earthly Paradise* (1868–70), was widely acclaimed in his day, while the earlier *The Defence of Guenevere* (1858) is a favorite of modern criticism. His *Sigurd the Volsung and the Fall of the Niblungs*, based on Icelandic sagas and rendered into a kind of Teutonic-English meant to capture a sense of the archaic, was seen as one of the greatest epic poems of the nineteenth century.[12]

RUSKIN AND THE ROMANTIC TRADITION

In all of his varied artistic and political endeavors, Morris drew inspiration from the English Romantic movement, associated with figures such as Thomas Carlyle and John Ruskin. Despising the possessive-individualism of bourgeois society, Carlyle declared: "Cash payment never was, or could except for a few years be, the union-bond of man to man. Cash never yet paid one man fully his deserts to another; nor could it, nor can it, now or henceforth to the end of the world."[13] For Carlyle, preaching in the manner of an Old Testament prophet: "All work . . . is noble." Industriousness was to be praised. But a society that reduced human relations to sordid "cash-payment," as "the sole nexus of man with man," was headed to a moral "Abyss and nameless Annihilation. . . . So scandalous a beggarly Universe deserves indeed nothing else; I cannot say I would save it from Annihilation."[14] Yet, for all the greatness of his criticism, Carlyle's perspective was, in the end, a reactionary one, negatively contrasting capitalism to the feudal obligations of an earlier hierarchical order, while rejecting any attempt to move forward in history.[15]

Although acknowledging his critical debt to Carlyle, it was through Ruskin, whom he described as "the first comer, the inventer," that Morris was able to obtain a clear conception, even prior to his acquaintance with socialist theory, of the estrangement of art and labor—and through this saw the alienation of nature.[16] As he declared in "How I Became a Socialist," "Ruskin. . . .before my days of practical Socialism, was my master towards the ideal [of art and labor]. . . . It was through him that I learned to give form to my discontent."[17]

Ruskin was a complicated, even enigmatic, figure. He described himself as "a violent Tory of the old school (Walter Scott's school, that is to say, and Homer's)," but he ventured far enough in the direction of a literary radicalism to support, at least initially, the Paris Commune.[18] Although in the main a conservative Romantic and supporter of a traditional hierarchical order, adopting a high Tory paternalism, Ruskin moved in his work from the position of art critic to social critic, approaching at times, but not entirely embracing, a genuine radicalism.[19] He provided a devastating critique of capitalism, although one that remained much closer to that of Carlyle than Marx. In "The Nature of the Gothic," part of his three-volume work *The Stones of Venice*, written in the early 1850s, he argued that medieval Gothic art, with its naturalism, spontaneity, and imperfection reflected the very different conditions of labor in late medieval times, in which workers were all craftsmen and artists. The artistic products of the period evoked "signs of the life and liberty of every workman who struck the stone, a freedom of thought, and rank in scale of being, such as no laws, no charters, no charities can secure; but which it must be the first aim of all Europe at this day to regain for her children." This was contrasted with the conditions of workers in the capitalist present where "the animation" of the "multitude is sent like fuel to feed the factory smoke, and the strength of them is given daily to be wasted." In a passage that was to have a direct influence on Morris, who discussed it excitedly with his friend Edward Burne-Jones in 1853, Ruskin wrote:

> It is verily this degradation of the operative into a machine, which, more than any other evil of the times, is leading the mass of the nations everywhere into vain, incoherent, destructive struggling for a freedom of which they cannot explain the nature themselves. . . . It is not that men are ill fed, but that they have no pleasure in the work by which they make their bread. . . . We have much studied and perfected of late the great civilized invention of the division of labor; only we give it a false name. It is not, truly speaking, the labor that is divided; but the men: Divided into mere segments of men—broken into small fragments and crumbs of life; so that all the little piece of intelligence that is left

> in a man is not enough to make a pin, or a nail, but exhausts itself in making the point of a pin, or the head of a nail.[20]

The political domination of the Middle Ages, in which "the feudal lord's lightest words were worth men's lives," was for Ruskin nothing to the slavery of the modern workforce under the capitalist present, where the worker is "to be counted off into a heap of mechanism, numbered with its wheels, and weighed with its hammer strokes."[21] In his analysis of what he saw as the genuinely free labor reflected in medieval art and the subsequent degradation of work under industrial capitalism, Ruskin developed an aesthetic theory of alienated labor. The irregular, roughly hewn character of the architecture of the late medieval era reflected the free, creative labor of the workers of that period. By the same token, the very precision of manufactured products in modern times was, he argued, an indication of the slavery of the modern worker. As E. P. Thompson explained, "Ruskin was not the first to protest against this 'degradation of the operative into a machine'; but he was the first to declare that men's 'pleasure in the work by which they make their bread' lay at the very foundations of society, and to relate this to his whole criticism of the arts."[22]

Beginning in 1857, Ruskin decided to take his criticisms to Dickens's Coketown itself.[23] He delivered lectures on "The Political Economy of Art" in Manchester, the center of industrial capitalism and home of classical-liberal political economy. Before an audience of industrialists and merchants, who no doubt reacted in shock and indignation, he questioned the moral basis of the entire system of cash nexus. In *Two Paths*, a series of five lectures delivered in London, Manchester, Bradford, and Tunbridge Wells in 1859, he provided a powerful critique of the deformation of use value under capitalism:

> You must remember always that your business as manufacturers, is to *form the market* as much as to supply it. . . . But whatever happens to you, this at least, is certain, that the whole of your life will have been spent in corrupting public taste and encouraging public extravagance. Every preference you have won by gaudiness must have been based on the purchaser's vanity; every demand you have created by novelty has fostered in the consumer a habit of discontent; and when you retire into inactive life, you may, as a subject of consolation for your declining years, reflect that precisely according to the extent of your past operations, your life has been successful in retarding the arts, tarnishing the virtues, and confusing the manners of your country.[24]

Ruskin systematically extended his criticisms of degraded art and degraded labor in capitalist society into a more systematic ethical questioning of bourgeois political economy in his book *Unto This Last* (1860), which he expected to stand "surest and longest" of all his work. Undeterred by the harsh reviews of *Unto This Last*, which castigated him for failing to understand the laws of political economy, Ruskin returned to lecture in Manchester in 1864, again sharply criticizing capitalist mores in what was to become *Sesame and Lilies*.[25]

Ruskin's Manchester lectures on "The Political Economy of Art" addressed the contradictions of an exchange-value economy that produced luxuries for the rich while neglecting useful things for the people. Lavender could be equated with oats, he said, only in political economy.[26] In *Unto This Last* he argued that "THERE IS NO WEALTH BUT LIFE," distinguishing wealth from mere pecuniary riches. Wealth was "the possession of useful things, which we can use," which was contrasted to "illth" or the production of useless and destructive things for purposes of profitable accumulation. The earth was not infinite; land, "pure air," and "pure water" were limited. Attacking the whole idea of industrialization as a universal object Ruskin wrote: "All England may, if it so chooses, become one manufacturing town; and Englishmen, sacrificing themselves to the good of general humanity, may live diminished lives in the midst of noise, of darkness, and of deadly exhalation. But the world cannot become a factory, nor a mine. No amount of ingenuity will ever make iron digestible by the million, nor substitute hydrogen for wine. Neither the avarice nor the rage of men will ever feed them."[27]

In a series of "Essays on Political Economy" written for *Fraser's Magazine* in 1862–63 (and subsequently revised as *Munera Pulveris* in 1872), Ruskin presented "valuable material things" as consisting of five categories, the first of which was "Land, with its associated air, water, and organisms." Land, he observed, had a twofold value associated with "food and mechanical power" and "as an object of sight and thought, producing intellectual power," that is, its relation to beauty. "Wealth," properly understood as such, he declared, "consists in an intrinsic value, developed by a vital power." It was sharply distinguished from mere exchange value and private riches.[28]

Ruskin detested the ugliness of the new industrial capitalism and the destruction of nature and order that it represented.[29] This came out forcefully in *Sesame and Lilies*, where he told his Manchester audience that the commercial economy despised science, art, nature, and human compassion. Indicting capital, he charged:

> You have despised Nature; that is to say, all the deep and sacred sensations of natural scenery. The French revolutionists made stables of the cathedrals of France; you have made race-courses of the cathedrals of the earth. Your *one* conception of pleasure is to drive in railroad carriages round their aisles, and eat off their altars. You have put a railroad-bridge over the fall of Schaffhausen.

> You have tunneled the cliffs of Lucerne by Tell's chapel; you have destroyed the Clarens shore of the Lake of Geneva; there is not a quiet valley in England that you have not filled with bellowing fire; there is no particle left of English land which you have not trampled coal ashes into—nor any foreign city in which the spread of your presence is not marked among its fair old streets and happy gardens by a consuming white leprosy of new hotels and perfumers' shops.[30]

In his major work of the 1870s and '80s, *Fors Clavigera*, subtitled *Letters to the Workmen and Labourers of Great Britain*, Ruskin complained that utilitarian civilization was "vitiating" the air "with foul chemical exhalations; and the horrible nests which you call towns are little more than laboratories for the distillation into heaven of venomous smokes and smells, mixed with effluvia from decaying animal matter, and infectious miasmata from purulent disease." Meanwhile, "every river of England" was being turned "into a common sewer, so that you cannot so much as baptize an English baby, but with filth, unless you hold its face out in the rain; and even *that* falls dirty."[31] Cleaning up such environmental pollution was well within the reach of science and society, but was never accomplished because doing so was not a source of profits to the capitalist owners. As he rhetorically asked in *The Crown of Wild Olive* (1866):

> Now, how did it come to pass that this [environmentally destructive] work was done instead of the other [environmental maintenance/restoration]. . . ? There is but one reason for it, and at present a conclusive one—that the capitalist can charge percentage on the work in the one case, and cannot in the other. If, having certain funds for supporting labor at my disposal, I pay men merely to keep my ground in order, my money is, in that function, spent once for all; but if I pay them to dig iron out of my ground and work it, and sell it, I can charge rent for the ground, and percentage both on the manufacture and the sale, and make my capital profitable in these three by-ways. The greater part of the profitable investment of capital, in the present day, is in operations of this kind, in which the public is persuaded to buy something of no use to it, on production or sale of which the capitalist may charge percentage; the said public remaining all the while under the persuasion that the percentages thus obtained are real national gains, whereas, they are merely filching out of partially light pockets, to swell heavy ones.[32]

It was in *Fors Clavigera*, at the time of the Paris Commune, that Ruskin came close to crossing what Morris was later to refer to as "the river of fire," separating middle-class radicals from straightforward identification with the struggles of the working classes.[33] In "Letter 6," written on June 1, 1871, he passionately defended the Commune on the basis of the class "cruelty [that] has been done by the kindest of us" and the "robbery" that had been "taught to the hands" by the present system. In "Letter 7," written a month later on July 1, 1871, he defended the Communards by pointing out that "the guilty Thieves of Europe, the real sources of all deadly war in it, are the Capitalists—that is to say, people who live by percentages on the labour of others, instead of by fair wages for their own." Yet he also acknowledged that in the previous month he had been at the point of declaring himself "a Communist—of the Old School" (though the meaning he gave to this was a highly idiosyncratic one), when news had come by telegram of the burning of the Tuileries Palace and the damage to the Louvre. Ruskin's "sympathies with workers," Thompson observes, were undoubtedly "sharply repressed" as a result of the damage to the Louvre. Consequently, he went no further than this in his identification with the working-class cause, intensely fearing this threat to the kingdom of order.[34]

Ruskin's argument that the ornamental art of the Gothic or Late Medieval age expressed the free, non-alienated condition of the medieval craftsmen—and that the loss of this was evident in the commercial present—was to exert a determining influence on Morris's own thinking. For Morris the Romantic movement was an attempt to bring to life the intrinsic human needs for creativity, change, and courage in life. He contrasted this to the mechanistic and pecuniary ends of capitalism. "What romance means," he wrote, "is the capacity for a true conception of history, a power of making the past part of the present." For Morris, Thompson writes, "The masterpieces of the past were not dead relics, but a living inspiration and warning to the present, a proof of qualities in man which—however suppressed and slumbering—could not be extinguished forever."[35]

CROSSING THE RIVER OF FIRE

The 1870s were a transitional period for Morris during which the critical Romantic heritage he inherited from Ruskin and others interacted with other influences—his Icelandic experiences; his role in founding the Society for the Preservation of Ancient Buildings; his growing struggles against British imperialism, and his rising dissatisfaction with catering his art to the idle wants of the rich—all of which served to push him toward socialism.[36] In the late 1860s he became interested in the old Icelandic sagas, and in 1871 and 1873 made trips to Iceland. What he found there was not only a heady mixture of history and myth, as represented by the Icelandic *Edda*, the product of the old Germanic and Norse traditions, but also a sense of courage and the virtue of simplicity.[37] He brought away the strong conviction that what in English terms would be considered dire poverty was easily supportable in a society of equality. The publication in 1876 of *The Story of Sigurd the Volsung and the Fall of the Niblungs*, based on Icelandic saga material, took place in the same year as Morris's resignation from the board of directors of the Devon Great Consols and literally sitting on his top hat—never to wear one again. These events also coincided with his active entry into political struggles: the Eastern Question agitation and the movement to conserve ancient buildings.[38]

A major factor in this transition in his forties to a life of political action was Morris's dissatisfaction with his artistic work at the Firm, as he increasingly despaired over the reality that the high cost of artistic productions, and the decadent purposes that they came to serve in the present social structure, meant that he was spending his life—as he was reported exclaiming at one point—"ministering to the swinish luxury of the rich." He deplored, as he said to Burne-Jones, doing artistic work that "will serve no human end but [the artist] amusing himself," while confessing to his socialist friend Andreas Scheu that both he and his artistic productions hung on "to the apron-strings of the privileged classes."[39]

It was at this point that Morris became more politically active. On October 24, 1876, a long letter by Morris appeared in the Liberal *Daily News* on what was known as the Eastern Question, opposing British imperial policy and its support of the Ottoman Empire of the Turks. The Eastern Question had arisen in 1875–76 when the Serbs, Montenegrins, and Bulgarians had risen in revolt against Turkish rule, resulting in reports of the savage suppression of the Christian population of Bulgaria. In direct line with the Romantic tradition of Lord Byron at the time of the Greek revolt against the Ottoman Empire in the 1820s, Morris demanded that the British government withdraw its support for Turkey. Matters were further complicated by Russia's entry into the conflict, using it as an excuse to push south toward the Mediterranean, with the danger that Britain would enter into the war on the Turkish side.[40] In May 1877, Morris, then Treasurer of the Eastern Question Association, wrote his famous Manifesto, *To the Working-men of England*, signing it "A Lover of Justice." He deplored the role of "irresponsible capital" that left workers enchained and the imperial policies tied to this oppression that were "driving us to an unjust war."[41]

With this *Manifesto* by Morris, Thompson was to write, "a new force had entered English public life." As Britain in the late 1870s and early 1880s proceeded to aid the Ottoman Empire, took control of Cyprus, warred in Afghanistan, fought the Zulus in Africa, engaged in the First Anglo-Boer War, and intervened militarily in Egypt, Morris was drawn more and more into the anti-imperialist struggle, on the side of worker internationalism. This struggle, more than any other, tore away his remaining illusions about Gladstonian Liberalism, which, while frequently anti-colonialist in its rhetoric, demonstrated beyond a doubt, once in office, that it served the same class interests and backed the same imperial expansion as the Tories. It was this, added to his deeper, class-based critique, that pushed Morris finally in the direction of socialism and the need for revolution.[42]

Morris's fusion of Romantic sensibilities with ever more radical political action was evident in the role he was to play in the Society for the Preservation of Ancient Buildings, founded under his instigation in 1877. Dubbed "Anti-Scrape" by Morris, the original sponsors of the organization, under his leadership, included such notables as Carlyle, Ruskin, Burne-Jones, Leslie Stephen, and John Lubbock. The organization was devoted particularly to preserving old churches as a manifestation not only of past architects but also past artisans. "All architectural work," Morris declared, "must be co-operative." Actual restoration of buildings, he insisted, was impossible. Victorian workers could no more restore the artistic production of Gothic workers than Gothic workers could restore the works of the ancient Greeks, since the social conditions affecting the art had changed. Preservation, rather than restoration, as it had come to be understood, should therefore be emphasized.[43] Arising out of Morris's developing socialist understanding was a sense of history as constituting endless strivings to create a new present. The precious remnants of the past, revealed in artistic production, were records of these strivings; speaking to us as a ghost of the present in spite of the irreversible changes that had taken place, and giving new life and inspiration to our own struggles as "the continuers of history."[44] Hence these cycles of historical struggle, traceable in art and architecture, should not be obliterated.

It was vital, Morris explained, to value past traditions and recognize that "the earlier order [is] never dead but living in the new. . . . How different a spirit such a view of history must create it is not difficult to see. No long shallow mockery at the failures and follies of the past, from a standpoint of so-called civilization, but deep sympathy with its half-conscious aims, from amidst the difficulties and shortcomings that we are only too sadly conscious of to-day."[45] For Morris, in terms that were close to those of Marx, present generations were mere "life-renters" of the environment (built and natural) around them and had a responsibility to "the humanity of unborn generations" to preserve what remained, while drawing on the vitality of the past to add anew to life.[46] This revolutionary historical (and implicitly ecological) attitude to art and labor, and to the role of working people as "the continuers of history," put him in sharp conflict with the existing property order of capitalist society, an order dedicated if anything to effacing the past.

Morris was to become a self-conscious socialist upon reading John Stuart Mill's posthumous *Chapters on Socialism*, published in the *Fortnightly Review* in February–April 1879. There Mill, in Morris's words, attacked "Socialism in its Fourierist guise," putting the utopian socialist "arguments, as far as they go, clearly and honestly." The effect on Morris, however, was the opposite of what Mill had intended: "The result, so far as I was concerned, was to convince me that Socialism was a necessary change, and that it was possible to bring it about in our own days. Those papers put the finishing touch to my conversion to Socialism."[47]

MARX AND THE CRITIQUE OF CAPITALISM

Morris commenced reading Marx's *Capital* in the French translation immediately after joining Hyndman's Democratic Federation in January 1883, and by late February of that year was enthusiastically discussing it with his friends.[48] Over the years he was to return to it over and over, taking detailed notes, particularly on the manufacturing division of labor, the labor process, and the general law of accumulation. A manuscript sheet of notes has been preserved in the William Morris Gallery at Walthamstow, which consists of free translations into English from the French edition of Marx's *Capital*—clearly intended for Morris's own use.[49] The notes center on chapter 14 of *Capital* on the "Division of Labour and Manufacture," and particularly on Section 5 on "The Capitalist Character of Manufacture."[50]

In one such note, Morris jotted down: "'It is not only the labour that is divided, subdivided, and portioned out betwixt divers men: it is the man himself who is cut up, and metamorphosised into the automatic spring of an exclusive operation.' Karl Marx."[51] For Morris, who had already explored the issue of the degradation of labor in similar terms via Ruskin, this constituted the essence of the Marxian critique. Indeed, what Morris was to bring most distinctively to historical materialism, as a product of his own prior development, was a deep understanding of the alienation of production and of the human relation to the environment. What in earlier times had been a "compulsion by Nature to labour in hope of rest, gain, and pleasure [had] been turned into compulsion by man to labour in hope—of living to labour," that is, a compulsion to work under alienated conditions that had become intrinsic to bourgeois society.[52] In words that resembled Marx's discussion of alienated labor in his 1844 *Economic and Philosophic Manuscripts* (not to become available for another four decades), Morris declared in his lecture "Art and Its Producers," delivered to the National Association for the Advancement of Art in 1888, that the interest of the factory worker's "life is divorced from the subject-matter of his labour"; the proletarian's "work has become 'employment,' that is, merely the opportunity of earning a livelihood at the will of someone else. Whatever interest still clings to the production of wares under this system has wholly left the ordinary workman, and attaches only to the organisers of his labour; and that interest commonly has little do with the production of wares, as things to be handled, looked at . . . used, in short, but simply as counters in the great game of the world market."[53]

Historian A. L. Morton remarked: "Through his reading of Ruskin Morris was able to arrive independently at something very close to the concept of alienation—an aspect of Marxism ignored, and indeed unknown at this time."[54] The significance of Morris's grasp of the reality of alienated labor can hardly be exaggerated. As Paul Thompson noted in *The Work of William Morris*:

> The question which has concerned so many Morris biographers until recently—whether Morris was a Romantic, an anarchist, a Marxist, or even a crypto-Fabian—now seems to miss the essential point. Morris was an *original* socialist thinker. At a time when orthodox Marxism took a narrowly constricted form and most of the early writings of Marx remained unpublished, Morris was able to create a socialist worldview of extraordinary richness. He took from Marx his economic and class interpretation of history. But Morris's understanding of the fundamental importance to mankind of fulfillment in work—of alienation—was an independent insight, parallel to that of Marx himself. It allowed Morris to fuse with his Marxism the moral power of the radical Romantic tradition. But Morris went much further than this. Although no successful socialist revolution had yet taken place, he was able to leap forward into an imaginative portrayal of the kind of society which could be created in the future. And unlike so many political idealists, Morris remained always strongly aware of the need in such a future to distinguish means from ends: to place at the forefront the realization, in a world freed of material inequality, asceticism and alienation, of a new consciousness of desire and fulfillment in mankind.[55]

If part of this power of revolutionary imagination was a product of Morris's previous Romantic revolt, it fused into a new synthetic vision as a result of his engagement with Marx's political economy. Morris referred frequently to Marx in his writings and constantly applied the adjective "great" when referring to Marx or his works.[56] In this respect, it would be a serious mistake to make too much of Morris's humorous, self-deprecating allusion in his 1894 article "How I Became a Socialist" to the "agonies of the confusion of the brain" he had encountered in his attempts to comprehend Marx's "pure economics"—as opposed to the more "historical parts" of *Capital*. Both his statement and his insistence in the same piece on the importance of culture for the struggle for socialism, were meant, Thompson notes, as "salutary rebuffs to the doctrinaire and mechanical outlook" adopted by the Social Democratic Federation, with its too facile understanding.[57]

Morris delved deeply into Marx's *Capital*, together with numerous other works in socialist political economy. T. J. Cobden-Sanderson observed in his diary in October 1884—when Morris sent his copy of *Capital* to him for rebinding—that "it had been worn to loose sections by his own constant study of it." "To read such a book to pieces in less than two years," Morton observed, "was no small feat!" Morris proceeded to reread *Capital* in 1887 at the time of the publication of the English edition, when he was preparing with E. Belfort Bax a series of *Commonweal* articles on "Socialism from the Root Up," later revised to constitute their book, *Socialism: Its Growth and Outcome* (1893).[58]

Morris's firm grasp of the core bases of Marx's political-economic argument was revealed throughout his later writings, and, in particular, in *Socialism: Its Growth and Outcome.* Engels thought well of this book and sent a copy to Friedrich Sorge.[59] In the concluding sentence of their chapter on "Scientific Socialism," Morris and Bax underscored the importance of Marx's *Capital* by referring to it as an "epoch-making work" that expounded the "salient principles" of the socialist critique of the capitalist economy.[60] In February 1885, Morris wrote to an unknown correspondent, "On the whole tough as the job is you ought to read Marx if you can: up to date he is the only completely scientific Economist on our side."[61] Later, in February 1887, when he was struggling at composing with Bax his first "Socialism from the Root Up" article on Marx, Morris wrote in his *Socialist Diary* of the difficulties in presenting Marx's abstract economics, indicating self-deprecatingly, "I don't think I should ever make an economist even of the most elementary kind: but I am glad of the opportunity this gives me of hammering some Marx into myself."[62] He was to persist, and his eventual comprehension of Marx's *Capital* was profound enough to allow him to perceive critical elements passed over by others and to develop distinctive themes, based on Marx, the full significance of which are only being fully recognized and appreciated today.

Some of the Fabians turned to William Stanley Jevons's marginal utility theory, in preference to Marx, presenting a problem for the nascent English socialist movement. Faced with the criticisms of Marx's value theory by figures like George Bernard Shaw and Sidney Webb, Morris wrote to a correspondent in December 1887, explaining that a debate simply about value theory

> was bound to be inconclusive, because Socialism does not rest on the Marxian theory; many complete Socialists do not agree with him [Marx] in this point; and of course the disproving of a theory which professes to account for the facts, no more gets rid of the facts than the mediaeval theory of astronomy destroyed the sun. What people really want to know is why they cannot get at the raw material & instruments of labour without being taxed for the maintenance of a proprietary class; and why labour is so disorganized that all the inventions of modern times leave us rather worse off than we were before. This can be shown them without pitting Marx against Jevons or vice versa.[63]

Yet it would be a serious error to presume, as Ruth Kinna and others have, that this very brief comment in an 1887 letter can be taken as evidence that Morris distanced himself from Marx's value theory, or sympathized with George Bernard Shaw and Sidney Webb's reliance on Jevons. There is much evidence to the contrary, most notably *Socialism: Its Growth and Outcome.*[64] Morris was simply stating that the broad political and moral case for socialism did not rest directly on any particular theory of economic value—however useful this was in understanding the internal laws of the system—but had its basis in the more general reality of the monopoly of the means of production by a single "proprietary class," able to exact tribute or monopoly rents for itself, with the obvious class exploitation that this entailed. If non-Marxist socialists and radicals shared many of these conceptions and took part in the movement on other bases, none of this negated the more specific results of "scientific socialism," on which Morris himself based his analysis. Indeed, Morris issued a trenchant 1890 critique of the 1889 *Fabian Essays in Socialism,* by Shaw, Webb, Annie Besant, and others, for its opportunism, charging that "the clear exposition of the first principles of Socialism . . . is set aside for the sake of pushing a theory of tactics, which could not be carried out in practice; and which, if it could be, would still leave us in a position from which we should have to begin our attack on capitalism over again."[65]

Morris continued to develop his deep grasp of Marx's political-economic critique, alongside the development of his own socialist practice, and to advance his arguments on that basis. In an 1890 interview printed in *Cassell's Saturday Journal*, Morris is quoted as saying: "It was Carl [*sic*] Marx, you know, who originated the present Socialist movement; at least, it is pretty certain that that movement would not have gathered the force it has done if there had been no Carl Marx to start it on scientific lines."[66]

"The effect of his [Morris's] study" of *Capital*, Thompson observed, "is obvious in all his writing" as a socialist in the 1880s and '90s.[67] Indeed, the immediate effect of Morris's reading of Marx coupled with his growing involvement in the socialist movement can be seen in a change in the growing sophistication of his critque of capitalism in this period. Whereas as late as March 1883 he was still writing positively of attempts to "fill up the gap that separates class from class," by the summer of that year he had adopted a revolutionary position of a fundamental class struggle between workers and capitalists, which was to constitute his political standpoint for the rest of his life.[68]

In his persistent efforts to probe Marx, Morris sought out others such as Bax, who had knowledge of Marx's works in German. Bax had been drawn to socialism at the age of sixteen, as a result of the Paris Commune. He studied musical composition in Stuttgart in 1875 and became a journalist in Berlin as well as a student of German philosophy, reading Marx's *Capital* as early as 1879.

He wrote an article on Marx (along with one on Hegel) for *Modern Thought* in 1881, while still in his twenties, enthusiastically introducing Marx to the English public. Marx sent Bax a number of appreciative comments but was too ill to meet with him, and it was only after Marx's death in 1883 that Bax met Engels and began to study Marxist works in earnest.[69]

Another of Morris's comrades in the Socialist League was Frederick Lessner, a German-born artisan-tailor and a dedicated German revolutionary who had emigrated to England in 1847, marching with the Chartists in 1848. It was Lessner who delivered the manuscript copy of *The Communist Manifesto* to the printer when it arrived in London from Brussels. He took an active role in the 1848 revolution in Germany, working with Marx on the *Neue Rheinische Zeitung*. He was arrested in 1851, in Cologne, and sentenced in the 1852 Cologne Communist trial against eleven members of the Communist League to three years in prison. He subsequently returned to England. He was to become a member of the General Council of the First International, and an intimate friend of Marx and the Marx family, attending Marx's funeral. He later became a stalwart supporter of Morris's Hammersmith branch of the Socialist League.[70]

The Austrian socialist Andreas Scheu was a political refugee who became a close associate of Morris. In addition to being a noted socialist orator, Scheu was a furniture designer, and took an active interest in Morris's work at the Firm, presumably sharing many of Morris's views on art and socialism. May Morris described Scheu as a "fiery and eloquent speaker of striking aspect in his brown close-fitting Jaeger clothing, his fine head like nothing less than one of Dürer's careful studies of a curly-bearded German warrior."[71]

More important, Morris was friends with Engels, whom he visited on occasion. He was also close to Eleanor Marx and (for a time) Edward Aveling, giving support to their open marriage and visiting them at their home.[72] Like Marx and Engels, Morris viewed himself as a Communist. As George Bernard Shaw famously declared in "Morris as I Knew Him": "Morris, when he had to define himself politically, called himself a Communist. . . . It was the only word he was comfortable with. . . . He was on the side of Marx *contra mundum*."[73]

When Morris joined the Democratic Federation, around a year and a half after its founding, the principal works on socialism available in English, apart from Marx's *Civil War in France*, originally published in English, and *The Communist Manifesto*, which had been translated in 1850, were Hyndman's two works: *England for All* (1881) and *The Historical Basis of Socialism in England* (1883). *England for All* drew heavily in two of its chapters on Marx's *Capital*, but without acknowledging Marx by name.[74] Hyndman had been something of a "Tory-Radical"—as Engels put it, "an ex-Conservative"—who, in an historical twist, was to become the founder of the Marxist-oriented social democratic movement in England.[75] After reading *Capital* in French, Hyndman met Marx, and had a number of discussions with him on political economy.

From a historical-materialist perspective, *England for All* was a deeply flawed work. Historian Chushichi Tsuzuki wrote that Hyndman's slim volume was "a text-book of English 'Tory Democracy' rather than Continental Social Democracy; and Marx's theory of Surplus Value seemed merely an intrusion."[76] Although sharply critical of British exploitation of the Colonies, Hyndman nonetheless made it clear that that he supported the continuation of the British Empire. Still, for those eagerly looking for a revival of British socialism and its advancement in historical-materialist terms, *England for All* was viewed as a useful wedge, making "good propaganda," Marx wrote to Engels, "although the man is a weak vessel."[77] It incorporated, if in a crude way, the labor theory of value and a class critique of capitalism. It gave to the English-reading public the first inklings of scientific socialism, and it played a large role in bringing together the group of individuals who were to struggle to develop a "practical socialist" movement in England. Edward Carpenter was so impressed by *England for All* that he donated £300 for the founding of *Justice*, the organ of the new movement and the first weekly socialist paper.[78]

Hyndman's *Historical Basis of Socialism in England*, in which he made a fuller acknowledgment of Marx (Hyndman presented himself, according to Thompson, as "the English inheritor of Marx's mantle"), was a better book in its treatment of the political economy and in the factual arsenal it offered. But it was sometimes inaccurate and was overall an eclectic and mechanical work. For example, Hyndman referred to the "iron law of wages" and the "perpetual degradation" of labor's wages (borrowing from Ferdinand Lassalle, Thomas Hodgskin, Henry George, and Karl Rodbertus) in ways that lacked the nuances of Marx. In a dramatic flourish in the conclusion to his book, he invoked the approaching centenary of the French Revolution, in 1889, as presaging a working-class revolt in England. Nonetheless, Morris thought well enough of Hyndman's *Historical Basis of Socialism* to recommend it in 1885 with qualifications to others who were restricted to works in English.[79]

In 1884, Hyndman and Morris co-authored a 64-page book, *A Summary of the Principles of Socialism*, which laid out a Marxian view of history and political economy. This short book had the added character, due to Morris's influence, of emphasizing the importance of art for free labor.[80]

The one work that Morris in 1885 believed was the best introduction to socialist political economy available in English, for those who could not read German or French and hence could not read *Capital* itself, was Laurence Gronlund's *The Co-operative Commonwealth in Its Outlines: An Exposition of Socialism*. It provided an accessible and sophisticated exposition for the time (using U.S. Census–based national income data) of Marx's value theory. In

Morris's view, Gronlund carried the argument "out further" than Hyndman's *Historical Basis*.[81] Born in Denmark in 1846, Gronlund had emigrated to the United States in 1867, where he taught German in Milwaukee schools and then became a practicing lawyer. In the 1870s he turned to socialism. He was arrested under the name Peter Lofgreen, as a leader in the Workingmen's Party of the United States and was implicated in the St. Louis General Strike. Afterward, he became a writer and journalist for the cause, writing a pamphlet titled *The Coming Revolution: Its Principles* in 1878 (reportedly sending copies to Marx). This was followed in 1884 by his major work, *The Co-operative Commonwealth*, which attempted to apply Marx's analysis in *Capital* to American conditions. Although drawing extensively on Marx's ideas and presenting a Marxist position, Gronlund refrained from referring to Marx in his work, except in one somewhat dubious passage about the "Jewish Age," where he alluded to Marx (not by name) as "a noble Jew." (In the 1890 edition of his book he inserted: "It is to. . . Karl Marx, that we owe the scientific basis of socialism.") *The Co-operative Commonwealth* was a huge success, selling a hundred thousand copies, influencing not only Morris and George Bernard Shaw, who wrote a preface to an 1885 English edition, but also Edward Bellamy and Eugene Debs in the United States.[82]

Gronlund traveled to England in 1884–85 and joined Morris's Socialist League. He was elected to the Council of the League at its first general meeting in July 1885, and worked for it as a lecturer, returning to the United States in the late 1880s. He gradually moved away from any connection to Marxian views, and increasingly from class struggle, associating with various ethical and nationalist versions of socialism, such as the Socialist Labor Party, Bellamy's Nationalist movement, and Populism. He later attempted to develop a Fabian-type organization in the United States.[83]

The American socialist Florence Kelley (Wischnewetzky), who was to translate Engels's *The Condition of the Working Class in England* into English, sent Engels a copy of Gronlund's *The Cooperative Commonwealth* in 1885. Engels, who said Gronlund's book raised various "speculative" issues, commented that Gronlund took "our views, to the extent that he understands them or not" as a basis for pushing "his own utopianism as real live German socialism." Kelley herself contended that Gronlund's book was a "would-be-popular-at-all-costs" work. Nevertheless, she considered it valuable enough to recommend it in the same way that Morris did, as an important "preliminary work" for those unable to read German or French. Gronlund in this way exercised an important influence on English-speaking socialists.[84]

There is no doubt about the broad range of Morris's own knowledge of the socialist literature, including political economy and Marxist theory. Works he read in English, in addition to Gronlund, included Robert Owen's *Book of the New Moral World*; John Stuart Mill's *Chapters on Socialism*; Alfred Russel Wallace's *Land Nationalisation*; Henry George's *Progress and Poverty*; and John Carruthers's *Communal and Commercial Economy*. Also available in English translations were Marx and Engels's *The Communist Manifesto*; pamphlets by Ferdinand Lasalle and Friedrich Sorge; Sergius Stepniak's *Underground Russia*; and Chartist leader Bronterre O'Brien's 1836 translation of Buonarroti's *History of Babeuf's Conspiracy of Equality*. Marx's *The Civil War in France* had been published originally in English based on his addresses to the International Working Men's Association and hence would have been readily available to Morris.

Morris was also familiar with August Bebel's *Woman and Socialism*, which was translated into English under the title *Women in the Past, Present and Future* in 1885, and which he immediately purchased. He read Edward Aveling and Eleanor Marx-Aveling's pamphlet *The Factory Hell*, published by the Socialist League in 1885. In February 1885, Morris introduced a series of lectures by Edward Aveling on Marx's *Capital*, which took place weekly through June 1885. The lectures, which were aimed at a detailed, step-by-step explanation of Marx's economics, were published monthly in *Commonweal*, edited by Morris, under the title "Lessons in Socialism." Morris was undoubtedly aware of Aveling and Eleanor Marx-Aveling's important article "The Woman Question," which appeared in the *Westminster Review* in 1886. The year 1886 also saw the publication of Bax's *The Religion of Socialism* with its important discussions of dialectics and historical materialism, which had a substantial impact on Morris's thinking.

Within three years or so of Morris having joined the socialist movement, more of Marx and Engels's classic works were available in English translation. *Wage-Labour and Capital* was translated into English in 1886. The English edition of *Capital*, translated by Samuel Moore and Aveling, appeared in 1887 (before which Morris, as noted, had relied on the French edition). Also in 1887 Engels sent Morris a copy of Florence Kelley's translation of Engels's *Condition of the Working Class in England*, excerpts of which Morris ran in *Commonweal*.

Moreover, Morris's knowledge of French gave him access to a much wider body of socialist literature, including Marx's *The Poverty of Philosophy*; the French edition of Engels's *Socialism: Utopian and Scientific* (the first English translation appeared in 1892); and works by Charles Fourier, Henri de Saint-Simon, Louis Blanc, and many others.[85]

Yet, for all of his exploration of Marx and socialist thought, Morris's approach to historical materialism was in many ways unique. As E. P. Thompson famously wrote: "Morris was a Communist Utopian, with the full force of the transformed Romantic tradition behind him."[86] He drew from Marx and Engels's writings penetrating insights that others had missed, while also developing critical concepts that paralleled some of Marx's own philosophical insights in unpublished manuscripts, unknown even to Engels. The more abstract value theory of Marx's *Capital* took second place in Morris's understanding to the degradation of work, and to the various qualitative transformations of working-class life and consciousness—together with changing relations to the environment.

As a mature thinker, embodying the full weight of the English Romantic tradition, and his not inconsiderable practical experience as a designer and manufacturer, Morris—engaged in synthesizing Ruskin with Marx's materialist conception of history—ended up presenting a new Marxian revolutionary vernacular suited to English conditions.[87] "The essence of what Ruskin then taught us," he stated, "was simple enough, like all great discoveries. It was really nothing more recondite than this, that the art of any epoch must of necessity be the expression of its social life."[88] But it was precisely here, as Morris well knew, that the Romantic tradition overlapped with historical materialism, allowing him to create a symbiotic unity. The result was one of the most vital, complex visions to emerge out of the historical materialist tradition, one in which the transcendence of alienation within production was understood in aesthetic and ecological, as well as economic, terms.[89]

ART AND THE LABOR OF PRODUCTION

Morris delivered one of his earliest lectures on socialism, "Art Under Plutocracy," at Oxford in November 1883 with John Ruskin as the chair. As Thompson noted with respect to Morris on this occasion: "Nothing was more appropriate in his whole life."[90] In a Ruskinian vein, Morris distinguished between two forms of art, one of which he characterized as "Intellectual," and which catered simply to the mental characteristics (exemplified by painting and sculpture), and the other which was seen as "Decorative." For Morris, decorative art was "always . . . a part of things which are intended primarily for the service of the body," and thus consisted in the ornamentation of material use values. There are societies, he argued, that lacked intellectual art, "but positively none which lacked the Decorative (or at least some pretence of it)."[91]

These two forms of art as manifested in modern society were a product of the class division that had become more acute under capitalist class society, during which decorative art hads declined, while intellectual art had been monopolized more and more for the sake of a wealthy few. In previous societies

> the humblest of the ornamental art shared in the meaning and emotion of the intellectual; one melted into the other by scarce perceptible gradations; in short, the best artist was a workman still, the humblest workman was an artist. This is not the case now, nor has been for two or three centuries in civilized

> countries. Intellectual art is separated from Decorative by the sharpest lines of demarcation, not only as to the kind of work produced under those names, but even in the social position of the producers; those who follow the Intellectual arts being all professional men or gentlemen by virtue of their calling, while those who follow the Decorative are workmen earning weekly wages, non-gentlemen in short.[92]

Morris insisted that "art is man's expression of his joy in labor." Whatever the hardships human beings encountered in earlier historical epochs, their work could be judged more or less free to the extent that this remained true, and "all men were more or less artists" adding that an "instinct for beauty" is essential in human beings, which they naturally incorporated into all that they produced. The power of artistic expression was most evident in Gothic or late-medieval architecture, the art form in which cooperation was most essential, and hence the one in which the "association" of the medieval period most clearly triumphed artistically over the competitiveness of modern times. But the same principle had a more universal application in medieval society and was reflected in the artistic compositions integrated into all goods produced, where the organization of work itself was unconstrained—however much medieval workers may have "suffered grievous material oppression" in other respects.[93]

It is here that Morris's deep reading of Marx came into play. Essential for Morris was Marx's clear demarcation of the historical development of the labor process beginning with the rise of capitalism in the fifteenth century, and the triumph of the "manufacturing" (or capitalist organization of handcraftsmanship) in the eighteenth century, prior to the Industrial Revolution. Morris saw the internal degradation of work associated with the development of the capitalist division of labor in these years as exemplified by the loss of artistic labor, and through that the loss of meaning in work. The result, he explained in "Art Under Plutocracy," was work that was degraded and "precarious," allowing little control over working conditions, or even secure access to work itself, thereby creating conditions of absolute alienation. Following Marx in *Capital*, he frequently quoted J. S. Mill's statement that machinery had never lightened the load of the worker.[94]

Throughout his socialist writings, Morris placed great stress in his analysis of the industrial reserve army on Marx's concept of a working class constantly in a "precarious" position, caught between the dual contradictions of work under conditions of exploited labor, on the one hand, or falling into the reserve army of the unemployed and underemployed on the other. Thus in "Useful Work *versus* Useless Toil" (first delivered as a lecture in 1883 and later incorporated into his 1888 book *Signs of Change*), he wrote of "the precariousness of life among the workers" resulting from the tendency toward an "increase in the number of the 'reserve army of labour.'" So important was the issue of the "precariousness" of workers under capitalism, that in his 1887 lecture, "What Socialists Want," Morris penciled "precariousness" in the margin.[95]

It was this precariousness of their conditions that reduced workers' control over their production, leading to the almost infinite degradation of their working conditions, in which they were relegated to the "one-sided dealing with a trifling piece of work." Lost, then, was that very "freedom for due human development" that work under unalienated conditions, conducive to artistic labor, had provided. Lost too was a "universal sense of beauty" exhibited "in the outburst of the expression of splendid and copious genius which marks the Italian Renaissance," but which faded suddenly with the growth of commercialism. With this came the general alienation of humanity from its artistic soul—to the point that "the romance of the arts died out." The decorative arts were reduced to a mere "phantom of that tradition which once bound artist and public together."[96]

This general alienation, which Morris saw as the internal degradation of working conditions, was also accompanied by what he called the "external degradation of the face of the country" and could be traced to the same cause. "That loss of the instinct for beauty which has involved us in the loss of popular art" was at the same time, he contended,

> surely and not slowly destroying the beauty of the very face of the earth. Not only are London and our other great commercial cities mere masses of sordidness, filth, and squalor, embroidered with patches of pompous and vulgar hideousness no less revolting to the eye and the mind when one knows what it means: not only have the whole counties of England, and the heavens that hang over them, disappeared beneath a crust of unutterable grime, but the disease, which, to a visitor coming from the times of art, reason, and order, would seem to be a love of dirt and ugliness for its own sake, spreads all over the country, and every little market-town seizes the opportunity to imitate, as far as it can, the majesty of the hell of London and Manchester. Need I speak to you of the wretched suburbs that sprawl all round our fairest and most ancient cities?... Our civilization is passing like a blight, daily growing heavier and more poisonous, over the whole face of the country, so that every change is sure to be a change for the worse in its outward aspect.[97]

In the face of such general alienation, which he attributed in "Art and Plutocracy" to the economic development of capitalist society, Morris was driven to outright rebellion and announced to his astonished audience at Oxford University: "For I am one of the people called Socialists." He followed this up by calling upon those in attendance to come to the aid and support a "reconstructive socialism."[98] The immediate reaction of the Oxford dons was anything but tranquil or supportive. The Master, Reverend Dr. James Franck Bright, publicly chastised Morris immediately following his talk, indicating that in inviting him to speak at Oxford it was not known that he would be promoting socialist propaganda. According to the *Times* the following day: "Mr. Morris announced himself a member of a socialist society and appealed for funds for the objects of the society. The Master of [the] University then said to the effect that if he had announced this beforehand it was probable that the loan of the College-hall would have been refused."

Ruskin's presence as chair helped to calm the proceedings. As always a loyal friend to Morris, Ruskin rose to his feet to smooth over the situation. Nevertheless, the drama was reported widely in the press and Morris was warned that his position as a man of eminence, one of England's greatest poets and artists, was not sufficient to abort establishment efforts to silence him once he had crossed over the "river of fire" from capitalism to socialism. As J. W. Mackail summed it up, "The meeting had, at all-events, a success of a scandal, and henceforth Morris was widely known as a declared Socialist."[99]

SIGNS OF CHANGE

No single lecture, even one as brilliantly developed as "Art Under Plutocracy," is sufficient to convey the extraordinarily complex vision that Morris crafted from the beginning of his career as a practical socialist. Grasping the totality of his vision has never been easy, since it has required bringing together the numerous, diverse, and scattered strands of his intellectual-artistic legacy. As Perry Anderson noted, Morris's

> thought was coherent enough in substance, by any standards. But its form was largely unsystematic—variously strewn through prose and verse romances, lectures and articles alike. Attractive yet *ad hoc*, this dispersal told against it afterwards. For the lessons of Morris to be learnt, either for emulation or amendment, they had first to be assembled. This they were not. Some of the major political texts themselves were not even readily available until the two supplementary volumes of his work were belatedly published by his daughter in 1936. . . . Systems have their costs, as [E. P.] Thompson has argued: but lack of system too has its price.[100]

As a result, only scattered attempts (most significantly in the work of E. P. Thompson and Paul Meier) have been made up to the present day to see Morris's work as a system. Usually what is captured in most analyses of his writings is the general tenor of his thought, the structure of feeling, and little more.

Nevertheless, it is Morris's unified vision, connecting his understanding of the dialectical relations between nature, labor/art, and humanity, that is of abiding interest today. To get at the systematic content of his work in this respect it is useful to focus on his 1888 book, *Signs of Change*, consisting of seven of his lectures from his first four years as a declared socialist. *Signs of Change* was, in Thompson's words, "one of his greatest achievements, the point of confluence of the moral protest of Carlyle and Ruskin and the historical genius of Marx, backed up by Morris's own lifetime of study and practice in the arts and in society."[101] Two of his lectures, "The Hopes of Civilization" and "Dawn of a New Epoch," were published in the book for the first time—the former, constituting a transitional chapter, preceding "The Aims of Art," and the latter standing in for a conclusion to the work as a whole.[102] The other five talks—in the order they appeared in the book, "Whigs, Democrats, and Socialists" (1886), "Feudal England" (1887), "How We Live and How We Might Live" (1887), "The Aims of Art" (1886), and "Useful Work *versus* Useless Toil" (1884)—had all appeared either in *Commonweal* or in pamphlet form.

As Morris noted in his Preface, these talks, taken together, were the outpouring of one who was "neither a professional economist nor a professional politician," whose "ordinary work" had forced upon him "the contrast between times past and the present day," and had made him "look with grief and pain on things which many men notice but little, if at all." The "repulsion to pessimism" so characteristic of one embroiled in the arts had eventually combined with his understanding of "the truths of Socialism" to provide a new hope for the historical development—the "dawn of a new epoch"—of humanity.[103]

Although in appearance, at least, a mere lecture collection, "delivered on various occasions," as he emphasized in the subtitle, *Signs of Change* nonetheless had a much greater significance because Morris culled these particular lectures from the much larger set of lectures he had given at the time, as representative of his overall views. Through this work it is therefore possible to see the main outlines of his outlook.

"How We Live and How We Might Live," which constituted an introduction to the book, commenced with an explanation of the meaning of revolution and then took as its main theme the "perpetual war" that capitalism represented, both in relation to other peoples through imperialism, and in terms of the class war internally. The following chapter, "Whigs, Democrats, and Socialists," provided his critique of liberal, radical, and mechanical socialist arguments, pointing to the need for a more revolutionary approach, and rejecting a false parliamentarianism. "Feudal England" revealed Morris's broad historical point of view, characteristically reaching back into the medieval era in order to provide the historical perspective for the critique of capitalism and the promotion of socialism. "The Hopes of Civilization" offered a long historical view of the development of capitalism and socialism in England. "The Aims of Art" advanced further Morris's central thesis on the role of art and labor and of the degradation of work under capitalism. "Useful Work *versus* Useful Toil"—the oldest lecture included in *Signs of Change*, and one that Morris had delivered on numerous occasions—extended this analysis of the degradation of art-labor to a critique of the alienated use-value structure of capitalist production, and the wasted, useless labor that resulted. "Dawn of a New Epoch," appearing for the first time, was aimed at the direct promotion of the socialist society of the future.

Morris clearly intended to bring these lectures together in the hope that the book would then serve as a more systematic introduction to his thinking as a whole, despite the "repetitions," which, as he confessed to the reader, arose from this kind of presentation—since in each of these lectures, delivered to "mixed audiences," it had been necessary to repeat certain basic points.[104] Nevertheless, it is useful to look at the argument lecture by lecture (or chapter by chapter).

The opening paragraph of "How We Live and How We Might Live" provided Morris's concept of revolution:

> The word Revolution, which we Socialists are so often forced to use, has a terrible sound in most people's ears, even when we have explained to them that it does not necessarily mean a change accompanied by riot and all kinds of violence, and cannot mean a change made mechanically and in the teeth of opinion by a group of men who have somehow managed to seize on the executive power for the moment. Even when we explain that we use the word revolution in its etymological sense, and mean by it a change in the basis of society, people are scared at the idea of such a vast change, and beg that you will speak of reform and not revolution. As, however, we Socialists do not at all mean by our word revolution what these worthy people mean by their word reform, I can't help thinking that it would be a mistake to use it, whatever projects we might conceal beneath its harmless envelope. So we will stick to our word, which means a change of the basis of society; it may frighten people, but it will at least warn them that there is something to be frightened about, which will be no less dangerous for being ignored; and also it may encourage some people, and will mean to them at least not a fear, but a hope.[105]

The revolutionary struggle against the war of all against all that constituted bourgeois society was nothing less than the struggle for a more rational and reconstructive order. It meant replacing a capitalist regime based on inequality of condition and perpetual war with a socialist commonwealth based on equality of condition and a climate of peace.[106]

The second lecture in *Signs of Change*, "Whigs, Democrats, and Socialists," provided Morris's critique of the existing parliamentary parties in England.

Condemning Tories, Whigs, Liberals, and Radicals, he claimed that each was a defender of capitalism and that even the last, despite its name, would not "go such a very short journey towards revolution as the abolition of the House of Lords . . . the abolition of the monarchy they would consider a serious inconvenience to the London tradesman." Outside these parliamentary parties, he contended, there were undoubtedly "genuine Democrats . . . who have it in their heads that it is both possible and desirable to capture the constitutional Parliament and turn it into a real popular assembly, which, with the people behind it, might lead us peacefully and constitutionally into the great Revolution which all *thoughtful* men desire to bring about."

However, a mere political-constitutional reform, he contended, would not touch the economic-class bases of society and would take those who carried it out right back where they started. In such a case, he told the Democrats of his day: "You would have made a revolution, probably not without bloodshed, only to show the people the necessity for another revolution the very next day. Will you think the example of America too trifle? Anyhow, consider it! A country with universal suffrage, no king, no House of Lords, no privilege as you fondly think; only a little standing army, chiefly used for the murder of red-skins; a democracy after your model; and with all that, a society corrupt to the core, and at this moment engaged in suppressing freedom with just the same reckless brutality and blind ignorance as the Czar of all the Russias uses." Morris went still further to attack those who advocated what he called a kind of "semi-State Socialism" characterized by nationalization, taxation of income, and factory legislation by such parliamentary means. At present, he suggested, socialists could only compromise themselves by playing the parliamentary game, while their real task, in existing conditions in England, was "to help to make the people *conscious*" of the class struggle and the great antagonism between the people and the existing state structure.[107] It is in Morris, as Anderson emphasized, that we find "the *first frontal engagement with reformism in the history of Marxism*," in a way not present even in Engels's work at the time Morris was writing, nor fully developed in Marx's earlier writings.[108] Attacking reformism straight on, Morris explained:

> Those who think that they can deal with our present system in this piecemeal way very much underrate the strength of the tremendous organization under which we live, and which appoints to each of us his place, and if we do not chance to fit it, grinds us down till we do. Nothing but a tremendous force can deal with this force; it will not suffer itself to be dismembered, nor to lose anything which really is its essence without putting forward all its force in resistance; rather than lose anything it considers of importance, it will pull the roof of the world down upon its head.[109]

In "Feudal England" and his various historical essays (most notably "The Development of Modern Society" in 1890 and the historical chapters in *Socialism: Its Growth and Outcome*), Morris presented his core argument that the medieval epoch, particularly in England, had culminated in the fourteenth century, the period of the "victory of the handicraftsmen."[110] Although the early fourteenth century is often associated with the Black Death, Morris argued that more significant than that, and completely overriding it, was the growth of freer and more egalitarian work relations. This was the period in which the development of free yeomanry in the rural areas and relatively egalitarian democratic guilds of free craftsmen in the cities were at their high point, as reflected in the achievements of the decorative arts.[111]

"Feudal England" began with the conquest of England by William the Conqueror and examined the changes in the organization of society and labor up to "the fully developed mediæval period of the fourteenth century," at the time of Edward III, who reigned from 1327 to 1377. In literature this was the time of Chaucer and William Langland's *Piers Plowman* and in the ballad poetry of the people, the "songs of the Foresters." It was also a time of the profusion of art of all kinds. "The life of the worker in it," Morris wrote, "was better than it ever had been." Many of the craftworkers in the town guilds and the yeomanry and other commoners in the rural areas were able to move up in status, spelling the end of serfdom and the culmination of the Middle Ages.

This ushered in a reaction. In response to the growing power of laborers in England—which had increased as a result of the massive depopulation associated with the Black Death and the associated shortage of labor—Edward III and Parliament attempted, through the Statute of Labourers in 1351, to repress the working population by establishing a maximum level of wages. This period of repression reached its height during the reign of his grandson and successor, Richard II, leading to the Peasant's Revolt in 1381 (celebrated in Morris's *A Dream of John Ball*). "The revolt," Morris wrote, "was put down . . . but nevertheless serfdom came to an end in England, if not because of the revolt, yet because of the events that made it, and thereby a death-wound was inflicted on the feudal system." Serfs were transformed into tenants.[112]

In "The Hopes of Civilization," Morris provided an evocative picture of fourteenth-century England, which for him represented the expansion of a non-capitalist system of production to its "utmost limit," and the rise of the free laborer with the demise of serfdom. At the same time, it was a period marked by class struggle and the first emerging signs, soon to come in the fifteenth century and after, of enclosures, so-called primitive accumulation, and the rise of commercial society. Yet, looking back at the fourteenth century, he was able to discover in living history the possibility of a more vital future after capitalism. Despite the manifold oppressions of the time, such oppression was grossly obvious and "external to the work of the craftsmen." Consequently, workers were relatively free in the conduct of their labor and the artistic contributions they embedded in it. "And when I think of this," Morris wrote, "it quickens my hope of what may be: even so it will be with us in time to come; all will have changed, and another people will be dwelling here in England, who, although they may be of our blood and bear our name, will wonder how we lived in the nineteenth century." Here was revealed the historical spirit that was later to infuse Morris's great utopian romance, *News from Nowhere*.

If the "hope" Morris referred to here was a product of history, and a recognition of a time in which labor had been freer, he nonetheless insisted that there was no going back historically, only forward. Still, the past pointed to the freedom to develop an active, creative relation between human beings and nature through production, one that was unalienated in the sense that it was imbued with the creativity and hope essential to human existence. In "Hopes of Civilization" he described the long process of primary accumulation, which began abortively in England in the fifteenth century, and then became more pronounced in the three centuries to follow, producing a country of "landless labourer[s]." Adopting Marx's terms, Morris explained that this meant "the expropriation of the *people* from the land" through a relentless process of enclosure. In the towns too there was a transformation with the rise of guild-less journeymen. Notwithstanding all the class struggles that took place, from the Levellers to the Chartists, the intensive division of labor and proletarianization that characterized capitalist commodity production came to dominate. The Industrial Revolution itself hardly benefited the workers, who worked longer hours and under more precarious and sordid conditions. "At no period of English history," he wrote, "was the condition of the workers worse than in the early years of the nineteenth century."[113]

Such conditions gave rise to socialism in England as well as on the Continent. Here Morris praised the utopian socialism of Robert Owen, Charles Fourier, and Henri de Saint-Simon. "Amongst these," he stated, "Fourier is the one that calls for the most attention: since his doctrine of the necessity and possibility of making labour attractive is one which Socialism can by no means do without." Utopian socialism gave way to the scientific socialism of Marx, who "made modern Socialism what it is. . . . The new school [of Marx], starting with an historical view of what had been, and seeing that a law of evolution swayed all events in it, was able to point out to us that the evolution was still going on, and that, whether Socialism be desirable or not, it is at least inevitable. Here then was at last a hope of a different kind to any that had gone before it." This new truth was evident in the Paris Commune. Moreover, the inevitability of socialism was revealed by its opposite. If one were to assume that some "unforeseen economical events . . . put off for a while the end of our Capitalist system, the latter would drag itself along as an anomaly cursed by all, a mere clog on the aspirations of humanity," until it were at last done away with.[114]

With "The Aims of Art," Morris returned to what was always his central Ruskinian theme, the role of art in free, unalienated production. It was an essential characteristic of human beings that they must "either be making something or making believe to make it." It was here that he arrived, independently, at the same general ontological foundations of human existence as Marx in *The Economic and Philosophic Manuscripts*, giving rise to a similar conception of alienated labor under capitalism—a conception that was not to enter centrally into Marxism, outside of Morris's thinking, for another half century.

Presenting an almost anthropological view of the connection of art and labor, Morris stated: "All men that have left any signs of their existence behind them have practised art." This followed from the fact that "the chief source of art is man's pleasure in his daily necessary work, which expresses itself and is embodied in that work itself." Consequently, art "has been and should be a part of all labour in some form or other." There was always a "definite sensuous pleasure" in labor insofar as it was art and art insofar as it was unalienated labor, and this pleasure increased "in proportion to the freedom and individuality of the work." Conversely, "labour degrading at once to body and mind, both by its excess and by its mechanical nature" lacked, according to Morris, this "sensuous pleasure" in labor, and hence was alienated and divided off from any genuine connection to art.[115]

Although he lacked a direct acquaintance with Hegelian philosophy, and knew next to nothing of Marx's treatment of the relation of art and the division of labor, Morris's understanding of artistic labor as *sensuous work*, constituting a distinctly human relation to nature—and as reflecting human self-consciousness and hope—can be usefully viewed in terms of Hegel's and Marx's writings on aesthetics. For Hegel, "the universal and absolute need out of which art . . . arises" has to do with "active self-realizedness" of human beings, both as conscious and as sensuous beings. In these terms, "the work of art" can be seen as presenting "itself to sensuous apprehension. It is addressed to sensuous feeling, outer or inner, to sensuous perception and imagination."[116]

For Marx, who developed Hegel's views and gave them a more materialist content, art was universal, and primarily a social rather than individual, productive activity. Marx and Engels's views on art and the division of labor can be seen most clearly in their response to Max Stirner, whose work emphasized the importance of the isolated ego. Stirner had insisted that no one could take the place of the individual work of a Mozart or a Raphael. Marx and Engels responded in *The German Ideology* that Stirner was "unlucky with his practical examples. He thinks that 'no one can compose your music for you, complete the sketches for your paintings. No one can do Raphael's works for him.'" He "could surely have known, however, that it was not Mozart himself, but someone else who composed the greater part of Mozart's Requiem and finished it, and that Raphael himself 'completed' only an insignificant part of his own frescoes." Marx together with Engels insisted that great art was a product of a historical age and of social labor, which did not mean that "everybody can work in Raphael's place, but rather that everybody who has a Raphael in him should be able to develop unhindered." Moreover, art was also social in the sense that "the works of Leonardo depended on the state of things in Florence, and the works of Titian, at a later period, depended on the totally different development of Venice."[117]

In their uncompromising historical-materialist critique of the estrangement of art and the alienated division of labor in bourgeois society, Marx and Engels went on to declare:

> The exclusive concentration of artistic talent in particular individuals, and its suppression in the broad mass which is bound up with this, is a consequence of division of labour. Even if in certain social conditions, everyone were an excellent painter, that would by no means exclude the possibility of each of them being also an original painter, so that here too the difference between "human" and "unique" labour amounts to sheer nonsense. In any case, with a communist organisation of society, there disappears the ... subordination of the individual to some definite art, making him exclusively a painter, sculptor, etc.; the very name amply expresses the narrowness of his professional development and his dependence on division of labour. In a communist society there are no painters but only people who engage in painting among other activities.[118]

Although unaware of Marx and Engels's writings in this area—*The German Ideology* was not published until well into the twentieth century—Morris not only advanced a similar argument but went further in emphasizing the *universal* character of art, by stressing its importance to *all* labor. As Caroline Arscott had argued in *Interlacings*, Marx's entire philosophical project embodied a critical aesthetic, which Morris, rooted in his own concrete experience as an artist-producer and the whole Romantic tradition he carried within him, somehow independently came to embrace.[119]

Morris and the other Pre-Raphaelites were engaged in a rebellion against the standards of bourgeois art. A young Oscar Wilde, the most gifted follower of Ruskin and Morris, wrote in 1882 in "The English Renaissance of Art" that the "Pre-Raphaelites," as "they called themselves," had "not imitated the early Italian masters at all, but in their work, as opposed to the facile abstractions of Raphael, they found a stronger realism of imagination. ... But above all things was it a return to Nature . . . they would draw and paint nothing but what they saw, they would try and imagine things as they really happened." Of Morris, Wilde said that "by the revival of the decorative arts he has given to our individualized Romantic movement the social idea and the social factor also."[120]

Like Ruskin, Morris used architecture to emphasize art's social character, exemplified by the innumerable craftworkers that had contributed to various architectural constructions and the extraordinary richness of their decorative designs. "No one knows," he said, "the name of the man who designed Westminster Abbey." And this was precisely because it was a social product of medieval craftworkers, requiring no "special reward" for the individual artist.[121] Like Marx, but based on his own line of thinking, Morris argued that the "trenchant line of demarcation" in the division of labor under capitalism between artist and artisan, and between elite art and society, was a product of the development of the detailed division of labor. It thus represented the degradation of work in an alienated society. Although the craftworkers of "the Middle Ages *were* all artists," in capitalism such mingling of work and art became rare. People, if they were to get art in their ordinary goods, could do so, though even then it was doubtful, only by "paying extra" for beauty, treated as an added cost.[122]

Morris's conception of art as *social* extended to his views on literature, where he placed the highest value on works that were the products of entire historic-cultural traditions. Asked to list what he thought were the one hundred essential works of literature, he emphasized "the kind of book which Giuseppe Mazzini called 'Bibles,'" and thus placed at the top of his list those literary works that were most clearly *social* rather than *individual* products, such as Homer's *Odyssey* (which Morris translated), the English (King James) Bible, the Norse *Edda*, and *Beowulf*. These books had "grown up from the very hearts of the people." They thus exemplified the dialectic of social aesthetics.[123]

None of this denied that in bourgeois society the laws of political economy had necessarily eradicated art in ordinary labor. Rather, Morris used this to criticize bourgeois society itself.[124] For capitalist factory owners, he explained, their employees are, "so far as they are workmen, a part of the machinery of the workshop or the factory." Their previous roles as "craftsmen, of makers of things by their own free will, is played out." They were no longer cost-efficient in capitalist commodity production. Hence, what art still existed tended to be sham, hollow, mechanical art, reflecting an age in which human beings had become slaves to machines. Art, "either . . . in its sincerity or its hollowness," he wrote, is "the expression of the society amongst which it exists."[125]

Although it was true that machinery frequently reduced the necessity of labor, it was not usually to the benefit of the laborer, and was determined by the speed with which poor quality, makeshift, and often useless goods could be turned out, generating an "artificial famine" associated with overproduction of commodities and the lack of attendance to real needs. Under the present system, workers were reduced to the status of slaves of machines, and to the system that those machines served. "I do not mean by this," Morris wrote in "Art and Its Producers," "that we should aim at abolishing all machinery: I would do some things by machinery which are now done by hand, and other things by hand which are now done by machinery: in short, we should be the master of our machines and not their slaves, as we are now." So-called free labor under the capitalist system meant simply labor open to exploitation by capital and not labor that was free to develop according to its own needs.

The result of this pattern of development, Morris stated in "The Aims of Art," would be either a revolutionary reconstruction of society, in which people took history into their own hands, or else some "terrible cataclysm," and in the end the collapse of civilization—that is, if the system were to be allowed to continue, while art perished and science became "more and more one-sided, more incomplete." Indeed, there was "no hope save in Revolution." In the end, the "springs of art in the human mind" could be seen as "deathless" and would be set free, as nothing could "take the place of art" in the fulfillment of human labor and human self-realization.[126]

"Useful Work *versus* Useless Toil," the sixth lecture included in *Signs of Change*, was the oldest lecture. It constituted what Morris considered to be the most important political-economic aspect of his argument, focusing on waste and useless or unproductive labor. "Capitalistic manufacture, capitalistic land-owning, and capitalistic exchange force men into big cities in order to manipulate them in the interests of capital; the same tyranny contracts the due space of the factory so much that (for instance) the interior of a great weaving-shed is almost as ridiculous a spectacle as it is a horrible one. There is no other necessity for all this, save the necessity for grinding profits out of men's lives, and of producing cheap goods for the use (and subjection) of the slaves who grind." There was no universal need, Morris argued, that factories be designed this way or that workers "be compelled to pig together in close city quarters." Production could be more dispersed and organized in such a way that workers were more creative and happier.[127]

Natural limits were clearly demarcated in Morris's analysis. Thus he wrote that there was "a certain amount of natural material and natural forces in the world, and a certain amount of labour-power inherent in the persons of the men that inhabit it." The expansion of labor productivity and the introduction of machinery had made it possible for human beings to satisfy their needs with less labor-power and more efficiently providing room for fuller, more meaningful lives. Yet, society had yet "made *no use*" of these enhanced powers, since "labour-saving machines" had not been used to reduce total labor or to make room for more creative labor. Instead, they had encouraged the growth of the reserve army of labor and general conditions of precariousness. Science, which had been incorporated into production, was used one-sidedly to enhance the exploitation of labor, rather than to create better laboring conditions and more ample room for the free development of human beings.[128]

The inferior articles turned out by such a society were what was to be expected, while the wasted lives that this entailed constituted the greatest condemnation of all. Consider, Morris said,

> the mass of people employed in making all those articles of folly and luxury, the demand for which is the outcome of the existence of the rich non-producing classes. . . . These things, whoever may gainsay me, I will forever refuse to call wealth: they are not wealth, but waste. Wealth is what Nature gives us and what a reasonable man can make out of the gifts of Nature for his reasonable use. The sunlight, the fresh air, the unspoiled face of the earth, food, raiment and housing necessary and decent; the storing up of knowledge of all kinds, and the power of disseminating it; means of free communication between man and man; works of art . . . all things which serve the pleasure of people, free, manly and uncorrupted. This is wealth. Nor can I think of anything worth having which does not come under one or other of these heads. But think, I beseech you, of the product of England, the workshop of the world, and will you not be bewildered, as I am, at the thought of the mass of things which no sane man could desire, but which our useless toil makes—and sells?[129]

It was impossible, he insisted in "Useful Work *versus* Useless Toil," to attain "attractive labour" under the capitalist system. Popular art, or the art embodied in use values, deteriorated and disappeared under such a system, and along with it the meaning and fulfillment provided by unalienated work itself. This could only be remedied under socialism. In the creation of a new society, it was possible for every individual to have "at least three crafts"—various forms of sedentary work combined with occupations "calling for the exercise of strong bodily energy," most especially the cultivation of the earth, "the most necessary and pleasantest of all work."[130]

The last of the lectures included in *Signs of Change* was "Dawn of a New Epoch." Here Morris focused on the need for epochal change. The "ideal of the new epoch," which was emerging out of "the old order which it [was] destined to supplant," was that of an unalienated society, or, as he put it, an "undegraded existence on the earth." Building on Marx's theory of the labor process and his analysis of the development of machinery, Morris argued that the new machinery of the system was used "in a threefold way: first they get rid of many hands; next they lower the quality of labour required, so that skilled work is wanted less and less; thirdly, the improvement in them forces the workers to work harder while they are at work, as notably in the cotton-spinning industry." As a result, work was degraded and the reserve army of labor increased. All of this reinforced the differences "between the two great classes of modern Society": "the possessing class," who owned the means of production and hired labor power, and the "non-possessing class," forced to sell their labor power.

"The natural desire of man" was "to be free." The "only reward that you *can* give the excellent workman is opportunity for developing and exercising his excellent capacity." What Morris referred to as "complete Socialism" or "Communism" was aimed at promoting an equality of condition that would allow for the "free development of each man's capacity." This required first and foremost the end of the monopoly of the means of production. The emancipation of labor constituted "the basis on which all Socialists may unite."[131]

In his 1885 lecture "Socialism," written during the same period as some of his *Signs of Change* lectures, Morris turned Marx's phraseology with respect to "labor power" around, stating that the workers "possess nothing except . . . the power of labour. . . . The rich," he explained, "can compel . . . the poor to sell that power of labour to them on terms which ensure the continuance of the rich class"—since the rich are able to appropriate the "surplus value" from the unpaid labor of the workers. Yet, by emphasizing *the power of labor* rather than labor power, Morris subtly drew attention to the power of the workers to "rebel against them [the capitalists]: indeed in one way or another they have rebelled even in our own times, and are organized, for rebellion (though but badly and loosely) into trade unions." Still, a genuine struggle for freedom would need to be aimed at "Revolution, the change in the basis of society," with hope it would occur "peaceably because . . . irresistibly."[132]

Signs for Change provided a powerful socialist aesthetic, tied to a historical materialist reading of changing conditions between feudalism and capitalism, and integrating within it Marx's critique of political economy. It envisioned a new epoch based on an understanding of historical conditions past and present. Morris emphasized in Ruskinian-Marxian fashion the social dialectic underlying all art. This was clear in his treatment of Gothic architecture, which was unquestionably social in character. But it was also apparent in his approach to the decorative arts, where he saw art as having been generated by *every worker* and in the most ordinary wares in the late-medieval era. "A work of art is always a matter of co-operation."[133] Hence, the meaning of art for humanity was social and its relation to the historical process dialectical.

Indeed, what brought Morris's immense intellectual corpus together and unified it was its underlying materialist conception of history and nature—"the cause and effect of material nature"—and the almost innate dialectic of art that pervaded his thinking.[134] His deep, materialist conception of history and nature was related to his own role as designer, artisan, and manufacturer, as well as his close relation to workers. "The exigencies of my own work," he explained in July 1884 to the Anti-Scrape Organization, "have driven me to dig pretty deeply into the strata of the eighteenth-century workshop system, and I could clearly see how very different it is from the factory system of to-day, with which it is commonly confounded; therefore it was with a ready sympathy that I read the full explanation of the change and its tendencies in the writings of a man, I will say a great man [Karl Marx], whom, I suppose, I ought not to name in this company, and who cleared my mind on several points (also unmentionable here) related to this subject of labor and its products."[135]

The revolutionary imagination pervaded Morris's thinking and derived from his deep historical sensibility, so unusual among socialists of his time, together with his own encounter with Marx and his materialist understanding. With his unique historical consciousness, he was able to explain that "the very designer [Morris's own occupation], be he never so original, pays his debt to . . . necessity in being in some form or another under the influence of *tradition*; dead men guide his hand even when he forgets they ever existed." So also with history in general.[136]

Morris's analysis was imbued throughout with complex notions of the changing pace of history, immanent contradictions and reversals, explosive new developments and crises, and emerging forces of epochal change, all propelling history from one period to another. This was most evident in his chapter on "How the Change Came" in *News from Nowhere*.[137] However, it was in *John Ball* (1886–87) that we find one of the best-known passages in all of Morris's work, set in the contest of the English Peasant Revolt of the fourteenth century: "I pondered all these things, and how men fight and lose the battle, and the thing that they fought for comes about in spite of their defeat, and when it comes turns out not to be what they meant, and other men have to fight for what they meant under another name."[138]

CHAPTER THREE

The Movement toward Socialism

In the weeks of late October and early November 1887, unemployed workers, waving black banners and red flags, marched repeatedly on Trafalgar Square in London, demanding that the government respond to their plight. Irish protesters in favor of home rule also marched to Trafalgar Square. A general atmosphere of unrest in London had been created by the sentencing and impending judicial execution, on November 11, of four Chicago anarchists, blamed for the so-called Haymarket riot.[1] On November 8, Sir Charles Warren, Chief Commissioner of the London Metropolitan Police, ordered a ban on all public demonstrations in Trafalgar Square, in what was then the favorite area of public assembly.

Alarmed by the police actions and the restrictions on free speech and the freedom to assemble, some twenty thousand unemployed workers, socialists, anarchists, radicals, and Irish nationalists gathered on November 13, on what was to become known as "Bloody Sunday." They gathered in different areas and marched in columns down the various streets to the sunken area of Trafalgar Square, an area capable of holding several thousand persons.[2]

"In the greyness of the chilly November afternoon," Morris and the Socialist League, along with other socialist groups (including a branch of the Social Democratic Confederation) gathered on Clerkenwell Green with numerous workers, mostly artisans, in preparation for the march to Trafalgar Square. Morris, who described himself on the occasion as "thickset and short and dressed in shabby blue," and the then-socialist Annie Besant addressed the crowd, upwards of 5,000 in total, from a cart, and then they all proceeded to march to the square.[3]

The marchers were unaware that Warren had deployed some 2,000 police along with four squadrons of cavalry and 400 foot soldiers—Guardsmen with fixed bayonets, each with twenty rounds of ammunition—to confront the strikers. The orders were to stop each column and to break it up before it reached the square. Police were stationed at strategic points within "a radius of about a quarter of a mile of the square," waiting for the columns to march into their net. The main body of the foot soldiers and the Guardsmen lined the sunken portion of the square.

The Clerkenwell contingent, with Morris at the head, leading the Hammersmith branch of the Socialist League, was "about to enter the Seven Dials streets to make our way to St. Martin's Lane" when they were flanked and attacked at both ends. The police struck hard, seeing the marchers as an enemy in the class war, and the workers and their allies, though resisting, were unable to maintain a line and the procession was broken up and scattered. The Socialist League banner was torn from the hands of its bearer, Mrs. Taylor, who resisted valiantly. Morris, who was in the middle of the attack, wrote: "I shall never forget how quickly these unarmed crowds were dispersed into clouds of dust," adding, "I found myself suddenly alone in the middle of the street, and, deserted as I was, I had to use all my strength to gain safety." Morris and a few others, such as Annie Besant (who is said to have flung herself at the solid wall of police lined up six deep in her attempt to get to the center of the square) and the artist Walter Crane, a member of Morris's Socialist League, made it somehow to the square. Crane wrote: "I never saw anything more like real warfare in my life—only the attack was all on *one* side." Other columns suffered even greater brutality before they reached the square. In the main contingent of the Socialist Democratic Federation, Cunninghame Graham, an aristocratic Radical-Socialist Member of Parliament from Scotland, attacked the police cordon, along with John Burns, later to become a leading figure in the British socialist movement (and a friend of E. Ray Lankester). Graham's head was cut open. Both were subsequently arrested, tried, convicted, and imprisoned for six weeks in 1888, for their role in confronting the police in the march. Three men died of their injuries at the hands of the police and hundreds more were wounded, many hospitalized. Three hundred people were arrested, and many of these were imprisoned. A policeman beat Eleanor Marx-Aveling across the arm with his baton and she was hit in the head, knocking her down, her hat and cloak torn to shreds. She managed to avoid arrest. Afterward she proceeded to Engels's house. He noted in a letter to Paul Lafargue: "Her coat [was] in tatters, her hat bashed and slashed by a staff blow."[4]

The following Sunday, on November 20, a sequel took place. A relatively minor demonstration was held in Hyde Park protesting the police brutality on Bloody Sunday. Warren stationed mounted police in Trafalgar Square, and police actively pursued anyone who appeared troublesome. Just south of the square the mounted police knocked down a young Radical law-writer named Linnell, who died on December 2 of his injuries. For Linnell's funeral, a procession of mourning and protest was organized in December, attended by over 10,000 people. Morris composed "A Death Song," the printed version of which sold for a penny and had a powerful Walter Crane woodcut, showing a mounted policeman with a truncheon attacking Linnell, with the words "Killed in Trafalgar Square." The song began:

> What commeth here from west to east a-wending?
> And who are these, the marchers stern and slow?
> We bear the message that the rich are sending
> Aback to those who bade them wake and know.
> Not one, not one, nor thousands must they slay,
> But one and all if they would dusk the day.[5]

With Morris as one of the six pallbearers, the funeral procession started in Soho, where the coffin was loaded into an open hearse. The coffin had on its top a black shield on which was inscribed, "Killed in Trafalgar Square," and with the shield were three flags, red, yellow, and green, for the Socialists, Radicals, and Irish, respectively. A tremendous number of people joined the procession, which stretched a mile long, enveloped in a mass of banners, mostly red. Once the coffin had been lowered into the grave, several speeches were made, of which Morris's was the most notable. H. A. Barker of the Socialist League was to recall that Morris "threw his whole soul into his speech. There was a fearful earnestness in his voice when referring to the victim he had just laid to rest. He cried out, 'Let us feel he *is* our brother.' The ring of brotherly love in it was most affecting." A choir then sang "A Death Song." As E. P. Thompson wrote, Morris "gained, for the first time in his political agitation, real stature and affection in the eyes of the Radical London masses. It was perhaps in these days, more than at any other time, that he laid the basis for the love—almost veneration—in which he was held by great sections of the Labour movement at the time of his death."[6]

Indeed, by the time of the Trafalgar Square conflicts in 1887, Morris, as leader of the Socialist League, and as poet, artist, and militant, had reached the apex of the revolutionary workers movement in Britain, while being recognized at the same time as one of the leading representatives of Marxian socialism worldwide. The year 1887 also marks a kind of transition point. The two years leading up to it had been dominated by Morris's break with Hyndman's Socialist Democratic Federation, while the following three years were to witness the slow demise of the League. This led him in subsequent years to expand his historical vision, taking into account the changing nature of capitalist society and the need for a deeper, more ecological, vision of socialism.

THE SOCIALIST LEAGUE

Morris's role in founding and leading the Socialist League from 1885 to 1890 was a product in part of the powerful synthesis between the English Romantic tradition and revolutionary Marxian socialism which he had come to embody. More than any other figure within English socialism, he created a distinctive revolutionary vernacular, wedding this to a socialist aesthetic and an ecological consciousness. The range of his vision made him an exceptionally resolute revolutionary figure, unwilling to make long-term compromises with what he regarded as short-term realities. For this reason, however, he was to find it difficult to develop a socialist praxis that fit the conditions of the present. The result was to give him an uneasy relationship to the other, less far-sighted socialist currents and leading representatives of his time, weakening his immediate effectiveness as a practicing socialist. Yet, these very same characteristics were to validate his vision over the long haul, making him one of the most inspiring socialist intellectuals of all time.

The break with Hyndman's Social Democratic Federation occurred in the last weeks of December 1884. On the surface, the dispute had to do with Hyndman's authoritarian, manipulative, and opportunistic personality, his tendency to hurl calumnies at certain members, such as Morris's friend Andreas Scheu, and his iron grip over the Social Democratic Federation's publication of *Justice*. But behind this were more substantial issues, separating the Hyndman-dominated Federation from the movement that Morris and others sought to create. These included (1) the neglect of socialist education; (2) an overemphasis on what Morris called "State Socialism," meaning the opportunistic promotion of the purely political mechanism and parliamentary form, which led in the direction of what Marxists were later to call "revisionism"; and (3) Hyndman's scarcely concealed jingoism and support of the British Empire. All these issues were to be emphasized by the Socialist League in its *Manifesto* and other initial documents, of which Morris was the chief author.

In response, Morris organized what he sardonically called "the cabal," challenging Hyndman within the leadership of the Social Democratic Federation. This led to a decisive vote in which Morris's group, which included Edward Aveling and Eleanor Marx-Aveling, E. Belfort Bax, Scheu, and six others, proved to be the majority. The cabal, rather than seeking control of the Social Democratic Federation, immediately announced their collective resignation from the Federation. On December 30, 1884, the Socialist League was officially founded.[7]

In all of this Morris had consulted on a number of occasions with Engels. Not only were the Avelings linked closely to Engels in a kind of "'Marx-Engels' family" relationship, but Bax too was a close associate of Engels at this time, a frequent participant in Engels's Sunday socialist gatherings at his home in Regent's Park Road. Morris was in and out of Engels's home, and they engaged in frequent animated conversations. On one occasion Morris was excited to see the old Norse *Edda* (presumably the *Poetic Edda*) on Engels's table, and he read to Engels from his great epic poem *Sigurd*.[8]

Engels was supportive but skeptical about Morris's leadership of the Socialist League, writing to Eduard Bernstein that in Morris, Bax, and Edward Aveling, the League had cornered "the only honest men among the intellectuals—but men as impractical (two poets and a philosopher)," referring respectively to Morris, Aveling, and Bax, "as you could possibly find."

It was a peculiar combination of individuals in other respects as well. Aveling was extremely talented: a popular university lecturer in biology; an exponent of secularism, which he had discussed with Darwin and Ludwig Büchner; and a prolific writer and poet. Yet he was untrustworthy both with respect to money and in other areas, and prone to sexual liaisons, leading eventually to the suicide of Eleanor Marx in 1898, two years after Engels's death, which resulted in Aveling being despised by all. Nevertheless, his considerable talents, exhibited in his works *The Student's Darwin* and *The Student's Marx*, his common law marriage with Eleanor Marx, and his friendship through the former with Engels, gave him a prominent role in the socialist movement.[9] His understanding of Marx was more schematic than critical, but it exceeded that of most others in the movement. He assisted Samuel Moore in translating Marx's *Capital*, known as the Moore and Aveling translation.

Bax, although gifted with a remarkable understanding of the main outlines of historical materialism, and one of the first of Marx's followers to explore the question of dialectics via both Hegel and Marx, was, in contrast to Aveling, somewhat dry and humorless. He was concerned primarily with ethical questions, and an adamant anti-feminist, which came out fully in his later years. This alienated him from Eleanor Marx-Aveling, who challenged him to a public debate, and from much of the socialist movement of that time—and since.[10] Bax's early work, notably *The Religion of Socialism*, generally avoided "the woman question," though even then contained some chauvinistic comments.[11] According to Morris's daughter May, Morris usually treated Bax's outbursts in this respect with "shouts of laughter," and bemused derision over their human folly, undoubtedly curbing Bax's excesses in this way.[12] No doubt Engels also played a restraining role. It was not until the fall of 1895, when Engels had died and Morris was seriously ill, that Bax was to engage in outright sexist attacks on the feminist movement, including criticisms of Marxists like Bebel who took a feminist stance. He was to continue this into the early decades of the twentieth century. Moreover, not content on those occasions to oppose the feminist movement itself, he extended his criticisms to misogynist comments about women in general, such as his insistence on their being "organically inferior" to men.[13] None of this, though, was present in the earlier works that Morris and Bax co-authored in the 1880s. Nor did it enter into the publications of the Socialist League. It was mainly taken up years later, after Bax had left the League and rejoined the Social Democratic Federation, where he expressed some of these views in its organ *Justice*.

Notwithstanding the transgressions (mostly later on) of a few of its key members, there was no doubt about the general theoretical position that the Socialist League represented when it came into existence at the very end of 1884, with Morris at its head. "We uphold the purest doctrines of Scientific Socialism," Morris told an interviewer from the *Daily News* shortly after the split with the Social Democratic Federation, thereby placing the League squarely in line with Marxism. He left little doubt that this meant a revolutionary movement of workers aimed at the creation of a society of equality.[14] Morris immediately began working on the new socialist monthly (soon to be weekly) *Commonweal*, which he was to edit, initially with Aveling as associate editor (the latter stepped down in 1886 when the publication became a weekly). Morris provided the necessary subsidy, beginning with a £300 "loan" at the outset, and continuing to subsidize it in the following years.

The first number in February 1885 carried *The Manifesto of the Socialist League*. It also included an important article by Bax titled "Imperialism *v.* Socialism," in which he presented the thesis that imperial "wars must necessarily increase in proportion to the concentration of capital in private hands." Eleanor Marx-Aveling initiated her series, "Record of the International Movement," in the same issue. The second number carried Engels's singular article "England in 1845 and in 1885," which was later to be incorporated into his preface to the English edition of *The Condition of the English Working Class*. It also included articles by Bax, Sergius Stepniak, George Bernard Shaw, Paul Lafargue, and Aveling, while Marx-Aveling's "Record" for that issue contained greetings from August Bebel, Wilhelm Liebknecht, Karl Kautsky, and others. Morris added his "Message of the March Wind," which was to be his prelude to *Pilgrims of Progress*. As E. P. Thompson noted, the second issue of *Commonweal* stood out as "one of the most remarkable issues of any British Socialist periodical."[15]

The Manifesto of the Socialist League, even in its original February 1885 version (before the second edition with annotations by Morris and Bax later that year), was an extraordinary document, exhibiting Morris's intelligence, straightforwardness of style, and fervency as a socialist political writer. It began with the words "Fellow Citizens—We come before you as a body advocating the principles of Revolutionary International Socialism; that is, we seek a change in the basis of *Society*—a change which would destroy the distinctions of classes and nationalities." It proceeded in just a few short pages to lay out in plain language the main thrust of a Marxian critique of capital: (1) the increasing class polarization of society; (2) the theory of surplus value; (3) the appropriation and amassing of capital by the rich; (4) competition and the world market; (5) economic waste and waste of labor; (6) "modern bourgeois property-marriage" and the oppression of women; (7) education caught in "the trammels of commercialism"; and (8) the state and class. It argued that "the *people*, who are the only really organic part of society, are treated as a mere appendage to capital—as part of its machinery."

It then proceeded to criticize various incomplete schemes of radical change, falling short of complete socialism, including (1) "Co-operation so-called," that is, competitive cooperative schemes; (2) "Nationalisation of land alone"; and (3) "State Socialism," meaning in this case any system "whose aim it would be to make concessions to the working class while leaving the present system of capital and wages still in operation."[16]

A more thoroughgoing theoretical critique was developed in a series of annotations by Morris and Bax to the second edition of the *Manifesto* in October 1885. The most significant of these was note C, which dealt with the issue of the equality of labor under socialism in its various phases, and ended with a statement on dialectics. At the beginning of this note it said: "The end which true Socialism sets before us is the realization of absolute equality of condition helped by the development of the variety of capacity, according to the motto, *from* each one according to his capacity, *to* each one according to his needs."[17] This was the first appearance of this memorable saying in English. Marx had famously employed this phrase in the *Critique of the Gotha Programme*, written in 1875, but not published until 1891, where it came to stand for communist society. But the phrase had an earlier and wider history.[18]

The origin of this idea, and its development in the socialist literature, is complex. It is often attributed to the 1840 edition of Louis Blanc's *Organization of Work*.[19] However, this is not correct. Blanc in the first edition of his book wrote something quite different, referring to "the St. Simonian doctrine . . . '*from each according to his ability, to each ability according to its works*.' "[20] It was not until nine years later that Blanc in *Le Nouveau Monde* no. 6 (December 15, 1849) coined the very different "from each according to his ability, to each ability according to his needs." He then inserted it into the ninth (1850) edition of his *Organization of Work*. Credit for the idea is also due to Etienne Cabet, who had inscribed on the title page of the 1840 Fourierist *Voyage en Icarie*: "To each according to his needs, from each according to his strength." And even more credit, as we shall see, goes to François-Noël Babeuf, in the late eighteenth century.[21]

Blanc's slogan was popular and was to be taken up by socialists generally. In 1851, Engels wrote an article on Proudhon in which he explicitly quoted: "From each according to his ability, to each according to his needs," attributing the saying to Blanc.[22] However, the idea actually appears earlier in volume 2, chapter 5 of Marx and Engels's 1845–46 *The German Ideology* (not published in full until 1932). In this chapter one finds the following extraordinary passage:

> But one of the most vital principles of communism, a principle which distinguishes it from all reactionary socialism, is its empirical view, based on a

> knowledge of man's nature, that differences of *brain* and of intellectual ability do not imply any differences whatsoever in the nature of the *stomach* and of physical *needs*; therefore the false tenet, based upon existing circumstances, "to each according to his abilities," must be changed, insofar as it relates to enjoyment in its narrower sense, into the tenet, *"to each according to his need"*; in other words, a *different form* of activity, of labour, does not justify *inequality*, confers no *privileges* in the respect of possession and enjoyment.[23]

Here we see already, more than a quarter-century before the *Critique of the Gotha Programme*, and prior to Blanc's 1849 article, the development of Marx's distinctive approach to human productivity and needs. Moreover, the emphasis is on needs. *The German Ideology* and the *Critique of the Gotha Program* both take their stand *contra mundum* with the deeper egalitarianism of Babeuf and his "conspiracy of equals." According to Babeuf: "Equality must be measured by the *capacity* of the worker, and the *need of the consumer*, not by the intensity of the labour and the quantity of things consumed."[24] This is clearly the broad tradition with which Marx (and also Morris) identified, and it is to Babeuf that we must ultimately attribute this deeply communistic view.

In fact, like all great ideas, the conception of "from each according to his ability, to each according to his needs" was a *social* or *collective*, not merely an *individual* product. In this respect it is significant that it was Moses Hess, a German socialist/communist thinker with whom Marx and Engels were closely associated in the early 1840s, and not Marx and Engels themselves, who it seems initially drafted chapter 5 in volume 2 of *The German Ideology*. The chapter appears to have been an adaptation of an earlier article by Hess, edited (and perhaps refined) by Marx. Hess's name is noted on the manuscript version of the chapter. This means that the core conception underlying the best-known description of communist principles can be said to have originated with Babeuf and Cabet, was elaborated by Hess and Marx-Engels (and inserted into *The German Ideology*), put into a slightly more succinct form by Blanc, and finally explored in depth decades later by Marx—in what was to be his most detailed expansion of the transition to socialism/communism.

Morris and Bax attached considerable importance to Blanc's phrase, not only referring to it in note C in the *Manifesto of the Socialist League*, but also quoting it in *Socialism: Its Growth and Outcome* where the phrase was attributed to Blanc. Morris also referred to it in his 1888 lecture, "Equality." In their annotations to the *Manifesto*, Morris and Bax indicated that this phrase was aimed at the "absolute equality of condition" that characterized complete socialism or communism. Morris admired Babeuf and frequently referred to the "Society of Equality" (or "society of equals").[25] Moreover, note C pointed to a two-stage theory of the transition to socialism and communism, of the kind later associated with Lenin's interpretation of Marx's *Critique of the Gotha Programme.* Such a two-stage theory was practically unknown in the socialism of their time.[26] In the first stage, neither the labor required of individuals nor earnings and consumption would be regulated by the principle of absolute equality. As Morris indicated elsewhere, "The old habit of rewarding excellence or special rare qualities with extra money payment will go on for a while, and some men will possess more than others." However, even this would constitute an advancement on the much greater inequality that had preceded it. In the second stage of communism, the principle of "*from* each one according to his capacity, *to* each one according to his needs" would pertain to working time equal for all individuals, machinery helping to decrease natural advantages, and distribution according to need.[27]

One influence on Morris and Bax in this respect was Gronlund's *The Cooperative Commonwealth*, published in 1884. There Gronlund had written: "The motto of socialism is: 'Everybody according to his *deeds*'; that of Communism is: 'Everybody according to his *needs*.'" (Gronlund himself insisted on following the first motto, not the second, thereby identifying himself with socialism rather than communism.)[28] Gronlund was in England working with the Socialist League at the time the second edition of the *Manifesto of the Socialist League* was written.

The other crucial element in note C of the second edition of the *Manifesto* was the direct allusion to the dialectical movement in history. Here they wrote:

> Finally, we look forward to the time when any definite exchange will have entirely ceased to exist; just as it never existed in that primitive Communism which preceded Civilisation.
>
> The enemy will say, "This is retrogression not progress"; to which we answer, All progress, every distinctive stage of progress, involves a backward as well as a forward movement; the new development returns to a point which represents the older principle elevated to a higher plane; the old principle reappears transformed, purified, made stronger, and ready to advance on the fuller life it has gained through its seeming death. As an illustration (imperfect as all illustrations must be) take the case of advance on a straight line and on a spiral—the progress of all life must be not on a straight line, but on the spiral.[29]

The characterization of the dialectic as a spiral was associated with Bax more than Morris. Indeed, Bax's demonstrated ability in his *Religion of Socialism* to present in concise fashion some of the principal elements of Hegel's dialectic was perhaps his greatest contribution to socialism in the British Isles, and certainly exercised a notable influence on Morris. Bax referred to "the dialectic movement"; the contradictory laws of history; the "negation of the negation" in which the "potential becomes the actual"; and to the complex, spiraling movement of history.[30] Yet it was Morris who gave real historical substance in an English context to this abstract product of German speculative philosophy, most notably in *A Dream of John Ball*, but also elsewhere. This can be seen in the presidential address he delivered four years later to the Applied Art section of the National Association for the Advancement of Art in Edinburgh, titled "The Arts and Crafts of To-day." There Morris stated:

> Nor can I altogether tell you how much of the past is really dead. I see about me now evidences of ideas recurring which have long been superseded. The world runs after some object of desire, strives strenuously for it, gains it, and apparently casts it aside; like a kitten playing with a ball, you say. No, not quite. The gain is gained, and something else has to be pursued, often something which seemed to be gained and was let alone for a while. Yet the world has not gone back; for that old object of desire was only gained in the past as far as the circumstances of the day would allow it to be gained then. As a consequence, the gain was imperfect; the times are now changed, and allow us to carry on that old gain a step forward to perfection: the world has not really gone back on its footsteps, though to some it has seemed to do so. Did the world go back, for instance, when the remnants of the ancient civilisations were overwhelmed by the barbarism which was the foundation of modern Europe? We can all see that it did not. Did it go back when the logical and orderly system of the Middle Ages had to give place to the confusion of incipient commercialism in the sixteenth century? Again, ugly and disastrous as the change seems on the surface, I yet think it was not a retrogression into prehistoric anarchy, but a step upward along the spiral, which, and not the straight line, is, as my friend Bax puts it, the true line of progress.
>
> So that if in the future that shall immediately follow on this present we may have to recur to ideas that to-day seem to belong to the past only, that will not be really a retracing of our steps, but rather a carrying on of progress from a point where we abandoned it a while ago. On that side of things, the side of art, we have not progressed; we have disappointed the hopes of the period just before the time of abandonment: have those hopes really perished, or have they merely lain dormant, abiding the time when we, or our sons, or our son's sons, should quicken them once more?[31]

What was most astonishing about Morris's dialectical approach was his extraordinary poetic ability to translate this into a concrete historical meaning, one that transcended usual ways of thinking about the past and future, opening the way to the appropriation of the ghostly presence of the past for the revolutionary re-creation of the living. Morris constantly pointed to "the change beyond the change," the dialectic of history created by human struggle. As Morris and

Bax stated in *Socialism: Its Growth and Outcome*, history moves forward only by means of the "negation of negation."[32] The Morris biographer and Marxist writer Jack Lindsay observed in the 1970s that Morris "was the first Marxist to put into print the concept of history as involving a spiral movement in which old forms returned, changed and [were] given a new force through the intervening period, their positive aspects now freed from the limiting elements."[33]

The most important economic statement by the League, made at the outset, and to have a considerable effect on Morris, was Engels's powerful argument on "England in 1845 and in 1885" in which he laid down the reasons for the downfall of socialism in England in the 1840s, particularly after 1848 with the demise of Chartism and Owenism—and the reasons why socialism was experiencing a revival in the late 1880s. In Engels's argument, the English manufacturing bourgeoisie had concluded that it was necessary to incorporate the working class to some extent into the polity, since it could not rule without it, resulting in the Factory Acts and the *de facto* enactment of the Peoples' Charter that the capitalist class had previously resisted. This was associated with the fact that England had emerged as the "workshop of the world" with a virtual monopoly on world manufacturing trade. Although it still experienced the ups and downs of the business cycle, the enormous expansion of the world markets for capital had moderated its effects, preventing severe overproduction. A section of factory workers and trade unionists were incorporated into the system under these conditions and were indirectly beneficiaries of the whole system of Empire, constituting "an aristocracy among the working class." Yet the general law of accumulation, involving the constant reproduction of the industrial reserve army of the unemployed, continued to operate and "the great mass of the working people," Engels wrote, were in a "state of misery and insecurity," which was as "low as ever, if not lower. The East-end of London is an ever-spreading pool of stagnant misery and desolation, of starvation when out of work, and degradation, physical and moral, when in work."

In fact, the years of prosperity associated with England's dominance of the world market was breaking up. Wherever coal was available, industrialization was possible and hence "France, Belgium, Germany, America, even Russia" were now industrializing at a rapid rate and freeing themselves from dependence on British manufactures—refusing to be "turned into Irish pauper farmers merely for the greater wealth and glory of English capitalists." And with the decline in England's domination of world markets, the economy of England subsided into a period of endless stagnation. In Engels's words, "But then a change came," breaking up the earlier capitalist prosperity:

> The crash of 1866 was, indeed, followed by a slight and short revival about 1873; but that did not last. We did not, indeed, pass through the full crisis

> at the time it was due, in 1877 or 1878; but we have had, ever since 1876, a chronic state of stagnation in all dominant branches of industry. Neither will the full crash come; nor will the period of longed-for prosperity to which we used to be entitled before and after it. A dull depression, a chronic glut of all markets for all trades, that is what we have been living in for nearly ten years.[34]

Engels went on to explain that these conditions were the reason for the new thrust of British imperialism into Africa:

> The manufacturing monopoly of England is the pivot of the present social system of England. Even while that monopoly lasted the markets could not keep pace with the increasing productivity of English manufacturers; the decennial crises were the consequence. And new markets are getting scarcer every day, so much so that even the negroes of the Congo are now to be forced into the civilisation attendant upon Manchester calicoes, Staffordshire pottery, and Birmingham hardware. How will it be when the Continental, and especially American goods, flow in ever increasing quantities—when the predominating share, still held by British manufactures, will become reduced from year to year? Answer, Free Trade, thou universal panacea?[35]

For the newly formed Socialist League, the critique of imperialism was no less important than the critique of capitalism itself. Hence, scarcely less important than the *Manifesto of the Socialist League* and Engels's landmark article in defining the position of the Socialist League at the outset was the "Manifesto of the Socialist League on the Soudan War," a four-page leaflet published on March 2, 1885, written primarily by Morris and signed by the members of the Provisional Council, including Aveling, Marx-Aveling, and Bax. In this manifesto, the Socialist League took a stand against the British invasion of Khartoum, thereby running athwart of the lamenting in the press over the fall of Khartoum and the death of General Gordon in February 1885. The "only crime" of the Sudanese, the manifesto stated, was that "they have risen against a foreign oppression." Caustically, referring to "the 'rebels' otherwise Sudanese," it said that the tragedy from the standpoint of imperialism is that Khartoum had "fallen . . . into the hands of the Sudanese themselves." The Socialist League courageously attacked the pervasive imperialism and jingoism of the time, making no concessions to hegemonic views, whether in print or in its rallies. It made it clear from the start that it considered the imperialist expansion into Africa as aimed at increasing the "new lands for exploitation; fresh populations for pillage." The Sudan War was aimed at gaining control of the region so that it could "be 'opened up' to the purveyor of shoddy wares." Morris declared in a speech (reported in the *Daily News*) that "capitalists and stock-jobbers . . . could not exist as a class without this exploitation of foreign nations to get new markets."[36]

In 1886–87 Morris wrote his classic, Romantic historical work based on the English Peasants Revolt of 1381, *A Dream of John Ball,* which was serialized in *Commonweal.* At its high point, it provided a discussion between John Ball and the nineteenth-century England character "Friend" (standing for the dreamer—Morris himself) comparing the position of workers' struggles in the two periods. Also serialized in *Commonweal* in 1886–87 was the series of articles by Morris and Bax run under the heading "Socialism From the Root Up" (later published in book form in 1893 as *Socialism: Its Growth and Outcome*), which explained the historical development of class struggles and the emergence of scientific socialism (Marxism).

The Socialist League was a heterogeneous organization that included Marxists, social democrats, Fabians, anarchists, and others, seeking, like Marx's First International, to create unity in the context of diversity.[37] It had around a thousand members at its peak in 1887. The League had an executive council but no chair. Morris, as treasurer and editor of *Commonweal* was the most influential figure in the executive and the effective head of the organization. The League had key branches in Leeds, Norwich, Bradford, Glasgow, Edinburgh, and a half-dozen provincial towns, as well as nine London branches, of which Hammersmith and Bloomsbury were the largest. Morris threw himself into the struggle, devoting his main efforts to the cause, both at the level of party-building and grassroots actions. He took on the hard toil of editing and writing for *Commonweal,* together with giving speeches at open air rallies and participating in mass demonstrations and strikes. He also engaged in the necessary mundane duties of handing out leaflets, taking collections, carrying banners, selling literature, writing letters to the newspapers, chairing meetings, and paying bills. Morris's role was so central that the organization was hardly imaginable apart from him. As Shaw was to write, the Socialist League was "entirely dependent on one of the most famous men of the nineteenth century, who was not only a successful employer and manufacturer in the business of furnishing and decorating palaces and churches, but an eminent artistic designer, a rediscoverer of lost arts, and one of the greatest of English poets and writers."[38]

The first two years of the Socialist League's existence were ones of building. *Commonweal* flourished, and the League was engaged in public protests, principally directed at free speech, since the authorities regularly disrupted public gatherings by socialists, radicals, workers, and the unemployed. Morris was in the thick of it. He was brought before a magistrate in Thames Police Court on September 21, 1885, for allegedly striking a police offer in an affray, when, in the words of Aveling, "a rush of police was made at those in court," and on Eleanor

Marx in particular, after they had loudly protested a verdict with the word "Shame!" Morris, who strongly remonstrated against the heavy-handedness of the police, threatening legal action, was singled out as the "chief thumpee" and detained. He was hauled before the magistrate two hours later. Upon being asked "What are you?" he replied, no doubt to the delight of those in attendance: "I am an artist, and a literary man, pretty well known, I think, throughout Europe." He was released. As E. P. Thompson explained:

> It was indeed an unlucky moment for the police when they singled out Morris for arrest. The scene, of course, was a three day wonder. No amount of editorials taxing Morris with "indiscretion" or worse could hide the fact that the police persecution was both unjust and unequal. *Funny Folks* carried a cartoon of the police blacking Morris's boots. The dovecotes of literature were thrown into a flutter. "Do you see the reports of the row the Socialists have had with the police in the East End?" George Gissing wrote to his brother: "Think of William Morris being hauled into the box for assaulting a policeman! And the magistrate said to him 'What are you' Great Heavens!"[39]

THE TWO-FRONT WAR

If the Socialist League achieved initial success organizationally and in terms of publicity, by 1887, in what proved to be a "watershed" in "the League's fortunes," it was facing a crisis associated with a conflict between its three principal factions: (1) parliamentary-oriented socialists, (2) non-parliamentary-oriented socialists, and (3) anarchists.[40] The struggle between the first two groups had commenced soon after the creation of the Socialist League in the first weeks of 1885. What distinguished the Socialist League from the Socialist Democratic Federation, from Morris's standpoint in particular, was the former's greater emphasis on education and its rejection of parliamentary opportunism. The struggle against parliamentary "Podsnaps" (from Charles Dickens's *Our Mutual Friend*) was therefore crucial to how he saw the new organization.[41] This view, however, was not held by all in the Socialist League, most notably not by Aveling and Marx-Aveling, setting up a conflict within the organization from the outset. Soon after the split with the Social Democratic Federation and the creation of the Socialist League, the Provisional Council of the League adopted a draft constitution, brought forward, in all likelihood, by the Avelings and no doubt representing Engels's views. According to this constitution, the main activities of the organization were to be:

1. Forming and helping other Socialist bodies to form a National and International Socialist Labour Party.

2. Striving to conquer political power by promoting the election of Socialists to Local Governments, School Boards, and other administrative bodies.
3. Helping Trade-Unionism, Co-operation, and every genuine movement for the good of the workers.
4. Promoting a scheme for the National and International Federation of Labour.[42]

This draft constitution was voted down, and, in the words of Thompson, marked "the defeat of the Avelings on the Provisional Council and the complete conversion of Morris to the 'purist' and anti-parliamentary position." Nevertheless, Morris's objection to the Socialist League engaging in parliamentary action was never absolute or based on some abstract "purist" principle. Nor did it arise simply from his distaste for the opportunism that he saw as so prevalent in Hyndman's Social Democratic Federation. Rather, it was rooted in strategic considerations and a longer, more critical historical view of the transition to socialism and of the pitfalls the movement would confront along the way. In a July 1885 article for *Commonweal* titled "Socialism and Politics," Morris explained that "the object of Parliamentary institutions" was "the preservation of society in its present form—to get rid of defects in the machine in order to keep the machine going." Using an analysis of the Factory Acts as his basis, he argued that the most that could be expected of Parliament was "the creation of a new middle class"—a division of workers whose toil had been alleviated somewhat and which received added benefits—"to act as a buffer between the proletariat and their direct and obvious masters; the only hope of the bourgeoisie for retarding the advance of Socialism lies in this device." In present circumstances, Morris argued the socialism movement in Britain was too weak, too unclear about its objectives, too removed from the needs of the working population as a whole to enter into the parliamentary fracas with any hope of not simply playing into the needs of the system, serving to provide fresh flocks of sheep to be sheered. The goal ahead required instead organization and education at the societal level rather than a focus on the state. "The real business of Socialism," he wrote, "is to impress on the workers the fact that they are a class, whereas they ought to be a society."[43]

In the struggle against those who wanted to focus primarily on a parliamentary course of action and the building of a Socialist Labor Party Morris welcomed the growth of an anarchist contingent within the Socialist League, which by 1887 began to take on coherence as a separate faction. This was boosted by the sympathy generated by the judicial murder of the American "anarchists" in Chicago on the eve of the Bloody Sunday protests in London. Despite his own adamant opposition to anarchism, Morris became dependent on these allies in his anti-parliamentary struggle. Hence, he was soon to be engaged in a two-front war with both parliamentary socialists and anarchists, a war that he was politically ill-equipped to wage.[44]

Engels, who had a history of fighting two-front wars—and who, together with Marx, had struggled with Continental anarchists over the control of the First International, all the while resisting reformist tendencies—was aware of the deepening conflict, but seemed unwilling to exert his influence to bring together the genuine Marxists among the parliamentarians and the Morris contingent, with its focus on building the conditions for revolution. Engels worried that Morris was a "sentimental Socialist" and saw danger in his increasing dependence on the anarchists in the anti-parliamentary struggle within the League. No doubt Engels, who was most concerned about the growth of anarchism in the League, remembering the events that had torn apart the First International, hoped for a meeting of the minds among the genuine socialists. Here a compromise on the issue of parliamentarianism would have been necessary. But his own family-like connection (through Eleanor) to Edward Aveling (who Morris by September 1887 had dismissed as a "disreputable dog") overrode any constructive role on Engels's part.[45]

Morris's own stance in this struggle, which has so often been dismissed as tactically unsound, was rooted in the strategic view that a focus on reforms or ameliorations in the system through parliamentarianism—or from too close an adherence to trade unionism—under the conditions that then prevailed in Britain, could only undermine the long-run prospects for building socialism and thus represented the single greatest threat to the movement. The alternative strategy was to build for the future outside the state. In this he took his place, in a way unique in his time, as a theorist of the long-run transition to socialism, or the building of a movement toward socialism. The effect of Bloody Sunday on his own thinking was not, as in the case of some others such as Shaw, to retreat from revolutionary action, but to reinforce his notion that the struggle required an extended period of education and building of the movement at the level of civil society. Rather than a direct, immediate involvement in the state—something that Morris always believed would come after the movement had grown in strength—what was needed now was the making of socialists. Morris also warned of too much absorption into a purely economic, mechanical view of socialism without considering its larger social, cultural, and educational aspects.[46]

As the conflict intensified within the Socialist League in 1887, Morris forcefully articulated his own view in his lecture "The Policy of Abstention," delivered at the Hammersmith and Clerkenwell branches that summer. He argued that the best and indeed the fastest way to build a powerful movement for socialism was to concentrate on making socialists through education and broader political activity, rather than direct entry into struggle over the bourgeois state. Socialism in Britain was still in "its intellectual stage" where the revolutionary ideas were being deepened and slowly diffused among the population. However strong the objective forces favoring revolution, the subjective forces remained weak. "If we neglect" socialist education "in our haste or impatience," Morris argued, "we shall never come to the point at which more definite action will be forced upon us."

Instead of falling into the parliamentary trap, he contended, "let us try rather . . . to sustain a great body of workers outside Parliament, call it the labour parliament if you will." This was definitely a dual power strategy, in which the "labour parliament" would be gradually counterpoised to the "Westminster Committee," as he called it. In such a battle Morris proposed a political "boycott," "a general strike," and the refusal to obey oppressive law as widespread weapons of the population. In the end, though, building the subjective conditions of revolution was most important: without that, socialism was but "the mill-wheel without the motive power."[47]

For Morris, this emphasis on a long-run vision of the making of socialists was a product of his deep historical sense of the subjective weakness of the forces of change. Even the economic stagnation then affecting Britain had not created a wellspring of revolt. Coupled to this subjective weakness of the movement was that the objective conditions would not necessarily continue to be so favorable in the future. The continued expansion of imperialism, with the division of Africa, and the possibility of a "great European war" might well give new life to the system. Those dedicated to the socialist cause, then, had to be prepared to so deepen the revolutionary understanding of the population that it could weather such untoward events and reemerge renewed. A socialism without such a long-term revolutionary perspective would find every reform, every upturn in economic activity, as a perpetual obstacle, weakening its motive power. Looking at the problem in 1888, he articulated a long preparatory struggle in the overall "movement toward Socialism":

> It is not our business merely to wait on circumstances; but to do our best to put forward the movement towards Socialism, which is at least as much part of the essence of the epoch as the necessities of capitalism are. Whatever is gained in convincing people that Socialism is right always, and inevitable at last, and that capitalism in spite of all its present power is merely a noxious obstruction between the world and happiness, will not be lost again, though it may be obscured for a time, even if a new period sets in of prosperity by leaps and bounds.[48]

In his critique of the *Fabian Essays in Socialism* in 1890, Morris wrote that the development of the machine industries might contribute to the "movement toward Socialism," but they are not its "essential condition," nor for that matter was the instrumentality of the state sufficient. Socialism thus could not be achieved by merely mechanical means and required the development of a whole culture.[49]

According to Thompson, it was Morris's "alarm at the vision of reformism," emerging in the socialist movement in Britain and even within the Socialist League—which could only undermine the effort to build a revolutionary movement toward socialism—that caused him to rely on the small group of anarchists for support, with the result that he was to fall "overbalanced backwards into their arms."[50] Morris's relation to anarchism was intensely negative as a whole. He always, and irrevocably, expressed his opposition to anarchism as such ("I distinctly disagree with the Anarchist principle"; "I am not an Anarchist as I understand the word"), including anarcho-communism. On another occasion he depicted anarchism as a "negation of society," even of direct democracy, and viewed it as tending to "spasmodic insurrectionary methods." His own conception of a long revolution in his later works led him to a notion of socialism developing as an irresistible mass movement, passing through various transitional stages and struggles, in which the shift toward a society of equality would at last become irresistible. In his 1895 speech on "What We Have to Look For," he referred to "the anarchists, who seem to have a strange notion that even equality would not be acceptable if [it] were not gained by violence only." Morris's three main criticisms of the anarchism of his time thus focused on its emphasis on violence; its emphasis on individualism rather than the kind of rich individuality that he saw as the natural outgrowth of a true egalitarian, communist society; and its lack of any kind of authority structure, even by means of direct democracy. Like most Marxists, he believed that anarchism lacked a coherent political-economic critique, and hence the necessary relation between theory and practice.[51]

Nevertheless, Morris clearly saw the possibility of limited, overlapping agreement in some areas with anarchist views (as distinct from methods), particularly in his preference for a "federation of communities" as the basis of socialism/communism. He was relatively comfortable with the more urbane anarchism of his friend Prince Pyotr Alexeyevich Kropotkin, although he saw it as a thing apart. Kropotkin later indicated that Morris was a socialist not an anarchist.[52]

However, it was the cruder form of anarchism, of the insurrectionary variety, that was to be associated with the Socialist League and gain strength within the organization as a result of the parliamentary/non-parliamentary split. Morris was not entirely unaware of the consequences for the League of the growth in power of the anarchist contingent. When in 1888 the final breach between the parliamentary and non-parliamentary factions occurred and the Bloomsbury branch (in which the Avelings were most prominent) was cast out of the organization,

Morris wrote in a letter to a socialist colleague: "We have got rid of the parliamentarians, and now our anarchist friends will want to drive the team. However, we have the Council and the *Commonweal* safe with us for at least a twelvemonth, and that is something to be thankful for."[53]

Indeed, there was plenty of reason for forebodings. Some of the most talented of the socialist intellectuals were lost to the League following the 1888 breach, including not only the Avelings, but also Bax, who rejoined the Socialist Democratic Federation in 1888. By the summer of 1890, Morris had lost the editorship of *Commonweal* and he left the organization on November 21, 1890, with the entire Hammersmith branch, which represented about half the League membership at that point. At age fifty-six he began to build a new socialist organization: the Hammersmith Socialist Society.

The Socialist League, now under anarchist control, entered a period of disintegration as a political organization, though it continued to exist for a number of years. In 1892, *Commonweal* advocated the assassination of a judge at the time of the Walsall bomb case in which a group of anarchists were arrested for bomb making. (No actual bombs were found, and the arrests were the work of an *agent provocateur*; nevertheless convictions were handed out of five to ten years in prison.) The authorities raided the *Commonweal* office, seizing its stock and printing press, jailing the organization's leaders. It was in the general context of these events that Morris made his sharpest criticisms of anarchism. "As a Socialist," he stated in an interview in *Justice*, "I regard the Anarchists—that is, those who believe in Anarchism pure and simple—as being diametrically opposed to us. . . . The negation of society is the position taken up by the logical Anarchists. . . . The real anarchists . . . are against society altogether. But then we have the so-called Anarcho-Communists, a term which seems to me a flat contradiction. In so far as they are Communists they must give up their Anarchism." The anarchist-dominated League continued on for a number of years, publishing *Commonweal* sporadically but lost all influence.[54] In "How I Became a Socialist," Morris made it clear that he had learned important lessons from the anarchist takeover of the Socialist League: "Such finish to what of education in practical Socialism as I am capable of I received afterwards from some of my Anarchist friends, from whom I learned, quite against their intention, that Anarchism was impossible."[55]

The Socialist League's decline had corresponded, ironically, to a burst of strike activity in England. In the late 1880s, there was a massive upsurge of trade union agitation in England. Never seeing itself as connected to trade unionism, the Socialist League was generally disconnected from these struggles. Nevertheless, in April 1887, Morris marched in solidarity with striking Northumbrian coal miners and gave a speech to some 6,000–7,000 in Horton, standing high up on a plank above a wagon on a "day that was bright and sunny, the bright blue sea forming a strange border to the misery of the land." He insisted that one local strike would lead simply to another unless the result was a "general workingmen's strike." He urged the miners to rebel against the upper classes but to do it in an organized fashion so as not to destroy the whole entire social-cultural order and, "in such a way that it would be a kind of insurance against the violent deaths of the members of the upper classes." He called upon the policemen and soldiers who were themselves working men, to sheath their weapons, and join the populace. His speech was listened to attentively by the miners and met with resounding cheers at the end.[56]

Yet the Socialist League, with its weak connections to trade unionism, was to play practically no direct on-the-ground role in the rising tide of strikes and agitations taking place in London in 1888–89—the London Match Girls Strike of 1888, the London Dock Strike of 1889, and the great Silvertown strike in 1889 in London's East End. In contrast, Eleanor Marx played a central organizing role in a number of these East End struggles.[57]

Morris of course gave what support he could to these struggles with his pen, writing in the pages of *Commonweal*. He saw the London dock strike as possibly evolving into a general strike and hoped for a wider unity among the workers. He explained that the Silvertown strike against Samuel Winkworth Silver's rubber and electrical factory was "a revolt against oppression: a protest against the brute force which keeps a huge population down in the depths of the most dire degradation, for the benefit of a knot of profit-hunters. . . . It is a strike of the poor against the rich."[58]

Morris's greatest active contribution to the international socialist movement in 1889 was his role in supporting the formation of the Second International. On July 14 (Bastille Day), 1889, two rival socialist congresses were held simultaneously in Paris. One was the Congress of Possibilists, led by the French Possibilists (a form of municipal socialism) with the backing of most of the French socialists, and many of the English socialists, including Hyndman's Social Democratic Federation, which played an active role—together with others, such as the increasingly anti-Marxist Besant.

The other Congress was the International Socialist Working Men's Congress, sometimes referred to as the International Socialist Congress of Marxists, out of which grew the Second International. Engels, though he did not attend, had played a role in organizing the latter, in which the German Marxists predominated. Morris, in his role as leader of the Socialist League, and the most prominent Marxist thinker in Britain, was the spokesperson for the English Marxists, and the "peer," as Thompson notes, of Bebel, Liebknecht, Bernstein, and Eleanor Marx. Carpenter left an account of Morris's speech, in which he was depicted as standing "in navy blue pilot shirt—fighting furiously there on the platform with his own words . . . hacking and hewing the stubborn English phrases out—his tangled grey mane tossing, his features reddening with the effort! But the effect was remarkable." Morris himself saw his distinctive contribution and that of the English Marxists as adding "the aesthetic side" to what otherwise was a one-sidedly political-economic outlook.[59]

Under the pressure of these events, there was a deepening and a broadening of Morris's outlook at the end of the 1880s, even as the Socialist League waned. He insisted more and more that his own position was that of communism, or complete socialism. He began to (1) take into consideration the shifts in capitalism toward monopoly capitalism (including the system of waste it brought into being) and a larger imperialism; (2) develop a notion of the "movement toward socialism" and of a long revolution, as well as the strategic aspects of revolutionary transitions, in which federations of workers, general strikes, and dual power all played their part; and (3) push socialist theory in a more universalistic ecological-aesthetic direction.

One of Morris's last contributions to *Commonweal* was the final installment of *News from Nowhere* on October 4, 1890.[60] It represented the evolution of his position and the development of a thoroughgoing revolutionary vision amid the decline of the Socialist League.

MONOPOLY CAPITALISM, WASTE, AND THE AGE OF EMPIRE

"The larger background to Morris's change in perspective" in the late 1880s, E. P. Thompson wrote in *William Morris: Romantic to Revolutionary*, "was in his growing realization of the resources of monopoly capitalism and of imperialism."[61] As early as 1884, Gronlund's *The Co-operative Commonwealth* had drawn extensively on Marx's notion of the concentration and centralization of capital. For Gronlund, the dominant tendency of capitalism was toward the growth of combination and monopoly. The chief example of this, beyond the railroads, was Standard Oil Company, which had become the single corporation monopolizing nearly all oil (kerosene) produced in the United States, and using this, as H.D. Lloyd famously explained in his March 1881 article "The Story of a Great Monopoly" for the *Atlantic Monthly*, as a way of "limiting the production and maintaining an artificial [monopoly] price." Referring to Lloyd's analysis of the growing monopolization in U.S. manufacturing by a handful of firms controlled by a few great capitalists, Gronlund wrote: "These gentlemen [the great capitalists] know practical dialectics. They know that, though Competition and Combination are opposites, they yet may come to mean the same thing—to them. They have already found that while Competition is a very excellent weapon to use against their weaker rivals, Combination pays the far better in relation to their peers. It is evident that it is combination they mainly rely upon for their future aggrandizement." Gronlund backed this up with information drawn from the U.S. Census, showing that the number of manufacturing establishments had not increased in recent years despite phenomenal increases in wealth. From this he inferred that assets were becoming much more concentrated in a few firms. Giant firms controlling large sections of the market were able to obtain "monopoly value." The result was an inexorable drive to socialism. "Is it Utopian," he asked rhetorically, "to expect that all enterprises will become more and more centralized, until in the fullness of time they will all end in *one* monopoly, that of Society?"[62]

It was Gronlund's contention in *The Co-operative Commonwealth* that all of these monopolistic corporations would evolve in the end into "*one* monopoly, that of Society" which became the theoretical premise for Edward Bellamy's 1888 utopian socialist novel, *Looking Backward: 2000–1887*, the most popular book of its day, selling millions of copies and translated into twenty languages. As Erich Fromm observed, "Three outstanding personalities, Charles Beard, John Dewey, and Edward Weeks, independently making a list of the twenty-five most influential books published since 1885, all put Bellamy's work in the second place, Karl Marx's *Das Kapital* being in the first."[63]

When Bellamy's late nineteenth-century protagonist Julian West miraculously wakes up at the beginning of the twenty-first century, he is greeted by Doctor Leete, who presents a history of the late nineteenth and twentieth centuries focusing on the development of monopoly capitalism. West is told that "the era of small concerns with small capital was succeeded by that of the great aggregations of capital" in the form of "the great corporation." The "concentration of capital" led to greater masses of capital in fewer hands and the rise of all-commanding enterprises. Given the "gigantic scale of its enterprises," the new monopolistic corporations were able to fix prices and to subordinate the remaining small capitals to their needs. The growing concentration and centralization of capital eventually led to one "Great Trust" as society nationalized the giant corporations and took over the management of the economy in the interest of all.[64] All the means of production were in the hands of the state. Although the utopian picture of the organized, egalitarian society that Bellamy painted for the year 2000 accounted for much of the attraction of Bellamy's novel, its influence in relation to the critique of the monopoly capitalism of his time was scarcely less important.

Morris's own argument on the concentration and centralization of capital and monopolization clearly owed much to Marx's *Capital* and Gronlund's *The Co-operative Commonwealth*. He also carefully studied the analysis of the U.S. economist David A. Wells in this regard. As early as his 1885 lecture "The Hopes of Civilization," which was to appear in *Signs of Change*, Morris wrote of "businesses growing bigger and bigger" and of "the aggregation of capital." Under these circumstances, he observed, "the productivity of labor [was] also increasing out of all proportion to the capacity of the capitalists to manage the market or deal with the labor supply: lack of employment therefore [was] becoming chronic."[65] In his 1885 lecture "Commercial War," he followed Marx in referring to the tendency "to accumulate capital in fewer & fewer hands."[66]

Morris relied on the second part of Wells's article on "The Great Depression of Trade" for *The Contemporary Review* (August and September 1887), in which Wells addressed the empirical treatment of monopolization tendencies in a running debate with Charles Braudlaugh. Braudlaugh was the leader of the British secularist movement and a Member of Parliament for Northampton; he was virulently anti-socialist. In a public debate with Bax, Braudlaugh had denied any tendency toward the concentration and centralization of capital. Morris responded in the pages of *Commonweal* in early October 1887 with evidence taken from Wells, who had pointed to the growing concentration in all areas of manufacturing and transportation. In a passage quoted by Morris, Wells wrote: "Thus, the now well-ascertained and accepted fact, based on long experience, that power is most economically applied when applied on the largest possible scale, is rapidly and inevitably leading to the concentration of manufacturing in the largest establishments, and the gradual extinction of those which are small." For Wells, the "great corporations or stock companies" were becoming altogether typical of modern industry. "The rapidity . . . with which such combinations of capital" were arising and the "scale" they assumed was "wholly unprecedented," leading to great syndicates and trusts. Focusing on Britain, the United States, and Germany, he pointed to rapid concentration not only in railroads and steamship lines but also in such areas as steel and iron, sugar, cotton, and banking (in Germany). All of this was taken in and emphasized by Morris.[67] "Monopolist competition," he argued in "Equality" in 1888, was giving way to forms of combination and trusts that reflected the system was "growing sick."[68]

In October 1887, Morris presented his lecture, "Monopoly: Or, How Labour Is Robbed," which some, like Ruth Kinna, have characterized as his main entry into the subject of "monopoly-capitalism." Here Morris emphasized that not only were the means of production monopolized by a particular class, but that the whole tendency was toward the development of monopolistic firms. The new giant firms were "selling . . . wares at an enhanced price" and were greatly expanding the realm of advertising.[69] He was sharply critical of attempts to create a British coal trust modeled after Rockefeller's oil trust in the United States. Such "a monopoly will have the whole public in its power" and "its effect" would be to increase coal prices—at the expense of workers and consumers, since the whole purpose of such "combinations of capitalists" was higher rates of return.[70] "Morris's denunciations of monopoly-capitalism," Florence Boos has written, "clearly foreshadowed . . . excoriations of the devastation wrought by market-driven monopoly and conspicuous consumption." Indeed, Morris was to exert a strong influence on Thorstein Veblen in this respect when the latter was writing his *The Theory of the Leisure Class*.[71]

"During 1888," Thompson writes, "there was a good deal of discussion in Socialist circles, Fabian and Marxist alike, of the phenomenon of the growing trustification of American Big Business, and Morris made reference to it in his *Commonweal* notes," where he wrote of "our modern monopolist society."[72] The effect of Bellamy's 1888 novel, which Morris did not read until May 1889, was to draw even greater public attention, particularly among socialists, to the issue of the rise of big business. For Morris, Bellamy's discussion of the role of monopoly and trusts was a welcome one, but Bellamy's naive "hope of the development of the trusts" in such a way that they would lead mechanically to socialism was something to be rejected. It was not in some new mechanism that the path to socialism was be found but in the struggle for a "true life," which meant a "free and equal life." And that meant an unalienated existence, which mere mechanical solutions—or the false promise that the monopoly economy would simply turn into a "huge national centralization"—could not possibly deliver.[73]

Morris's main contribution to the understanding of monopoly capitalism was to perceive at the outset the very deep consequences that such a concentrated economic regime would have on the organization of labor and generation of waste. In "The Revival of Handicraft" in November 1888, he relied not only on Marx but also drew on Wells's description of the effect of increasingly mechanized and automatized industry. Here Morris distinguished three separate "epochs of production." The first of these was the medieval era, in which production lacked a developed division of labor beyond the division into crafts, even when workers were drawn into associations or guilds. The second was the early capitalist manufacturing era (in Marx's terminology), where "workmen were collected into workshops," beginning in the sixteenth century, with the growth of the enclosures, and developing fully by the late eighteenth century. Here workers were increasingly subject to a detailed division of labor, leading to the factory system. Labor was thus degraded; its potential for life wasted. The third epoch was "machinofacture" or capitalist industrialism. In Morris's words:

> The latter half of the eighteenth century saw the beginning of the last epoch of production that the world has known, that of the automatic machine which supersedes hand-labour, and turns the workman who was once a handicraftsman helped by tools, and next a part of a machine, into a tender of machines. And as far as we can see, the revolution in this direction as to kind is complete, though as to degree, as pointed out by Mr. David A. Wells last year (1887), the tendency is toward the displacement of ever more and more "muscular" labour, as Mr. Wells calls it.[74]

Via Wells, Morris came to the conclusion that the new monopolistic corporations were introducing more and more the age of the "automatic machine," altering the conditions of the labor process, in ways that could lead to a more automatized existence for most people under capitalism—or else to new developments of human freedom and new options for human labor under revolutionary socialism.[75]

The deepening contradictions of the system were evident in the manifold forms of waste that it generated, including (1) useless goods; (2) useless labor; (3) whole new layers of supernumeraries required by the new stage of the system; (4) the degradation of human life; and (5) a destructive relation to the environment. Although this critique of what he called a "system of waste" had been central to Morris's socialist critique from the beginning, it took an expanded form in his analysis of the large-scale industry of the monopoly era with its extreme mechanism. Linking such pervasive waste to monopoly, he told his audience in his 1893 lecture "Communism":

> Remember what the waste of a society of inequality is: 1st: The production of sordid makeshifts for the supply of poor folk who cannot afford the real article. 2nd: the production of luxuries for rich folk, the greater part of which even their personal folly does not make them want. And 3rdly: the wealth wasted by the salesmanship of competitive commerce, to which the production of wares is but a secondary object, its first object being the production of a profit for the individual manufacturer. You understand that the necessary distribution of goods is not included in this waste; but the endeavour of each manufacturer to get as near as he can to a monopoly of the market which he supplies.[76]

The significance of waste for the critique of capital was treated in an even more expansive way in his lecture "Makeshift," delivered in 1894:

> For I say the cause of the disease of poverty, from which not only all the nations but the whole of each nation suffers, is just that very war between the have-alls and the lack-alls of which I spoke of a minute ago: the have-alls perpetually fortifying their position, for they have no idea how to live out of it: the lack-alls perpetually struggling to gain a little *more*, and yet a little more if they only can. Take note also that the result of this war is necessarily waste. I noticed that the other day Mr. Balfour was saying that Socialism was impossible because under it we should produce so much less than we do now. Now I say that we might produce half or a quarter of what we do now, and yet be much wealthier, and consequently, much happier, than we are now: and that by turning whatever labour we exercised, into the production of useful things, things that we all want, and . . . by refusing to labour in the producing useless things, things

which none of us, not even fools want. What a strange sight would be a great museum of samples of all the market-wares which the labouring men of this country produce! What a many of them there would be which every reasonable man would have to ticket as useless!

My friends, a very great many people are employed in producing mere nuisances, liked barbed wire, 100-ton guns, sky signs and advertising boards for the disfigurement of the green fields along the railways and so forth. But apart from these nuisances, how many more are employed in making market wares for rich people which are of no use whatever except to enable the said rich to "spend their money" as 'tis called; and again how many more in producing wretched makeshifts for the working classes because they are so poor that they can afford nothing better?[77]

A crucial aspect of this argument was that the amount of luxury and waste in the society was evidence of the enormous economic surplus being generated and the capacity of society to meet the genuine needs of all within the context of a society of equality. In his 1888 lecture on "Equality," Morris insisted that "complete equality of condition for all" was "the aim of Socialism stated in the fewest possible words . . . no further mastery over the powers of nature that we may gain can be a substitute for it; without it freedom, education, happiness, in one word, progress is impossible."[78]

Morris recognized more fully than anyone else in his day that the capitalist system in its developed monopoly stage relied more and more on the production of "artificial" or specifically capitalist use values that were necessary to keep the system going but no longer constituted real wealth (as distinct from mere riches). Adulterated and makeshift wares sold to the workers, together with the entirely useless luxury "goods" bought by the rich, served to impoverish the population, not only failing to fulfill their needs but constituting "useless toil." "The essence of their reason for production," he declared in 1894, with particular regard to the sham commodities foisted on workers, "is not the production of *goods* but of *profits* for those who are privileged to live on other people's labour."[79] Morris presented his basic thesis in this respect in a letter to the *Daily Chronicle* in May 1895, where he explained: "The truth is that our system of Society is essentially a system of *waste*."[80]

The adulteration of goods, particularly for the workers but extending more broadly, was exemplified in the case of bread and butter. "You have all heard of the thing called *bread*," Morris exclaimed in "Makeshift,"

but I suspect very few of those here present have ever tasted the real article, although they are familiar enough with the makeshift. A makeshift which I have no doubt is of somewhat long standing. In my youth genuine bread was

> usually eaten in the country-sides, but was not for the most part sold in the big towns; but now the country bread made by the bakers in the small towns is worse than the town bread. For the country-people, at all events in the country I know, have quite given up baking at home and buy of the small town baker. . . . Perhaps you will say, but people can bake at home if they like still. No, they cannot. For to bake a good loaf you must have good flour, and that is unattainable; the ideal of the modern miller (imported from America, I believe, that special land of makeshift) seems to be to reduce the rich oily wheat grains into a characteristic white powder like chalk. Whiteness and fineness are what they seem to aim at, at the expense of the qualities that are discoverable by the palate.
>
> So you see, bread is not to be had now by anybody almost; and this you must understand is an essential characteristic of the Social makeshift; it is forced on the whole population, and in a very short time supplants the original and genuine article entirely.[81]

He went on to discuss as another makeshift the displacement of butter by margarine, primarily for economic motives: "Save trouble, make money, and who cares for the rest?"[82]

All of this went hand in hand, in Morris's view, with growing monopolization of industry and increasing commercialism. His last public address, on January 31, 1896, was, significantly, presented to a meeting of the Society for Checking the Abuses of Public Advertising at the Society of Arts. Already in 1880, he had protested against "the daily increasing hideousness of the posters of which all our towns are daubed," insisting that those concerned with "the beauty of life" should resolve "never to buy any of the articles so advertised." He saw the rapid growth of advertising as a product of the need to sell useless or makeshift goods, representing wasted labor, to people who did not for the most part need or even want them: exemplifying the penetration of waste into every niche and cranny of society. "Our newspaper and periodical press," he declared, "are little more than puffing sheets when they are successful, sugared with a little news, a little politics & sometimes a little literature."[83]

From his very first acquaintance with socialist doctrines, Morris was concerned with the wasted labor associated with the processes of commercial exchange and distribution under capitalism. He had, as noted earlier, first become aware of the political economic debate surrounding socialism from his reading of Mill's posthumously published *Chapters on Socialism* in the *Fortnightly Review* in 1879, in which Mill attacked "Socialism in its Fourierist guise." Mill's intention was to critique socialism. But in the process, as Morris explained, he drew on actual writings from Fourierist thinkers, thereby convincing Morris for his part of the necessity of socialism.

Since at least 1849, Mill had been interested in the work of Victor Considérant, Fourier's leading follower. Mill quoted at length from Considérant in *Chapters on Socialism*, emphasizing in particular Considérant's emphasis on wasted labor in distribution, along with "the adulteration of products," the waste associated with the accumulation of profits, etc. For Considérant, following Fourier, the system "robs society by the subtraction of its productive forces; taking off from productive labour nineteen-twentieths of the agents of trade who are mere parasites. Thus, not only does commerce rob society by appropriating an exorbitant share of the common wealth, but also by considerably diminishing the productive energy of the human beehive." As Mill himself put it, "one of the leading ideas of this [Fourierist] school is the wastefulness and at the same time the immorality of the existing arrangements for distributing the produce of the country among the various consumers, the enormous superfluity in point of number of the agents of distribution, the merchants, dealers, shopkeepers and their innumerable employés, and the depraving character of such a distribution of occupations."[84]

It was this same conception that entered into the *Manifesto of the Socialist League*, which stated: "The whole method of distribution under this system is full of waste; for it employs whole armies of clerks, travellers, shopmen, advertisers, and whatnot, merely for the sake of shifting money from one person's pocket to another's; and this waste in production and waste in distribution, added to the maintenance of the useless lives of the possessing and non-producing class, must all be paid for out of the products of the workers, and is a ceaseless burden on their lives."[85] In "Art and Socialism" in 1884, Morris was to write:

> It would be an instructive day's work for any one of us who is strong enough to walk through two or three of the principal streets of London on a week-day, and take accurate note of everything in the shop windows which is embarrassing or superfluous. . . . I beg you to think of the enormous mass of men who are occupied with this miserable trumpery, from the engineers who have had to make the machines for making them, down to the hapless clerks who sit daylong year after year in the horrible dens wherein the wholesale exchange of them is transacted, and the shopmen who, not daring to call their souls their own, retail them . . . to the idle public which doesn't want to buy them, but buys them to be bored by them and sick to death of them. I am talking of the merely useless things; but there are other matters not merely useless, but actively destructive and poisonous, which command a good price in the market; for instance, adulterated food and drink. Vast is the number of slaves whom competitive Commerce employs in turning out infamies such as these.[86]

To produce useless, destructive, ugly goods, the product of human alienation, was to waste, degrade, and contaminate both work and life. Such "non-artistic human work," Morris stated in his lecture "The Arts and Crafts of Today" in 1889, "bear with them the same sort of harm as blankets infected with small-pox or the scarlet-fever"—a reference to the British use of these techniques to kill off Indian populations in Colonial America—"and every step in your material life and its 'progress' will tend towards the intellectual death of the human race."[87]

The broad theme of useless employment, reflecting a waste of the economic surplus of society, was also evident in *Signs of Change*, where Morris wrote of those "who follow occupations which would have no place in a reasonable condition of society, as, e.g., lawyers, judges, jailers, and soldiers of the higher grades, and most Government officials," representing the servile hangers-on to the capitalist class. Generally above this, in terms of the extraction of tribute, were the major commercial speculators fighting for "individual shares of the tribute" taken from the working class: "the group that one calls broadly business men, the conductors of our commerce."[88]

Morris and Bax argued in the *Manifesto of the Socialist League* that some of those workers who had, by dint of hard labor, raised themselves up to the level of "small capitalists," constituted "aristocrats of labour." Such small businesspeople occupied a contradictory class location—"both slave-drivers and slave-driven." At the same time, some ostensibly "middle class" members of the poorly paid medical and literary professions, whose income was often not much more than that of the skilled worker, could be seen as constituting "an intellectual proletariat."[89]

In the phase of monopolistic industry, Morris was to observe in 1889, the "*professional* middle-class men" were characterized by their "complicity with the monopolist class" and could be viewed as mere hangers-on in the rising corporate universe, subordinate to the "triumphant bourgeoisie."[90] In general, the more centralized capitalism became, and the more the sphere of commercial sales and distribution expanded, the greater the amassing of waste. As he further observed in May 1896 (only a few months before his death), under such a system, "Nothing better will happen than more waste and more, only perhaps exercised in different directions than now it is. Waste of material, and waste of labour (for few indeed even of the genuine wage-earners are engaged in the production of utilities). Waste, in one word, of LIFE."[91]

For E. J. Hobsbawm "the era of the Great Depression," as the 1873–96 economic period was referred to in Europe, brought on "the era of imperialism; the formal imperialism of the 'partition of Africa' in the 1880s, and the semi-formal imperialism" that followed. These changes were connected to economic concentration and attempts of newly arising giant corporations to widen profit margins: "Between 1876 and 1915 about one-quarter of the globe's land surface was distributed or redistributed as colonies among a half-dozen states."[92]

Morris in his time correctly perceived the economic stagnation of this period, together with the growth of monopolistic firms, as giving rise to the scramble for Africa and the imperialist movement generally. In response to an article by Bax in *Commonweal* in 1888 on the partition of Africa, he adopted Bax's thesis that such expansion might revive the European capitalist system, putting off the day of revolution. Morris's response to this new challenge was that the "movement toward Socialism" must not "wait on circumstance" and should continue to move forward.[93] Imperialism, he had stated in his 1885 lecture "The Commercial War," was "simply the agony of capitalism driven by a force it cannot resist to seek for new & ever new markets at any price, at any risk. . . . And if by chance the great capitalist & despotic communities are to meet in a huge all-embracing conflict, I don't believe for one that the new heavens and the new earth that will arise from Ragnarók or Twilight of the Gods will turn out to be the paradise of exploitation which the Imperialist liberals have figured to themselves."[94]

On May Day 1896 he declared that imperialism was for the time being the way out for the system threatened by socialism and economic crisis, but a way out that needed to be stopped:

> The capitalist classes are doubtless alarmed at the spread of Socialism. . . . They have at least an instinct of danger; but with that instinct comes the other one of self-defence. Look how the whole capital world is stretching out long arms towards the barbarous world and grabbing and clutching in eager competition at countries whose inhabitants don't want them; nay, in many cases, would rather die in battle, like the valiant men they are, than have them. So perverse are these wild men before the blessings of [bourgeois] civilization which would do nothing worse for them (and also nothing better) than reduce them to a propertyless proletariat.
>
> And what is all this for. . . . It is for the opening of fresh markets to take in all the fresh profit-producing wealth which is growing greater and greater everyday; in other words, to make fresh opportunities for *waste*; the waste of our labour and our lives.

Morris's answer was an international movement toward socialism, based on a "hunger for freedom and fair play for all, both people and peoples."[95]

CHAPTER FOUR

An Earthly Paradise

During a lecture tour in Scotland in the 1880s, William Morris, together with several companions, walked two miles through the coal mining district on the way from Whifflets railway station to Coatbridge. Along the way he inquired into all aspects of the miners' lives, commenting on the bleak condition of the "colliers' rows" (or miners' housing, consisting of stone row houses ofen constructed near the mouth of the pit) and how the ironworks had affected the vegetation in the area. Upon arriving in Coatbridge he delivered a lecture to the workers gathered there. After he finished speaking, a miner asked him, "Does the lecturer propose to do away with coal-mining, and, if so, what would we do for fuel?" According to the necessarily imperfect but seemingly authentic recollections of John Glasier many years later, Morris replied that coal production should be sharply cut due to environmental factors and the effects on workers' lives, but that need not involve hardship in a more rational society:

> For myself, I should be glad if we could do without coal, and indeed without burrowing like worms and moles in the earth altogether; and I am not sure but we could do without it if we wished to live pleasant lives, and did not want to produce all manner of mere mechanism chiefly for multiplying our own servitude and misery, and spoiling half the beauty and the art of the world to make merchants and manufacturers rich. In olden days the people did without coal, and were, I believe, rather more happy than we are to-day. . . .
>
> But without saying we can do without coal, I *will* say we could do with less than half of what we use now, if we lived properly and produced only really useful, good, and beautiful things. We could get plenty of timber for our domestic fires if we cultivated and cared for our forests as we might do; and with the water and wind power we now allow to go to waste, so to say, and with or without electricity, we could perhaps obtain the bulk of the motive power which might be required for the essential mechanical industries. And anyway, we

> should, I hope, be able to make the conditions of mining much more healthy and less disagreeable than they are to-day, and give the miners a much higher reward for their labour; and also—and this I insist is most important—no one ought to be compelled to work more than a few hours underground, and nobody ought to be compelled to work all their lives, or even constantly week by week, at mining, or indeed any other disagreeable job. Everybody ought to have a variety of occupation, so as to give him a chance of developing his various powers, and of making his work a pleasure rather than a dreary burden.[1]

On numerous other occasions, Morris was to emphasize the importance of limiting coal production because of its environmental harms, as well as the need for limiting industrial production itself when it did not contribute to the fulfillment of human needs and was destructive of human health, nature, and beauty.[2] The material waste that capitalism produced through the manufacture of useless and ugly goods had its counterpart in the waste and ugliness imposed on human lives. Such ecological views induced him to develop a wider conception of socialism/communism encompassing humanistic, naturalistic, and aesthetic values that were starkly opposed to capitalism's Gradgrind philosophy.[3]

Unless this wider meaning of socialist struggle was gradually incorporated into the movement toward socialism, and its current mechanistic character abandoned, the struggle would be unable to overcome either its own subjective limitations or the objective obstacles that would be placed in its way. As Morris explained in "The Revival of Handicraft," the task was to determine how the human freedom and artistic creativity that had been lost as a result of transformations in the mode of production could be re-created on another plane as part of a more "dynamic," more culturally expansive and collective future.[4]

An ecological aesthetic thus pervaded Morris's thinking. All of his later romances, such as *A Tale of the House of the Wolfings* (1888), *The Roots of the Mountains* (1889), and *The Sundering Flood* (1897), revolve around the historical or mythic concept of a "sundering" of love, community, art, and nature—each of which is surmounted in subsequent struggles over the course of the romance.[5] This was fundamental to Morris's Romantic aesthetic and is embedded in his socialist lectures as well, representing a critique of the pervasive estrangement or alienation generated by capitalist society.

As Morris wrote in 1891 in "The Socialist Ideal: Art": "The sundering of the ways between the Socialist and the commercial [or capitalist] view of art lay in the fact that "to the Socialist a house, a knife, a cup, a steam engine, or whatnot, anything, I repeat, that is made by man and has form, must either be a work of art or destructive to art." The capitalist severs this relationship, alienating art and community, by dividing "'manufactured articles' into those which are prepensely works of art, and offered for sale in the market as such, and those which have no pretence to artistic qualities." Rather than based in the atomistic individual, art, in Morris's conception, was in its essence collective, and was a product of the work of a community. "The great mass of effective art, that which pervades all life, *must* be the result of the harmonious cooperation of neighbours." The sundering of community, of love, of nature (of which humanity is part), through utilitarian capitalism, was therefore the sundering of humanity's own "aesthetic": the alienation of life.[6] "The advance of the industrial army under its 'captains of industry'. . . is traced, like the advance of other armies, in the ruin of the peace and loveliness of earth's surface and nature."[7]

THE SUNDERING OF TOWN AND COUNTRY

In an 1895 lecture titled "What We Have to Look For" Morris spoke of the need to "restore what of the earth's surface is spoilt and keep that which is unspoilt."[8] This required a restoration and transformation of the entire urban-rural landscape. The key question, posed in his 1894 lecture "Town and Country," was "whether it may not be possible in the long run to make the town a part of the country and the country a part of the towns." The town (in England represented by London in particular) was the center of intellectual life, while the country, despite its "superintendent beauty," was caught up in "the makeshift-stupidity of the epoch."[9]

The real division between town and country arose in the eighteenth century with the Industrial Revolution—manifested both in London and the new manufacturing towns. Morris therefore argued for the dispersion of the population into the countryside from the overdeveloped urban centers, while not eliminating the great towns. Urban centers were to be surrounded by greenery. "I want neither the towns to be appendages of the country, nor the country of the town. I want the town to be impregnated with the beauty of the country, and the country with the intelligence and vivid life of the town."[10]

This argument closely paralleled that of Karl Marx and Frederick Engels. Engels's 1844 *Condition of the Working Class in England* had discussed the growth of the "Great Towns" in similar fashion. In *The Communist Manifesto* Marx and Engels wrote of how the towns had "rescued a considerable part of the population from the isolation of rural life," which is removed from the major forces and cultural influences shaping the epoch, while at the same time subjecting the close-packed urban population to conditions of machine-like exploitation and physical degradation. They went on to argue for the "gradual abolition of the distinction between town and country by a more equable distribution of the population over the country," a position not unlike the one that Morris was to take.[11] Marx drew a similar distinction in *Capital*, where he said that capitalism "destroys at the same time the physical health of the urban worker, and the intellectual life of the rural worker."[12]

Laurence Gronlund too was to insist that the answer to the contradiction between town and country was for a good part of the population of "overgrown cities" to disperse to the countryside. Yet, to do so, production had to some extent move as well, and the distinction between the cities as the sole intellectual centers and the rural areas with their cultural "isolation" had to be overcome. All of this required socialism or a cooperative commonwealth.[13]

In the final chapter of *Socialism: Its Growth and Outcome*, Morris and E. Belfort Bax presented three different ideas of how "the transformation of the modern town"—"industrial," as in the case of Manchester, or a "capital," as in the case of London—might be effected under socialism:

> The first would leave the great towns still existing, but would limit the population on any given space; it would insist on cleanliness and airiness, the surrounding and segregation of the houses by gardens; the erecting of noble public buildings; the maintenance of educational institutions of all kinds—of theatres, libraries, workshops, taverns, kitchens, etc. This kind of town might be of considerable magnitude, and the houses in it might not be very different in size and arrangement from what they are now, although the life lived in them would be transformed. It is understood, of course, that any association in dwelling in such places would be quite voluntary, although . . . no individual or group could be allowed to engross an undue area.
>
> The second method of dealing with the unorganized and anarchic towns of to-day proposes their practical abolition, and the supplanting of them in the main by combined dwellings built more or less on the plan of the colleges of our older English universities. As to the size of these, that would have to be determined by convenience in each case, but the tendency would be to make them so large as to be almost small towns of themselves; since they would have to include a large population in order to foster the necessary give and take of intellectual intercourse, and make them more or less independent for ordinary occupation and amusement.
>
> It is to be understood that this system of dwellings would not necessarily preclude the existence of quite small groups, and houses suitable to them, although we think that these would tend to become eccentricities.
>
> Yet another suggestion may be sketched as follows:—a centre of a community, which can be described as a very small town with big houses, including various public buildings, the whole probably grouped around an open space. Then a belt of houses gradually diminishing in number and more spaced out, till at last the open country should be reached, where the dwellings which would include some of the above-mentioned colleges, would be sporadic.

It was clear that in practice Morris and Bax saw the arrangement of cities utilizing to some extent all of these approaches: all three were evident in part in *News for Nowhere*, written three years earlier, though the description there was closest to the first method above. The one principle that would govern all these arrangements, they stated, would be "the doing away of all antagonism between town and country, and all tendency for the one to suck the life out of the other."[14]

The ecological critique of the town and country under capitalism did not derive simply from aesthetic concerns but had a more directly ecological form as well. In *Capital*, Marx, inspired in part by the German soil scientist Justus von Liebig, wrote of the depletion of soil nutrients, due to the shipment of the "constituent elements" of the soil from the countryside to the city. This led simultaneously to the despoliation of the land and the pollution of the cities, rupturing "the metabolic interaction of man and the earth." He concluded: "Capitalist production . . . only develops the techniques and the degree of combination of the social process of production by simultaneously undermining the original sources of all wealth—the soil and the worker."[15]

Laurence Gronlund wrote of the concentration and centralization of capital within agriculture, leading to "bonanza farms," and the rift in the reproduction of the soil, as soil nutrients were sent in the form of food and fiber to the city. As he put it, "Our present mode of farming impoverishes the soil; 'bonanza' farming does so to a still greater extent. Every bushel of wheat sent to our large cities or abroad, robs the soil of a certain amount of nutriment. And next to nothing—in fact, on the bonanza farms nothing at all—is done to reimburse the soil for that loss. The object of the bonanza farmers is simply to plunder the soil as much as possible in order to fill their own pockets. When it becomes no longer profitable to work the land with even the most extensive machinery, they will be left mere deserts."[16]

In *Woman and Socialism* August Bebel underscored the ecological rift associated with industrial agriculture. "The ground," he noted,

> must receive exactly the same chemical ingredients as those which have been extracted by the previous crops, and it must especially receive those chemical ingredients which the crop to be next sown requires. . . . This rule is being constantly transgressed at the present day, especially in large towns, which receive enormous quantities of food, but restore only a small portion of the valuable refuse and excrements to the land. The consequence is, that all farms at a distance from the towns to which they annually send the greater part of their produce, suffer considerably from want of manure . . . and a ruinous system of cultivation ensues, by which the soil is impoverished.[17]

Bebel went on to connect this, as with Marx, with sewage problems in the city. Only under socialism and the dispersal of population would these problems be alleviated.[18]

It is hardly surprising, then, given his familiarity with the works by Marx, Gronlund, and Bebel, in which these observations occurred—as well as the general Victorian debate on this subject unleashed by Liebig—that the same general critique of the ecological rift of town and country entered into Morris's thinking as well. As he stated in his 1885 lecture on "The Depression of Trade": "While I speak to you London is practically undrained; a huge mass of sewage, which should be used for fertilizing the fields of Kent and Essex now and especially the latter actually passing out of cultivation, a wall of filth is accumulating at the mouth of the Thames garnering up for us who knows what seeds of pestilence and death."[19]

What made the division between town and country under capitalism so acute was the uncontrolled industrialization, concentration of capital, and concomitant effects on cities like London and Manchester. Taking the terrible conditions of capitalist machinofacture almost for granted, Morris wrote relatively little about the sordid environmental conditions within *The Factory Hell*, as Edward Aveling and Eleanor Marx-Aveling called it. In such factories the lack of sanitation and adequate ventilation, plus the overall congestion, extreme-exploitative work conditions, and almost total absence of safety measures to protect workers created a situation that was almost indescribably bad, the source of all sorts of diseases, respiratory ailments, lead poisoning, and accidental death. As Aveling and Marx-Aveling wrote: "No one has heart in the work done in our hideous factories, whose chimneys rise up like curses from earth to heaven."[20]

On one occasion Morris highlighted the horror of these conditions, referring to a case in which

> a man was killed by being compelled to work in a place where white-lead was flying about, and . . . no precautions were taken to prevent his dying speedily. . . . It is quite impossible that the man's employers did not know the risk he ran of this speedier death, and the certainty of his being poisoned later. . . . This is only an exaggerated example of the way in which the lives of working-people are played with. Under present conditions, almost the whole labour imposed by civilisation on the "lower classes" is unwholesome; that is to say that people's lives are shortened by it; and yet because we don't see people's throats cut before our eyes we think nothing of it.[21]

Morris's answer to such problems was laid out in his remarkable essay "The Factory as It Might Be," published in *Commonweal* in three short parts, where he presented a new vision of the factory, no longer toxic to the workers and their surroundings. "A socialist factory, just like a capitalist factory, could support gardens as at present, but not in this case the lavish gardens twenty miles away from the factory smoke at the great houses of the capitalists, but instead gardens for workers in the vicinity of the factory itself. Our factory," he wrote, "must make no sordid litter, befoul no water, nor poison the air with smoke. I need say nothing more on this point, as 'profit' apart it would be easy enough."[22]

If the capitalist factories in in England in which workers were being exploited daily were hellacious, their housing conditions were just as inhuman, the product of poverty mingled with environmental contamination. In an article on "The Housing of the Poor" in *Justice* in 1884, Morris, outraged, wrote of a letter written to the *Pall Mall Gazette* in which the author, in Morris's words, claimed, "It is not so bad as one might think for a whole family to live in one room; by a *room* of course meaning the ordinary 12 ft. sq. hutch of an East End [London] house."[23] Capitalism in general threatened to drag the "working classes" into "that hell of irredeemable degradation."[24]

Most of his condemnations of the environmental degradation of capitalism, however, had as their setting not the factory, or the housing of the poor, but the larger architecture and geography of the capitalist city, and the extension of its ugly, polluted, and pestilential deformations into the country on an ever-widening basis. In "Why Not?," written for *Justice* in 1884, Morris asked, "Why should one third of England be so stifled and poisoned with smoke that over the greater part of Yorkshire (for instance) the general idea must be that sheep are naturally black? Profit would have it so: no one any longer pretends that it would not be easy to prevent such crimes against decent life: but the 'organizers of labour,' who might better be called 'organizers of filth,' know that it wouldn't pay."[25] He complained in *Signs of Change* of a system of "profit which won't take the most ordinary precautions against wrapping a whole district in a cloud of sulphurous smoke; which turns beautiful rivers into filthy sewers."[26]

Morris celebrated the beauty of nature and the love of nature in almost everything he wrote. The famous "Prologue" to *The Earthly Paradise* begins with the words:

> Forget six counties overhung with smoke,
> Forget the snorting steam and piston stroke,
> Forget the spreading of the hideous town;
> Think rather of the pack-horse on the down,
> And dream of London, small and white and clean,
> The clear Thames bordered by its gardens green.[27]

In "Under an Elm Tree, or Thoughts in the Countryside," published in *Commonweal* in 1889, we find Morris evoking the White Horse of Uffington in Berkshire, a 360-foot-long, 160-foot-high image cut into the chalk downs some 2,000 to 4,000 years ago. In Morris's day it was thought to have been of much more recent origin and to have commemorated King Alfred's victory in the Battle of Ashdown in 871. Morris saw it as representing the defense of the "peace and loveliness of this very country where I lie." But if the battle needed to be fought again, he commented, it would be "against *capitalist* robbers this time."[28]

Morris passionately defended not only the rural countryside but argued for the preservation of rivers and wooded areas. He called for restraints on the horrendous capitalist intrusions into nature, designed to turn it into a commodity, a market, or a plaything for the idle rich. Although referring at times to the superabundance of nature and frequently celebrating, as was common in his day, the conquest or "victory over nature," putting society in command over natural forces, he also recognized definite natural limits. As he wrote in *Signs of Change*: "There is a certain amount of natural material and natural forces in the world."[29] The question then became how they were used for the benefit of all.

Morris faulted class-based luxury consumption, greed, and waste of nature's resources for the advent of the stupendous flood in Johnstown, Pennsylvania, in 1889, which killed over 2,000 people. The "jerry-built dam, was in fact a pleasure lake, the property of a fishing club; so that this gigantic threat of sudden death to thousands was simply one of the means of wasting the riches that the idle class wring by force from the workers, and which they cannot *use* but only waste. I do not wonder at the anger of the survivors from this artificial deluge, this subsidized terror, against the owners or holders of the pleasure-lake."[30]

In general, the pastimes of the idle rich tended toward ecological excess and destruction. In his foreword to More's *Utopia*, Morris proposed the banning of upper-class hawking and hunting, characterizing these and other similar forms of so-called sportsmanship as "butchery."[31]

Morris wrote three passionate letters to the *Daily Chronicle* in 1895 in defense of Epping Forest on the outskirts of London, near where he had grown up. As in other writings, he argued against cutting down and excessive thinning of the woods, contending that it was necessary to leave it as a "thicket," and as near as possible in its natural state. In this respect, he challenged the authority of so-called experts on forest management bought out by commercial interests.[32]

These problems were not simply confined to capitalism; they would continue even in the "federation of communities" that constituted Morris's preferred form of communism. He insisted that there had to be some kind of sovereign authority or compact going beyond the individual and even beyond mere plebiscite, which would help ensure the common interest. He illustrated this by pointing out that the "grievous flood of utilitarianism," which would continue to haunt society to some extent even with the advent of a society of equality.

"The public opinion of a community" might be "in favour of cutting down all the timber in England, and turning the country into a big Bonanza farm [of the kind referred to by Gronlund] or a market garden under glass." Hence, there needed to be some sovereign public constitution or system of authority, erected on a democratic foundation, but representing the longer, more collective interest or "common bond" of the people (taking into account future generations)—able to restrain both the single individual and the mass of individuals in favor of the long-term ecological needs of the associated producers.[33]

But though Morris was a strong advocate for conservation and even preservation, and argued for the dispersion of population as well as an end to the division of town and country, he did not—despite the claims of such scholars as Peter Gould—adopt a "back to nature" outlook of the kind advocated, for example, by his friend and fellow socialist Edward Carpenter, a follower of Henry David Thoreau and Walt Whitman. Morris read Thoreau's *Walden* and visited Carpenter on his largely self-sufficient estate. He even, Gould noted, wrote a December 1884 letter indicating how he had listened with "longing heart" to Carpenter's description of life on his farm, all of which sounded "very agreeable." But these few words in Morris's letter hardly bear the weight of the conclusion that Gould draws from it. For Gould, Morris's "ideal life continued to bear a close similarity to that of Carpenter on his smallholding of Millthorpe." Yet, Morris, more so than Carpenter, as Sheila Rowbotham acutely observed, "was sceptical about a Thoreau-style detachment, politically and personally. . . . Renunciation did not figure in Morris's socialism unless it was forced on him by the exigencies of struggle." Morris stressed on numerous occasions: "Do not think I am advocating asceticism," proposing rather a "non-ascetic simplicity of life."[34]

If we examine the letter that Morris wrote on this particular occasion, we find that he was then low in spirits (the reason for visiting Carpenter in the first place) due to the impending split in the Social Democratic Federation. He followed up his statement of a vague "longing" to be out of it all, removed from the direct struggle over bourgeois civilization, with the sort of end resolve characteristic of him, saying simply it would be "dastardly to desert."[35] He immediately went on in the following weeks to play the principal role in the founding of the Socialist League, hardly an indication of the desire to pursue a life of self-sufficient farming. Nor is there any indication elsewhere in his work that a secluded existence in the countryside constituted Morris's ideal, which always started with the town, not with the country. Although Morris admired the countryside, what he continually sought, as expressed in *News from Nowhere* and elsewhere, was not a retreat to some abstract nature, but a much more complex, dialectical integration of town and country. This was far removed from Carpenter's own Arcadian vision articulated in his 1883 book, *Co-operative Production*. Rather, Morris took his stand directly with the working class and socialism, addressing factory production and the urban environment, but all the while seeking to merge this with an ecological vision of sustainable existence for society as a whole.

It is true that Morris's deep dislike of bourgeois civilization was such that he obtained considerable pleasure and inspiration from reading Richard Jefferies's post-apocalyptic fictional work, *After London*, published in 1885. Jefferies presented a picture of some indeterminate catastrophe that had destroyed civilization, not only in England but in other countries as well. The first part of his book consists of a narrative by some unknown historian who describes the catastrophic environmental changes that have destroyed civilization and speculates on the possible causes (such as the tilting of Earth altering the climate). London has been reduced to a vast pestilential swamp in its lower regions and is completely overgrown in its higher regions. A vast depopulation of the country has occurred and those who have departed are never heard from again. All modern technology is lost. Almost all communication with the outside world has been cut off. The Welsh and the Irish from the Celtic fringe have invaded and conquered much of England in what is seen as a kind of "divine vengeance." A feudal system characterized by continual warfare ensues, coupled with a kind of return to nature. The second part of the book consists of an adventure story set in the "after London" world, in which the youthful protagonist Sir Felix Aquila undergoes an odyssey fraught with dangers and battles, and the hope of triumph over unrequited love.[36]

Morris regarded *After London* as a "queer book" but indicated in a letter to his close friend Georgiana Burne-Jones that "I rather like it: absurd hopes curled round my heart as I read it." A month later, apparently with Jefferies's book still at the back of his mind, and in a depressed state, Morris wrote to her:

> I have [no] more faith than a grain of mustard seed in the future history of "civilization," which I *know* now is doomed to destruction, and probably before very long: what a joy it is to think of! and how often it consoles me to think of barbarism once more flooding the world, and real feelings and passions, however rudimentary, taking the place of our wretched hypocrisies. With this thought in my mind all the history of the past is lighted up and lives again in me. I used really to despair once because I thought what the idiots of our day call progress would go on perfecting itself: happily. I know now that all that will have a sudden check—sudden in appearance I mean—"as it was in the days of Noë."[37]

In his historical romances and his lectures on art and socialism, Morris frequently glorified the Goths, and even "barbarism," albeit in the Fourierist sense in which barbarism was less "barbaric" than the bourgeois civilization that succeeded it. Thus he told his socialist audiences: "So shall we be our own Goths, and at whatever cost break up again the new tyrannous Empire of capitalism." For those with a knowledge of classical history, the mark of an educated person in Morris's day, the meaning was obvious. The heroic role of "external proletariat" (to adopt the later Toynbian language) represented by the invading Goths of old, who had vanquished the Empire of Rome, was to be carried out in a modern times by the "internal proletariat," whose job was to dispense with "the Empire of capitalism."[38]

Yet, though Morris derived satisfaction from the notion of the downfall for one reason or another of capitalist civilization, leading to a retrogression of a kind, even to a new "healthy barbarism," he generally conceived this resurrection of an earlier cultural mode in a dialectical sense, as a way forward to a higher, communist society.[39] As Morris and Bax observed in *The Manifesto of the Socialist League*, referring to the revolutionary overthrow of bourgeois society, "The new development returns to a point which represents the older principle elevated to a new higher plane; the old principle reappears transformed, purified, made stronger, and ready to advance on the fuller life it has gained through its seeming death."[40]

There is nothing, in fact, in Morris's entire corpus that suggests he seriously adopted nineteenth-century Romantic notions of a *return to nature*—or of a return to medieval society.[41] "We cannot turn our people back into Catholic English peasants and guild-craftsmen, or into heathen Norse bonders," he wrote, "much as may be said for such conditions of life: we have no choice but to accept the task which the centuries have laid on us of using the corruption of 300 years of profit-mongering for the overthrow of that very corruption."[42] Rather he stood wholeheartedly for the *return of nature* and of unalienated human values as part of a revolutionary-dialectical movement of society, rejecting the exclusions and enclosures of a one-sided, distorted capitalist development. The radical conception for which he fought thus grew out of a complex notion of historical change in which the past became a force in transforming the future.

Morris's organic dialectic taught him that complete socialism and communism—the struggle for which constituted the whole reason and necessity for the movement toward socialism—required the transcendence of both the division between town and country and the rift between capitalist society and nature. Art meant for him unalienated production, and thus an active, creative existence in unity with both humanity and nature. Nature, he believed, in a manner that paralleled Epicurus and Marx, must be recognized as "a friend." Through association it was possible to create a more "harmonious whole" of nature and human community.[43] In terms of the socialist movement of his time, this meant that he hoped for the development, for which there were already some bases in his time, of an environmental proletariat, concerned with safeguarding and sustaining life, creativity, beauty, and the earth itself. As he stated in his lecture "Art: A Serious Thing" in 1882: "I have taken note of many strikes, and I must needs say without circumlocution that with many of these I have heartily sympathized: but when the day comes that there is a serious strike of workmen against the poisoning of the air with smoke or the waters with filth, I shall think that art is getting on indeed."[44]

But such a transformation of the struggle for socialism into a struggle for an aesthetically and ecologically sustainable social life required a conscious transcendence of prevailing productive relations far beyond the socialist movement of Morris's day. It required, he recognized, that society consciously "forgo some of the power over Nature won by past ages in order to be more human and less mechanical."[45] This vision meant forging a truly revolutionary utopian-Romantic consciousness, reaching beyond contemporary material conditions; one that would be able to use the past and historical understanding to reshape the image of what was possible and necessary in the future.[46]

NEWS FROM NOWHERE: NATURE, LABOR, AND GENDER

William Morris's celebrated utopian romance *News from Nowhere or An Epoch of Rest: Being Some Chapters from a Utopian Romance* constituted his most singular attempt to present a revolutionary ideal aimed at inspiring a movement toward socialism.[47] Centering on the overcoming of human alienation in relation to the three primary forms of the division of labor—social production, town and country, and gender relations—it provided a holistic, ecological outlook extending far beyond most nineteenth-century socialist views. Although *News from Nowhere* was subtitled *Being Some Chapters from a Utopian Romance*, it followed a pattern that left it free from the criticisms that Marxian thinkers, including Morris himself, had leveled at utopian socialism, since its role was didactic rather than prophetic. The object was not to forecast the victory of socialism as a superior way of organizing the mechanism of production, but rather one of radically refashioning the movement toward socialism in the present by widening the conception of the revolutionary project, building on the Romantic tradition.

The key chapter, "How the Change Came," was set in the England of the early twenty-second century,[48] but contained a vivid historical treatment of the mid-twentieth-century revolution that separated the England of old from the new communal order of Nowhere. The text presented a society of equality that was geographically and historically connected to Morris's own life environment. *News from Nowhere* was a "romance" in the double sense in that it took from the past to reimagine the future, while inscribing within it a relationship of love and recognition between William Guest, the protagonist, and Ellen, the text's most fully developed character, the embodiment of the complex dialectic of labor, ecology, and gender.

Morris's utopian romance was structured as a vivid dream, with William Guest, representing a fictionalized Morris, awakening at the end to the new needs of the struggle and the importance of imparting the glimpse of the utopian future to others. It ends with the words: "And if others can see it as I have seen it, then it may be called a vision rather than a dream."[49]

The chief inducement to write *News from Nowhere* was Morris's dissatisfaction with Edward Bellamy's extremely popular 1888 utopian novel *Looking Backward*, in which Bellamy's hero Julian West wakes up in the year 2000 to discover society entirely transformed along socialist lines.[50] "The only safe way of reading a utopia," Morris observed in his review of Bellamy's book, "is to consider it as the expression of the temperament of its author."[51] And it was Bellamy's temperament as revealed in his book that Morris objected to, since it projected an altogether too mechanical version of socialism. *Looking Backward* focused almost exclusively on the *mechanism* of change. The great monopolies metamorphosed peacefully into a new realm of centralized state-organized production. Technological improvements allowed for enhanced production and increased leisure. The historical, human, or aesthetic elements of a completed socialist (or communist) society were downplayed or missing. Hence, Bellamy's "temperament," Morris wrote, "may be called the unmixed modern one, unhistorical and unartistic; it makes its owner (if a Socialist) perfectly satisfied with modern civilization, if only the injustice, misery and waste of class society could be got rid of; which half-change seems possible to him." The book was a good example of "the economical semi-fatalism of some Socialists," which was "deadening and discouraging."

All individuals in Bellamy's utopian Boston were required to begin work at twenty-one, spend three years as a laborer, and then move on to some skilled occupation, retiring at forty-five. Work was pain, not pleasure. The point was to enjoy a life of leisure beginning in one's mid-forties. Bellamy's novel, Morris argued, gave the impression of "a huge standing army, tightly drilled." Bellamy had "no idea beyond existence in a great city." The future Boston that formed the background to *Looking Backward* was "beautified" in a purely utilitarian fashion, with huge aggregations of population. Yet, from Morris's perspective, such a mechanical socialism was an iron cage.[52]

News from Nowhere, which first began to appear in serial form in *Commonweal* in January 1890, was an attempt to provide a utopian romance reflecting Morris's own very different, artistic temperament. Nevertheless, in writing it, Morris was responding not simply to Bellamy's *Looking Backward* but also to the two factions of the Socialist League with which he had been struggling: the parliamentarians, who like Bellamy tended to focus on the mechanism of change and not the substance, and the anarchists, who in Morris's interpretation saw the change as requiring the actual dissolution of society.[53] Significantly, *News from Nowhere* opened with the reference to a meeting of the Socialist League in which four anarchists were disputing with two others, one of whom was clearly meant to represent Morris, "as to what would happen on the Morrow of the Revolution."[54]

Seen in this way, Morris's utopian romance sought to provide a wider cultural description of the revolutionary ideal of a socialist/communist society, and in that way to address what he perceived as the narrowness and deficiencies in the visions currently being projected within the socialist movement. For this reason, he concentrated on those aspects distinguishing his views from others, putting most of the emphasis in his romance on town and country (the ecological problem), work and art (social labor), and men and women (gender relations).[55] Much less attention was given to the socialization of production, beyond the withering away of state and the demise of the world market. His famous chapter "How the Change Came" was meant to counter Bellamy's notion of a purely mechanical change via monopolies, and to substitute a realistic historical conception of revolution, without which the larger transformations that Morris perceived would not have been possible.

The structure of *News from Nowhere* is fairly simple and takes the form of two journeys. William Guest, representing Morris, wakes up in the early twenty-second century in what is now a guest house but which is on the spot once occupied by Morris's home, Kelmscott House in Hammersmith.[56] He soon learns to his surprise that there are salmon in the Thames and that he is in a dreamlike future. On his first day in Nowhere, Guest travels by carriage through London with his friend Dick, a young boatman. They more or less follow the line of the Thames from Hammersmith to Bloomsbury, ending up at the British Museum, where he is to have a long discussion with old Hammond, Dick's 105-year-old great grandfather, a former librarian. This journey involves traveling through urban London, seeing the many changes that have taken place: the decrease in congestion and the freeing up of parts of the city to greenery; the open markets divorced from selling; the conversion of the Parliamentary buildings to a dung warehouse; the new, architecture-resurrecting fourteenth-century forms, blending this with new forms of decorative art; the more artistic nature of work in general; the happy, attractively clad populace; and the absence of the London poor. Nevertheless, the city remains populous, with "the ghost of London still asserting itself as a centre."[57]

After returning to the Guest House at the end of the day, William Guest journeys on the second day up the Thames toward the source of the river and Kelmscott Manor in Oxfordshire (Morris's summer home). If the first excursion is a one-day journey through the city, the second occupies several days in a leisurely, 137-mile expedition in the countryside via the Thames. The first journey, as Krishan Kumar has pointed out, can be seen as urban-intellectual, the second as rural-erotic. It is only in the second journey—following the route of a boat trip that Morris made with a number of friends in the summers of 1880 and 1881—that some of the deeper truths of Nowhere are revealed, with respect to the relationships between town and country, art and labor, as well as gender and earthly love. Traveling up the river, Guest is introduced to the haymaking festival in the country; the new age of handicraft; a countryside no longer sacrificed to railroads and factories; the new women of the new age; and sensuous and earthly love. It is a romantic journey, but one tinged with the new socialism of substantive equality.

Although old Hammond is the pivotal character in the first journey through London, the young woman, Ellen, Guest's love interest, is the central figure in the second journey through the countryside. The second journey ends with William Guest's departure: that is, the end of the dream; and, as Morris indicates in the final lines, the hopeful vision of complete socialism that his readers will share—and not merely a dream.[58]

The long, remarkable treatment of "How the Change Came" in which the venerable Hammond, during the stop at the British Museum, tells the story of the mid-twentieth-century revolution, plays a key role in the utopian romance. Here Morris imparts a sense of historical realism and a connection to the nineteenth century. He borrows concrete elements from the main European revolutions of the eighteenth and nineteenth centuries, primarily in France: the revolutions of 1789, 1830, 1848, and 1871. Aspects of the English Civil War can also be perceived, and the chronicle of events is rendered more vivid through inclusion of Morris's experience of Bloody Sunday on November 13, 1887, in Trafalgar Square.[59]

The English Revolution of the 1950s depicted in vivid colors in *News from Nowhere* is a complex, spiraling dialectical process of change in which reforms, economic crisis, repression, struggles of the press, dual-power relations, massacres, organized resistance, right-wing vigilantes, guerilla warfare, and the final triumph of socialism all form a part. As Perry Anderson wrote: "The care and depth of thought that Morris devoted to the nature of a computable revolutionary process in Britain—with its dialectic of social reforms and economic crisis, political moves and counter-moves by capitalist and popular centres of sovereignty, brusque pauses and accelerations in mass mobilization, oscillations by intermediate forces, military actions unleashed within and outside the State apparatus—represents an extraordinary *theoretical* feat, in historical retrospect. There is nothing like it in any other national literature of the time or since."[60]

Despite old Hammond's vivid historical account of the tempestuous revolutionary struggle of the 1950s, William Guest is told that all of this was now distant, having occurred around a century and a half before. The bulk of Morris's utopian romance is thus free to focus on describing the world of the early twenty-second century, now long removed from that struggle. Moreover, the romance centers not on the mechanisms of this new society of equality so much as its effects on the healing of the main nineteenth-century estrangements of town and country, art and labor, men and women. It is through the transcendence of these various alienations that the main rewards of complete socialism, or "pure Communism," as he called it in *News from Nowhere*, are to be found.[61]

Morris's utopian romance extends well beyond a socialist political-economic critique, borne of the revolt against capitalism. Its focus is rather on the next stage of post-revolutionary society (the morrow of the revolution), and the making of complete socialism or communism. The object is to provide an extended, but still open-ended, vision of an ideal, humanistic world: the structure of feeling in a long revolution.[62] In Morris's two-stage view, the socialist insurrection, the Great Change or civil war in *News from Nowhere*, brings into being a transitory society full of possibility, although one that will abort if it does not continue on the journey to full communism, eradicating first and foremost capitalist labor relations, along with all of its other alienations.[63] *News from Nowhere* is mainly concerned with *the change beyond* the Great Change, on the long-term effects, a century and a half further down the road, with the advent of pure communism.

Writing in *Socialism: Its Growth and Outcome*, Morris and Bax explain: "It is essential that the ideal of the new society should be always kept before the eyes of the mass of the working classes, lest the *continuity* of the demands of the people should be broken, or lest they should be misdirected."[64] Complete socialism is thus not envisioned in Morris's utopian romance simply in terms of the mechanisms of the state, economy, science, and technology. All of these are present but are pushed into the background, in order to focus on life itself. Morris's attitude to technology was expressed in his talk on "Art, Wealth, and Riches" in March 1883, where he declared, "I want modern science, which I believe to be capable of overcoming all material difficulties, to turn from such preposterous follies as the invention of anthracene colours and monster cannon to the invention of machines for performing such labour as is revolting and destructive of all self-respect to the men who now have to do it by hand."[65]

News of Nowhere is also about an *Epoch of Rest*. Morris depicts a "life of repose amidst energy," using the word *repose* in the sense of meanings of tranquility and harmony—or the *ataraxia* of Epicurus.[66] He creates in the twenty-year-old Ellen the very embodiment of Nowhere as an earthly society: "She smiled with pleasure, and her lazy enjoyment of the new scene seemed to bring out her beauty doubly as she leaned back amidst the cushions, though she was far from languid; her idleness being the idleness of a person, strong and well-knit both in body and mind, deliberately resting."[67]

This emphasis on a pause in the material development of society, a moment of peace and repose within a longer historical process, is crucial to the description of Nowhere. It is an age in which invention of new productive machinery is less emphasized, as compared with the quality of human existence. Nevertheless, the society rests in part on "immensely improved machinery" that reduces irksome labor. The real age of revolution and reconstruction, as Henry Morsom (an antiquarian working at a museum of relics dating back to the age of machines) informs Guest during the journey up the river, occurred only *after* the civil war. The machine-determined age was at its worst immediately following the Great Change. It was only gradually, after the workers had triumphed, that a new handicraft movement emerged. This constituted the central element in the long revolutionary transformation that followed, changing work into art and art into work, to the point that they could practically no longer be separated. And it was here, through the passion for unalienated, creative, artistic work, as Hammond had earlier intimated in the discussion in the British Museum, that the incentive for labor in the new society arose.[68]

Morris stresses the importance of the utopian socialist Charles Fourier rather than the historical materialist Marx in *News from Nowhere*, despite Morris's deeper overall reliance on the latter. (Marx's *Critique of the Gotha Programme* had not yet been published and he had left few clues otherwise about the morrow of the revolution.) Fourier was to be commended since he saw the necessity of making work pleasurable.[69] In Morris's modified Fourierist vision, what drives people in their everyday creative activities is the maximization of pleasure and the fulfillment of genuine human needs, together with the approbation of the society regarding work well done. This is the argument Morris had outlined the year before in his lecture "The Revival of Handicraft." In the new society machinery exists, but it is utilized exclusively to eliminate the worst kinds of work. On his journeys, Guest encounters at a distance a revolutionary form of energy, replacing steam power, which propels "force vehicles," used on both land and water, and presumably within production itself. The result is that the smoke from burning coal that so dominated Victorian London is gone.

The role of technology has been altered in the century and a half since the Great Change. The machine is now viewed as an appendage to human labor, not human labor as an appendage to the machine. It is this central transformation of labor, as the historian Hammond explains, that forms the basis of the society of equality. A community of associated producers nurtures the creativity of each individual, while dull, utilitarian individualism and capitalist exploitation have vanished.[70]

In Nowhere, science, which under capitalism had been commercialized and made a mere instrument of the industrial system, is now turned to the benefit of human beings. People are free to choose old ways where they are deemed better, such as an old-fashioned lock for going up river rather than a new mechanical lock, which "would have been ugly and would have spoiled the look of the river." Mere economic productivity and the resulting technological determinism no longer rule all. Yet science, now that it has been put in the service of humanity, is clearly respected. Old Hammond characterizes art and science as the two "inexhaustible" forms of human endeavor. What is no longer in evidence is the alienated science of Victorian England, which Morris associated with the utilitarianism and dualism/agnosticism of Thomas Huxley. In his 1890 essay, "Capital—The Mother of Labour," Huxley had sought to reintegrate materialist science with the bourgeois order, legitimizing the latter. For this Morris exhibited nothing but scorn. The socialist society of Nowhere, in contrast, celebrates "science for science's sake," and science standing on the same side as art, unsullied by the ends of profit-grinding.[71]

Labor in Nowhere is free to be artistic due to an abundance that comes from historical gains in productivity and a transformation of both use and want. There is no longer useless labor devoted to useless and destructive commodities, driven by pure pecuniary gain. As Hammond explains: "It would be mere insanity to make goods on the chance of their being wanted; for there is no longer any one who can be *compelled* to buy them. . . . All work which would be irksome to do by hand is done by immensely improved machinery; and in all work which it is a pleasure to do by hand machinery is done without."[72] Where actual want is not the chief concern, art triumphs.

If the pivotal change in Morris's revolutionary utopia is the transformation of alienated mechanical labor into unalienated artistic labor, its overarching manifestation is the metamorphosis of town and country, standing for the new relation to the earth, no longer the object of mere conquest. In the beginning of the new epoch, townspeople had dispersed into the countryside, causing much disruption, but eventually a new equilibrium was created. Population too had stabilized, though partly through emigration to aid people in other parts of the world. As old Hammond said to Guest: "The town invaded the country; but the invaders, like the warlike invaders of early days, yielded to the influence of their surroundings, and became country people; and in their turn, as they became more numerous than the townsmen, influenced them also; so that the difference between town and country grew less and less; and it was indeed this world of the country vivified by the thought and briskness of town-bred folk which has produced that happy and leisurely but eager life of which you have had the first taste." The slums of the East End of London had been demolished in what was called the Clearing of Misery and replaced with more and ample housing, better spaced, surrounded by gardens. Predominantly industrial cities like Manchester had largely disappeared as industrial work was dispersed.[73] The factories or mills in which people still labored were less machine-dominated, organized around collective labor, located in communities, and made attractive—surrounded by gardens, as Morris had written in "The Factory as It Might Be."[74]

Towns in Nowhere are dominated by their "streets and squares and market-places." Life in the country villages, in particular, is centered in the "mote," or assembly house. But in the city too, the mote is preeminent, since the most important form of public management of daily life—though not the only one—is the commune, in which "the Mote" looms large, with decisions being made by democratic, majoritarian means. Just as Kensington Gardens had been turned into a wood, so had "wild nature," in addition to gardens and farms, been encouraged in the countryside. Urban suburbs are no more, having vanished in the blending together of town and country.[75]

In the socialist civilization of Nowhere, the country has been repopulated as the city has been depopulated, marking a return of nature in the society as a whole. The second journey up the Thames by boat to Oxfordshire, in which William Guest travels with the two reunited lovers Dick and Clara, highlighted the changed relations in the countryside in minute detail. Much of the journey is a celebration of nature's beauty all along the river. But it is also a story of recovery, reconstruction, and ecological revolution. Old iron bridges are torn down and stone ones put in their place. All signs of the railroad vanish. The mills that remain are beautified. The oldest architecture remains. The ugly nineteenth-century brick is mostly gone, while a new modern architecture more reminiscent of the fourteenth century emerges. The river in the upper waters, as in London itself, is a bright blue, rather than a muddy brown. Beauty has replaced the Victorian age of coal and soot.

In the chapter on "The Upper Waters," the Baconian metaphors of the conquest of nature and the making of nature into a slave, viewed as constituting the governing mores of the former capitalist civilization, come in for sharp criticism:

> Clara broke in [on the discussion] here, flushing a little as she spoke: "Was not their mistake [of seeing work as onerous] once more bred of the life of slavery that they had been living?—a life which was always looking upon everything, except mankind, animate and inanimate—'nature,' as people used to call it—as one thing, and mankind as another. It was natural to people thinking in this way, that they should try to make 'nature' their slave, since they thought 'nature' was something outside them."[76]

Near Runnymede, during the haymaking festival, Guest and his two companions become acquainted with Ellen, a "slim girl," "grey-eyed," the new woman of the novel, with her intelligence, vivaciousness, and "wild beauty."[77] Soon she joins them on their river journey, and a strong attachment between Ellen and Guest arises based on a common attraction.

Ellen, we learn, comes from "the once-poor," her father a tiller of the earth, which in nineteenth-century England would have meant a life of drudgery, exploitation, and early death. In her first appearance in the romance, she enters into a dispute with her grandfather who idealized the capitalist Victorian age and disliked the new revolutionary communal order:

> "But in those past days, you Grandfather, would have had to work hard after you were old; and would have been always afraid of having to be shut up in a kind of prison along with other old men, half-starved and without amusement. And as for me, I am twenty years old. In those days my middle age would be beginning now, and in a few years I should be pinched, thin, and haggard, beset with troubles and miseries, so that no one could have guessed that I was once a beautiful girl."[78]

Later, near the end of the novel, she declares to Guest:

> "My friend, you were saying that you wondered what I should have been if I had lived in those past days of turmoil and oppression. Well, I think I have studied the history of them to know pretty well. I should have been one of the poor, for my father when he was working was a mere tiller of the soil. Well, I could not have borne that; therefore my beauty and cleverness and brightness" (she spoke with no blush or simper of false shame) "would have been sold to rich men, and my life would have been wasted indeed; for I know enough of that to know that I should have had no choice, no power of will over my life; and that I should never have bought pleasure from the rich men, or even opportunity of action, whereby I might have won some true excitement. I should have wrecked and wasted in one way or another, either by penury or luxury. Is it not so?"[79]

In the sensuous trip up the Thames, Guest's attraction to this irrepressible young woman and his love for the earth merge together and become one. When Kelmscott Manor is at last reached, Ellen is ecstatic: "She led me up close to the house, and laid her shapely sun-browned hand and arm on the lichened wall as if to embrace it, and cried out, 'O me! O me! How I love the earth, and the seasons, and the weather, and all things that deal with it, and all that grows out of it,—as this has done!'"[80] It was Ellen, Morris's finest creation in the novel, who represented the highest level of human development in Nowhere, in terms of intelligence, revolutionary commitment, beauty of body and soul, and the organic connection of humanity to the earth. Morris intimates that the revolution is still not complete, and that Ellen has a future of struggle ahead of her.

Morris's views on women, however, were complex and at times contradictory. It is clear that his utopian romance was meant primarily to extend the revolutionary ideal of socialism to the artistic conception of labor, the substantive equality of women, and the ecology of the earth itself. In all of this the transformation of gender relations occupied a central place. If the society of Nowhere had solved some of the problems, the issue of gender equality still in some respects remained, and this was the measure of not only how emancipated the society had become, but also of its limitations and the need for future emancipation. In his *Theory of the Four Movements*, Fourier had declared: "*The extension of the privileges of women is the basic principle of all social progress*." As Engels put it in *Socialism: Utopian and Scientific*, Fourier "was the first to declare that in any given society the degree of women's emancipation is the natural measure of the general emancipation."[81] Throughout his writings, and particularly *News from Nowhere*, Morris sought to give concrete meaning to this principle, initiated by Fourier. In 1885 he told George Bernard Shaw that he did not "consider a man a socialist at all who is not prepared to admit the equality of women as far as condition goes," and added that "as long as women are compelled to marry for a livelihood real marriage is a rare exception and prostitution or a kind of legalized rape the rule."[82]

Complete socialism or communism was only possible by means of equality of condition of the sexes. Like Marx and Engels, Morris insisted that this would require the complete dissolution of bourgeois marriage, based as it was on relations of property and patriarchy. He argued that "genuine unions of passion and affection" were denied women (and men also) due to women's lack of economic security and the double standard, which supported a patriarchal system of adultery and female prostitution. Marriage itself under such a system was little more than "legal prostitution," and thus a mechanism for the enslavement of women. What was needed in place of such a "venal" marital system, he raged, was a more natural set of relations, consisting of "decent animalism . . . plus human kindness."[83]

Marriage continues to exist in Nowhere, but there are no divorce courts, and Dick and Clara, who had divorced in the past due to Clara's attraction to someone else—an indication of greater sexual freedom for women—are driven by their renewed love to remarry. This sequence of events is seen as perfectly natural and easy, in the sense of being free from legal obstacles. The absence of private property relations and of hopeless marriages from which parties cannot escape, along with the general equality of condition of men and women, has eradicated the fundamental basis of bourgeois patriarchy, and with it much of the conflict between the genders. But Morris nonetheless emphasizes throughout his utopian romance that many of the trials and tribulations of love between men and women (he does not consider relations other than heterosexual ones), associated with uncontrolled passions remain—and continue to generate conflicts. "Love," Dick tells us, "is not a very reasonable thing."[84]

The position of children in such marital breakups is unclear, but it is specified that neither parent has the right to tyrannize over them. Children are generally brought up collectively, and the education of the genders is the same. They are free of the rigid forms of schooling that characterized the life of boys in the Victorian upper classes. They are able to move around with considerable freedom, following their interests, within the context of a more communal upbringing.[85]

The strict, forced division of labor between the sexes (genders) has disappeared in twenty-second-century Nowhere. But Hammond tells Guest that if women turn out to be especially good at and disposed toward managing the household and wish to do so, then they should be allowed to follow that path like any other. In the third chapter, we find the women in the Guest House serving the meal to Guest and the men he was visiting with—yet in a joyous and playful way that tends to dispel the sense that they are engaging in mere servile work based on rigid distinctions in status.[86]

A number of feminist critics have understandably centered on this chapter in his book, suggesting that the condition of women in Morris's utopia remained fundamentally unchanged from the Victorian reality of his day. But much of the rest of the book raises challenges for such an interpretation. Indeed, Morris not only showed women serving the men in the Guest House in an early scene, but then went on to question that directly, and to pose several different—not altogether consistent—answers with respect to women and labor in the course of the novel, thus highlighting it as an issue that is not fully resolved in the society, and therefore subject to change.[87]

There is no doubt that Morris was struggling within himself here, caught in seemingly contradictory sentiments, the tangled product of his Victorian patriarchal upbringing and his revolutionary socialist values. In his weaker moments he suggested that women were especially suited by innate gifts or inclinations, to work as household managers, but even then they should be free to choose their occupations.[88] At the same time he contended that childbearing generally made women more dependent on men and even "inferior" to men from the standpoint of the material-work world of a capitalist society.[89] Such positions were close to those of Gronlund in *The Co-operative Commonwealth*.[90] In alluding on a number of occasions in interviews and correspondence to some kind of natural sexual division of labor—though impacted by an alienated capitalist society—Morris appears to have fallen somewhat short of the more advanced views propounded in his day by Engels, August Bebel, and other contemporary socialists, including Clara Zetkin and Eleanor Marx. For Bebel "the argument that it is a woman's natural vocation to be housekeeper and nurse" had no basis in science or history and was the result of a patriarchal view equivalent to the divine right of kings.[91]

Nevertheless, Morris made it clear that he believed in "absolute equality of condition" of men and women, and that he did not think that women should be restricted to any particular role. Women as well as men should be allowed to develop their talents fully. There were "many things," he argued, "which women can do equally as well as men, and some a great deal better." Women, he suggested in an 1894 interview with *Woman's Signal*, were especially gifted in such areas as the "medical profession" and "business affairs." Indeed, women have "a born faculty for business," in that "they can hold their own, too, in the intellectual field"—if not in "the arts or in inventive power." Morris, like Ray Lankester, pointed to the phenomenal Philippa Fawcett (who had been E. Ray Lankester's student at Universiy College, London, in the first class of women permitted to attend, in 1882) as definitive proof that women could excel in mathematics, going beyond men. Morris was a strong advocate of women's trade unions and the demand for equal pay for equal work, as well as for universal suffrage.[92] If not "a thoroughgoing feminist" by today's measure, he ranks, according to Fiona MacCarthy, as a kind of "semi-feminist."[93] And in his art and his most advanced ideas he arguably surpassed that.

Indeed, Morris's position on gender was considerably more nuanced, progressive, and dialectical than may appear at first glance, since his model was ultimately one of revolutionary transformation, requiring a changed society, a changed relation to labor and the earth, and a changed humanity. Thus, though adhering at least in part, as we have seen, to the view that women were especially suited for (but should not by any means be confined to) domestic work, Morris gave to such work a much more central importance and a larger scope in the unalienated society of the future, hearkening back to a time when the household was the center of production. He argued that men could not altogether refrain from domestic work in a society of equality without being maldeveloped and contributing to the "enslavement of women." In his March 1889 lecture "How Shall We Live Then?," delivered at a meeting of the Fabian Society, he stated emphatically, with regard to the future socialist society, that "the domestic arts" consisted of "the arrangement of a house in all its details, marketing, cleaning, cooking, baking, and so on: sewing with its necessary concomitant of embroidery and so forth. . . . Whoever was incapable of taking interest and a share in some parts of such work would have to be considered diseased; and the existence of many such diseased persons would tend to the enslavement of the weaker sex."[94] As Paul Meier noted, "In no other of his writings is Morris so positive and practical in his advocacy of sex-equality."[95]

Nevertheless, a direct evocation of the need for men as well as women to engage in the domestic arts is missing from Morris's *News from Nowhere*, written only a year later. As Ady Mineo, a professor of English at the Insttute Universitario Orientale in Naples specializing in utopian traditions, has pointed out, Morris's failure to "translate these propositions" on gender equality directly "into fiction can be imputed to two main reasons," related both to his own time and readership and to the complex structure of his novel, which represents an incomplete ideal:

> Firstly, his disagreement with some of his comrades, especially Belfort Bax, who held very traditional views about women's role, and secondly his concern about the response of his reading public, who might be shocked by the depiction of men engaged in household tasks and thus be diverted from the core of his message: the radical dismantling of the patriarchal order. As is well known, the uprooting of deep-seated cultural habits, which challenges one's own interiorized identity, creates a feeling of dislocation *both* in women and in men.
>
> However, since *News from Nowhere* is not a detailed blueprint of a future society, its open-endedness and dialogism suggest further development in every arrangement of human life. . . . The reader can therefore envision a further stage when the young man laying the table in Chapter XXVI will not be an isolated figure but a common sight.[96]

It was precisely in this chapter XXVI of *News from Nowhere*, "The Obstinate Refusers," and in his depiction of Ellen as the embodiment of the highest values, that the artist Morris most clearly triumphed over his own inner hesitations with respect to gender. If the first journey by carriage along the Thames focuses on the coming to be of twenty-second-century London, and on the sociology of Nowhere, it is only in the journey up the Thames that Guest's observations take on an active, living form, raising the question of a long, continuing revolution, extending to more earthly concerns.

It is significant that it is in Morris's addition of the important chapter "The Obstinate Refusers," representing a key passage in that upriver journey, that the published book version of *News from Nowhere* differs most from the version serialized in *Commonweal*. This was the new chapter he introduced when his serialized 1890 utopian romance was released in book form in 1891. Here he upends almost completely the division of labor between the genders. "The Obstinate Refusers" chapter offers the only instance of a master craftsperson seen at work in his story—representing the most esteemed role in Morris's utopia, and the one corresponding most closely to his own role in nineteenth-century society. When we are introduced for the first and only time in the novel to an example of higher craftsmanship, and of the most strenuous kind, it is an occupation filled by a woman. Mistress Philippa, the stonemason, is engaged in carving with mallet and chisel, indicating strength and dexterity as well as artistic sense. She is sculpting "a kind of wreath of flowers and figures all round it." So singly dedicated is she to her work that she, along with her fellow workers, are good-humoredly jeered at by others as the "Obstinate Refusers" of the chapter's title, since not joining in the communal haymaking. Phillipa, just as obstinately refuses to interrupt her work with a meal. Previously the work on finishing and decorating the new house had to wait, affecting the entire work crew, because Philippa was ill, and they were not able to continue without her—so great was their dependence on her craft. Her gruffness and obstinacy is clearly a parody of Morris himself. The other apprentice stonemason is a young woman, Philippa's daughter. In contrast, a young man sets the table for the meal. The foreman, as if in concession to the male ego, is a man but clearly has a secondary role to Philippa as the master mason.[97]

Here Morris dramatically reverses the dominant gender roles of his time. There is little doubt that the sculptor Philippa is named after the phenomenal mathematician Philippa Fawcett.[98] In this case, though, the strength, intelligence, and artistry of women craftworkers, particularly masons, is displayed.

Morris strongly admired Clara Zetkin's speech at the International Socialist Congress in Paris in 1889, when she declared: "While women fight side by side with the Socialist workers, they are ready to share all sacrifices and hardships, but they are also firmly resolved to take as their due after victory [in the struggle with bourgeois society] all the rights that belong to them." The "Obstinate Refusers" chapter in *News from Nowhere* seems to reflect this view of a transformation of gender relations developing out of revolutionary struggle, playing out over a long period of time.[99]

Women in *News from Nowhere* are not depicted as the languid, idle ladies, or the gaunt, working-class drudges, so familiar in the Victorian novels of Morris's day. Instead they are physically, intellectually, and artistically vibrant. They no longer wear massive layers of clothing characteristic of Victorian women's fashions—as if they were "upholstered" furniture rather than human beings—but lighter clothes that allow them to move. Ellen is tanned on her face, arms, and feet. She dresses in a way that emphasizes freedom of movement, while walking barefoot in the fields. The free women of Nowhere engage in labor like men, participating in the haymaking festival. Ellen takes part in the work in the fields, as well as being an excellent sculler, able to row much more efficiently in terms of strength and skill than William Guest (Morris)—none of which takes away from the fact that she is perhaps the most powerful critical-intellectual voice in the text as she argues with her grandfather on literature and history (a fact highlighted by her close connection to the British Museum historian Hammond).[100] Ellen's considerable charm derives from her independence, spontaneity, confidence, intelligence, and clear sense of her own value, combined with a love for the world of nature all around her. It is she who, in a departure from Victorian mores, takes the sexual initiative, overwhelming Guest, who is unaccustomed to this from women.[101]

This is in line with Morris's historical romances, set in primitive communist society and among Germanic peoples, in which women are presented as taking on the role of warriors, wearing armor and fighting side by side with the men. In *The Roots of the Mountains*, Bow-may, whose archery is unrivaled, and Bride, who could wield sword, spear, and bow, are at the forefront of the battle for Silverdale—while the former was also a leader in the guerrilla war that preceded it. Here Morris's clear intention was to strike directly at Victorian notions of "the weaker sex."[102]

In *News from Nowhere* and Morris's other romances, women (and also men) express their emotions and sensuousness in direct, relatively uninhibited ways that break radically with the frozen mores of the Victorian age. Women are relatively free to express open physical affection for men. Men are allowed to weep in public, to blush, and to wear gaudy clothes. As Mineo has argued in "Beyond the Law of the Father," Morris "prefigured the changes envisaged by post-feminism" in which both femininity and masculinity are opened up, allowing for more expansive, overlapping gender roles: "In syntony with the destructuring of the traditional male identity, Morris . . . also deconstructed the female model as it was inscribed in Victorian collective imagery. In depicting the new woman, Morris erases every form of discrimination based on the criterion of the double standard."[103]

Morris's goal, though not in all respects successful, was to portray an equality of condition between men and women, as a reflection of the ideal of substantive equality.[104] In this respect his greatest, most generous literary creation, Ellen, stands out as a "new woman," giving credence to the notion that "The Emancipation of Women," as stated by Hammond, is no longer the central question that it once was—and that society in the century and a half since the Great Change has moved substantially forward. Ellen's role as William Guest's love interest is secondary to her larger role as the embodiment of all that is most healthy and revolutionary in the new society. It is Ellen who recognizes the vital importance of the recovery of a historical perspective that has been largely lost in Nowhere, in order to ensure the future development of the new society.[105] As a prospective mother—in a world where motherhood has lost much of its burden with society collectively caring for children—she insists that she intends to pass on her critical knowledge and her whole essential being to her children. As someone close to the sages of her time (she has embraced the knowledge obtained directly through dialogue with old Hammond and others—preferring that to mere book learning); as the only person in the book said to have traveled abroad (she had been on the Rhine); and as the embodiment of love and beauty and the love of the earth itself, Ellen symbolizes the romantic-socialist utopia that is Nowhere. It is in Ellen, who stands for all that is most complete in Nowhere, that Morris's art reaches the furthest, telling us that equality between men and women goes hand in hand with the creation of an ecosocialist society. She personifies the whole movement toward *complete socialism*, the struggle for which extends to future ages *beyond the epoch of repose*, when "times may alter."[106] Mere emancipation of labor is not sufficient, it must embrace substantive equality, including full gender equality, the flourishing of art and beauty at all levels of society, and the sustaining of the earth itself.

Indeed, in a relatively few brief pages in the last third of the novel, centered on this twenty-year-old woman, Morris seems to have embodied his full revolutionary vision of communism, the earth, and love, challenging the predominantly mechanistic views of socialist thought in his age. For Morris, only such an ideal can animate the necessary revolution and carry it forward.

Guest's dream ends with Ellen's last words floating in his mind as he fades away from Nowhere, challenging him to go back and continue the struggle:

> "No, it will not do; you cannot be of us; you belong so entirely to the unhappiness of the past that our happiness even would weary you. Go back again, now you have seen us, and your outward eyes have learned that in spite of all the infallible maxims of your day there is yet a time of rest in store for the world, when mastery has changed into fellowship—but not before. Go back again, then, and while you live you will see all round you people engaged in making others live lives which are not their own, while they themselves care nothing for their own real lives—men who hate life though they fear death. Go back and be the happier for having seen us, for having added a little hope to your struggle. Go on living while you may, striving with whatsoever pain and labour needs must be, to build up little by little the new day of fellowship, and rest, and happiness."[107]

KELMSCOTT PRESS

The engraved frontispiece that Morris designed for the 1893 Kelmscott Press edition of *News from Nowhere* depicted the sixteenth-century stone house, Kelmscott Manor, Morris's country home from 1871 to his death in 1896. Morris's London home, Kelmscott House in Hammersmith, was named after the manor. Both were on the Thames. In *Nowhere*, the Kelmscott House is no more, and a Guest House now occupies the spot. Kelmscott Manor, however, still exists, and represents the endpoint of the journey up the Thames, in the "epoch of repose."

It was in 1888–89, during the crisis of the Socialist League, and Morris's growing recognition of the need for a long-term movement toward socialism, that he began to envision his last great artistic adventure, the creation of Kelmscott Press, founded in 1890. As he explained in 1895: "I began printing books with the hope of producing some which would have a definite claim to beauty, while at the same time they should be easy to read."[108] In many cases, it was as easy, in production, to give "a beautiful form" to the things produced as one that was "ugly and not the beautiful," especially once the waste in capitalist production was taken into account.[109] With the Kelmscott Press, Morris sought to bring back much of the beauty of the books of the fifteenth century. At a time "when written literature was still divine, and almost miraculous to men," he wrote, "it was impossible that books should fail to have a due share in the epical-ornamental art of the time."[110]

Such a move toward a more beautiful book need not be more costly, since much of it involved merely the changing "architecture" of the book, that is, the typography, the spacing of words and letters on the page, margins, etc. Questions of binding, the quality of paper, and like issues, were part and parcel of the durability of the product: a product made for use and not to sit on a shelf. As Morris put it: "A book quite unornamented can look actually and positively beautiful, and not merely un-ugly, if it be, so to say, architecturally good, which by the by, need not add much to its price (since it costs no more to pick up pretty stamps than ugly ones) and the taste and forethought that goes to the proper setting, position, and so on, will soon grow into a habit, if cultivated, and will not take up much of the master-printer's time when taken with his other necessary business."[111]

Morris thus sought to bring back beautiful typography, drawing on the late fifteenth-century printers, particularly Nicholas Jenson, of the Venice of the 1470s. Borrowing in part from earlier forms, Morris developed his own successful and influential typefaces: his famous Golden type (a variation of Roman) and his Troy and Chaucer types (semi-Gothic). Margins, lettering, spacing, and all the other architectural aspects of a book were reinvented in Kelmscott Press books, with an emphasis on beauty, legibility.[112] Kelmscott Press books, however, went beyond the normal book architecture to the making of the paper, which had to be handwoven out of linen, and to the adding of decorative illustrations in the margins and pictures from woodcuts, after the manner of medieval illuminated manuscripts and the work of the fifteenth-century printers. The Kelmscott edition of Chaucer contained eighty-seven illustrations from woodcuts by Edward Burne-Jones along with title, initials, and borders designed by Morris. It was bound in pigskin and printed in red and black on hand-woven paper.[113]

Altogether the Kelmscott Press published fifty-three separate books, including nine of Morris's works, with *The Earthly Paradise* published in eight separate volumes. Nineteenth-century works included volumes of poetry by Percy Bysshe Shelley, John Keats, Samuel Taylor Coleridge, and Alfred

Tennyson, along with John Ruskin's *Nature of the Gothic* from *The Stones of Venice*. A Kelmscott edition of Shakespeare's *Poems and Sonnets* was published, as well as More's *Utopia* and the famous Kelmscott edition of *Chaucer's Works*. Morris's translation of *Beowulf* was included. Overall the press emphasized medieval works. The only explicitly nineteenth-century socialist work published by the Kelmscott Press was Morris's own *News from Nowhere*, printed in Golden type in black and red. The most vivid and startling use of the red typeface in *News from Nowhere* was in the inscription on the side of the old Guest House in Hammersmith: "*Guests and neighbours, on the site of this Guest-hall once stood the lecture-room of the Hammersmith Socialists. Drink a glass to the memory! May 1962.*"[114]

Morris's involvement in the Kelmscott Press, in fact, heightened the contradiction between the egalitarian objectives of England's leading socialist and his expensive, artistic productions, available only to the wealthy, raising questions about his whole vision of society. He clearly believed that the resurrection of unalienated, artistic, decorative production of all kinds, devoted to creating things of beauty could only serve to enhance the socialist future—however limited the access was to such works in the society of the day. In an interview with the *Daily Chronicle* in 1893, Morris commented on some of his own concerns in this respect, saying: "True, the prices are not the prices which Tom, Dick, and Harry can pay. I wish—I wish indeed that the cost of the books was less, only that it is impossible if the printing and the decoration and the paper and the binding are to be what they should be."[115] As he told the *Pall Mall Gazette* two years earlier:

> You see if we were all Socialists things would be different. We should have a public library at every street corner, where everybody should read all the best books, printed in the best and most beautiful type. I should not then have to buy all these old books, but they would be common property, and I could go and look at them whenever I wanted them, as would everybody else. Now I have to go to the British Museum, which is an excellent institution, but it is not enough. I want these books close at hand, and frequently, and therefore I must buy them. It is the same with everybody else, and if they have not money enough to buy them they must go without. Socialism would alter all that.[116]

These contradictions entered into the relations of Morris and Thorstein Veblen. In the summer of 1896, Veblen, then about thirty-nine years old, and working on the ideas that were to appear in *The Theory of the Leisure Class* three years later, traveled to England to visit Morris. Veblen was a close reader of Morris's works, including *Sigurd* and the prose romances, which were in his personal library. He would quote from Morris to his students at the University of Chicago and liked to quote from the prologue to *The Earthly Paradise*:

> Dreamer of dreams, born out of my due time,
> Why should I strive to set the crooked straight? [117]

Like Morris, Veblen believed in "the instinct of workmanship," that is, the need of human beings to engage in meaningful, unalienated, and above all, useful work. Veblen was particularly concerned with issues of waste and developed a powerful economic critique of monopoly capitalism.[118] He visited Morris when the latter was seriously ill—he was to die a few months later, on October 3—but still able to meet guests. Veblen was undoubtedly astonished by Kelmscott House with its medieval and workmanlike air, full of tapestries, bronzes, Rossetti paintings, and a profusion of rare manuscripts, along with furniture designed by Morris.[119]

Veblen clearly saw Morris's Kelmscott Press as something of a throwback and as dependent on the growth of the leisure class. He devoted a considerable part of *Theory of the Leisure Class* to lambasting the Kelmscott Press as representing the "exaltation of the defective." Such operations led to an increase in the value of the goods due to their lack of machine perfection and their accompanying higher price was associated with limited editions. They were marketed to the rich as items of "conspicuous waste." Not denying the outstanding beauty of the Kelmscott Press books, Veblen nonetheless contended, "The Kelmscott Press reduced the matter [of production-consumption] to an absurdity—as seen from the point of view of brute serviceability alone—by issuing books for modern use, edited with the obsolete spelling, printed in black-letter, and bound in limp vellum fitted with thongs." Veblen, though a severe critic of the economic waste of modern industry, was enough of a utilitarian, with an emphasis on productivity as the determining character of modern life, to ridicule artistic creations that cost more time and money, and hence, in the present society, took the form of luxury products for the leisure class.[120]

Veblen took up the issue of Morris again several years after the publication of *Theory of the Leisure Class* in a 1902 review essay on "The Arts and Crafts" movement. Here he claimed that Morris had renounced the machine—but less so than in the case of Ruskin—making his ideas for the most part impracticable. But here, perhaps more than anywhere else in his writing, Veblen seems to have revealed his own soul. Criticizing the pure arts and crafts movement, he nonetheless commended the industrial arts version of that movement, represented by Oscar Lovell Triggs, the leading follower of Morris in the United States, arguing that in attempting to blend art with machine-civilization in order to make work less alienating, Triggs's Industrial Art League represented an important advance. Quoting from *The Earthly Paradise* and referring to Morris, based on the poem, as "the Dreamer," Veblen showed his own concern with the alienation of monopoly capitalist society, and the importance of a change beyond the change:

> But however impracticable, within the frontiers of a democratic culture, may be the (substantially aristocratic) ideals and proposals of the "Dreamer of dreams, borne out of his due time," it does not follow from all this that the movement initiated by the Dreamer need be without salutary effect upon the working life of the workmen or the artistic value of their output of goods. Indirectly these ideals, romantic or otherwise, have already had a large effect, and there is every reason to hope that the propaganda of taste carried on by organizations like the Industrial Art League and its congeners will count for much in checking the current ugliness of the apparatus of life.[121]

Morris no doubt would have agreed with some of this criticism, just as Veblen sympathized with Morris's ultimate objectives. Both sought in different ways for a more socialist, more ecological world. For Morris, aesthetic value often superseded machine productivity, insofar as the quality of life was concerned. If this put the artist in a peculiar, contradictory position in capitalist society, making art the plaything of the rich, this only meant that the existing order itself needed to be transcended. Veblen, despite his bitterly ironic use of the Kelmscott Press to illustrate "the law of conspicuous waste," was undoubtedly more sympathetic with Morris's Romantic-Marxian socialism than his analysis on the surface suggested. Both had a conception of use value and need that transcended capitalist society.[122]

Yet it was Morris, the Romantic artist and Marxian socialist, who was able to draw upon history for a vision of the future as the negation of the negation—the *change beyond the change*.[123] The upriver journey in Morris's great socialist romance *News from Nowhere* ends not with a bigger and better factory, as in some mechanistic socialist visions of his day (and our own), but with a sixteenth-century stone manor, which is said to have grown out of the earth.[124] Morris presents an ecological vision of socialist revolution designed to heal the rift generated by capitalist modernity, by resurrecting the ghosts of the past struggles and the history that will not die. As Jack Lindsay observed in his biography of Morris, "Marx and Engels were aware of the disastrous effects on nature that a society of commodity-production was liable to inflict; but for Morris . . . the awareness of this destructive tendency was central."[125]

On May Day 1896 Morris wrote in *Justice* that capitalists were dealing with the crisis of the age by striving for

> the opening of fresh markets to take in all the fresh profit-producing wealth which is growing greater and greater every day; in other words, to make fresh opportunities for *waste*; the waste of our labour and our lives.
>
> And I say this is an irresistible instinct on the part of the capitalists, an impulse like hunger, and I believe that it can only be met by another hunger, the hunger for freedom and fair play for all, both people and peoples. Anything less than that the capitalist power will brush aside. But they cannot; for what will it mean? The most important part of their machinery, the "hands" becoming MEN, and saying, "Now at last we will it; we will produce no more for profit but for *use*, for *happiness*, for LIFE."[126]

Yet, there were fears as well as hopes. Rather than arguing for an inexorable progress, Morris pointed to the contingencies of history contrasting such optimistic views, which depended on a working-class revolt, to more pessimistic ones, in which the revolt would fail. In *Signs of Change* he stated:

> I can conceive that the revolt against Artificial Famine or Capitalism, which is now on foot, may be vanquished. The result will be that the working class—the slaves of society—will become more and more degraded. . . . Nor will their masters be much better off: the earth's surface will be hideous everywhere, save in the uninhabitable desert; Art will utterly perish, as in the manual arts so in literature, which will become, as it is indeed speedily becoming, a mere string of orderly and calculated ineptitudes and passionless ingenuities; Science will grow more and more one-sided, more incomplete, more wordy and useless, till at last she will pile herself up into such a mass of superstition, that beside it the theologies of old time will seem mere reason and enlightenment. All will get lower and lower, till the heroic struggles of the past to realize hope from year to year, from century to century, will be utterly forgotten, and man will be an indescribable being—hopeless, desireless, and lifeless.[127]

Such an utterly degraded capitalist society Morris strongly implied would be so destructive of the environment around it as to lead toward universal disaster. And in this way a kind of "deliverance" might take place, but in a destructive fashion. "Man may, after some terrible cataclysm," he wrote, "learn to strive towards a healthy animalism, may grow from a tolerable animal into a savage, from a savage into a barbarian, and so on; and some thousands of years hence he may be beginning once more those arts which we have now lost." This reflected the view, put forward in his 1888 lecture on "Equality," that "if the present state of Society merely breaks up without a conscious effort at transformation, the end, the fall of Europe, may be long in coming, but when it does come it will be far more terrible, far more confused and full of suffering than the period of the fall of Rome." Yet, even if humanity were to struggle back over centuries and millennia from such a "terrible cataclysm," ultimately brought on by capitalism's destruction of the world around it, it would—in the pessimistic view—constitute no true deliverance, since the whole cycle would have to be gone over again.[128]

"That pessimism," Morris stated, "I do not believe in, nor, on the other hand, do I suppose that it is altogether a matter of our wills as to whether we shall further human progress or human degradation."[129] Revolutionary change was a product of a dialectic of subjective and objective conditions. The only rational course for humanity under these circumstances was to pursue the aims of art, beauty in nature, and unalienated human labor—and to organize a movement toward socialism.

> Not one, not one, nor thousands must they slay,
> But one and all if they would dusk the day.[130]

PART TWO

Engels's Ecology

CHAPTER FIVE

Environmental Conditions of the Working Class

Frederick Engels was in his early twenties when he wrote *The Condition of the Working Class in England*, and over the next few years he co-authored *The Holy Family*, *The German Ideology* (which remained unpublished in his lifetime), and *The Communist Manifesto* with Karl Marx. However, his principal direct influence on the development of Marxism, and the main basis of his lasting fame as a thinker in his own right, was not to come for another three decades or more.[1] In 1878, when he was fifty-eight, he completed his most influential theoretical work, *Herr Eugen Dühring's Revolution in Science* (better known as *Anti-Dühring*). It wasn't until well into the late 1880s and '90s that *Anti-Dühring* was to have its major impact. As Franz Mehring observed, "The culmination" of Engels's "historical influence came with his old age."[2]

The influence of the later Engels thus traversed the great gulf that Raymond Williams has called "The Interregnum" of 1880–1914, separating the Victorian Age from what we commonly think of as modernity.[3] Unlike Morris, for example, whose Romanticism was very much a nineteenth-century phenomenon, one has no difficulty thinking of Engels as belonging (through his work) as much to the twentieth century as the nineteenth, even though his own life span fell five years short of the new century's beginning. Indeed, in the eyes of many Western Marxists, part of the objection to the later Engels has always stemmed from his having lived to grapple with the historical contradictions associated with the rise of monopoly capitalism, imperialism, and the new scientific-technical age that Marx himself had not lived to see and that were to bedevil twentieth-century Marxism.

In his final decades Engels was to take on his shoulders not only the responsibility for editing the second and third volumes of *Capital*, but also for undertaking the integration of the dialectical conception of science and nature with the broad philosophical basis of historical materialism. This was a task that had emerged as a central aim of both Marx and Engels beginning in the 1860s and '70s, due to the changing conditions of the late nineteenth century and the growing role of natural scientists in society (and social science). Engels's major efforts in this regard were to remain preliminary and unfinished. Indeed, such incompleteness was inherent in the overall dialectical project that Engels, like Marx, envisioned.[4] In Engels's case, it represented what Nikolai Bukharin, following the lead of Engels, was later to call an endless "philosophical arabesque": the struggle to grasp within a scientific worldview the curvilinear movement of change and development, in nature as well as history.[5] Engels's mature works, coupled with his youthful investigations into the conditions of the working class, are in fact best seen as constituting the essential elements of an ecological dialectic, the full significance of which is only becoming apparent today.

Engels can be seen as an individual in constant motion, both physically and intellectually, in many ways the embodiment of an active, and reflexive, socialist praxis. However, he was also a figure, who, though he sought to change history, was notably unable to do so under conditions of his own choosing, and who for a large part of his life was compelled by circumstances to live out his true revolutionary nature as a kind of a shadowy existence, behind a solid front of bourgeois respectability.

In December 1842, at age twenty-two, Engels arrived in Manchester from Barmen (having met Marx for the first time during a brief stop in Cologne along the way). During what was to be a 21-month stay in Manchester, he was given the task of learning the business at his father's cotton textile plant (founded in 1837 by Friedrich Engels Sr. together with a number of Ermen brothers).[6] The Chartist leader Julian Harney, to whom Engels paid a visit in Leeds soon after arriving in Manchester, remembered him from this time as "a tall, handsome, young man" with an almost "boyish" countenance, speaking an astonishingly accurate English.[7] Engels was soon engaged in the research for *The Condition of the Working Class in England* (1845). It was this work, along with his 1843 "Outlines of a Critique of Political Economy," that would play a crucial role in inspiring Marx's own critique of political economy.

As Steven Marcus writes in *Engels, Manchester, and the Working Class*, Engels walked incessantly "at all times of the day and night, on weekends and holidays," up and down the crowded, refuse-strewn streets and alleys of industrial Manchester, guided on numerous occasions (or so it is believed) by his companion, Mary Burns, the lively, pretty twenty-one-year-old daughter of Michael Burns, a textile dye worker and factory laborer, and Mary Conroy, both Irish immigrants from Tipperary. The Burns family lived in Deansgate, which was then an extremely poor area of narrow alleys and fetid courts.

Mary Burns was born in 1822 and by the early 1840s had secured a domestic service position in a master painter's household. She may have been a factory operator in her younger years, and there were vague suggestions—chiefly in the form of a ribald poem by Engels's friend George Weerth, who was clearly enamored with Mary, describing her more than once as a "wild rose"—that she may have engaged in prostitution, using her proceeds to support the Irish nationalist cause. Mary was known for her ebullient spirit and was a strong supporter of Chartism. Engels met her in 1843 not long after arriving in Manchester. A Mary Burns was registered as living in a small cottage in the working-class suburb of Hulme, a mile or two walk from where Engels was working in Manchester in 1843, suggesting that Mary and Engels may have already "set up home together" at that time. Certainly, as Tristram Hunt writes, they were "in each other's arms over 1843–44."

With Burns at his side and playing the role of guide, Engels traversed the streets and alleys of working-class Manchester, entering the hidden recesses of the city. In the process he carried out the social and environmental investigations that were to make *The Condition of the Working Class* the classic description of the nineteenth-century industrial proletariat and its built environment. Many of the intimate details of working-class life that made Engels's study so powerful were likely derived in part from Burns.

The two were separated when Engels left Manchester in 1844. However, in the summer of 1845 Engels returned to Manchester along with Marx to collect materials for their research on classical political economists, and he and Burns were reunited. Engels persuaded her to accompany him to Brussels. Karl and Jenny Marx were fond of her, and, according to their daughter Eleanor, found her "pretty, witty, and charming." From then on, Mary and Frederick were companions/partners, in a free union. As historian Roy Whitfield tells us, "For twenty years [until Mary's Burns' death in 1863] she was his wife in all but name."[8]

Three years later, in October 1848, in the midst of the 1848 Revolution, we again see Engels, now age twenty-eight, on the move, making his way on foot out of a conquered Paris on a long meandering journey to Switzerland.[9] In the travel diary *From Paris to Berne*, kept during his marathon, 300-plus-mile walk, Engels describes in loving detail the countryside, the vineyards, and the peasants, clearly enjoying life on the way but always on the lookout for hidden revolutionary potential, the spark of revolt. At every step he displays a deep appreciation of the French landscape and the "variety of its gifts of nature." He writes at one point of "huge blue rocks, between which green shrubs and saplings grow," and at another of an "avenue . . . lined with elms, ashes, acacias, or chestnuts," while "the valley floor" below "comprises luxuriant pasture and fertile fields."[10]

From Switzerland Engels dispatched articles to the *Neue Rheinsche Zeitung*, at that time edited by Marx in Cologne. In January 1849 he reentered Germany, and in June–July fought as the aide-de-camp to August Willich (associated with the Communist League) in the military campaigns in Baden and the Palatinate against the Prussians, participating in four battles.

Horseless for several days during the fighting, Engels nevertheless carried out his adjunct duties—on foot.[11]

Following the 1848 Revolution, Marx and Engels both settled in England, where Engels's time was mostly taken up working as a corresponding clerk and general assistant—and later, beginning in 1864—as a partner in the Ermen and Engels manufacturing business in Manchester. Ermen and Engels produced sewing thread, a highly specialized component of the cotton industry. They were also engaged in cotton spinning and bleaching. They had mills, warehouses, and offices in Manchester and in the surrounding towns of Salford, Eccles, and Bolton.[12]

Engels used his earnings through Ermen and Engels to support both his respectable public lodgings in town, essential for business and his class position, and his real private home with Mary Burns outside of town. Mary, together with her younger sister Lydia (Lizzy), ran private boarding houses, in which Engels was often listed as a lodger but under different names to discourage the prurient. During this period, Engels and Mary Burns moved from residence to residence, taking on different aliases, including Mr. and Mrs. Burns and Mr. and Mrs. Boardman. At one point, they were forced to change lodgings, because, as Engels put it, "The philistines have got to know that I am living with Mary." Marx teased Engels in 1851, in light of his scientific pursuits, for "studying physiology on Mary Burns," and later characterized her as "good-natured, witty" and devoted to Engels. All the while Engels, despite having to maintain two residences, was regularly sending money to Marx to address his financial exigencies.[13]

In May 1856, less than a decade after the Great Irish Famine, Engels and Mary Burns made a tour of Ireland, traveling hundreds of miles and traversing around two-thirds of the country, including Tipperary, from which Burns's parents had come. They covered the regions most hard hit by the famine, and were shocked by its still visible effects, including the hunger and destitution of the population and the reduction of much of the land to "utter desert, which nobody wants." It was at this time that Engels remarked, "Ireland may be regarded as England's first colony."

Mary Burns was to die suddenly and tragically in January 1863, leaving Engels broken-hearted. He wrote to Marx: "Mary is dead. . . . Heart failure or an apoplectic stroke. . . . I simply can't convey what I feel. The poor girl loved me with all her heart."[14] Mary's sister Lizzy, who was five years her junior, and had been living with Engels and Mary, gradually took over the vacant place in his life left by Mary's death.[15]

Engels left few traces of his true feelings, though acknowledging Mary's love for him, and, indirectly, his own love for her, as well as his feelings that with Mary his youth was gone.[16] In his unfinished *History of Ireland*, written in 1870, he poetically declared of Ireland: "The weather, like the inhabitants, has a more acute character, it moves in sharper, more sudden contrasts: the sky is like an Irish woman's face: here also rain and sunshine succeed each other suddenly and unexpectedly and there is none of the grey English boredom."[17] Undoubtedly in these lines he was picturing the two Irish women he loved, not simply commenting on the beauties and vagaries of the Irish climate.

Engels's double life in Manchester in these years required him, as a respectable bourgeois gentleman, to partake in social activities typical of his class, extending even to aristocratic pursuits, far removed from his political commitment to the working class, such as fox hunting, which in this case allowed him to maintain his horsemanship. Engels kept a horse of his own—a hunter the costs of which were at least initially assumed by his father, who was willing to finance bourgeois pursuits associated with increasing one's class standing. Engels regularly participated in the Cheshire Hounds, the famous fox-hunting meet, sometimes spending seven hours in the saddle. He was often among those leading the field, clearing ditches, and taking his horse on one occasion over a hedge measuring five feet and some inches.[18]

It was not until 1869–70 that Engels was finally able to retire from the firm in Manchester, selling his share in the business and moving to London, and along with Lizzy (now no longer needing to disguise his household relationships and openly referring to her as his wife), took up residence within a quarter-hour's walk from Marx, whom he visited every day. In 1869 he visited Ireland with Lizzy and Eleanor Marx, inspiring him to write his *History of Ireland*, which he began but never completed.[19] Again we find Engels at this point in his life in continual motion, this time with Marx at his side, wandering together on Hampstead Heath or pacing up and down in Marx's study. As Eleanor Marx-Aveling recalled in 1890:

> During the following ten years [after Engels's move from Manchester to London] Engels came to see my father every day; they sometimes went for a walk together but just as often they remained in my father's room, walking up and down, each on his side of the room, boring holes with his heel as he turned on it in his corner. In that room they discussed more things than the philosophy of most men can dream of. Frequently they walked up and down side by side in silence. Or again, each would talk about what was then mainly occupying him until they stood face to face and laughed aloud, admitting that they had been weighing opposite plans for the last half hour.[20]

It was in this period, when Engels was in his fifties and early sixties, that his constant restless energy was to be channeled into an outpouring of his mature work, including *The Housing Question* (1872); the major part of the draft manuscripts and notes for his unfinished *Dialectics of Nature* (largely complete by

1878); *Anti-Dühring* (1878); *Socialism: Utopian and Scientific* (taken from *Anti-Dühring*) (1880); the remaining drafts and notes to the *Dialectics of Nature* (1880–82), and *The Origin of the Family, Private Property, and the State* (1884).

In all of these writings, and in a number of other books written by Engels well after Marx's death—*Ludwig Feuerbach and the Outcome of His Philosophy* (1888), and *Can Europe Disarm?* (1893)—what emerged was a broad ecological perspective toward the world and human interactions, already present in the 1840s in *The Condition of the Working Class* but developed further by Engels in his mature period. For Engels all was motion, interconnection, contradiction, and spiraling change. The world exhibited a natural dialectic, that is, from the standpoint of reason it could be comprehended as embodying dialectical relations—a complex evolutionary process of continuing flux and spiraling development (and sometimes retrogression). Recognition of this was integral to his entire revolutionary praxis.

Engels's later work represented in many ways the *return of nature* in Marxian theory. For both Marx and Engels, the materialist conception of nature and the materialist conception of history were inextricably connected, just as the alienation of nature and the alienation of labor were.[21] But in their later years, following the publication of Marx's *Capital*, volume 1, they were compelled to develop their ideas regarding the materialist conception of nature more systematically in order to strengthen their understanding of the materialist conception of history. This return of nature in their thought represented a process that Marx had already commenced in part in *Capital*, the threads of which are being gradually rediscovered in our time.[22] Significantly, it was in its character as work on the *human ecology* and *urban environment* of the proletariat, reflecting the antagonism of nature and society in the new industrial towns, that Engels's early *Condition of the Working Class* was to have its greatest impact, when it appeared for the first time in an English-language edition in 1887. The translator, Florence Kelley (Wischnewetzky), was to emerge as perhaps the leading protagonist in the early socialist environmental justice movement in the United States.

A DIALECTICAL HUMAN ECOLOGY

An ecological worldview, David R. Keller and Frank B. Golley write in their introduction to *The Philosophy of Ecology*, includes a commitment to such theoretical principles as (1) "ontological interconnectedness," (2) "internal relations"—seeing the "essence or identity of a living thing" as the product of complex connections and processes, (3) holism, (4) naturalism, (5) non-anthropocentrism, and (6) a recognition of the "negative impacts" of humans on the earth.[23] Ecology transcends the boundaries between society and extra-human nature. Looked at from this standpoint, human social systems are both inescapably part of the natural world, and, insofar as they reflect specifically *social* determinants, are relatively independent from it. This creates both the possibility for the human-generated ecological disruption that characterizes our times and also for its opposite in the form of sustainable human development. Social systems thus become human ecologies. Such varied thinkers as William Blake, Percy Bysshe Shelley, Charles Dickens, Marx, Engels, John Ruskin, and William Morris saw the Industrial Revolution as a violation of nature, presenting a contradiction between town and country. It is no accident, then, that some of the most influential, early descriptions of "ecology" had to do with urban systems.

From the viewpoint of Europe and North America, it was undoubtedly more obvious in the nineteenth century than it is today that the new urban megalopolises were in antagonistic relation to the natural environments from which they emerged and to which they remained connected.[24] Perhaps the most dramatic indication of the antagonistic relation between the new industrial towns and what Marx was later to call the "universal metabolism of nature" was the spread of contagious diseases, namely, cholera, typhus, typhoid fever, tuberculosis, diphtheria, and scarlet fever.[25] Although little was known at the time about the etiology of such diseases, the fact that they were associated with a fundamental transformation of the nature-society relation was widely perceived. In *Bleak House* Charles Dickens wrote of "malignant diseases" that were "a shameful testimony to future ages, how civilization and barbarism walked this boastful island together."[26]

Looked at from this broad perspective, Engels was an early exponent of an ecological worldview, particularly of the dialectical relation between human beings and nature. He was a lifelong student of a broad range of sciences and one of the most erudite figures of his age, speaking as many as twenty languages, revered by Marx for his encyclopedic knowledge.[27] In his "Letters from Wuppertal," published when he was only eighteen, he wrote of the deplorable health conditions of factory work in his native region: "Work in low rooms where people breathe in more coal fumes and dust than oxygen—and in the majority of cases beginning already at the age of six—is bound to deprive them of all strength and joy in life." He contrasted this to the free, unbounded air of the countryside.[28] Engels's first book, *The Condition of the Working Class in England* (1845), was concerned with this town-country division and pioneered in the study of social epidemiology. His last book, *Can Europe Disarm?* (1893), commented on the consequences of the destruction of the soil. In between, he addressed the dialectic of nature-ecology in nearly all of his major works.

Engels's situating of his work in the broad context of capitalism, nature, and socialism was evident as early as his 1843 "Outlines to a Critique of Political Economy." Here he argued that there were "two elements of production . . .

nature and man." Alienation served to sever these. "The immediate consequence of private property," he wrote, "was the split of production into two opposing sides—the natural and the human sides, the soil which without fertilisation by man is [soon] dead and sterile, and human activity, the first condition of which is that very soil." Under capitalism the robbery of the earth became a governing principle of accumulation: "To make land an object of huckstering—the land which is our one and all, the first condition of our existence—was the last stage towards making oneself an object of huckstering."[29]

Engels's view of nature was not a reified one associated with economic categories of capitalist commodity production, where nature was reduced to something to conquer and exploit. Rather, from the start, he recognized the intrinsic value of nature and hence the tragedy of its estrangement under capitalism. This appreciation of the natural environment was evidenced by Engels's loving descriptions, for example in his 1840 article "Landscapes," where he captured the natural beauty displayed by the countryside in Greece, Germany, and England, and his constant evocations throughout his writings in his twenties to Shelley's *Queen Mab*, in which he highlighted in particular Shelley's vivid poetic descriptions of the natural environment, referring to "a tenderness and originality in depiction of nature such as only Shelley can achieve."[30]

This acute Shelleyan love of life coupled with a sense of the alienation of nature and humanity in bourgeois society is evident in *The Condition of the English Working Class in England*, where Engels writes of "Shelley, the genius, the prophet Shelley, and Byron, with his glowing sensuality and his bitter satire upon our existing society."[31] References to poetry, often revolutionary in nature, loom sporadically in Engels's early work, standing for an irrepressible, luminous natural and social reality outside and opposed to the bleak world and degraded existence imposed by industrial capitalism. Engels was already developing the notion of the division of town and country that was to become a central theme in Marx and Engels's *German Ideology*. "Town and country," he wrote, "are in constant competition" under capitalism. "The greater the town the greater its advantages," arising from its infrastructure, existing establishments, its ready market, and its skilled labor. In contrast, the country has as its main advantage low wages. "But the centralizing tendency of manufacture continues in full force, and every new factory built in the country bears in it the germ of a manufacturing town."[32]

Engels's *Condition of the Working Class* was to play a formative role in the construction of Marxian political economy, and was to attain historical significance, as Eric Hobsbawm stressed, as "the earliest large work whose analysis is systematically based on the concept of the Industrial Revolution." It was also, though often less appreciated, a foundational environmental work. It was concerned above all with the physiological conditions of the working class in the environs of the "great towns," and particularly industrial Manchester, though there are brief excursions into the conditions of the agricultural and mining proletariats outside of the large cities.[33] Only a small amount of the book considered actual factory conditions, and in these cases the focus is almost exclusively on the environmental conditions within the workplace and their effects on the health of the workers.

To be sure, *The Condition of the Working Class* provides powerful insights into surplus-value relations, and it is here that we first see a systematic development of the theory of relative surplus population or the industrial "reserve army," a concept that Engels introduced here as well as in his earlier "Outlines of a Critique of Political Economy." Yet it is the environmental conditions of the working class that pervaded the work as a whole and constituted the youthful Engels's chief concern. Most of the book is devoted to the social epidemiology of working-class life in the industrial towns and with the etiology of disease. The combination of the critique of political economy with his critique of environmental and epidemiological conditions and their relation to the reproduction of the laboring class under capitalism, is what gives Engels's work its material power and its astonishing ability to evoke our emotions and our conscience even today.

The everyday lives of proletarians in Manchester and other industrial towns in the 1840s were filled with smoke, filth, overwork, disease, work degradation, crippling injury, and of course, premature death. Engels's expressed aim in *The Condition of the Working Class* was to provide a detailed description of these conditions in the lives of the workers, and to point systematically to the political economy of capitalism as the source. As Howard Waitzkin observed in *The Second Sickness*, "Engels's theoretical position was unambiguous. For working-class people the roots of illness and early death lay in the organization of economic production and in the social environment. British capitalism, Engels argued, forced working-class people to live and work under circumstances that inevitably caused sickness; this situation was not hidden but was well known to the capitalist class. The conflict between profit and safety worsened health problems and stood in the way of necessary improvements."[34]

Engels's treatment of the Industrial Revolution, which sets the stage for his book, begins with what has become by now a fairly standard discussion of the main inventions—beginning with the spinning jenny—associated with the stupendous growth of cotton (and wool) textile manufacture. However, he quickly moves on to examine the basis of this in the production of iron and coal and the larger question of energy. Here he places a heavy emphasis on the eighteenth-century transformation of iron smelting, from wood-based charcoal to coke (derived from coal). This resulted in a vast increase in iron production by the late eighteenth century and a much-reduced need for wood imports—given the prior decimation of English forests as a consequence of charcoal-based iron smelting. In 1720, sixty British furnaces, producing 17,000 tons of pig iron, required (when forging was added) around 830,000 tons of charcoaling wood for the smelting. The result was the extensive destruction of English forests. As Vaclav Smil explained, "Already in 1648 anguished inhabitants of Sussex wondered how many towns would decay if the iron mills and furnaces were allowed to continue (people would have no wood to build houses, watermills, wheels, barrels, and hundreds of other necessities), and they asked the king to close down many of the mills."[35]

Indeed, what largely deforested England was not so much population growth as supposed in the standard Malthusian interpretation according to which too many people led inexorably to too much wood consumption and hence wood scarcity.[36] Rather, the massive deforestation in the seventeenth and eighteenth centuries was predominantly the consequence of an early stage of proto-industrialization in which the manufacture of iron was dependent on charcoal smelting. So serious, Engels explained, was the shortage of wood for charcoal in the early eighteenth century, until the means of smelting iron with coal became widespread, that the English were forced, when the environmental crisis peaked, "to obtain all their wrought iron from abroad," particularly from Sweden. Engels further observed that the shift from wood-based charcoal to coal-based coke smelting of iron in 1788 led to a six-fold increase in iron production in six years.[37] It was this that led Max Weber, with his eye on the environmental history of England, to declare that the discovery of the coking process for smelting iron with coal had saved the German forests.[38]

From the standpoint of the industrial takeoff, the expansion of coal production was initially aimed at boosting the production of iron. As Engels observed in *The Condition of the Working Class,* the rapid introduction of improved forms of iron smelting from coke in the form of puddling—"withdrawing the carbon which had mixed with the iron during the process of smelting"—in late eighteenth-century England gave an enormous impetus to the production of iron. The sheer size of smelting furnaces grew fifty times in a matter of decades. The Industrial Revolution was in many ways symbolized, as he noted, by Thomas Paine's design for building the first iron bridge in Yorkshire.[39]

By the mid-1830s, Engels underscored, some 700,000 tons of iron were produced, which consumed each year more than 3 million tons of coal for the smelting of pig iron alone.[40] In 1869, at the very height of the Industrial Revolution, more coal in England was used for smelting iron than for firing all the steam engines of general manufactures and trains combined. Indeed, the demand for coal for iron smelting (along with the demand for tin, copper, and lead) led to development of the steam engine, which then increased the demand for coal in a positive feedback mechanism of the sort that characterized the whole industrial takeoff. Thus, it was the steam engine in the end that was to give "importance to the broad coal-fields of England." This was inextricably linked, via the coking process, to "the iron mines which supplied raw material" for the production of machine industry.[41]

Industrialization was not simply about machinery and factories, but included a whole new transportation infrastructure, railways, the digging of canals, and the introduction of steamships. Agriculture too was revolutionized as capital was applied to the soil via novel fertilizing processes and as new agricultural methods were developed, due to the advances in chemistry associated with figures such as Humphrey Davy and Justus von Liebig. England, which shifted its agriculture to meat and wool production, became a net importer of grain even as its agriculture expanded.

Displacement of labor in agriculture led to the rise of an enormous industrial proletariat, the key element in the development of modern industry. "Population," Engels explained, "becomes centralised as capital does," that is, increasingly located in the great towns. It was in *The Condition of the Working Class* that he systematically introduced the concept of relative surplus population or the industrial "reserve army" of labor, which became the linchpin of the Marxian critique of political economy, and its answer to crude Malthusian notions in which poverty was the product of population growth. Under capitalism, accumulation was made possible by the existence of a vast army of unemployed workers, allowing production to be shifted rapidly into new areas during periods of expansion, while also holding wages down during periods of contraction. Accumulation of capital, as Marx later wrote, was at the same time the accumulation of a laboring population, much of which remained unemployed and underemployed. Accumulation of wealth at the top of society was thus mirrored in the relative misery, toil, and dispossession at the bottom of society, upon which the entire system of capital rested.[42] Engels ended his chapter on "The Industrial Proletariat" in *The Condition of the Working Class* with the words: "But in these [great manufacturing] towns the proletarians are the infinite majority, and how they fare, what influence the great town exercises upon them, we have now to investigate."[43]

In carrying out his investigation, Engels made use of an array of important governmental reports. In 1832, in the midst of the second great cholera pandemic and the inevitability of a "cholera visitation" in Manchester, "a universal terror," he wrote, "seized the bourgeoisie of the city" as "the epidemic was approaching." It was in these circumstances that "people remembered the unwholesome dwellings of the poor, and trembled before the certainty that each of these slums would become a centre for the plague, whence it would spread desolation in all directions through the houses of the propertied class." In this context a public health commission was created under

Dr. James Phillips Kay, who scrutinized all aspects of the living conditions of the workers in his 1832 report on *The Moral and Physical Condition of the Working Classes in the Cotton Manufacture in Manchester.* Although Engels pointed out that "Dr. Kay confuses the working class in general with the factory workers," he nonetheless considered it "an excellent pamphlet." Engels also made use in his study of Edwin Chadwick's influential 1842 report to the Poor Law Commissioners, *Report on the Sanitary Conditions of the Labouring Population of Great Britain*, as well as a number of key parliamentary reports focused principally on children's employment.[44]

However, *The Condition of the English Working Class* was based fundamentally on Engels's interactions with workers and on his own observations. In many ways it reflected the working-class consciousness that he found in Manchester shortly after the 1842 General Strike—also known as the Plug Plot riots—when the working class was actively involved, in E. P. Thompson's terms, in its own *making*. In the General Strike of 1842, centered in Manchester during the August before Engels's arrival, workers had marched from factory to factory, pulling the plugs from the boilers to shut down the mills, demanding that the Six Points of the People's Charter be adopted as the law of the land. Repression and hunger, however, drove the strikers back to work by September.[45]

Together with Mary Burns, Engels attended mass meetings of workers held at the House of Science, founded by Owenites (it has been suggested that they may actually have met there).[46] Along with his interactions with the national Chartist leader George Julian Harney, Engels drew heavily on the work of his friend the Manchester Chartist leader James Leach, who had been employed in a variety of working-class occupations, including coal mining and power-loom weaving, and probably hand-loom weaving, and who had led the 1839 resistance of Manchester workers to cuts in their wages. Leach was one of the principal figures behind the idea of the National Charter. He argued that labor was the source of wealth (value) and that workers were being robbed of the product of their labor—an argument presented in his remarkable 84-page work, *Stubborn Facts from the Factories by a Manchester Operative* (1844). In Leach's words, "Working people" are "rendered *surplus in the labour market by the machines*." Hence, the owners were able to exploit the fact that they had "two sets of labourers at command, one in work and the other out"—creating a favorable condition for lowering wages and "taking away from Labour its due reward." Elsewhere Leach was to argue "as manufactories increased, the value of labor diminished." Engels quoted from and cited Leach's *Stubborn Facts* at a number of points in *The Condition of the Working Class in England*. Engels also drew on statistics that workers themselves had collected on factory work as part of the Chartist movement and that were incorporated in Leach's book. Leach had a bookshop less than ten minutes' walk from the Southgate office where Engels worked, and where Engels purchased the *Northern Star* and the *Miners' Advocate*. They first met in early 1843. It was most likely through Leach's agency that Engels met Harney. Since Leach was writing *Stubborn Facts* at the very same time as Engels was investigating working-class conditions in Manchester, the two undoubtedly had intense, productive exchanges.[47]

Indeed, "Engels," as Paul Pickering noted in *Chartism and the Chartists in Manchester and Salford*, "shared the views of the working people he befriended. . . . Engels's working-class friends, who had ushered him into their councils, meetings and community networks, were living proof that a strong close-knit culture existed in spite of, and in opposition to, the hellishness of the environment."[48] Engels also benefited from his knowledge of Chartist literature, from which he derived the concept of "social murder."[49]

But Engels also carried out his own firsthand investigations on foot. Industrial Manchester was "built" in such a way, he claimed, that "a person may live in it for years, and go in and out daily without coming into contact with a working-people's quarter or even with the workers, that is, so long as he confines himself to his business or to pleasure walks. This arises chiefly from the fact that by unconscious tacit agreement, as well as with outspoken conscious determination, the working-people's quarters are sharply separated from the sections of the city reserved for the middle class; or if this does not succeed, they are concealed with the cloak of charity."[50]

It was exactly these areas of the city that Engels sought to explore. A German acquaintance who visited him at the time was astonished by his constant excursions into the working-class sectors of the city. It was the thoroughness of his labors in this respect that led Engels to declare that he knew Manchester "as intimately as my own native town, more intimately than most of its residents know it." He added, "If any one wishes to see in how little space a human being can move, how little air—and *such* air! —he can breathe, how little of civilization he may share and yet live, it is only necessary to travel hither" to the working-class quarters of Manchester.[51]

Manchester, Engels observed, was at that time the "the first [that is, most important] manufacturing city in the world." It had a population, including its suburbs, of around 400,000 people, the vast majority of whom were working class. Like other industrial cities, it had expanded rapidly with virtually no controls on building and no overall system of sanitation. Engels made drawings of the arrangement of streets and housing, showing the overcrowded and degraded conditions in which people lived. The main means of disposal of human and other wastes in cities at the time, save the homes of the wealthy, which were sometimes connected to sewers, was in the form of cesspools (enclosed pits that were dug into the ground). Theoretically these were periodically emptied, but in many cases, particularly in the poorer districts, this seldom occurred, resulting in overflow. Deep cesspools sometimes leaked into ground water with a minimum of biological cleansing.[52]

In exploring the environmental conditions of the working class in Manchester, Marcus writes, Engels made "pertinent observations about the ecological relations" of the various districts of the city, connecting them "to the rivers, streams and flats" in which they were situated.[53] Three rivers, the Irk, Irwell, and Medlock, formed the environs of the new industrial "Cottonopolis," as Manchester came to be known. In describing Manchester's urban environment, he examined successively the general system of building; the Old Town and the New Town; the method of construction of the workers' quarters; alleys, courts, and side streets; Little Ireland; the surrounding districts; lodging houses; overcrowded populations; cellar dwellings; the workers' clothing; food and nutrition; and disease. He started out in Old Town and took the reader in a circuit of the city moving in a clockwise direction, on foot, through the working-class districts of the city.[54] Eric Hobsbawm evoked the emotional current that runs through Engels's book: "If we follow Engels as he walks through Manchester cotton-mills and slums . . . we shall have no difficulty in generating horror and fury" even today, at well over a century's "distance."[55]

From the Ducie Bridge high above the city, Engels mapped out the urban landscape for all to see:

> At the bottom flows, or rather stagnates, the Irk, a narrow, coal-black, foul-smelling stream, full of *débris* and refuse, which it deposits on the shallower right bank. In dry weather, a long string of the most disgusting, blackish-green, slime pools are left standing on this bank, from the depths of which bubbles of miasmatic gas constantly arise and give forth a stench unendurable except on the bridge forty or fifty feet above the surface of the stream. But besides this, the stream itself is checked every few paces by high weirs, behind which slime and refuse accumulate and rot in thick masses. Above the bridge are tanneries, bonemills, and gasworks, from which all drains and refuse find their way into the Irk, which receives further the contents of the neighbouring sewers and privies. It may be easily imagined, therefore, what sort of residue the stream deposits. Below the bridge you look upon the piles of *débris*, the refuse, filth, and offal from the courts on the steep left bank; here each house is packed close behind its neighbor and a piece of each is visible, all black, smoky, crumbling, ancient, with broken panes and window-frames. The background is furnished by old barrack-like factory buildings. On the lower right bank stands a long row of houses and mills; the second house being a ruin without a roof, piled with *débris*; the third stands so low that the lowest floor is uninhabitable, and therefore without windows or doors. Here the background embraces the pauper burial-ground, the station of the Liverpool and Leeds

railway, and in the rear of this, the Workhouse, the "Poor-Law Bastille" of Manchester, which, like a citadel, looks threatening down from its high walls and parapets on the hilltop upon the working-people's quarter below.[56]

Enclosed within a bend of the Medlock River on the Manchester side was the low-lying district known as Little Ireland. Of this district and its environs, Engels wrote in disgust and outrage:

> Here flows the Medlock. . . . Along both sides of the stream, which is coal-black, stagnant and foul, stretches a broad belt of factories and working-men's dwellings, the latter all in the worst condition. . . . But the most horrible spot . . . lies on the Manchester side, immediately south-west of Oxford Road, and is known as Little Ireland. In a rather deep hole, in a curve of the Medlock and surrounded on all four sides by tall factories and high embankments, covered with buildings, stand two groups of about two hundred cottages, built chiefly back to back, in which live about four thousand human beings, most of them Irish. The cottages are old, dirty, and of the smallest sort, the streets uneven, fallen into ruts and in part without drains or pavement; masses of refuse, offal and sickening filth lie among standing pools in all directions; the atmosphere is poisoned by the effluvia from these, and laden and darkened by the smoke of a dozen tall factory chimneys. A horde of ragged women and children swarm about here, as filthy as the swine that thrive upon the garbage heaps and in the puddles. In short, the whole rookery furnishes such a hateful and repulsive spectacle as can hardly be equaled in the worst court on the Irk. The race that lives in these ruinous cottages, behind broken windows, mended with oilskin, sprung doors, and rotten doorposts, or in dark, wet cellars, in measureless filth and stench, in this atmosphere penned in as if with a purpose, this race must really have reached the lowest stage of humanity. This is the impression and the line of thought which the exterior of this district forces upon the beholder. But what must one think when he hears that in each of these pens, containing at most two rooms, a garret and perhaps a cellar, on the average twenty human beings live; that in the whole region, for each one hundred and twenty persons, one usually inaccessible privy is provided; and that in spite of all the preachings of the physicians, in spite of the excitement into which the cholera epidemic plunged the sanitary police by reason of the condition of Little Ireland, in spite of everything, in this year of grace 1844, it is in almost the same state as in 1831! Dr. Kay asserts that not only the cellars but the first floors of all the houses in this district are damp; that a number of cellars once filled up with earth have now been emptied and are occupied once more by Irish people; that in one cellar the water constantly wells up through a hole stopped with clay, the cellar lying below the river level, so that its occupant, a

> hand-loom weaver, had to bail out the water from his dwelling every morning and pour it into the street![57]

Human beings had been forced back into living in damp holes and cattle sheds. Some 12 percent of the working-class portion of the city lived in cellars. In the larger metropolitan area, including the suburbs, this meant, Engels noted, that some 40,000 to 50,000 people resided in damp, overcrowded cellars, prone to flooding and in close contact with cesspools. "These filthy holes" were the dwelling places for "a ragged, ill-fed population." In the Old Town district of Manchester, he wrote, "I found a man, apparently about sixty years old, living in a cow-stable. He had constructed a sort of chimney for his square pen, which had neither windows, floor, nor ceiling, had obtained a bedstead and lived there, though the rain dripped through his rotten roof. This man was too old and weak for regular work, and supported himself by removing manure with a hand-cart; the dung-heaps lay next door to his palace!"[58] At another point he gives a picture of a microcosm of the tragedy he saw everywhere in the Manchester slums:

> Passing along a rough bank, among stakes and washing-lines, one penetrates into this chaos of small, one-storied, one-roomed huts, in most of which there is no artificial floor; kitchen, living and sleeping-room are all in one. In such a hole, scarcely five feet long by six broad, I found two beds—and such bedsteads and beds!—which, with a staircase and chimney-place, exactly filled the room. In several others I found absolutely nothing, while the door stood open and the inhabitants leaned against it. Everywhere before the doors refuse and offal; that any sort of pavement lay underneath could not be seen but only felt, here and there, with the feet. This whole collection of cattle-sheds for human beings was surrounded on two sides by houses and a factory, and on the third by the river, and besides the narrow stair up the bank, a narrow doorway alone led out into another almost equally ill-built, ill-kept labyrinth of dwellings.[59]

Engels's firsthand descriptions of these conditions corroborated the official reports, such as Chadwick's 1842 *Report on the Sanitary Condition of the Labouring Population of Great Britain* delivered to the Poor Law Commission, while going beyond them. Chadwick's report made him overnight the leading figure in public health and sanitation in the 1840s and early 1850s. A utilitarian thinker and follower of Jeremy Bentham and John Stuart Mill, Chadwick's emphasis was on the replacement of the old cesspool approach to sanitation, which was no longer adequate in the great towns, such as London and Manchester, with a water carriage system of disposing of wastes through an enormous expansion of sewers. He based his argument on the then dominant miasmatic theory of infectious disease, which argued that epidemic diseases such as cholera, typhus, and typhoid fever, which plagued the industrial cities, were the result of gases released into the air by decaying organic matter, which could be detected through the stench they created. The answer was therefore a sanitation system that rapidly removed wastes from the cities through sewers.[60] Other theories of epidemic disease at the time included the notion that such diseases arose by spontaneous generation (a view disproven by Louis Pasteur in a famous experiment in 1859) and the germ theory of disease.[61]

The miasmatic theory of disease, also sometimes referred to as the "filth theory" or the pythogenic theory, is a case where an incorrect theory of the etiology of disease nonetheless produced remarkably improved results, since it captured some of the crucial environmental factors of the problem, thereby giving it considerable credence and surprising persistence. Sometimes referred to as a "sociological" theory of disease, it tended to emphasize a broad array of factors, often connected to poverty, rather than disease-specific factors, as in the more exact germ theory that succeeded it.[62] Yet, its very weakness in terms of the etiology of disease, at a time when knowledge of bacterial pathogens was so inadequate, encouraged broad sociological changes in municipal water and sanitation systems, housing, and hygiene, which ended up alleviating some of the causes. As Charles-Edward Amory Winslow wrote in *The Conquest of Epidemic Disease* (1967):

> It was the intestinal diseases with which the sanitarians of the early nineteenth century were chiefly concerned; and these, of course, were precisely the diseases in which environmental sanitation was of fundamental importance. Therefore the concept of local miasms fitted the case remarkably well. As we shall see, however, the nineteenth-century Filth Theory of Disease was a relatively precise and scientific form of the old doctrine of miasms. It was backed up by statistical and epidemiological evidence; and it actually accomplished results in the practical control of epidemic disease.[63]

Engels's exploration of the etiology of disease in *The Condition of the Working Class* exhibits the influence of the dominant miasmic theory of his day. For example, he declared, "All putrefying vegetable and animal substances give off gases decidedly injurious to health, and if these gases have no way of escape, they inevitably poison the atmosphere. The filth and stagnant pools of the working people's quarters in the great cities have, therefore, the worst effect upon the public health, because they produce precisely those gases which engender disease; so, too, the exhalations from contaminated streams."[64] Nevertheless, while drawing on the miasma theory in *The Condition of the Working Class*, Engels refrained from promoting a single-factor epidemiological explanation, and his overall account was thus remarkable in its attention to numerous environmental factors and conditions with respect to their influence on public health.

In the very same paragraph, Engels provided a powerful description of the air pollution threatening the populations of the large cities, and the lack of oxygen from which the population suffered: "The centralisation of population in great cities,"

> exercises of itself an unfavourable influence; the atmosphere of London can never be so pure, so rich in oxygen, as the air of the country; two and a half million pairs of lungs, two hundred and fifty thousand fires, crowded upon an area three to four miles square, consume an enormous amount of oxygen, which is replaced with difficulty, because the method of building cities in itself impedes ventilation. The carbonic acid gas, engendered by respiration and fire, remains in the streets by reason of its specific gravity, and the chief air current passes over the roofs of the city. The lungs of the inhabitants fail to receive the due supply of oxygen, and the consequence is mental and physical lassitude and low vitality. . . . And if life in large cities is, in itself, injurious to health, how great must be the harmful influence of an abnormal atmosphere in the working-people's quarters, where, as we have seen, everything combines to poison the air.[65]

Engels was not alone in making such observations, though he was more concerned than most contemporary commentators about the health effects on the population. Leon Faucher, visiting Manchester from France in 1844, wrote of "the clouds of smoke that vomited forth from the numberless chimneys," comparing the effect of the air pollution on the town to that of an active volcano.[66]

A particular problem, Engels stressed, was the lack of the "means of cleanliness" on the part of the poor, "since pipes are laid only when paid for, and the rivers so polluted that they are useless for such purposes; they are obliged to throw all offal and garbage, all dirty water, often all disgusting drainage and excrement into the streets, being without other means of disposing of them; they are thus compelled to infect the region of their own dwellings."[67]

Engels was particularly concerned with tuberculosis, then known as consumption or "phthisis." (The cause of tuberculosis was then unknown. Robert Koch discovered the tuberculosis bacillus, *Mycobacterium tuberculosis*, in 1882.) "The bad air of London," Engels wrote, "and especially of the working-people's districts, is in the highest degree favourable to the development of consumption" and other lung diseases, along with "scarlet fever, a disease which brings most frightful devastation into the ranks of the working-class." In the 1880 epidemic in Edinburgh, scarlet fever was found to have killed nearly 20 percent of the children who contracted it. It is caused by the bacterium

Streptococcus pyogenes (group *A. streptococci*) transmitted by air droplets when someone coughs or sneezes. It was not fully identified until the late 1880s.[68]

The cause of typhus (the bacteria *Rickettsia prowazekii* spread in the feces of lice) was also unknown at the time. It was not clearly distinguished from typhoid fever until 1869. Typhoid fever is caused by the ingestion of water or food contaminated by feces of an infected person containing the bacterium *Salmonella enterica subsp. enterica*, Typhi. Engels, following the parliamentary reports of the day, attributed typhus to "the bad state of the dwellings in the matter of ventilation, drainage, and cleanliness," particularly where "the inhabitants are greatly crowded." It was, he noted, "found in the working-people's quarters of all great towns and cities," while "in Scotland and Ireland . . . it rages with a violence that surpasses all conception."[69]

Cholera, in particular, struck terror in the ranks of the upper classes and was regarded as a greater danger than typhus and other contagious diseases, beyond its statistical significance for the society as a whole. This is so because while the epidemic always centered principally in the poorer regions of the urban geography, it crossed class lines more readily than other contagious diseases of the day, sometimes infecting the well-to-do. Terror therefore struck the ranks of the bourgeoisie, as Engels emphasized, whenever a cholera epidemic approached.[70] Indeed, the speed with which cholera seemed to migrate from the slums of the poor to the much better habitations of the rich imparted to it a frightening aspect in the eyes of the better-off.

In 1845, when *The Condition of the Working Class* appeared, it was not yet suspected that cholera was due to a water-borne pathogen (the bacteria *Vibrio cholerae*). Nevertheless, Engels quoted a remarkable passage from the classical political economist Nassau Senior's 1837 *Letters on the Factory Act as It Affects the Cotton Manufacturer*, in which Senior wrote of the working-class quarters in Manchester in this respect:

> These towns [the working-class districts such as Irish Town, Ancoats, and Little Ireland], for such they are in extent and population, have been erected by small speculators with an utter disregard to every thing except immediate profit. . . . In one place we saw a whole street following the course of a ditch, in order to have deeper cellars (cellars for people, not for lumber) without the expense of excavations. *Not a house in this street escaped cholera.* And generally speaking, throughout these suburbs the streets are unpaved, with a dunghill or a pond in the middle; the houses built back to back, without ventilation or drainage; and whole families each occupy a corner of a cellar or of a garret.[71]

That a whole street of people came down with cholera, where housing had been built along the path of a sewage ditch so that deeper cellars could be dug there for human occupation, was an important empirical observation at the time. In these damp, porous cellars mingled with cesspools, people were destined to die in great numbers. There was no doubt about the unhealthiness of such housing for the poor in the minds of Senior or Engels. And both knew the political economic reasons for these conditions—although Senior, as Engels noted, was "a fanatical opponent of all independent movements of the workers."[72]

Engels underscored that many of the workers were reduced to living in "damp dwellings, cellar dens that are not waterproof from below." In Manchester one-tenth of the families lived in cellars, in Liverpool one-fifth. Brought into the world under such horrendous conditions more than half of working-class children in Manchester at the time died before the age of five.[73] As public-health historian Anthony S. Wohl has written of the cellars in which so many of the workers lived in the large towns in the Victorian era:

> It is hardly necessary to dwell upon the insanitary nature of cellar dwellings—at the best damp, at the worst oozing with raw sewage and ill-ventilated, they were the perfect nexus for disease. For those suffering from pulmonary illnesses and for those who contracted typhus and other fevers they were often death-traps, to those suffering from arthritis or rheumatism the cellars were cells which aggravated and perpetuated their discomfort. Few precise analyses of the connection between cellar dwelling and mortality were taken in the nineteenth century—although George Buchanan argued from his survey of Liverpool undertaken in 1864 for the Privy Council that the general death rate in the cellars was some 35 percent higher than among the working classes in general—and, given the pythogenic theory, no such analyses were necessary in the minds of reformers. That the lower classes were often, in their habitations, literally lower, and that they were denied the purifying and cleansing power of fresh air was in itself an affront to Victorian sensibilities. . . . The continued existence of cellars for dwelling places down into the 1860s and after served to publicize the severity of the "housing question."[74]

Issues of nutrition also drew Engels's attention. There he pointed to the artificial food scarcity and inflated prices that contributed to the poor nutritional intake of urban workers, along with problems of contamination and spoilage. He treated scrofula as a disease arising from nutritional deficiencies—an observation that, Waitzkin explains, "antedated the discovery of bovine tuberculosis as the major cause of scrofula and pasteurization of milk as a preventive measure." Likewise, Engels discussed the skeletal deformities associated with rickets as a nutritional problem, long before the medical discovery that it was due to deficiencies in vitamin D.[75] A key problem in nutrition, Engels argued, was the frequent adulteration of food. He quoted an article from the *Liverpool Mercury* which explained that a chemical substance from soap factories was mixed with sugar; cocoa was adulterated with dirt mixed with mutton fat; pepper was "adulterated with dust from husks," etc.[76] As Wohl was to write of the adulteration of food in Victorian England:

> Much of the food consumed by the working-class family was contaminated and positively detrimental to health. . . . The list of poisonous additives reads like the stock list of some mad and malevolent chemist: strychnine, cocculus indicus (both are hallucinogens) and copperas in rum and beer; sulphate of copper in pickles, bottled fruit, wine, and preserves; lead chromate in mustard and snuff; sulphate of iron in tea and beer; ferric ferocyanide, lime sulphate and turmeric in chinese tea; copper carbonate, lead sulphate, bisulphate of mercury, and Venetian lead in sugar confectionary and chocolate; lead in wine and cider; all were extensively used and were accumulative in effect, resulting, over a long period, in chronic gastritis, and indeed, often fatal food poisoning. Red lead gave Gloucester cheese its "healthy" red hue, flour and arrowroot a rich thickness to cream, and tea leaves were "dried, dyed, recycled again and again." As late as 1877 the Local Government Board found that approximately a quarter of the milk it examined contained excessive water or chalk, and ten per cent of all butter, over eight per cent of the bread, and over 50 percent of all the gin had had copper in them to heighten the colour.[77]

Engels provided a meticulous description of the social forces leading to endemic alcoholism. All the factors that affected the worker's condition, the demoralization, the injuries, the need for some social intercourse (often to be found only in pubs), the desire for inexpensive pleasure provided by cheap liquor, all contributed to widespread intemperance. The result, however, was injurious to the extreme. "But as inevitably as a great number of working-men fall prey to drink, just so inevitably does it manifest its ruinous influence upon the body and mind of its victims. All the tendencies to disease arising from the conditions of life of the workers are promoted by it, it stimulates in the highest degree the development of lung and digestive troubles, the rise and spread of typhus epidemics."[78]

The fact that medical help was largely unavailable to the working class because of the high cost of doctors meant that they were prey to all sorts of charlatans and "patent medicines" promoted by all means of advertising. Infamous among these was "Morrison's Pill," which was promoted as a cure to all maladies. "One of the most injurious of these patent medicines," Engels wrote, "is a drink prepared with opiates, chiefly laudanum, under the name of Godfrey's Cordial," which people were encouraged to take in large amounts and give to children, even infants. The result of such remedies was often to increase mortality and to further worsen the physical and mental conditions of the workers.[79]

Beyond these general illnesses, Engels investigated occupational diseases and accidents associated with factory work and other working-class occupations. Many of "the physiological results of the factory system," as he called them, did not come under intensive study until the second half of the twentieth century. Engels paid particular attention to orthopedic disorders due to long periods of standing and the physical requirements of production. As Waitzkin notes, "He discussed curvature of the spine, deformities of the lower extremities, flat feet, varicose veins, and leg ulcers as manifestations of work demands that required long periods of time in an upright posture." He also examined the damaging effects of repetitive motions on the workers.[80] In some cases the analysis was based on Engels's personal observations in Manchester. A worker of his acquaintance suffered from a fairly common distortion among operatives—Engels remembered running into numerous such cases as he "traversed Manchester"—which took the form of a distinctive distortion of "the spinal columns and the legs" resulting from overwork, long periods standing in one position, and repetitive motions. Often workers filing lathes, he wrote, had "crooked backs and one leg crooked, 'hind leg' as they call it, so that the two legs have the form of a K."[81]

Factories were both warm and damp and characterized by a "bad atmosphere," "deficient in oxygen, filled with dust and the smell of the machine oil." Many of the cotton mills, Engels noted, were

> filled with fibrous dust, which produces chest affections, especially among workers in the carding and combing-rooms. . . . The most common effects of this breathing of dust are blood-spitting, hard noisy breathing, pains in the chest, coughs, sleeplessness—in short, all the symptoms of asthma ending in the worst cases in consumption. Especially unwholesome is the wet spinning of the linen-yarn which is carried on by young girls and boys. The water spurts over them from the spindle, so that the front of their clothing is constantly wet through to the skin; and there is always water standing on the floor. This is the case to a less degree in the doubling-rooms of the cotton mills, and the result is a constant succession of colds and affections to the chest. A hoarse, rough voice is common to all operatives but especially wet spinners and doublers.[82]

Engels explained that the grinders of knife blades and forks, commonly performing their work with a dry stone, could normally expect an "early death." This involved a "bent posture" accompanied by the inhalation of the fine metal dust particles freed by the grinding, resulting in what was called "grinders' asthma."[83]

Workers in the pottery industry were subject to severe lead poisoning. Such workers, he explained,

> dip the finished article into a fluid containing great quantities of lead, and often of arsenic, or have to take the freshly dipped article up with the hand. The hands and clothing of these workers, adults and children, are often wet with this fluid, the skin softens and falls off under the constant contact with rough objects, so that the fingers often bleed, and are constantly in a state most favourable for the absorption of this dangerous substance. The consequence is violent pain, and serious diseases of the stomach and intestines, obstinate constipation, colic, sometimes consumption, and, most common of all, epilepsy among children. Among men, partial paralysis of the hand muscles, colica pictorum, and paralysis of whole limbs are ordinary phenomena.[84]

According to Waitzkin:

> [Engels's] observations of occupational lead poisoning again are startling because this disease has evoked wide concern in modern industrial hygiene. . . . The consequences Engels described included severe abdominal pain, constipation, and neurologic complications like epilepsy and partial or complete paralysis. These signs of lead intoxication occurred not only in workers themselves, according to Engels, but also in children who lived near pottery factories. Epidemiologic evidence concerning the community hazards of industrial lead has gained appreciation in environmental health since 1970, again without recognition of Engels's observations.[85]

Lace-making, a manufacturing operation carried out chiefly by young women and children, led to severe eye disorders, Engels explained, including increased myopia, corneal inflammation, cataracts, and temporary blindness. This resulted from the fine close-up work, requiring visual concentration, usually under conditions of poor lighting, overcrowded conditions, and long hours. Extreme exploitation and "total exclusion from fresh air," he observed, also accompanied dressmaking and needlework professions. Women and girls were often forced to work endless hours under excruciating conditions, with inadequate diet and poor sleeping quarters, in order to provide the gowns and finery the upper classes needed on short notice for some ball or gala. (The horrible conditions in dressmaking would be publicly revealed in the 1860s by Edwin Lankester and discussed in Marx's *Capital.*)[86]

Engels also explored the various pulmonary disorders that plagued coal miners, including "black spittle," later in the twentieth century to be referred to as black lung syndrome. "Every case of this disease," he declared, "ends fatally. . . . In all the coal-mines which are properly ventilated this disease is unknown, while it frequently happens that miners who go from well- to ill-ventilated mines are seized by it. The profit-greed of mine owners which prevents the use of ventilators is therefore responsible for the fact that this working-men's disease exists at all." Engels goes on to note:

> In the whole British Empire there is no occupation in which a man may meet his end in so many diverse ways as this one. The coal-mine is the scene of a multitude of the most terrifying calamities, and these come directly from the selfishness of the bourgeoisie. The hydrocarbon gas which develops so freely in these mines, forms, when combined with atmospheric air, an explosive which takes fire upon coming into contact with a flame, and kills every one within its reach. Such explosions take place, in one mine or another, nearly every day.[87]

Accompanying such conditions in industrial workplaces, as a mere matter of course, was death on the job and maiming due to accidents. Engels discussed the continual deaths from being caught in the machinery, and maiming in the loss of fingers and limbs. Maiming, he indicated was frequently followed by "lockjaw" (tetanus). All of this was the result of the lack of even the most minimal safety precautions on the part of factory owners, and by the conditions of exploitation and overwork that they promoted—an almost complete disregard for the lives of the factory operatives.[88]

An indication of the diminishing health of the working class as a whole, Engels observed, was the fact that the military could not find sufficient soldiers without reducing the height requirements, and even then, a growing percentage of men were "little adapted for military service, looked thin and nervous, and were frequently rejected by the surgeons as unfit."[89]

Engels provided along with these assessments of the environmental and health conditions of the working class a series of mortality tables, relating these to social class, and to industrial versus agricultural conditions. His mortality tables for cities were divided into geographical districts in order to distinguish the working class from middle- and upper-class sections of the cities. He indicated that child mortality was highest in the working-class quarters. In Manchester well over half of working-class children died before they reached their fifth birthday, compared to 20 percent of the higher classes. Fatalities from smallpox, measles, whooping cough, and scarlet fever, among "small children" (presumably referring to children under five) were four times higher in Manchester and Liverpool than in country districts. He was also able to demonstrate with respect to Carlisle, the one town for which he had such data, that the mortality rate had increased dramatically for those under forty years of age after the introduction of factories. Comparing the mortality rates of North England miners with Swedish mortality tables, considered the best of the day, he concluded that "the North of England miners are robbed by their work of an average of ten years of life," even when compared with a sample that mainly consisted of Swedish workers, that is, not compared against the life spans of the bourgeoisie.[90]

When a society and a ruling class permits such conditions to exist, he wrote, "knowing that . . . thousands of victims must perish, and yet permits these conditions to remain, its deed is murder just as surely as the deed of the single individual; disguised, malicious murder, murder against which none can defend himself, which does not seem what it is, because no man sees the murderer, because the death of the victim seems a natural one, since the offense is more one of omission than commission. But murder it remains." He continued:

> I have now to prove that society in England daily and hourly commits what the working-men's organs, with perfect correctness, characterize as social murder, that it has placed the workers under conditions in which they can neither retain health nor live long; that it undermines the vital force of these workers gradually, little by little, and so hurries them to the grave before their time. I have further to prove that society knows how injurious such conditions are to the health and the life of the workers, and yet does nothing to improve these conditions. That it *knows* the consequences of its deeds; that its act is, therefore, not mere manslaughter, but murder.[91]

"Social murder" in this sense, raised accusingly by the English working class and emphasized by Engels, was also to be understood as *environmental murder*. "The bourgeoisie," he explained, "reads these things every day in the newspapers," for example, the death of children as a result of the toxic industrial system, "and takes no further trouble. But it cannot complain if, after the official and non-official testimony here cited which must be known to it, I broadly accuse it of social murder."[92]

In many ways the greatest loss experienced by the workers, though, was the separation from meaningful, unalienated life activity. Engels captured this through continual references to the "demoralization" of workers and the "degradation" of their labor. "The descriptive or characterizing term used with the greatest frequency throughout *The Condition of the Working Class*," Marcus tells us, "consists of variations of the word 'demoralize'—demoralized, demoralizing, demoralization and so on."[93] It is in this sense that Engels writes of the worker's laboring experience that it was,

> properly speaking, not work, but tedium, the most deadening, wearing process conceivable. The operative is condemned to let his physical and mental powers decay in this utter monotony. . . . Moreover, he must not take a moment's rest; the engine moves unceasingly; the wheels, the straps, the spindles hum and rattle in his ears without a pause, and if he tries to snatch one instant, there

> is the overlooker at his back with the book of fines. This condemnation to be buried alive in the mill, to give constant attention to the tireless machine is felt as the keenest torture by the operatives, and its action upon mind and body is in the long run stunting to the highest degree.[94]

Yet, it is precisely here that Engels went on to say: "If the operatives have nevertheless, not only rescued their intelligence, but cultivated and sharpened it more than other working-men, they have found this possible only in rebellion against their fate and against the bourgeoisie, the sole subject on which under all circumstances they can think and feel at work." Engels's book proceeded to a chapter on "The Labour Movements," and particularly Chartism, which was still strong at this time. He quoted in full the poem "The Steam King" by the Chartist poet Edward P. Mead, representing the voice and views of the working class, who wrote of the industrial capitalists: "For filthy gain in their servile chain / All nature's rights they bind."[95]

In the same vein, Engels bitterly denounced the separation of the workers from the natural environment and hence from much of the import of the natural sciences. As he put it, "It too often happens" that the worker "never gets the slightest glimpse of Nature in his large town with his long working-hours." Hence, in these circumstances "the natural sciences" appear "utterly useless" to the worker.[96] In focusing on the working class under capitalism in all of its forms—industrial, agricultural, mining—and on the overall environmental conditions of the proletariat, Engels was developing a concept of the working class that was environmental in character, rather than the narrower notion of an industrial proletariat of purely factory workers that was later to prevail among many socialists—and their critics.

CAPITAL AND THE "SECOND SICKNESS"

The dominant capitalist medical model, in the nineteenth and twentieth centuries and today, promotes a narrow, reductionist approach to the causation of disease that focuses on factors that are subject to direct medical treatment, largely ignoring the wider social determinants. In opposition to this model, Norman Bethune, the world-famous Canadian surgeon who came to the aid of the Spanish Republic in the Spanish Civil War and then aided the Chinese Communists in their revolutionary struggle, referred to the social causes of illness as the "second sickness." Waitzkin was to adopt this phrase from Bethune as the title of his incisive work on the "contradictions of capitalist health care." According to Waitzkin, Engels's *The Condition of the Working Class in England* was one of the great foundational analyses of the second sickness, tracing it to the development of capitalism. But "despite later writings on natural and physical sciences," Engels, in his mature writings, "never returned to the social origins of illness as a major issue in its own right."[97]

Yet, while Engels did not revisit the issue of the environmental causes of illness systematically and comprehensively in his later writings, he did continue to refer to the environmental conditions of the working class in a number of his later works, such as *The Housing Question* (1872). Moreover, *The Condition of the Working Class in England* had a direct impact on Marx's own discussions of these issues in *Capital*, which took over where Engels had left off in this respect, particularly where issues of overcrowding, poor housing, unsanitary conditions, contagion, occupational illness, and the adulteration of food were concerned. It is therefore possible to reconstruct their views on these issues into the 1870s and after.

Marx never tired of emphasizing the importance of Engels's *Condition of the English Working Class* in the development of his own critique of political economy, particularly as related to the socio-ecological conditions of urban workers. In April 1863, he reread Engels's book and wrote to the latter:

> How soon the English workers will throw off what seems to be a bourgeois contagion remains to be seen. So far as the main theses in your book are concerned . . . they have been corroborated down to the very last detail by developments subsequent to 1844. For I have again been comparing the book with the notes I made on the ensuing period. Only your small-minded German philistine who measures world history by the ell and by what he happens to think are 'interesting news items,' could regard 20 years as more than a day where major developments of this kind are concerned, though these may be again succeeded by days into which 20 years are compressed.
>
> Re-reading your work has made me unhappily aware of the changes wrought by age. With what zest and passion, what boldness of vision and absence of all learned or scientific reservations the subject is still attacked in these pages! And then, the very illusion that, tomorrow or the day after, the result will actually spring to life as history lends the whole thing a warmth, vitality, and humour with which the later 'grey on grey' contrasts damned unfavourably.
>
> *Salut.*[98]

Marx's main direct statement on Engels's *Condition of the Working Class* in *Capital* came in his chapter on "The Working Day," where he was addressing the English Factory Acts and the introduction of the ten-hour day. Marx presented the problems of the regulation of the duration of labor, and of the worker's health, as ecological or metabolic relations, akin to that of the replenishment and recuperation of the soil. "Apart from the daily more threatening advance of the working-class movement," he wrote, "the limiting of factory labor was dictated by the same necessity as forced the manuring of English fields with guano. The same blind desire for profit that in the one case exhausted the soil had in the other case seized hold of the vital force of the nation at its roots. Periodical epidemics speak as clearly on this point as the diminishing military standard of height in France and Germany."[99] He then drew on Liebig's notion (already prefigured by Engels) that physical height and fitness for military service were decreasing, an indication of the diminishing physical condition of the working population associated with early industrialization.

It was in this context that Marx turned explicitly to Engels's analysis in *The Condition of the Working Class*. Engels's book was written, Marx noted, before the introduction of the Factory Acts. These reforms had altered in part the conditions that Engels had described, since it became necessary for capital to intervene up to a point to protect the reproduction of labor power, and to ensure its availability in sufficient quantity and quality—as well as altering housing and sanitary conditions to the degree necessary to prevent the spread of disease, which threatened the ruling class itself. Nevertheless, Marx wrote:

> I only touch here and there on the period from the beginning of modern industry in England to 1845, concerning which I would refer the reader to *The Condition of the Working Class in England*, by Frederick Engels. How well Engels understood the spirit of the capitalist mode of production is shown by the Factory Reports, Reports on Mines, etc. which have appeared since 1845, and how wonderfully he painted the circumstances in detail is seen on the most superficial comparison of his work with the official reports of the Children's Employment Commission, published eighteen or twenty years later (1863–67). These deal especially with the branches of industry in which the Factory Acts had not, up to 1862, been introduced, and in part remain unintroduced to the present. Here then, little or no alteration had been enforced by authority in the conditions depicted by Engels.[100]

The environmental considerations that Marx is concerned with here, and their close relation to Engels's *Condition of the Working Class*, is highlighted by his reference to the Children's Employment Commission, the reports of which he frequently relied on in *Capital*. The Children's Employment Commission was the product of John Simon, the chief medical officer of Britain, who also had responsibility for the government's periodic *Public Health Reports*, to which he wrote the introductions from 1858 to 1876. Marx frequently quoted these reports and Simon's in particular, considering him to be the greatest epidemiologist of the age and a dedicated opponent of capital. In August 1881 Engels was to write to Karl Kautsky about the speech "State Medicine":

> In *Nature* you will find a speech made by John Simon before the International Medical Congress here in which *the bourgeoisie is virtually put on the mat by medical science*. J. Simon is *Medical Officer to the Privy Council*, virtual head of Britain's entire public health inspectorate, and the same who is frequently and approvingly quoted by Marx in *Capital*, a man—perhaps the last of the old really professional and conscientious officials of the 1840–60 period who, in the performance of his duty, everywhere found that bourgeois interests were the first obstacle he was obliged to combat. Hence, his instinctive hatred of the bourgeoisie is as violent as it is explicable.[101]

In 1848 Simon had been elected as the first Medical Officer of Health of the City of London. It was in this capacity that he issued his 1856 *Report on the Last Two Cholera Epidemics of London, as Affected by the Consumption of Impure Water*, which came out in support of the research of John Snow, Henry Whitehead, and Edwin Lankester into the 1854 cholera epidemic in the Vestry of St. James in Soho, in which it was concluded that cholera was due to a waterborne pathogen of some unknown nature (discussed in chapter 1).[102] This helped solidify Simon's reputation, and in 1855 he became the Medical Health Officer for the General Board of Health and then assumed the same role in relation to the Privy Council after the General Board of Health was dissolved in 1858. He retained this position until his retirement in 1876. All of this made him the leading public health authority in Britain.

Simon represented a shift from the early period of sanitary reform, led by Chadwick, to the governance of public health by professional medical health officers—a brief period that came to an end in the late 1870s in Britain with the growth of an entire state bureaucracy in its place. Simon's ascendance in public health represented the gradual displacement of the miasma theory by the germ theory in the etiology of disease, a shift that he himself began to make following the 1854 cholera epidemic and the new discoveries centered on the cholera investigations of Snow, Whitehead, and Lankester. Simon was inclined toward the "progressive" side in the etiology of disease, represented by figures like Snow and William Farr, and concerned with the "sociological" elements that had been emphasized by the earlier, consensus miasmic theory.

It was Simon's bringing together of professional scientific research with an underlying pragmatism, and a recognition of the detrimental effects on the public health of commercial interests, which made him so central to the effecting of progressive change. Known for his strongly worded, often caustic, reports, Simon unleashed a torrent of criticisms of commercial interests for their violation of the basic conditions of public health and their general inhumanity. Beyond the investigation into sanitary conditions and disease, he organized investigations into the environmental conditions of all laboring populations in Britain, in agriculture as well as industry.

In 1854, arguing for the establishment of a Ministry of Health, Simon declared emphatically:

> If there be citizens so destitute, that they can afford to live only where they must straightway die—renting the twentieth straw-heap in some lightless fever-bin, or squatting amid rotten soakage, or breathing from the cesspool and the sewer; so destitute that they can buy no water—that milk and bread must be impoverished to meet their means of purchase—that the drugs sold them for sickness must be rubbish or poison; surely no civilized community dare avert itself from the care of this abject orphanage. . . . If such and such conditions of food or dwelling are absolutely inconsistent with healthy life, what more final test of pauperism can there be, or what clearer right to public succor, than that the subject's pecuniary means fall short of providing him other conditions than those? It may be that competition has screwed down the rate of wages below what will purchase indispensable food and wholesome lodgment. . . . All labour below that mark is masked pauperism. Whatever the employer saves is gained at the public expense. . . . It is the public that, too late for the man's health or independence, pays the arrears of wage which should have hindered this suffering and sorrow.[103]

Simon and John Ruskin were close friends. Ruskin was influenced by Simon's annual *Public Health Reports* and quoted them in his own work questioning the reigning political economy. They shared a dislike of the Manchester school of free trade—Simon from a public health standpoint and Ruskin in his aesthetic-ecological critique of political economy. Simon also shared a friendship with William Morris and the Pre-Raphaelites. He had a close working relationship with Edwin Lankester, who became editor of the *Journal of Social Science*, the official publication of the Social Science Association, an organization that Simon co-founded.[104]

In Marx's view, Simon was not only the leading pathologist in Britain, but also the most important scientific commentator on the environmental condition of the working class in the 1860s (at the time that Marx was writing *Capital*). He referred to Simon's analysis extensively in his discussions of "The Working Day," "Machinery and Large-Scale Industry," and "The Absolute General Law of Accumulation," in volume 1 of *Capital*, and in his treatment of "Savings on the Conditions of Work at the Workers' Expense" in volume 3. Writing of the growth of the industrial towns and the overcrowding and decline of sanitation, which had transpired since Engels's discussion of this in the early 1840s, Marx explained:

> The antagonistic character of capitalist accumulation, and thus of capitalist property-relations in general, is here so evident that even the official English reports on this subject teem with heterodox onslaughts on "property and rights." This evil makes such progress alongside the development of industry, the accumulation of capital and the growth and "improvement" of towns that the sheer fear of contagious diseases, which do not spare even "respectable people," brought into existence from 1847 to 1864 no less than ten Acts of Parliament on sanitation, and that the frightened middle classes in certain towns, such as Liverpool, Glasgow, and so on, took strenuous measures to deal with the problem through their municipalities. Nevertheless, Dr. Simon says in his report of 1865 "Speaking generally, it may be said that the evils are uncontrolled in England."[105]

Marx was so impressed by a table that Simon constructed on the mortality rate of tailors and printers in London due to overcrowding, poor ventilation and sanitation, and disease, that he reproduced the same table in both volumes 1 and 3 of *Capital*.[106] As he wrote in volume 1, "Dr. Simon, the chief medical officer of the Privy Council and the official editor of the *Public Health Reports*, says among other things":

> In my Fourth Annual Report [1861; published in 1862] I showed, how practically impossible it is for the workpeople to insist upon that which in theory is their first sanitary right—the right that, whatever the work their employer assembles them to do, shall, so far as depends upon him, be, at his cost, divested of all needlessly unwholesome circumstances; and I pointed out that, while workpeople are practically unable to exact that sanitary justice for themselves, they also (notwithstanding the presumed intentions of the law) cannot expect any effectual assistance from the appointed administrators of the Nuisances Removal Acts. . . . And in the interests of myriads of labouring men and women, whose lives are now needlessly afflicted and shortened by the infinite physical suffering which their mere employment engenders, I would venture to express my hope, that universally the sanitary circumstances of labour may, at least so far, be brought within appropriate provisions of law.[107]

A major killer under such conditions was the class of "lung diseases" of various sorts, as Simon argued in passages quoted by Marx. Speaking as England's chief medical officer, he stated: "In proportion as the people of a district are attracted to any collective indoor occupation, in such proportion, other things being equal, the district death-rate by lung disease will be increased." In these circumstances, he added, "the increased mortality of the workpeople is such as to colour the death-return of the whole district with a marked excess of lung disease." Beyond this, Simon emphasized on all occasions the prevalence of unhygienic conditions, overcrowded housing, and poor nutrition. Marx used Simon's tables showing inadequate nutritional intake by workers and quoted him as saying:

> That cases are innumerable in which defective diet is the cause or the aggravator of disease, can be affirmed by any one who is conversant with poor-law medical practice, or with the wards and out-patient rooms of hospitals. . . . Yet in this point of view there is, in my opinion, a very important sanitary context to be added. It must be remembered that privation of food is very reluctantly borne, and that, as a rule, great poorness of diet will only come when other privations have preceded it. Long before insufficiency of diet is a matter of hygienic concern—long before the physiologist would think of counting the grains of nitrogen and carbon which intervene between life and starvation—the household will have been utterly destitute of material comfort; clothing and fuel will have been even scantier than food; against inclemencies of weather there will have been no adequate protection; dwelling space will have been stinted to the degree in which over-crowding produces or increases disease; of household utensils and furniture there will have been scarcely any,—even cleanliness will have been found costly or difficult; and if there still be self-respectful endeavours to maintain it, every such endeavour will represent additional pangs of hunger. The home, too, will be where shelter can be cheapest bought—in quarters where commonly there is least fruit of sanitary supervision, least drainage, least scavenging, least suppression of public nuisances, least, or worst, water supply, and, if in town, least light and air. Such are the sanitary dangers to which poverty is almost certainly exposed, when it is poverty enough to imply scantiness of food.[108]

Like Engels in *The Condition of the Working Class*, Marx provides a holistic notion of the working class that takes in its entire environmental condition both within production and without. This is not, as has often been mistakenly characterized, a narrow theory of the industrial proletariat. Instead what we find is a larger theory of an environmental working class, considering the entirety of its conditions and relations. He devoted more than fifteen pages in *Capital* to the housing and general environmental conditions of the working class, relying mainly on the *Public Health Reports* and related reports by medical officers. Marx quoted from these reports where it was suggested that typhus, the most devastating contagious disease mainly affecting the working class—the actual cause of which, the bacteria *Rickettsia prowazekii* transmitted by the feces of lice was then unknown—was associated with extreme overcrowding, with numerous people occupying the same rooms, and poor sanitation.

In the late summer of 1866, when Marx had at last all-but completed the first volume of *Capital* and was promising to provide the printer's sheets within two months, another major cholera epidemic hit the impoverished, working-class East End of London. At the peak of the epidemic in early August, more than nine hundred people were dying a day. According to Simon, "Of the mortality of 5,915" from the cholera epidemic in London in 1866, "no less than 4,276 occurred in the east districts of the metropolis and adjacent suburban districts of West Ham and Stratford. . . . There is but one condition known which might become capable of propagating cholera common to the whole area of the outbreak, namely, the water-supply."[109]

William Farr, the Register-General, who had pioneered in the development of health statistics and who had adopted the waterborne pathogen theory of cholera, following figures like John Snow and Edwin Lankester, played a central role in addressing the epidemic. Going over the death rolls, Farr pinpointed the source of the epidemic as water coming from the East London Water Company. Edwin Lankester wrote his 1866 pamphlet *Cholera: What It Is and How to Prevent It* in response to the epidemic. Simon's public response was characteristically incisive, blaming the role of commercial interests, and drawing the important historical lesson in that respect: "The colossal power of life and death in commercial hands is something for which, till recently, there has been no precedent in the history of the world."[110]

ENVIRONMENTAL JUSTICE AND THE WORKING CLASS IN IRELAND AND ENGLAND

For Engels, the condition of the Irish working class remained a vital issue. Along with Mary and Lizzy Burns, he supported the nationalist (in the 1860s and 1870s, the Fenian) struggle in Ireland. In September 1869, in celebration of his freedom at last from Ermen and Engels, he decided to take Lizzy Burns and the young Eleanor Marx on a trip to Ireland. They traveled much less extensively than he and Mary Burns had in 1856, less than a decade after the Great Irish Famine, but nevertheless seeing the country from Dublin to Killarney and Cork in the southwest. It was this experience that led Engels to begin his *History of Ireland* addressing the material conditions of the Irish people—a project which he never completed.[111]

Still, the manuscript gave an indelible indication of Engels's method, which necessarily considered natural-physical as well as social conditions. The first half of the extant 40-page manuscript of his *History of Ireland*, begun in 1869 but never pursued after that, consisted of a section on "Natural Conditions," which started with a detailed excursion into the geological history and proceeded from there to the natural condition of the soil, prior to cultivation.

Discussing Engels's treatment of Irish natural conditions, prior to the entry of social processes, in his important essay "Engels on Ireland's Dialectics of Nature," sociologist Eamonn Slater explains that in Engels's method "the ecological base of a social formation involves unravelling a maze of metabolising processes, both natural and social, and figuring out how those processes interact with each other."[112] By starting out geologically and historically with an attempt to look at the natural preconditions of human development, Engels believed it was possible to conceive more accurately the roles of the natural and social and avoid a naturalistic determinism. The aim of his unfinished work was thus to develop a more complex understanding of the metabolism of nature and society through the prism of Irish history.

Engels proceeded from his opening chapter on "Natural Conditions" to a critical exploration of the investigations into the Irish soil and climate by figures like Arthur Young and Edward Gibbon Wakefield. Here he sought to establish that the natural fertility of the soil in Ireland was equal or superior to that of England. Likewise, Engels argued, in contrast to Goldwin Smith, professor of history at Oxford, and others, that Ireland's climate was no worse from the standpoint of agriculture than that of England. On this basis, he suggested, the Irish famine of 1847 and Irish hunger was due to the poor *social productivity* of the soil in Ireland, that is, the capitalist-induced ecological rifts plaguing Ireland, and not to a lack of *natural fertility*. It had its roots, in particular, in the greed of the large Irish landowners and English colonial rule.[113]

Attempts to transform Ireland into a giant pasture for raising cattle for England and to justify this on so-called natural grounds refused to acknowledge the social conditions that had compromised Irish agriculture. "Compared to England," he wrote,

> Ireland is more suited to cattle-rearing on the whole; but if England is compared with France, she too is more suited to cattle-rearing. Are we to conclude that the whole of England should be transformed into cattle pastures, and the whole agricultural population be sent into the factory towns or to America—except for a few herdsmen, to make room for cattle, which are to be exported to France in exchange for silk and wine? But that is exactly what the Irish landowners who want to put up their rents and the English bourgeoisie who want to decrease wages demand for Ireland: Goldwin Smith has said so plainly enough. . . . It would mean the transplantation of four million: the extermination of the Irish people.[114]

Hence, "even the facts of nature," Engels wrote, "become points of national controversy between England and Ireland. . . . Today England needs grain quickly and dependably—Ireland is just perfect for wheat-growing. Tomorrow

England needs meat—Ireland is only fit for cattle pastures. The existence of five million Irish is in itself a smack in the eye to all the laws of political economy, they have to get out but whereto is their worry!"[115] Indeed, such "facts of nature," Engels was clear, were actually created by capitalist political economy. As he had earlier noted, paraphrasing Marx, "*The robbing of the soil*: the acme of the capitalist mode of production is the undermining of the *sources of all wealth*: the soil and the labourer."[116]

If in Ireland the question of the environmental condition of the working class was overwhelmingly an agricultural and hence rural one, in England it was industrial and urban. Engels took up the question of the environmental conditions of the working class in England once again in *The Housing Question* (1872). Originally written for *Volksstaat*, the organ of the German Social Democratic Party, *The Housing Question* was responding to articles on urban housing reform that had appeared there. Specifically Engels was concerned with countering the schemes of (1) Arthur Mülberger, a follower of the French anarchist Pierre-Joseph Proudhon, who believed that it was possible to transform the entire working class, including the propertyless poor, into "free owners" of housing through direct reforms in legal title, ending the exploitative relation between landlord and tenant; and (2) Emil Sax, who argued for various moral and philanthropic reforms, and insisted that the attachment of gardens to houses would transform workers into independent proprietors able to obtain income from real estate.

In a series of logical and historical responses, Engels showed that the contradictions of capitalist housing were insurmountable within the system, and that bourgeois reforms at most consisted of (1) the replacement of working-class housing in inner cities with that of more expensive housing for the middle and upper classes, displacing working-class neighborhoods and simply situating them in new, often more out-of-the way locations (in this argument Engels used the term "Haussmann," after the French civic planner under Napoleon III, to refer to what we now call gentrification), or (2) small-scale philanthropic or model communities that in no way comprehensively addressed the core problem. In relation to Sax's proposal for the attachment of gardens to houses to elevate workers to the status of individual proprietors, Engels pointed out in the preface to the second edition of *The Housing Question* that such gardens had allowed German capitalists to pay workers lower wages—a form of profit by deduction.[117]

Indeed, the housing problem, Engels observed, was secondary to, and indirectly related to, the capital-labor relationship, and ultimately derived from the division between town and country, which was a fundamental feature of capitalism. It was thus impossible to solve the housing problem in the context of a capitalist society. At most, the better-off workers would be drawn from traditional rental arrangements to mortgage arrangements that left them deeply in debt and further compromised their independence. Even in the 1870s, housing was not so much lacking in the major cities in Britain, France, and Germany, as distributed in accordance with market principles and class terms. Poor housing and homelessness were the inevitable fate of the more pauperized sectors of the working class.[118]

In developing this critique, Engels returned to the central thesis of his *The Condition of the Working Class*, nearly three decades before, in which he had argued that the main motivation for housing and sanitary reform in London and other large British cities from the 1840s to the 1860s, prefiguring reforms elsewhere, was the threat of disease. As he put it in *The Housing Question* in the early 1870s:

> The big bourgeoisie is also very much interested in it [the housing question], even if indirectly. Modern natural science has proved that the so-called poor districts, in which the workers are crowded together, are the breeding places of all those epidemics which from time to time afflict our towns. Cholera, typhus, typhoid fever, smallpox and other ravaging diseases spread their germs in the pestilential air and the poisoned water of these working-class quarters. Here the germs hardly ever die out completely, and as soon as circumstances permit they develop into epidemics and then spread beyond their breeding places into the more airy and healthy parts of the town inhabited by the capitalists. Capitalist rule cannot allow itself the pleasure of generating epidemic diseases among the working class with impunity; the consequences fall back on it and the angel of death rages in its ranks as ruthlessly as in the ranks of the workers.
>
> As soon as this fact had been scientifically established the philanthropic bourgeois became inflamed with a noble spirit of competition in their solicitude for the health of their workers. Societies were founded, books were written, proposals drawn up, laws debated and passed, in order to stop up the sources of the ever-recurring epidemics. The housing conditions of the workers were investigated and attempts made to remedy the most crying evils. In England particularly, where the largest number of big towns existed and where the bourgeoisie itself was, therefore, running the greatest risk, extensive activity began. Government commissions were appointed to inquire into the hygienic conditions of the working class. Their reports, honourably distinguished from all continental sources by their accuracy, completeness and impartiality, provided the basis for new, more or less thoroughgoing laws. Imperfect as these laws are, they are still infinitely superior to everything that has been done in this direction up to the present on the Continent. Nevertheless, the capitalist order of society reproduces again and again the evils to be remedied, and does

> so with such inevitable necessity that even in England the remedying of them has hardly advanced a single step.[119]

Later, Engels reiterated that the sanitary reform laws "as a general rule" were introduced (or effectively implemented) "only as the result of the outbreak of some epidemic, such as in the case of the smallpox epidemic last year [1871] in Manchester and Salford."[120]

In these passages Engels shows his attentiveness to scientific developments in epidemiology. He has now clearly embraced the germ theory of disease, and the transmission of viruses through water as well as air, adopting an approach that was still not dominant in the scientific community.[121] Typhus and typhoid fever are clearly distinguished. Likewise, he recognizes that germs leading to epidemics may persist in an urban environment, becoming endemic, failing to die out altogether. Engels's approach is fully in accord with and in some respects in advance of Simon's, who was to prepare an article on "Contagion" six years later for *Quain's Dictionary of Medicine* in which, though still avoiding references to germs and bacteria, he referred to "the true or metabolic contagia" associated with such diseases as smallpox, scarlet fever, and typhus.[122] Like Snow, Lankester, Simon, and Farr, Engels saw this in terms of the larger social epidemiology, of which *The Condition of the Working Class* was a pioneering example.

Engels's discussion of housing was no less advanced. Putting particular emphasis on what he called the "Haussmann" method (that is, gentrification), Engels referred to:

> The practice, which has now become general, of making breeches in the working-class quarters of our big cities, particularly in those which are centrally situated, irrespective of whether this practice is occasioned by considerations of public health and beautification or by the demand for big centrally located business premises or by traffic requirements, such as the laying down of railways, streets, etc. No matter how different the reasons may be, the result is everywhere the same: the most scandalous alleys and lanes disappear to the accompaniment of lavish self-glorification by the bourgeoisie on account of this tremendous success, but—they appear again at once somewhere else, and often in the immediate neighbourhood.[123]

Engels illustrated this point by going back to the impoverished, environmentally hazardous working-class area of Manchester called Little Ireland, "as it looked in 1843 and 1844," described in *The Condition of the Working Class*. Little Ireland, he explained in *The Housing Question*, had long since vanished, with a railway station standing where it had been located. This was presented as a great success on the part of the well-to-do. But in 1871 a "great inundation" had occurred from summer floods. Manchester's *Weekly Times* then revealed, as Engels explained, that "Little Ireland had not been abolished at all, but had simply been shifted from the south side of Oxford Road to the north side, and that it still continues to flourish." In these areas, the *Weekly Times* explained, inhabited by the poor along the Medlock River's lower valley, the floods, combined with the general unsanitary conditions, threatened "the danger of epidemic," thus making it an issue for the vested interests of the city. In Engels's words:

> This is a striking example of how the bourgeoisie settles the housing question in practice. The breeding places of disease, the infamous holes and cellars in which the capitalist mode of production confines our workers night after night, are not abolished: they are merely *shifted elsewhere*! The same economic necessity which produced them in the first place produces them in the next place also. As long as the capitalist mode of production continues to exist it is folly to hope for an isolated settlement of the housing question or of any other social question affecting the lot of the workers. The solution lies in the abolition of the capitalist mode of production and the appropriation of all the means of subsistence and instruments of labour by the working class itself.[124]

For Engels the entire question of the urban environment of the city was tied to the division between town and country and the analysis of Marx, based on Liebig, of the metabolic rift in the relation between humanity and nature in general.[125] As Engels famously wrote in *The Housing Question*:

> The abolition of the antithesis between town and country is no more and no less utopian than the abolition of the antithesis between capitalists and wage-workers. From day to day it is becoming more and more a practical demand of both industrial and agricultural production. No one has demanded this more energetically than Liebig in his writings on the chemistry of agriculture, in which his first demand has always been that man shall give back to the land what he receives from it, and in which he proves that only the existence of towns, and in particular big towns, prevents this. When one observes how here in London alone a greater quantity of manure than is produced by the whole kingdom of Saxony is poured away every day into the sea with an expenditure of enormous sums, and what colossal structures are necessary in order to prevent this manure from poisoning the whole of London, then the utopia of abolishing the distinction between town and country is given a remarkably practical basis. And even comparatively unimportant Berlin has been suffering in the malodours of its own filth for at least thirty years.[126]

In 1892, almost fifty years after he had first walked the streets of Manchester examining the situation of the workers there (and twenty years after the publication of *The Housing Question*), Engels wrote a preface to the second German edition of *The Condition of the Working Class in England*, in which he looked back on the environmental conditions of the working class as they appeared in 1844, and how they had changed since. Once again, he emphasized the role that epidemic disease had played in the creation of the public health movement:

> Again, the repeated visitations of cholera, typhus, smallpox, and other epidemics have shown the British bourgeois the urgent necessity of sanitation in his towns and cities, if he wishes to save himself and family from falling victim to such diseases. Accordingly, the most crying abuses described in this book have either disappeared or have been made less conspicuous. Drainage has been introduced or improved, wide avenues have been opened out athwart many of the worst "slums." "Little Ireland" had disappeared, and the "Seven Dials" [seven streets at the center of London populated by the working class] are next on the list for sweeping away. But what of that? Whole districts which in 1844 I could describe as almost idyllic have now, with the growth of towns, fallen into the same state of dilapidation, discomfort, and misery. Only the pigs and the heaps of refuse are no longer tolerated. The bourgeoisie have made further progress in the art of hiding the distress of the working class. But that, in regard to their dwellings, no substantial improvement has taken place is amply proved by the Report of the Royal Commission "On the Housing of the Poor," 1885.[127]

The state of the working class, Engels continued to argue in the 1890s, was most evident in its overall environmental conditions and not simply the conditions of the labor process, although ultimately it was a question of the alienation of the means of production from the workers and their monopolization by the capitalists. The principal answer therefore was "to place the means of production in the hands of the community."[128]

THE RESURRECTION OF A HALF-FORGOTTEN BOOK

Engels's *The Condition of the Working Class in England* was a half-forgotten book when, in 1887, an English-language translation by Florence Kelley (Wischnewetzky) was finally published in the United States, where growing struggles over the factory and overall environmental conditions of the working class were taking place. This was followed by the publication of an edition of the Kelley translation in England in 1892. As Hobsbawm was to note, it had taken "the best part of a half-century for this masterpiece about early industrial

England to reach the country which was its subject," but after that it remained in print and exerted a considerable influence, "familiar to every student of the Industrial Revolution, if only by name."[129] The same year the English edition appeared, a second German edition was published, reflecting that the growth of capitalism in Germany was producing many of the same bleak conditions as in early industrial Britain. Engels wrote new prefaces for all three editions. The overall impact of his book in this era on socialists and social reformers engaged in the struggle over the conditions of the working class in the 1890s and after was to be substantial in all three nations: England, Germany, and the United States.

The 1892 English edition of *The Condition of the Working Class* sold well, and was to have a significant impact on the development of British socialism. The impact of Engels's book when it finally appeared in English can be seen in the way in which Engels's analysis obviously affected figures like Morris, to whom Engels gave a copy of the American edition, when it appeared in 1887, and who published extracts in *Commonweal.*

The salience of Engels's work can also be seen in the views of John Simon about the time that the English edition of *The Condition of the Working Class* finally appeared. It is unlikely that Simon saw the American edition of Engels's book, and thus he was probably not directly aware of it when he wrote his *English Sanitary Institutions* (1890), which referred to some of the history that Engels had covered and included favorable references to the proletariat and socialism.[130] Nevertheless, Simon's work reminds us just how Engels's *The Condition of the Working Class*, and particularly its epidemiological discussion, still remained directly relevant in late nineteenth-century Britain. Although then long retired, Simon remained the most eminent figure in public health in England in the late nineteenth century. Not only did he count among his friends Ruskin and Morris, but he had read and was influenced by Prince Pyotr Alexeyevich Kropotkin's articles on "mutual aid" in *Nineteenth Century*, a journal to which Simon also contributed. Simon also cited favorably the research of Beatrice Potter (later Webb) on dock labor in East London, published in *Nineteenth Century*, and Charles Booth's *Labour and Life of the People in London* (1885)—works falling within the general Fabian socialistic reform movement.

In the conclusion to his landmark book on *English Sanitary Institutions* (1890, 1897), which followed the penultimate chapter on "The Politics of Poverty," Simon did not hesitate to state that the fundamental issue was that of "the general prosperity of the proletariat," for which "the proletariat must itself struggle"—though he put this in terms of individual struggle rather than the struggle of the class. The question of public health in capitalist commercial society, he argued, came down to the question of "the state of the proletariat as to the conditions of labour and living"—in the face of almost unspeakable hardships and conditions where "labour is redundant." The proletariat, he insisted, was driven to the wall by "*over-competition* for *employment* and *house-room*." The question of the housing accommodation of the "poorer laboring classes," thus necessarily came down in great part to "how far poverty can be turned into non-poverty, *how far the poor can be made less poor*."

Simon insisted that the answer was "socialism of the sort which consists with social justice and tends to social consolidation." This included "additional socialistic taxation" to promote greater equality. Always careful to confine his sharp criticisms of the existing order to the edge of what could be considered the boundaries of respectable opinion, Simon, nonetheless, ended his crucial historical retrospective of the development of sanitary reform in England with a call for a moderate "socialism" in answer to the all-important question of the "proletariat."[131]

Simon's arguments in 1890 on behalf of "the proletariat," and in favor of "socialist" style social justice—motivated by his deep concerns over poverty and the deplorable conditions of public health—are all the more remarkable since they were emanating from the man who had been the chief medical officer in England from the 1850s to the mid-1870s, and who, in the 1890s, was still the most respected figure in his field. It was in the context of such authoritative views by the leading public health specialist in England that Engels's book appeared in the 1890s, giving it immediate salience in the debates then occurring, despite his book being almost a half-century old. In the decades to follow, it was to gain a reputation as the classic description of conditions in the early Industrial Revolution. It was the foremost work of its era on the socioecological effects of industrial capitalism in manufacturing towns and a forerunner of what today is called the environmental justice movement.

In Germany, *The Condition of the Working Class* exercised an influence that extended well beyond socialist circles. Rudolf Virchow, the German doctor and pathologist, famous as the author of *Cellular Pathology* (1858)—a work described by Waitzkin as "the first comprehensive exposition of the cell as the basic unit of physiologic and pathologic processes"—referred favorably to Engels's book in his work on social epidemiology.

A contradictory figure, Virchow had been influenced by Hegel's philosophy and by Marx's former co-editor of the *Deutsch-Französische Jahrbücher*, Arnold Ruge. (In the 1860s Ruge had moved to the right, becoming a vigorous supporter of Bismarck.) Virchow participated in the 1848 Revolution and later became a liberal statesman of science, involved in the formation, in 1861, of the German Party of Progress. He opposed the teaching of Darwinism in German schools on the reactionary grounds that "the Darwinian theory leads to Socialism."[132]

Although a scientific materialist of the mechanistic variety, Virchow was not above drawing fairly explicitly at times on dialectical thinking. His approach to disease and illness emphasized cell pathology and social conditions rather than the germ theory, though not rejecting the latter outright. Instead, he adopted a more dialectical approach in which bacteriology was only one aspect. His virtue as an epidemiologist, in Waitzkin's words, lay in his reliance on a "multifactorial etiology," combining "social, political, economic, geographic, climatic, and physiological factors" that were seen as interacting with one another in the promotion of disease.[133]

Virchow studied Engels's *The Condition of the Working Class* closely, and utilized some of Engels's statistics on the class basis of mortality to advance his own arguments. He blamed the dire cholera epidemics in Berlin in his time on the failure to address poverty. Designating epidemics of cholera and typhus as "crowd diseases," he played a leading role in sanitary reform in Berlin.[134]

In the United States, Engels's *The Condition of the Working Class* found a genuine proponent in Florence Kelley, who began translating it into English in 1885, with the final version (approved by Engels and accompanied by a new preface and appendix for American readers) published in 1887.[135] Kelley, as U.S. Supreme Court Justice Felix Frankfurter recalled in 1953, was "a woman who had probably the largest single share in shaping the social history of the United States during the first thirty years of this century. . . . During that period hers was no doubt a powerful if not decisive role in securing legislation for the removal of the most glaring abuses of our hectic industrialization following the Civil War."[136] Kelley, however, started out as a Marxian socialist, was a friend of Engels, and remained committed to socialism in one form or another all her life.[137]

Florence Kelley was born in Philadelphia, where her father, William D. Kelley, was a lawyer and a noted abolitionist. He was one of the founders of the Republican Party, a strong supporter of Lincoln, and a longtime member of the U.S. House of Representatives. In economics he was a protectionist and a follower of Henry C. Carey. Unusual for a woman in her day, Florence studied at Cornell University, delving into Greek, Latin, and algebra, and obtaining her B.A. She pursued postgraduate studies at the University of Zurich. During her time in Zurich she became a socialist, reading Marx's *Capital* in 1883–84. She and her husband, Lazare Wischnewetzky, were to meet Engels in London on their way from Zurich to New York in 1886.[138]

In 1887, soon after the publication of her translation of Engels's *The Condition of the Working Class*, Kelley wrote her major article, "The Need of Theoretical Preparation in Philanthropic Work." She insisted that Engels's book was "the best introduction to the study of modern scientific political economy." This was not simply because of its theoretical critique of capitalism, its support of the proletariat, and its case for socialism, but because of its concrete exploration of the actual conditions of the working class. Here she pointed, like Engels, to the question of the sanitary conditions of the cities, affecting the impoverished working class especially, which only became an issue for the vested interests when epidemic disease threatened their own privileged existence. "Epidemic disease, as murderous to the ruling class as to the workers," she wrote, "must be prevented in [the] self-defense" of the latter. Nevertheless, the real causes, rooted in exploitation and poverty, were never fully addressed, and reform stopped short of what was necessary from the standpoint of a "common humanity," remaining within the limits of "the accepted usage of the business world." If Engels's work was the best *introduction* to political economy, Marx's *Capital*, in Kelley's view, represented its developed science, standing in the same relation "to political economy" as "the works of Darwin are to the natural sciences. . . . She who has mastered this work thoroughly finds a wholly new standpoint from with which to judge the society of today, with its good and its evils."[139]

"From Engels," historian Katherine Kish Sklar noted, Kelley "learned a truth later expressed in her measurement of the bodies of child laborers and her invasion of sweatshop homes: since the new order of industrial capitalism reconfigured personal as well as public life, any effort to challenge the hegemony of industrial capitalism had to do the same."[140] As early as 1887, Kelley wrote to Engels indicating that she was focusing her efforts on the problem of child labor and the conditions of the working class in the United States. Taking her three children with her, she left her abusive husband at the end of 1891 to take up residence at Hull House in Chicago with Jane Addams and others. In making the move, she was supported by her friend Caroline Lloyd and her brother Henry Demarest Lloyd, a progressive and a muckraker. Henry Demarest Lloyd had a socialistic outlook and was famous for his 1881 article "The Story of a Great Monopoly" in the *Atlantic Monthly* (which Marx had read) and his 1890 book *A Strike of Millionaires Against the Miners*—a copy of which he had sent to Engels. Lloyd was personally acquainted with Engels, having interviewed him in London in 1891. He later wrote *Wealth Against Commonwealth* (1894), one of the great early critiques of monopoly.[141]

Kelley, with Lloyd's support, was hired in 1892 as a special agent for the Bureau of Labor Statistics in Illinois, investigating the needle trades in the tenements of Chicago, and was appointed by the Illinois Governor, John P. Altgeld, the following year as chief inspector of factories. In the years of her work investigating the needle trades in Chicago and then as chief inspector of factories, she corresponded regularly with Engels up to his death in 1895 on her experiences, including her battles against child labor, for the eight-hour day, and the fight against sweathouses and tenements. Following the lead of Charles Booth, she constructed maps of the impoverished areas of Chicago, coding the maps in color for ethnicity and class, representing the state-of-the-art graphics for the social geography of class in her day.[142]

Kelley's small staff of twelve (including herself) was responsible for investigating tens of thousands of factories, shops, and rooms where garment production took place. As she herself observed in one of her reports, there were up to a thousand licensed clothing manufacturing establishments along with "about 25,000 other rooms in which garments are manufactured." In 1893, as a result of an outbreak of smallpox (there were a total of 1,407 documented cases), she was able to give force to the factory legislation law for the first time, pushing for the transfer of unregulated tenement house work to factories, where more effective regulation of labor conditions could take place. "Nowhere in the civilized world," she grimly noted in her factory inspection report for 1894, "has it been made a crime to endanger life and limb of employees in a factory or workshop by a failure to supply safeguards."[143] With regard to the inhuman conditions of child labor that she discovered in Chicago, she decried: "The child who handles arsenical paper in a box-factory long enough becomes a hopeless invalid. The boy who gilds cheap frames with mercurial gilding, loses the use of his arm and acquires incurable throat troubles." Meanwhile, Kelley, with an eye to the future, was introducing children in her English classes at Hull House to Engels's *Socialism: Utopian and Scientific* and William Morris's *News from Nowhere*.[144]

In 1894 Kelley wrote to Engels that she thought that they had won the eight-hour day in Illinois. However, the next year the law was struck down by the Illinois Supreme Court. Kelley lost her position as chief inspector of factories in 1897, following a change in administration. She went on to become the leading founder and general secretary of the National Consumers League, and from there she fought for factory regulation, a shorter working day, minimum wage legislation, and related labor causes. She occupied this position from 1899 until her death in 1932 at the trough of the Great Depression, only months before the election of Franklin Roosevelt as president. In one of her very last letters she attacked Herbert Hoover's "shallow economics."[145]

Engels sent regular remittances to Kelley from the sale of the English edition of *The Condition of the Working Class*. In his will, the final codicil of which was drawn up on his deathbed, he left her all of the royalties for the English edition of his book—his most successful, in terms of sales.[146]

CHAPTER SIX

The Dialectics of Nature

On July 2, 1858, a distraught Karl Marx wrote to Frederick Engels explaining that he had been unable to correspond for some time or to concentrate on his work because he and his wife, Jenny, were deeply worried over the condition of their daughter Eleanor, then three years old, who had come down with whooping cough, and had been suffering from this "most alarming" disease "for weeks." Jenny too had been feeling weak.

Whooping cough or pertussis was one of the most dangerous contagious diseases in Victorian times, particularly threatening to young children. Arising from the bacilli *Bordetella pertussis*, first isolated in 1906—although recognized as early as the Middle Ages, where it was known as "the kink"—pertussis spreads from person to person by means of coughing or sneezing. It was not until the 1930s that a vaccine was finally developed.[1]

Engels apparently sent Marx a brief reply immediately, which has not survived, and on July 14 wrote back "at greater length," having first sought out medical information, in a letter that opened with an inquiry after Eleanor's condition. He noted that his close friend and medical adviser Dr. Eduard Gumpert, who worked at the Clinical Hospital for the Diseases of Children in Manchester, had said that whooping cough was seldom fatal in the English climate, and, though chronic, was generally benign. "All the cases they've had in the hospital so far have ended well."[2] Yet, while doing all he could to reassure Karl and Jenny Marx with regard to Eleanor's case of whooping cough, Engels himself was all too aware of the possible dangers of the disease. In *The Condition of the Working Class in England,* thirteen years before this, he had noted that fatalities from whooping cough were all too frequent in Manchester in the 1840s, and that whooping cough was among a group of diseases particularly threatening to the children of the poor. It followed—although the etiology of the disease was then unknown—that it was less likely to prove fatal in cases where there was proper nutrition, sanitation, and housing. In this regard, Eleanor would have been considered comparatively safe.

Nevertheless, in his concern for Eleanor and her parents, Engels was drawn back once again to the kind of environmental analysis that had played a prominent part in his 1845 book. He referred Marx to two medical reports released in 1856 and 1857 by the Clinical Hospital for the Diseases of Children in Manchester. The reports were co-authored by the two doctors who had founded the hospital, August Schoepf Merei and James Whitehead. These reports addressed whooping cough along with other diseases striking children. The first report analyzed the nearly 800 diseases discovered in its first 530 patients, mostly very young working-class children, and the causes and effects of these diseases among the children. The second report examined a similar list of diseases among 1,584 children. So striking were these two reports that Engels indicated he was having them copied to send on to Marx. "They are highly scientific," he told Marx, "and I wish I had had material of this kind when I was writing my book."[3]

The first report of the Clinical Hospital for the Diseases of Children, which Engels had transcribed for Marx, indicated that while four children had died of whooping cough together with other complications, only one as old as three (Eleanor's age) had died. Beyond the question of whooping cough, which Eleanor's condition had raised, the two reports together were extraordinary in the data they provided. This included information on the actual occupations of the parents of the patients, including how many shillings (or less) per week they earned, the number of patients with families living in substandard conditions, along with attempts to connect such material conditions to the etiology of disease. "A considerable proportion of the children of the poor," the first report noted, "die here of bronchitis," which was seen as related to atmospheric conditions. All told, some 33 percent of the patients covered in the second report suffered from bronchitis. A very high percentage of deaths of children under five were due to complications with breastfeeding and early weaning, plus poor quality of cow's milk—a problem that the wealthy, the second report noted, did not suffer from because of the ability to procure wet nurses. There was no doubt that the Children's Hospital reports contained a serious condemnation of the class system, laid bare by their in-depth consideration of the dismal social-environmental conditions, the reality of which was made incontrovertible by the concrete data that these reports provided.[4]

Few would have appreciated the significance of such epidemiological data as much as Engels. Engels's interest in developments in physiology and medical science reflected his deep interest in natural science in general. Thus, it was in this very same letter, of July 14, 1858, perhaps inspired in part by the reports of the Clinical Hospital for the Diseases of Children, that we find the first strong indication of Engels's systematic engagement with the philosophy and history of science. This eventually led to his conception of the dialectics of nature, and the development of an ecological view. Moreover, his research and conclusions were already at this point remarkably well advanced. His letter continued:

> Kindly let me have Hegel's *Philosophy of Nature* as promised. I am presently doing a little physiology which I shall combine with comparative anatomy. Here one comes upon highly speculative things, all of which, however, have only recently been discovered; I am exceedingly curious to see whether the old man may not have already had some inkling of them. This much is certain: were he *today* to write a *Philosophy of Nature*, subjects would come flocking in on him from all directions. One has no idea, by the way, of the progress made in the natural sciences during the past 30 years. Two things have been crucial where physiology is concerned: 1. the tremendous development of organic chemistry, 2. the microscope, which has been properly used only during the past 20 years. This last has produced even more important results than chemistry; what has been chiefly responsible for revolutionising the whole of physiology and has alone made comparative physiology possible is the discovery of the cell—in plants by Schleiden and in animals by Schwann (about 1836). Everything consists of cells. The cell is Hegelian "being in itself" and its development follows the Hegelian process step by step right up to the final emergence of the "idea"—i.e. each completed organism.
>
> Another result that would have delighted old Hegel is the correlation of forces in physics, or the law whereby mechanical motion, i.e. mechanical force (e.g. through friction), is, in given conditions, converted into heat, heat into light, light into chemical affinity, chemical affinity (e.g. in the voltaic pile) into electricity, the latter into magnetism. These transitions may also take place differently, backwards or forwards. An Englishman whose name I can't recall [James Joule] has now shown that these forces pass from one to the other in quite specific quantitative proportions so that e.g. a certain quantity of one, e.g. electricity, corresponds to a certain quantity of each of the others, e.g. magnetism, light, heat, chemical affinity (positive or negative—combining or separating) and motion. The idiotic theory of latent heat is thus disposed of. But isn't this splendid material proof of how the reflex categories [Hegel's reflection determinations] dissolve one into the another?
>
> This much is certain—comparative physiology gives one a healthy contempt for man's idealistic arrogance in regard to other animals. At every step it is forcibly brought home to one how completely his structure corresponds to that of other mammals; he has basic features in common with all vertebrates and even—if less distinctly—with insects, crustaceans, tapeworms, etc. Here too Hegel's stuff about the qualitative leap in the quantitative sequence fits in very nicely. Finally, with the most primitive infusoria, one reaches the original form, the single cell existing independently, which again is not perceptibly

> distinguishable from the lowest vegetable life (single-celled fungi such as those causing disease in potatoes, the vine, etc., etc.) or, at a higher stage of development, from the germ right up to and including the human ovum and spermatozoon, and is identical in appearance to the separate cells in the living body (blood corpuscles, the cells of the epidermis and mucous membrane, secreting cells in the glands, kidneys, etc., etc.).[5]

Engels's brief exegesis here highlighted the simultaneous breakdown of both religious or teleological views of nature, and of the rigid, mechanistic view of the universe. Everything could be seen in a complex flux. The clear implication for both Engels and Marx was that science, through its development, was unconsciously demonstrating the existence of natural relations that could only be comprehended in historical and dialectical terms, as evidenced in areas as distinct as physiology (including discoveries in organic chemistry and cellular analysis), thermodynamics, and comparative anatomy. This was to form the basis for the argument Engels was later to develop in such works as *Dialectics of Nature*, *Anti-Dühring*, and *Ludwig Feuerbach and the Outcome of Classical German Philosophy*, written in the 1870s and '80s.

THE DARWINIAN REVOLUTION AND THE DIALECTICS OF NATURE

Engels's observations concerning the close morphological relation of the human species to other species, down to insects and, indeed, at the cellular level, connected to all life, in his July 1858 letter to Marx, are all the more remarkable when placed in the context of an historic event—almost certainly unknown to him at the time—that had taken place only thirteen days before, on July 1, 1858. On that day, the secretary of the Linnaean Society of London had read to an audience of "thirty-odd nonplussed fellows," a set of scientific papers/abstracts written by Charles Darwin and Alfred Russell Wallace, providing evidence of their separate discoveries of natural selection by innate variation—the first announcement of the new theory of evolution. The Darwin and Wallace papers were to be published together on August 20, 1858. This was followed, the next year, by the landmark publication of Darwin's *The Origin of Species*.[6]

As the noted British scientist J. D. Bernal was to observe in 1935 in his *Engels and Science*, commenting on Engels's July 14, 1858, letter to Marx, Engels had shown "himself prepared to accept beforehand the idea of transformation of species which Darwin was to publish in the next year." According to Bernal, Engels, in emphasizing the notion of the morphological similarities between species, which he extended to humans with Georg Wilhelm Friedrich Hegel's notion of small quantitative changes leading to qualitative transformation, was thinking in many ways along the same general lines as Darwin.[7]

Engels's receptiveness to Darwin's breakthrough in the development of evolutionary thought was intertwined with both his general materialist outlook and the impact that Hegelian dialectics had exerted on his thinking. Both Marx and Engels were actively reconsidering Hegel's legacy at this time, determining how best to make use of it in their own analyses: for Marx in relation to political economy, for Engels in relation to natural science. On January 16, 1858, Marx wrote to Engels that a return to Hegel's *Logic* had helped him work out certain questions related to the theory of profit in his critique of political economy.[8] Engels meanwhile had begun to think about the relation of Hegel's philosophy of nature to the dialectical understanding of natural-scientific phenomena, as exhibited in his July 14 letter to Marx.

Engels brought the question of Hegel's dialectics, which had long since lost its popularity in Germany, out into the open in a review of Marx's *Contribution to the Critique of Political Economy* for *Das Volk* (the London organ of the German Workers Educational Association) on August 20, 1859. Here he confronted the rigid, metaphysical-mechanistic scientific philosophy then prevalent. What was needed, he argued, was a materialist reappropriation of the dialectical outlook of Hegel (and before Hegel, Immanuel Kant) within the sciences. The value of this for the social sciences had already been demonstrated by Marx's work under review. But Engels insisted that a similar critical reappropriation of the dialectical method of German idealism was also needed in the natural sciences, and that Marx's materialist dialectical method had, indeed, helped pave the way. Marx's work thus represented not simply a critical economics but a new approach to science.[9]

The decline of Hegelian philosophy in the late 1840s and 1850s had led to a weakening of the critical nature of German thought following the 1848 Revolution. "Hegel was forgotten and a new materialism arose in the natural sciences" in place of philosophy—a materialism that "differed in principle very little from the [mechanical] materialism of the eighteenth century." This new scientific materialism was of course superior to the materialism of the eighteenth century, as represented by figures such as Denis Diderot and Julien Offray de la Mettrie, insofar as it rested on "a greater stock of data relating to the natural sciences, especially chemistry and physiology." This reflected the revolutions initiated by such figures as Theodor Schwann and Matthias Schleiden in cell physiology and by Antoine-Laurent de Lavoisier, John Dalton, and Justus von Liebig in organic chemistry, Yet, the new scientific materialist worldview was often accompanied by a poverty in its philosophical presumptions, which took a rigid, mechanistic form. This was particularly evident in the work of such naturalists and physicians as Ludwig Büchner, Karl Vogt, and Jacob Moleschott.[10]

Even though they were materialists (albeit of the mechanistic variety) and influential among social democrats, Büchner, Vogt, and Moleschott represented, in Marx and Engels's view, a retrograde movement philosophically, insofar as they had reverted to the rigid, sterile metaphysics exemplified by the German rationalist philosopher Christian Wolff (1679–1754), who Kant had characterized, in his preface to the second edition of *The Critique of Pure Reason*, as "the greatest of all dogmatic philosophers." Engels contended that Kant, and "more particularly," Hegel, left the prior Wolffian system theoretically demolished. However, with the demise of Hegelian philosophy, the narrowly metaphysical Wolffian-style thinking, Engels contended, was again reasserting itself in German science.[11] Here he clearly had in mind Büchner's *Force and Matter* (*Kraft und Stoff*), the most influential work on materialism of the day. First published in 1855, it went through twenty-one different German editions and was translated into seventeen languages. Later, Engels was to focus on Büchner's *Man in the Past, Present, and Future*, published in 1869. Büchner (like both Vogt and Moleschott) claimed to have inherited the materialist philosophical mantle of Ludwig Feuerbach, while basing his analysis on natural science alone, and on Spencerian notions of linear progress. The critique of such mechanistic views would be central to Engels's attempt in his mature works to reconstruct the dialectics of nature and science in ways that lent themselves to the eventual development of a critical ecological analysis.[12]

The key to developing a critical method applicable to science in general, in Engels's view, was to return to Hegel's dialectic "divested of its idealist wrappings." Rather than a call for a renewal of speculative philosophy, the emphasis here was on the coevolution of ideas and material processes in history. "It was the exceptional historical sense underlying Hegel's manner of reasoning," Engels wrote, "which distinguished it from that of all other philosophers. However abstract and idealist the form employed, yet his evolution of ideas runs always parallel with the evolution of universal history." Following this complex, parallel development required an examination of contradictions and discontinuities. "The fact that it is a *relation* already implies that it has two aspects which are *related to each other*. Each of these aspects is examined separately; this reveals the nature of their attitude to one another, their reciprocal action. Contradictions will emerge which will require a solution."[13]

"History," Engels observed, "often moves in leaps and bounds and in zigzags."[14] The recognition of complex processes and the emergence of new forms—the irreversibility of contingent developments and the introduction of new properties, often representing qualitative leaps—was crucial to such a historical understanding of what Marx was later to call "the universal metabolism of nature" and what Engels himself was to refer to as "a metabolism" that "occurs everywhere," related in different ways to organic and inorganic bodies.[15] What was required was systematic thinking, but not that of a static, mechanical order, but one of change.

"The True is the whole," Hegel had written. "But the whole is nothing other than the essence consummating itself through its development."[16] In other words, the whole can only be understood through its becoming. Such a conception meant that nature and humanity had to be conceived in historical terms, that is, in their *making*, with humanity to be viewed in large part in terms of its *self-making*. Engels clearly argued for what is now known as "ontological emergence," in which the question of a higher level is not simply one of non-predictability or "epistemological emergence," but a change in the whole "causal landscape" representing a fundamental transformation.[17] Here he was pointing to a conception of integrative levels or emergent evolution, as integral to a dialectical worldview.[18]

Due to this complex philosophical and scientific outlook, Engels, like Marx, was by 1859 exceptionally well placed to grasp the revolutionary nature and significance of Darwin's argument, which pointed to the historical evolution of living species. The first copies of the *Origin of the Species* came off the press in early November 1859. Around 1,170 copies, out of a total print run of 1,250, were offered to the public for sale on November 24, 1859, and were quickly purchased.[19] One of these soon found its way into the hands of Engels, who wrote to Marx on December 12, 1859: "Darwin, by the way, whom I'm reading just now, is absolutely splendid. There was one aspect of teleology that had yet to be demolished, and that has now been done. Never before has so grandiose an attempt been made to demonstrate historical evolution in Nature, and certainly never to such good effect."[20]

Engels's letters of July 14, 1858, and December 12, 1859, as well as his August 1859 review of Marx's *A Contribution to the Critique of Political Economy*, clearly demonstrate that he had had already arrived at the broad conception of the historical-dialectical development of nature (and science) that was to constitute the core of his later *Dialectics of Nature*. As Ilya Prigogine, winner of the 1977 Nobel Prize in Chemistry, observed:

> The idea of a history of nature as an integral part of materialism was asserted by Marx, and, in greater detail, by Engels. Contemporary developments in physics, the discovery of the constructive role played by irreversibility, have thus raised within the natural sciences a question that has long been asked by materialists. For them, understanding nature meant understanding it as being capable of producing man and his societies.
>
> Moreover, at the time Engels wrote his *Dialectics of Nature* [the 1870s], the physical sciences seemed to have rejected the mechanistic worldview and drawn closer to the idea of an historical development of nature. Engels

> mentions three fundamental discoveries: energy and the laws governing its qualitative transformations, the cell as the basic constituent of life, and Darwin's discovery of the evolution of species. In view of these great discoveries, Engels concluded that the mechanistic worldview was dead.[21]

Here it is significant that the core proposition that Prigogine associates with Engels's *Dialectics of Nature*, including the stipulation of the three key scientific discoveries—those associated with the cell, thermodynamics, and Darwinian evolution—were all points that Engels had outlined in letters to Marx by the end of 1859, the same year as the publication of Marx's *Contribution to a Critique of Political Economy* and Darwin's *Origin of Species*.

Although Engels's conceptual breakthrough cannot be compared to that of Marx or Darwin, its significance nonetheless stands out markedly in our time. Few at that time recognized at so general a level what Prigogine has called the materialist proposition that "understanding nature meant understanding it as being capable of producing man and his societies." That is, that nature and history had to be understood dialectically as a product of contradictory developments, and the emergence of entirely new forms. Moreover, Engels was to extend this logic further in his subsequent work, recognizing that humanity, though seemingly triumphant, was capable of producing its own antithesis in capitalist society by undermining its fundamental relation to nature, of which it was merely a part.

GERMAN SCIENTIFIC PHILOSOPHY AFTER HEGEL

It was not until 1873, a number of years after Engels had freed himself from his business responsibilities and relocated to London, that he began to work on what was to become *Dialectics of Nature*. The opening notes to *Dialectics of Nature*, starting on the front of the first sheet, were headed "Büchner" and were directed at Büchner's *Man in the Past, Present, and Future: A Popular Account of the Results of Recent Scientific Research as Regards the Origin, Position, and Prospects of the Human Race*, a second edition of which appeared in 1872. Meanwhile, the discussion of matter and motion was related, though in a more complex, dialectical way, to the opening subject of Büchner's earlier book, *Force and Matter*. From this it seems clear that Engels's motivation to begin writing *Dialectics of Nature* in 1873, and to try to articulate the scientific-philosophical basis for his and Marx's views, was an immediate response to the work of Büchner, as well as other scientific materialists, such as Vogt and Moleschott.[22]

For Marx and Engels, the so-called scientific materialists Büchner, Vogt, and Moleschott, from the 1850s to the 1870s, represented a serious challenge to their own position within the growing socialist movement in Germany, in which the scientific materialists exerted a strong influence due to their adamant materialism and atheism, their association with Feuerbach, and their sympathies with the 1848 Revolution. Vogt popularized the view that "ideas stand in the same relation to the brain as bile does to the liver or urine to the kidneys."[23] The difficulty for Marx and Engels was to separate their own conception of materialism from that of the scientific materialists, and from the political ideas with which their mechanistic materialism was associated, which on the surface seemed to dovetail with scientific socialism. This was all the more difficult as their critique in *The German Ideology* (and in Marx's *Theses on Feuerbach*, not known even to Engels until after Marx's death) had not yet been published. The philosophical bases of historical materialism thus remained unclear to most of their followers. According to the great Russian Marx scholar David Riazanov, Marx and Engels's follower Wilhelm Liebknecht, who played a key role in the development of the German Social Democratic Party, was taken in by the work of the scientific materialists: "Liebknecht himself so little grasped the Marxian philosophy that he confused the dialectical materialism of Marx and Engels, with the natural-historical materialism of Jacob Moleschott (1822–1893), and Ludwig Büchner (1824–1899)."[24]

Politically, Vogt had participated in the 1848 revolution as a liberal democrat (a member of the Frankfurt National Assembly), while Büchner and Moleschott both sympathized with republican tendencies in the revolution. Moleschott was the least socially and politically oriented of the three. His central, reductionist notion was that human beings were what they eat. Büchner and Vogt, however, both presented themselves at times as political-philosophical revolutionaries. Büchner, in particular, was a left democrat, to the right of Ferdinand Lassalle (but sometimes supporting the latter), opposed to an independent working-class movement. He was a delegate to the 1867 conference of the International Working Men's Association. Marx spent about a year writing his book *Herr Vogt*, which was an attempt to reply to calumnies that Vogt had hurled at him. (Later, government records revealed that in 1859 Vogt received 40,000 francs from the secret funds of Napoleon III, associated with propaganda on the latter's behalf.)[25]

Büchner, Vogt, and Moleschott thus constituted political as well as scientific rivals of Marx and Engels. Their theoretical significance lay in their claim that they based their ideas exclusively on natural science, rejecting all speculative philosophy, along with historical analysis and political-economic critique. Büchner was a particularly sharp critic of Hegel.[26] They sought to use the huge prestige of natural science, particularly following Darwin, to outflank the socialist-communist critique of capitalism. There is no doubt that, for Engels, Büchner was the most significant of the scientific materialists in Germany, both theoretically and in terms of his direct influence on the growing social democratic movement.[27]

Büchner was almost always listed first when Engels referred to scientific materialists; and it was Büchner's work that Engels took as his general yardstick for the non-dialectical, "metaphysical" materialism to which his and Marx's more dialectically oriented materialism was opposed.

Büchner was a serious, if mechanical, materialist. "Nature," he wrote in *Force and Matter*, "knows neither a supernatural origin nor a supernatural continuation; she, the all-bearing and the all-devouring, is her own Alpha and Omega, her own generation and death."[28] He lauded the ancient materialist philosophers, particularly Democritus, Epicurus, and Lucretius, whom he saw as the founders of the natural scientific view. The materialist tradition in philosophy, he believed, stretched up through Feuerbach, "the philosopher *par excellence* of emancipated and self-contained humanity." At that point, materialism was taken over entirely by natural science, as philosophy, particularly speculative philosophy—as Feuerbach himself argued—had lost all real value. The heroes of materialism in the nineteenth century, according to Büchner (as indicated in the later editions of *Force and Matter*), were figures like Julius Robert von Mayer, one of the discoverers of the conservation of energy, Charles Lyell, the discoverer of the modern geological view, and above all Charles Darwin, the discoverer of evolution.[29]

At the core of Büchner's argument was the depiction of matter as consisting of two things, stuff and force, generating a dualist ontology.[30] In the Cartesian tradition, matter was seen in terms of extension, and was inert, except when two material objects collided with each other. Büchner, however, summarizing the tendencies of science in his time, saw matter as inseparable from force. In this view, the barrier between the inorganic and organic broke down, passing into each other, a development arising out of organic chemistry and the study of hydrocarbons.[31]

In *Man in the Past, Present and Future*, Büchner derided what he called the "so-called dialectical method," which "attained its climax in the great Hegel, that 'deluge of words poured over a desert of ideas' as Helvetius so suitably described the results of the scholastic philosophy of the Middle Ages which is still far from being extinct." For Büchner, the mechanical laws of science had triumphed over "meaningless words or phrases." Science had removed "the veil of the mystery and found nothing there except the effete skeleton of philosophical emptiness of spirit and thought, clothed with the motley rags of a philosophical terminology or mode of expression. There is not now and never was or will be a possibility of enlarging human knowledge beyond experience, or human philosophy beyond the conclusions drawn from experience."[32] Denying the role of Kant's critical epistemology, Büchner went so far as to claim crassly that there was no "scientific foundation for the doctrine of Kant, which is derived from pure speculation. Kant's 'thing in itself' is a purely ideal entity, or a logical and empirical nonentity." In this way, Büchner simply denied all philosophical problems, relying simply on crude, positivistic assumptions.[33]

Büchner's positivistic perspective pointed to progress as the law of science and the universe. Unending forward motion on earth would come to an end, it was true, in the extinction in the far distant future of Earth's inhabitants. But this, he contended, would coincide in time with the appearance of other life-forms with similar intellectual and physical properties on "thousands upon thousands" of other planets throughout the universe. Inorganic and organic existence, life, society, and the even eventual destruction of life on Earth, due to the waning of the sun, were all in accord with an overall progressive movement within Earth, and ultimately the universe, that arose simply from the combined action of matter and force as the "indestructible basis" of all reality. The world could be explained in terms of mere "*mechanical* laws which lie in the very nature of things" and on a purely empirical basis, with no need for speculative hypotheses characteristic of philosophy. "The strength of its [science's] 'proofs,'" Büchner wrote, "lies in *facts*, and not in unintelligible and meaningless phrases. . . . 'Nature and experience' is the watchword of the age. . . .'Speculation,' says Ludwig Feuerbach, 'is philosophy intoxicated.'"[34]

Man in the Past, Present, and Future constantly referred in Spencerian fashion to "the great organic law of development and progress"; "nature's great 'progression'"; "the common and uniform progress of humanity" brought on by the Darwinian "struggle for existence." The struggle for existence became the universal explanation for all organic development. It dominated human development from the moment that the transformation from ape to man occurred, with the development of a more erect posture, "the increased usefulness of the hands" and the emergence of speech (here Büchner followed the argument of Ernst Haeckel). Büchner, although recognizing at one point that human beings were social beings and that sociality was crucial to this developmental process, nonetheless reverted constantly to the Darwinian struggle for existence as the being and end-all. Was not society, he asked, quoting Hobbes, "a *bellum omnium contra omnes* [a war of all against all]?" This self-same struggle of existence that explained the rise of society would lead, in the end, to "the struggle *against* the struggle for existence, or *the replacement of the power of nature by the power of reason*." Out of this would rise a good, rational, harmonious government.[35]

Although sometimes presenting himself as a socialist, Büchner argued explicitly for the supremacy of capital, even saying that the workers or "work-takers" should adopt the slogan "Long live capital!" recognizing the beneficial role played by the "work-givers." In Büchner's words, those who decried "the so-called capitalistic mode of production," which was "only a necessary and inevitable result of our given social relations," were essentially guilty of looking a gift horse in the mouth; since "wherever a business or factory depends on the creative activity, the inventive genius, the industry or any other special faculty of its undertaker, or even upon the particular goodness of the whole organization, the increased gain, falsely called the premium on capital of the undertaker or organizer, *is very well earned*."[36]

On the question of the emancipation of women, Büchner was somewhat more progressive, arguing against the intellectual inequality of the genders, and defending women's rights. On race, however, his deep prejudices came to the fore. Like Vogt, though somewhat more hesitantly, he promoted the thesis of polygenesis in the origin of the human races, deriding Wallace's notion of a common origin for all humankind. In line with his mechanical notion of progress, Büchner insisted that in the end there would be "greater uniformity" of humankind, as a result of "the destruction of the weaker and a constant increase of the stronger or more intelligent races." The "non-Caucasian" races would either be entirely supplanted by the European race or would in some way blend with it to the advantage of the Europeans, given the "more highly developed brain of Europeans." Like Haeckel, Büchner was eventually to adopt an explicit monism with racial overtones.[37] Such propositions, he believed, were simply straightforward results of "scientific materialism," arising out of the mechanical properties of matter and force, empirically ascertained through our senses.[38]

Engels did not view Büchner, Vogt, and Moleschott as major scientific figures—though giving the most credit to Büchner among the three. Rather they were popularizers of materialist scientific doctrines, mere "caricature-like itinerant preachers"—referring to the lecture circuits that they were constantly engaged in, speaking to audiences in England as well as on the Continent.[39] They were mechanistic philosophers of science devoid of any genuine philosophy except of the most unreflexive, positivist kind. Why then was it so important to engage with such thinkers at all? Addressing this question, Engels wrote: "One could let them alone and leave them to their not unpraiseworthy if narrow occupation of teaching atheism, etc., to the German philistine but for: 1, abuse directed against philosophy . . . and 2, the presumption of applying the theories about nature to society and of reforming socialism. Thus, they compel us to take note of them."[40]

Although Engels acknowledged that the materialist teachings of these thinkers had some value, he regarded their views as too simplistic due to their active neglect of philosophy, which led them down the road to metaphysical (in the Hegelian sense) fixity of thought and mechanism. Their monistic (and dualistic) tendencies were consistently opposed by Engels who strongly insisted on the manifoldness of nature/reality.[41] Moreover, attacks on the dialectic made them opponents of genuine critical thought. Finally, their attempts to transform socialism along lines of survival of the fittest doctrines made them opponents of historical materialism. Darwinism, in its crudest form, Engels argued, "was immediately monopolised by these gentlemen," that is, by Büchner, Vogt, and Moleschott, constituting a threat to scientific socialism.[42]

It was therefore necessary to take up the challenge represented by the new mechanistic scientific materialism by providing a more powerful alternative in the form of a dialectics of nature and history, connecting the materialist conception of nature to the materialist conception of history. This required a similar overall range of analysis to that of Büchner in *Force and Matter* and *Man in the Past, Present, and Future*.

The manuscript, fragments, and notes that made up Engels's *Dialectics of Nature* were arranged in individual sheets contained in four folders, numbered 1–4, and titled, respectively, "Dialectics and Natural Science," "The Investigation of Nature and Dialectics," "Dialectics of Nature," and "Mathematics and Natural Science. Miscellaneous." The original sheets were subsequently numbered according to the order in which they were found in the folders. The front of the first sheet of the first folder began with the heading "Büchner" and was concerned with the rise of scientific materialism in Germany. The back of that first sheet consisted of notes on matter and motion, corresponding to the general range of inquiry that distinguished the main part of Büchner's *Force and Matter*. It was undoubtedly based directly on these notes that Engels wrote his celebrated May 30, 1873, letter to Marx, who was then in Manchester.[43] Here Engels laid out what he saw as the main "dialectical points" involved in the analysis of the natural sciences. He began with what was a short abstract, mainly on physics and chemistry:

> The subject matter of natural science—matter in motion, bodies. Bodies cannot be separated from motion, their forms and kinds can only be known in motion; one cannot say anything about bodies without motion, without relation to other bodies. Only in motion does a body reveal what it is. Natural science therefore knows bodies by examining them in relation to one another, and in motion. To understand the different forms of motion is equivalent to understanding bodies. The investigation of these different forms of motion is therefore the chief subject of natural science. . . .
>
> 1) the simplest form of motion is change of *place* (in terms of time—to please old Hegel)—*mechanical* motion. . . .
> 2) *Physics proper*, the science of these forms of motion, establishes the fact, after investigation of each individual form of motion, that under certain conditions they *pass into one another* and ultimately discovers that all of them—at a certain degree of intensity which varies according to the different bodies set in motion—produce effects which transcend physics, changes in the internal structure of the bodies—*chemical* effects.

3) *Chemistry*. For the investigation of the previous forms of motion it was more or less immaterial whether it dealt with animate or inanimate bodies. The inanimate bodies even exhibited the phenomena in their greatest *purity*. Chemistry on the other hand can distinguish the chemical nature of the most important bodies only in substances which have arisen out of the process of life; its chief task becomes more and more to produce these substances artificially. It forms the transition to the science concerned with organisms, but the dialectical transition can be produced only when chemistry has either made the real transition or is on the point of doing so.
4) Organism. Here I will not embark on any dialectics for the time being.[44]

In contrast to Büchner's *Force and Matter*, there can be little doubt that Engels was here planning an alternative conception of the development of natural science, on a far greater scale, rooted in dialectical conceptions. To develop such an analysis thoroughly would require many years of work. Although the analysis would culminate in an analysis of the organic world, the precondition for developing a meaningful philosophy-history of science in this respect was to provide a dialectical conception of the basic scientific viewpoint underlying developments in physics and chemistry. This was then a crucial starting point for Engels's entire project.

No doubt Engels had already begun to discuss the project in outline with Marx before he left for Manchester. Here, though, was the first concrete description of the premises with regard to the understanding of inorganic and organic phenomena. Engels remarked to Marx, "Since you are there at the centre of the natural sciences you will be in the best position to judge if there is anything to it."[45] By this, Engels was referring to the fact that Marx was in Manchester, a noted center of science and technology, where he could consult with Engels's scientific friends Carl Schorlemmer and Gumpert, and also Samuel P. Moore, who was interested in the natural sciences, particularly geology. (Another of Engels's and Marx's friends in the Manchester area, living on a farm nearby, was the noted geologist John Roche Dakyns, who was for many years a member of the International Working Men's Association.)[46] However, it was Schorlemmer, Engels's very close friend, a member of the Royal Society and one of the world's leading chemists, who was the chief authority being referred to here. Marx, during his visit to Manchester, was staying at the rooming house where Schorlemmer resided.[47] Engels added at the bottom of his letter, in order to underscore that all of this was extremely preliminary and should be judged in that way: "Working it all out will take a long time yet."[48]

Marx wrote back to Engels on May 31 that the letter had "edified me greatly. However, I shall venture no judgment until I have had time to reflect on the matter and consult the 'authorities.'" When Schorlemmer arrived shortly after, Marx added, at the end of the same letter, that "Schorlemmer read your letter and says he is essentially in agreement with you but reserves his judgment on points of detail." Schorlemmer then wrote some marginal notes on Engels's letter, agreeing with Engels's first paragraph in his abstract on bodies and motion. In relation to Engels's paragraph on chemistry, Schorlemmer exclaimed, "That's the point!"[49]

With that response, Engels seemed to be on his way, and the research and writing of *Dialectics of Nature* could proceed in earnest. At the outset, he sought to work out more fully the significance of the dialectics of matter and motion, and the relation of physics and chemistry, which were to guide his study, and which would culminate, as his general plan for the book would show, in a conception of the evolution of human beings and their relation to their natural environment. Such a project was extraordinarily ambitious. A dialectical view of the philosophical method of the natural sciences, he was aware, had to address in its most general forms, physics (bodies, motion, energy), followed by organic chemistry. Only then could it explore cells, comparative anatomy, the whole of the development of organic forms, including evolution, and with human evolution the development of society and what we now refer to as human ecology.

Underlying Engels's argument in his Büchner notes was the view that natural science was already pointing to dialectical conceptions, breaking down all previous, fixed, frozen conceptions, requiring a more fluid analysis. This was true, he pointed out, even though "the bulk of natural scientists are still held fast in the old metaphysical categories and helpless when these modern facts, which so to say prove the dialectics in nature, have to be rationally explained and brought into relation with one another." In this way, Engels presented early on what was to be his core thesis in *Dialectics of Nature*, later articulated in *Socialism: Utopian and Scientific*, that "nature is the proof of dialectics." In this view, it was the complex, spiraling process of contingency, change, interpenetration, contradiction, negation, mediation, transcendence, and emergence within the natural world itself (and also history), which generated, at the highest level of human consciousness, fluid, dialectical conceptions of reality. Such conceptions arose at the level of thought once humanity emerged as thinking, self-conscious nature, *nature aware of itself* and of its own history, and thus conscious for the first time of its potential for self-actualization in accordance with nature's laws. At the same time, what Hegel called "bad infinity," the principle of infinite merely quantitative and linear expansion, excluding qualitative transformation, asserted itself more and more in the capitalist world, which was increasingly in conflict with the very principles of change, placing humanity at odds with the natural world, history, and its own existence.[50]

All of this suggests that *Dialectics of Nature* was conceived in its initial phase as a response to the scientific materialists. No sooner had he begun, however, than Engels was confronted with other challenges. In the years that Engels was conceiving *Dialectics of Nature* as a project, neo-Kantian philosophy was emerging as the primary philosophical tradition in Germany, in the work of figures such as Friedrich Albert Lange, Eduard Zeller, Alois Riehl, and Hermann Cohen, as well as German scientists with close affinities to neo-Kantianism, such as Hermann Helmholtz, Emil Du Bois-Reymond, and Carl Wilhelm von Nägeli. These thinkers—for which such self-designated "agnostics" as Thomas Huxley and John Tyndall were to be the British counterparts—adopted a mechanistic materialism in science while dualistically insisting that there were areas beyond science, represented by Kant's "thing in itself" (*noumena*), which lay completely outside the realm of materialist analysis.

In the neo-Kantian view, the role of philosophy became principally an epistemological one of demarcating the logic and limits of science, while also incorporating ethics and aesthetics. Science was unquestioned and philosophy was no longer seen as providing it with foundations. Indeed, ontological questions were no longer taken up by philosophy, and were relegated to science with its materialist conceptions or subsumed within epistemology. Thus the dominant emphasis of neo-Kantianism, as represented in particular by Lange's *History of Materialism*, became one of systematically curtailing the influence of materialism, even while celebrating its role in the development of science.[51] It is no accident that Lange, who had been in correspondence with Marx and Engels, sought to limit the influence of historical materialism by means of a neo-Kantianism meant to reestablish and defend the bourgeois worldview.

In Engels's view of these developments, leading scientific figures either distorted materialism, reducing it to a mechanistic-metaphysical form, or fought against it altogether. The forms of attack varied. Haeckel promoted a philosophical "monism," or what Engels also termed "moral materialism." Both Haeckel and Oscar Schmidt explicitly promoted social Darwinism as the leading defense against socialism. Rudolf Virchow argued that Darwinism was simply a *theory* (to be rejected), that it should not be taught in schools, and that it promoted socialism (a view in opposition to Haeckel and Schmidt). Neo-Kantian epistemology erected a wall between what could be known and the world beyond human perception. Liebig, prone to vitalism, argued that life was eternal, like matter.[52]

These various mechanistic materialist, social Darwinist, neo-Kantian, and vitalistic theories all reflected, from Engels's standpoint, the inner contradictions of bourgeois society and could be combatted effectively only by means of a thoroughgoing *materialist conception of nature and of history, incorporating a dialectical logic*. What was called for, in response to these various challenges, was a "return to dialectics," opening the way to revolutionary praxis.[53]

THE RETURN TO DIALECTICS

Engels's research into dialectical naturalism was an attempt to reintegrate the materialist conception of nature, which Marx and Engels shared with the science of their day, with the materialist conception of history, which had been their distinctive contribution to social thought. The *Dialectics of Nature*, although never completed, is considered one of Engels's major works. It was an enormous undertaking, which initially occupied him for six years, 1873–79, during which the more important historical and philosophical parts of the work (and the great mass of the notes) were composed—overlapping at the end of this period with the writing of *Anti-Dühring*, which was published in a series of articles in 1877 and 1878, with the book version of *Anti-Dühring* appearing in the summer of 1878. He continued to work on *Dialectics of Nature* in 1880–82, in the period after *Anti-Dühring* and following the publication of *Socialism: Utopian and Scientific* (which reproduced parts of *Anti-Dühring* in revised form), drafting in this period a number of additional chapters to the *Dialectics of Nature* mainly concerned with the illustration of dialectics via physics and energy.[54] These last chapters are now quite dated, and are of secondary importance, although they reveal the wide extent of Engels's knowledge of science and his integration of thermodynamic principles into his analysis.

Engels, by his own testimony, in the preface to the second edition of *Anti-Dühring*, was only about halfway through the "moulting" process with respect to natural science and the completion of the *Dialectics of Nature* when he was compelled by circumstances to turn to writing *Anti-Dühring*.[55] Chapters 1 to 3 of *Dialectics of Nature* as it has come down to us (the "Introduction," the "Old Preface to *Anti-Dühring*," and "Natural Science in the Spirit World"), as well as the concluding chapter ("The Part Played by Labor in the Transition from the Ape to Man"), were drafted in this early moulting process before the appearance of *Anti-Dühring*. Chapter 4, "Dialectics," was drafted in the year following the publication of *Anti-Dühring* while Engels was preparing *Socialism: Utopian and Scientific* based on *Anti-Dühring*. Following this short chapter on "Dialectics" (which remained incomplete, about a third finished), the only other major parts of *Dialectics of Nature*—all drafted in 1880–82—were the five physics chapters on "The Basic Forms of Motion," "The Measure of Motion: Work," "Tidal Friction," "Heat," and "Electricity."[56] The chapter on "Electricity" was about a third of what is considered the main text of the work as a whole, but is relatively distant from the philosophical issues that dominate the manuscript as a whole and the most dated part of the manuscript, since Engels was dealing with developments in science and technology that were still in their very early stage.

Where the broader historical and philosophical issues in relation to nature and science are concerned, *Dialectics of Nature* can therefore be seen as a work the composition of which partly preceded and partly overlapped with the publication of *Anti-Dühring*. The general historical and philosophical conceptions of the work were by that time mainly sketched out. However, the extension of the analysis to physics was not carried out until the early 1880s, while the planned sections on chemistry, biology, and knowledge were never composed (and exist only in the form of scattered notes).

With Marx's death in 1883, Engels was forced to curtail altogether his research and writing for *Dialectics of Nature* and to confine his main intellectual efforts to the massive task of editing and publication of volumes 2 and 3 of Marx's *Capital*, based on the voluminous notebooks Marx had left behind, and to writing *The Origin of the Family, Private Property and the State*, which he regarded as carrying forward Marx's project in his *Ethnological Notebooks*. In his 1885 preface to *Anti-Dühring*, he indicated that he still hoped to draw on his notes for the *Dialectics of Nature* in the context of preparing an edition of Marx's mathematical notebooks.[57] Nevertheless, the closest he came to returning to the themes of *Dialectics of Nature*, in the dozen years in which he outlived Marx, was in the 1888 *Ludwig Feuerbach and the Outcome of Classical German Philosophy*, where he briefly explored some core issues of the decline of speculative philosophy and the rise of a crude and unphilosophical scientific materialism in its place, a critical assessment that demonstrated the necessity of a resurrection of conscious dialectics if socialist theory was to advance.

Following Engels's death in 1895, the manuscripts of *Dialectics of Nature* were held for thirty years in the archives of the German Social Democracy. In 1924, Eduard Bernstein asked Albert Einstein to look at the work—presumably the ten chapters and articles, consisting of about 150 pages in all—which were relatively intact. Einstein responded that the work was worth publishing for historical reasons but that it had limited significance for contemporary science, particularly physics, more than four decades after it was written. Einstein, it can be assumed, was commenting much more on the natural science than on the philosophical aspects of the work.[58] *Dialectics of Nature* was finally published in Russia (both in the original German and Russian translation) in 1925. It was translated into English in 1940.[59]

For Riazanov and his team of editors, putting together the manuscript to *Dialectics of Nature* in the third decade of the twentieth century was certainly not an easy or straightforward task. Although Engels left a schematic general plan for the work, it was impossible to know precisely how he himself would have put the book together in the end, for it remained far from complete, whether in its entirety or in its separate parts. The ten chapters/sections/articles that had been drafted did not all correspond to the general plan, and substantial parts of the general plan, including the entirety of Engels's intended illustration of the dialectic through an examination of the organic world, had no counterparts in the drafted material, and had their traces only in the voluminous preparatory notes. In addition to about 150 pages of text, there were around 150 pages of preparatory material and scattered notes, which were included in the published version and categorized under various topics. These notes are invaluable in providing insights into what Engels intended to do, especially in those parts of the planned manuscript that remain unpublished. But they also point to the indefiniteness of the whole.

No single part of *Dialectics of Nature* can be seen as entirely finished. The famous "Introduction" was referred to by Engels himself as "The Old Introduction," presumably to be extensively rewritten, no doubt in connection with the "Old Preface to *Anti-Dühring*," which occupies second place in the published *Dialectics of Nature*. Only about a third of the chapter on dialectics was drafted. Almost all of the other pieces that make up the core text were incomplete in various ways and often were cut off at the end, indicating that Engels had not entirely worked out the connections and conclusions to which the argument was directed. The most complete pieces were "Natural Science in the Spirit World" and "The Part Played by Labour in the Transition from Ape to Man," which appear originally to have been drafted as articles (the latter intended as part of a larger work on *The Three Basic Forms of Slavery*), but remained unpublished.[60] In contrast to "The Part Played by Labour," "Natural Science in the Spirit World" was not included in the original general plan for the work, and is largely extraneous to the main argument.[61] If we therefore exclude that chapter, which Engels apparently never intended to include in the book, and consider the four later chapters on physics and energy (beyond the chapter on "The Basic Laws of Motion") to be mainly illustrative materials directed at motion in the inorganic world—intended to illustrate the salience of a method that views nature dialectically, but of little interest today in terms of their substantive scientific content—then the core elements of Engels's *Dialectics of Nature* that chiefly concern us here amount to a mere sixty pages or so, mostly written before (or simultaneous with) the appearance of *Anti-Dühring*.[62] The *Dialectics of Nature* will therefore be treated as a work that primarily precedes *Anti-Dühring*.

Since it was an actual published work and for the most part was written later, *Anti-Dühring* can be seen as more definitive in some of its particular formulations than *Dialectics of Nature*, in those areas where the two works overlap. Nevertheless, the *Dialectics of Nature* represented Engels's larger project, which was meant to carry forward his inquiry with respect to nature-science at a much higher, more ambitious level. It is here that we find his most penetrating ecological understandings, in the "The Part Played by Labour in the Transition from the Ape to Man" and his deepest ecologically rooted critique of capital's "bad infinity" in the introduction to his work. The significance of *Dialectics of Nature* as it has come down to us thus lies less in the form of a completed treatise on natural science, and more in terms of the new forms of dialectical questioning that it introduced, leading in the direction of what we know today as Earth System analysis, or systems ecology. It proved to be an immense source of inspiration to those struggling to comprehend ecological complexity and human-environmental impacts.[63]

Although the *Dialectics of Nature* was not published until the 1920s, and not available in an English edition until 1940, the analysis that Engels developed in his "half moulting" was to enter partially into the argument in *Anti-Dühring*, having a profound impact on Marxian theory in his lifetime. He contributed in significant ways to a growing understanding of nature and history in terms of complexity, change, contradiction, and coevolution—representing a dialectical and ecological point of view that has now, in our time, become an absolute requirement of human survival.

The intent of the "Introduction" to *Dialectics of Nature*, as Engels explained in his "Outline of the General Plan," written in late summer 1878, was to provide a historical argument demonstrating that "the metaphysical conception [of rigid, immutable relations] has become impossible in natural science owing to the very development of the latter."[64] The "brilliant natural-philosophical intuitions of antiquity," which had produced, in the work of figures such as Heraclitus, Epicurus, and Lucretius, a dialectical conception of the whole of nature in a process of flux, was replaced, after the important additions made by the Arab world, with a kind of medieval stasis, where the social and religious ideologies of the Christian Middle Ages limited scientific progress. It was only with the bourgeois revolution and the rise of capitalism that science reemerged in full force, breaking through these religious constraints, in the Renaissance and the succeeding Enlightenment. This was manifested in the breakthroughs in cosmology, physics, mathematics, and biology associated with Nicolaus Copernicus, Galileo Galilei, Gottfried Wilhelm Leibniz, Johannes Kepler, Isaac Newton, and Carl Linnaeus. Indeed, "natural science . . . developed in the midst of the general revolution" of these times "and was itself thoroughly revolutionary." Yet, in spite of the revolutionary discoveries of the new science, which freed it in part from rigid religious doctrines, still, in a kind of compromise, it continued to uphold the established order by postulating "the absolute immutability of nature."

In the Newtonian view, "the planets and their satellites, once set in motion by the mysterious 'first impulse,' circled on and on in their predestined ellipses for all eternity, or at any rate until the end of all things. The stars remained forever fixed and immovable in their places, keeping one another therein by 'universal gravitation.'" The same was true of all other areas of science, thus the geology and geography of the world had always been the same, and "species of plants and animals had been established once [and] for all when they came into existence.

. . . All change, all development in nature, was denied. Natural science, so revolutionary at the outset, suddenly found itself confronted by an out-and-out conservative nature, in which even today everything was as it had been from the beginning and in which—to the end of the world or for all eternity—everything would remain as it had been since the beginning." Nature was thus dehistoricized and made passive: "In contrast to the history of mankind, which develops in time, there was ascribed to the history of nature only an unfolding in space." In this period, "the highest general idea to which . . . natural science attained was that of the purposiveness of the arrangements of nature, the shallow teleology of Wolff, according to which cats were created to eat mice, mice to be eaten by cats, and the whole of nature to testify to the wisdom of the creator."[65] Nature thus remained fixed, passive, and preordained, excluding all active, dialectical evolutionary and ecological conceptions.

Such paradigms were dominant in the seventeenth and eighteenth centuries and extended even into the nineteenth. "The first breach in this petrified outlook on nature," Engels explained, "was made not by a natural scientist but by a philosopher," in the form of Kant's 1755 formulation of the nebular hypothesis on the origins of the solar system, which was to be expounded definitively decades later by Pierre-Simon Laplace. This was followed by a revolutionary advance in physics in the form of the theory of the conservation of energy and the interchangeability of its forms, developed simultaneously by Mayer and James Joule, whereby "the special physical forces, the as it were immutable 'species' of physics, were resolved into variously differentiated forms of the motion of matter." Lavoisier and Dalton in chemistry demonstrated that the laws of chemistry were equally applicable "for organic as for inorganic bodies," bridging what had hitherto been seen as an unbridgeable gap. Georges Cuvier and Charles Lyell showed geology to be historical. While in zoology and botany, the discovery of the cell, following upon that of the microscope and the development of the comparative method, produced a mass of empirical results under which "the rigid system of an immutably fixed organic nature crumbled away." Despite the resistance to materialism, the development of the evolutionary theory that emerged full force only with Darwin's *Origin of Species* was inevitable. Nature in all its forms had become historical.[66]

In this way, over the course a century, science had returned objectively to a mode of outlook with respect to the world as a whole that invited comparison with the brilliant dialectical (and ecological) intuitions of the ancient Greeks in which "the whole of nature, from the smallest element to the greatest, from grains of sand to suns, from Protista to man, has its existence in eternal coming into being and passing away, in ceaseless flux, in unresting motion and change." Even the theory of the heat death of the universe arising from thermodynamics,

Engels argued, could not halt this process since our "island universe" must give rise to others among "innumerable worlds in infinite space." Nevertheless, it was clear that the solar system itself came into being and passed away, as must humanity itself along with it.[67]

Such a historical-dialectical and ecological understanding was needed most of all in approaching human development itself. In the "Introduction" to *Dialectics of Nature*, Engels outlined his argument on the origins of the human species through the development "of the *hand*"—human labor and the related development of articulate speech and the brain—a coevolutionary analysis that was to be developed more fully and in ecological terms in what was to be the closing section of *Dialectics of Nature*, composed around the same time: "The Part Played by Labour in the Transition from Ape to Man."

It was here too in his "Introduction" to *Dialectics of Nature* that Engels makes his famous observation:

> Darwin did not know what a bitter satire he wrote on mankind, and especially on his countrymen, when he showed that free competition, the struggle for existence, which the economists celebrate as the highest historical achievement, is the normal state of the *animal kingdom*. Only conscious organisation of social production, in which production and distribution are carried on in a planned way, can lift mankind above the rest of the animal world as regards the social aspect, in the same way that production in general has done this for mankind in the specifically biological aspect. Historical development makes such an organization daily more indispensable.[68]

The reason that such social planning is necessary, Engels insisted, is the increasing scale of "the unforeseen effects" and "uncontrolled forces" of human production, leading to increasing ecological contradictions both between individual- and class-based production and the needs of society and a whole, and between social development and the larger natural environment. The introduction of the "conscious organization of social production," which, if not inevitable, is at least "with every day more possible," will represent a new "epoch of history" comprising an advance for humanity that "will put everything preceding it in the deepest shade."[69]

In "The Old Preface to 'Anti-Dühring,'" which made up the second chapter of *Dialectics of Nature* in the published version, Engels was concerned with the rise of metaphysics and mechanical materialism following the demise of Hegelian speculative philosophy, and therefore the necessary "return to dialectics" that was occurring "unconsciously" in natural science, "hence contradictorily and slowly."[70] Here he argued that conscious dialectics constituted "the analogue for, and thereby the method of explaining, the evolutionary processes occurring in nature, inter-connections and general, and transitions from one field of investigation to another." Arising in its formal, intellectual characteristics within the human mind, dialectics nonetheless was a manifestation of the real, objective dynamism of nature, on the one hand, and the intellectual means of understanding that dynamism, on the other. Once again, the "atomic philosophy of Ancient Greece," exemplified by Epicurus and Lucretius, was coming to the fore in science.[71] The conception of the whole of reality introduced by the Greeks, and the forms of scientific inference they had pioneered on this basis, were being rediscovered in science in the form of "so-called objective dialectics." What impeded this development, represented above all by Hegel, was the subsequent regression to a crude materialist view, characterized by fixity and absolute opposition, in the crudities of thinkers like Büchner, Vogt, and Moleschott, preventing the evolution of "so-called subjective dialectics."[72]

What was needed, then, was "a return, in one form or another, from metaphysical to dialectical thinking," a return to more dialectical, evolutionary and ecological perspectives (as in the ancient Greeks) that science's spontaneous development was making possible, but that needed to attain a much more conscious form.

A significant development in philosophy, in this respect, was that Kant had become fashionable again, by means of the neo-Kantianism of thinkers like Lange. Unfortunately, this revival was based on a fetishism of Kant's notion of the *noumena* or thing-in-itself, in Engels's view the least important aspect of Kant's immense legacy, and a means of attacking a consistent, critical materialism. Hence, only a revival of Hegelian dialectics, but in a form related to realism and materialism, offered real hope for the resurrection of critical reasoning with respect to natural history, providing the basis of a dialectical and evolutionary-ecological view. It was precisely this emphasis on nature as historical that opened the way to what we today call ecological thinking, and which was embedded in Engels's focus on nature as dialectic.

This central theme of the *return to dialectics*, animating Engels's whole argument in *Dialectics of Nature*, was to form the basis more than a decade later of *Ludwig Feuerbach and the Outcome of Classical German Philosophy*. Engels in fact omitted a four-page section from *Ludwig Feuerbach* and placed it in the second folder of materials for *Dialectics of Nature* next to "The Part Played by Labour in the Transition from Ape to Man," clearly indicating that he meant it to be included in some form in the published work. However, the editors placed the "Omitted from 'Feuerbach'" section instead in the notes to the volume, outside the main text. It was here in "Omitted from 'Feuerbach'" that Engels returned to the three great discoveries in natural science that he had raised as early as 1858–59 in correspondence with Marx: the discovery of the conservation of energy by Mayer and Joule, the discovery of the organic cell by

Schwann and Schleiden, and the discovery of evolution by Darwin. "By means of these three great discoveries, the main processes of nature were explained and referred to natural causes." A materialism in which the world was in a process of flux and change, of the kind that had characterized the innate dialectics of the ancient Greeks, was reemerging on a firmer foundation after "more than two thousand years of an essentially idealist outlook on the world."

Yet, the objective triumph of materialism in natural science was caught in a contradiction in which scientists were "inexorable materialists within their science but outside it . . . not merely idealists, but even pious and indeed orthodox Christians." The same dualism could be seen in Feuerbach himself. "In the field of nature he is a materialist, but in the human field" he is otherwise. For Engels, it was the rejection of dialectics that had led to a dualistic split between the natural-scientific and human worlds, which was so evident in the crude metaphysics of the scientific materialists, and in another and more sophisticated way in neo-Kantianism. Implicit in his view was the notion that a dialectical perspective was more useful than Enlightenment rationalism in interrogating the world since it offered a more realistic representation of nature's complexity, as manifested as well in the thinking mind.[73]

Standing against the numerous criticisms of Engels for promoting a metaphysical conception in his well-known three laws of dialectics, is the reality of this sophisticated approach, akin to dialectical critical realism, which, in contrast to the Western Marxist philosophical tradition, allows us to think of humanity as part of nature while exploring the interaction.[74] "Dialectics," Engels observed in his provisional notes for *Dialectics of Nature,* "is conceived as the science of the most general laws of *all* motion. This implies that its laws must be valid just as much for motion in nature and human history as for the motion of thought."[75] Dialectical reason was seen by Engels, along with Marx, as crucial for apprehending nature because it was itself a refracted, reflexive part of nature's complex process of change mediated by historical society. The dialectical development of thought thus went hand in hand with our developing human interactions with the natural world through production. Nature could never be treated as fixed or passive but was in contrast fluid and characterized by complex, developing interconnections and change.

"Dialectics," viewed in this way, was "the science of interconnections."[76] In the unfinished draft titled "Dialectics" that became the fourth chapter of *Dialectics of Nature*, Engels argued that "the laws of dialectics" were "abstracted" from "the history of nature and society," and represented the human effort to understand its own experience and relation to nature in critical-rational form. This was depicted in the form of general laws. The most general dialectical laws of nature and history together, "as well as of thought itself," could be "reduced in the main to three": "the law of the transformation of quantity into quality and vice versa; the law of the interpenetration of opposites; the law of the negation of the negation."[77] In his general plan to *Dialectics of Nature*, Engels depicted these laws as "transformation of quantity and quality—mutual penetration of polar opposites and transformation into each other when carried to extremes—development through contradiction or negation of the negation—[leading to the] spiral form of development."[78] The notion of development in nature and history as occurring in the form of a spiral rather than in linear form or in a circle, was a way of illustrating the general movement of the dialectic represented especially by the principle of the negation of the negation.

All three "laws" of the dialectic could be attributed to Hegel, who had introduced the first of these tendencies in the first subdivision of his *Logic* (the Doctrine of Being), the second in the second subdivision of the *Logic* (Doctrine of Essence)—which encompassed such objective phenomena as attraction and repulsion—while the third law, related to sublation, was the fundamental basis of the construction of Hegel's entire system.[79] Each of these dialectical laws, though presented in very general terms, was subject to enormous elaboration.

Hegel's mistake, Engels stressed, had been to foist "these laws . . . on nature and history as laws of [abstract, speculative] thought," whereas they emanated from human attempts to understand *objective processes and complex evolutionary developments* manifested in nature and history themselves. From a realist and materialist perspective, it was no longer necessary to force nature and history within the Procrustean bed of what turns out to be simply "a definite stage of development of human thought." Rather, it was possible to understand the development of thought as a process that is designed to capture the actual movement of matter, that is, of nature and history themselves, including human history. "Dialectical laws" were thus for Engels "real laws of development of nature, and therefore are valid also for theoretical natural science."[80]

It was no doubt Engels's intention to illustrate each of these laws by means of theoretical natural history. He managed to go a considerable way in his unfinished chapter on "Dialectics" toward illustrating the law of the transformation of quantity into quality by means of chemistry, comparing various carbon molecules, and discussing Mendeleyev's periodic classification of the elements. Quantitative changes, Engels argued, produce various "nodal points," a concept he drew from Hegel, wherein qualitative transformations occur. "The so-called physical constants are for the most part nothing but designations of the nodal points at which quantitative addition or subtraction of motion produces qualitative change in the state of the body concerned, at which, therefore, quantity is transformed into quality." Indeed, "the discrete parts [of matter] at various stages (ether atoms, chemical atoms, masses, heavenly bodies)," he pointed out, "are various *nodal points* which determine the various *qualitative* modes of existence of matter in general."[81]

In a letter to Marx on June 16, 1867, Engels referred directly to Hegel's "nodal points" in which quantitative change turned into qualitative change. Marx replied on June 22, 1867, indicating how in *Capital*, vol. 1, "I quote Hegel's discovery regarding the *law that merely quantitative changes turn into qualitative changes* and state that it holds good alike in history and natural science." In a footnote to *Capital*, Marx referred to "the law discovered by Hegel, in his *Logic*, that at a certain point merely quantitative differences pass over by a dialectical inversion into qualitative distinctions." Elaborating later on Marx's footnote here, in an annotation to the third edition of *Capital*, volume 1, Engels explained this in terms drawn from his discussion of carbon molecules in *Anti-Dühring* and in his unpublished chapter on "Dialectics" in *Dialectics of Nature*, referencing Schorlemmer's 1879 *Rise and Development of Organic Chemistry*.[82]

In the *Anti-Dühring* chapter "Dialectics. Quantity and Quality," which Engels had read to Marx along with the rest of the draft manuscript prior to publication, he strongly defended Marx's use in *Capital* of the Hegelian law of the transformation of quantity into quality, arguing against Dühring's criticisms of Marx in this regard. There he commented on the development of paraffins: "Each new member is brought into existence by the addition of CH_2 to the molecule of the preceding one, and this quantitative change of the molecule produces every time a qualitatively different body." Schorlemmer was to quote this sentence from Engels in the revised (1894) version of *The Rise and Development of Organic Chemistry*. For Schorlemmer, one of the foremost chemists of the day and a member of the Royal Society, organic chemistry demanded "a dialectic treatment of the subject and justified even for molecules the axiom of Heraclitus that everything is in eternal flux."[83]

The general principle or law of the transformation of quantity into quality (that is of emergence or integrative levels) has to do with levels of *organization* in material reality and is fundamental to all contemporary science. New forms of organization of the same elements, often by mere changes in quantity (or through variation), lead to qualitatively different results. The application of this same principle to society can also be perceived. In an attempt to demonstrate this, Engels drew in *Anti-Dühring* on the memoirs of Napoleon Bonaparte, who "describes the combat between the French cavalry, who were bad riders but disciplined, and the Mamelukes," an Arab military caste descended from slaves whom Napoleon encountered in Ottoman Egypt, who were "undoubtedly the best horsemen of their time for single combat, but lacked discipline." In Napoleon's words: "Two Mamelukes were undoubtedly more than a match for three Frenchmen; 100 Mamelukes were equal to 100 Frenchmen; and 1,000 Frenchmen invariably defeated 1,500 Mamelukes." At a certain quantitative level, organization trumped individual skill, and created a qualitative shift, even though the basic elements constituting the two forces had not changed.[84]

The unfinished chapter on "Dialectics" for *Dialectics of Nature*, however, cuts off after only a few pages of discussion of the law of the transformation of quantity into quality—and well before the interpenetration of opposites, the negation of the negation (and the spiral process of development), are concretely addressed.[85] Nevertheless, dialectical principles in the interpretation of the latter two "laws" were treated in *Anti-Dühring*, written about the same time.

Engels continually points in *Anti-Dühring* and elsewhere to the interpenetration or unity of opposites and the fallacy of the "metaphysical" frame of thought, which generates fixed polarities, and "eternal" distinctions, at the expense of dialectical interconnections and contradictions.[86] "The first elements of dialectics," he wrote, "deal precisely with the inadequacy of all polar opposites," such as being and nothingness, subject and object, mind and matter, repulsion and attraction, quantity and quality, and nature and society.[87]

In this dialectical conception, for example, there can be no absolute opposition between nature and society; rather, human beings are a *part* of nature, while society is an *emergent form* within the universal metabolism of nature, the product of material evolution, operating according to its own laws, but still subject to natural laws, such as the laws of physics.

Engels's third dialectical law is dealt with most comprehensively in his chapter "Dialectics: The Negation of the Negation" in *Anti-Dühring*, where his main concern again is defending Marx's own references to the negation of the negation in *Capital* against Dühring's criticisms.[88] The negation of the negation was an integral part "of a whole series . . . of dialectical turns of speech [such] as Marx used: processes which in their nature are antagonistic, contain a contradiction; transformation of one extreme into its opposite; and finally, as the kernel of the whole thing, the negation of the negation." A concrete example was the evolution of materialism:

> The philosophy of antiquity was primitive, spontaneously evolved materialism. As such, it was incapable of clearing up the relation between mind and matter. But the need to get clarity on this question led to the doctrine of a soul separable from the body, then to the assertion of the immortality of the soul, and finally to monotheism. The old materialism was therefore negated by idealism. But in the course of the further development of philosophy, idealism, too, became untenable and was negated by modern materialism. This modern materialism, the negation of the negation, is not the mere re-establishment of the old, but adds to the permanent foundations of this old materialism the whole thought-content of two thousand years of development of philosophy and natural science, as of the history of these two thousand years. It is no longer a philosophy at all, but simply a world outlook which has to establish its validity and be applied not in a science of sciences standing apart, but in the

> real sciences. Philosophy is therefore "sublated" here, that is, "both overcome and preserved"; overcome as regards its form, and preserved as regards its real content.[89]

Although a product of the "Hegelian jargon" the negation of the negation could be seen again and again in the complex evolutionary process, combining both progression and regression, and including in its development what was surpassed, so that that "progress" contains "antagonism" and is "at the same time retrogression."[90] In this way, Marx and Engels often remarked that capitalist civilization also advanced barbarism, generating contradictions that required a further advance.[91]

"What" then, Engels asks,

> is the negation of the negation? An extremely general—and for this reason extremely far-reaching and important—law of development of nature, history, and thought; a law which, as we have seen, holds good in the animal and plant kingdoms, in geology, in mathematics, in history and in philosophy. . . . It is obvious I do not say anything concerning the *particular* process of development of, for example, a grain of barley from the germination to the death of the fruit-bearing plant, if I say it is a negation of the negation. . . . When I say that all these processes are a negation of the negation, I bring them all together under one law of motion, and for this very reason I leave out of account the specific peculiarities of each individual process. Dialectics, however, is nothing more than the science of the general laws of motion and the development of nature, human society, and thought.[92]

Numerous critics have of course derided Engels's dialectical "laws," which he saw as standing for "form[s] of universality" and change in nature, but which they see as mere mechanical or metaphysical formulations.[93] Such critics have seldom looked beyond the brief presentation of the transformation of quantity into quality, however, and the allusions to the identity/unity of opposites, and the negation of the negation provided in Engels's incomplete chapter on "Dialectics" in his unfinished *Dialectics of Nature*—without rigorously following out their more complex development in *Anti-Dühring* and his thought as a whole.[94] Yet, for Engels, these were not simply laws of nature, but as he repeatedly emphasized, also laws of human history.[95] Thus the negation of negation represented a complex process of negation and sublation (transcendence) that was "operative in nature and history, and . . . in our heads"—unconsciously at first, and then, consciously, with the development of science.[96]

In developing his analysis of dialectics via the famous three laws, Engels gave the dialectic a much greater range than has been characteristic of contemporary

Marxian theory, where there has been a tendency to reduce it simply to the law of the interpenetration of opposites or the unity of opposites. In contrast, a far more sophisticated response to Engels's three laws is represented by Roy Bhaskar's dialectical critical realism. In *Dialectic: The Pulse of Freedom*, Bhaskar emphasizes that Engels's law of transformation of quantity into quality corresponds to what is now known as the dialectics of emergence, the law of the interpenetration of opposites to what is frequently referred to today as the dialectics of internal relations, and the law of the negation of the negation to the dialectics of absence (or the absenting of absence), the key contribution of Bhaskar's own dialectic.[97] Without all of these dimensions of dialectic, it is hollowed out as a critique and as a specifically *dialectical logic*.[98] Engels's three laws can thus be seen as a brilliant, nascent attempt at charting the development of dialectical thought as a whole.

REFLECTION DETERMINATIONS

Of even greater significance than the direct criticisms of Engels's dialectical laws is the common charge, made by adherents of the so-called Western Marxist philosophical tradition (defined primarily by its rejection of the dialectics of nature) that his dialectical naturalism simply disguised an underlying positivism. Behind Engels's three dialectical laws, it is contended, was a mechanistic view of the world or a crude metaphysics that downplayed the role of human thought. Engels, we are frequently told, was epistemologically naive, seeing the human mind as a mere *reflection* of the external world, in accordance with a crude correspondence (or reflection) theory of knowledge, in which the mind merely mirrored reality. It is characteristic of such criticisms that they are typically presented in vague, general terms without any specific references or citations to back them up, which would be open to close examination and dispute.[99] Hence, any recognition of the value of Engels's dialectical naturalism (and of the ecological conceptions to which they give rise) depends on transcending these criticisms, which fail to recognize the dialectical character of reflection, in the thinking of Hegel, Marx, and Engels.

Although Engels often referred (as did Marx) to the "reflection" within thought of dialectical processes of matter in motion, mind was never conceived by him as a passive mirroring of external reality.[100] As S. H. Rigby usefully notes in *Engels and the Formation of Marxism*:

> It is often argued that Engels's metaphor of "reflection" implies an empiricist passivity of mind in the production of knowledge; yet there is no reason why this should necessarily be the case. After all, the image of an object reflected in a mirror is not solely dependent upon the properties of the object reflected,

> but also upon the surface of the mirror: the reflection is the product of the interaction of the two. As Engels said in his draft version of *Anti-Dühring*, "All ideas are taken from experience, are reflections—*true or distorted*—of reality." . . . Engels, however, rejected the possibility of pure empirical knowledge, stressed the limits of inductive thought and insisted upon the centrality of theory in the production of knowledge.[101]

But the category of reflection was far from being a mere "metaphor" in Engels's dialectical view, as Rigby supposes here. Rather, it had a complex theoretical meaning in Hegel's philosophy, which formed the logical context in which Marx and Engels employed the term.[102] The Latin root of the word *reflect* meant "to bend back" and in Hegel it was used to convey both (1) "*pure identity*-with-self, unity of *reflection-into-self*," as in light, in which the immanent essence of an object is posited and bends back or is refracted through some prism; and (2) reflection in the sense of interrelation, similar to "reflexive," a term which was coined only later, in the 1890s. According to Christopher Yeomans in *Freedom and Reflection: Hegel and the Logic of Agency*, "Hegel characterizes reflection in terms of a difference that is also a reflexive relation." A reflection thus expressed the complex relation between the object in its free, self-subsistent state and as an external object of thought in which it exists for us.[103]

In his *Phenomenology of Spirit*, Hegel wrote: "The True [is] a result, but it is equally reflection that overcomes [*aufheben*] the antithesis between the process of its becoming and the result." So crucial was reflection to the whole process of human reason, in Hegel's dialectical perspective, that "self-consciousness" was defined as "reflection into self," through which "the object has become Life."[104]

Engels pointed out that at the very heart of Hegel's *Logic*, as depicted in "The Doctrine of Essence," were the "determinations of reflection" (or reflection determinations), which stood for the dialectical movement from essence to appearance to actuality (the real). In these reflection determinations, related to essence, "everything," Engels emphasized, "is *relative*," having "meaning only in their relation[s]," that is, in complex reflections and mediations, and "not each for itself."[105]

Likewise, Georg Lukács was to explain in his *Ontology of Social Being* that the "centre of the dialectic," for Hegel, was the concept of "reflection determinations," through which the contradictions between ontology and epistemology manifested themselves. A reflection determination, in Hegel's conception, represents a complete "turning back" of a subject (or an object) on itself, deriving its meaning through the unity of opposites—for example, identity and difference, attraction and repulsion, internal and external, positive and negative. This conforms with Benedict de Spinoza's great principle of "*Omnis determinatio est negatio*" (Every determination is a negation).[106] No wonder that Lukács in *The*

Young Hegel declared: "Philosophical reflectivity is the most important driving force of the dialectic, of his [Hegel's] system, it is the methodological foundation both of the dialectic and of his view of history as a moment of the dialectic."[107]

The concepts of reflection and mediation, as Raymond Williams argued in *Marxism and Literature*, are tightly interwoven in any dialectical view. Mediation represents a kind of "sophistication of reflection. . . . 'Mediation' is always the less alienated concept" pointing to the role of a "constitutive consciousness."[108] As Hegel put it, mediation is "a *becoming-other* that has to be taken back . . . a reflection into self" and thus represents self-consciousness asserting itself in relation to the world of objects.[109]

What may seem, then, in a cursory reading of Engels, to be a crude notion of reflection, as simple mirroring or correspondence, becomes something altogether different when reflection is understood as also encompassing the *bending of thought-reality*, or, in Engels's words, the "mediation of ideas." The real, objective complexity of nature itself (as grasped by the mind) is not to be denied since it consists of opposing, contradictory forces and relations, part of an ever-changing, emerging existence. It is these constant metamorphoses in material reality, the result of the opposition between essence and appearance—mediated via human thought and action—that constitute the complex set of "reflection determinations" that lead to the realm of "so-called objective dialectics"—along with "so-called subjective dialectics."[110] This is what Lukács called "the dialectical conception of the reflection of objective reality."[111]

All of this indicates that the mere use of the word *reflection* by Engels (along with Marx) in relation to the sensual perception and cognition of natural objects cannot immediately be taken as referring to a one-dimensional mirror image, or the action of "mere reflexes," and therefore as evidence of his adherence to a simple one-to-one correspondence or, in this sense, a crude "reflection" theory of knowledge.[112] Rather, Engels saw reflection as a process of dialectical mimesis, embodying contradiction and the constitutive role of the intellect.

This view was perhaps best captured by Lenin, who wrote in his *Philosophical Notebooks*: "The reflection of nature in human thought is not 'dead,' not 'abstract,' *not without movement*, not without contradictions, but is to be comprehended in the eternal process of movement, in the emergence and resolution of contradictions."[113] In the words of French Marxist sociologist and philosopher Henri Lefebvre, "Civilization 'reflects' nature, material or living; but the relationship involved is radically different from a passive reflection. It extracts natural elements from nature in order to profoundly metamorphose them into forms: into a human order."[114]

For Bhaskar, in *Dialectic: The Pulse of Freedom*, Marx and Engels could be seen as employing the concept of reflection primarily in Hegel's developed sense related to reflexivity and cognitive activity, and not in the simple mirror-image sense, that is, "immediate form," which was widely attributed to them—and to Engels in particular. If this was in some sense a "correspondence theory" of truth, then it was a "deep correspondence theory," one that was aimed, as in Hegel, at the comprehension of what constituted "essential relations"—a comprehension possible only through the active agency of thought, or in Marx and Engels's more materialist terms, through human praxis.[115] As Hegel observed: "Of a metaphysics prevalent today, which maintains that we cannot know things because they are absolutely shut to us, it might be said that not even the animals are so stupid as these metaphysicians; for they go after things, seize and consume them." Only an understanding of the world and of thought as dialectically related could explain how nature could exist for us in terms of universals, and also constitute "free, self-subsistent being."[116]

Rejecting the notion that thought was simply outside nature, and thus was in opposition to objective being, Engels said that if we ask "what thought and consciousness really are and where they come from, it becomes apparent that they are products of the human brain and that man himself is a product of nature, which has developed in and along with its environment; hence it is self-evident that the products of the human brain, being in the last analysis also products of nature, do not contradict the rest of nature's interconnections but are in correspondence with them."[117]

In using the term *correspondence* here Engels did not mean a one-to-one correspondence, but rather a correlation of growth in the products of the mind and the objective material environment, of which human consciousness was itself (reflexively) the product. Following Kant and the entire critical tradition in German philosophy, Engels insisted that such concepts as matter and motion (like space and time) must be understood as abstractions, or concepts of the understanding, which are necessary if we are to know nature at all.[118] Knowledge could never be based simply on the empirical perception of finite phenomena immediately available to us through the senses, but had to rely ultimately on *a priori* categories, logically independent of experience, that is, abstract universals. Nevertheless, an extreme "apriorism," as in neo-Kantianism, that attempted to deduce relations from concepts alone, inevitably fell prey to reification.[119]

Our perceptions about the world, Engels posited more definitively, arise "not from our minds, but only *through* our minds from the real world."[120] But this only took place as a result of human activity or praxis. As he stated in the *Dialectics of Nature*:

> Natural science, like philosophy, has hitherto entirely neglected the influence of men's activity on their thought; both know only nature on the one hand and thought on the other. But it is precisely *the alteration of nature by man*,

> not solely nature as such, which is the most essential and immediate basis of human thought, and it is in the measure that man has learned to change nature that his intelligence has increased. The naturalistic conception of history, as found for instance to a greater or lesser extent in [J. W.] Draper and other scientists, as if nature exclusively reacts on man, and natural conditions exclusively determined his historical development, is therefore one-sided and forgets that man also reacts on nature, changing it and creating new conditions of existence for himself.[121]

All scientific knowledge, Engels insisted in line with Hegel, consisted of going beyond the particular (the finite) to the universal (the infinite). It was therefore incompatible with the "shallowest empiricism," which denied the active role of thought.[122] Nor was a critical scientific understanding facilitated by a neo-Kantian dualism, which sharply divided off the transitive (mind-dependent) realm from the intransitive (mind-independent) realm, thus denying the possibility of knowledge in certain areas. In his critique of the neo-Kantian Swiss botanist Nägeli's celebrated 1876 lecture on the limits of scientific knowledge (part of the famous *Ignorabimus* controversy), Engels declared:

> Nägeli first of all says that we cannot know real qualitative differences, and immediately afterwards says that such "absolute differences" do not occur in nature! . . . In accordance with the prevailing mechanical view, Nägeli regards all qualitative differences as explained only in so far as they can be reduced to quantitative differences. . . . "We can only know the finite," etc.
>
> This is quite correct in so far as only finite objects enter the sphere of our knowledge. But the proposition needs to be supplemented by this: "Fundamentally we can know *only the infinite*." In fact, all real exhaustive knowledge consists solely in raising the individual thing in thought from individuality into particularity and from this into universality, in seeking and establishing the infinite in the finite, the eternal in the transitory. . . . The form of universality in nature is *law,* and no one talks more of the *eternal character of the laws of nature* than the natural scientists. Hence when Nägeli says that the finite is made impossible to understand by not desiring to investigate merely this finite, but instead adding something eternal to it, then he denies either the possibility of knowing either the laws of nature or their eternal character. All true knowledge of nature is knowledge of the eternal, the infinite, and hence essentially absolute.[123]

Scientific knowledge therefore requires that "we transform things into universals, or make them our own."[124] Nägeli's failure was not to discern how Kant, and then Hegel, had emphasized the critical and dialectical bases of knowledge in contravention to Wolffian metaphysics and Humean empiricism. Nägeli was thus unable to perceive that scientific knowledge required *a priori* universals, without which there could be no real knowledge, no real science. Dialectics was a necessary element in this process of scientific inference, without which causal laws, complexity, and the concrete conditions of change could not be fully comprehended.[125]

Related to this was the rejection of all fixity and finitude that stood in the way of the analysis of motion, change, and universal processes, including the realm of evolutionary ecology. Engels emphasized that a dialectical view was "incompatible" with the kinds of "hard and fast lines" that characterized the metaphysical-mechanistic outlook. Dialectics was antagonistic toward all forms of rigidity and reductionism. He frequently illustrated this with references to changes in the classification of species, which were then undergoing radical changes as a result of the development of evolutionary perspectives. Here he singled out E. Ray Lankester's remarkable discovery, in which, by means of a study of the development of homologous organs, he had determined that the king crab (*Limulus*) was an arachnid, part of the spider and scorpion family, a revelation that startled the scientific world and threw previous biological classifications askew. Evolutionary theory thus quickly broke down hard and fast lines between species, showing complex and contingent lines of descent and transmutations.[126] "From the moment we accept the theory of natural evolution," Engels wrote, "all our concepts of organic life correspond only approximately to reality. Otherwise there would be no change. On the day when concepts and reality completely coincide in the organic world development comes to an end."[127] There could be no fixity in the perception of evolutionary reality.

It was in the chapter of *Dialectics of Nature* on "The Basic Laws of Motion" that the dialectical conception of the physics of matter and motion that Engels had first laid out in his May 30, 1873, letter to Marx came into play. The chapter strongly criticized Helmholtz's (and by implication Büchner's more popular and derivative) use of the concept of "force" to explain the basic physical laws of motion. The concept of "force," Engels argued, was treated as a reified concept for unspecified physical actions of attraction and repulsion and added nothing but mystification to the understanding of general scientific laws. Instead, Engels insisted on the use of the concept of "motion," or the newly emerging scientific notion of "energy," both of which were conceived in a dialectical way in terms of polarities of attraction and repulsion—basing his analysis in particular on Mayer's 1845 *Organic Motion in Its Connection with Metabolism* (1845).[128] So important was Engels's position in this regard that Haldane, writing a half-century later in the preface and notes to the English-language edition of *Dialectics of Nature* he edited, pointed repeatedly to the significance of Engels's critique of "force" and its replacement with "motion" and increasingly "energy," as evidence of his comprehension of the only sound, scientific-dialectical concepts.[129]

What this meant, Engels explained, was that "motion [energy] in the most general sense, conceived as the mode of existence, the inherent attribute, of matter, comprehends all changes and processes occurring in the universe from mere change of place right up to thinking." All of material reality was to be conceived as process. Physics was the science of that motion or energy inherent in matter in its most general physical form. "Only after these different branches of the knowledge of the forms of motion governing non-living nature had attained a degree of development could the explanation of the processes of motion representing the life process be successfully tackled." Too little was known, as of yet, of the physio-chemical aspects of organic motion, however, to provide a general account beyond the mechanics of physical motion.[130]

Nevertheless, it was indisputable, Engels insisted, that motion was the "mutual reaction" between bodies. Moreover, "Matter is unthinkable without motion. And if, in addition, matter confronts us as something given, equally uncreatable as indestructible, it follows that motion also is as uncreatable as indestructible." Dialectics demonstrated that any conception of the cessation of motion in the universe was "excluded from the outset." Furthermore, "Dialectics has proved from the results of our experience of nature so far that all polar opposites in general are determined by the mutual action of the two opposing poles on each other, that the separation and opposition of these poles exist only within their mutual connection and union, and conversely, that their union exists only in the separation and their mutual connection only in their opposition. This once established, there can be no question of a final canceling out of repulsion and attraction." The investigation of the world and the universe was an investigation of the forms of motion, which could be perceived in hierarchal terms as extending from atoms all the way to the "heavenly bodies," and from inorganic to organic forms. This was consistent with notions of emergence that were to be developed within science, and particularly ecology.[131]

In a passage that was intended for *Dialectics of Nature*, but was left out of the published version, Engels stated that the most general approach to the "system of the universe" takes the form of analyzing "its origin to its passing away, hence . . . a history in which at each stage different laws, i.e. different phenomenal forms of the same universal motion, predominate, and so nothing remains as absolutely universally valid except—motion."[132]

In this context, ecosocialist Ted Benton observed that Engels provided what "can be understood as a 'first approximation' to a concept of emergent qualities and laws, consequent upon a given level of organization. . . . The explanation of higher-level laws and properties in terms of lower ones is a feature of many of the epoch-making new developments in science."[133] For Engels, such hierarchies in integrative levels or emergent realities, were a product of historical development, including nature's own evolution over time. "The introduction into his [Engels's] characterization of the historical process of the notion of levels of complexity," Benton stressed, "also suggests a historicization of the problem of 'emergence.'...Historicity in nature [the essence of the ecological worldview] is ... the emergence, in temporal succession, of new levels of complexity in forms of motion."[134] Similarly, Z. A. Jordan, though often critical of Engels, explained that it "cannot be denied that the central idea of emergent evolution is to be found in *Anti-Dühring* and *Dialectics of Nature*. ... Engels's doctrine of emergent evolution is part of his dialectical conception of nature."[135]

ECOLOGY IS THE PROOF OF DIALECTICS

If the *Dialectics of Nature* was Engels's most ambitious attempt to address the dialectics of nature and society, raising all sorts of ecological issues, it was nonetheless, as we have seen, an unfinished work. Not only were most of the drafted chapters unfinished, with the key chapter on "Dialectics" only just begun, but the general outline that Engels drew up for the book indicates that five of the six concluding chapters (the final chapter, "The Part Played by Labour in the Transition from the Ape to Man," being the exception), in which he had intended to address such questions as the limits of scientific knowledge and the rise of the Darwinian theory, were never even drafted.

Nevertheless, it is evident from Engels's plans for the later and greater part of the book that he intended to enter into two overlapping debates dominating German philosophical and scientific controversy in the late 1870s: (1) the role of Darwinism in Germany, and particularly the emergence of social Darwinism in opposition to socialism; and (2) what was known as the *Ignorabimus* (We will be ignorant) controversy, associated with the rise of neo-Kantianism, and focusing on the inherent limits of scientific knowledge. The chief figures in the Darwinism and socialism controversy were German naturalist Virchow, famous for his theory of cellular pathology; German zoologist Schmidt, often seen as the earliest proponent of social Darwinism; and Haeckel, Germany's leading evolutionary theorist and proponent of Darwinism.[136] The principal protagonists in the closely related *Ignorabimus* controversy were German physiologist Du Bois-Reymond, Büchner, Lange, Swiss botanist Nägeli, and Virchow. Both controversies arose at the time that Engels was in the process of writing *Anti-Dühring*, and in both cases his analysis there helps us understand how he would have responded to these debates, as well as the development of his overall conception of nature and history. It is therefore crucial to turn to that work.

Engels began writing *Anti-Dühring* (the full title of which was *Herr Dühring's Revolution in Science*) in May 1876, after considerable hesitation.[137] At the time he was deeply engrossed in his research and writing of *Dialectics of Nature*, and he did not welcome the interruption. Nor did he see the work of Eugen Dühring, which at the time had considerable influence, as worthy of a full-scale critique. It soon became apparent, however, that many of the younger German Social Democrats with whom Marx and Engels were associated, including August Bebel and Eduard Bernstein, and even to a certain extent Liebknecht, were being taken in by Dühring, who declared himself a socialist in 1875. At that time the two rival factions within German Social Democracy—the "Eisenachers" (those closest to Marx and Engels) and the General German Workers Union, or the "Lassalleans"—had come together in their 1875 conference in Gotha, forging a common program. This resulted in what Marx and Engels considered serious mistakes associated with concessions made by the "Eisenachers" to the "Lassalleans." It was this that led to Marx writing *Critique of the Gotha Programme* (circulated privately at the time and only published years later by the German Social Democratic Party at the urging of Engels).[138]

It was in this context that Dühring threatened the still fragile unity of the factions by, in Engels's words, openly proceeding "to form around himself a sect, the nucleus of a separate party."[139] Dühring was a lecturer at the University of Berlin with an eclectic mixture of positivist, materialist, and idealist (neo-Kantian) views, whose criticisms of the cultural hegemony and seeming defense of the oppressed was attracting a strong following among German workers.[140]

Dühring's published work was peppered by vituperative rhetoric against Hegel, Marx, and Darwin, among others. Dühring referred to the "Hegel pestilence," and the "crudities" of the Hegelian method. Marx's analysis was said to full of "barren conceptions," "undignified affectation of language," "anglicised vanity," and "deformity of thought and style," as well as characterized by "snotty" and "vile mannerisms . . . buffoonery . . . philosophical and scientific backwardness." In general, Marx was accused by Dühring of having a "narrowness of conception" and an "impotence of the faculties of concentration and systematisation." Marx's critique of the individual capitalist, considered as a personification of capital, was, according to Dühring, full of "venomous hatred." Likewise, what was "specific to Darwinism," distinguishing Darwin's work from that of his Lamarckian forerunners, in Dühring's terms, was simply that it constituted "a piece of brutality directed against humanity." Dühring was also to pen three of the most vicious anti-Semitic tracts of the nineteenth century. "Along with Heinrich von Treitschke," Frederick Beiser writes, "Dühring has the dubious distinction of being a founder of the anti-Semitic movement in the late nineteenth century."[141]

Nevertheless, Dühring's work had all the pretensions of constituting a complete "world schematics" of thought in all of its areas.[142] Its attraction to socialists lay in its apparently comprehensive worldview, while Marx and Engels's work in comparison seemed to be lacking in philosophical and general-scientific perspective. Most of Marx's more philosophical works, evolving out of the critique of Hegelianism, including Marx and Engels's *German Ideology*, had never been published, giving the impression, even among some of their followers, that their work was almost exclusively political-economic. Even on political-economic grounds Dühring challenged their perspective, rejecting Marx's value theory, calling it a "hazy conception," though also drawing on it and presenting it as his own.[143]

Marx and Engels reluctantly concluded that there was simply no alternative to a full-scale critique of Dühring's system, "criticising Dühring without any compunction," as Marx insisted in his letter to Engels of May 25, 1876.[144] Given Marx's occupation with *Capital* and their general division of labor, the necessary critique was to be carried out by Engels alone, but with Marx's support. Dühring's extensive attacks on Marx had centered on the latter's dialectics and use of Hegelian concepts, and hence Engels was compelled to respond to Dühring point by point.

Marx was deeply involved in the nature of Engels's response, including the chapters on dialectics where Marx's own work was directly concerned. Engels read the entire draft manuscript of *Anti-Dühring* to Marx, no doubt incorporating some of Marx's observations into the final version. Marx himself contributed the chapter "From the Critical History," the longest chapter in the book, addressing Dühring's view of the evolution of economic thought. In addition, Marx provided notes on the Greek atomists, on which it appears Engels relied in *Anti-Dühring* (these excerpt notes in Marx's handwriting were later published as part of the notes on the history of science attached to Engels's *Dialectics of Nature*).[145] Marx's brief Introduction to the French edition of *Socialism: Utopian and Scientific* (the contents of which were taken from *Anti-Dühring*) emphasized the "great success" of *Anti-Dühring* and referred to the part excerpted from the "theoretical section of the book" as "an *introduction to scientific socialism*."[146]

In *Herr Eugen Dühring's Revolution in Science*, or *Anti-Dühring*, Engels was replying specifically to three works by the prolific Dühring that had appeared in the 1870s: *Critical History of Political Economy and Socialism* (1871), *Course of Philosophy* (1875), and *Course of Political and Social Economy* (1876). Since much of Dühring's writing here criticized Hegel, Marx, and Engels, as well as the utopian socialists, Robert Owen, Charles Fourier, and Saint-Simon—and thus sought to redefine the entire intellectual basis of socialism, as well as its connection to philosophy and science—Engels constructed *Anti-Dühring* as a kind of *anti-critique*, a term that Marx and Engels had employed in *The German Ideology*.[147]

Engels specifically denied the intention of creating an all-encompassing system of thought pertaining to all areas of knowledge. Nevertheless, in responding to Dühring's reflections on "all things under the sun," he was compelled to enter into areas in which he was, as he said, only a "semi-initiate" and in which he had no particular expertise, as well as other areas where he had much more comprehensive knowledge, and even expertise. In each case he tried to draw on principles of general dialectical analysis, as well as recognizing the need to consider the specific results of each area of knowledge. It was necessary at all times to isolate and analyze the concrete details—the task of the natural sciences and historical studies—as a means to understanding the specific mediations that constituted the actual whole, which otherwise would succumb to mere idealization.

The result of Engels's attempt to counter Dühring's all-encompassing "world schematism" was thus the development, if only provisionally, of a broad historical materialist approach to a wide array of areas, applying a dialectical-realist standpoint, not just in regard to political economy, history, and the development of socialism, but also in relation to the philosophy of science and naturalistic dialectics. As Engels put it, "My negative criticism became positive; the polemic was transformed into a more or less connected exposition of the dialectical method and of the communist world outlook championed by Marx and myself—an exposition covering a fairly comprehensive range of subjects."[148] What emerged was a complex, holistic, and broadly ecological point of view.

In addition to a Preface and Introduction, *Anti-Dühring* was divided into three parts: Philosophy, Political Economy, and Socialism. In Part One, which focused in particular on the philosophy of nature and science, Engels developed his broad, ecological dialectic, to the degree that natural science and philosophy allowed at the time. "Nature," he argued, "is the proof of dialectics."[149] In other words, it is nature that teaches us to comprehend things (and the mind itself can be considered a part of nature) "in their essential connection, concatenation, motion, origin, and ending." Today we would say, elaborating on Engels's argument, that *ecology is the proof of dialectics*.

Dialectical reason demands that we think about the world of nature as including both nature as external to human action and the human place *within* nature. There is no contradiction here, since to say that something is a mere part of a whole means that there are other parts that are external to it. As Marx wrote, "*Man* is directly a *natural being*. . . . That is to say, the *objects* of his drives exist outside him as *objects* independent of him. . . . To say that man is a *corporeal*, living, real, sensuous, objective being with natural powers means that he has *real, sensuous* objects as the object of his being."[150] Conversely, to speak of internal relations in the dialectical sense is to point to the integral and interdependent *relations* between the various *relata*. Such a view does not logically deny difference or reduce all opposition to simple identity.

Society or the human historical realm can be viewed as an emergent form within nature, with its own laws, irreducible to the natural world (or what Henri Lefebvre usefully called *physis*).[151] Reason, as opposed to mere understanding, Engels suggested, is essentially dialectical, a product of the complexity of natural relations themselves. It thus stands opposed to the narrow, motionless thought, caught in "irreconcilable antitheses," which he characterized as "metaphysics" in the Hegelian sense (encompassing rationalistic philosophy, mechanistic science, and positivism), and which is unable to perceive the fluidity of natural relations, and indeed of thought itself.[152] The complex, ever-changing character of material existence is most immediately apparent in life itself. "Every organic being," Engels wrote, "is every moment the same and not the same; every moment it assimilates matter supplied from without, and gets rid of other matter; every moment some cells of its body die and others build themselves anew; in a longer or a shorter time the matter of its body is completely renewed, and is replaced by other atoms of matter, so that every organic being is always itself, and yet something other than itself." Every organic being, in other words, participates at each and every moment in what Marx called "the universal metabolism of nature" and what Engels called the "metabolism" that "in the long run occurs everywhere," affecting both inorganic and organic existence. All life is in "*continual metabolic interchange with the natural environment*" that surrounds it.[153]

In the two chapters on "Dialectics: Quantity and Quality" and "Dialectics. Negation of the Negation" in *Anti-Dühring*, Engels came to Marx's defense, countering Dühring's harsh criticisms of the use of dialectical laws in *Capital*.[154] Yet Engels's distinct dialectical approach to nature/ecology is most evident not in his defense of Marx, but rather in his defense of Darwin's evolutionary theory against Dühring's attacks. Moreover, it is this critical defense of Darwin, when supplemented by notes for *Dialectics of Nature*, that allows us to understand the basis of Engels's response to the rise of the debate over socialism and Darwinism, and particularly social Darwinism, which was then arising in Germany.

Engels's best-known statement in *Anti-Dühring* (and also *Socialism: Utopian and Scientific*) was, as we have noted, that "nature is the proof of dialectics, and it must be said for modern science that it has furnished this proof with very rich materials increasing daily." "In this connection," Engels wrote, "Darwin must be named before all others. He dealt the metaphysical conception of nature the heaviest blow by his proof that all organic beings, plants, animals, and man himself, are the products of a process of evolution going on through millions of years." Darwin thus implicitly built his evolutionary analysis on a dialectical view, recognizing "innumerable actions and reactions . . . of progressive and retrogressive changes." Nevertheless, Darwin, Engels contended, remained an exception, even among Darwinists: "The naturalists who have learned to think dialectically are few and far between, and this conflict of the results of discovery with preconceived modes of thinking explains the endless confusion now reigning in theoretical natural science, the despair of teachers as well as learners, of authors and readers alike."[155]

Although he would hardly have characterized Dühring as a naturalist, Engels contended that Dühring misunderstood both Darwin and natural history. Dühring criticized Darwin for (1) taking his ideas from Malthus; (2) adopting the naïve view of a breeder; (3) filling his work with a kind of "semi-poetry" about nature; (4) producing an analysis that offered nothing beyond Lamarck (and Malthus) but an emphasis on "brutality" in nature; (5) failing to show the sources of the variability (innate variation) which is the basis of his theory; and (6) not solving the problem of the origins of life and specifically human life.[156] Engels strongly defended Darwin in all of these respects, showing in the process his deep understanding of Darwin's theory of evolution. He demonstrated that Dühring contradicted himself innumerable times, taking on Darwin's theory at one point, relying implicitly on a Creator at another.

Although Darwin noted the importance of Malthus's overpopulation theory for his notion of the struggle for existence as well as the general impact of Malthus on his ideas, and although both Marx and Engels had themselves criticized the intrusion here of bourgeois notions of competition into Darwin's theory, Engels insisted that Darwin's praise for Malthus did not go so far as to contend that Malthus was the source of his ideas. Darwin would "not dream," Engels wrote, of saying that the "*origin*" of the theory of natural selection by innate variation is to be found in Malthus. Nor were "Malthusian spectacles" necessary to (or particularly useful) in arriving at such an analysis. In point of fact, Darwin had become deeply engaged in the analysis of natural variation within and between species and its causes in the context of his voyage on the *Beagle*. Upon returning home, he had studied animal breeding in England, the country which had developed it to the highest industrial art, as a means of further inquiry into the problems of variation and inheritance and how artificial selection might throw light on natural selection. The arduous intellectual path by which Darwin arrived at his conclusions, sifting through an immense amount of data, ordering it, and coming to theoretical conclusions, was evident in the totality of his work and could not be dismissed as the product mainly of Malthus's ideas or of animal breeding.[157]

Similarly, the dismissal of Darwin as an author of semi-poetry, Engels contended, was simply a refusal to understand the nature of such scientific discoveries or the elegance with which they were presented in Darwin's "epoch-making work." The notion that Darwin had taken his ideas from Lamarck was evidence of Dühring's absolute failure to understand Darwin's theory. Lamarck's work had been important but had developed at a time before either embryology or paleontology had emerged as systematic fields, and thus lacked the preconditions of Darwin's own evolutionary theory. Lamarck thus relied simply on the inheritance of acquired characteristics.[158]

For Engels, Dühring's charge that what Darwin had provided (beyond Lamarck and in line with Malthus) was merely a notion of "brutality," in the form of the struggle for existence, demonstrated a complete failure on his part to comprehend the complex, dialectical (and ecological) character of Darwin's evolutionary theory. Rather, Dühring saw things in the simplistic terms of a crude "bourgeois Darwinian," a view that Engels distinguished from Darwin's own theory, and was synonymous with what was later to be called "social Darwinism."[159] Here Darwin's dialectical conception of evolution was reduced to a mechanical, animal-like competition, leaving out the world of plants altogether, as well as the relation to nature as a whole, inorganic as well as organic. In Dühring's analysis, according to Engels, the idea of "the struggle for existence"

> is arraigned again and again. It is obvious, according to him, that there can be no talk of a struggle for existence among unconscious plants and good natured-plant eaters: "In the precise and definite sense the struggle for existence is found in the realm of brutality to the extent that animals live on prey and its devourment."
>
> And after he has reduced the idea of the struggle for existence to these narrow limits he can give full vent to his indignation at the brutality of this idea, which he himself has restricted to brutality. . . . [Yet] it is . . . not Darwin who "sought the laws and understanding of all nature's actions in the kingdom of the brutes."
>
> Darwin had in fact expressly included the whole of organic nature in in the struggle [for existence]. . . . That the *fact* exists also among plants can be demonstrated to him by every meadow, every cornfield, every wood; and the question at issue is not what it is to be called, whether "struggle for existence" or "lack of conditions of life and mechanical effects," but how far this fact influences the preservation or variation of species.[160]

Dühring, in his gross, uninformed distortions of Darwin, according to Engels, not only criticized Darwin moralistically for the "brutality" of his theory, but also, in a contradictory way, gave support to bourgeois Darwinian (or social Darwinist) notions of the struggle for existence as "the survival of the fittest," and the merging of this with Malthusian notions of society—to which Darwin in his weaker moments gave some limited credence but which had nothing to do with his science.

Dühring's criticism of Darwin for not discerning the source of natural variation—genetics as a science did not yet exist, and Mendel's work, although published in 1866, was unknown—was dismissed by Engels on the grounds that it was precisely Darwin who had given the impetus to such an investigation, which would eventually bear fruit. Darwin, moreover, demonstrated the dialectical nature of his thinking by basing his analysis on the maximum of chance, connecting this to necessity, in a manner analogous to Hegel's dialectic of chance and necessity.[161] In Darwin's evolutionary theory, as Haeckel had shown, innate variation constituted evolutionary potential; preservation of such variations by means of the struggle for existence meant the realization of a part of this potential.

Likewise, the fact that Darwin did not explain the origins of life—which must have occurred, Engels argued, by some kind of chemical action, though science had not yet solved this problem—only served to underscore that Darwin had done the most to extend evolutionary views to all of organic existence, or the ecological world, including the evolution of human beings themselves. To fault Darwin for not having solved all the mysteries of organic existence was sheer nonsense, a failure to understand the way science itself evolved.

In one of his most trenchant points, Engels argued that there were laws of population that widely differed for all "the organisms of nature," pointing to the need for inquiries in this area, a subject that was later termed population ecology. This too was an area to which Darwin had given impetus.[162]

Engels was equally critical of Dühring's attempt to define life as metabolism (*Stoffwechsel*), viewed simply as the exchange of matter, since such exchange of matter was common to both the inorganic and organic world, as explained by modern chemistry. A meaningful, fixed, singular definition of life, Engels argued, was not then possible and had generated untold problems for naturalists making the attempt. Moreover, such a definition of life would have to consider the entire range of living species, the development of cells, including single cell-organisms, and the elements making up cells, all of which had to be seen in evolutionary (and totalistic or ecological) terms.[163]

SOCIAL DARWINISM AND NEO-KANTIANISM

While Engels was writing *Anti-Dühring* the great controversy over Darwinism and socialism burst out in Germany, leading to the first explicit formulations of what we now know as social Darwinism. In September 1877, Virchow gave a speech at the 50th Congress of the German Association of Naturalists and Physicians on *The Freedom of Science in the Modern State* in which he attacked the Darwinian theory of evolution and argued against the teaching of it in the schools on the grounds that it was only an unfounded hypothesis and that it opened the way to socialism and would generate insurrections such as the Paris Commune. "Imagine, then," he exclaimed, "the shape which the evolution theory assumes at the present day in the brain of the Socialist! . . . Notice that Socialism has already established a sympathetic relation with it."[164]

Virchow's remarks touched off a debate on socialism and Darwinism, giving rise to reactionary social Darwinist notions. Haeckel, Virchow's former student and the leading Darwinian evolutionist in Germany, who was the subject of many of Virchow's barbs, wrote his *Freedom in Science and Teaching* in response. In a preface to the English edition, Huxley claimed that the attempt on Virchow's part to claim that Darwinism aided the socialist cause was simply "an attempt to frighten sober people."[165]

Haeckel himself took a much stronger stance than Huxley, arguing that socialism and the doctrine of descent were like "fire and water." Supporting similar criticisms of Virchow by Schmidt, Haeckel pronounced that "socialist ideas" were "impracticable" since based on the premise of greater equality. "For the theory of descent," he observed,

> proclaims more clearly than any other scientific theory, that the equality of individuals that socialism strives after is an impossibility, that it stands, in fact, in irreconcilable contradiction to the inevitable inequality of individuals which actually and everywhere subsists. Socialism demands equal rights, equal duties, equal possessions, equal enjoyments for every citizen alike; the theory of descent proves, in exact opposition to this, that the realization of this demand is a pure impossibility. . . . The more highly political life is organized, the more prominent is the great principle of the division of labour. . . . The evolution hypothesis in general [is] the best antidote to the fathomless absurdity of extravagant socialist leveling. . . .
>
> Darwinism, I say, is anything rather than socialist! If this English hypothesis is to be compared to any definite political tendency . . . that tendency can only be aristocratic, certainly not democratic, least of all socialist. The theory of selection teaches that in human life, as in animal and plant life everywhere, and at all times, only a small and chosen minority can exist and flourish while the enormous majority starve and perish more or less prematurely. . . . The cruel and merciless struggle for existence which rages throughout all living nature, and in the course of nature *must* rage, this unceasing and inexorable competition of all living creatures is an incontestable fact; only the picked minority of the qualified "fittest" is in a position to resist it successfully, while the great majority of the competitors must perish miserably . . . [according to the law of] "the survival of the fittest" . . . "the victory of the best."[166]

However, it was Schmidt's earlier claim, in response to Virchow, that Darwinism generated a social perspective diametrically opposed to socialism, which was to be the first systematic invocation of social Darwinism. In the July 18, 1878, issue of the British journal *Nature*, Engels saw a notice that Schmidt intended to read a paper on "On the Relation of Darwinism to Social Democracy" at the 51st Congress of the German Association of Naturalists and Physicians to be held in Kassel that year.[167] Engels wrote to Schmidt on July 19, indicating he planned eventually to subject Schmidt's views, of which he already had an inkling, to a healthy critique and sent Schmidt a copy of *Anti-Dühring*, then fresh off the press, pointing to the passages on Darwin. In a reply to Engels soon after, Schmidt promised to send his report to the German Congress of Naturalists and Physicians to Engels. In a letter to Pyotr Lavrov in Russia in August 1878, Engels noted that "the German Darwinians," in response to Virchow's criticism of Darwinism as socialism, had "come out unequivocally against socialism." Mentioning Haeckel and Schmidt, he indicated, "I shall take it upon myself to reply to these gentlemen."[168]

Schmidt's presentation to the Congress of German Naturalists and Physicians, which began with a reply to Virchow, was published in November 1878 in *Deutsche Rundschau* (and also as a pamphlet under the title of "Darwinismus and Socialdemocratie"). It is here that Schmidt offered what was the first systematic statement of social Darwinist ideas, though his ideas paralleled those of Haeckel developed at about the same time.[169] Most of Schmidt's fire in promoting social Darwinism, significantly, was directed explicitly against Marx and Engels.

Schmidt explored what he called "the actual relations of sociology to Darwinism," or what might be better referred to as the social implications of Darwinism, offering this as the scientific basis for a critique of Marxian social democracy, focusing particularly on Marx's *Capital* and even more on Engels's *Anti-Dühring*.[170] Schmidt told the assembled German scientists that Engels had been wrong in referring to (ecological) laws of population pertaining to each species. Instead Schmidt argued on positivistic grounds that one could not properly talk of laws in cases such as that of differing species, which were the result of various contingent events, and thus went against any inference of fixed laws. This did not, however, prevent Schmidt from claiming that there was one single Darwinian proposition or law applicable to all species, including humans: the "struggle against the environment."[171]

It was the law of the stronger, or "the question . . . of might," according to Schmidt, that refuted the idea of socialism: "The Socialist's 'aspiration toward perfection' is associated with his ideal of the equality of mankind. Now, *this illusion Darwinism utterly demolishes*. The very principle of development negatives the principle of equality. So far does Darwinism go in denying equality, that even where in idea we should have equality, Darwinism pronounces its realization an impossibility. *Darwinism is the scientific establishment of inequality*."[172]

The more advanced socialists like Engels, Schmidt argued, recognize that all individual inequalities will not be eliminated with class, but nevertheless falsely contend that socialism could promote social equality. Darwinism, he contended, refuted this as well. Inequality is an inescapable reality that "man inherits from his brute origin." The fundamental principle of Darwinism is competition, that is, the struggle for existence. Denying altogether any difference between animal labor and the social labor of humanity in this respect, Schmidt offered as a trenchant criticism of equality of labor under socialism the (questionable) observation that "most animals labour [simply] for themselves."[173]

In a passage referring to class mobility, Schmidt declared on pseudo-scientific social Darwinist grounds that since "the organism that makes the struggle adapts itself to the environment," human society was therefore the direct product of natural history. "The doctrine of development teaches the brute origin of man," and for Schmidt this represented not simply the origin but the inalterable law of human existence.[174]

As Schmidt further contended in 1873 in *The Doctrine of Descent and Darwinism*, "The vehemence of the struggle" in the kingdom of the brutes "rises with the closeness of the kindred," producing "a rapid war of extermination" between closely related species, and this warfare extends to different species that live in the same vicinity. The same clearly applied to the various human races, where the stronger would annihilate the weaker. This inevitable "destruction in the struggle for existence" of the weaker races (which Schmidt said were also different "human species") was a natural "consequence of their retardation."[175] On issues of gender Schmidt was equally blunt, contending that, women, due to their "abnormal brain structure," must always remain "a subordinate part" of humanity, along with the stratification of races, and human population as a whole.[176]

We know from Engels's letters to Schmidt and Lavrov that he intended to reply to Schmidt's social Darwinist attack on Marx and himself. Engels made it clear, however, that he intended to do so in his own time and as part of his larger work. Such a response to Schmidt and Haeckel was meant to close *Dialectics of Nature*, according to the "Outline of the General Plan" of that work.[177] As late as November 1882, in a letter to Karl Kautsky, who was requesting an article on Darwinism, Engels indicated that he was not prepared to write the requested article, as he intended to delve more deeply into Darwin's work and the development of subsequent Darwinian notions, as part of his work on *Dialectics of Nature*, and that it would have to await the point at which he reached that stage in his work. Marx, however, died only four months after this letter was written, and Engels never went forward with his research in this area, since his efforts shifted to editing volumes 2 and 3 of Marx's *Capital*.[178]

Still, based on *Anti-Dühring* and the notes to *Dialectics of Nature*, we can get some idea of the larger socio-ecological and dialectical approach that Engels was developing in his unfinished work. This involved five areas of research: (1)

the relation of Darwin's theory to Hegel's dialectic of chance (contingency) and necessity; (2) a critique of the idea of the double transference of Hobbesian/Malthusian ideas to the biological realm and then back to the social realm;[179] (3) an examination of the notion of the survival of the fittest (and its confusion with Darwin's struggle for existence); (4) an emphasis on cooperation as the counterpart of competition in natural history; and (5) a stress on how the history of the division of labor, property, and class represents an emergent social reality that cannot be reduced to natural evolution. Together, these various points stressed in Engels's notes make it clear that, in line with his "General Plan," he was concerned with reemphasizing the dialectical nature of Darwin's ideas, and more important, the critique of "bourgeois Darwinian" or social Darwinist notions. In his notes, Engels becomes increasingly critical of "Darwinists" (such as Haeckel) and incipient social Darwinists (such as Schmidt), but seldom has anything but praise for Darwin himself.[180]

Indeed, Engels indicated that the "Darwinian theory" was "to be demonstrated as the practical proof of Hegel's account of the inner connection between necessity and chance."[181] In this respect, Darwin's reliance on the maximum chance or contingency in order to establish evolutionary necessity was crucial to his discovery. Here he opposed the non-dialectical character of eighteenth-century French materialism that had "tried to dispose of chance by denying it altogether." Hegel, on the contrary, indicated in his *Logic* that "necessity determines itself as chance." For Engels, in setting "out from the widest existing basis of chance," Darwin emphasized the "infinite, accidental differences between individuals within a single species," differences that then become the cause of evolution, in the context of the complex, mutually interdependent interactions of organisms and their environments.

It was Darwin's dialectical brilliance in his theory of natural selection, Engels suggested, that was missing in subsequent Darwinism, which becomes once again metaphysical, mechanistic, and monistic—the last two terms being used interchangeably by Haeckel in defining his approach. The result was a set of extremely reductive views, in which Darwin was turned into Hobbes (the war of all against all), on the one hand, and into Malthus (whose population-food argument was designed to justify class distinctions) on the other.[182] In the name of natural science, a crude Hobbesian-Malthusian view was thus smuggled into society (a kind of double "transference" or "re-extrapolation").[183] "Bourgeois Darwinians" like Schmidt and Haeckel were able to reduce society to "survival of the fittest" on supposedly Darwinian grounds.

Engels's singling out of "bourgeois Darwinism," or what is now called "social Darwinism," is important. As Alfred Kelly has noted, "No one in the late nineteenth century called himself a Social Darwinist."[184] Yet, they already existed, and the first recognizable statements of the creed, in the work of Schmidt and

Haeckel, were explicitly directed against German Social Democracy, particularly Marx and Engels.

In this, Darwin himself had no direct part. At most he had, by accepting the Spencerian term "survival of the fittest" and emphasizing the importance of Malthus's work, inadvertently encouraged such ideas. "Darwin's mistake," going against his own ideas, Engels observed, was in allowing the "lumping together" of "natural selection" with "survival of the fittest" as categories, though they were clearly different. This opened the way to social Darwinism. Darwin's natural selection, Engels underscored, could not be seen as necessarily favoring the strongest over the weakest in adaptation, even in relation to overpopulation pressures. In a case where the force behind selection was changing environmental conditions, "adaptation as a whole can mean regress just as well as progress (for instance adaptation to parasitic life is *always* regress)." Moreover, "each advance in organic evolution is at the same time a regression, fixing *one-sided* evolution and excluding the possibility of evolution in many other directions. This [is] a basic law."[185] Here Engels adopted a view similar to that of E. Ray Lankester's *Degeneration*.[186] In Darwin's case, such a complex, non-linear view of evolution that recognized the possibility of regress as well as progress was clearly evident, though he occasionally opened the way to more reductive views, which encouraged crude, mechanistic forms of "Darwinism."

Equally significant, Engels observed, was a tendency in cruder versions of Darwinian theory to emphasize competition in a narrow sense (survival of the fittest) without recognizing that evolutionary theory was just as compatible with cooperation. Animals do not simply adapt; they actively change their environments. Ironically, as Engels stressed on more than one occasion, those mechanistic materialists, such as Vogt, Büchner, and Moleschott, who talked about nothing but the struggle for existence, which they interpreted in the most reductive fashion possible, had formerly written of cooperation and the interconnection of nature. Liebig's analysis, in particular, with its emphasis on metabolism and the interconnection of all inorganic and organic life, represented an element of a wider dialectical view that got lost when Darwinian evolution was reduced to crude, one-sided Hobbesian/Malthusian terms, rather than reflecting a complex, open system.[187]

Further, social-historical systems could not be viewed as just different forms of natural-historical systems since they entailed the emergence of modes and relations of production, class, the state, etc., which mediated between human beings and nature and generated new integrative levels and laws. Social Darwinism, which reductionistically denied this, whether in Dühring, Haeckel, Schmidt, or Büchner, was thus a regression and reactionary in its implications. Engels was especially critical of those supposed socialists, like the Italian theorist Enrico Ferri (later to become a supporter of Fascism and Mussolini), who took on a pseudo-Darwinian approach, embodying aspects of social Darwinism. For Engels, Ferri's *Darwin, Spencer, Marx* was to be dismissed as "an atrocious hotchpotch of insipid rubbish."[188]

Engels thus saw Darwin's "epoch-making" work as the key to an understanding not only of natural evolution, but also a more complex view of the interconnections between nature and society.[189] Nature in Darwin was the proof of dialectics, as society was in Marx. Indeed, ecology, we would now say, elaborating on Engels's famous phrase was the proof of dialectics. The materialist conception of history and nature could be unified within a wider dialectical vision of a spiral form of development, one of regress as well as progress. Such an outlook was fully cognizant of the dangers in the attempted domination of nature, as well as the domination of humanity.

Darwinism for some, of course, became the basis for a new imperialist view. Vogt, Büchner, Haeckel, Dühring, Schmidt, and Ferri were all to be known, particularly in relation to their later works, for their promotion of monist views, merging racist and social Darwinist ideologies, a development that would have surprised Engels least of all. Thus, Schmidt opined: "Inferior human races exist—we may also call them human species—which are related to others, as are lower animals to higher. . . . If we contemplate the ethnology and anthropology of savages, not from the standpoint of philanthropists and missionaries, but as cool and sober naturalists, destruction in the struggle for existence as a consequence of their retardation (itself regulated by the universal conditions of development), is the natural course of things." Büchner, meanwhile, asserted: "The white or Caucasian human species is ordained to take dominion of the earth, while the lowest human races, like Americans, Australians, Alfuren, Hottentots, and such others, are proceeding toward their destruction with huge steps."[190] Nothing could have been more opposed to Engels's or Marx's views with respect to human equality.

Just as crucial in highlighting the significance of Engels's claim that "nature is the proof of dialectics" was the *Ignorabimus* controversy associated with the rise in the 1860s and '70s of neo-Kantianism in Germany and its penetration into science. Neo-Kantianism was a response within liberal philosophy to the crude scientific materialism of thinkers like Büchner, Vogt, and Moleschott, and represented a different and more complex challenge to historical materialism. Neo-Kantians accepted a rigid mechanistic interpretation of science (within its own proper realm), but placed their emphasis on Kant's unknowable "thing-in-itself," and the reality of *a priori* knowledge, in order to emphasize the epistemological limits of knowledge. On this basis, neo-Kantianism sought to carve out a separate sphere of meaning and ethics, thereby leaving room for the reentry of religion. The earliest and most influential systematic treatise in the neo-Kantian tradition was Lange's 1866 *History of Materialism*. Lange, as Marx and Engels acutely observed in their correspondence, sided with Büchner, Vogt, and Moleschott in the absolute rejection of Hegelian speculative philosophy and in viewing nature in mechanistic terms, but he coupled this with a dualistic conception that divided off materialist science from philosophy. All attempts at general systems, in the manner of German idealist philosophy that sought to transcend the multiple dualisms of quantity and quality, nature and history, empiricism and *a priori* knowledge, materialism and religion, as well as chance and necessity, were to be rejected. Engels, in particular, saw this emerging neo-Kantianism in Germany as closely connected to the "agnosticism" of scientists like Huxley and Tyndall in Britain.[191]

The neo-Kantianism that emerged primarily in Germany in the last third of the nineteenth century sought to erect epistemology into a separate science dominating over philosophy as a whole, sharply curtailing all conceptions based on materialism/realism or a wider dialectical logic. As the great Soviet philosopher Evald Ilyenkov critically observed, the "special feature [introduced by neo-Kantian epistemology] was not at all, of course, the discovery of knowledge as the central philosophical problem, but the specific form in which it was posed, which boiled down" to the question of existence of definite boundaries to human knowledge based on "the eternal and immutable nature of man's psycho-physiological peculiarities through which all external influences were refracted (as through a prism)."[192] As he went on to explain, epistemology was distinguished as a special science in this broad neo-Kantian

> tradition only on the grounds of *a priori* acceptance of the thesis that human knowledge was not knowledge of the external world (i.e. existence outside consciousness) but was only a process of ordering, organisation, and systematisation of facts of "inner experience," i.e. ultimately of the psycho-physiological states of the human organism, absolutely dissimilar to the states and events of the external world.... "Epistemology" was thus ... counterposed to "ontology" (or "metaphysics'"), and not at all [conceived] as a discipline investigating the real course of human knowledge of the surrounding world; quite the contrary, it was born as a doctrine postulating that every form of knowledge without exception was not a form of knowledge of the surrounding world but only a specific schema of the organisation of the "subject of knowledge."[193]

Neo-Kantians thus sought to promote a strict epistemology establishing the boundaries of "the subject of knowledge," which could not extend to the Kantian thing-in-itself. Although natural science (usually viewed in mechanical terms) was frequently accorded its own distinct worldly realm in this conception, its actual knowledge claims were thrown into doubt. Scientific realism was thus often criticized as based on "metaphysical" propositions that were inherently "positivistic."[194] Moreover, neo-Kantianism was adamant in rejecting the possibility of a more complex dialectical conceptions linking natural-material existence and human knowledge, that is, "the possibility of naturalism."[195] The specific role given to epistemology under the influence of neo-Kantianism was to have enormous influence on the development of philosophy as a profession, extending into our time.

Engels was attentive to developments in neo-Kantian philosophy, focusing not just on Lange but also on related thinkers such as Du Bois-Reymond, Nägeli, and Virchow among the scientists, and figures such as Riehl, Cohen, and Paul Natorp among the philosophers. Neo-Kantianism in Germany frequently overlapped with the so-called "philosophy of realism" associated with positivists like Dühring, who relied on similar dualistic conceptions. Thus Riehl, who argued that "all quality . . . is alien to science as such," saw his work arising in important ways out of that of Dühring.[196]

Neo-Kantianism, however, represented a serious challenge to historical materialism in its rejection of dialectics and in its entrenched dualism. The difficulty lay in neo-Kantianism's *Ignorabimus* claims, which were meant to cordon off materialism. The neo-Kantian view turned fundamentally on Nägeli's argument on infinity, which conflicted with a dialectical approach to the material world, and with an understanding of the earthly limits of humanity itself. For Engels, Nägeli's argument, like bourgeois ideology itself, represented a "bad infinity," in its reductive quantitative approach and its related metaphysical dualisms. As indicated in his plan for the later chapters of *Dialectics of Nature*, he clearly intended to challenge these perspectives from the standpoint of the dialectic of nature and society.[197]

The *Ignorabimus* controversy arose in 1872 with a speech by Du Bois-Reymond, then rector of Berlin University, and one of Germany's most prestigious physiologists. He claimed that although one could imagine an ideal Laplacian scientist who was able to extend quantitative knowledge to its furthest limits, scientific knowledge nonetheless was presented with two insurmountable, largely qualitative limits: (1) the actual development of consciousness (sensations, thought) out of the physiology and chemistry of the brain; and (2) the underlying nature of matter (Du Bois-Reymond dismissed atoms as a philosophical fantasy). Neither of these points were new, but given Du Bois-Reymond's prestige within the scientific establishment and the turn toward neo-Kantian dualism and skepticism, they created quite a stir. Büchner, as a representative of scientific materialism, sharply criticized Du Bois-Reymond's claims, arguing that neither of the two realms he singled out were beyond the potential progress of mechanistic science. In contrast, Lange as the founder figure in neo-Kantianism, came to Du Bois-Reymond's defense, emphasizing the inherent limits of knowledge.[198]

More important even than Du Bois-Reymond's address in the *Ignorabimus* controversy was that of Nägeli's speech to the German Congress of Natural Scientists and Physicians in Munich in 1876. Nägeli adopted the Humean empiricist position that knowledge is obtained from the senses but that the senses are limited, and, although empirically based knowledge can be extended through scientific inference, the capacity to know the universe decreases with time and space. In this respect, Du Bois-Reymond, he contended, had failed to consider the full limits of knowledge, which extended beyond the inability to comprehend the nature of the realms of matter and consciousness, to the inability to comprehend the infinite. For Nägeli, "We can know *only the finite*." Adopting a Humean view, Nägeli claimed that we cannot explain constant causal connections in nature since our observations lack universality. Space is infinitely divisible and infinitely extendable and thus beyond universal comprehension. Time too showed the same infinite divisibility and extension. Qualities in general defied our ability to grasp them since they were beyond quantitative measure. In fact, Nägeli reinforced Humean empiricism and skepticism, introducing into the neo-Kantian and positivist thrusts in German philosophy views that were in fact pre-Kantian (Humean).[199]

It was this argument of Nägeli's that, for Engels, most clearly demonstrated the growing failure to recognize the dialectical character of both reason and nature *as comprehended by self-conscious reason* and from a materialist perspective. Nägeli's error started with his contention that we cannot know the qualitative, since only quantitative knowledge is valid. Such views of the qualitative as somehow constituting an altogether separate reality, Engels insisted, were wrong for at least four reasons. First, every qualitative difference had "infinitely many quantitative gradations" that could therefore be measured quantitatively. Second, qualities do not only exist in themselves but only in relation to things. Although things with widely different qualities may seem very distinct, it is always possible to put other things with varying qualities in between and thus by classification show that things stretching from "meteorite to man" belong to "a series" and thus "to allocate to each its place in the interconnection of nature and thus to *know* them." Third, the correlation of our senses allows us to detect interconnected qualities. Fourth, organic chemistry demonstrates that what are sometimes considered to be absolute qualities are themselves the product of quantitative changes (or the lack of them), so that with certain molecular changes, entirely new qualities *emerge* (qualitative leaps). Nägeli's argument for absolutely distinct qualitative differences outside quantitative determinations, together with his notion that knowledge consisted simply in the quantitative, indicated his inability to think dialectically where both quantity and quality constitute necessary and interconnected aspects of knowledge.[200]

More important was Nägeli's contention that knowledge was simply the comprehension of the finite and that the infinite was by definition unknowable. It was here, in countering Nägeli (and also in contradicting Dühring who had advanced similar arguments), that Engels drew explicitly on Hegel's critique of "bad infinity," which was to be a key concept unifying his entire conception of the dialectics of nature and history, grounding it in an ecological worldview. In Hegel's philosophy, if the infinite is viewed as separate from the finite then it is limited by the finite, which would contradict the notion of the infinite, hence the finite must be viewed as a moment in the infinite. An infinite, moreover, that was seen as an infinite progress(ion) or extension, a mere 1 + 1 + 1, was a "bad infinity," intellectually self-defeating, and essentially meaningless. True infinity, for Hegel, was the universe as a whole turning back on itself, assuming a self-contained circular form. True infinity does not go on forwards or backwards forever. It is as infinite as the world and operates in cycles of life and death and negation of the negation. In the face of the bad infinity of the Enlightenment concept of progress where all boundaries were barriers to be surmounted by an endless progress, Hegel thus sought to resurrect on a higher plane the self-contained circular understanding of ancient Greek dialectics. If bad infinity was simply an abstract 1 + 1 + 1, true infinity carried the finite within itself and was thus filled with differentiated content, exhibiting real transformations.[201]

As Engels put it, "True infinity was already correctly put by Hegel as *filled* space and time." In this respect, nature was seen as historical, with content, and natural history differed from social history only in the sense that the latter was self-conscious. Here, bad infinity, or the notion of infinite progression, was necessary at a certain level for the development of thought, but offered only a partial, one-sided conception. This had to be sublated through a conception of true infinity, breaking away from such linear, merely add-on conceptions. The concept of true infinity pointed to "the infinite complexity of nature" and the "practically infinite diversity of phenomena and natural knowledge." It was on this conception, in our little corner of the universe, "more or less restricted to our little earth," that universal natural laws were devised.

Engels thus argued that true infinity was not endless repetition, nor a circle as in Hegel, but a kind of spiraling "development," in which both progression and regression had their part. Hegel was himself mistaken in arguing, as his idealist system demanded, that "development was excluded from the temporal history of nature." Rather, the more we learn about "*the eternal laws of nature*" referred to by (positivistic) science, the more we learn that they have "become transformed . . . into historical ones." Indeed, nothing "remains as absolutely universally valid except—motion." As Marx, quoting Lucretius (Epicurus), put it, the only immortal thing is mortality (death the immortal); change is all. But such true infinity has content, development is "filled space," that is, space with determinate content. We can know the universe, Marx and Engels suggested, because we are a moment within it and partake of its universality in our own finite existence.[202]

Engels's critique, inspired by Hegel, of the sterile bourgeois notion of progress, that is, bad infinity, was central to all of his writings on nature and science, and constituted the foundation of his overall ecological perspective. "According to Hegel," Engels wrote, "infinite progress is a barren waste." Rather than an "eternal repetition" or a linear notion of upward progress, as in the Enlightenment perspective, nature and history were characterized by "development, and advance or regression." Indeed, "the end of the earth's lifetime," Engels observed, "can already be foreseen. But then, the earth is not the whole universe."[203] Engels commended Fourier for having "introduced into historical science" the idea of "the ultimate destruction of the human race."[204]

The Introduction to *Dialectics of Nature* ends by pointing to the absolute destruction of terrestrial nature. There was no getting around the eventual demise of the earth (tied to the demise of the sun, at that time believed to be much closer):

> "All that comes into being deserves to perish" [Mephistopheles's words in Goethe's *Faust*, Act I, sc. 3]. Millions of years may elapse, hundreds of thousands of generations be born and die, but inexorably the time will come when the declining warmth of the sun will no longer suffice to melt the ice thrusting itself forward from the poles; when the human race, crowding more and more about the equator, will finally no longer find even there enough heat for life; when gradually even the last trace of organic life will vanish; and the earth, an extinct frozen globe like the moon, will circle in deepest darkness and in an ever narrower orbit about the equally extinct sun, and at last fall into it. Other planets will have preceded it, others will follow it; instead of the bright warm solar system with its harmonious arrangement of members, only a cold dead sphere will pursue its lonely path through universal space. And what will happen to our solar system will happen sooner or later to all the other systems of our island universe.[205]

Yet, materialist and dialectical logic teaches us that the same universal laws of the natural world that will, through their action, "exterminate on the earth its highest creation, the thinking mind" will "somewhere else and at another time again produce it."[206] In Engels's ecological view the universe was open and change was universal.

CHAPTER SEVEN

The Ecology of Human Labor and Social Reproduction

A thick fog has always obscured the origins of "The Part Played by Labour in the Transition from Ape to Man," Engels's most specifically ecological work. It was first drafted in May–June 1876 as the introductory portion of a planned work originally titled *The Three Basic Forms of Slavery* (later changed to *The Enslavement of the Worker*). The book was never completed beyond the introduction, which itself breaks off mid-sentence, and no plan of the work as a whole exists. Engels later gave the incomplete introduction its present title, "The Part Played by Labour in the Transition from Ape to Man," and incorporated it into the plan for the *Dialectics of Nature* as part of the concluding section of that work (Part 11), which was meant to address the interrelations between nature, society, and human evolution and the social Darwinism of Ernst Haeckel and Oscar Schmidt.[1] The "Part Played by Labour" was first published as a separate article in 1896 in *Die Neue Zeit*, shortly after Engels's death.[2]

All of this leaves a host of unanswered questions: How are we to understand the original context in which "The Part Played by Labour" was written? What was the likely intent of the larger work, *The Three Basic Forms of Slavery*, for which it was originally planned as the introduction? How was that work related to Engels's *Dialectics of Nature* which was then his main focus? What are we to make of the fact that Engels was writing "The Part Played by Labour" in May 1876 at the very time that he finally committed to putting aside his work on *The Dialectics of Nature* to write *Anti-Dühring*?[3] How was all of this related to Darwin's *The Descent of Man*, published in 1871, with a second edition in 1874? Finally, what did Engels mean by the "three basic forms of slavery" and how is this connected to his conception of human origins, human ecology, and the oppression of women? Answering these questions requires that we look at both "The Part Played by Labour" and at Engels's later 1884 work, *The Origin of the Family, Private Property, and the State* so we can grasp his wider anthropological and historical objectives.

What Engels meant by the title *The Three Basic Forms of Slavery* or servitude, constituting the overall context in which the "The Part Played by Labour" was written, is obvious from his wider writings. In *The Origin of the Family, Private Property, and the State* he wrote:

> With slavery, which attained its fullest development under civilization, came the first great split of society into an exploiting and an exploited class. This split has continued during the whole period of civilization. Slavery was the first form of exploitation, peculiar to the world of antiquity; it was followed by serfdom in the Middle Ages, and by wage labour in modern times. These are the three great forms of servitude, characteristic of the three great epochs of civilization; open, and latterly, disguised slavery, are its constant companions.[4]

Following Charles Fourier, Engels saw civilization, which he associated with the development of monogamy and private property, as based on the development of slavery and class society in general. The emergence of "slave labour as the prevailing form of production" in civilization following the development of economic surplus was correlated from the first, in his thought, with a definite "form of family," namely "monogamy, the supremacy of the man over the woman, and the individual family as the economic unit of society."[5]

From all of this it seems clear that Engels's original intention in *The Three Basic Forms of Slavery* was to address the emergence of human beings through labor, in a process of metabolic interaction with external nature, leading to the development via human ecology of human society. Originally communal forms and a more generalized equality predominated but with the growth of an economic surplus class society emerged, taking the form of three great eras of servitude/slavery: ancient slavery, serfdom, and wage slavery. Moreover, class bondage in history, including capitalism, had its origins and basis in the first, and most fundamental form of oppression: "monogamy, the supremacy of the man over the woman, and the individual family as the economic unit of society." Human history at every stage of the development of class society was characterized by widening contradictions associated with the domination of nature together with the domination of human beings, forcing, in the end, a revolutionary shift toward a planned, sustainable, collective, and egalitarian form of production. This was the overall argument, which no doubt would have pervaded *The Three Basic Forms of Slavery*, as foreshadowed by "The Part Played by Labour."[6]

Engels appears to have been seeking to provide a more coherent answer to the Darwinian theorizing then going on with respect to human evolution and its relation to the evolution of human society, especially with regard to its neglect of labor and its treatment of slavery.[7] As anthropologist Eleanor Leacock writes, Engels was concerned with providing a materialist alternative to the views propounded by Darwin's followers who were "so caught up in idealistic modes of thinking as not to perceive the centrality of labor—as expressed in tool-making in human evolution. Darwin himself was more concerned to prove man's kinship to the higher primates than to define basic differences, and to demonstrate this for human development in such things as their sociability, curiosity, and display of emotion."[8]

Darwin was particularly concerned in *The Descent of Man* with combatting the then prevalent polygeny or the notion of the separate origin of the human races, in which they were viewed in effect as different species, rather than races or sub-species. Polygeny was commonly used as a racial justification for slavery. But while strongly insisting on common descent, extending this to the human races, and while adamantly opposing slavery, Darwin nonetheless contended that contact between different races would necessarily lead the "civilised races" to "exterminate" the "savage races," resulting in the "extinction"—partial or complete—of the latter, a view that seemed to justify as inevitable the extirpation of human populations then going on in the era of European conquest and colonization.[9]

In his rejection of polygeny and slavery, Darwin sought to account for human races based on sexual selection, which was to constitute a core argument of *The Descent of Man*. The human races were the product of different conceptions of beauty manifesting themselves in peoples in different geographical areas. This argument on race, however, carried with it a conception of sexual inequality characteristic of Victorian society. The male part of the species, Darwin argued, had inherited the greater "energy and perseverance" required by the incessant competition among males for the most attractive women. Turning to barnyard analogies, such as the stallion and the mare, he argued that males in their competition for females had inherited greater intelligence as well.[10]

Engels, as a dedicated materialist and egalitarian, sought to counter all such views of inherent human inequality with a materialist anthropological approach emphasizing labor as the basis of human self-creation, and slavery/servitude as a product of the development of class society. Insisting on the innate equality of women, he accounted for male domination in social rather than biological terms. Hence, *The Origin of the Family* was to focus on the historical development of patriarchal forms and oppression of women. Attempts to explain human evolution by purely biological factors and its relation to the development of moral faculties, left out, he argued, what was most important, the active role of human beings in their self-creation through the transformation of nature and their relation to nature by means of labor. This, however, raised issues of human ecology. As Leacock observed, "The Part Played by Labour" was directed at an issue "most pertinent today: the complete interdependence of human social relations and human relations to nature." In this wider human-ecological perspective, a purely biological approach that excluded the social was undialectical and wrong. Nor could a social analysis idealistically exclude human corporeal existence.[11]

What is clear is that (1) for Engels the dialectics of nature argument culminated in a complex conception of the *dialectics of nature and society*;[12] and (2) there is a continuity between Engels's "The Part Played by Labour in the Transition from Ape to Man" and his anthropological arguments almost a decade later in *The Origin of the Family, Private Property and the State.*

AN ECOLOGICAL ANTHROPOLOGY

The "Part Played by Labour" opens by emphasizing, as in all of Marx and Engels's political economic works, that wealth (as opposed to value) is a product of both nature and labor. Engels goes on to observe that labor "is the prime basic condition for all human [that is, social] existence, and this to such an extent that, in a sense, we have to say that labour created man himself."[13] From there he proceeds to sketch out a distinctive theory of the evolution of the human species from its pre-human primate ancestry.[14]

Engels's research in this area was undoubtedly thorough. As Paul Heyer wrote in his *Nature, Human Nature, and Society: Marx, Darwin, Biology and the Human Sciences*, with respect to "The Part Played by Labour in the Transition from Ape to Man": "Engels's description of the behavior of modern anthropoid apes, which he used for comparative purposes, is quite accurate and indicates a thorough familiarity with the available primate literature. Perhaps like Darwin and the anthropologist E. B. Tylor, Engels made sojourns to the London Zoo to observe anthropoid behavior."[15]

Even more explicitly than Haeckel in *The History of Creation* (1868) and Darwin in *The Descent of Man* (1871), Engels argued that the descent of human ancestors (hominins) from the trees and the development of erect posture had resulted in the gradual evolution of the hands and the making of tools, constituting the key to human evolution. Engels's argument on the evolution of the hand seems to have been closer to Darwin's than Haeckel's, given Darwin's emphasis on the evolution of the hand. Yet Darwin, true to his notion of the struggle of existence, stressed the appearance of weapons, as opposed to tools and thus labor.[16]

For Engels it was clearly the development and gradual perfection of the hand, following upon the bipedal motion of human beings, that was most important.

"It stands to reason," Engels wrote,

> that if erect gait among our hairy ancestors became first the rule and then, in time, a necessity, other diverse functions must, in the meantime, have devolved upon the hands. . . . Before the first flint could be fashioned into a knife by human hands, a period of time probably elapsed in comparison with which the historical period known to us appears insignificant. But the decisive step had been taken, *the hand had become free* and could henceforth attain ever greater dexterity. . . . Thus the hand is not only the organ of labour, *it is also the product of labour*. Labour, adaptation to ever new operations, through the inheritance of muscles, ligaments, and, over longer periods of time, bones that had undergone special development and the ever-renewed employment of this inherited finesse in new, more and more complicated operations, have given the human hand the high degree of perfection required to conjure into being the pictures of a Raphael, the statues of a Thorwaldsen, the music of a Paganini.[17]

As Engels explained in the Introduction to *Dialectics of Nature*, "The specialization of the hand . . . implies the *tool*, and the tool implies specific human activity, the transforming reaction of man on nature, production." With the evolution of the hand, "and partly owing to it, the brain of man . . . correspondingly developed" as a consequence of human labor.[18] Demonstrating a complex notion of coevolutionary processes, Engels explained that the impetus of labor, in the form of work with the hand, and the resulting increased (if still crude) mastery of the immediate environment, placed a premium on the development of articulate speech and intelligence, leading to the enlargement of the brain and further development of human labor—through mutual interaction and positive reinforcement.[19] "The hand did not exist alone." Rather, "it was," he emphasized, "only one member of an integral, highly complex organism. And what benefited the hand, benefited also the whole body it served." Here he turned to "the law of correlation of growth, as Darwin called it" in *The Origin of Species*. In Engels's words: "This law states that the specialized forms of separate parts of an organic being are always bound up with certain forms of other parts that apparently have no connection with them. . . . The gradually increasing perfection of the human hand, and the commensurate adaptation of the feet for erect gait, have undoubtedly, by virtue of such correlation, reacted on other parts of the organism."[20]

Nevertheless, of greater importance was the "direct, demonstrable influence of the development of the hand on the rest of the organism" through the development of human culture and sociability, and the effect on speech (requiring the evolution of the larynx) and the development of language. "Mastery over nature began with the development of the hand, with labour, and widened man's horizon at every new advance." Humanity's hominin ancestors were "continually discovering new, hitherto unknown properties in natural objects" by means of their increased interaction with their environment through their labor. Concurrently,

> the development of labour necessarily helped to bring the members of society closer together by increasing the cases of mutual support and joint activity, and by making clear the advantage of this joint activity to each individual. In short, men in the making arrived at the point where *they had something to say* to each other. Necessity created the organ; the underdeveloped larynx of the ape was slowly but surely transformed. . . .
>
> First labour, after it and then with it speech—these were the two most essential stimuli under the influence of which the brain of the ape gradually changed into that of the man. . . . The reaction on labour and speech of the development of the brain and its attendant senses, of the increasing clarity of consciousness, power of abstraction and of conclusion, gave both labour and speech an ever-renewed impulse to further development.[21]

According to Stephen Jay Gould, what Engels presented here was "the best nineteenth-century case for gene-culture coevolution," that is, the best general explanation of human evolution in Darwin's own lifetime, since gene-culture coevolution is the form that all coherent theories of human evolution must take. Commenting on Engels's theory, Gould noted that with the development of the hand, tools, and labor, "an enlarging brain (biology, or genes in later parlance) then fed back upon tools and language (culture), improving them in turn and setting the basis for the further growth of the brain—the positive feedback loop of gene culture coevolution."[22] The evolution of "human corporeal organization" that leads to the development of the brain was, as anthropologist Thomas Patterson notes, a complex process; one that began with human interaction with the environment in a fundamentally new way through the development of *the hand* and tools.[23]

Engels's speculation in the 1870s, like that of Haeckel and Darwin upon whom he relied, was based largely on deduction and the results of comparative anatomy rather than anthropological evidence. Apart from Neanderthals (first discovered in 1856, three years before the publication of Darwin's *Origin of Species*), no fossils of early hominins had been found. Engels's argument was therefore necessarily developed deductively along the lines of historical materialism, which suggested that it was the physical interaction with the environment resulting from the freeing of the hands that gave the primary impetus to human evolution.

Engels not only pointed clearly to the most likely development of human evolution, he also highlighted why the process of human evolution seemed so mysterious and convoluted in current accounts. With the development of tribe, nation, and class, religion had more and more come to dominate over human minds, inverting the real relations, in the form of a "fantastic reflection," in which everything was attributed to the mind in idealist fashion, while the "productions of the working hand retreated into the background." Consequently,

> men became accustomed to explain their actions as arising out of thought instead of their needs (which in any case are reflected and perceived in the mind); and so in the course of time there emerged that idealistic world outlook which, especially since the fall of the world of antiquity, has dominated men's minds. It still rules them to such a degree that even the most materialistic natural scientists of the Darwinian school are still unable to form any clear idea of the origin of man, because under this ideological influence they do not recognize the part that has been played therein by labour.[24]

Gould argued that Engels's critique of "cerebral primacy" in the dominant treatment of human evolution was one of his most brilliant insights. The "idealist tradition," Gould wrote, had "dominated philosophy right through to Darwin's day. Its influence was so subtle and pervasive that even scientific, but apolitical, materialists like Darwin fell under its sway," preventing them from seeing the centrality of labor, and thus the hand, in human evolution.

Darwin was not the first thinker of his school to address human evolution. During the intervening years between his publication of *The Origin of Species* in 1859 (which carefully avoided the issue of human evolution) and his publication of *The Descent of Man* in 1871, works on the subject had been produced by Thomas Huxley, Haeckel, Alfred Russel Wallace, John Lubbock, Ludwig Büchner, Carl Vogt, and others. But Darwin's own account, which placed considerable emphasis on the hand, seems to have influenced Engels the most. Still, even in the case of Darwin, a cerebral emphasis was present, while the role of labor in human evolution was largely excluded from his conception of evolution.[25] Hence, Engels's analysis stands out in its clarity and its consistent materialist perspective.

Engels's contention that conceptions of human evolution were dominated by a kind of cerebral primacy borne of idealist discourse was to receive strong, if indirect, confirmation in the notorious Piltdown Man fraud that hindered the understanding of human evolution for decades. In 1912, Charles Dawson, a successful solicitor and amateur archaeologist, supposedly uncovered fossil fragments of a skull and the jaw of what became known as Piltdown Man (*Eoanthropus dawsoni,* Dawson's "Dawn Man"). The Piltdown skull was indistinguishable from a modern human, while the jaw appeared to be apelike (it was to be discovered many years later to be from an orangutan). Flint implements were found nearby.

Leading figures in the British anthropological establishment, including Arthur Smith Woodward and Arthur Keith, accepted the authenticity of the find, and the *Eoanthropus* was for decades recognized as the "missing link" in human evolution. It was only in the late 1940s and early 1950s that the physical anthropologist Kenneth Oakley was able to use chemical (fluorine-dating) analysis to demonstrate definitively that the fossils were not from the Lower Pleistocene at all but of recent origin. In 1953 the question arose as to whether the fossils were actually a consciously perpetrated fraud. Upon examining them from that standpoint, Oakley, together with Joseph Weiner and Wilfrid Le Gros Clark, discovered evidence of deliberate deception throughout, for example, coloring and filing of teeth. In the end, it turned out that the specimens associated with the Piltdown finds, including the various flints found, were all fraudulent, either a forgery or an authentic item deliberately put in place to deceive.[26]

As Engels's argument suggested, there is little doubt that it was the assumption of cerebral primacy, and the desire to perceive human evolution in these terms, that contributed to anthropologists and paleontologists being fooled for so long by this deliberate fraud. Grafton Elliott Smith, one of the principal scientific figures in the Piltdown find, argued on the basis of this supposed paleontological evidence for cerebral primacy in human evolution, stating in *The Evolution of Man*:

> The outstanding interest of the Piltdown skull is the confirmation it affords of the view that in the evolution of Man the brain led the way. It is the veriest truism that Man has emerged from the simian state in virtue of the enrichment of the structure of his mind. It is singular that so much biological speculation has neglected to give adequate recognition to this cardinal fact. The brain attained what may be termed the human rank at a time when the jaws and face, and no doubt the body also, still retained much of the uncouthness of Man's simian ancestors. In other words, Man at first, so far as his general appearance and 'build' are concerned, was merely an Ape with an overgrown brain. The importance of the Piltdown skull lies in the fact that it affords tangible confirmation of these inferences.[27]

Smith went so far as to argue that the erect posture that characterized human beings was itself a result of the development of the brain.[28]

However, not only those who believed in cerebral primacy were deceived by Dawson. One figure who was fooled, and whose being taken in by the fraud was essential to the hoax's whole success (since he was so closely associated with Darwin and Huxley) was Marx's friend and Engels's acquaintance, E. Ray Lankester. Although not one of the principal figures associated with the "discovery," Lankester, next to Arthur Keith (who was to devote about half of his 1915 book *The Antiquity of Man* to Piltdown), was clearly crucial to its acceptance.[29] In John Cooke's famous 1915 painting *A Discussion of the Piltdown Skull*, Lankester was pictured as sitting to the side, while Keith sat looking directly at the skull, and Dawson, Smith, and Arthur Smith Woodward all stood.[30] In this way the two main scientists, Lankester and Keith, were presented as verifying the discovery, with the discoverers themselves in the background observing the process. Lankester was a strong materialist. Ironically, in his 1915 *Diversions of a Naturalist*, in which he addressed the Piltdown "discovery," he presented perhaps the closest argument to that of Engels on the course of human evolution. In the chapter "From Ape to Man" he wrote, in a manner very similar to Engels's by then published, "The Part Played by Labour in the Transition from Ape to Man" (though there is no indication that Lankester would have read it or even known about it) that it was the hand, following erect posture and a bipedal gait, that was crucial to human evolution and that led the way:

> I think we are justified in taking the large opposable thumb and fingers as the starting-point in man's emergence from the ape stage of his ancestry. The exploring hand, with its thumb and forefinger, is the great instrument by which the intelligence, first of the monkey and then of man, has been developed. The thumb of the gorilla is, in proportion to the size of the fingers, very much smaller than that of man, but bigger than that of the chimpanzee, and much bigger than that of the orang and of lower monkeys. It is evident that the thumb has increased in size in the man-like apes, and in man himself this increase has been carried much further, and led to the perfecting of the hand as an instrument of exploration and construction. Contributory to the perfecting of the hand has been the gradual attainment of the upright carriage, and the use of the feet alone for walking . . . The upright carriage enabled the early ancestors of man to survey, and so to judge the conditions of safety or danger at a distance from them, as well as to devote their hands to new and special uses.[31]

Lankester thus avoided falling prey to the notion of cerebral primacy in the origin of hominins, in spite of the Piltdown hoax, which was designed to suggest cerebral primacy in the evolution from ape to human ancestors, thereby contradicting the materialist interpretation of human evolution. Nevertheless, he was enormously excited by the announcement of the Piltdown discoveries and visited the pit in the company of Dawson. He wanted to see about obtaining a government grant to carry out systematic digging. "I feel sure," he wrote in his enthusiasm, "the whole family [of *Eoanthropus*] are there, leg bones and all of a dozen individuals!"[32] No doubt Lankester thought that the discovery of fossils of entire individuals would verify the materialist thesis, presented in *Diversions of the Naturalist*, that the development of the hand was "the starting point in man's emergence." Yet, he went on in his discussion of human evolution in that book to write a chapter on Piltdown Man titled "The Missing Link." Lankester was clearly disturbed by the paradox of Piltdown Man, with its developed skull, pointing to a brain the size and shape of modern humans, together with an ape-like jaw. "If it had been found under other circumstances," he noted, the jaw "might quite well have been described" as that of "a simiid—a large ape." The skull was human-like. "In fact," he concluded, "the only ground which at present justifies the association of *Eoanthropus* with the Homindae or human series rather than the Simiidae or ape series—derived from a common ancestry—is the man-like rather than ape-like size of the brain, which we must attribute to Eoanthropus on the assumption, which is at present a reasonable one, that the half-jaw and the incomplete skull found near each other at Piltdown are parts of the same individual." Lankester, the dedicated materialist and opponent of cerebral primacy, nonetheless accepted the authenticity of Piltdown Man merely on the word of Dawson, who claimed to have found the jaw and the skull fragments in close proximity to each other. He certainly did not suspect an elaborate fraud. Hence, he concluded that the supposed *Eoanthropus* represented "a real 'missing link,' an animal intermediate in great and obvious features between the two stocks [*Simiidae* and *Homindae*] and either to be described as an ape which had become man-like or a man who still retained characteristic ape-like features."[33] Lankester, who was known as perhaps the greatest detector of spiritualistic frauds in his day, fell prey to the greatest scientific fraud in history.

The bias toward cerebral primacy and the supposed confirmation in that respect provided by the false *Eoanthropus* meant that when Raymond Dart discovered the first of the australopithecines (*Australopithecus africanus*, the first word standing for Southern Ape) in South Africa in 1924, it took two decades before they were accepted as human ancestors by the anthropological establishment. The reason is that the australopithecine fossils that began to be found, including quite distinct species within the genus, pointed to beings of erect posture with more developed hands but brain sizes that were still akin to those of apes, precisely what Engels had strongly hypothesized, and Haeckel and Darwin suggested. Yet, there was enormous resistance to such conclusions due to notions of cerebral primacy, and due to the African origin of humanity that such fossils suggested. Arthur Keith, who had made his reputation based on Piltdown, immediately announced that Dart's *Australopithecus africanus* was nothing more than a "remarkable" ape. As S. L. Washburn and Ruth Moore were later to explain, it was assumed that "a human brain might go with a sub-human body, but surely it could not be the other way around."[34]

It was not until more discoveries of australopithecines were made in Africa, and *Eoanthropus* had become more and more of an anomaly (followed by the discovery of the fraud), that the myth of cerebral primacy in human evolution began to break down.[35] Even then, some prominent paleontologists like Louis Leakey, who had studied with Arthur Keith, continually leaned toward the view that the small-brained australopithecines could not have made tools, and with the discovery of *Homo habilis* in 1964 viewed all signs of tool making as evidence of the genus *Homo*, a supposition that has now broken down due to subsequent paleontological finds.[36]

Still, the discovery of the australopithecines, and the acceptance of them as human ancestors would so alter evolutionary theory that Oakley, best known for uncovering the Piltdown fraud, wrote *Man the Tool-Maker* in 1950, summarizing the evidence that human evolution had primarily occurred through tool making and the evolution of the hand. Writing in a manner reminiscent of Engels's argument, Oakley stated, "Man is a social animal distinguished by 'culture': by the ability to make tools and communicate ideas. . . . When the immediate forerunners of man acquired the ability to walk upright habitually, their hands became free to make and manipulate tools—activities which were in the first place dependent on adequate powers of mental and bodily co-ordination, but which in turn perhaps increased those powers." The discoveries of Louis and Mary Leakey in Olduvai Gorge in East Africa in 1959 further raised the question as to whether the australopithecines were tool users with hands developed beyond those of the apes. The key to human evolution, once erect posture freed the hands, it was increasingly believed, was tool using/making and the effect that this had on the hands, language, the brain, etc., in a feedback process. As Gould declared, this was a view best described in the nineteenth century by Engels. This was encapsulated in Washburn and Moore's famous phrase, "Tools Makyth Man."[37] The Soviet anthropologist V. Jakimov, in 1964, drew the conclusion that the discovery of various hominin species pointed to the Engelsian conclusion that "the most progressive bipedal fossil anthropoids were those that systematically employed various objects as tools and weapons which became the basis of their ecology," distinguishing them from all other animals. This systematic tool-making "took man's ancestors out of the framework of purely biological adaptation," constituting "the forerunner of human labor."[38]

Today the overall story with regard to human evolution has shifted somewhat. Paleoanthropologists have for some time focused, in their accounts of the origin of the first hominins some 6 to 7 million years ago, on the advent of bipedalism itself, and less on the relation of this to the evolution of the hands and tool making, although the evidence of stone tools dates back as much as 3.4 million years. It is still assumed that the evolution of the hand, the making of tools, language, and the development of the brain were related, but bipedalism, it is thought, may have anticipated tool making by a considerable lag. The evolution of bipedalism has most recently been explained by climate change and by alterations in the ecology associated with tectonic geological shifts, particularly in an evolutionary hotspot stretching north from Gona to Ledi-Geraru in Ethiopia, part of the Great Rift Valley in East Africa (where *Homo habilis* was found). In the context of such immense environmental changes, it is believed, natural selection took over and led to more efficient and varied forms of movement among human ancestors.[39]

Nevertheless, it is now recognized that stone tools extend back 3.4 million years, long before genus Homo, in the time of the late australopithecines. Hence, it is now thought likely that *Australopithecus afarensis* (Lucy's species), with their developed hands but apelike features and relatively small brains, were tool makers—although other australopithecine species are also possible candidates.[40] In 2015 stone tools 3.3 million years old were found in Kenya. Indirect evidence of stone tools has been found in Ethiopia dating back 3.4 million years, the evidence consisting of marks on bones, pointing to stone-tool use in the butchering of meat. These early tools took the form of flaked implements with sharp edges, made from hitting stones against each other, which could be used for cutting. It then became possible to cut through even the toughest animal hides and meat eating became possible, adding to the diet and making it more secure. As Richard Leakey wrote in *The Origin of Humankind*, those hominins "who made and used these simple stone flakes thereby availed themselves of a new energy source—animal protein," which would not be otherwise available. Around this time the brain expanded substantially in size. Labor, which Marx and Engels saw as material exchange with and transformation of the environment, thus becomes the key to a process of gene-culture coevolution.[41]

The argument of many contemporary anthropologists is thus similar in this respect to that made by Engels in "The Part Played by Labour." For Engels, it was the growth of a "meat diet" made possible by tool making that enhanced the overall nutritional intake by providing "in an almost ready state the most essential ingredients required by the organism for its metabolism. . . . Adaptation to a meat diet, side by side with a vegetable diet, greatly contributed towards giving bodily strength and independence to man in the making."[42] Contemporary anthropologists likewise argue that the added nutrition made possible by tool making played a key role in the evolutionary track. Further tool development, particularly the stone hand ax, was associated with the emergence of *Homo erectus* around two million years ago.[43]

With the emergence of *Homo sapiens* some 300,000 years ago, there was a tripling of the size of the brain in relation to the earliest australopithecines.[44] This increase in brain size was associated with the development of language. For Engels, writing in the nineteenth century, language along with the associated development of the brain was the result of natural selection tied to human sociability arising in conjunction with labor.[45] In contrast, today's anthropologists commonly see theories of the evolution of language in terms of either "man the toolmaker" or "man the social animal"—technology or sociability.[46] Nevertheless, such distinctions are rooted on reified notions, in which technology and sociability are seen as ideal activities separate from each other and human labor. As Engels insisted, the evolution of the hand implies tool making, tool making implies labor, labor implies social cooperation, and this leads over evolutionary time to the development of language and the brain. It is the process of labor, associated with the increasing mastery of the environment, that constitutes the dynamic natural-material explanation for human evolution and human history. What contemporary anthropology has shown us is that this evolutionary process occurred over millions of years. Nevertheless, there is every reason to suppose that it was the human interaction with the environment through labor, that is, the development of a distinct human ecology, that was the central factor setting off gene-culture coevolution.

Building on his discussion of human evolution through labor, Engels went on to distinguish human ecology from animal ecology. Departing from simpler forms of Darwinian "survival of the fittest" notions in which animals merely adapt to their environment, he argued that animals too "change their environment." Animals, he insisted, have a kind of consciousness, have been known in the higher primates to use simple tools, and sometimes engage in patterns of behavior that appear to be "planned, premeditated. . . . In animals, the capacity for conscious, planned action is proportional to the development of the nervous system, and among mammals it attains a fairly high level." Non-human animals, Engels contended, "have in common" with humans

> all activity of the understanding: *induction, deduction,* and hence also *abstraction* (Dido's [Engels's dog] generic concepts: quadrupeds and bipeds), *analysis* of unknown objects (even the cracking of a nut is a beginning of analysis), *synthesis* (in animal tricks), and, as the union of both, *experiment* (in the case of new obstacles and unfamiliar situations). In their nature all these modes of procedure—hence all means of scientific investigation that ordinary logic recognizes—are absolutely the same in men and the higher animals. They differ only in the degree (of development of the method in each case).[47]

Animal ecology was a complex process of two-way interaction, in which the environment impacts animal life, and animal life alters the environment:

> Animals . . . change the environment by their activities in the same way, even if not to the same extent, as man does. . . . But all the planned action of all animals has never succeeded in impressing the stamp of their will upon the earth. That was left for man. In short, the animal merely *uses* its environment, and brings

> about changes in it simply by its presence; man by his changes makes it serve his ends, *masters* it. This is the final, essential distinction between man and other animals, and once again it is labour that brings about this distinction.[48]

Engels's analysis here was dependent on an understanding of the dialectical complexity of the environment. "In nature," he wrote, "nothing takes place in isolation." An example of this weblike ecological interdependence could be seen in the effects of the introduction of goats and pigs into St. Helena, which in the nineteenth century was one of the best-known cases of ecological destruction of colonialism. In 1839, in his *Journal of Researches into the Geology and Natural History of the Various Countries Visited During the Voyage of the HMS Beagle*, Darwin had commented on the devastating deforestation wrought since the introduction of goats and hogs to the island at the beginning of European settlement in 1502. "So late as the year 1716," he wrote, there were many trees in the area previously called the Great Wood,

> but in 1724 the old trees had mostly fallen; and as goats and hogs had been suffered to range about, all the young trees had been killed. . . . The extent of surface, probably covered by wood at a former period, it is estimated at no less than two thousand acres; at the present day scarcely a single tree can be found there. It is also said that in 1709 there were quantities of dead trees in Sand Bay; this place is now so utterly desert, that nothing but so well attested an account [records left by Alexander Beatson] could have made me believe that they could ever have grown there.[49]

On such bases, Engels observed that the "goats and pigs brought by the first arrivals" to St. Helena "have succeeded in exterminating its old vegetation almost completely, and so have prepared the ground for the spreading of plants brought by later sailors and colonists" to replace the established species. This demonstrated three things: (1) how animals change the environment, sometimes irreversibly; (2) how this effect on the environment is altered and made invasive by human intervention, and especially colonization of remote areas; and (3) how "the flora and fauna" of islands and indeed "whole continents" are thus changed through the combination of human and other animal action, often with devastating ecological consequences—as suggested by Darwin, in the form of desertification.[50]

This leads to the wider ecological critique to which the entire argument in "The Part Played by Labour" is directed. For Engels, labor is the key to human evolution and to the subsequent development of human society. It leads the way from natural history of human beings to their social history. From the mastery of tools, hunting and gathering, the domestication of animals, the planned cultivation of crops, to tribe, nation, state, and the development of modern human society with its developed science and technology, all human development is in the final analysis dependent on the development of the labor process and production in their widest senses. Like Marx, Engels saw the labor process as the interdependent social metabolism between human beings and nature. But if humanity, in contrast to animals, was distinguished by its capacity to "master" as opposed simply to "use" nature, this mastery had its limits in the social, economic, and ecological construction of human society itself. As he famously put it:

> Let us not, however flatter ourselves overmuch on account of our human victories over nature. For each such victory nature takes its revenge on us. Each victory, it is true, in the first place brings about the results we expected, but in the second and third places it has quite different unforeseen effects which only too often cancel out the first. The people who, in Mesopotamia, Greece, Asia Minor, and elsewhere, destroyed the forests to obtain cultivable land, never dreamed that by removing along with the forests the collecting centres and reservoirs of moisture they were laying the basis for the present forlorn state of those countries. When the Italians of the Alps used up the pine forests on the southern slopes . . . they had no inkling that by doing so they were cutting at the roots of the dairy industry in their region; they had still less inkling that they were thereby depriving their mountain springs of water for the greater part of the year, and making it possible for them to pour still more furious torrents on the plains during the rainy seasons. . . . Thus at every step we are reminded that we by no means rule over nature like a conqueror over a foreign people, like someone standing outside of nature—but that we, with flesh, blood, and brain, belong to nature, and exist in its midst, and that all our mastery of it consists in the fact that we have the advantage over all other creatures of being able to learn its laws and apply them correctly.[51]

Engels here raises the question of how the generation of ecological catastrophes, in areas such as Mesopotamia, resulted from the unforeseen long-term consequences of human production. In this respect, he was strongly influenced, like Marx, by the work of the German agronomist Carl Nikolas Fraas's book *Climate and the Plantworld* (1847), which focused on the human destruction of the forests of Mesopotamia, Persia, Palestine, Egypt, and southern Europe. Arguing against seeing such environmental change as simply due to natural causes, Fraas emphasized the importance of human beings in generating more arid climates in these regions. "The developing culture of people," he wrote, "leaves a veritable desert behind it."[52] As Engels observed in his notes on Fraas, this desertification constituted "the main proof that civilization is an antagonistic process that, in its form up to the present, has exhausted the land, devastated the forests, rendered the land unfertile for its original crops and made the climate worse. Prairies and the increased heat and dryness of the climate are the consequences of culture [civilization]."[53]

At around the same time as Fraas published his book, the German biologist Matthias Jakob Schleiden, one of the pioneers of cell theory, published *The Plant: A Biography* (1848), which also influenced Engels.[54] Schleiden was particularly concerned with regional climate change in historical times, and saw humanity as a factor in triggering such changes. "Man," he argued, "brings about results which surprise even himself, because he does not at the moment mark the gradually accumulating consequences of his labours, nor, led by necessary knowledge, foresee the final results." There were strong indications in the historical records, Schleiden declared, "that those countries which are now treeless and arid deserts, part of Egypt, Syria, Persia, and so forth, were once thickly wooded, traversed by streams," but were later "dried up or shrunk within narrow bounds" and exposed to the full force of the sun. He attributed these changes to the environment *in historical time* primarily to the disappearance of forests by human hand. "Behind him," Schleiden concluded, "he [man] leaves the Desert, a deformed and ruined land" and is guilty of the "thoughtless squandering of vegetable treasures. . . . Here again in selfish pursuit of profit, and consciously or unconsciously, following the abominable principle of the great moral Vileness which one man has expressed, '*après nous le déluge*,' he begins anew the work of destruction."[55]

Marx, like Engels, was strongly influenced by the arguments of Fraas and Schleiden, pointing to the catastrophic effects on entire civilizations resulting from the undermining of the environmental conditions of human development, what Marx called "the whole gamut of permanent conditions of life required by the chain of human generations."[56] In the classical Marxian critique, desertification (dustbowlization) was a natural result of the course of "civilization," meaning historical class societies, with the destructiveness of capitalism in this respect far greater than in any previous society.[57] Underscoring the short-term aims and long-term irrationality of bourgeois society, particularly in its most destructive colonial forms, Engels, in "The Part Played by Labour," exclaimed:

> What cared the Spanish planters in Cuba who burned down forests on the slopes of the mountains and obtained from the ashes sufficient fertilizer for *one* generation of very highly profitable coffee trees—what cared they that the heavy tropical rainfall afterwards washed away the unprotected upper stratum of the soil, leaving behind only bare rock! In relation to nature, as to society, the present mode of production is predominantly concerned only with the

> immediate, the most tangible result; and then surprise is expressed that the more remote effects of actions directed to this end turn out to be quite different, are mostly quite the opposite in character.[58]

In all of this Engels had in mind Francis Bacon's famous scientific maxim that "nature is only overcome by obeying her," that is, by discovering and conforming to nature's laws.[59] In Marx's and Engels's view, the Baconian principle, to the extent that it was applied in bourgeois society, was primarily a "ruse" for conquering nature so as to bring it under capital's laws of accumulation and competition. Science itself was made into a mere appendage of profit-making, treating nature's boundaries as mere obstacles to overcome, rather than rationally mastering the human metabolic relation to nature—in conformity with genuine human needs and potentials, and the requirements of long-term reproduction. This pointed to a contradiction between, on the one hand, science's own dialectic, which more and more recognized, in Engels's words, our "oneness with nature," and, on the other hand, capital's myopic drive to accumulation *ad infinitum*.[60]

What finally distinguished human ecology from animal ecology was thus "the fact that we have the advantage over all other creatures of being able to learn its laws and apply them completely." It was this that removed human beings from the mere struggle for existence. But all progress was also regression, and society was constantly being thrust back into the Hobbesian war-of-all-against-all that characterized capitalist society. Under prevailing social conditions, no rational long-term course of action was possible for humanity. For the human "oneness with nature" to be realized, there needed to be a "regulation," not only of the short-term effects, but also "the indirect, more remote social [and environmental] effects, of our production activity. . . . This regulation, however, requires something more than mere knowledge. It requires a complete revolution in our hitherto existing mode of production, and simultaneously a revolution in our whole contemporary social order." Without this, Engels believed, society would be prone to long-term ecological catastrophe, metaphorically expressed as the "revenge" of nature.[61] The English capitalists in conquering India, he observed, had failed to do what every other conqueror before them had done—they had failed to take responsibility "for the collective maintenance of irrigation throughout the river valleys, without which no agriculture was possible there. . . . The enlightened English . . . let the irrigation canals and sluices fall into decay, and are now at last discovering, through the regularly recurring famines, that they have neglected the one activity which might have made their rule in India at least as legitimate as that of their predecessors."[62]

It is this perspective, which denies the bad infinity of infinite linear-quantitative progress, mere 1+1+1, that informs Engels's discussion of the human destruction of ecological systems in "The Part Played by Labour in the Transition from Ape to Man," along with the introduction to the *Dialectics of Nature*.[63] Humanity is capable of destroying the natural bases of its own existence, which are not permanent, and need to be sustained. However, in order to generate a sustainable social metabolism it is necessary to create a productive mode that breaks with this bad infinity (metaphorically represented, as in Friedrich Schelling, by the English national debt) and with a system of unplanned competition for unlimited capital accumulation. Instead, society needs to be organized on a planned basis by the associated producers regulating our productive relation to nature on a sustainable basis, recognizing our coevolution with nature and our place within its universal metabolism. Such "regulation," Engels argues, "requires something more than mere knowledge. It requires a complete revolution in our hitherto existing mode of production, and simultaneously a revolution in our whole contemporary social order."[64]As Leacock observed, Engels's brilliance in "The Part Played by Labour" is that he pointed to "the destructiveness of nature as a result of man's profit-making course and the necessity for revolutionizing society in order to arrest its pernicious effects."[65]

Engels drew hope at every point from the communal past of humanity. In *The Mark*, written in 1882, he delved into the early German commune. The demise of the Mark (the early German system of communal association) came with the loss of the commons on which the peasants had grazed their cattle. Hence, there was no longer any manure with which to fertilize their small plots of land, resulting in the decline of the soil, peasant agriculture, and their means of subsistence. All of this fed the so-called primitive accumulation and the rise of the large estates. The remaining peasants were thus gradually squeezed out of existence. What Marx called the social metabolism between the population and the land was disrupted—a crisis of peasant agriculture that constituted a precondition of capitalism itself.[66]

ENGELS AND THE ORIGIN OF THE FAMILY

Engels's works on *The Origin of the Family, Private Property, and the State* and "The Mark" are explorations in prehistory associated with the emergence of anthropology as a discipline, and hence are closely connected to his argument on "The Part Played by Labour in the Transition from Ape to Man."[67] *The Origin of the Family, Private Property and the State* was published in 1884, the year after Marx's death, and was based in part on Marx's *Ethnological Notebooks*. It represented Engels's attempt (like Marx) to build on the early anthropological work of Lewis Henry Morgan, particularly in his *Ancient Society* (1877).[68] As Engels's title indicates, the purpose of this work was to point to the *historical origins* of the family (particularly the patriarchal family), private property, and the state. The intent was to demonstrate that the central bulwarks of modern class society had not existed throughout human anthropological development but had arisen *in historical time* (although before written history).

Much of the early anthropology on which Engels (and before him Marx) relied was mistaken on crucial points. For example, the emergence of an economic surplus and crucial changes in the division of labor between men and women are now seen as arising at an earlier stage, in gatherer societies. Yet, the basic character of his argument with respect to the historical origins of patriarchy can still be seen as holding, in broad outline.[69]

Engels thus provided a radical extension of historical materialism, focusing on the intersections of gender and class, of production and reproduction, viewed as dialectically related. "According to the materialist conception," he observed in the Preface to his book,

> the determining factor in history is, in the last resort, the production and reproduction of immediate life. But this itself is of a twofold character. On the one hand, the production of the means of subsistence, of food, clothing and shelter and the tools requisite therefore; on the other, the production of human beings themselves, the propagation of the species. The social institutions under which men of a definite historical epoch and of a definite country live are conditioned by both kinds of production: by the stage of development of labour, on the one hand, and of the family on the other.[70]

The emphasis of the book was on how the early kinship group known as the clan or *gens* (from "to beget") associated with matrilineal descent, collective production, and communal property, had preceded the development of the patriarchal (monogamous) family as the "individual economic unit of society."[71] This was part of the "revolution in ethnological time," giving rise to anthropological studies in the early 1860s, at around the same time as Darwin's theory of natural selection. It emphasized the similarity in the processes of development within early human society, reflecting the interaction of chance and necessity in a manner similar to Darwinian natural selection.[72] This social evolution of kinship and property relations was the result of changing conditions of subsistence and their effect on kinship rules governing sexual relations and group marriage. Basing his analysis on the research not only on Morgan, but also such figures as Johann Bachofen, Lubbock, Maxim Kovalevsky, and John McLennan—all of whose ideas were dealt with in detail in Marx's *Ethnological Notebooks*—Engels pointed to the combined "progressive-retrogressive" origins of the monogamous family:

> Monogamy does not by any means make its appearance in history as the reconciliation of man and woman, still less as the highest form of such a

> reconciliation. On the contrary, it appears as the subjection of one sex by the other, as the proclamation of a conflict between the sexes entirely unknown hitherto in prehistoric times. In an old unpublished manuscript, the work of Marx and myself in 1846 [*The German Ideology*], I find the following: "The first division of labour is that between man and woman for child breeding." And today I can add: The first class antagonism which appears in history coincides with the development of the antagonism between man and woman in monogamous marriage, and the first class oppression with that of the female sex by the male. Monogamy was a great historical advance, but at the same time inaugurated, along with slavery and private wealth, that epoch, lasting until today, in which every advance is likewise a relative regression, in which the well-being and development of the one group are obtained by the misery and oppression of the other. It is the cellular form of civilized society, in which we can already study the nature of the antagonisms and contradictions which develop fully in the latter.[73]

Seeing monogamy, therefore, as both "the first class antagonism" and "the cellular form" of all oppressions built up over the course of civilization, meant that Engels gave an importance to the historical origin of gender oppression that went far beyond that of most of today's gender researchers in this respect. Highlighting the historicity of the family, Engels abandoned the view of all prior "written history," which had taken as its "point of departure the absurd assumption, which became inviolable in the eighteenth century, that the monogamous individual family, an institution scarcely older than civilization, is the nucleus around which society and the state gradually crystallized." Rather than viewing the monogamous family in this way, as constituting the original "natural" condition, Engels insisted that "it was the first form of the family based not on natural but on economic conditions, namely, on the victory of private property over original, naturally developed common ownership." Following Marx, he gave priority to the "genetic constitution" as a stage in human development, representing the phase of group marriage, and preceding the pairing family and the monogamous family.[74] It was Morgan, who had, through his research into the Iroquois and other American Indian tribes, pointed to the kinship relations associated with the ancient gens (each tribe consisting of a number of gentes or gens related by blood on the mother's side). Here lineage was traced through the female line. Although marriage existed within tribes, sexual relations with partners within the same gens were prohibited.[75]

Relying on a large number of sources—including, in addition to Morgan, the full range of Greek and Latin literature on the ancient gens, as well as Tacitus, Caesar, and the Icelandic *Edda* on the Germanic gens—Engels highlighted the relative equality between the sexes/genders, communal property relations, and egalitarian political institutions associated with the original genetic constitution based on mother-right. "That woman was the slave of man at the commencement of society," he wrote, "is one of the most absurd notions that have come down to us from the period of the Enlightenment of the eighteenth century."[76] However, the relative equality of women nurtured in the earliest societies had broken down in Lower and Middle Barbarism, particularly in Europe and Asia, with the widespread domestication of animals and the development of cattle (a new form of mobile, exchangeable wealth).[77] Women's domestic work, which under communal production and the genetic constitution had equal importance as a form of public industry carried out in common, lost its public character and receded in relative status. The economic basis of the society thus shifted more to the province of men, resulting in the institution of patriarchal family-based relations along with male-dominated property relations.[78] Cultivated land eventually came to be "alienated" and treated as private property, the economic surplus grew, concomitant with slavery once the scale of production grew. The state originated in this context as an institution over and above society to protect private property.[79]

Hence, for Engels, the fall of the early genetic constitution represented a "revolution," the "world-historic defeat" or "overthrow" of the system of mother-right embodied in the gens—a revolution that fell entirely in "prehistoric times," and "with the patriarchal family we enter the field of written history." The individual family gradually becomes "the economic unit of society" displacing communal life and production. According to Marx, "The modern family contains within itself in *miniature* all the antagonisms which later develop on a wide scale within society and its state."[80]

Engels's designation of the monogamous family as the "cellular form" of class society gave a much more coherent materialist basis to Marx and Engels's repeated references to the class divisions within the family—with the patriarchal relation between men and women variously described in their work as relations between master and slave, bourgeois and proletarian. In this framework, the reference to class divisions within the family were not to be seen as constituting a "sex-gender analogy" as some socialists were later to argue.[81] Rather, class relations, as Engels explained (and Marx too had concluded), had emerged out of patriarchal relations with the displacement of the genetic constitution.[82] As Marx put it in his *Ethnological Notebooks,* "The modern family contains in embryo not only slavery, but also serfdom."[83] Class society not only developed simultaneously with, but was also, in important ways, *based upon* the patriarchal family, viewed as the "individual economic unit of society" and as the "cellular form" of class divisions. As Tristram Hunt put it in his Introduction to the *Origin of the Family, Private Property and the State*, Engels went further in this work than he and Marx had previously gone in suggesting that "antagonism between the social classes was first predicated upon male oppression of the female within the monogamian family." Indeed, in its etymological origins, Engels pointed out that the word "*famulus* means household slave," while "*familia* signifies the totality of slaves belonging to one individual."[84]

In the monogamous-patriarchal family that emerged with civilization, inequality, not equality, is established as the basis of the family, as it is rooted in the "economic oppression of women." Equality before the law in the marriage contract, Engels argued, is hitherto mainly a way of disguising "*on paper*" this real inequality.[85] The essential basis of the patriarchal family is the fact that women's household work, which in early modes of production had the character of public industry, has now become private:

> In the old communistic household, which embraced numerous couples and their children, the administration of the household, entrusted to the women, was just as much a public, a socially necessary industry as the providing of food by the men. This situation changed with the patriarchal family, and even more with the monogamous individual family. The administration of the household lost its public character. It was no longer the concern of society. It had become a *private service*. The wife became the first domestic servant, pushed out of participation in social production. Only modern large-scale industry again threw open to her—and only to the proletarian women at that—the avenue to social production; but in such a way that, when she fulfills her duties, in the private service of her family, she remains excluded from public production and cannot earn anything; and when she wishes to take part in public industry and earn her living independently, she is not in a position to fulfill her family duties. What applies to the woman in the factory applies to her in all the professions, right up to medicine and law. The modern individual family is based on the open or disguised domestic enslavement of the woman; and modern society is a mass composed solely of individual families as its molecules. Today, in the great majority of cases, the man has to be the earner, the breadwinner of the family, at least among the propertied classes, and this gives him a dominating position which requires no special legal privileges. In the family he is the bourgeois; the wife represents the proletariat.[86]

Engels concluded from this that *full equality before the law* made materially possible by "the re-introduction of the entire female sex into public industry" constituted "the first premise for the emancipation of women . . . and that this demands that the quality possessed by the individual family of being the economic unit of society be abolished." The full emancipation of women, he argues, requires that household work again be transformed into a public industry, not a private service within the family, and that women be enabled to pursue a full public role in all endeavors. Indeed, "The emancipation of women and their equality with men are impossible and must remain so as long as women are excluded from socially productive work and restricted to housework, which is private."[87] Needless to say, the free entry of women into industry as the *first premise* of their full emancipation was to be regarded simply as a necessary step in a long struggle for substantive equality.

Along with the abolition of "private domestic work," it would also be necessary to do away with the special male privileges of adultery and the accompanying institutions of prostitution that had characterized the hypocritical, patriarchal family during the entire period of civilization. The new form of the marriage contract (or cohabitation agreement) must be "sex love" between men and women, a form more characteristic of the property-less proletarian family than that of the propertied bourgeoisie.[88]

As Eleanor Leacock wrote in the 1970s, in support of Engels's analysis:

> It is crucial to the organization of women for their liberation to understand that it is the monogamous family as an economic unit, at the heart of class society, that is basic to their subjugation. Such understanding makes clear that child-bearing itself is not responsible for the low status of women, as has been the contention of some radical women's groups. And more important, it indicates the way in which working-class women in their obviously basic fight on the job but also in their seemingly more conservative battles for their families around schools, housing, and welfare, are actually posing a more basic challenge than that of the radicals. By demanding that society assume responsibility for their children, they are attacking the nature of the family as an economic unit, the basis of their own oppression and a central buttress of class exploitation.[89]

Engels's achievement was thus to undermine all theories of biological determinism used to justify the social inequality of men and women, eliminating any notion that the patriarchal-monogamous family was the original, natural form of human society. In the words of Peter Aaby, "Engels's problematic was the transition from a complementary relation between the sexes to the reification of women."[90] In this respect, Engels contradicted socialists like August Bebel who, in his work *Woman and Socialism* (1879), saw women's oppression as a primordial condition, a position that remains dominant within anthropology with its androcentric biases, despite conflicting evidence. Thus, in his influential 1967 *Kinship and Marriage*, Robin Fox flatly declared in reference to men controlling women: "One does not need to recapitulate the evolutionary history of man to see why. For the greater part of human history, women were getting on with their highly specialized task of bearing and rearing the children. It was the men who hunted the game, fought the enemies, and made the decisions. This is, I am convinced, rooted in primate nature."[91]

In sharp contrast to such views, commonly voiced both in his day and ours, Engels *historicized* women's oppression, a position that was to be reinforced around a century later with the development of feminist anthropology in the 1970s.[92] Like Fourier before him, Engels argued that the periods of barbarism and civilization (that is, the forms of society from the point of the domestication of animals and the development of agriculture) had introduced inequality in the family and in industry that broke with the longer history and evolution of humanity. Human "progress" with respect to the monogamous family was at the same time a "regression"; the full emancipation of women was central to the emancipation of society as a whole. Nature did not establish any fundamental inequality within humanity.[93] Writing in 1986, Stephanie Coontz and Peta Henderson declared: "A growing body of evidence supports the broad evolutionary perspective first suggested by Engels: relations between the sexes seem to be most egalitarian in the simplest foraging societies and women's position worsens with the emergence of social stratification, private property, and the state."[94]

Rejecting essentialist, biological-determinist views of gender relations, Engels also strongly rejected all essentialist, biological-determinist views of race. The aversion to social Darwinism and essentialism with respect to human populations, evident throughout his thought, could be seen in his praise of indigenous peoples in the Americas and Africa in relation to their social organizations, and even civilizations. The early "gentile constitution," of the Iroquois, he observed,

> is wonderful in its childlike simplicity! Everything runs smoothly without soldiers, gendarmes, or police; without nobles, kings, governors, prefects or judges; without prisons; without trials. All quarrels and disputes are settled by the whole body of those concerned—the gens or the tribe or the individual gentes among themselves. . . . All are free and equal—including the women. There is as yet no room for slaves, nor, as a rule for the subjugation of alien tribes. When the Iroquois conquered the Eries and the "Neutral Nations" about the year 1651, they invited them to join the [Iroquois] Confederacy as equal members; only when the vanquished refused were they driven out of their territory. And the kind of men and women that are produced by such a society is indicated by the admiration felt by all white men who came into contact with uncorrupted Indians, admiration of the personal dignity, straightforwardness, strength of character and bravery of these barbarians.
>
> We have witnessed quite recently examples of this bravery in Africa. The Zulu Kaffirs a few years ago, like the Nubians a couple of months ago [referring to the Zulu-British War of 1879 and the Nubian-British War of 1883]—in

> both of which tribes gentile [that is, related to gens or clan] institutions have not yet died out—did what no European army can do. Armed only with pikes and spears and without firearms, they advanced, under a hail of bullets and breechloaders, right up to the bayonets of the English infantry—acknowledged as the best in the world for fighting in close formation—throwing them into disorder and even beating them back more than once; and this despite the colossal disparity in arms and despite the fact that they have no such thing as military service, and do not know what military exercises are. Their capacity and endurance are best proved by the complaint of the English that a Kaffir can move faster and cover a longer distance in twenty-four hours than a horse. . . .
>
> This is what mankind and human society were like before class divisions arose.[95]

This analysis by Engels, lacking any trace of the racist and imperialist values of most Europeans of his day, but rather emphasizing the social institutions and material conditions that govern humanity, was quite unlike virtually any analysis of his time, in its exhibition of a strong affection for humanity as a whole, extending to the Zulus in their war on the British. As Heyer has observed, "Nowhere in the nineteenth century has greater admiration for non-Western society been expressed than in *The Origin of the Family*."[96]

Unlike most prominent authorities on human evolution in his day, figures as varied as Lyell, Louis Agassiz, Charles Darwin, and Wallace—representing a variety of views on the origins of the races, slavery, etc. and the relations of these to human evolution, but all believing in the biological fact of race and in racial inequality (extending even to the extirpation of so-called savage races)—Engels's analysis is almost completely devoid of any treatment of biological race whatsoever.[97] Here his analysis seems to prefigure the principle, later enunciated by Gould, that the reality of "human equality is a contingent fact of history."[98] In this area too, Engels demonstrated his revolutionary and egalitarian materialism.

Engels's argument at the outset of *The Origin of the Family, Private Property, and the State* that "the determining factor in history is, in the last resort, the production and reproduction of immediate life," which he interpreted as having a "twofold character" in "the production of the means of subsistence, of food, clothing and shelter and the tools requisite therefore," on the one hand, and "the [re]production of human beings themselves, the propagation of the species," on the other, set up a complex ecological relation between labor and social reproduction.[99] The metabolism of human life was one of both production and reproduction. Although this "twofold character" of the human social metabolism was not fully developed in his thought, it nonetheless established an essential unity crucial to the development of any future ecological critique. For

Engels, not only production but also social reproduction within the family were necessary objects of revolutionary change.

In 1890 Paul Ernst, an editor of the German Social Democratic Party journal *Die Neue Zeit*, was caught in a dispute with the Austrian dramatic critic Hermann Bahr. Ernst had initially engaged in a debate with a writer from the German naturalist magazine *Freie Bühne für modernes Leben*, where Bahr was an editor. Ernst strongly criticized Henrik Ibsen's plays, including *A Doll's House*. For Ernst women's liberation had to await the inevitable development of the material means of production. At the same time, he ridiculed Ibsen as a "petty bourgeois" figure who concentrated on moral and psychological issues. Bahr proceeded to attack Ernst in two installments of an article on "The Epigones of Marxism," presenting what he saw as a more authentic Marxist view. Ernst then appealed to Engels for support, as the authority on Marxism. In a private letter in reply, in which he explicitly declined to enter the fray, Engels refused to support Bahr's interpretation of Marx's views (which stripped away all historical evolution in the treatment of women and the women's question), but more important, he indicated his strong disagreement with Ernst with respect to Ibsen and the women's movement.

Engels made it clear that it was wrong to criticize Ibsen or the Norwegian women's movement along the lines that Ernst had advanced. Specifically, the nascent women's movement could not be denounced on the basis of a mechanical argument on the necessary prior development of the material means of production. As Engels put it, "The materialist method is converted into its direct opposite if, instead of being used as a guiding thread in historical research, it is made to serve as s ready-cut pattern on which to tailor the historical facts." Moreover, to deride Ibsen and the Norwegian women's movement on the grounds that they represented petty-bourgeois views ignored the historical specificity of the development of the petty bourgeoisie in Norway in particular, where it had come to play a more progressive role. Nor was the women's question to be shortchanged or treated as a minor matter. "The field covered by what is generally designated as the woman question," he wrote, "is so vast that one cannot, within the confines of a letter, treat this subject thoroughly or say anything half-way satisfactory about it." What was needed was deep analysis of historical evolution. "Whatever weaknesses" there were in Ibsen's plays from the standpoint of a class critique, Engels indicated, they nonetheless pointed to the possibility of progressive action not determined simply by class relations. This reflected the fact that the condition of Norwegian women, with which Ibsen was especially concerned, had reached a "superior" level of liberation as compared with their German counterparts.[100]

Engels's sensitivity to the issues raised in Ibsen's plays (some of which he knew) were no doubt deeply affected by his deep affection for Eleanor Marx and his involvement in socialist circles where there was an enormous enthusiasm for Ibsen. Eleanor Marx-Aveling was the first translator into English in 1888 of Ibsen's plays *An Enemy of the People* and *The Lady of the Sea*. Eleanor was a great Ibsen enthusiast. In 1884 Edward Aveling read part of *Ghosts* to Eleanor and Olive Schreiner. In 1885 there was a performance of *A Doll's House*—the first ever in England—at Eleanor's residence, with Eleanor as Nora Helmer, Aveling as Torvald Helmer, George Bernhard Shaw as Nils Krogstadt and May Morris (William Morris's daughter) as Kristine Linde. Engels was likely present, as was Helene Demuth, on such occasions. For socialists, Ibsen and the issues that he raised about women's conditions were central.[101]

After the death of Mary Burns, Engels had taken up a common-law marriage with her younger sister, Lizzy. He openly referred to her as his "wife" and they lived together until her death in September 1878. As Gustav Mayer refers to their relationship and of Engels's attitude toward marriage, "Neither his conviction nor his sentiments would allow the claim of state and church to legitimize his closest human relationship." Nevertheless, standing for the second time before "the deathbed of comrade and lover" Engels chose, at Lizzy's request, to honor her by marrying her in a legal ceremony.[102]

Later in 1891, writing to Julie Bebel, the wife of August Bebel, who was known for his *Women and Socialism*, and who had found in Julie a proletarian companion, Engels said of his wife Lizzy—with his own parallel work on the *Origin of the Family, Private Property and the State* clearly in mind, though written years after her death: "My wife was also of genuine Irish proletarian blood and her passionate feeling for her class, a feeling that was inborn, was of immeasurably greater value to me and has been a greater standby at all critical junctures than anything of which the priggishness and sophistry of the 'heddicated' and 'sensitive' daughters of the bourgeoisie might have been capable. But my wife has now been dead for twelve years and more, while August is fortunate enough to have you still at his side; that is the difference."[103]

ENGELS AND THE NEW MATERIALISM

Engels's dialectical argument with respect to nature and society, along with production and reproduction, taken as a whole, arose, as with Marx, from his materialist dialectics. Its inspiration thus went back to Hegel and Feuerbach, a topic that Engels returned to in his *Ludwig Feuerbach and the Outcome of Classical German Philosophy*, published in 1888. In *The Essence of Christianity*, Feuerbach had led the way in the critical revolt against Hegelian idealism. Thus Feuerbach, and those immediately influenced by him in the period leading up to the 1848 revolution, "placed materialism on the throne again" recognizing that "nature exists independently of all philosophy," that "nothing exists outside nature and man."[104]

The most active and critical of those who separated themselves from Hegelian idealism, including Marx and Engels, were therefore driven back to the tradition of "Anglo-French materialism." Here materialism, in its widest and only meaningful sense, could be seen as related, most fundamentally, to the critique of religion—and to the rejection of teleological thinking or final causes:

> The question of the relation of thinking to being, the relation of spirit to nature—the paramount question of the whole of philosophy . . . could achieve its full significance, only after European society had awakened from the long hibernation of the Christian Middle Ages. . . .
>
> The answers which philosophers gave to this question split them into two great camps. Those who asserted the primacy of spirit to nature, and, therefore, in the last instance, assumed world creation in some form or other—(and among the philosophers, Hegel, for example, this creation often becomes still more intricate and impossible than in Christianity)—comprised the camp of idealism. The others who regarded nature as primary, belong to the various schools of materialism.
>
> These two expressions, idealism and materialism, primarily signify nothing more than this; and here also they are not used in any other sense.[105]

Materialism without a dialectical understanding of nature as forever in motion was, however, in part a regression. Thus, there reemerged in German philosophy after Hegel the tendency to see materialism in mechanistic terms, related to eighteenth-century metaphysics, which created a narrow, reductionist, static set of views that divorced materialism from the comprehension of the real complexity of a natural world in ceaseless motion, and hence interconnected and forever changing. Philosophy, which was at the center of this regressive movement, was transformed into a self-supporting, if contradictory, amalgam of skepticism/dualism (or neo-Kantian philosophy) and of crude empiricism/mechanism (or positivism/monism).

What all such analyses had lost, according to Engels, was the dialectical outlook that classical German philosophy had enunciated at its highest level (if in inverted, idealist form) in Hegel's philosophy. Neo-Kantian philosophers raised the "question of the possibility of any cognition (or at least of any exhaustive cognition) of the world," while mechanistic materialists and crude empiricists in the philosophy of science, represented most clearly by Büchner, Vogt, and Moleschott, interpreted nature in lifeless, fixed, mechanical terms, simultaneously denying the complexity of both thought and reality.[106] Such perspectives were, for Engels, antagonistic to the more dialectical understanding of nature propounded in Darwin's evolutionary theory and Marx's and his own historical materialism. Mechanistic materialism, although capable of important insights, ultimately contradicted genuine history since nature was reduced to mere passivity, thereby undermining any realistic foundation from which to understand either human praxis or natural evolution.

The proof of the centrality of the dialectical method to science, and the complex reflection determinations tying thought to objective reality, Engels argued in *Feuerbach*, lay in the three great scientific revolutions of the 1840s–1860s: (1) the discovery of the cell; (2) the development of thermodynamics and the understanding of the laws of the transformation of energy; and (3) the Darwinian theory of evolution through natural section of innate variations. These three revolutions in science, he contended, demonstrated the interconnected, contingent, transitory, transformational—in short, the dialectical—character of natural necessity. Moreover, as opposed to those who argued from the standpoint of the inherent limitations in the human cognition of the natural world, what such scientific revolutions proved was that human understanding arose through *praxis*, as part of the development of human society, industry, and science.[107] Humanity could know the natural world, and establish universal propositions with regard to it, because it was *part of it*, able to comprehend the conditions of its existence rationally and through social action, that is, *dialectically*.[108]

PART THREE

Toward a Critical Human Ecology

CHAPTER EIGHT

Ecology as a System

In 1889, the students in Professor E. Ray Lankester's course on zoology at University College, London, led by a young, eighteen-year-old Arthur George Tansley, presented Lankester with a petition. Lankester's lectures were celebrated at the time. Each was a carefully staged event. Before the lecture commenced in a large theater lit by a skylight, the elderly laboratory steward would set the stage, hanging up various diagrams. "Promptly at one, greeted by applause, the Professor entered—well-dressed, a powerful confident figure with strong black hair and muscular torso, his height harmonizing his bulk—in no way the learned man of popular conception." He supplemented his prepared diagrams, of which he had around five hundred, by drawing with colored chalks on specially designed sliding chalkboards. His treatment of zoology did not begin and end with the comparative anatomy of dead animals, in the manner of his own mentor, Thomas Huxley, who had been frequently criticized for being a mere "necrologist" or laboratory anatomist. Instead, he emphasized animal life in its environment and living interconnections, in the context of what he called "bionomics" or ecology. Lankester thus provided his students with a depth and breadth of analysis that was breathtaking.[1]

Lankester's students were entranced.[2] But they were also hungry. Lankester lectured at 1:00 p.m. and invariably continued well beyond 2:00 p.m., and sometimes until 2:40. Most of the students had been attending lectures and working in laboratories continuously since 9:00 a.m. The practical explorations in zoology were supposed to take place from 2:00 to 5:00 p.m. and the students desperately wanted a few minutes for lunch and relaxation. Arthur Tansley thus wrote a petition asking that Lankester stop his lectures at 2:00 p.m., and got most of his fellow students to sign it. Lankester, obviously taken aback by this student rebellion, responded with something about allowing for a "light lunch," indicating that he would endeavor to stop at 2:00. But after a few days he fell back into his old habits.[3]

This was the first known interaction between Lankester—the protégé of Charles Darwin and Huxley, and friend of Karl Marx, the leading British zoologist of his time and a major figure in the development of materialist ecology—and Tansley, who was to be the founder of the British Ecological Association, and the originator of the concept of ecosystem.

The young Tansley's boldness in confronting Lankester was no doubt due to his own experience growing up in the environment of higher education in London, albeit of an unconventional sort. His father, George Tansley, was a very wealthy businessman (a "ball and rout furnisher"), who had made his money selling "high-class" furnishings, such as polished dance floors, to the wealthy for Victorian social events. He became a volunteer teacher and the managing director of the Working Men's College, London, and a supporter as well (along with Tansley's mother, Amelia Tansley) of the Working Women's College, London. George Tansley had himself been a student at the Working Men's College, where such figures as John Ruskin and William Morris, and Pre-Raphaelites like Dante Gabriel Rossetti taught. It was also where John Lubbock, the close friend and colleague of Darwin, and an anthropologist (one who had influenced Marx and Frederick Engels) was to be the principal from 1883 to 1898.

The founder and first principal of the Working Men's College, from when it was established in 1854 until his death in 1872, was Frederick Denison Maurice, a minister in the Church of England and a Christian socialist. The Working Men's College was reputedly Europe's first higher education institution devoted to adult education. The intellectual atmosphere was materialist and broadly socialist, mostly of a Fabian variety. Many of the teachers in the school were part of a Fabian socialist group organized by Frank Galton, but socialists of other varieties taught at the school as well. Morris, by then a follower of Marx, taught classes at the College. In October 1885, he delivered a lecture titled "Socialism." Marx's friend Edward Spencer Beesly, a professor of history at University College, delivered a series of lectures at the Working Men's College, which were turned into his book *Catiline, Clodius, and Tiberius*.[4] A Comtian positivist rather than a historical materialist, Beesly was nonetheless a strong fighter for worker rights and chaired the inaugural meeting in 1864 of the International Working Men's Association. Beesly's fellow positivist, Frederick Harrison, of the Church of Humanity, also taught at the college. Engels's friend, Eugene Oswald, who, along with Engels, had taken part in the Baden-Palatinate uprising in the 1848 revolution and had been a member of the Revolutionary Provisional Government, taught French at the school.[5]

Arthur Tansley, born in 1871, the second child and only son of Amelia and George Tansley, was clearly influenced by this intellectual atmosphere, one that was part of his everyday life growing up. It provided an early acquaintance with materialist, radical, and socialist, as well as freethinking and humanist ideas. The Tansley home was a center of continual discussion and social intercourse related to the Working Men's College (and the Working Women's College). The working-class and socialist orientation of the college, and the focus on science, gave it a strongly materialist ethos. As Tansley's biographer, Peter Ayres, writes, "An ancient philosophy originating with the Greek philosopher, Epicurus, materialism was being re-affirmed both by new discoveries in chemistry, geology, and biology, and by new necessities in politics and economics." The intellectual life at the Working Men's College was governed by the relation between theory and practice. An associate of the College, who was a woodturner by trade and an enthusiastic amateur field botanist, helped the young Tansley discover his scientific vocation. George Tansley took a cottage high up in West Malvern, and his son was entranced with the flora and fauna of the Malvern Hills.[6] In Ayres's words:

> In an age when much was talked and written about socialism, Arthur Tansley was able to grow up in an environment where socialism was practiced, albeit of a gentle, Fabian kind. The expansion of educational opportunities was generating an awareness among ordinary men and women that they had a right to share in, and even take some responsibility for, the countryside and the natural world. The Working Men's College may have stolen too much of his parents' attention, and encouraged what became a lifetime's habit of introspection, but in other ways it left him a rich legacy that included not merely a love of botany but first-hand evidence that the world could be changed by someone like him.[7]

In 1889, after several years at Highgate School in London, Tansley began his studies in intermediate science at University College, London, taking courses with both Lankester, as professor of zoology, and Francis Wall Oliver, lecturer, and soon professor, in botany. University College had been founded as London University in 1826 and incorporated in 1836, together with King's College, as the University College, London. University College was also the first institution to admit women students on an equal basis with men in 1878, after absorbing the London Ladies' Educational Association.[8]

University College encouraged innovative approaches to learning, which Lankester took over from his mentor, Huxley. The latter introduced a novel form of teaching at the Science School in South Kensington, where laboratories were included, so that students could get firsthand experience with the anatomy of animals and plants. When Lankester was appointed Chair of Zoology at University College, he immediately went about introducing these same methods, incorporating experience with specimens and laboratory work directly into the classroom experience. These methods were then taken up by Oliver in botany, who brought six specimens to every class. Tansley was later to recall that the lectures in these years were the high point of his entire student life.

Lankester, who insisted on the need to view species in their entire environment, and placed emphasis on bionomics (ecology) and such issues as nutrient cycling, was unique in his time. Ironically, Darwin's evolutionary theory, though the product of the work of a great field naturalist, encouraged biologists to retreat into laboratories and museums to explore comparative anatomy and morphological characteristics, allowing them to delineate evolutionary lineages. Lankester, like Huxley, a specialist in comparative anatomy of invertebrates, contended that the future lay in understanding life in its natural systems, and in relation to species interactions. Lankester's insistence on the need for a more bionomical approach to the study of marine animals had led to the creation of the Marine Biological Association under his leadership in 1883, and the establishment in 1888 of the Plymouth Marine Laboratory under his supervision. The Plymouth Marine Laboratory had just opened when Tansley was studying with Lankester, and the force of the professor's wider ecological initiative, representing a radical departure at the time, was undoubtedly deeply impressed on his students, including Tansley.[9]

Lankester was a charismatic figure, infectious in his radical commitment to science—not only for its own sake, but as a better way of living, forming the basis of an alternative to the dominant commercial ethos. In "Biology and the State," his 1883 presidential address to the Biological Section of the British Association at Southport, he had declared, "Good as Science is in itself, the desire and search for it is even better, raising men above vile things and worthless competitions to a fuller life and keener enjoyments. Through it we believe that man will be saved from misery and degradation, not merely acquiring new material powers, but learning to use and guide his life with understanding."[10] There is no doubt that Tansley, who recalled the brilliance of Lankester's lectures, was affected by his materialist approach to science and society; by his systematic, environmental approach to the study of life forms; and by his strong commitment to natural preservation.

Oliver, a botanist who shared Lankester's wider ecological concerns, would exert a more direct influence on Tansley's intellectual development. Oliver had been appointed to a lectureship in 1888 and in 1890 was given a full professorship. Tansley took Oliver's advanced botany course, which he later recalled as the single most important course in his training as a botanist. In October 1890, Tansley entered Trinity College, Cambridge, where he studied botany, zoology, physiology, and geology. There he struck up a lifelong friendship with Bertrand Russell, with whom he shared interests in socialism, science, and philosophy, as well as a common love of Shelley's poetry.

In 1893, while in his final year at Cambridge, Tansley accepted an offer of an assistantship with Oliver at University College, London, rising to the position of assistant professor (1895–1903) and then lecturer (1904–1906). In 1907, he secured a lectureship at Cambridge. In 1903 he married Edith Chick, the daughter of a lace merchant, who was a trained botanist and Oliver's assistant. Chick and Tansley had co-authored two articles (in the second of which she was the first author), but after they were married, Edith abandoned her career as a botanist to take care of household duties. They had three daughters, all of whom became professionals: a physiologist, an architect, and an economist.[11]

Tansley's evolving role as assistant to Oliver, assistant professor, and lecturer at the University College during these years was largely determined by his work with Oliver, who encouraged him to shift his research from plant anatomy to the nascent field of ecology. Oliver had a wide vision of the development of botany as a science, having studied in Germany and briefly held a fellowship in the United States. He was known as a radical and rebellious figure. He transformed his department into one of the most progressive sites for botanical research and analysis. Plant ecology, in his view, grew out of studies of plant geography. He was especially interested in the effects of pollution on botanical life and conducted studies into the effects of urban smog on cultivated plants, setting up pollution monitoring sites around London. Urban air pollution, he declared, was "an increasing source of dismay," requiring action. "A winter never passes now without one or more prolonged spells of fog, contaminated with the products of coal combustion. For weeks at a time, during the winter, the London suburbs are enshrouded in semi-darkness, whilst the air is tainted with foreign and offensive matter."

In 1903–1904 Oliver introduced England to the practice of botanical field excursions, which had already commenced in the United States, during which he stressed the importance of understanding botanical life in terms of dynamic systems. Under his tutelage, Tansley came to see ecology as a practical subject based on field exploration, leading to the analysis of plant communities (biomes), and what Tansley was later to call ecosystems.[12]

In 1894 Tansley taught himself German. He was thus able to read Danish botanist Eugenius Warming's great conceptual work, *Plantesamfund: Grundtræk af den økologiske Plantegeografi* (1895) in the 1896 German translation. Warming's work was later translated into English as *Oecology of Plants* in 1909. The word *ecology*, although introduced by Ernst Haeckel in 1864 to refer to what Darwin had called the "economy of nature," had previously attracted little attention. It was thus Warming's book that more than anything else led to the development of plant ecology as a discipline. Warming contrasted traditional "floralistic plant geography," or the taxonomic listing of plants growing in distinct areas, to "oecological plant geography" concerned with the relation of species to habitats, communities of species, and the physiognomy of plant communities.[13]

In 1900 and 1901, Tansley spent about three months on two botanical excursions in Ceylon and in the Malay peninsula and visited Egypt. He was thus introduced to both the wet tropics and desert environments. When he arrived back from the East, he started a new botanical journal, *The New Phytologist*, which he financed and edited for the next thirty years. The goal of the journal was to emphasize botanical discussions and push forward new approaches. Tansley's paper "Problems of Ecology," presented to the British Association for the Advancement of Science in 1904, became British ecology's founding statement. In 1908, at the International Geographic Congress in Geneva, Tansley proposed a series of international meetings inspired by Warming's work in plant ecology. This became the International Phytogeographic Excursion, organized by Tansley in Britain in 1911. That same year, Tansley edited the first systematic survey of British vegetation, titled *Types of British Vegetation*, authoring a theoretical introduction. The Vegetation Committee behind the project shortly metamorphosed in 1913 into the founding Council of the British Ecological Society, the world's first ecological association, with Tansley as its first president. He became editor of the new society's *Journal of Ecology*, a position he occupied from 1917 to 1938. In 1915, Tansley was made a Fellow of the Royal Society. All of this led the leading U.S. ecologist, Frederic Clements, to declare in a letter to Tansley in 1915: "You not only are the managing director, so to speak, of British ecology, but you are the outstanding (European) figure . . . and thinker, which is much more important."[14]

Tansley's introduction to *Types of British Vegetation* laid out some of the conceptual elements of the new ecology. He contrasted the taxonomic study of the distribution of plant species, which he referred to as "*floristic* plant-geography," to "*ecological plant-geography*, from the Greek *oikos*, a house (habitat)." Adopting the notion of "plant communities"—a concept he would later largely reject—Tansley wrote that "ecology includes more than the study of vegetation-units or plant-communities; it deals with the whole of the relations of individual plants to their habitats."[15]

THE TANSLEY MANIFESTO

The rise of ecology under Tansley's leadership created conflict with the botanical establishment, consisting mainly of figures who, in the aftermath of the Darwinian revolution in biology, had come to specialize in the comparative morphological structure of plants and their evolutionary lineages. For these thinkers, the new emphases on ecology, plant physiology, and genetics, seeking a wider balance, were threatening. The two key figures in this respect were Frederick Orpen Bower, Regius Professor of Botany at Glasgow University, and Isaac Bayley Balfour, Regius Professor of Botany at Edinburgh. Balfour had been one of the two translators of Warming's book, published in English in 1909 as the *Oecology of Plants*. But the English edition was in fact a different book with a much greater emphasis on morphology.

Despite Tansley's successes in establishing ecology as a discipline with the founding of the *New Phytologist*, the formation of the British Ecological Society, and the rise under his editorship of the *Journal of Ecology*, ecology remained a small affair, dominated by the older traditions of British botany. Tansley himself, though the leading figure in ecology, was still a mere Cambridge lecturer, not yet having attained a chair as a professor. Balfour had played a leading role in the founding and editing of the *Annals of Botany*, established in 1887, and no doubt saw Tansley's *New Phytologist* as an upstart rival.

An open conflict emerged between the two in 1917–19, beginning with the December 1917 publication of a twelve-page article, "The Reconstruction of Elementary Botany Teaching," signed by F. F. Blackman, V. H. Blackman, F. Keeble, F. W. Oliver, and A. G. Tansley.[16] So dominant was Tansley's role at this point, that the article quickly came to be referred to by its opponents as the "Tansley Manifesto"—despite that it had been a jointly initiated article, and Tansley, in drafting it, had done so in mutual agreement with the other signatories. The "Tansley Manifesto" (as the "Reconstruction" article will heretofore be called, though its signatories preferred to refer to simply as an article or a memorandum) created a rift with the old guard of botany, ensconced most powerfully in the Scottish universities, dividing the parties on both political and intellectual grounds.

The political aspect was the support the *New Phytologist* and the Tansley Manifesto gave to the National Union of Scientific Workers, a new radical-led organization in which the Marxian mathematician and physicist Hyman Levy played a significant role. Its goal was to organize scientific and technical workers into a broad union. On March 11, 1918, the following spring (prior to the publication of Bower's "Botanical Bolshevism" letter), the *New Phytologist*, under Tansley's editorship, published a memorandum by the nascent National Union of Scientific Workers, providing tentative support to its proposals. In the Tansley Manifesto, such economic issues related to the economic demands of scientific workers had already been raised. This, then, divided off the signatories and the *New Phytologist* from the more conservative elements of the scientific establishment. Moreover, it encouraged the view of them as representing radical, socialist interests within the profession.[17]

However, most of the discussion in the Tansley Manifesto and in the subsequent dispute had to do with the intellectual and pedagogical orientation of botany itself. Botany as comparative morphology in the period after Darwin had been largely concerned with phylogenetic relations, or the evolutionary branching process of the "phylogenetic tree." The physiological processes within botany, along with such emerging areas as ecology and genetics, tended to be subordinated to morphology. As the Manifesto stated:

> Botany in this country is still largely dominated by the morphological tradition, founded on an attempt to trace the phylogenetic relationships of plants, which began as the result of the general acceptance of the doctrine of descent. Elementary teaching (as well as a very large part of advanced teaching) is mainly occupied with the endless facts of structure and their interpretation from a phylogenetic standpoint. Side by side with this there generally goes a discussion which is often limited to a crude Darwinian teleology. Plant physiology is relegated in most cases to a subordinate place and is taught as a separate subject. The newer studies of ecology and genetics play a very small part in the curriculum. The result is that the student's introduction to the study of plant life is unbalanced and has a definite morphological bias. He inevitably comes to regard the most vital parts of the subject—those dealing with the plant as a living organism—as specialized studies of subordinate importance. The elementary student is not clearly shown the essential basic importance of these studies, which should be fundamental, because his teaching is mainly in the hands of men who are primarily morphologists.[18]

In a statement that represented a crossing of swords, the five authors wrote: "Comparative morphology should be reduced to a subordinate position [in the curriculum] and should be used primarily to illustrate the principle of division of labor and the progressive ecological adaptation of the great phyla." The reasons for this they made clear: "What is maintained is that morphological botany *ought not* to be made the main topic of elementary education in botany, because, in its current form at least, it is sterile and leads to little but further refinements of itself, and because it has no outlets on practical life."[19] Balfour, as noted, was one of the translators of Warming's *Oecology* into English, which had also been revised extensively by Warming at the same time to incorporate a much greater emphasis on morphology. The Tansley Manifesto was thus an attempt not only to alter the botany curriculum, but also to define, in dynamic, physiological terms, the emerging field of ecology. The "credo" of the five authors, as A. D. Boney called it in his discussion of "The 'Tansley Manifesto' Affair," was to be found in the following declaration: "There should be a treatment of the physiological as well as the structural life history of the individual plant, passing on to different ecological types with the physiological as well as their structural characters and leading to an elementary treatment of competition and the social life of plants. The field of ecology should thus be developed on a physiological basis."[20]

The emphasis on physiology and its relation to ecology, on the one hand, and genetics, on the other, was meant to promote a more comprehensive materialist perspective. The Tansley Manifesto highlighted the growing awareness of the close relations between "metabolism in plants" and "similar problems in animals," and the need to bring them together within a common ecological perspective. All physiology, whether of plants or animals, ultimately had "biophysical" and "biochemical" bases, out of which broader ecological relations of "competition" and "social life" were derived. What was being proposed, therefore, was the shift of botany toward a more systemic ecological analysis.[21]

The reaction of the botanical establishment, surrounding Balfour and Bower in particular, as evident both in their direct replies in the *New Phytologist* and in their private correspondence, was one of outrage. The best-known intervention was by Bower in a letter published in the *New Phytologist* titled "Botanical Bolshevism." Bower was explicit in charging Tansley and his co-authors with socialistic objectives: "The signatories appear to advocate immediate *Botanical Bolshevism*. They propose that in order to secure improvement 'comparative morphology should be reduced to a subordinate position.'... In order to secure their own Utopia they propose to 'subordinate' something which they admit is a good in itself. That is the spirit that has ruined Russia and endangered the future of civilization. Are the signatories prepared to follow a like course?" Bower characterized the "Reconstruction" article as both a "manifesto" and an "encyclical." Arguing that it was the signatories who were narrow in their conception, since they wanted to "subordinate" morphology, rather than pursue a more coordinated approach, Bower opined: "I would say 'Physician heal thyself.'"[22]

Although numerous figures openly entered into the Tansley Manifesto/Botanical Bolshevism debate, Balfour, one of the key players, did not. Rather, his views were conveyed in correspondence with Bower. The first draft of Bower's letter to the *New Phytologist* has not survived. We do have, however, the response of Balfour to the draft, in which the first extant mention to "botanical

Bolsheviks" is made—a term that may or may not have been in Bower's original draft. In his April 17, 1918, letter to Bower, responding to the latter's draft, Balfour wrote:

> You may well ask who makes them lords over us? Their pigeonholed brains seem unable to understand that the work of nature can only be understood if the construction is known and conversely . . . . I am not at all sure that it is wise to accept the challenge on the grounds put forward by the Bolsheviks. We are not morphologists with the limited outlook suggested. . . . I think your excellent counterblast would be stronger if in refusing to admit the Bolshevik's position you pointed out . . . that it is impossible to discuss a matter of this kind on such false premises.[23]

The conflict over the Tansley Manifesto had an aftermath that carried with it serious consequences for Tansley's career. In 1918, the Chair of Botany opened up at Oxford University. Tansley at that time was forty-seven years old and still occupied a mere lectureship at Cambridge, having not yet attained a position as professor. Chairs were hard to come by in the British system. Yet Lankester, Oliver, Bower, and Balfour, figures with whom Tansley might have reasonably compared himself, had first gained their chairs as professors at ages 26, 27, 30, and 26, respectively. Although Lankester was made a Fellow of the Royal Society at age 28 and Oliver at age 33, Tansley did not receive this honor until he was 44. Despite his enormous reputation and importance as the founding figure of British ecology, he undoubtedly felt himself to have been held back in his career.

Balfour, along with A. C. Seward and D. H. Scott, were the botanical representatives in the selection for the Oxford chair. Balfour, in his correspondence in relation to the chair, left no doubt about his strong personal bias against Tansley, describing the latter in a letter as a "*persona irritans.*" F. W. Keeble, who was one of the five signatories of the Tansley Manifesto, but was disliked less by Balfour, got the Oxford chair. Seward went so far as to tell Keeble that, in his opinion, Tansley's qualifications were greater but that he was outvoted.[24] In a letter to Bower in 1921, Balfour referred to the Tansley Manifesto and said, "I laughed in my sleeves when at the election of the Oxford Professorship Seward, solemnly and at great length, gave as one of Tansley's chief claims to the appointment 'his signal services as a reformer on botanical teaching.'. . . My word, Bower, how I chuckle when I think what a bombshell your *Botany of the Living Plant* must have been to the coterie" of botanical Bolsheviks.[25]

The effect of his being turned down for the Oxford chair was devastating for Tansley. It contributed to a remarkable turn in his intellectual development. In 1915, Tansley had a dream in which he was in Africa, surrounded by "a number of savages armed with spears" with no way of escape, and as his wife approached him unhindered dressed in white. Before she reached him, however, his rifle somehow went off. It was this dream that led Tansley to study Sigmund Freud's work intensely. No doubt because of the obstacles he was facing in his chosen profession, but also responding to a society in the grips of war, he turned to psychology with a vengeance. He quickly completed a book interpreting Freud's analysis, *The New Psychology and Its Relation to Life* (1920). *The New Psychology* was an instant best-seller, and Tansley's first huge public success. Ernest Jones, Freud's English collaborator, wrote a highly favorable review of the book. In 1922 Tansley spent three months undergoing analysis with Freud and played an important role in the 1922 meetings of the British Psychological Association. In late spring 1923, he resigned from his position at Cambridge and moved with his wife and daughters to Vienna with the intention of resuming his analysis with Freud. Upon returning to London six months later in 1924, he took on a psychoanalytic case that Freud referred to him in order to further acquaint himself with the discipline, and in 1925 was elected to full membership in the British Psychoanalytic Society. He had indicated in a letter to Clements that he intended to switch his career from botany to psychoanalysis.[26]

Tansley's *New Psychology* was an extraordinary work for its time, seeking to synthesize the social psychology of William McDougall, as presented in his highly influential *An Introduction to Social Psychology* from 1908, with the ideas of Freud, while also drawing heavily on Wilfred Trotter's "Herd Instinct and Its Bearing on the Psychology of Civilized Man," first published in the *Sociological Review* in 1908. Tansley approached these issues from a materialist standpoint, drawing on Freud's notion of the libido and the framework of psychic energy and moving to issues of herd instinct and the herd complex.[27] His object was to comment on the social psychology and increasing social tensions associated with the First World War and its aftermath, and the growth of the proletarian movement and feminism. The actual borrowings from Freud were fairly thin, for although Tansley addresses the unconscious mind, repression, sublimation, and dream therapy, the treatments for these are very general and, in many ways, circumspect. Such crucial areas as the Oedipus Complex and the Electra Complex were relegated to brief mentions in footnotes. Nor was there much discussion of particular psychological-sexual problems, although insanity and hysteria receive brief mention. Rather, the emphasis of the book was toward the construction of a social psychology that addressed the major movements of the time via Trotter's treatment of the herd instinct.

Two key issues in Tansley's book were the rise of proletarianism and feminism, both of which (the former more than the latter) engendered his sympathy. Class consciousness and class struggle were seen as growing out of the herd instinct and leading to the development of "partial herds" in the form of classes or national groups. With respect to the proletariat he wrote:

> Finally, we have the great partial herd of the proletariat itself, whose "class consciousness" has increased so enormously, and is still increasing with every step in better education, improved means of intercommunication and more clearly realized demands in the society at large. Trade unionism, of course, has been the most potent instrument in this development, which took place at first on occupational lines, creating a number of highly and deliberately organized partial herds. Lately these have reached out in different ways so as to embrace the whole, or nearly the whole, of the wage-earners of the country; and although this universal proletarian organization is not yet complete, it is rapidly becoming so. At the present time the proletariat is certainly the most intensely class conscious of all the social classes; and this, apart from its preponderating numbers, means that it is much the most powerful and important of all existing partial herds—potentially at least, for it has, of course, by no means reached the zenith of its political power.[28]

The defeat of "the programme of the 'Internationale'" in favor of the organization of the proletariat on national bases, marked by the failure of the working class to "throw down their arms and refuse to fight against their brothers" in the First World War marked, in Tansley's view, a setback to the world proletarian movement, and meant that the move toward a more egalitarian society needed to be waged on a more national basis for the time being. He held out the prospect of the growth of a more "universal herd" based in the formation of the working class that could lead in the direction of "the brotherhood of man" and "world federation."[29] Society thus had to be ready for radical change:

> The license of individualism must be curbed .... The upheaval of the proletariats of many countries as a result of the Great War, and the increasing sense of solidarity between them are working in this direction, though the loosening of the bonds of the old social order has set free many untamed instincts which have caused and are causing much damage and destruction. The path towards the goal will inevitably be marked by many set-backs, by bitter conflicts, and much confusion, even by temporary chaos. The refusal of many to believe that we shall get any sort of stable progress towards a better social order, or that the destruction of the old forms of society is anything but an unmixed evil, is natural enough. The human mind is seldom willing to believe in the accomplishment of the next step towards which the trend of evolution points .... In the existing condition of the world the path of sanity is the path of increasing objective knowledge and of increasing solidarity of the human race.[30]

For Tansley, who had been exposed in his early years to radical and socialist ideas, and to working-class education through his parents' involvement in the Working Men's College and the Working Women's College, the idea of a more egalitarian society based on the rise of workers was viewed as a welcome reality rather than a threat to be warded off.

At the same time, Tansley carefully considered various feminist views. He argued that women, like men, had sexual instincts and drives, and that women's sexual freedom would need to grow along with the "increase in [women's] material resources" and their expanding role in public life. The expression of love, he argued, should be free from the extreme restrictions of the current marriage laws, which limited divorce, and from the chains of contemporary sexual morality. In that way it would be possible to "do away" eventually with the main constraints imposed by the idea of "illicit character of extramarital sexual intercourse." Tansley referred critically to "what feminists call a 'man-made world.'" Although he rejected "the conviction of some feminists," citing Cicely Hamilton's 1909 *Marriage as a Trade*, that "the confinement of women to the domestic sphere is wholly the result of a sort of conspiracy on the part of men to keep them there," he recognized that many feminists' claims were just, and criticized the repression of women in contemporary society. As a result, *The New Psychology* was widely acclaimed by feminists as well as socialists.[31]

One of the most prominent authorities on hysteria at the time, and a critic of both Freud and Tansley, was the physician and neurologist H. B. Donkin. He was E. Ray Lankester's lifelong friend and formerly Karl Marx's doctor (as well as the doctor of Jenny Marx, Eleanor Marx, and Olive Schreiner). He was a former member of the Men and Women's Club, together with Karl Pearson and Schreiner, in which Lankester and Eleanor Marx had also participated indirectly. At the time that he wrote his famous article on "Hysteria" for Tuke's *Dictionary of Psychological Medicine*, Donkin was not only a Fellow of the Royal Society of Physicians but also physician to the East London Hospital for Children, and lecturer at the London School of Medicine for Women.

Donkin's work on hysteria is often referred to by feminist scholars and critics of Freud today as having offered an interpretation that was especially sympathetic with the plight of women, emphasizing the costs of the repression of their sexuality in Victorian society, and the role of patriarchal institutions in frustrating women's ambitions, and their development as free individuals. Donkin, when compared with Freud, thus provided a more directly social analysis of women's position and the psychological costs of their social repression. In acknowledging that "the subjects of hysteria are, in a very larger proportion, the female sex," he attributed this primarily to social conditions, including not simply "educational repression and ignorance as regards sexual matters of which the girl is the subject ... but [also] all kinds of other barriers to the free play of her powers ... set up by ordinary social and ethical customs." Young women were therefore confronted with an inability, as compared with young men, to engage in worldly activity and thus obtaining an outlet for their abilities and emotions. They were thus met with "far more obstacles" to their "development." They were faced in their daily lives with restrictive customs surrounding sex that entailed "enforced abstinence" and led to "dammed-up sexual emotions." The typical female hysteric was therefore reduced by society to an asocial individuality, constituting "an unsocial unit" cut off from her larger "organic surroundings," and caught in the trap of the "multiform anxieties of home life." Donkin's argument was clearly one of suggesting that the answer to the "hysteria" so commonly associated with women, was to create a world in which women were free to develop equally with men. The contrast to Freud, who tended to ignore (or even suppress in his research) the terrible family situations of his patients, such as Dora, and to base his analysis on interpretations of their fantasies, is quite evident.[32]

In July 1925 Tansley wrote a review of volume 3 of Freud's *Collected Papers* for *The Nation and Athenaeum*. This occasioned a number of responses and a hot debate between Tansley and Donkin, who objected to psychoanalysis on the grounds that no one was allowed to criticize it "unless they had previously practiced it" on Freud's own terms, including subjecting themselves to psychoanalysis. Tansley sought to defend this as sound scientific practice, while Donkin retorted that psychoanalysis was a "a truly mystic dogma" protected by the "Freudian fortress." He contended that its imperviousness to normal scientific inquiry established it as a "Freudian cult."[33]

The New Psychology demonstrated the breadth of Tansley's social commitments but had little direct relation to ecology. At most, one can see in it his later emphasis on the human dimensions of an ecological worldview. Some, however, have suggested a closer relation. Historian Peder Anker has put forward the intriguing argument that Tansley developed his ecosystem analysis of the mid-1930s during his brief time studying Freud's psychoanalysis and social psychology, and particularly in his *New Psychology*.[34] But there is no meaningful basis for this inference as direct connections are absent; the two intellectual developments in Tansley's life are separated by more than a decade; and the sources upon which Tansley erected the ecosystem concept are presented in his 1935 article, and were distant from the investigation of mental phenomena. Tansley approached basic psychic phenomena from a mechanistic-materialist perspective, like Freud, emphasizing energetic phenomena, specifically psychic energy and questions of equilibrium. Hence there are formal similarities between Tansley's analysis in psychology and ecology, stemming from basic materialist methods of inquiry. Nevertheless, the notion that Freud's concept of the libido led to Tansley's notion of ecosystem, however intellectually appealing such an idea may be to some, is devoid of foundation.

Even while he was pursuing his interest in psychoanalysis, Tansley did not ignore his ecological studies. He engaged in them concurrently, but without a direct relation between the two pursuits. Thus, he continued to edit the *New Phytologist* and the *Journal of Ecology*. And in 1923 he wrote *Practical Plant Ecology*, followed in 1926 by *The Aims and Methods in the Study of Vegetation* (a dual-edited, multi-authored volume in which Tansley had the leading role).

In *Practical Plant Ecology*, Tansley declared: "In its widest meaning ecology is the study of plants and animals *as they exist in their natural homes*," aimed at the "*study of the living populations of the globe*." It was closely related, he emphasized, to what Lankester had termed bionomics. "Ecology," he wrote, "is nature study *par excellence*." However, as in his other works up to this point, Tansley largely adhered to notions of plant community, succession, and climax, as developed by Clements, the doyen of plant ecology in the United States, as represented by his two major works, *Research Methods in Ecology* (1905) and *Plant Succession* (1916). Tansley was critical of Clements's more teleological concepts and would break fully with Clements in the 1930s, with the development of the ecosystem concept.[35]

In 1927 the Chair of Botany at Oxford again opened up, and this time Tansley was offered it. For the next two and a half decades, until his 1952 book *Mind and Life*, he rededicated his career to ecology almost entirely.

OXFORD AND THE MAGDALEN PHILOSOPHY CLUB

In obtaining the Botany chair at Oxford, Tansley was finally able to organize botany in his department in line with the philosophy enunciated in the Tansley Manifesto. He thus emphasized the development of a very broad range of studies with ecology at its fulcrum. At Oxford he became part of a larger ecological culture, which encompassed not only botany and zoology but a number of fields, including wide-ranging philosophical discussions in the Magdalen Philosophy Club on materialism versus idealism and the relation of nature and society.

A frequent presence at Oxford was Julian Huxley, Thomas Huxley's grandson and Lankester's friend. Huxley had left his position at Oxford in 1925 for King's College, London. But he remained a significant presence in and out of Oxford. In leading the first Oxford expedition to the Arctic island of Spitsbergen in northern Norway in 1921, Huxley had chosen as his assistant Charles Elton, who was to emerge as the principal figure in the development of animal ecology. In 1923, following the completion of his dissertation, Elton was made a "departmental demonstrator" (departmental lecturer) at Oxford, and in 1929 was appointed "university demonstrator" (university lecturer). In 1925 Elton became a consultant for the Hudson's Bay Company, which was interested in the systematic examination of fluctuations in fur-bearing animals. As a result, he obtained the records of trappers going back to the early eighteenth century. All of this was to lead to his well-known research on the fluctuations in mouse and vole populations. Huxley provided the introduction to Elton's classic work *Animal Ecology* in 1927, which Elton wrote in eighty-five evenings while he was teaching at Oxford during the day. Elton's book introduced many of the staple concepts of ecology, such as ecological niche, the food chain, the food cycle, and the pyramid of numbers (referring to the fact that the relative few animals at the top of the food chain relied on larger numbers at the bottom). In all, Elton presented a complex, dynamic, and dialectical view of ecology.[36]

In his 1930 work *Animal Ecology and Evolution*, Elton argued, "'The balance of nature' does not exist and perhaps has never existed." His emphasis on migration of species led him to conclude that animals, in large part, "select" their environments, rather than simply adapting to them, as in the standard theory of natural selection. "Selection of environment by migration," he wrote, "allows of a certain choice on the part of animals... animals also possess a fund of characteristics, which may on the one hand remain unborn for many years and then suddenly possess the value of a casting vote at some novel environmental crisis, and result in the preservation of one section of the population rather than another."[37] His later influential works, *Voles, Mice and Lemmings: Problems in Population Dynamics* (1942) and *The Ecology of Invasions by Animals and Plants* (1958), exhibited similar dialectical tendencies.

Elton began his *Animal Ecology* with accolades for Tansley's work in plant ecology, while Tansley wrote a very favorable review of *Animal Ecology*, in which he referred to Elton as "one of the keenest and most successful of our very small band of animal ecologists." Animal ecology, however, grew by leaps and bounds from this point and, by 1932, the number of articles in animal ecology had grown to such an extent that Tansley and Elton recommended, on behalf of the British Ecological Association, the founding of a new *Journal of Animal Ecology*, which was to be edited by Elton.[38]

Another figure at Oxford, from 1934–36, was the Nobel-winning physicist Erwin Schrödinger, who in 1944 was to write his little book *What Is Life?*, relying centrally on the concept of metabolism. Tansley and Schrödinger were apparently well acquainted.[39]

In 1931–33 Tansley participated in the Magdalen Philosophy Club at Oxford. The Magdalen Philosophy Club was unique in that it included extensive discussions and debates between idealists and Romantics, mostly in philosophy and literature on the one hand, and materialists, mostly in the physical sciences, on the other. Both groups, moreover, were interested in issues of nature and ecology. The idealists were led by John Alexander Smith, best known for his twelve-volume commentary on Aristotle. Smith argued that reality at its core was the creation of the self-conscious mind, a view he put forward in his Gifford

Lectures on "The Heritage of Idealism," presented in the academic years 1929–31. Smith had served as the peer reviewer of Jan Christiaan Smuts's *Holism and Evolution*, a work that was later to be the subject of Tansley's critique of idealist approaches to ecology leading to his development of ecosystem theory. Next to Smith was Robin George Collingwood, who presented a series of lectures at Magdalen in the 1930s that were later published as *The Idea of Nature.* Collingwood's treatment of the issue of nature took the form of a strong defense of idealist views, including Smuts's *Holism and Evolution*, and a condemnation of all realist and materialist views, which he associated with technological determinism and a retreat from Christian values.[40]

Others sitting around the Magdalen dinner table and connected, at least indirectly, to these discussions were the literary Romanticists Clive Staples Lewis and John Ronald Reuel Tolkien.[41] Lewis was an Oxford tutor who converted to theism and then Christianity in 1929–31. In the late 1930s, '40s, and '50s he was to write *The Screwtape Letters*, the "Narnia" series, and the famous Space Trilogy (*Out of the Silent Planet*, *Perelandra*, and *That Hideous Strength*). J. R. R. Tolkien was an Oxford philologist, professor of Anglo-Saxon, and later author of *The Hobbit* and *The Lord of the Rings.* Tolkien had been directly inspired by Morris's epic poem from the Icelandic Sagas, *The Story of Sigurd the Volsung and the Fall of the Niblungs*, and by Morris's historical fantasies, *The House of the Wolfings* and *The Roots of the Mountains*, based on Germanic prehistory. These works by Morris played a considerable role in inspiring Tolkien's *The Lord of the Rings.* Morris wrote his historical romances as a socialist attempting to explore the historical-aesthetical roots that would inspire a revolt against the capitalist society of his day. Tolkien, from a conservative Romantic perspective, was also rebelling against capitalist modernity and technology. "It may seem odd," Meredith Veldman has written, "that Tories such as Lewis and Tolkien should find Morris, the revolutionary Marxist, so appealing, but the common quest for community overcame these political barriers and drew Lewis and Tolkien to Morris." Both Morris and Tolkien drew heavily on ecological themes. Tolkien was quite explicit about the nature-loving character of his work, telling the *Daily Telegraph* in 1972, "In all my work I take the part of trees against their enemies. Lothlorien is beautiful because the trees were loved." With respect to England of the 1970s, he wrote: "The savage sound of the electric saw is never silent wherever trees are still found growing." *The Hobbit* and *The Lord of the Rings* referred to sixty-four species of wild plants, as well as a number of invented varieties.[42] How much figures like Lewis and Tolkien interacted with Tansley is unknown, but it is clear that both idealists and materialists around the Magdalen dinner table were discussing nature and ecological ideas, whether by way of Romantic culture or materialist science. Typically, there was a strong affinity in their views when it came to nature conservation.

The materialists/realists at the Magdalen dinner table included the Nobel Prize-winning neurophysiologist Charles Sherrington. In addition to his pioneering work on the nerve systems, Sherrington had an interest in philosophy nurtured by the Magdalen Philosophy Club. In 1937–38 Sherrington delivered the Gifford Lectures, published in 1940 as *Man on His Nature*.

John Zachary Young, a tutor in zoology, took a strong materialist stance.[43] Young was a neurophysiologist. He was to become an influential scientist and scientific publicist, who broadcast the Reith Lectures on "Doubt and Certainty in Science" in 1950. He eventually became president of the Marine Biological Association established by Lankester. One of his last works, in 1987, was *Philosophy and the Brain*.

Tansley's main contribution to the Magdalen Philosophy Club discussions, and his most ambitious effort in the philosophy of science, was a paper he delivered at the Magdalen dinner table in May 1932 titled "The Temporal Genetic Series as a Means of Approach to Philosophy."[44] This paper, which was not actually published until 2002, seventy years after it was written, and nearly half a century after his death, was Tansley's response to the philosophical discussions with respect to *emergence*, associated in particular with C. Lloyd Morgan's theory of *Emergent Evolution* (1923). The concept of emergence, which was to become an essential element of modern science, was aimed at providing a philosophical-scientific explanation of the rise within material existence of whole new levels of organization, and novel forms, constituting at each successive level of reality fundamentally different orders of scientific law. The higher levels in this sequence were products of and yet irreducible to the lower levels, since they gave rise to qualitative novelty and whole new principles. In Lloyd Morgan's work, the various levels of existence were presented as a "pyramidal scheme," pointing from matter, to life, to mind.[45] In the work of Samuel Alexander, author of *Space, Time and Deity*, with whom Lloyd Morgan's work was closely associated, the base of the pyramid was designated as "Space-Time."[46] "Emergent evolution," as the philosopher of science David Blitz explained in the 1990s, is associated with three general propositions: "Firstly, that evolution is a universal process of change, one which is productive of qualitative novelties; secondly, that qualitative novelty is the emergence in a system of a property not possessed by any of its parts; and thirdly, that reality can be analyzed into levels, each consisting of systems characterized by significant emergent properties."[47] What was meant by emergence, he explained, was the rise of qualitatively new relations.[48]

Within the British tradition, the idea of emergence is usually traced to John Stuart Mill's distinction in his *A System of Logic* (1843) between homeopathic and heteropathic laws. Mill had observed:

> All organized bodies are composed of parts, similar to those composing inorganic nature, and which have even themselves existed in an inorganic state; but the phenomena of life, which result from the juxtaposition of those parts in a certain manner, bear no analogy to any of the effects which would be produced by the action of the component substances considered as mere physical agents. To whatever degree we might imagine our knowledge of the several ingredients of a living body to be extended and perfected, it is certain that no mere summing up of the separate actions of those elements will ever amount to the action of the living body itself.[49]

It was to deal with this problem that Mill introduced the distinction between homeopathic laws operating horizontally within some sphere and heteropathic laws that arose at a new level, and represented processes that were discontinuous with the lower level of material reality.[50]

The general problem was taken up in the 1870s in the work of philosopher and critic George Henry Lewes, who introduced the term "emergence" for the qualitatively distinct laws at a new level, leading to Lloyd Morgan's adoption of the concept of "emergent evolution" in 1915.[51] A central element in Lloyd Morgan's analysis of emergence was the notion that a higher emergent reality could react on a lower level, affecting processes from which the new emergent level had arisen—a phenomenon to which he gave the term "supervenience." As he put it: "When some new kind of relatedness is supervenient (say at the level of life [as opposed to mere matter], the way in which the physical events which are involved run their course is different in virtue of its presence—different from what it would have been if life had been absent."[52] Emergence as an evolutionary process occurred *over time*, reflecting irreversible change.

Because it was aimed at integrating evolutionary theory with what could be considered to be fundamental dialectical conceptions, the theory of emergent evolution was attractive to both idealists and materialists, who engaged with each other in quite remarkable ways in the development of the concept. Lloyd Morgan, like Alexander, conceived the theory of emergent evolution in idealist terms, culminating in God. Although emergent evolution, particularly in Lloyd Morgan's work, was generally couched in a way consistent with Darwinian evolutionary theory, explicitly rejecting vitalism as in the case of Bergson, it generally sought to superimpose on this idealist notions such as an inexplicable "all-embracing Activity" of a teleological nature. "We acknowledge God," he concluded his book, "as above and beyond. But unless we also intuitively enjoy his Activity within us . . . we can have no immediate knowledge of Causality or of God as the Source of our own existence and emergent evolution."[53] Alexander insisted that emergent evolutionary processes be viewed with "natural piety," a notion that Morgan also took up. In his *Life, Mind and Spirit* (1926), Lloyd Morgan wrote: "There is no disjunctive antithesis of evolutionary progress and Divine purpose." Indeed, "The acknowledged activity in Divine Purpose is monistic to the core. It is that activity which is manifested in *all* action—in that which obtains in the atom as in that which obtains in man, each according to its status."[54] But he indicated that a consistent naturalism, that is, materialism, needs no divine activity to explain emergence, and hence the inclusion of God within the schema was more a preference than a logical necessity.[55]

In *Emergent Evolution*, Lloyd Morgan devoted a lengthy appendix to the ideas of the U.S. socialist and materialist philosopher Roy Sellars, author of *Critical Realism* (1916) and *Evolutionary Naturalism* (1922), and later *The Principles and Problems of Philosophy* (1926).[56] As a critical realist, Sellars argued: "No motive has entered to cause us to doubt the existence of physical things co-real with the percipient, but reflection has discovered that the objective content with which we at first clothe these acknowledged realities is intra-organic. In other words, we can no longer believe that we can literally inspect, or intuit, the very external existent itself. The content of which we are aware is clearly distinct from the physical existent with which it was erstwhile identified, though it is in causal relation to it."[57] In order to explain the temporal increase in complexity, Sellars incorporated a notion of emergence, or of evolutionary levels, into his materialist philosophy. He accepted Lloyd Morgan's fundamental notion of emergent evolution, although in entirely materialist-naturalist terms. Lloyd Morgan declared that he and Sellars were in "substantial agreement" with respect to the naturalistic basis of emergent evolution, but not with respect to "the supplementary concept of Activity," whereby Lloyd Morgan reintroduced teleology and God.[58]

Although emergent evolution found its most influential early proponents in the idealist camp, the general concept was ultimately to be far more important to critical (or dialectical) materialists, allowing them to surmount mechanistic and reductionist forms of materialism and crude positivism. In Sellars's critical realism, the different evolutionary levels reflected in the phenomenon of emergence were associated with increasing organizational complexity over time.[59] Such a broad concept of emergence has always been implicit in Marxian theory, with its Hegelian heritage, and had been developed further by Engels in his exploration of the dialectics of nature. This dialectical emergentism was to be carried forward by Joseph Needham in the late 1930s. Needham valued the evolutionary naturalism of Sellars but saw it as falling short of Marx and Engels. Instead, Needham was to develop the Marxian approach in line with materialist science as one of integrative levels, involving levels of organization, which encompassed both envelopes and succession.[60] Emergence was to be reappraised and to play a central role in the dialectics of the critical-realist Marxian philosopher Roy Bhaskar in the 1990s.[61]

Today a distinction is often made in the philosophy of science between ontological emergentism and epistemological emergentism, with the former insisting that there is a change in laws at the new level due to changes in organization, and the latter arguing simply that the higher level is not predictable based on the conditions of the lower one; this is often characterized as well as "strong emergentism" and "weak emergentism," respectively. Strong emergentists argue for a kind of "downward causality" (in addition to upward causality) in which the new relations and processes at the higher level can turn back and affect the lower.[62]

Tansley's own contribution to this discussion in his 1932 presentation to the Magdalen Philosophy Club, "The Temporal Genetic Series as a Means of Approach to Philosophy," was intended as a materialist-ecological approach to the question of emergence—at one and the same time rejecting both idealism and mechanical materialism. Tansley began by modestly emphasizing his lack of credentials for the grand subject he was to approach, indicating that he was not an experimentalist in biology. He stated: "I fully realize that I have missed the chance of contributing humbly to the progress of biology in any significant sense, though this does not in fact greatly distress me." He designated himself as an "amateur" in psychology (despite his work with Freud), and an "ignoramus" in philosophy, in spite of his close association with Bertrand Russell and familiarity with his ideas. His goal in his paper, he stated, was to depict what he called the "temporal genetic series" from inorganic matter to living organism to mind. In Tansley's argument there were three gaps that needed to be examined: between the inorganic and the organic, between the physiological and the psychical, and between psychical activity in general and judgments of value involving the intellectual, aesthetic, and ethical realms. His analysis of the temporal genetic sequence thus sought to follow each of these out successively along materialist lines. He insisted that there are no "phenomena of life (leaving 'mind' for the moment out of consideration) that are not theoretically capable of 'explanation' in terms of chemistry and physics." Moreover, there was "no sharp boundary," he insisted, "between organic and inorganic compounds." Here he referred to the materialist theory of the origin of life developed simultaneously by J. B. S. Haldane in Britain and A. I. Oparin in the USSR in the 1920s. A materialist approach, in order to avoid reductionism, thus required the notion of emergent evolution as introduced by Morgan, emphasizing the qualitative differences in existence, despite what Tansley called "continuity throughout the universe" in its basic physic-chemical-material character. The origin of organisms could be seen, in accordance with the Haldane-Oparin theory, Tansley claimed, as an "excellent example of emergent evolution," in the sense that something "new" had appeared, which was nonetheless "implicit in previous inorganic development." If organisms were "unique," it was therefore a "limited uniqueness."[63]

Similar problems were presented by the gap between the physiological and the psychological. Tansley, based on his knowledge of psychology from William James to Freud, and his biological training, explored the extent to which the mental (neurological) activity could be seen in physiological terms. He emphasized the similarity of the mental processes of humans and higher animals. "We cannot escape the fact," he wrote, "of the continuity of life and organic structure with which in its higher ranges, mental phenomena are associated .... But supposing awareness, and therefore mind, have arisen in this way, it must be quite freely conceded that when they have arisen they are something new—something *sui generis* in a sense in which physiological perception is not, something of which we cannot give a clear account of in terms of anything else." Again, Tansley insisted that the "continuity throughout the universe" was reflected in the lack of any real material discontinuity "between the physiological and the psychical, which again had to be seen as a qualitative leap or emergence."[64]

In approaching the issue of mind itself, Tansley argued that "self-consciousness" was really a social product and hence could not be approached primarily from the standpoint of the individual ego. The human mind developed only in society (a fact he would have applied to the higher mammals as a whole). This was related to the third gap in his temporal genetic series, between psychical activity in general and the development of values of an intellectual, aesthetic, and ethical nature, which could only occur within society. "We cannot," he wrote, "conceive of values created in minds of a much lower degree of complexity than our own. Values are a new kind of attribute arising from the specific activity of the human mind, though like all other phenomena we have been considering, they are not without antecedents." What is "good," Tansley insisted, was in no way transhistorical. It arose out of definite material social relations. "Each society forms its own ideas of the good life according to its own nature and circumstances .... That is why it is difficult to be satisfied that one is leading the good life in the modern world of the 20th century." Freedom and determinism both existed in this view of the world, with freedom consisting of each thing being allowed to develop according to its own intrinsic nature, and determinism consisting in the fact that the complex of relations and interactions meant that freedom in this sense was always limited. For Tansley, the world as a whole could be seen as evolutionary in the sense that it represented "the progressive appearance of integrated systems, successively in the inorganic, the organic, the psychical, and finally in the intellectual, the aesthetic, and ethical spheres." But like other sophisticated theorists of material evolution, he insisted that this "progressive appearance" did not necessarily imply, especially in the higher realms, the achievement of "the good life," and that the struggle of freedom-in-determination would continue.[65]

Tansley's entire analysis, although it remained unpublished, was consistent with the argument on emergence that Needham was to introduce five years later at Oxford in his Herbert Spencer Lecture, "Integrative Levels."[66] Like figures such as J. S. Mill, Engels, and Needham, Tansley's perspective pointed to a strong emergentism. This was to play a role in his later development of the ecosystem concept.

THE NATURE OF LIVING MATTER

More important than Oxford ecology and the Magdalen Philosophy Club in determining Tansley's ecological thinking and the rise of ecosystem analysis were the debates taking place internationally over the questions of materialism versus idealism, and the nature of ecology. Here too the main lines drawn were between conservative, idealist, and vitalist views, on the one hand, and socialist and materialist ones, on the other, with the Romantic tradition often seemingly straddling the two. A kind of showdown occurred at the meetings of the British Association for the Advancement of Science in the summer of 1929, which Tansley attended.[67] The British Association meetings were to be the site of the now famous "Nature of Life" debate between idealists, in which General Jan Christiaan Smuts, philosopher of holism; physiologist John Scott Haldane (father of J. B. S. Haldane); philosopher H. Wildon Carr (author of books on Bergson and Croce); physicist and astronomer Arthur Eddington (author of *The Nature of the Physical World,* which argued for a shift from materialism to idealism); and socialist biologist and mechanistic materialist Lancelot Hogben, all took part. However, it was the stark conflict between Smuts and Hogben that was to stand out and to be remembered as constituting the core of the debate, and which was to impact the development of ecology. Smuts, though primarily an army general, statesman, and public philosopher, was also a gifted amateur botanist, and had been on several major botanical expeditions. Smuts's knowledge of botany was substantial, and he was recognized worldwide as an expert on the savanna grass.[68]

Smuts claimed that his philosophy of holism was an outgrowth of science, and indeed represented a major contribution to the philosophy of science. A number of influential figures in the scientific community, such as John Scott Haldane, agreed. Haldane, who arranged the Nature and Life debate, saw the promotion of Smuts's holism as its principal goal, and chose Hogben as a strong mechanist-materialist and socialist, simply for contrast, and to attract attention.

That Hogben spoke so effectively and subsequently developed his ideas into a major work in response, was no doubt unexpected.[69]

Commonly referred to as General Smuts because of his military role in the Boer War (he fought on the side of the Afrikaners), Smuts had also been a legal adviser to Cecil Rhodes and was one of the principal figures in establishing the apartheid system. In 1915, during the First World War, as South African Minister of Defense, he conquered German Southwest Africa (Namibia) and German East Africa (Burundi, Rwanda, and mainland Tanzania). It was Smuts who coined the word *apartheid* (meaning literally apartness) in 1917—almost a decade before he coined the word *holism*. Though Smuts is often ironically viewed as a "moderate" in the history of white South African racial politics, he is also referred to as the real "architect" of apartheid.[70] He was a strong advocate of the territorial segregation of "the races" and what he called "a grand [white] racial aristocracy."[71] He indicated at one time that he had a simple message: to "defy negrophilists," a derogative term used to refer to a person (usually white) who was supportive of the rights of black people. He is perhaps best remembered worldwide as the South African general who arrested Gandhi. Smuts tried to impede the flow of immigrants from India to South Africa, imposed martial law against labor strikers, and deported labor leaders from the country.[72]

Smuts was the South African minister of defense from 1919 to 1929, and prime minister and minister of native affairs from 1919 to 1924 and 1939 to 1948. He was to be a longtime leader of the Union Party (the liberal, pro-British Empire party, opposed to the Nationalist Party). He was a figure soaked in blood. In 1920, when the Native Labour Union demanded political power and freedom of speech, Smuts crushed it with violence, killing sixty-eight people in Port Elisabeth alone. In 1921, when a black religious group referring to themselves as "Israelites" in Bull Hoek (near Queenstown), squatting on land surrounding their place of worship, and refused to relocate, Smuts deployed regiments armed with artillery and machine guns and close to two hundred people were killed. In 1922, when the Bondelswarts, a group of Khoikhoi, the nomadic non-Bantu populations in South West Africa (now Namibia), refused to pay their dog tax and complained about white penetration of their lands, Smuts sent four hundred troops armed with four machine guns supported by two bombing planes. As Edward Roux wrote in *Time Longer than Rope*, "To the mechanised slaughter that then took place even the determined Bondelswarts could offer no manner of resistance. Over 100 men, women, and children were killed outright and many more mutilated or seriously injured. No white man died."[73] Horrified by these actions, the South African poet Roy Campbell wrote the poem "HOLISM," which included the following lines:

The love of Nature burning in his heart,
Our new Saint Francis offers us his book—
The saint who fed the birds at Bondleswaart
And fattened up the vultures at Bull Hoek.[74]

The "new Saint Francis" was Smuts; "his book" was his 1926 *Holism and Evolution*. Although Smuts asserted that "we do not want to re-create Nature in our own image," his concept of holism was grounded in the social-political climate of South Africa and it represented a transfer of social relations to nature and back again to society (of the kind criticized by Engels as a sort of double transference).[75] It embodied issues of domination and control. He argued that life is a process of change and that evolution is a creative process (in the sense of the vitalist Henri Bergson). Rejecting the perceived rigidity of mechanism or mechanical materialism, Smuts sought a universal principle to explain the organization of both nature and society. The whole is a self-generating cause. For Smuts, the world comprised an ongoing, evolving series of wholes, which were constantly interacting. For each whole, the parts are in constant reflexivity sustaining a dynamic equilibrium. The parts act to fix and repair any damage to the whole, because they are subordinate to the whole. "The new science of Ecology," he wrote, "is simply a recognition of the fact that all organisms feel the force and moulding of their environment as a whole. There is much more in Ecology than merely striking down of the unfit by way of Natural Selection."[76]

Holism and Evolution began with three premises. First, life evolved from matter. Thereafter matter as life (reflecting its emergent evolution) is no longer bound by mechanistic principles of motion and energy. Instead, matter has become a realm of life and the entire world is alive through progressive developments. Second, the natural world is essentially beneficent and moving teleologically toward constant improvement, which involves cooperation, service, and order. Third, the universe is concerned and guided by the principle of holism. The production and advancement of wholes is part of the essence of life. For instance, "wholeness generally as characteristic of existence, is an inherent character of the universe."[77] Indeed, "Evolution of the universe, inorganic and organic," he wrote, "is nothing but the record of whole-making in its progressive development." As for holism as a philosophy, Smuts rhetorically asked, "What else is Holism but . . . an attempted ground-plan of the universe?" In its wider sense, "holism is really no more than an attempt to extend the system of life and mind . . . to inorganic Evolution."[78]

In arguing that evolution was a process of creating ever more complex and important wholes and establishing that there was a hierarchy of wholes, some of which were more exalted than others, Smuts was able to organize, order, and divide the world, from high to low species. He assumed, in contradistinction to materialist thinkers, that evolution was a series of ordered advances toward perfection. The organism was the center of control, given that this was the site of the development of personality. As opposed to Darwinian natural selection, Smuts contended that the higher, teleological process of "Holistic Selection is much more subtle in its operation, and is much more social and friendly in its activity. . . . Its favours go to those variations which are along the road of its own development, efficiency, and perfection." Nature's hierarchy was then seen as directly "social and friendly"—or cooperative.[79]

Within the hierarchy of wholes, there was a hierarchy of personalities (reflecting the different levels of wholes). This was Smuts's famous concept of "personology," which he related to ecology. The notion of superior personalities as the highest form of life was a view that seemed to present an almost religious striving.[80] Smuts declared that "man is in very truth an offspring of the stars," a quasi-religious view that was meant to be counterposed to materialism.[81] Smuts's outlook was influential with Alfred Adler, Freud's great opponent within psychology. Adler argued that "a body shows a struggle for complex wholeness" and saw this as connected to Smuts's emphasis on personality and holism.[82]

The most advanced, complex wholes (personalities), in Smuts's view, had greater independence (freedom) from the immediate environment. The less advanced did not have the same degree of freedom and control over their environment, which they could not socially construct to meet their needs and ends. Such people remained at the mercy of nature; they were seen as "children of nature." The hierarchy in the natural and social worlds was, he argued, the result of natural inequalities rather than social structures and social history.[83]

Although *Holism and Evolution* was primarily abstract in its discussion, its concrete meaning was not hard to discern. The lectures on Africa that Smuts presented at Oxford in the fall of 1929 (with Tansley again present), a few months after the Nature of Life debate in South Africa, were much more explicit with respect to his position on natural and racial relations and the meaning of his holism. He had been invited to speak on holism at Oxford with the idealist John Alexander Smith playing a leading role in the invitation. Instead, Smuts chose to speak more concretely on Africa in the context of his holist philosophy.[84] The views that Smuts presented help to explain the depth of the conflict that emerged in the Nature of Life debate in South Africa between Smuts and Hogben, and the subsequent politicization of the whole question of ecology. In these lectures he made explicit connections between his hierarchical, teleological ecology, in which nature is turned into a hierarchy of wholes and the system of racial stratification, based on his notion of personology, justifying the construction of the apartheid system in South Africa.

Indeed, from the late 1920s on, in the words of South African Marxist ecologist Edward Roux and his wife, mathematician Winifred Roux, "segregation" in South Africa, while always present, "was raised to a philosophy."[85] Smuts prepared his Oxford lectures to counter those who questioned the dominant presence of Europeans in Africa and their right to influence African development along imperial lines. As a politician centrally involved in the organization of the League of Nations, he framed white European interest in naturalized, "humanitarian" interventionist terms, even when advocating outright racism. W. E. B. Du Bois, many years later, when Smuts pleaded for an article on "human rights" to be adopted by the United Nations, did not miss the "twisted contradiction of thought" being revealed, given that Smuts had "once declared that every white man in South Africa believes in the suppression of the Negro except those who are 'mad, quite mad.'"[86]

In his Oxford Lectures, published as *Africa and Some World Problems*, Smuts presented the colonial explorations of David Livingstone and Henry Morton Stanley as those of early Europeans seeking to bring civilization to the people of Africa. He asserted that their historic mission must be continued to save Africa from barbarism. Smuts argued that Britain must take a humanitarian and commercial interest in Africa. Labor would be recruited from various African nations. But this development would also raise new questions regarding what happens "whenever a superior culture came in contact with a lower, more primitive. We cannot mix the two races, for that means debasement of the higher race and culture."[87]

In accord with these views, Smuts insisted that blacks naturally lacked an internal impetus for creating the world. The "Bushman" was, in his words, "a mere human fossil, verging to extinction."[88] In his ecological theory, they were seen as lacking the evolutionary development of a complex (climax) personality, a notion that represented a convulsed, double transfer from society to nature (via Smuts's holism) and then back again. Thus, it was the duty and right of Europeans to organize the social and natural structure of Africa. In an account that drew on the concept of "recapitulation" (ontogeny follows phylogeny) introduced by Ernst Haeckel, and heavily relied upon by nineteenth-century biological racism, Smuts wrote:

> It is even possible, so some anthropologists hold, that this [the African] was the original mother-type of the human race and that Africa holds the cradle of mankind. But whether this is so or not, at any rate here we have the vast result of time, which we should conserve and develop with the same high respect which we feel towards all great natural facts. This [racial] type has some wonderful characteristics. It has largely remained a child type, with a child psychology and outlook. . . . There is no inward incentive to improvement,

> there is no persistent effort in construction, and there is complete absorption in the present, its joys and sorrows. Wine, women, and song in their African forms remain the great consolations of life. No indigenous religion has been evolved, no literature, no art since the magnificent promise of the cave-men and the South African petroglyphist, no architecture since Zimbabwe (if that is African). Enough for the Africans the simple joys of village life, the dance, the tom-tom, the continual excitement of forms of fighting which cause little bloodshed. They can stand any amount of physical hardship and suffering, but when deprived of these simple enjoyments, they droop, sicken, and die. . . . These children of nature have not the inner toughness and persistence of the European, nor those social and moral incentives to progress which have built up European civilization in a comparatively short period. . . . It is clear that a race so unique, and so different in its mentality and its cultures from those of Europe, requires a policy very unlike that which would suit Europeans.[89]

Smuts's reference to adult Africans as "children" drew, as noted, on the recapitulation theory in biology, which was already falling out of favor at the time Smuts was writing and has long been rejected by modern biologists.[90] Recapitulation was the notion that each individual of a species in its development passes through (recapitulates), in telescoped fashion, the main stages that the entire species over historical time had previously passed through. It argued that the children of higher races passed through and went beyond in their development the stage in which adults of lower races were permanently stuck, making the latter in effect equivalent to permanent children. In Stephen Jay Gould's words, "The 'primitive-as-child' argument stood second to none in the arsenal of racist arguments supplied by science to justify slavery and imperialism."[91]

On this basis, Smuts proposed that separate and parallel institutions and segregation were required to save and retain African wholeness. He argued that this policy of nascent apartheid would maintain a healthy, good society. Any unnatural mixing of the races, contravening the natural, hierarchical principles, would lead to the moral deterioration of the species:

> The old practice mixed up black with white in the same institutions; and nothing else was possible, after the native institutions and traditions had been carelessly or deliberately destroyed. But in the new plan there will be what is called in South Africa "segregation"—separate institutions for the two elements of the population, living in their own separate areas. Separate institutions involve territorial segregation of the white and black. If they live mixed up together it is not practicable to sort them out under separate institutions of their own. Institutional segregation carries with it territorial segregation. The new policy therefore gives the native his own traditional institutions on land

> which is set aside for his exclusive occupation. . . . For urbanized natives, on the other hand, who live, not under tribal conditions but as domestic servants or industrial workers in white areas, there are set aside native villages or locations, adjoining the European towns. . . .This separation is imperative, not only in the interests of a native culture, and to prevent native traditions and institutions from being swamped by the more powerful organizations of the whites, but also for other important purposes, such as public health, racial purity, and public good order. The mixing up of two such alien elements as white and black leads to unhappy social results—racial miscegenation, moral deterioration of both, racial antipathy and clashes, and to many other forms of social evil.[92]

In Smuts's intellectual system of natural hierarchy, the concept of ecological holism was seen as justifying racial segregation. His notion of a complex or climax personality and of natural holism emerged as a kind of integrated, ecological racism. Nevertheless, Smuts's views had a wider attraction, divorced from this aspect of his thought. His emphasis on wholes was seen as a more sophisticated scientific-idealist replacement for Bergsonian vitalism, and even for Lloyd Morgan's notion of emergent evolution, and as justified by the breakdown of traditional mechanistic physics. Yet, Smuts's teleological conception of wholes, though viewed by some, like Karl Popper, as a new Hegelianism, and condemned as such, lacked the concepts of totality and mediation that characterized dialectics. In the end, holism was used to provide teleological, quasi-religious justifications for hierarchy in both the natural and social worlds, though Smuts coupled with this a defense of "human rights," which led Du Bois to characterize him as "that great hypocrite." Smuts's philosophy was to give rise to a whole school of ecological racism within the botanical sciences in South Africa.[93]

Eleanor Marx's friend Olive Schreiner was a close friend of Smuts, both in their early support of the Boer cause, and later. Schreiner frequently indicated her "love" (friendship) for Smuts but was later critical of his more conservative racial policies. Schreiner was a supporter of the Russian Revolution and in her last year, 1920, she was elated by the triumph over the White Army. In October 1920 she wrote to Smuts: "The next few years are going to determine the whole future of South Africa in 30 or 40 years time. As we sow we shall reap. We may crush the mass of our fellows in South Africa today, as Russia did for generations, but today the serf is in the palace and where is the Czar? . . . *This is the 20th century*; the past is past never to return, even in South Africa. The day of princes, and Bosses is gone forever: one must meet the incoming tide and rise on it, or be swept away 'forever.'"[94]

Lancelot Hogben was thirty-two years of age at the time of his arrival in Cape Town in 1927. Born in 1895, the son of a Methodist preacher, Hogben was educated at Cambridge and quickly emerged as a productive scientist and prolific scientific writer, as well as a socialist with a strong Marxian bent. Although distinguishing his view from the Marxism of the Communist Party of Great Britain (and thus sometimes counterposing his views to those of the dominant Marxism), and extremely skeptical about dialectical materialism as a philosophy and scientific method, Hogben was strongly attracted to historical materialism, and counted among his close friends Marxian scientists Levy, Haldane, and J. D. Bernal, as well as Marxian classicist and philosopher Benjamin Farrington and social archaeologist V. Gordon Childe. He saw the progress of science and humanism as making possible for the first time the kind of utopian developments identified with William Morris and Edward Carpenter. Hogben insisted, "as did Lucretius," that "not the least" of "the benefits of science" was "to liberate mankind from the terror of the gods," that is, from organized religion.[95]

Hogben was equally critical of state worship as he was of religious worship. When "God Save the King" was played, he would invariably refuse to stand and go on doing whatever he was doing. On one occasion he was caught on the dance floor when the orchestra struck up "God Save the King." He immediately abandoned his partner and walked across the room and sat down. On a journey on a luxury liner, he so enraged some of the more patriotic passengers by repeatedly refusing to stand when "God Save the King" was played, and instead continuing deep in conversation as if nothing was happening, that the enraged passengers planned to abduct him from his cabin and give him a dunking in a swimming pool on the ship. A number of his university students were on board the ship, and they got wind of the plan to attack him. They established themselves as a bodyguard, protecting him when he was on deck and taking turns standing in front of his cabin at night.[96]

Hogben's appointment to the Chair of Zoology at the University of Cape Town in 1927, a position he was to retain until 1930, was his first professorial chair. Hogben arrived with his wife, Enid Charles, an ardent socialist, feminist, and trade unionist, who was to receive a PhD in physiology from the University of Cape Town and became a statistician and demographer. They were immediately caught up in the political as well as scientific culture in South Africa.[97] One of Hogben's first acts in his new position was to invite the young English zoologist G. Evelyn Hutchinson, who had been a student of Needham and Haldane at Cambridge, and had been teaching in a two-year position at the University of Witwatersrand in Johannesburg, to come down to Cape Town to do research in the summer (the Northern Hemisphere's winter) of 1927–28. Hogben, who had a deep interest in ecology, encouraged Hutchinson and his wife and co-researcher Grace Pickford, also a biologist, to study the shallow lakes in the region, which had a diverse flora and fauna that were tightly connected. This was Hutchinson's introduction to limnological research (from the Greek word *limne* for pool or lake), which became the basis on which Tansley's ecosystem analysis was later to be operationalized in the United States. When Hutchinson's temporary position at the University of Witwatersrand ended, Hogben wrote a letter to the chairman of the Zoology Department at Yale and largely through his influence was able to secure Hutchinson an instructorship there. Hutchinson was to remain at Yale for the next sixty years and became known as "the Father of Ecology," famous for developing the metabolic and biogeochemical conceptions of systems ecology. Hogben and Hutchinson were to remain in contact over the years.[98]

Much of Hogben's time while in South Africa was taken up by political and philosophical studies, and confrontation with the increasingly institutionalized South African system of racial segregation, which soon hardened into apartheid. This diverted him from his strict scientific studies. Under the influence of the Irish Marxist Benjamin Farrington, then a senior lecturer in Classics at the University of Cape Town, Hogben became interested in the ancient Greek materialists, particularly Epicurus, in search of a more radical materialism. He read everything accessible about the Greek atomists, including Marx's doctoral dissertation, to which Farrington had introduced him.[99]

Hogben also developed a close friendship with the South African ecologist and Marxist Edward Roux. Roux's mentor was Frederick Frost Blackman, a good friend of Tansley, and along with the latter, one of the authors of the Tansley Manifesto and thus branded by critics a "Botanical Bolshevik." Roux was a strong proponent of materialist dialectics, a member of the Communist Party of South Africa (before being expelled in 1936 for taking what was considered too much of a black nationalist line). His most famous book, written in 1948, was *Time Longer than Rope: A History of the Black Man's Struggle for Freedom in South Africa*. One of South Africa's leading botanists, Roux emerged as an indefatigable defender of ecology and sustainable community, criticizing capitalism's destruction of the environment. In opposition to the biological community presented by Smuts's follower John Phillips, with his philosophy of racial holism, Roux saw the protection of the environment as the key to an egalitarian social development, one in which the black struggle for freedom could be achieved. Roux was also an outspoken opponent of Smuts's holism. Roux met his future wife, socialist mathematician Winifred Lunt, at Hogben and Charles's home, and would remain closely tied to Hogben throughout the latter's Cape Town years. Like Farrington and Hogben, Roux, a materialist and rationalist, admired Epicurean philosophy and subscribed to Epicurus's views on death, quoting Lucretius. He concluded his short 1946 book *The Veld and the Future: A Book on Soil Erosion for South Africans* with the hopeful words, "To save the soil we must all work together, the black man and the white man, the man and the woman . . . . The soil does not really belong to this person or that who has the right to use a bit of land. It belongs to the nation and the children who are yet unborn."[100]

Hogben and Charles's home, Xenopus (named after the South African clawed toad they both studied), became a social hub for left intellectuals, such as Farrington and Roux, a place where it was possible to be outspokenly anti-apartheid. Hogben opened his classes to significant numbers of students of non-European descent and refused to accept the color bar. "At the time of my arrival," Hogben wrote in his autobiography, "one could not remain long in Cape Town without feeling the impact of the mounting pressure for apartheid." By early 1929, it was no longer safe for a university staff member who opposed the emerging apartheid policy, particularly a radical who was the president of the students' Rationalist Society, and Hogben felt increasingly vulnerable.[101]

Hogben watched in dismay and growing anger while the iron vise began to close on the black population: "The most dramatic of all provisions of the new legislation," he wrote, "abolished the Cape native franchise and withdrew from the native anywhere in the Union the right of free assembly. . . . The sentiments expressed by the [opposition] followers of the incorrigibly equivocal Smuts differed little from those of government supporters."[102]

In the midst of this growing climate of apartheid, at Roux's urging, Lancelot and Enid rescued two black protesters from a lynch mob, concealing them in the trunk of their car (a bright blue Nash). As Hogben recounted the story in his autobiography:

> There followed a personally memorable incident in 1930. During the week before free assembly of natives became illegal, a conference of natives called to protest the new legislation met in Worcester, about a hundred miles north of Cape Town. Whereupon local farmers who had formed a posse of *vigilantes*, dispersed the gathering and forced into hiding two leaders they were out to lynch. A white man sympathetic to the native cause appealed for help to bring them to safety in District Six, the native and coloured quarter of Cape Town. Both Enid and I had learned to drive since our arrival, and our second-hand car had a capacious boot. The emissary of the natives assured us that the vigilantes would not allow without search a car driven by a male to enter or leave the district where the leaders were hiding. On the other hand, they would not entertain the possibility that a white woman could have any truck with a Bantu male. Enid offered to drive by night over the range known as the Hottentots Holland to the place of hiding of the two native leaders and to smuggle them in the boot of the car through the outposts of the vigilantes. She brought them safely back to Cape Town by daybreak.[103]

Lancelot and Enid had a secret cellar in their house in which they offered to conceal Communist Party members and others fleeing the South African racial system. The entrance to the cellar could be obtained by lifting a rug in the dining room and removing two planks below it, to reveal the "unattractive cavern."[104] Hogben wrote poetry under the pseudonym of Kenneth Calvin Page, in which he promoted ecological values and attacked the South African racial system.[105] In his poem "To William Blake," written in Cape Town, and opening his *A Journey to Nineveh and Other Poems*, he compared the Nineveh of capitalism to Blake's prophetic New Jerusalem:

But still amidst the clamour of
The merchandise of Nineveh,
When factory chimneys tower above,
Jerusalem is here with me.

Factory chimneys lift upright
Phallic shapes against the night:
Giant cranes of steel forlorn
Loom like gallows in the dawn

Chimneys with the might of Mars
Belch forth crimson to the stars:
Cranes as pitiless as shares
Would hang a thousand millionaires.[106]

In leading off the Nature of Life debate at the British Association for Advancement of Science meetings in South Africa in 1929, Smuts, in his words, "gave the audience a good dose of Holism," presenting the ideas in *Holism and Evolution*, particularly the notion that there is an innate "tendency in nature to form wholes that are greater than the sum of the parts through creative evolution."[107] Hogben countered with a mechanistic materialism that, though not denying emergence, objected to all teleological (final-cause) thinking, and attacked the more idealistic and vitalistic aspects of Smuts's creed. In developing his talk, Hogben had tried out a number of approaches, leading to several different essays, which became the basis of his 1930 book *The Nature of Living Matter*. His actual Nature of Life presentation was published as chapter 3, under the title "The Nature of Life—An Introduction to the Theory of the Public World."[108]

Although Hogben started out with criticisms of John Scott Haldane, whose work *The Sciences and Philosophy* had strongly praised Smuts, it was Smuts who was the principal object of his critique. "Holism, the newest form of Vitalism," he wrote, "claims to have found an alternative or supplementary principle that is essentially teleological. The holist does not specify by reference to any single concrete situation how he proposes to use his principle." In trying to demonstrate the abstract and useless character of holism, Haldane polemically queried in utilitarian terms: "Does the holist wish us to believe that we can help anyone to drive a car by assuring him that at every level of complexity between the internal structure of the atom and the newly licensed automobile there merges an ever-increasing urge to wholeness or unity which is somehow indefinably different than the interaction of the parts?" The cleverness of Smuts's holism argument, Hogben insisted, was that it did not deny materialist principles at any given level, but argued rather that in the innate tendency to wholeness, there was a surplus reality emerging that no analysis of parts, interactions, and material processes could comprehend. This occurred principally at the levels separating Matter, Life, and Mind in Smuts's connection where he postulated radical discontinuities.[109] (This was quite different than the universal continuity dialectally postulated by Tansley about the same time in his unpublished "Temporal Genetic Sequence.")

Hogben countered with a mechanistic materialism, which, however, was as a philosophy sufficiently dialectical (though he formally rejected dialectical materialism) to elude simple reductionism. In the conclusion to his book, he thus sought to provide a more complex understanding. He was not willing, he stated, "to be responsible for the billiard ball theory of matter which both Dr. Haldane and General Smuts have identified with the mechanistic conception of life. I am content to foresee enormous possibilities for the extension of physical interpretations of the properties of living matter." For Hogben, the reality of different levels of existence did not contradict materialism in the least. Moreover, there was "no difference of opinion concerning the statement that there emerge at different levels of complexity in natural phenomena specific properties which cannot yet be deduced from a knowledge of simpler systems." Yet, he believed that the application of the scientific method would continually enhance our understanding of such complex systems, unfolding their genetic qualities.[110]

In *The Nature of Living Matter*, Hogben referred to the help he had received in the preparation of the book from Levy. The strength of Hogben's view was his uncompromising materialism, which he associated with nineteenth-century socialism, and with the ancient Greek materialists. All teleological principles dissociated from materialism were to be denied. "The benign and tolerant humanism" which the ancient Greek materialist "Epicurus grafted on the soil prepared by the atomists," Hogben wrote in *The Nature of Living Matter*, influenced by Farrington and by Marx's doctoral dissertation, "was ill suited to flourish in the stern climate of the [Hellenistic] military state. Like [Smuts's] holism, Aristotle's [Hellenistic] system was a shrewd blending of science and statesmanship. It enabled its author to combine a personal predilection for natural history with a political partiality for slavery."[111]

In contrast to the views of Levy, Hogben was to adopt a somewhat ambivalent approach to "dialectical materialism," which he pointed out was a term introduced by Joseph Dietzgen and not Marx or Engels. Like Bernal, Needham, Levy, and others, Hogben was enormously impressed by the ideas of the 1931 delegation of Soviet scientists, led by Bukharin, who were to arrive unexpectedly at the Second International Congress of the History of Science and Technology in 1931. In response, Hogben wrote a lengthy and complex analysis of dialectical materialism and its overlap with a critical mechanism published under the title "Contemporary Philosophy in Soviet Russia" in *Psyche* in 1932. No less a figure than Needham thought it worth citing as one of the most important discussions of the subject. A central aspect of the paper was his criticism of Dietzgen for smuggling idealism back into materialism and the alienation of Marxism from natural science. Hogben strongly supported Bukharin's basic position in his paper at the 1931 Congress and emphasized the importance of dialectical materialism, overlapping with notions of holism and emergent evolution, in describing "different levels of complexity of phenomena with laws of their own." Yet, for Hogben any sense of idealism or mysticism within dialectical materialism (particularly of the Dietzgen variety) was to be rejected.[112]

Although Hogben was to distance himself formally from dialectical materialism as a philosophy, he continued to employ dialectical insights—contradiction, integrative levels, qualitative transformation—shorn of the more Hegelian vocabulary, throughout his work. Hence, his seeming departure from Marxian orthodoxy in this respect was more a matter of form than substance and was not of the sort to create any real barriers between him and the other Marxian scientists in Britain with whom he remained closely associated. Indeed, Needham saw Hogben's argument in his *Psyche* article as crucial: "English scholars," he wrote, "owe a debt to Lancelot Hogben, who was one of the first about this time to try to translate dialectical materialism (more or less successfully) into English idiom."[113] For Needham, what was most important was Hogben's declaration that dialectical materialism was similar to the tenets of emergent evolution in recognizing the importance of complexity and integrative levels.[114]

Despite his commitment to a seemingly mechanistic (if critical) materialism, Hogben was a radical humanist in orientation, deeply attracted to the vision of Morris. He argued that improvements in science had led to the possibility of what he called "the bio-aesthetic design of human life." This view was distinguished from a "back to nature" philosophy and associated with such early proponents of the human betterment of nature as the seventeenth-century Baconian John Evelyn, author of *Sylva* and *Fumifugium*. Advocating for "the social use of science" so as to harmonize human life with the natural landscape was, Hogben declared, "at least as rational" as aiming "at housing everybody in skyscraper tenements with ferroconcrete scenery."[115] He proposed "a biologically planned ecology of human satisfactions. A co-operative commonwealth could efface the skeleton grin of silk stocking and soap advertisements along our boulevards by vegetation flowing throughout the seasons." Turning to a utopian and ecological strand of socialism, he declared: "Free trade accepted the urban squalor of a coal economy as the price for its own definition of prosperity. Today scientific knowledge offers us the possibility of a new plan of social living more akin to the Utopia of a William Morris or an Edward Carpenter."[116] In presenting this vision Hogben insisted:

> It is important to emphasize that the distribution of purchasing power to increase the volume of effective demand is essentially different from the view held by the pioneers of Socialism fifty or a hundred years ago. *It* would have been regarded by them as a capitulation to the prevailing doctrine of *laissez-faire*, against which they revolted. Men like Owen and Morris were far less taken in by the glamour of capitalism than we are. They were not content to criticize it because it distributed its products unjustly or because it was incapable of producing as large a quantity of goods as a planned economy could deliver. They also, and more especially, attacked it because it was not producing the kind of goods which are good for people to want and to strive for. They were not hypnotized by the liberal delusion that things people have been educated to demand by capitalist advertisement are necessarily the things they need most.
>
> To-day we are apt to dismiss their lament on the ugliness which capitalist enterprise has bequeathed us as mere aestheticism with no significance for a realistic political programme. What is called realism implied a servile acceptance of the three cardinal errors of the capitalist ideology. The first is the assumption that the greatest good of the greatest number is achieved by producing the greatest number of saleable goods and ensuring that the greatest number of people can take their choice. The second is that the large community is a necessary condition of high productive capacity. The third is that peace between nations can only be insured by a maximum division of labour with free trade. I believe that each of these postulates is sociologically false.[117]

It was Morris, Hogben insisted, who had pointed to a wider, more coherent socialist strategy, more attuned to people's real needs:

> Morris contended that the drabness of capitalism is its chief condemnation. . . . Morris was a sound social psychologist in recognizing that a Socialist programme cannot afford to neglect the fact that people want their lives to be

> picturesque. . . . He was a sound biologist in believing that we could make Britain so beautiful that people would neither need nor wish to travel. If we are to plan for survival our first aim must be to create a social environment in which the setting of the family is satisfying because it is picturesque. It may be that the mere survival of Socialism will demand the same reorientation of social values.[118]

Like Morris, Hogben contended that socialism must reject the prevailing "pattern of *passive satisfaction* and *conspicuous expenditure* encouraged by an increasing multiplicity of useless commodities and new distractions," or else socialism would undermine the reason for its own existence. "There is no reason why Socialism should identify scientific planning with an exclusively mechanical technology." Again, like Morris, Hogben supported "the feminine point of view" that the future required "a much closer approximation to equality of wealth"—between men and women as well—"than most Socialists now advocate."[119]

In his 1938 *The Retreat from Reason*, Hogben took the side of William Blake and Morris against the "dark Satanic mills" and the dictatorship of production and consumption. "It is now the fashion," he stated, "to regard men like Morris and Edward Carpenter as charming but ineffective cranks." Yet, their ecological concerns, like those of Blake before them, pointed to the most urgent needs in the twentieth century, and reflected a wisdom transcending economic utilitarianism and "urban socialism." "The England which Blake loved was a land in which the energy of wind and water was replacing the slave labour of classical civilisation. . . . The discovery of electricity and of the light metals has now shown us how the power which drove those old water-wheels could do all the work of the dark Satanic mills, and do it better." An ecological society, Hogben insisted, would not see "the standard of living" as "defined in terms of the varieties of commodities which are produced," but would be concerned with genuine human needs and the wider environment of human community. Why else "has Blake's poem been sung and quoted until we are almost tired of it, if the masses really prefer the passive enjoyment provided by cheap gramophones in a labour-saving flat" to a life in touch with the world of nature?[120]

Likewise, in his 1943 *Dangerous Truths,* Hogben was to make a strong case for following the "other socialism"—not concerned simply with economic expansion—represented by Robert Owen and Morris. What made this approach to socialism so vital was its wider environmental perspective. It saw the "hypertrophied metropolitanism of capitalist evolution" with its "urban congestion" as a major problem. In opposition to "the Liberal doctrine that prosperity is being able to choose the greatest variety of goods," this other socialism, most clearly defined by Morris, "asserted the need to decide whether the dark satanic mills were making things which are good for men to choose" and the effects on the environment.[121]

Hogben's social-ecological perspective was especially evident in his treatment of race. "The racialist doctrine," he wrote in *The Retreat from Reason*, "has no serious title to be accepted as a biological interpretation of history, until the ecological factors in cultural differentiation have been explored exhaustively." What was needed was the development of human ecology as a field. "Man is bringing into being a world-wide ecology of his own. This world-wide ecology means that geographical localised communities are not more interdependent. They are less so." Any attempt to examine race independent of social and ecological conditions, that is, environmental factors, was bound to fail.[122] As he was to declare decades later in an address on "The Race Concept": "Human society is a unique ecological system," or a "human ecological system" in which elements of its environment are cumulatively transformed and transmitted by cultural-historical means. Mere acknowledgment of that fact proved fatal to the race concept.[123]

Beginning in 1930, when he took up the Chair in Social Biology at the London School of Economics, Hogben devoted his efforts to combatting biological racism and in criticisms of apartheid. Prior to the 1930s, biologist critics of eugenics in Britain, such as E. Ray Lankester, were extremely rare, and among geneticists only William Bateson seems to have exhibited doubts. All of this changed with Hogben's return from South Africa, determined to oppose biological racism, eugenics, and apartheid. A number of figures in the eugenics community, such as the biochemist Frederick Mott, had laid stress on the role of the environment (social as well as natural) as a major factor in the development of human beings. But there was no clear division between nature (innate) and nurture (social-environmental) advocates. As Pauline M. H. Mazumdar noted in her 1992 work, *Eugenics, Human Genetics and Human Failings*, it was at this time that "the link between the left and environmentalism was forged. . . . The explicit use of environment as a means of attacking eugenics began [in Britain] in 1931 with the work of Lancelot Hogben." In that year Hogben published his *Genetic Principles in Medicine and Social Science* concerned with racism, dedicating it to Levy and explicitly referring to Marx's socioeconomic analysis. Along with the direct introduction of environmental factors, Hogben, a sophisticated mathematician, employed various new mathematical techniques used by German geneticists. As Mazumdar explains, "Hogben took up German mathematical Mendelism and the blood-group studies that went with it as a means of attacking British eugenics for its naïve procedures, its neglect of the environment and above all for its subservience to class interests."[124] For these reasons, he is said to have "pioneered the genetic critique of race concept."[125] It was this work that was to inspire anthropologists such as Ashley Montagu, who, based primarily on Hogben's work, denied the significance of the biological concept of race in his *Man's Most Dangerous Myth: The Fallacy of Race.*[126]

Hogben's attack was viewed by many at the time as having "knocked the bottom out of eugenics," raising the ire of figures like Carlos Blacker, general secretary of the Eugenics Society and a strong advocate of "voluntary sterilization" of inferior groups. Hogben's argument had drastically undermined the work of even the most respected eugenicists, such as R. A. Fischer and Pearson, both from the standpoint of bringing in the environment and mathematical technique. Revealing the class as well as racial bias of eugenics, Hogben indicated In *Nature and Nurture* in 1933 that hope for the future lay not in changing the genotype of the human being but in altering social relations. He presented the Eugenics Society's sterilization program with contempt and characterized eugenics in general as "an apology for snobbery, selfishness, and class arrogance." One of the first figures to back Hogben's analysis was the socialist geneticist J. B. S. Haldane. Haldane's new approach to human genetics and the question of race beginning in 1932, in which he too brought in social and environmental influences in a more complex, dialectical analysis, followed closely on Hogben. After that, eugenics was never the same. As Mazumbar concludes, "It was the Marxist scientists who forced the change in the ideology and methods in human genetics. . . . The attackers were left-wing radicals and sharply sensitized to the part played by class in the eugenist problematic."[127]

Nevertheless, Hogben was critical of the failure of the British left in general to take up the question of racism and apartheid in Germany and South Africa. He was especially concerned with Smuts's return to power in 1939. South Africa's alliance with Britain in the Second World War was, in Hogben's view, based on a "tacit understanding" that this would give South Africa continuing control of Namibia.[128] All of this was to generate in Hogben's work a concerted attack on biological racism, as well as an explanation of the social causes of racism. Given this context, it is hardly surprising that his analysis of "the interdependence of nature and nurture," arising out of his critique of eugenics, has been credited with launching the modern emphasis on gene-environment interaction in human development (or gene-culture coevolution).[129]

In addition to resisting all forms of racism and of biological race, Hogben was known for what Werskey called "his lifelong adherence to feminist ideals." He was adamant that his colleagues not refer to his wife, Enid Charles, as Mrs. Hogben, and was critical of the notion that women, even in progressive Sweden, were seen as destined to be cooks and domestic servants for the household. All forms of the social demotion of women were to be condemned, and, for Hogben, the material bases of the prejudices that designated women as inferior.[130]

Ecology was a theme running throughout Hogben's writings. He argued in *Science for the Citizen* for "a planned ecology of human life," evoking the utopian spirit of Morris. Science had created a more global civilization, but it had also enhanced "the potential for local self-sufficiency."[131]

THE BATTLE FOR ECOLOGY

In the early 1930s ecology was being promoted by reactionaries as well as radicals, and the former seemed to be gaining the upper hand.[132] Smuts's holism was receiving growing support in the scientific community. Albert Charles Seward, who occupied the chair as Professor of Botany at the University of Cambridge, and was president of the International Botanical Congress, saw Smuts's holism as a key to the study of the evolution of plant life. At the Fifth International Botanical Congress in Cambridge in August 1930, Smuts's views were represented by John Frederick Phillips, Smuts's leading South African follower within the botanical community. A big push was made at the conference to work out an agreed set of concepts for plant sociology, as part of an International Commission on Concepts in Plant Sociology that was set up at the same time, leading to disagreements between Phillips and Tansley, who played leading roles in the International Commission. Phillips read a paper on "The Biotic Community" in which he argued that "in accordance with the holistic concept of Smuts, the biotic community is something more than the mere sum of its parts: it possesses a special identity—it is indeed a mass-entity with a destiny peculiar to itself." Phillips also criticized Tansley for adopting a narrow perspective to ecology that left out animals and inorganic nature.[133]

Of greater overall significance was General Smuts's election as president of the British Association for the Advancement of Science in 1931. The election was unusual, as Smuts was not a practicing scientist. Ostensibly this was due to the influence within the British scientific community of Smuts's holism philosophy. But it also had to do with the attempt of the British Association to extend its sphere of influence to the entire British Empire, of which Smuts was a symbol. Nevertheless, Smuts used the occasion to argue full bore for his holistic standpoint. In his presidential speech at the Association in London in September 1931, Smuts attacked the physicist John Tyndal's famous 1874 address to the Association (which was much admired by Marx and Engels) as an "unrestrained expression" of the "materialistic creed." Nature in any truly meaningful sense (beyond mere "brute fact") was to be seen as a construction of the mind:

> Great as is the physical universe which confronts us as a given fact, no less great is our reading and evaluation of it in the world of values. . . . Without this revelation of inner meaning and significance the physical universe would be but an immense empty shell or crumpled surface. The brute fact here receives its meaning, and a new world arises which gives to nature whatever

> significance it has. As against the physical configurations of nature we see here the ideal patterns or wholes freely created by the human spirit as a home and an environment for itself.[134]

"A crude materialism," Smuts declared, had "swamped biology for a generation," meaning the period subsequent to Darwin. Now "materialism has . . . gone by the board" to be succeeded by "a new monism" in the form of holism. "In this holistic universe," he concluded, "man is in very truth the offspring of the stars."[135]

As Peder Anker writes in *Imperial Ecology*, "Smuts's holism was by now on everybody's lips as the darling of contemporary intellectual debate. For some his philosophical slogan 'the whole is more than the sum of its parts' represented 'a new synthesis' of precise sciences, evolutionary biology, and psychology."[136]

Smuts's ecological holism was enormously influential in ecology.[137] Phillips, in particular, incorporated Smuts's as well as Clements's holism into his own ecological studies. In Phillips's construction of the natural world, humans were part of a biotic community that was filled with cooperation and harmony. At the same time, human beings were naturally organized in a racial hierarchy. That these two ideas coexisted within a single construction is no accident, since, as Anker notes, "Phillips coined the term 'biotic community' to designate this ecocentric ethics and environmental social policy of segregated ecological homelands." He argued in his scientific writings on ecology that natives should not be granted any autonomy or freedom because it would violate the relations of races within the community. The "ruling races" were to regulate the stock of natives to prevent excess grazing and degradation of the environment. In Phillips's racist biocentrism, miscegenation between the lower European stock and the natives was to be avoided to prevent the degeneration of biological diversity. Women's desire for freedom should be constrained and large families among whites should be encouraged.[138]

In his *Human Ecology*, John William Bews, another South African ecologist and follower of Smuts, contended that some humans were determined by the conditions of their environment, whereas other humans were more independent of their environment. This argument developed out of Smuts's theory regarding certain organisms and personalities being more independent and stronger, versus those that were affected by the environment. Bews spoke of "the ecological division of mankind" as "necessitating the segregation of the races." In his 1931 article on the "Ecological Viewpoint," he transferred the concept of natural hierarchy modeled on Smuts's holism back to human society, speaking of a "climax type of men" exemplified by "the small white population in South Africa." Those primitive peoples who were still tied to the "Earth-mother," he argued, should be left as much as possible in their proper biotic communities.

Underlying society was an ecological division of labor that, for Bews, justified the economic division of labor and the class structure of society, which should not be altered. Bews also insisted that marriage was the only natural relation between men and women and that homosexuality was ecologically and morally wrong. Smuts's holism thus reinforced naturalized ecological-racist views. At the same time, Clements and other ecologists in the United States, though free of such explicit racism, became strong defenders of Smuts's and Phillips's ecological holism.[139]

Bews's 1935 book on *Human Ecology* was explicit on race. "Racial characteristics," he wrote, "while not supremely important in human ecology, cannot be altogether neglected any more than plant taxonomy can in plant ecology. It is important to know one's men just as it is to 'know one's plants.' While the majority of the typical food-gatherers are to be regarded as ethnologically primitive from the racial point of view, it remains difficult to decide to what extent their racial characteristics are the result of a process of degeneration and how far they represent true primitiveness."[140]

For Julian Huxley and H. G. Wells, the ecological racism propounded by Smuts and his followers was to be strongly opposed. Huxley, a left-liberal figure, declared in his *African View* that it was "impossible not to sympathize in many ways" with Smuts's proposal to establish a "white backbone," that is, an extended settlement of white populations, predominantly at higher elevations from South to Central Africa. Nevertheless, he insisted that the aim should be to develop equality. He thus rejected Smuts's policy of promoting "territorial segregation . . . of the races in close proximity," claiming that this would lead to growing racial discrimination.[141]

Wells, as a socialist, was sharply critical, writing in *The Fate of Man*:

> It is one of the good marks in the checkered record of British Imperialism that in Nigeria it has stood out against the development of the plantation system and protected the autonomy of the native cultivator. . . . But against that one has to set the ideas of white-man-mastery associated with Cecil Rhodes and sustained today by General Smuts, which look to an entire and permanent economic, social, and political discrimination between the lordly white and his natural serf, the native African. And this in the face of the Zulu and the Basuto, the most intelligent and successful of native African peoples. The ethnological fantasies of Nazi Germany find a substantial echo in the resolve of the two and a half million Afrikanders to sustain, from the Cape to Kenya, an axis of white masters . . . with a special philosophy of great totalitarian possibility called holism, lording it over a subjected but much more prolific, black population.
>
> That racial antagonism makes the outlook of South Africa quite different from that of most of the other pseudo-British "democracies." Obviously, it is

> not a democracy at all, and plainly it is heading towards a regime of race terrorism on lines parallel and sympathetic with the Nazi ideal.[142]

The strength of Wells's objection to Smuts's holism was undoubtedly heightened by its peculiar combination of racism with ecology, a field with which Wells had an early association. Wells had been a student of both Thomas Huxley and Ray Lankester. The latter had examined Wells four times for his Bachelor of Science degree. Wells's 1895 *Time Machine* was based on Lankester's *Degeneration*. Beginning in 1900 they became close friends, constantly exchanging ideas, until Lankester's death in 1929. Wells was to draw constantly on ecological themes in Lankester's work. Lankester helped Wells in the writing of his 1920 *Outline of History*, overseeing the extensive introductory part on early human evolution. In his 1934 autobiography, Wells said that "the exactest" title for the kind of synthesis he had in mind in his 1931 work, *The Work, Wealth, and Happiness of Mankind* (connected to the other works in his trilogy: *The Outline of History* and *The Science of Life*) would have been "the Outline of Human Ecology. But I did not call it that because the word Ecology was not yet widely understood."[143]

In 1923 Wells wrote his social-ecological utopia, *Men Like Gods*, perhaps the most important attempt at a genuine utopian novel in Britain since Morris's *News from Nowhere* in 1890. In it he depicts a parallel world so advanced in physical-chemical science that it has become possible at last to create a more humanized natural world, while at the same time subordinating machines to the needs of humanity. In a kind of green Baconianism, humanity in this parallel universe has subjected nature, eliminating all of its "ugliness" and "horribleness," while nurturing its beauty, creating a kind of garden existence. As the character Urthred, one of the Utopians, tells visitors from twentieth-century Britain: "With Man came Logos, the Word and the Will into our universe, to watch it and fear it, to learn it and cease to fear it, to know and comprehend it and master it. So that we of Utopia are no longer the beaten and starved children of Nature, but her free and adolescent sons. We have taken over the Old Lady's [Mother Nature's] Estate. Every day we learn a little better how to master this little planet."[144]

In Wells's utopia the entire landscape has been altered by the management of plant life and new and beautiful flora. Men and women are free from many of the previous restrictions with respect to sexual relations. No longer ashamed of the human body they wear few clothes. At the same time, population has been limited by birth control. This reflects a theme of Lankester's who had written in his notes for his 1905 Romanes Lecture that humanity tends to cross all natural limits, insisting: "This cannot go on; man must have a limit. Then the real science can come in." Presumably this related to both population and economics. In 1909, Lankester wrote to Wells that his vision of a future world republic would have to find a way of controlling population. Solving problems of energy through atomic motors and ecological restoration such as the reclamation of deserts would not be enough, if the human population and the growing human pressure on the environment were to continue. Wells, however, like Morris (and Lankester), rejected eugenics as an answer to the future of humanity. Rather, the beautiful people that appear in *Men Like Gods* are the product of healthy living and Darwinian sexual selection. Wells envisioned the triumph of humanity over noxious bacteria and other sources of disease allowing for longer, fuller lives. Improvements in the condition of humanity are achieved not through eugenics, but, as Lankester had argued, through education. Such issues like invasive species and the destruction of habitats required that human beings adopt a conscious attitude toward the ecological ramifications of their actions.[145]

In his 1923 review of *Men Like Gods*, "Biology in Utopia," Julian Huxley attributed Wells's vision to "the rise of ecology." Humanity as depicted in Wells's novel has moved on from science to the fuller cultivation of its artistic sensibilities. Thus, in *Men Like Gods* humanity has moved on to a more complex, dialectical, and sustainable relation to nature. The people in Wells's utopia, as Huxley put it, are "interested primarily in two things—the understanding of Nature for its own sake, and its control for the sake of humanity." According to Huxley, the underlying vision of Wells's novel was that of a new, emerging relation between humanity and nature in "the idea that man is master in his own house of Earth, as opposed to the idea which, with few exceptions, has until now dominated his history—the idea that he is the slave, sport, or servant of an arbitrary personal Power or Powers." But this notion of humanity also required the growth of a humanistic-materialistic attitude recognizing the need for the creation of a more rational relation to the natural world.[146]

H. G. Wells and Julian Huxley became close friends in 1925. It was Wells who persuaded Huxley to give up his academic position to pursue full-time writing. They were to undertake, together with Wells's son, G. P. Wells—a former student of Hogben and an instructor in biology at the University College, London—a massive popular work, *The Science of Life*. The Wells, Huxley, and Wells's book was more than 1,400 pages long. It was written rapidly and serialized in thirty fortnightly installments beginning in March 1929 and ending in May 1930. It began to appear at the very moment that the debate over the Nature of Life between Smuts and Hogben was taking place in South Africa, and was completed, with the final installment appearing less than nine months after Smuts gave his lectures on Africa and Oxford, with its publication in book form coinciding with Hogben's *Nature of Living Matter*.

"The Science of Ecology" and "Life Under Control," the two closing chapters of Book 6, were crucial, constituting in many ways the core argument of the book, as intimated in the book's introduction and conclusion. In addition to being drafted by Huxley, and worked over by both H. G. and G. P. Wells, this entire section, in particular, was scrutinized by Elton prior to publication. It drew on the work of Tansley, Elton, and J. B. S. Haldane.[147]

The Science of Life opened by defining life in terms of metabolism, emphasizing that life could not be seen apart from its interactions. "The process of taking in, assimilating and using matter," Wells, Huxley, and Wells wrote, "is called *metabolism*. Metabolism and spontaneous movement are the primary characteristics of living things."[148]

The key chapter on "The Science of Ecology" began with the heading "Ecology Is Biological Economics." A didactic approach clearly adopted in the work was to take scientific terms and convert them into more familiar phrases, more conducive to a popular audience, so Lankester's *bionomics* became *biological economics*, which was seen as equivalent to ecology, while *biocoenosis*, then frequently used by ecologists on the Continent, became simply "life community." The term *ecology* was explained in terms of its etymological roots from the Greek *oikos* or household, from which the term economics had also been derived. Ecology as biological economics (bionomics) was merely the extension of political economy to the rest of life. But the broadening of the principles of political economy in this way altered the whole nature of the problem of economics. "Ecology," the three authors wrote, "lays the foundations for a modern, a biological . . . treatment of what was once very properly known as the 'dismal science' of economics." As distinct from economics, in their view, ecology dealt with "accumulation and consumption in every province of life." Economics was thus narrower, and was in fact, in their terms, mere "human ecology."[149]

There followed a discussion of "the chemical wheel of life," the photosynthetic role of plants as "pioneers" of the ecological community, ecological succession regulated by climate, the emergence of a relatively stable climax in plant life, life communities, dominant species, evolutionary equilibriums, food chains, etc. The force behind the "wheel of life" was "solar energy." Energetics allowed the analysis of how various chemicals and energy were utilized by the ecological system, and leakages in the process. It also provided the basis for understanding the human role and its disruptive influence. Much solar energy was locked up or stored in various ways (for example, as hydrocarbons), while human beings learned to release it. Carbon was essential to all life and a crucial issue was the carbon cycle. "The fireplace, the factory, and the automobile," they wrote, perhaps ironically (though the irony would take on a somewhat different meaning in our own time), "are doing all they can to restore this deposited carbon to a state of gaseous accessibility."[150]

A pivotal ecological contradiction, associated with environmental crises and the disruption of "the balance of nature," was the mining of the soil. In an argument related to Marx's discussion of the metabolic rift, they wrote:

> When man comes on the scene, matters are altered. He crowds the country with animals. He hurries up their growth and increases the demands they make on the soil. A modern cow gives about a thousand gallons of milk at one lactation period, and produces her first calf at about three years; the native cattle of Africa do not breed till they are six, and yield at most three hundred gallons of milk at one lactation. And too often he ships off the meat, bone-meal, cheese leather, and wool without putting anything back in the soil. He forgets that all their mineral ingredients have come out of the soil. A country that is exporting grassland products is also exporting grassland fertility. There are large areas which are naturally deficient in minerals; but man has been creating mineral-deficiency over other and vaster areas.[151]

Capitalist societies faced with problems of soil fertility in the nineteenth century turned to guano, primarily from Peru, as a way of replacing the nitrogen and phosphorous lost to the soil. "Guano, a deposit consisting of the excrement of bats and birds, is another example," Wells, Huxley, and Wells argued, "of locked-up material" that humans learned to release. "Most excrement serves to enrich the soil on which it falls, but on the Southern islands where guano is found the manure has been unused and has merely accumulated. Here again man comes to the rescue, and by using guano as a fertilizer, restores its nitrogen and phosphates to the soil."[152]

The ecological problem facing humanity then becomes a question of releasing nature's locked-up powers, avoiding leakages in energy flows, and ensuring that humanity does not heedlessly cross natural limits or break nature's laws. Evolution is presented as a slow, inherently progressive process. Humanity is able to speed this process, but it is also faced by ecological contradictions of its own creation. The final section of the chapter "Life Under Control," titled "The Ecological Outlook," explores the problem of anthropogenic ecological crises and the possible means of addressing them. Thus, we are told, in line with Lankester, that civilization's spread has been accompanied by a "trail of plagues." Colonization has gone hand in hand with the intended and unintended spread of invasive species, crowding out and killing off native habitat and species. Industrial agriculture leads to the systematic disruption of the soil cycle, robbing the soil of its nutrients. "To make good these losses of the soil, he [the human being] has crushed up the nitre [nitrates] of Chile, the guano of Peru, the stores of phosphate rock in various parts of the earth's crust. But these too are [natural] capital and the end of them is in sight. Linnaeus gave man the title of *Homo sapiens*, Man the Wise. One is sometimes tempted to agree with Professor [Charles] Richet, who thinks that a more suitable designation would have been *Homo stultus*, Man the Fool."

Describing this folly, Wells, Huxley, and Wells wrote:

> In the last couple of centuries he [humanity] has accelerated the circulation of matter—from raw materials to food and tools and luxuries and back to raw matter again—to an unprecedented speed. But he has done it by drawing on reserves of capital. He is using up the bottled sunshine of coal thousands of times more quickly than Nature succeeds in storing it; and the same rate of wastage holds for oil and natural gas. By reckless cutting without re-afforestation, he has not only been incurring a timber lack which future generations will have to face, but he has been robbing great stretches of the world of their soil and even of the climate which plant evolution has given them. . . .
>
> By over-killing, man has exterminated magnificent creatures like the bison as wild species. Less than a century ago herds numbered by the hundred thousand covered the Great Plains. Buffalo Bill killed 4,280 bison with his own rifle in a year and a half; and that was far from being a record. The United States Government detailed troops to help in the slaughter, in order to force the Indians, by depriving them of their normal subsistence, to settle down to agricultural life on reservations. Today there remain a few small protected herds.
>
> By over-killing, he has almost wiped out whales in the northern hemisphere, and unless some international agreement is soon arrived at, the improvement of engines of destruction is likely to do the same for the Antarctic seas. If he is not careful, the fur-bearers will go the same road; the big game of the world is doomed to go, and to go speedily, unless we take measures to stop its extinction. By taking crop after crop of wheat and corn out of the land in quick succession, he exhausted the riches of the virgin soils of the American west; and is now doing the same for the grasslands of the world by taking crop after crop of sheep and cattle off of them.[153]

The essential problem in all of this was the human economy, its speed of expansion, its ruthless acquisitiveness, its waste of resources, and its lack of planning. In the final section of the chapter on "Life Under Control," titled "The Ecological Outlook," the three authors argued:

> The cardinal fact in the problem of the human future is the speed of change. The colonization of new countries, the change from forest to fields, the reclamation of land from sea, the making of lakes, the introduction of new animals and plants—all these in pre-human evolution were the affairs of secular time, where a thousand years are but as yesterday; but now they are achieved in centuries or even decades. One cannot estimate such changes exactly, but we shall not be far out if we say that man is imposing on the life of the world a rate of change ten thousand times as great as any rate of change it ever knew before.[154]

Human beings were able to transform nature radically in the interest of the expansion of the human economy, but they did so under conditions in the dominant economic order, conditions that were unplanned and that showed a lack of concern and foresight for the long-term ecological consequences of such actions. Humanity is "very unlikely by the light of nature to see all the multifarious consequences" of such economic actions, "and too often the consequences will be quite different" from what was anticipated.[155]

"From the standpoint of biological economics, of which human economics is but a part, man's general problem is this: to make the vital circulation of matter and energy as swift, efficient, and wasteless as it can be made; and since we are first and foremost a continuing race, to see that we are not achieving an immediate efficiency at the expense of later generations." The issue then became one of long-term sustainable development.[156]

Wells, Huxley, and Wells explained that due to agricultural chemists such as "Liebig, Lawes, and Gilbert, the employment of chemical fertilizers has become almost universal. But up till quite recently man has taken little thought for the morrow beyond the single crop. It is true . . . that he has been forced by the demands of his wheat and corn to let his land lie fallow from time to time, or to introduce nitrogen-catching crops, like clover or lupins, into his rotation; but that is only a beginning." Nitrogen-based fertilizer was now available in unlimited supplies, making the loss of Chilean nitrates no longer a problem. But other limits were quite severe. They wrote: "We are using up our coal and oil." Fossil fuels would eventually have to be replaced by alternative energies: "Water-power is always with us, and there are tide-power and sun-power and wind power for us to tap. We are using up our oil; but sooner or later we shall replace it satisfactorily by power-alcohol made from plants."[157]

The most serious problem was phosphorus:

> Phosphorus is an essential constituent of all living creatures. It is, however, a rather rare element in nature, constituting only about one seven-hundredth part of the earth's crust. . . . From the soil of the United States alone the equivalent of some six million tons of phosphate is disappearing every year; and only about a quarter of this is put back in fertilizers. Meanwhile the store of fertilizers is being depleted, and man . . . is sluicing phosphorus recklessly into the ocean in sewage. Each year, the equivalent of over a million tons of phosphate rock is thus dumped out to sea, most of it for all practical purposes irrecoverable. The Chinese may be less sanitary in their methods of sewage disposal, but they are certainly more sensible; in China, what has been taken out of the soil is put back into the soil. It is urgently necessary that Western "civilized" man shall alter his methods of sewage disposal. If he does not, there will be a phosphorus shortage, and therefore a food shortage, in a few generations. But

> even if he does that he will still have to keep his eye on phosphorus; it is the weak link in the vital chain on which civilization is supported.[158]

The conclusion was that "man's chief need to-day is to look ahead. He must plan his food and energy circulation as carefully as a board of directors plans a business. He must do it as one community, on a world-wide basis, and as a species, on a continuing basis."[159]

ECOSYSTEM ECOLOGY

Tansley's landmark introduction of the ecosystem concept in 1935, in "The Use and Abuse of Vegetational Concepts and Terms," was a product of (1) the discussion that had emerged over the proper conceptual terms with which to define ecology; (2) the intensified debate within science over materialist and idealist (including vitalistic, organismic, and Smutsian "holistic") conceptions; and (3) the contentious introduction of concepts of racial hierarchy into ecological science.[160] Tansley had gained his reputation primarily as an organizer, editor, and taxonomist, as what Clements called the "managing director" of British ecology. Now well into his sixties, and secure at least in his Oxford Chair, he felt obliged to engage in a critique aimed at ensuring the materialist foundations of ecology and preventing what he referred to in the title of his article, as the "abuse" of ecological concepts.

Tansley, as we have seen, was in South Africa for the British Association for Advancement of Science meetings in the summer of 1929, when the Nature of Life debate took place between Smuts and Hogben over idealism/holism and materialism/realism. He would have been present when Phillips, Smuts's leading botanical follower, read a paper at the same conference.[161] Shortly after, Tansley was in the audience at Smuts's Oxford lectures on holism and Africa in September 1929. In the following year, at the Fifth International Botanical Congress in Cambridge in August 1930, Phillips read his paper on "The Biotic Community" (a concept to which Tansley strongly objected). In his paper Phillips directly criticized Tansley for neglecting inorganic factors in his ecological research. During the conference, Tansley and Phillips entered into a heated debate over the appropriate conceptual terminology to be universally adopted for ecology.[162] In 1932, Tansley was undoubtedly in the audience when Smuts gave his address as president of the British Association. Tansley was also unquestionably affected by the criticisms leveled by such figures as Wells, Huxley, Hogben, and Levy at Smuts's racist "holism." In the Magdalen Philosophy Club, with which Tansley was associated, Smuts's holism was being strongly promoted by some of the idealists, such as Collingwood, with whom Tansley debated. Tansley, meanwhile, was deeply engaged with the concept of emergence from a materialist standpoint as evident in his Magdalen paper on "Temporal Genetic Series as a Means of Approach to Philosophy."[163] If anything, Tansley's encounter with Freud's psychoanalysis had strengthened his commitment to materialism. Ecology, meanwhile, as exemplified by Wells, Huxley, and Wells in *Science of Life*, was taking on a whole new intellectual significance within the public sphere and science in general. All of this "overdetermined" Tansley, therefore, for a major confrontation with Smuts and Phillips.

In developing his critique of holism and its influence in ecology, Tansley, as we shall see, was to rely on the 1932 work, *The Universe of Science*, written by mathematician, physicist, and Hogben's close friend Hyman Levy. Levy was born in Edinburgh, Scotland, to an impoverished Jewish family. His father, Marcus, an exile from tsarist Russia, was a self-employed picture framer. The family was so poor that some of the children, including Hyman, were forced to sleep in the shop, which was across the street from a public house. His mother had a working-class consciousness and took the young Levy to hear socialist orators, leading to an early acquaintance with the ideas of Marx. Obtaining a scholarship to the University of Edinburgh through competitive examination, Levy studied mathematics and physics, going on to the University of Göttingen in Germany, followed by studies in aerodynamics at Oxford. For four years, from 1916 to 1920, he worked at the National Physical Laboratory outside of London as a rank-and-file scientist. During this time, he became active in the formation of the National Union of Scientific Workers and wrote *Aeronautics in Theory and Experiment* (1918), perhaps the first British text to provide the entire advanced theory of both airplane design and operation. In 1920 he attained the position of assistant professor in mathematics at the Royal College of Science of the Imperial College of Science and Technology, London, and was promoted to full professor three years later. At the time he completed *The Universe of Science* Levy was already a Marxist, having joined the Communist Party of Great Britain around 1930.[164]

The Universe of Science, as Levy indicated at the outset, was expressly intended as a materialist counter to the idealist views of thinkers such as Eddington and Smuts.[165] At the same time, it was a careful exposition of the scientific method and of systems thinking. The analysis focused on the roles of "isolation and isolate" or the processes of "abstraction and exclusion" in science. Scientific inquiry, Levy explained, is conducted by abstraction, in which various isolates or isolated systems neutral to their environment are generated as the basis for inquiries (empirical or otherwise) into particular phenomena. "The truth about the universe" is derived "by examining it in chips."[166] But this process of abstraction and isolates is not the same as mechanical reductionism. Rather, isolates may be whole complexes or systems and be aimed at understanding interactions, processes, and change, with the goal of ascertaining larger systems and emergent levels of reality. For Levy, in a botanical example that directly influenced Tansley's ecosystem concept,

> a tree is virtually an isolated system as long as we are concerned with the lesser systems we can derive from it by further analysis—the bark, the shape and color of the leaves, its fruit, its girth, its age, and the number of its annular rings. As soon as are concerned with its growth process, however, we have to take into account its roots and the atmosphere in which it grows. We have to widen the system so as to embrace more of that environment that previously was regarded as neutral to it. We have to take in sufficient of the soil in the region of the roots to provide us with another neutral system. Not all the atmosphere of the universe is needed for this purpose, and not all the soil of the earth. The vital question of course is how much precisely of each has to be included. . . . *The first function of experimental inquiry is, if possible, to find precisely how little of an environment need be included to render a system neutral.*[167]

That is, relatively neutral in relation to its environment, and thus a meaningful isolate. Such isolates or abstractions should not, Levy insisted, be given ontological status or be approached in an atomistic, reductionist fashion, where one expects to add up all the partial elements so discovered in order to arrive at the whole. It is precisely this misconception of science, he argued, that was the source of Smuts's error, which led him to believe that there is some surplus reality, encompassed in "wholes" as ontological realities distinct from atoms, which are then given a false ontological reality. The materialist-scientific method uses abstraction as a method for ascertaining scientific laws whereby nature's complexes can be isolated for analysis and investigated. Moreover, if there is any meaningful approach to examining nature it lies in recognizing that the world is in a constant state of flux, so that knowledge of it at best is concerned with processes and laws, which hold only at given levels of abstraction. "The environment of which we are an integral part, of which we are a chip, so to speak, is itself in a continuous state of flux."[168]

In Levy's view, a crude holistic philosophy such as that of Smuts, which simply claims that "nature does not proceed by atomic action" but in "wholes," leads nowhere. "How a self-contained 'whole' is not an atom of a larger 'whole' it is not easy to see, nor how, with a continuously interrelated changing environment, there can be either wholes or atoms *absolutely* isolated from the rest of the universe and functioning on their own." Instead, "to each class of question belongs its appropriate isolate."[169]

Emergence in the sense presented by Lloyd Morgan made sense in Levy's analysis precisely because it recognized that qualitative changes occur through the changing organization of material reality. Here Levy drew on an argument made in ancient times by Epicurus, and made familiar through Lucretius, whereby a literary work was "not . . . a mere collection of [alphabetical] letters. . . . [But] as elements are added to elements there emerges from the combination something new." In another example of emergence Levy pointed out how out of the combination of one atom of oxygen with two atoms of hydrogen there "emerges" a molecule of water, with new characteristics independent of the original gases.[170]

The analysis of reality in terms of isolates thus requires examining certain levels of organization, or levels of abstraction in which a relatively determinate entity can be ascertained. Knowledge thus tends to be directed at examining "internal relations" within a given isolate or how different systems with different internal relations come to interact. In contrast, "Holists endeavor to bolster an absolutist philosophy of Wholes merely by exposing the inadequacy of Atomism" and thinking that what is needed is the negation of the atom. They are thus "inevitably driven to postulate a mystical and emergent 'more coming out of the less,' within the body of these wholes." There is "a mystical birth" of such wholes "at each stage in the process of aggregation." In Smutsian holism, the internal relations that result in determinate entities (isolates) are thus lost in a myriad of abstracted "wholes."[171] It was this investigation of internal relations (within isolates) that Levy was famously to develop further in 1938 in his *A Philosophy for a Modern Man* as a dialectical outlook in line with historical materialism.[172]

Tansley's ecosystem article, although arising out of the complex debate between materialism and idealism, was primarily a response to a long, three-part treatment of plant succession, climax, and complex organism designed to forward the outlook of Smutsian holism, which Phillips had published in the *Journal of Ecology* over the course of 1934–35. In this series of articles, Phillips, building on his earlier work, argued that it was possible to speak of a "biological community" that included all biota, both plants and animals. Like Clements, Phillips viewed succession in the plant community as constituting a "complex organism," a notion that Phillips extended to the entire biological community. Such "wholes" in formation were themselves causes, determining biological processes. "Retrogressive development" was to be viewed as "impossible" in both the evolution of individual organisms and in the biological community. The evolution of the biological community insofar as the normal processes of succession and development were concerned was thus unidirectional, "progressive only; all examples of apparent retrogression are explicable in terms of some disturbing agency." Natural succession had an internal, continuous logic that could not be substantially subverted by outside forces, including human beings. Human societies as reflections of biotic communities were themselves a product of this same holistic logic. "Societies, nations, and Nature" were all part of this grand, unfolding holistic process.[173]

Tansley wrote "The Use and Abuse of Vegetational Concepts and Terms" as an explicit critique of Smuts's ideas, and more directly, Phillips's. At the same time, he was concerned that the work of Clements, whom Tansley considered the most important figure in plant ecology, was being unduly influenced by Smuts and Phillips. Tansley's critique extended to Clements himself, but not as an absolute rejection of Clementsian ecology. Rather, he clearly sought to persuade Clements to withdraw from his more teleological conceptions and to dissuade him from coquetting with Smutsian holism, a tendency that Clements had recently exhibited.[174]

Tansley began the "Use and Abuse" article with a clear crossing of the swords with Phillips and Clements, striking a combative tone that was far removed from his earlier ecological work:

> My return to the subject [of ecological concepts and terms] today is immediately stimulated by the appearance of Professor John Phillips's three articles in the *Journal of Ecology* which seem to me to call rather urgently for comment and criticism. . . . If some of my comments are blunt and provocative I am sure my old friend Dr. Clements and my younger friend Professor Phillips will forgive me. Bluntness makes for conciseness and has other advantages, always provided that it is not malicious and does not overstep the line which separates it from rudeness. . . . Phillips's articles remind one irresistibly of the exposition of a creed—of a closed system of religious or philosophical dogma. Clements appears as the major prophet and Phillips as the chief apostle, with the true apostolic fervor in abundant measure. . . . He is occupied for the most part in giving us the pure milk of the Clementsian word, in expounding and elaborating the organismal theory of vegetation. . . . The three articles [by Phillips] are respectively devoted to "Succession," "Development and the Climax," and "the Complex Organism." The greater part of the third article [by Phillips] is mainly concerned with the relation of this last concept to the theory of "holism" as expounded by General Smuts and others, and is really a confession of holistic faith. As to the repercussions of this faith on biology I shall have something to say.[175]

Phillips's idealist, organicist, and Smutsian holist constructions raised the ire of Tansley.[176] Hence, in one fell swoop in his *Ecology* article, he proceeded to attack a whole set of teleological notions propagated by Clements, Smuts, and Phillips: (1) that ecological succession was inherently progressive and developmental, leading invariably to a climax; (2) that retrogressive succession and external disruptions in the succession process were not possible; (3) that vegetation could be seen as constituting a "superorganism"; (4) that there was such a thing as a literal "biotic community," encompassing both plants and animals; (5) that an "organismic philosophy," postulating a holistic universe, was a way to understand ecological relations; and (5) that wholes, in the sense of Smuts's holism, could be seen as both cause and effect of everything in nature—and extended to society.

Much of Tansley's argument was a simple rejection of idealistic, teleological conceptions. A notion of unilinear progress leading to climax as the intrinsic outcome of all biological processes was to be rejected as in conflict with materialism, realism, and evolutionary theory. Even more objectionable was the Clementsian notion that the plant community could be viewed, in the context of the succession process, as a real organism, or that Phillips's "biological community" (or "biotic community") could be treated as a real organism. Such views led to Clements's "superorganism" and to Phillips's "complex organism," standing for the climax of the biological process of succession. To use the notion of organism in this sense, Tansley argued, was to confuse ecological complexes with real living organisms. Likewise, the idea of a "biological community" consisting of both plants and animals was, for Tansley, a misnomer, since there was no physical basis in which both plants and animals could properly be said to constitute a "community." Smutsian idealism, in which mystical "wholes" were the causes of all things, which was the ultimate justification provided by Phillips for his theory of biological community and complex organism, was, in Tansley's terms, a direct violation of materialist- scientific-ecological principles. Objecting to the growth of organicism, he pointed to "Professor Whitehead's 'Philosophy of Organism' and a whole school of 'organicist' philosophers: many [of whom] have not hesitated to call the universe an organism."[177]

In all of this, Tansley sought to be reasonable. He did not object to treating the plant community as a "quasi-organism." And rather than utilize "biological community," he thought that the concept of the "biome," which Clements had introduced, could be used to refer to the biota associated with a particular landscape or set of habitats, constituting "whole webs of life" or "the nuclei of *systems* in the sense of the physicist." The notion of a climax in process of a succession or development was certainly a meaningful concept, in Tansley's terms, as long as it was not converted into an absolute, teleological principle, representing the movement toward a single, ultimate climax (the monoclimax theory), one that excluded "retrogressive succession," or the possibility that "*catastrophic* destruction" from external forces might interrupt succession, and initiate new processes. Similarly, he indicated that he had no objection to the concept of emergence, which he thought necessary, if understood in materialist terms, in relation to changing levels of organization, in which something qualitatively new arises. As Tansley succinctly put it, summing up, "I plead for empirical method and terminology in all work on vegetation, and avoidance of general interpretation based on a theory of what *must* happen because "vegetation is an organism."[178]

Tansley concluded his critique of Phillips's (and more indirectly Smuts's) holistic, teleological view by intimating it was "at least partly motivated by an imagined future 'whole' to be realised in an ideal human society whose reflected glamour falls on less exalted wholes, illuminating with a false light the image of the 'complex organism.'" This was a subtle way of referring to the hierarchical system of racial stratification, which was built into Smutsian holistic ecology. Tansley clearly did not miss Phillips's pointed reference in Part 3, "The Complex Organism," of his article to "more primitive habitats under control of lower level wholes." As Anker contends, Tansley, in the passage from him quoted above, was "referring to Phillips's racist biocentrism and the politics of holism . . . with its treatment of 'less exalted wholes' at, for example . . . Bondlewaart, and Bull Hoek"—the sites of massacres of black populations ordered by Smuts.[179]

It was at this point, around three-quarters of the way into his article, that Tansley introduced the concept of "ecosystem" as a way of moving forward in ecological analysis without giving way to idealism, mysticism, and teleology.[180] Here he turned to Levy's *The Universe of Science* as a key to describing the scientific method and systems theory. The object, he insisted, must be to conceive

> the whole *system* (in the sense of physics), including not only the organism-complex, but also the whole complex of physical factors forming what we call the environment of the biome—the habitat factors in the widest sense. Though the organisms may claim our primary interest, when we are trying to think fundamentally we cannot separate them from their special environment, with which they form one physical system. . . . These *ecosystems*, as we may call them, are of the most various kinds and sizes. They form one category of the multitudinous physical systems of the universe, which range from the universe as a whole down to the atom. The whole method of science, as H. Levy . . . [*The Universe of Science*] has most convincingly pointed out, is to isolate systems mentally for the purposes of study, so that the series of *isolates* we make become the actual objects of our study, whether the isolate be a solar system, a planet, a climatic region, a plant or animal community, an individual organism, an organic molecule or an atom. Actually the systems we isolate mentally are not only included as parts of larger ones, but they also overlap, interlock, and interact with one another. The isolation is partly artificial, but is the only possible way in which we can proceed.[181]

Such systems (or mental isolates directed at what Levy called "chips" of physical reality) had to be seen as varying in their level of autonomy and in the degree to which they could be said to represent a stable equilibrium, reflecting internal integration, within a constantly changing, dynamic process. "The universal tendency to the evolution of dynamic equilibria," Tansley noted, has long been recognized. A corresponding idea was fully worked out by Hume and even stated by Lucretius (Epicurus). "The more relatively separate and autonomous the system, the more highly integrated it is, and the greater stability of its dynamic equilibrium."[182]

"The great regional climatic complexes" and "the soil complex" (with the subsoil and physiography varying more than the climate) were, in Tansley's analysis, "important determinants of the primary terrestrial ecosystems" and could be considered "parts" of these systems, just like the "organism-complex or biome." An important, dialectical aspect of Tansley's approach was the reciprocal action of different components. Thus "the climatic complex has more effect on the organisms and on the soil of an ecosystem than these have on the climatic complex, but the reciprocal action is not wholly absent. . . . What we have to deal with is a *system*, of which plants and animals are components, though not the only components. The biome is determined by climate and soil and in its turn reacts, sometimes and to some extent on climate, always on soil."

Relative to more stable physical systems such as chemical elements, Tansley observed, ecosystems consist of "components that are themselves more or less unstable—climate, soil, and organisms." They are therefore "extremely vulnerable. . . . nevertheless some of the fully developed systems—the 'climaxes'—have actually maintained themselves for thousands of years. In others there are elements whose slow change will ultimately bring about the disintegration of the system." External, more catastrophic change can also have an effect in drastically altering the system. "Owing to the position of the climatic-complexes as primary determinants of the major ecosystems, a marked change of climate must bring about the destruction of the ecosystem of any given geographical region, and its replacement by another. . . . If . . . a whole continent desiccates or freezes many of the ecosystems which formerly occupied it will be destroyed altogether."[183]

Bringing historical societies into his analysis, Tansley argued that humanity was to be "regarded as an exceptionally powerful biotic factor which increasingly upsets the equilibrium of preexisting ecosystems and eventually destroys them, at the same time forming new ones of very different nature. . . . *Anthropogenic ecosystems* differ from those developed independently of man. But the essential formative processes of vegetation are the same, however the factors initiating them are directed." Tansley argued against restricting ecology to the study of natural conditions independent of human beings, since this would unduly limit the range of ecology and remove it from practical problems. Rather, "ecology must be applied to conditions brought about by human activity."[184]

Four years later, in 1939, Tansley made another attempt to promote the ecosystem concept, both in his presidential address to the British Ecological Association that year, and also, briefly, in his 900-page magnum opus, *The British Islands and Their Vegetation.* In his 1939 presidential address, "British Ecology during the Past Quarter-Century: The Plant Community and the Ecosystem," he repeated, shorn of all polemic, some of the points he had made in his "Use and Abuse" article, rejecting the notion of the "complex organism" and suggesting that "the ecosystem," addressing a combined organic and inorganic complex in relative equilibrium, "is the most fundamental synecological [concerned with whole plant communities] concept." He also argued for the integration of plant and animal ecology around the category of ecosystem as a future project in which ecologists should be engaged. In *The British Islands and Their Vegetation,* he wrote: "My own view is that the position of relative equilibrium, corresponding with what I have called the mature 'eco-system' is the fundamental concept."[185]

The destructive role that human beings had played in relation to ecosystems was emphasized by Tansley throughout. Discussing the decline of "virgin" ecosystems in *The British Islands* he poignantly observed:

> With his increasing control over "nature" the human animal became a unique agent of destruction of the original ecosystems, as he cleared and burned natural vegetation and replaced it with his pastures, crops, and buildings. Limited at first to the regions where civilisation originally developed, this destructive activity has spread during recent centuries, and at an increasing rate, all over the face of the globe except where human life has not yet succeeded in supporting itself. It seems likely that in less than another century none but the most inhospitable regions—some of the more extreme deserts, the high mountains and the arctic tundra—will have escaped. Even these may eventually come, partially if not completely, under the human yoke.[186]

Tansley indicated that such alterations, for example, draining fens and deforestation to create pastures, though destructive of the original ecosystem, led to "the establishment of a new ecosystem [which was] the result of the original factors of climate and soil together with the modifying factors which [humans] introduced." Yet, there was also an intimation in his analysis that humans might undermine the original factors of the climate and the soil as well, raising more extensive ecological issues. This was made clearer in the last major attempt Tansley made to address the question of ecosystems, in his 1951 pamphlet *What Is Ecology?* written for the Council for the Promotion of Field Studies (later the Field Studies Council). Here he wrote that in a given area "the entire complex of natural plant and animal life (so long as it is not interfered with by man), together with the physical factors of climate and the soil which permit its existence, form, when mature, an integrated and balanced 'system' which may be called an *ecosystem*, and can sometimes maintain itself, apparently indefinitely, so long as the conditions which determine it continue." In designating such natural ecosystems, Tansley was not, however, denying his earlier consideration of the human relation to ecosystems. "Much natural vegetation," he wrote, "is annually destroyed by human agency, intentionally or carelessly, and not replaced, leaving great areas derelict, or the method of cultivation is ill-judged, or an area is abandoned after crop failure. Any of these mistreatments may lead to extensive erosion by rain or wind or to 'dust bowl' formation, according to the climate," constituting a "careless and disastrous exploitation of man's natural heritage." The complexities of the systems analysis required by ecological research meant that the field could not be drawn too narrowly, thus he specified: "There are certain non-biological subjects of great importance to the ecologist—*climatology* and *meteorology*, *geology*, *physiography* and *soil science*." Ultimately, the growth of human population and the destruction of ecosystems required the development of the field of "human ecology."[187] It was in fact the level of human ecological destructiveness that eventually catapulted the concept of ecosystem into one of the core critical concepts of the twentieth and twenty-first centuries.[188]

According to the ecologist E. P. Odum, whose *Fundamentals of Ecology* drew wide attention to Tansley's ecosystem concept, the main barrier to its widespread adoption had been the reductionism that prevailed at the time in science, and the lack of widespread recognition at that time of the concept of "emergent properties," which gave the ecosystem category its theoretical and practical importance.[189] Significantly, Nicholas Polunin, who was working under Tansley at the time the latter introduced the ecosystem concept, later emerged as a major ecological theorist and environmentalist. He played a key role both in extending the definition of ecosystem in spatial terms (similar to the Soviet ecologist Nikolaevich Sukachev's biogeocoenosis), and in integrating it with Vernadsky's concept of the biosphere. This pointed to the development of today's concept of the Earth System.[190]

CHAPTER NINE

The Return of Engels

The Second International Congress on the History of Science and Technology was held from Monday, June 29 to Saturday, July 4, 1931, at the Science Museum in South Kensington in London, attracting some of the leading figures in the history of science of the day. Yet what would otherwise have undoubtedly been a standard, even somewhat dreary and forgettable academic conference turned into an extraordinary historical event with the unexpected arrival in a transcontinental flight—at that time a rare occurrence—of a major Soviet delegation, led by Nikolai Bukharin, one of the major figures in the October Revolution. Only one Soviet speaker had been expected, the geneticist, B. M. Zavadovksy, known for his discoveries in endocrinology. Instead eight Russian scholars arrived, including Bukharin, then president of the Commission of the Academy of Sciences for the History of Knowledge, and director of the Industrial Research Department of the Supreme Economic Council, and they all insisted on presenting papers. For British scientists it represented the first major introduction to the new radical ideas on science and philosophy emanating from the revolutionary Soviet Union.

As late as Monday, June 22, only a week before the international congress in London was to start, the Soviet speakers had not themselves known they would be attending. This was altered when Joseph Stalin, the next day, issued a major change of policy, allowing greater academic freedom to scientists, concluding a year and a half of conflict between the Soviet state and intellectuals. Bukharin, who had been thrown out of the Politburo by Stalin, but who still had a leadership role within the Soviet Academy of Science, had handpicked the Soviet delegates, gathering together a brilliant group of natural scientists and historians/philosophers of science, including the USSR's best-known physicist, A. F. Joffe, and its best-known biologist and geneticist, N. I. Vavilov. Receiving the notification on June 23 that they were free to attend the conference, they threw themselves into three days of frantic activity getting ready to leave and rushed to the Moscow airport. So hasty was their departure that they were in the air before Bukharin discovered that he had left behind the paper he planned to present. The plane had to turn around and return to Moscow so he could retrieve it. They arrived in London on Saturday, June 27, to the complete astonishment of the conference organizers, which included Lancelot Hogben and biochemist and embryologist Joseph Needham. They met with the conference president, Professor Charles Singer of the University of London, just two days before the international congress was to begin.

Accommodations were soon found for the Soviets and they were integrated into the conference, with a further half-day of presentations added onto the last day, Saturday, July 4. Yet, the difficulties of translation of the lengthy Russian-language papers and the obstacles posed by the new revolutionary concepts the Soviet speakers offered presented a major challenge to the conference organizers. Hogben asked Bukharin if it were possible for the Soviet participants to get their unabridged addresses translated, edited, printed, and published as a book within a week's time. Bukharin was immediately taken with the audacious suggestion. In what the press described as "The Five-Day Plan," the Soviet Embassy was converted into a publishing house and authors worked side by side with translators. Provisional manuscripts were rushed to compositors who worked round-the-clock. The galleys were hastily edited to convert new Russian concepts into English. Page proofs were produced and frantically gone over. "Printer's boys" stood ready to rush the copy and proof pages between the Soviet Embassy and the printer. When the conference attendees filed into the lecture hall of the Science Museum on the morning of July 4, they were able to pick up the translated Soviet papers. Ten days later, the entire collection of papers appeared in a single volume under the title *Science at the Cross Roads*. On the following Saturday, a review by crystallographer and molecular biologist J. D. Bernal appeared in the *Spectator*.[1]

Vavilov, director of the Lenin All Union Academy of Agricultural Sciences, provided a stirring address on the Soviet discovery of the world centers of germplasm of the major cultivated plants. Soviet scientists, under Vavilov's leadership, had organized a search for the earliest areas of agricultural cultivation on every inhabited continent, based on the theory that this was the key to finding the areas of greatest genetic diversity of the major cultivated crops. This led to the discovery of what are now known as the Vavilov centers of genetic diversity. It represented an astounding demonstration of the power of historical materialist approaches to the evolution of the humanity-nature relations.

However, it was not Vavilov's great achievement so much as the philosophical and historical papers presented by Bukharin, along with Zavadovsky (director of the Institute of Neurohumoral Physiology) and Boris Hessen (director of the Moscow Institute of Physics and a Member of the Presidium of the State

Scientific Council) that came to exercise a dominant influence on younger socialist-oriented British scientists at the international conference.

Bukharin's paper, "Theory and Practice from the Standpoint of Dialectical Materialism," offered an epistemological critique of idealist views, particularly the subjective idealism of Berkeley so influential in the British empiricist tradition, and of mechanistic materialism. His analysis was mainly directed at the dialectics of science. But he took as his starting point Karl Marx's 1879–80 *Notes on Adolph Wagner*. There Marx had observed that Wagner perceived "the relations of man to nature" not as "*practical* from the outset, that is, relations established by action," but rather as "*theoretical* relations." Marx countered by stating:

> But on no account do men begin by "standing in that theoretical relation to the *things of the external world*." They begin, like every other animal, by *eating*, *drinking*, etc., hence not by "standing" in a relation, but by *relating themselves actively*, taking hold of certain things in the external world through action, and thus satisfying their need[s]. (Therefore, they began with production.) Through the repetition of this process, the property of those things, their property "to satisfy needs," is impressed upon their brains; men, like animals also distinguish "theoretically" from all other things the external things which serve for the satisfaction of their needs.[2]

With Marx's argument as his basis, Bukharin contended that although it was crucial to "adopt the standpoint that sensuality, sensual experience, etc., having as their source the material world existing outside our consciousness, constitute the point of departure and the beginning of cognition," nonetheless this objective world is known only through human practice and interaction with the objective world. And this occurs, not by means of "epistemological Robinson Crusoes" or "the first created Adam," and thereby abstracted from society, but through human society and the social history, that is, *historical human practice*. "Historically there is *no* absolutely unmixed individual sensation, beyond the influence of external nature, beyond the influence of other people, beyond the elements of mediated knowledge, beyond historical development, beyond the individual as the *product* of society—and society in active struggle against nature." In this view, then, Bukharin laid out, in line with Marx, an approach that was materialist, rooted in the senses and in human practice, and that recognized the complex relations between human beings and external nature.[3]

Building in this way on Marx's *Notes on Adolph Wagner*, Bukharin emphasized the objective nature of human beings as beings with their objects outside of themselves, meaning that they were sensuous beings, inherently interacting with and dependent on external nature, but also engaged in practice and thus an expanding knowledge of nature in relation to themselves—leading to a changing relation to nature, as they developed their own powers through production. In this regard he wrote, after the fashion of the times, that "society is in active struggle against nature." But this struggle was one of the development of human practice, instruments, and technology, a transformation of the human relation to nature and the relation of humanity to itself. "The objective world," he wrote, "is changed through practice and according to practice, which includes theory: this means that practice verifies the truth of theory; and this means that we *know* to a certain extent (and come to know more and more) objective reality, its qualities, its attributes, its regularities." In a statement that no doubt had an enormous impact on the young British socialists in the audience, Bukharin declared: "Theory is accumulated and condensed practice."[4]

This view, he insisted, made a mockery of Karl Pearson's notion in *The Grammar of Science* that knowledge of the world through our senses resembled a telephone exchange (an updating of Plato's cave metaphor). This constituted an idealist notion, characteristic of neo-Kantianism, in which the real, objective interrelations between humanity and nature were eliminated. Instead, Bukharin argued, humanity through social practice, was changing "the face of the whole of the earth. Living and working in the biosphere, social man has radically remoulded the surface of the planet." In his use of Vladimir Ivanovich Vernadsky's concept of the biosphere in defining the materialist conception of nature of historical materialism, Bukharin was making a fundamental departure, in line with what was later to emerge as systems ecology.[5]

In Bukharin's terms, "dialectical materialism" drew its essential meaning from its rejection of "all species of idealism and agnosticism," overcoming "the narrowness of mechanical materialism (its ahistoricism, its anti-dialectical character, its failure to understand problems of quality, its contemplative 'objectivism,' etc)." The emphasis was on a materialist approach to science that was also dialectical, and thus directed against both the teleology of idealism/vitalism and the crude mechanistic materialism represented by thinkers such as "Büchner-Moleschott."[6] He followed Frederick Engels's argument in the *Origin of the Family, Private Property, and the State* in emphasizing that historical materialism was concerned with both material production and also the reproduction of the family and life.[7]

The real essence of the dialectical view toward nature, Bukharin argued in the 1920s in his *Historical Materialism: A System of Sociology,* was to be found in Marx's concept of social and ecological metabolism. As he put it in his book: "This material process of 'metabolism' between society and nature is the fundamental relation between environment and system, between 'external conditions' and human society." Similarly, in his 1931 address at the International Congress on the History of Science and Technology, he declared: "In the process of production there takes place a 'metabolism' (Marx) between society and nature." Materialist dialectics was pointing to a more holistic and dynamic, less individualist and static, approach to human-nature and nature-nature relations. Referring to the development of ecology and its central notion, then, of plant "communities" or plant and animal "society," he stated: "In zoology and botany (the doctrine of heterogeneous 'societies' of plants and animals)," that is, ecology as then conceived represented a more complex, systemic or metabolic view of organic existence.[8]

Bukharin was to develop these ideas further six years later in his extraordinary, but still largely unknown philosophical treatise, *Philosophical Arabesques*, written in 1937 while he was being held prisoner in the depths of Lubyanka Prison in Moscow. It was completed on the twentieth anniversary of the October Revolution, five months before his execution on Stalin's orders. The title of the work was clearly meant as an ironic response to Eugen Dühring's satirical reference to Marx and Engels's work as consisting of "dialectical frills" and "conceptual arabesques."[9] Bukharin's approach in *Philosophical Arabesques* was deeply affected by V. I. Lenin's *Philosophical Notebooks*, and was designed to remove from the philosophy of historical materialism any trace of crude positivism. The natural-dialectical laws that Engels had pointed to were themselves historical laws. "These laws exist if certain natural-historical conditions are present. In their essence, these laws are just as historical as any law of society, only the time scale is different." At the same time, such natural laws, as we commonly describe them, are products of cognition, and should be viewed as "cognized laws of nature."[10]

Bukharin argued in *Philosophical Arabesques* that "philosophy has often been Janus-faced; one of its faces has been turned to humanity, the other to nature." The promise of the dialectic was to transcend this dualism by means of an understanding of the developmental and contradictory nature of existence in the world. With respect to external nature, Bukharin declared: "There exists a huge complex, organic world; there exists what Academician Vladimir Vernadsky termed the earth's biosphere, full of infinitely varied life, from the smallest microorganisms in water, on land, and in the air, to human beings." Human beings were to be seen as belonging to and affecting the biosphere. But this also raised, particularly in capitalist society, complex issues related to human alienation from nature:

> If human beings are both products of nature and part of it; if they have a biological basis when their social existence is excluded from account (it cannot be abolished!); if they are themselves natural magnitudes and products of nature, and if they live within nature (however much they might be divided from it by particular social and historical conditions of life and by the so-called "artistic

> environment"), then what is surprising in the fact that human beings share in the rhythm of nature and its cycles?... The feeling of a bond with nature is present in human beings in the most diverse forms, and there is nothing accidental about the longing of townsfolk for sunshine, green fields, flowers, and stars.[11]

The concept of continual "progress"—pointing to where Bukharin was headed following his 1931 paper—was rejected by both Marx and Engels. They had written in *The Holy Family*, "In spite of the pretensions of 'Progress,' continual *retrogressions* and *circular movements* occur." In the *Dialectics of Nature*, Bukharin observed, Engels, following the path set out by Charles Fourier, "considered inevitable both the decline of humanity and its extinction, together with the ending of life on the earth, on the planet. In other words, human history cannot be divorced in any way from the history of the earth as the base, *locus standi* and source of nourishment of society." Although Bukharin thought human beings might eventually move out into the cosmos, he was far from certain, writing: "Whoever lives will see." There was no smooth upward path in human history. The development of socialism would, he hoped, "free progress from the hobbles which decaying capitalism has placed upon it." The kind of "gloomy" pessimism of a Spengler was not justified. Nevertheless, "dialectics" constituted a warning against "immoderate worshippers of the god of progress." This followed from the complex relation of human beings (*homo faber*) to nature, according to which humanity is not only part of nature but also often finds itself "in opposition" to it, requiring that the associated producers learn to regulate their metabolism with nature in a rational way.[12]

These were important reflections, pointing to where Bukharin was headed following his 1931 paper before the International Congress on the History of Science and Technology. However, with Bukharin's execution, the 310 handwritten pages of *Philosophical Arabesques* were locked away in Stalin's secret vault and not made available (though their existence was discovered under Gorbachev) until the fall of the Soviet Union more than a half-century later. *Philosophical Arabesques* was published soon after in Russian, with an English-language edition appearing for the first time in 2005.

Bukharin's 1931 address in London was complemented by that of Zavadovsky, who astonished his audience by introducing a powerful critique of the sterile debate between mechanists and vitalists, then occurring within science. Zavadovsky sought to transcend both mechanistic materialism and vitalism by means of a "theory of organic evolution" rooted in materialist dialectics.[13] Drawing on Engels's then little-known *Dialectics of Nature*, he stressed the importance of dialectics in allowing Marxian materialism to take an active, dynamic form that was missing in mechanistic materialism but captured by vitalism. At the same time a dialectical conception of materialism allowed for the rejection of the idealist, teleological approach of vitalism.

A dialectical and materialist analysis began with "the fact of development." Darwinian evolutionary theory was viewed as "the expansion of the dialectical process," embodying materialist thinking. Zavadovsky thus argued for a strong Darwinian view, explicitly rejecting what he called "neo-Lamarckianism"—or attempts to depict evolution in terms of the inheritance of acquired characteristics, which he associated with the vitalist rejection of Darwinism.

The key to a meaningful dialectical approach in this sphere, Zavadovsky explained, was to focus on the complex relation between the "'biophysiological' as a factor that chiefly determines the processes of individual development, of metabolism and the regulation of the activity of organisms, and the 'biohistorical' as a factor in the formation of species and phylogenesis."[14] Mechanists were often weak when it came to the understanding of historical development, going so far as to reduce human history to mere mechanistic biological principles, ignoring questions of history and emergence. Such barren notions played into the hands of "social Darwinism," with its attempts to justify racism and capitalism. The vitalists, for their part, tended to associate the biological with "internal" development, seeing the "external" as the physical, non-biological factors, and forgetting that "physico-chemical factors" were conditions not only of inorganic but also organic nature. The result was mysticism and abandonment of the materialism essential to science. These divisions, so characteristic of bourgeois thought, generated "endless contradictions" reflecting the absence of a sufficiently realistic and critical method and the inability to distinguish between "the laws characteristic of the different stages [levels] of matter." This led to "the equally barren attempts to embrace all the complexity and multiformity of the world through a single mathematical formula of the mechanical movement of molecules, or through the vitalistic idea of a single 'principle of perfection,' in effect representing an attempt to know and explain the world through the inexplicable and unknowable."[15]

What was absolutely essential in biological work, Zavadovsky contended, was a dialectical-ecological approach in which "the 'external' is composed not only of the physical conditions of the external surroundings [of an organism], but also of the biological encirclement by a milieu of other organisms, and also—in the case of the evolution of man—the social-economic relations prevailing within human society." Only in this way was it possible to examine complex, organic relations. A rational materialist explanation of "the formation of species," incorporating "the most complex phenomena of biological adaptation (such as protective colouring, mimicry, care for the progeny and the other instincts, parasitism, symbiosis, etc.)," could thus be facilitated by a dialectically enhanced materialist philosophy. From such a methodological standpoint, he wrote, "the biological is considered in its indissoluble historical connection with physical phenomena (as a higher form of motion, originating out of lower inorganic forms of motion of matter), and also its dynamic connection (metabolism)." In this analysis, higher levels of organization were irreducible to material properties and relations of lower levels of organization.[16]

But it was Hessen's paper on "The Social and Economic Roots of Newton's 'Principia' " that was to have the greatest direct impact on the attendees to the International Congress and on the future of the history and sociology of science. Hessen proceeded to explain systematically and with an enormous wealth of detail the extent to which Newton's *Principia* was to be understood not simply as the internal product of a great brain and of pure science, but one that also grew out of the socio-economic problems of the time, and the mechanistic challenges facing science and technology—generating an-all pervasive philosophy of mechanism. As the noted science journalist, J. G. Crowther, present at the conference, explained:

> The most remarkable paper delivered at this congress was that of B. Hessen, on *The Social and Economic Roots of Newton's 'Principia.'* It had never occurred to me, or to most other people, that Newton's *Principia* had any social and economic roots. I knew from Marxist thought the principle that all science had its roots in society, but I had not perceived or looked for this in any concrete and particular case, especially not in the greatest case of all: Newton's *Principia*. I had assumed in the conventional manner that it was a purely intellectual creation.
>
> Hessen sketched an outline of the social origins of this greatest of scientific works. The argument of his paper was quite simple, and it was obvious to British historians that there was much relevant information which he did not quote and, indeed, of which he appeared to be ignorant. But the limitation of the scope of Hessen's knowledge was irrelevant; he was a professor of physics in Moscow university, not a British historian. It was the penetration of his thought, arising from his command of both mathematical physics and Marxism, that enabled him to reach new depths in the understanding of Newtonian science which intellectually superseded other historical analyses, however much more learned.[17]

Hessen's paper went on to discuss the limitations of mechanistic materialism, as it had emanated from Newton in particular, a principal weakness of which was that "all historical outlook on nature is missing." Moreover, "not only is the historical view of nature lacking in Newton," he wrote, "but in his system of mechanics the law of conservation of energy does not exist."

At the end of the nineteenth century, Engels had grasped, with the aid of the more developed science of his day, the need for a more complex materialist analysis of the natural world and of science. One of the virtues of Engels's approach to such issues, Hessen explained to those attending the congress, is that in adopting a more dialectical approach "he considered the process of the movement of matter as eternal transition from one form of material movement to another. This enables him not only to establish one of the basic theses of dialectic materialism, i.e., the inseparability of movement from matter, but also to carry the conception of the law of conservation of energy and quantity of movement to a higher level."[18] This of course was not the product of any particular genius on Engels's part but the result of a historical moment, a new revolutionary phase in history, when the limitations of mechanistic materialism were becoming more apparent. Emphasizing the relation between the quantitative and qualitative as seen by dialectics and its relation to thermodynamics, Hessen wrote:

> This treatment of the law of the conservation and conversion of energy given by Engels, raises to the forefront the qualitative aspect of the law of conservation of energy, in contradistinction to the treatment which predominates in modern physics and which reduces this law to a purely quantitative law—the quantity of energy during its transformations. The law of the conservation of energy, the teaching of the indestructability of motion has to be understood not only in a quantitative but also in a qualitative sense. It contains not only a postulation of the indestructibility and the increatibility of energy, which is one of the basic prerequisites of the materialist conception of nature, but a dialectical treatment of the problem of the movement of matter. From the aspect of dialectical materialism the indestructibility of motion consists not only in the circumstances that matter moves within the limits of one form of motion, but also in the circumstance that matter itself is capable of all the endless variety of forms of motion in their spontaneous transitions one into another, in their self-movement and development.[19]

Needham depicted Hessen's paper as "perhaps the outstanding Russian contribution," and almost "sacrilegious" in its argument with respect to Newton, who had previously been presumed to be so godly a figure as to be immune to his environment. (As Alexander Pope wrote in a famous couplet, "Nature and nature's laws lay hid in night; / God said 'Let Newton be!' and all was light.") Hessen, however, had removed the spell. Hessen's work encouraged Needham to revise and adapt the first volume of his *Chemical Embryology*, converting it into a *History of Embryology* in 1934. Bernal described Hessen's paper as "the starting point of a new evaluation of science" in England. Similar views on the breakthrough represented by Hessen's work were provided by Hogben, who invited Bukharin and his associates to an evening's discussion at his home; he was to describe Bukharin as a "charming and humane man." Crowther recorded that he had many discussions with Bukharin and Hessen and took them to the National Physical Laboratory as well as the Patents Office Library.

Altogether, the role of the Soviet delegation to the congress was summed up by Hymen Levy as "epoch-making." A strong bond was established between the British socialist scientists and the Soviet scientists who had attended the 1931 conference. It was to have an extraordinary and lasting effect on the future work of such figures as Hogben, Needham, Levy, and Bernal, all of whom were in attendance. It thus emerged as a formative event in the development over the next several decades of what came to be known as the "social relations of science" tradition rooted in a materialist dialectic. Crowther was to write of the warmth with which he and Julian Huxley were greeted by Bukharin and Hessen in a subsequent visit to the USSR.[20]

Yet, the fates of Bukharin, Hessen, Vavilov, and Zavadovsky were soon sealed in the purges of the Stalin era. As Needham later wrote, "It would hardly be possible in a foreword such as this [written for the 1971 edition of *Science at the Cross Roads*] to ignore the tragic fact of the disappearance of so many of these delegates in the years after the Congress, according to the dreadful principle that 'all revolutions devour their own children.'" Hessen and Bukharin, who were close allies, were both executed, in 1936 and 1938, respectively, as traitors to the revolution—in Bukharin's case under Stalin's direct orders. Vavilov and Zavadovsky had opposed Trofim Denisovich Lysenko, who had the backing of Stalin, on genetics. Vavilov was arrested in 1940 and died in prison of malnutrition in 1943. Zavadovsky, who was directly attacked by Lysenko, was removed from his post as director of the Timiryazev Biological Museum. He died shortly afterward.[21] Although Bukharin's execution was known, the fates of the other three emerged only decades later.[22]

In the meantime, the ideas presented at the 1931 Congress by these luminous thinkers, the product of the Russian Revolution up through the early 1930s, continued to inspire intellectual developments among Marxists in the West, leading to important new insights into dialectical naturalism, environmental systems theory, and socialist practice. For the British socialist scientists this was to spark an intense interest in Engels's *Dialectics of Nature*, in particular, more than a half-century or more after it was written.

PECULIARITIES OF THE BRITISH SOCIALIST SCIENTISTS

Ironically, it was in Britain, rather than the USSR, that the critical ideas of the Soviet delegates to the 1931 International Congress in London were to exert major, continuing influence. Gary Werskey observes that Bernal and the other Marxist scientists in Britain represented an approach to the role of science in society that was closely connected to that of Bukharin, emphasizing scientific humanism as the key to socialism—one that was to be largely extinguished in the USSR. Bukharin and the other British Marxian scientists he had handpicked as the Soviet participants to the International Congress were "the personification of the path not taken" in the USSR. In this sense, the fact that Bernal, Needham, Levy, Hogben, and J. B. S. Haldane were directly influenced by a genealogical line of descent in critical-dialectical materialism soon to be largely extinguished in the Soviet Union, meant that their attempts at a new socialist synthesis followed a path unlike that of anywhere else.[23] Moreover, they developed their views of historical materialism in relation to their own, primarily British, conditions, their strong Darwinian backgrounds, and their own distinctive interpretations, particularly of the classical historical materialist approach to science. "Most Marxists," Haldane was to write in the 1940s, "are Darwinists," something that applied to British Marxists perhaps most of all.[24] What emerged in Britain was thus a version of dialectical naturalism that was *sui generis*, with its own vernacular and its own important discoveries. Nowhere, outside of the Soviet Union itself, were science and Marxism, evolutionary theory and historical materialism, so closely connected. Moreover, the crisis of the sciences, particularly in areas related to genetics and Lysenkoism, sharply circumscribed progress in the USSR from the late 1930s on, making the discoveries of socialist scientists in Britain that much more important in terms of the evolution of historical materialist views.[25] These thinkers were full of creativity, reflecting the scientific and cultural revolutions occurring in their times. As Eric Hobsbawm wrote, "They tended to combine the imaginations of art and science with endless energy, free love, eccentricity and revolutionary politics."[26]

These thinkers of course have not been without their critics, even on the left. The whole problem of determining the meaning of what was popularly referred to as "red science" in Britain in the 1930s can be seen via political theorist Neal Wood's harsh assessment in his 1959 book, based on his Cambridge University doctoral thesis, *Communism and British Intellectuals*. Wood traced the foundations of this whole tradition of thought to what he called "the Baconian strand in Marxism," extending all the way back to Marx himself. Unaware that Marx had studied Francis Bacon directly, Wood asserted (citing H. B. Acton's *The Illusion of the Epoch*) that Marx had acquired this "Baconian strand" in his thought from Ludwig Feuerbach.[27] Yet, both Bacon in the seventeenth century and Feuerbach in the nineteenth had self-consciously reached back to earlier materialisms. Marx had traced out this development in his own work, and in his response to Georg Friedrich Hegel, writing his doctoral dissertation on Epicurus and the question of Epicurus's famous swerve—in his attempt to chart a dialectical course that avoided the Scylla of absolute idealism and the Charybdis of mechanistic materialism.[28]

In seeking to justify his classification of the British red scientists as Baconian Marxists, Wood pointed to the fact that the left classical scholar and historian of science Benjamin Farrington had written a small book on Bacon, some of whose work Farrington had translated from Latin into English.[29] However, Wood failed to notice that Farrington had, much more importantly, emerged as one of the major interpreters within British classicism of Epicurean philosophy. Indeed, this constituted the contribution for which Farrington was to be most esteemed, as evidenced in such works as *Science and Politics in the Ancient World* (1939), *Head and Hand in Ancient Greece* (1947), and *The Faith of Epicurus* (1967).[30] Other British Marxist classicists provided similar approaches to materialism, focusing on Epicurus, for example, George Thomson in his *The First Philosophers* (1955). Thomson claimed, "Epicurus is the culmination of ancient philosophical materialism. His sense of dialectics, revealed in his conception of the interdependence of necessity and chance, of the relation between man and nature, and of the uneven development of human progress, invites comparison with the intuitive dialectics of Ionian materialism, which culminated in Herakleitos."[31]

In Needham's case, Epicureanism was so closely related to the method of modern science that they could be referred to interchangeably as "the Epicurean or scientific attitude."[32] In his introduction to *Time: The Refreshing River* (1943), Needham wrote: "I look back with pleasure on my enthusiasm for Epicurus and Lucretius, from which I have never seen any reason to depart." Moreover, the most crucial part of Epicurus for Needham (no doubt influenced by Marx's dissertation), and for Marx himself, was the concept of the swerve, which opened the way to conceptions of contingency and organization.[33]

Bernal emphasized that Epicurus applied the materialism and atomism inherited from Democritus "to humanist ends. . . . The pleasure of Epicurus was an extremely refined kind of pleasure—he was called the Garden Philosopher. He spent his time discussing and enjoying a very simple life." The great didactic poem, *On the Nature of Things,* by Epicurus's Roman follower Lucretius, Bernal argued, poetically and philosophically prefigured "the gene theory of inheritance mixed up with the theory of atoms and, of course, the full essence of that mix-up has only been revealed to us in the last few years with the elucidation of the nature and actions of the molecules of DNA."[34]

Haldane observed that Charles Darwin's great discovery that today's animals had evolved from simpler forms by means of natural selection was prefigured in Epicurus and Lucretius.[35] While Hogben recalled how Farrington early on had gotten him to read Marx's dissertation on Epicurus, and the importance it had assumed in the development of his thought.[36]

If it is true that the British Marxist materialists of this period represented in a very qualified way a *Baconian* strand of Marxism, and thus were related to a distinctively English tradition, it would be much more accurate and meaningful to see them as representing an *Epicurean* strand of Marxism via Marx himself, reflecting a more fundamental and critical, as well as more ancient, version of materialist thought, attuned to dialectics, and the struggle for human freedom.[37] Indeed, materialist philosophy itself, Marx pointed out, lay in a line that extended from Epicurus to Bacon, to Feuerbach, out of which historical materialism was to emerge as a critical perspective.[38]

These lines of intellectual descent, derived from ancient materialism, converged in important ways within the Darwinian and Marxian traditions, to which all of these thinkers critically subscribed. The new innovations in the dialectics of science that leading Marxian-oriented scientists sought to promote were aimed principally at developing a wider, more dynamic materialist synthesis, extending to the interrelations between natural-historical and social-historical systems. That they were materialists and not idealists was not at all shocking in the context of the time. What they sought to combat, however, was a mechanical materialism, or crude mechanism, within science, and to replace it with a more active, dialectical, and praxis-related form.

Wood went on to characterize these so-called Baconian Marxist thinkers as "sympathetic interpreters of Soviet Communism."[39] Yet, although they were all to varying degrees favorable to the Russian Revolution, and to Soviet socialism, to see these Anglo-Marxist thinkers as mere fellow travelers belies their complex outlooks, their distinctive vernaculars arising from historically specific circumstance, the conflicts within Soviet Marxism itself, and the fact that their major investigations took all sorts of creative directions. Thus, their sympathy for the new revolutionary attempts in the construction of society and science in the USSR tells us very little in itself, since it ignores the enormous intellectual independence demonstrated by each of these scientists, who were among the most important of their time. In presenting dialectical materialism, for example, Haldane was sharply critical of what he called the "utter nonsense" in this regard often coming out of the Soviet Union, and self-consciously developed his views of the dialectics of nature directly on Engels, Marx, and Lenin (with some references to Bukharin, Vavilov, Hessen, etc.).[40]

Hence, the frequent suggestions of Wood and others that scholars like Bernal, Haldane, and Levy became "sympathetic interpreters" of Soviet-style dialectical materialism only serve to blunt our awareness of (1) the suppression in the Soviet Union from the late 1930s on of the critical views that these thinkers expressed; (2) the distinctiveness of the dialectical vernaculars that they promoted in the British context; and (3) the extent to which almost all of them openly broke with the ruling Soviet line, particularly after the invasion of Hungary in 1956.[41] Of the leading British social scientists, it was Bernal, as we shall see, who for a short period in the early Cold War years was most vulnerable to criticism for an uncritical adherence to the then rigid Soviet ideology. But this hardly explains his relation to Marxism in the 1930s and '40s—or indeed in the late 1950s and '60s. Nor would it be reasonable on that basis to overlook his legendary originality as a thinker, the immense impact of his ideas, his rebelliousness in many areas, or his leadership in the Cold War–era peace movement.

The 1930s and early 1940s were a time in which scientists in Britain became increasingly radical in their political orientation, reflecting the battle against fascism. C. P. Snow estimated that of the two hundred brightest young physicists in Britain, around three-quarters considered themselves left of center. Being an advocate of "complete socialism" in the case of a figure like Patrick Blackett, who received the Nobel Prize in Physics in 1948, tended, if anything, to enhance his public prestige among scientists, until the Cold War produced the opposite effect.[42] Many of the intellectuals operating within the "Old Left" introduced their own critical judgments. Indeed, there were, as E. P. Thompson (himself a product of the Old Left as well as an initiator of the New) declared, all sorts of "proto-revisionists in the Communist Party in those days," which for all of its increasing rigidity was also a sphere in which much of the most creative, critical activity was taking place.[43] This was true not only of philosophers, like Christopher Caudwell and David Guest (both of whom were killed in their twenties in Spain fighting for the Republican cause) and historians like Thompson, Hobsbawm, and Christopher Hill, but also applied to the red scientists, none of whom restricted their judgments to a party line.

Nevertheless, for Wood, as for numerous other Cold War–era critics, the leading red scientists, such as Bernal and Haldane, were to be especially marked for condemnation. "The extreme views of these communist sympathizers," Wood charged, entailed "the insatiable impulse . . . to control nature and society." Pointing almost exclusively to the young Bernal's early Wellsian, futuristic analysis in *The World, the Flesh, and the Devil* (1929), Wood argued that the goal of such red scientists was "dictatorship by the scientist" as "the apotheosis of control, complete and totalitarian." Here "science would become the absolute director of human destiny." Yet, this was a studied overreaction to Bernal's first book, written in his twenties, in which he had sought to be fanciful and provocative, in the spirit of Haldane's *Daedalus* and Bertrand Russell's *Icarus*. It was an important book. But it had no real relation to Marxism or "dialectical materialism" (which Bernal at this point was still only beginning to grasp) other than a reference to the possibilities opened up by Soviet planning in a future where the Soviet Union was "no longer in danger of capitalist attack."

It is true that the young Bernal's argument raised the idea of "an aristocracy of scientific intelligence" in a world where the peace and prosperity of humanity were secured. Yet, his work at that time was oriented more to the reform of capitalism than the development of socialism, suggesting that "the idea of private interest" be broadened in order to "include, almost necessarily some consideration of humanity," something missing in the capitalist reality of the time. The argument of *The World, the Flesh, and the Devil* was, as the British left scientists Hilary and Steven Rose later wrote, that of a twenty-eight-year-old thinker "becoming a Marxist"—but one far from there yet. The fact that Bernal, in his mature work, came out resolutely in opposition to such absolute control of society by scientists, as in his landmark *The Social Function of Science*, did not go unnoticed by Wood, but was consigned to a mere footnote.[44]

Such harsh criticisms leveled at the red scientists of the 1930s, of which Wood's was typical, were largely propagandistic in nature. They did not attempt to examine, but simply dismissed out of hand, what from another point of view would be regarded as the courageous attempts of these leading left scientists and historians of science to develop a non-mechanistic, non-reductionist materialism, which would serve as a theoretical guide to empirical investigations and social practice.

Historically, this radicalization of scientists was occurring in the context of the Great Depression, with millions of workers unemployed and the rise of the fascist threat, two overarching historical phenomena that propelled these thinkers to action. These same left scientists were to support peace efforts in the early 1930s, and—once the Spanish Civil War and the rise of fascism had proven peace to be impossible—were to commit themselves to what was known as the great Anti-Nazi War.[45] In 1939, John Anderson, the British minister for civil defense planning, declared of Bernal, "Even if he is as red as the flames of hell, I want him."[46] Bernal was to emerge as the leading scientific adviser of the combined military operations in the D-Day invasion.[47] Haldane became the foremost scientific authority on civil defense, aiding the British government during the Nazi Blitzkrieg. Needham was sent as a scientific advisor/diplomatic figure to the Chinese government during the war.

Inspired by the new possibilities opened up by the revolutionary science of the Soviet Union in the 1920s and early 1930s, the British Marxian-oriented scientists of the time undertook an extraordinarily audacious set of investigations into the complexity and dynamism of natural processes—along with the developing rifts in the human relation to nature. Recognizing, with the clouds of war already approaching, that the future was increasingly dependent on the development of science and technology, they nevertheless saw this as producing frightening results in a society dominated by the profit motive. For Blackett, capitalism was a "retrograde movement" that shaded over into fascism. For Levy the dangers of *Science in an Irrational Society* were enormous. Collectively, these thinkers were to stand out in their insistence on the need for greater social foresight and control, to be introduced by means of revolutions in the "social relations of science" and in society itself.[48]

Underlying all of this was the idea of a new scientific philosophy developing in the twentieth century. Hessen's work on Newton and the seventeenth-century scientific revolution gave rise to the idea of a similar scientific revolution in the twentieth century. Just as mechanism had dominated all materialist science since Newton, so it was suggested, in the analysis of thinkers such as Hessen, Bukharin, and Zavadovsky, and carried over into the work of Bernal, Haldane, Needham, and Levy, that materialism was at long last freeing itself from its overly mechanistic and reductionist past. The historical context in which science and society were now developing was increasingly a consciously dialectical one, in the sense of pointing to complexity, dynamics, relativity, interdependence, emergence, qualitative transformations, and integrative levels. Socialist revolution, like the bourgeois revolution before it, these thinkers believed, was opening the way to new transformative views of reality. The diachronic, or historical, reality of the physical world was now at long last coming to the fore, leading to the deep conviction that history, with its punctuated equilibriums, governed all of existence, both natural and social, in endlessly complex, still to be ascertained, ways.

BERNAL: THE DIALECTICS OF SCIENCE

Among the British socialist scientists, leading roles in developing what was commonly referred to in line with Soviet philosophy as "dialectical materialism," were taken by Bernal, Haldane, and Needham. Although aware of Soviet contributions in science and philosophy, particularly the more revolutionary ideas of the 1920s and early 1930s, they drew almost all their inspiration with respect to the application of dialectics to the material world from Engels's four later works, written in the 1870s and '80s—*Anti-Dühring*; *The Origin of the Family, Private Property, and the State*; *Ludwig Feuerbach*; and, after its publication in German in 1925 and in English in 1940, *The Dialectics of Nature*.[49]

Beyond Engels's works, references were primarily to Marx's *Capital* and Lenin's *Materialism and Empirico-Criticism*.[50] Although Marx's contributions to the critique of political economy and to the critique of science were studied closely, as were Lenin's early contributions to philosophy (his *Philosophical Notebooks* became available only later), it was to Engels that intellectuals like Bernal and Haldane primarily turned for inspiration in the attempt to connect materialist natural science and dialectics.

At the time, Marx's *Economic and Philosophical Manuscripts* were virtually unknown—only becoming available as a result of the efforts of David Riazanov in Russia, and were not widely available in the West until after the Second World War. (Although Bernal was one of the earliest to draw on Marx's early manuscripts in the British context, translating important passages from the German.) Hence, Marx's philosophical views, in the eyes of the British socialist scientists, were largely seen—in what was a distinctive approach to Marx's philosophy, mainly influential in the sciences—as related to Epicurus's resolutely non-mechanistic materialism, to which dialectical notions derived from Hegel were attached as a corrective to contemplative materialism. The role of Epicurus constantly reappeared, reflecting the publication of Marx's doctoral dissertation, and the discovery that Marx had anticipated modern Epicurean scholarship by almost a century in his treatment of Epicurus's swerve (the unpredictable swerve of an atom from a linear path), which, with its emphasis on contingency, broke with all mechanical, passive conceptions of nature, and all rigid determinisms, while pointing to the possibility of human freedom.[51]

Nevertheless, for those seeking to understand the relation of science and philosophy within classical historical materialism, the main guide was Engels. It was Engels, in his major works, who had directly connected dialectics to materialist science. Moreover, this was only to gain further impetus with the publication in English of *The Dialectics of Nature* in 1940. The renewed appreciation of Engels, which now began in the 1930s to exert an influence on some of the most prominent scientists of the day, particularly in Britain, can be seen especially in Bernal's writings in the early 1930s, which exhibited a deep appreciation of Engels's contributions to the dialectics of nature, science, and society.

John Desmond Bernal's father, Samuel Bernal, was an Irish-Catholic small farmer in the county of Tipperary. He had traveled widely, living for fourteen years in Australia. In 1900 he married an American, Elizabeth Miller, one of the first women to attend the then new Stanford University in California, and who had attended lectures at the Sorbonne, traveling widely in Europe and working as a journalist for such papers as the *San Francisco Argonaut*. She was, as C. P. Snow remarked, "a woman who was a little like a character out of Henry James—expatriate, literary, cultivated." Desmond, their first child, was born in 1901.

Desmond's brilliance was apparent early. His first solo chemistry experiment, which he initiated after reading a lecture that Michael Faraday had written for children on "the chemistry of the candle," took place when he was seven, and resulted in "a most magnificent explosion." His mother insisted that he be educated in England, where she believed the schools were better. He attended Bedford School, beginning at age thirteen, and in 1919 obtained a scholarship at Emmanuel College, Cambridge University, excelling in science and mathematics.

As a young man, Bernal, in the words of Werskey, was a "wiry, red-haired, audacious Irishman, with a quicksilvery brilliance" and had a capacious imagination. His friends and followers knew him in the 1930s as "Sage." At Cambridge he took up physics and x-ray crystallography. In 1927 he was appointed first lecturer in structural crystallography at Cambridge. A decade later, in 1937, he was made a Fellow of the Royal Society and was appointed professor of physics (later physics and crystallography) at Birkbeck College in the University of London, a post he was to retain throughout his career.[52]

Bernal became widely recognized by his colleagues as one of the most outstanding scientists of his day, a figure who was at one and the same time a crystallographer, physicist, molecular biologist, social scientist, planner, Marxian theorist, visionary, and peace campaigner. Joseph Needham referred to Bernal as one of the greatest minds of his generation. C. P. Snow wrote: "He is the most learned scientist of his time, perhaps the last of whom it will be said, with meaning, that he knew science." Snow's novel *The Search* focused on the brilliant crystallographer Constantine, who inspired everyone around him, modeled on Bernal.

Bernal's major specialty in x-ray crystallography was to give him a central role in the development of physics, chemistry, and molecular biology. He was "at the center of the revolution which was . . . to carry physics and chemistry into biology."[53] Crystals and crystalline solids are common in nature, with a crystalline structure composing most natural solid substances with which we come into regular contact. Familiar large simple crystals like snowflakes, table salt, and diamonds, exhibit the common crystalline form, characterized by flat faces and sharp angles (though not all crystalline substances take this form), with a crystalline *lattice* or periodic arrangement extending in all directions. The scientific understanding of crystals, however, had to await the development of John Dalton's atomic theory in the early nineteenth century, in which it was recognized that atoms combined in larger structures that are now called molecules. The better-known crystals were thus macromolecules, arising from the building up of the same structural arrangements of atoms repeated over and over. The key to analyzing such substances was thus understanding the atomic structures making up the individual cellular molecule. Polycrystalline substances, including metals and most inorganic substances, were made up of numerous crystals. The discovery of x-rays in the late nineteenth century led to the development beginning in 1912 of x-ray crystallography, which provided a way (through the analysis of diffraction patterns) of ascertaining the arrangement of atoms within a crystalline structure, and thus the structure of molecules. Suddenly there was a process, as Bernal himself put it, "comparable only with the analysis of molecules by the chemists in the nineteenth century but far quicker," for the "the analysis of the structure of solid materials by x-rays. . . . The methods of x-ray analysis are essentially those of optics. If we had eyes that could see x-rays the atomic structure of matter would itself be visible to us; lacking those eyes we can supplement them by photographic detection and mathematical calculation."

Bernal's work in x-ray crystallography began with the examination of graphite, considered the most stable form of carbon. He then turned to copper and tin. In the 1930s, he turned to biochemistry with the idea of delving into the physical basis of life. The complexity of arrays in biological substances was the result of the fact that biological molecules can be composed of hundreds of thousands of atoms. He began with substances of biological significance such as amino acids, sterols, and vitamins. He then turned to water since this was the key to most organisms, and then pioneered in protein crystallography and the molecular structure of proteins. This helped establish the basis for some of the great discoveries in molecular biology that were to follow. He argued that proteins were the stuff of life, always emphasizing the intuitive brilliance of Engels's insights in that respect. With the use of these new methods, "the structure of matter," Bernal contended, was finally revealed in physics, as well as chemistry, and increasingly in biology. This played a major role in the discovery of DNA.[54]

At Cambridge, Bernal had gone in a decisively radical direction, picking up socialism at the instigation of his friend Henry Dickenson, later a noted professor of economics, famous for his *Economics of Socialism* (1939). Bernal's initial introduction to Marxism in 1920, however, was a deterministic and heavily distorted one, judging from the first work he read in the area that had a considerable influence on him, Enrico Ferri's social Darwinist tract, *Socialism and Positive Science*, which Engels had detested. That same year, however, he read Leon Trotsky's *History of the Russian Revolution*. He joined the National Union of Scientific Workers and the Communist Party of Great Britain (CPGB) in 1923. In his Cambridge years, he was friends with Marxist economist Maurice Dobb. Still, Bernal's 1929 work, *The World, the Flesh, and the Devil*, referred to by science-fiction writer Arthur C. Clarke as "the most brilliant attempt at scientific prediction ever made," showed an interest in socialist and Soviet planning but little real knowledge of Marxism.[55] Bernal's intense scholarly interest in Marxism was to await the 1930s, following his encounter with the Russian delegation led by Bukharin at the International Congress to the History of Science in 1931, and Bernal's visit to the USSR for the first time that year.

In his early Cambridge years, Freud actually trumped Marx in Bernal's interests for a while, due to his awakening interest in sexuality, which was to characterize his life. He studied feminist works, beginning with Olive Schreiner's *Women and Labour* and Cicely Hamilton's *Marriage as a Trade*. He was later to be deeply influenced by Engels's argument and the discoveries in anthropology with respect to original matrilineal families and the historical emergence of patriarchy tied to relations of private property. He backed feminist struggles and was a strong supporter of the progress of women in science.[56]

In 1922 Bernal married Eileen Sprague, a graduate of Newnham College, University of Cambridge, then working for a secretarial agency in Cambridge, where she had transcribed Keynes's *Economic Consequences of the Peace*. They both agreed prior to the wedding that it was to be an open marriage. They had two children in what was to be a stormy if strong relationship. Bernal was far from monogamous and went on to have numerous intimate relationships. He was both a proponent of and an active participant in the new ideas of free sexuality. He saw the liberation of women as tied to the growth of birth control, which made sexual intercourse more a matter-of-fact occurrence, while also making it possible for women to break from domestic life and pursue careers, including science.

Some of these ideas, widely held among leftists at the time, were of course naïve, and rightly open to criticism later on, as all too convenient for males and underestimating the challenges women faced. Opinion was divided even among Bernal's friends on how responsive he was to his many lovers' needs. Yet, there is no doubt that Bernal was enormously attractive to his many women partners, as much for his ideas as his personality. He had long-term relationships, not only with his wife, Eileen, but also with two other women, Margaret Gardiner and Margot Heinemann, with whom he was to set up households. All three women would often appear together with him, apparently without rancor.

Part of this attraction was undoubtedly the sense of community and equality that were part of his being. He told a friend: "No love affair . . . will ever work where there isn't a community of social feeling."[57]

In the 1930s Bernal's studies in Marxism became increasingly evident. In 1934 he wrote his important essay on "Dialectical Materialism" as part of a lecture series organized by the Society of Cultural Relations, which resulted in a short collection of essays under the title *Aspects of Dialectical Materialism* that included Levy, Bernal, and others. This was followed by Bernal's key work, *Engels and Science*, the year after—first as a *Labour Monthly* article and then released as a pamphlet.[58]

Bernal's essay on "Dialectical Materialism" was an extraordinary attempt to explain the significance of dialectics for a scientific worldview, based on his reading of Engels and Marx. It was also a unique interpretation of dialectics that reflected Bernal's originality as a thinker. He started out by declaring: "Dialectical Materialism is the most powerful factor in the thought and action of the present day." What distinguished his analysis, though, was a strong emphasis on the limitations of the dialectic. "Dialectical Materialism," he wrote, "is not a formula to be applied bluntly either in the natural or the human world." Rather it was aimed at issues of complexity and "transformation." Dialectical analysis was no substitute for materialism or the scientific method but added coherence to scientific investigation.[59]

The materialist dialectic was particularly significant, in Bernal's sense, in that it allowed science to escape idealism in the form of "God or any of his more concealed equivalents" such as "emergence, or vitalism . . . or an agnostic skepticism," without falling prey to mechanical materialism or reductionism. As opposed to idealist thinking, "Dialectical Materialism," in Bernal's sense, was non-teleological, except in its recognition of the entropy law: "All the teleology in modern physics," he wrote, "is included in the second law of thermodynamics, and it is only in this sense that 'Dialectical Materialism' is teleological." Materialism was essential to meaningful scientific analysis, but mechanical materialism, despite its strengths, was based on "a reduction of all the universe to a number of separate abstract categories: space, time, matter, motion." Yet, science in practice, he argued, was forced to depart from this, due to various "impassable breaks" that occurred in any such rigid perspective. In contrast, dialectical thought was a way of intellectually "attacking the universe at all points."[60]

In Bernal's view, the scientific method built on materialism and empirical analysis was correct, but dialectics, or rather dialectical materialism, achieved importance precisely where the standard mechanistic approach ran into dead ends. Dialectical thinking broke through the specialization that compartmentalized science (Bacon's idol of the den) and dealt with the world as an integrated whole and as a process, describing the complex relation (or mediations) between any part and the whole. "From the most general standpoint," he wrote, "the only field for operation of the dialectic is the universe as a whole."[61]

As a supplement to standard science, dialectical analysis was concerned primarily with "the origin of the new." Indeed, "the essential task of the materialist dialectic is the explanation of the appearance of the qualitatively new" in a world where "static systems are mere abstractions," and in any process it was important to take into account "residual effects" and "oscillating changes," movement beyond mere "cyclic change," encompassing "new and qualitatively different" conditions. Continuous change, as pictured in Darwinian evolution, is envisioned in dialectical analysis "as an important, even essential forerunner of discontinuous change." For Darwin, Bernal noted, "evolution was a matter of continuous, imperceptible variation; now it appears as genetic mutations."[62]

The role of dialectics in envisioning the new was evident in Engels's "materialistic inversion" of Hegelian thought in the analysis of natural processes. Thus, Engels had pointed to general abstract "laws"—or cognitive principles standing for complex natural processes—such as the transformation of quality into quantity, the identity or interpenetration of opposites, and the negation of the negation. Ultimately, the dialectic for Bernal was a means of discovery. Methodologically, Marx, according to Bernal, had been "working on a . . . wider generalization. What he was seeking was essentially the origin of origins." This was an outlook that was radically materialist, historical, and one that employed dialectical forms of reasoning to understand the origin of the new—of the continuous/discontinuous change that was integral to the material world.[63]

Transformative change resulted from the internal contradictions in a developmental process and was precipitated by some critical "event." This was not unique to human beings, although human history was replete with such transformations, but was evident as well in the biological world as a whole by the relation of "organism and environment," considered as a "dialectic pair." But dialectics, in the sense of the complex, changing relation associated with matter and motion, went beyond the organic world, and was applicable to the universe as a whole—inorganic and organic.[64]

In one of his most pregnant notions, Bernal pointed to the residual elements associated with any given process that, if they take a cumulative form, can lead to opposing tendencies and a new synthesis. Explaining how changes at one stage are due to inner contradictions of the previous stage, he wrote:

> It is possible to state this part of the dialectic in a more or less physical and mathematical way, though, as we shall see later, this is a very partial statement. Given any system whatever—not a static system, because . . . static systems are mere abstractions—given any system, then, besides the main activity of the system, there will always be left certain cumulative, residual effects. Now, these residual effects can be divided into those that contribute to the main activity and those that oppose it. The former may be reckoned as simply part of the main activity; but the latter are bound in sufficient time and in the absence of external disturbances to accumulate to such an extent that the whole nature of the system and its activity are transformed. In the simplest possible case this is merely an explanation of the universally recurring oscillatory changes. Any process, once set going by an initial impulse, continues in the absence of external forces until, passing its equilibrium position as a result of its own momentum, it is brought to a stop and reversed. But in more complicated cases, instead of mere oscillatory back-and-forth movement as the type of cyclic change everywhere, we get as the result of the opposition and stopping of the primary activity a new and qualitatively different one.[65]

In *Engels and Science,* Bernal emphasized Engels's role as both a philosopher of science and a historian of science. Based primarily on his reading of Engels's *Dialectics of Nature* (the German edition; the English translation did not appear for another five years), Bernal argued that Engels was clearly far beyond the professional philosophers of science of his day such as Herbert Spencer and William Whewell in England and Friedrich Lange in Germany.[66] Behind Engels's extraordinary understanding of the historical development of science in his time was a dialectical perception in which the "concept of nature was always as a whole and as a process." In this, Engels had borrowed critically from Hegel, recognizing that behind the latter's idealist presentation of dialectical change in his *Logic* were processes that could be said to inhere objectively in nature itself, as captured in human cognition. These constituted, in Bernal's words, movements that were complex "reflections of those in the objective world." Indeed, "much of Engels's studies were devoted to exemplifying the Hegelian [dialectical] modes."[67]

Bernal particularly stressed Engels's emphasis on changes in quantity leading to changes in quality, that is, qualitative transformations. "With remarkable insight," Bernal wrote, "Engels says—'The so-called constants of physics are for the most part nothing but designations of the nodal points where quantitative addition or withdrawal of motion calls forth a qualitative change in the state of the body in question.'" Bernal also stated, "We are only now beginning to appreciate the essential justice of these remarks and the significance of such nodal points. The whole theory of quanta depends, like the theory of acoustic vibrations with which it has formal relations, on the distribution of nodes which mark out two qualitatively and quantitatively different sets of vibrations." Bernal stressed Engels's reference to Mendeleev's Periodic Table as exemplary of qualitative transformations arising from continuous quantitative change.[68]

The interpenetration of opposites was a more difficult concept in an operational sense, though of supreme importance in the process of scientific inquiry. In Bernal's explanation of Engels's analysis, this stood for two related principles: (1) "everything implies its opposite," and (2) there were "no hard and fast lines in nature." With respect to the former, Bernal contended, "Engels approached very close to the modern ideas of relativity."[69]

The negation of the negation, which, as Bernal indicated, seems so paradoxical in terms of mere words, was meant to convey that in the course of its historical development or evolution over time, anything within the objective world is bound to generate something different, a new emergent reality, representing new material relations at new levels of reality. Material existence as a whole was reflected in a hierarchy of organizational levels, and transformative change often meant the shift from one organizational level to another, as in the seed to the plant.[70]

Referring to the "Omitted Fragment" of Engels's *Ludwig Feuerbach*, intended for the *Dialectics of Nature,* Bernal celebrated Engels's remarkable insights into the three great scientific revolutions of the nineteenth century, namely: (1) thermodynamics—the laws of the conservation of forms of energy and entropy; (2) the analysis of the organic cell and the development of physiology; and (3) Darwin's theory of evolution.[71] Among Engels's concerns, according to Bernal, was pursuit of "the synthesis of all the processes affecting life, animal ecology, and [biological] distribution."[72]

More significant for Bernal, in pointing to Engels's dialectical perspective, was the progress that Engels made with respect to all four materialist problems of "origin" that remained after Darwin: (1) *the origin of the universe* (which Engels insisted was a self-origin as envisioned in the nebular hypothesis of Kant and Laplace); (2) *the origin of life* (in which he refuted Liebig and Helmholtz's notion of the eternity of life, and pointed to a chemical origin focusing on the complex of chemicals underlying the protoplasm); (3) *the origin of human society* (in which Engels went further than any other thinker in his time in explaining the evolution of the hand and tools through labor, and with them the brain and language, anticipating the later discoveries of paleoanthropology); and (4) *the origin of the family* (in which he explored the matrilineal basis of the family and the rise of the patriarchal family with private property).[73]

It was the socialist and Marxian thinkers Alexander Oparin in the USSR and Haldane in Britain who, independently in the 1920s, developed the modern materialistic theory of the origins of life, known as the "primordial soup theory," which arose virtually in tandem with Vernadsky's development of the biosphere concept. As summed up by Harvard biologists Richard Levins and Richard Lewontin, "Life originally arose from inanimate matter, but that origination made its continued occurrence impossible, because living organisms consume the complex organic molecules needed to re-create life *de novo*. Moreover, the reducing atmosphere [lacking free oxygen] that existed before the beginning of life has been converted, by living organisms themselves, to one that is rich in reactive oxygen." In this way, the Oparin-Haldane theory explained for the first time how life could have originated out of inorganic matter, and why the process could not be repeated. Equally significant, life, arising 3.5 billion years ago, could be seen as the creator of the biosphere.[74] These developments were to be critical in the later emergence of systems ecology. Bernal was himself to take this up in *The Origin of Life* in 1967.[75]

It was clear that Engels's method of dialectical inquiry had anticipated or prefigured many of the developments in materialist science. Moreover, "Engels, who welcomed the principle of the conversion of one form of energy into another," Bernal observed, "would equally have welcomed the transformation of matter into energy," that is, Einstein's great discovery. "Motion as the mode of existence of matter," Engels's great postulate, "would here acquire its final proof."[76]

"The central idea in dialectical materialism," Bernal wrote, "is transformation. . . . The essential task of the materialist dialectic is the explanation of the appearance of the qualitatively new." In this sense dialectics was aimed at the understanding that the conditions governing the emergence of a new "organizational hierarchy," as the interaction between chance and necessity, generated "critical events" that heralded qualitative change.[77]

As a physical scientist, Bernal was naturally drawn to Marxism at first via Engels, and only later engaged in a study of Marx's own outlook. This was to lead to his 1952 pamphlet *Marx and Science*, of which Farrington rightly said, "I do not think that Bernal has ever written better than here."[78] Here Bernal drew on Marx's early writings: his doctoral thesis on Epicurus, his *Economic and Philosophical Manuscripts of 1844* (from which Bernal translated long passages), his *Theses on Feuerbach*, and *The German Ideology*, as well as *The Communist Manifesto* and *Capital*. Marx in his doctoral dissertation, Bernal observed, "although still [writing] in Hegelian terms, was beginning his exploration of the social and political implications of materialism. Marx preferred Epicurus to Democritus because Democritus appeared to him as merely a naturalist-materialist philosopher, reducing everything to atoms and void, whereas Epicurus wished to make this atomic philosophy, with certain variations, the basis of a moral and political theory." Marx's thesis had recognized

> the limited and unsatisfactory character of pure natural science, and . . . the importance of Epicurus's law of atomic deviation in which chance is introduced into the rigid atomism of Democritus. The purport of the thesis, however, was by no means academic. It was to set out the liberating role of Epicurean ideas, particularly in the struggle against state-supported religion. Recent researches have shown how far Epicureanism was considered a subversive philosophy in ancient Greece and Rome and how it had largely been destroyed by the efforts of the official Platonic and Stoic philosophers.[79]

Bernal traced this materialist scientific orientation, which pointed to the eventual development of "one science," reflecting "the unity of man with nature"—if presently "alienated"—through the whole course of Marx's theoretical development.[80] Great emphasis was placed on the mature Marx's admiration for Darwin. By the time Bernal was writing, the broad idea of an evolutionary dialectic had "spread beyond the world of organism to the earth and the whole universe. In the light of recent discoveries scientists are now more willing to accept the phenomena of nature as *processes* not things, given or created. Intellectually, therefore, Marx who saw it all over a hundred years ago, stands revealed as a [scientific] mind of the first caliber."[81]

Bernal dramatically concluded *Marx and Science* with Engels's speech at the grave of Marx, where Engels had juxtaposed Marx and Darwin. For Bernal, a staunch Darwinian and no less staunch Marxist, such a comparison was entirely fitting. "The great discovery of Marx was that the ultimate motive force of human social development was not to be found in abstract ideas or mystical intuition. It lay in the very . . . productive process by which they [human beings] got food, clothing, and shelter. Production, social from the outset, brought with it social productive relations leading to the appearance of rival classes. Their conflicts, which form the significant part of history, can be followed in unbroken sequence to the present day and beyond it, and are the source of the intellectual productions of human culture." As Engels had put it, "Just as Darwin discovered the law of evolution in organic nature, so Marx discovered the law of evolution in human history."[82]

HALDANE: THE CONVERGENCE OF GENETICS AND ECOLOGY

Like Bernal, Haldane drew his inspiration with respect to the dialectics and nature chiefly from Engels. Haldane was one of the leading figures in the neo-Darwinism or the "modern synthesis," that linked Mendelian genetics to Darwinian evolutionary theory. In the 1970s, Stephen Jay Gould wrote that "English biologist J. B. S. Haldane probably anticipated every good idea that evolutionary theorists will invent during this century."[83] Much of this had to do with the inspiration associated with his dialectical approach to natural (and social) phenomena.

John Burdon Sanderson Haldane was born on November 5 (Guy Fawkes Day) 1892, into the British intellectual aristocracy. His father, John Scott Haldane, was a famous physiologist, Fellow of the Royal Society, and philosopher of science (originally a mechanist and later an idealist). When J. B. S. Haldane was a boy, his father took him down into coal mines to study coal gas (principally carbon monoxide) and its physiological effects. This gave the young Haldane an early sympathy for miners. One of his uncles, John Burdon Sanderson, Fellow of the Royal Society (FRS), had been a colleague of E. Ray Lankester at University College, London, in the 1870s, and was Wayneflette Professor of Physiology at Oxford. Another uncle, Richard Burdon, Viscount of Cloan, was a distinguished Liberal and (later) Labour cabinet member, twice Lord Chancellor. He was a devotee of Hegel and Schopenhauer and translated the latter's *The World as Will and Representation*.

J. B. S. Haldane had all the benefits of this background, coupled with his own natural gifts. He could read English at three and could speak German by five. He was educated at the Oxford Preparatory School (later the Dragon School), Eton, and at New College, Oxford. Haldane's initial break with his family's political values (his father was an urbane liberal, his mother a strong supporter of Joseph Chamberlain's imperialist policies) came with the First World War. Haldane served as an infantry officer on the front line and was wounded twice in the war.

Following the introduction of chlorine gas in the war in 1915, J. B. S. joined his father, the physiologist John Scott Haldane, who had been sent on a mission to France by Lord Haldane (Richard Burdon Haldane Viscount of Cloan—J. B. S.'s uncle), a member of the War Cabinet, to investigate the situation. The Haldanes discovered that gas masks that were utterly useless in protecting against poison gases of any kind were being widely distributed to the troops.

Their report revealed that a more effective respirator was needed and that the soldiers were being put into needless danger. Nevertheless, the General Staff did not proceed immediately to implement their recommendations. The result was the enormous British casualties, amounting to some 2,600 at Loos in September 1915. The British released 140 tons of chlorine gas, but the wind changed direction and it blew back on the British troops. When an incensed Lord Haldane made the issue into a crusade, he was removed from the leadership of the Liberal Party for his efforts. Outraged, J. B. S. Haldane was driven by these events to condemn the entire political establishment. He later fought in the Middle East during the war, where a British shell wounded him, resulting in several months of convalescence in India. The entire experience of the First World War had the effect of driving him in the direction of socialism, much to the shock of some members of his family.[84]

Haldane was a Fellow of New College, Oxford between 1919 and 1922, where he worked primarily in physiology and biochemistry. In 1924, he was appointed the Dunn Reader in Biochemistry at Cambridge University. However, he soon strayed into the relatively new field of genetics, specializing in the highly mathematical area of population genetics, and in 1926 agreed to also head the Genetics Department of the John Innes Horticultural Institute. Between 1924 and 1934, he wrote a series of papers in genetics, mathematizing Darwinian natural selection and establishing him as Britain's most illustrious figure in this realm. In 1930 to 1932 he was Fullerian Professor of Physiology at the Royal Institution in London. In 1932 he was elected a Fellow of the Royal Society. In the following year he accepted a position as professor of genetics at University College, London, where he was to remain until 1956.

In 1924 Haldane met Charlotte Burghes, a newswoman and novelist. They soon became attached to each other. However, Burghes was already married and had a son. In order to obtain a divorce for her, which required cause, they arranged to be discovered committing adultery (in a hotel). However, they decided to change hotels midstream, and went so far as to ask the private detective, who had been hired to catch them in the act (and whose identity they had detected) to carry one of their suitcases to their new hotel, lest he lose sight of them. It went off "without a hitch" and the next day the detective, according to Haldane, "appeared in our bedroom with the morning papers." The hoped-for exposure led to Haldane's formal dismissal as a reader at Cambridge by a body called the *Sex Viri* (referring to the six men that composed the body), a name that encouraged much jocularity among those observing the scandal. Haldane immediately took his case to the National Union of Scientific Workers, and with their help managed to have the decision immediately overturned. The consequence was that "Haldane's name was now firmly placed in the vanguard of sexual emancipation."[85] The two married in 1926.

Working in the orthodox Darwinian mode, Haldane emerged as one of the principal figures in what Julian Huxley famously called the "modern synthesis," which merged Darwinian theory and Mendelian genetics, accounting for evolutionary change by "mathematizing Darwin's metaphor of natural selection."[86] Haldane's 1925 paper on "The Causes of Evolution," delivered to the Rationalist Political Association, induced the elderly E. Ray Lankester to write to H. G. Wells saying that Haldane was the "model" of a well-trained materialist evolutionary theorist in his generation, incorporating a powerful "critical method." It was here that Haldane first incorporated the concept of degeneration, as pioneered in evolutionary theory by Lankester, to question the notion of progress and to raise issues of ecological complexity and ecological catastrophe.[87] These themes were to carry over into his great book of the same title, which helped to restore the prestige of Darwinism. In *The Causes of Evolution* (1932), Haldane reached as far back as Lucretius in pointing to the strengths of a materialist approach to evolution, and incorporated, as in many of his works of the period, Charles Elton's ecological writings (referring also to Wells, Huxley, and Wells's *The Science of Life*). He was forthright in questioning Bergsonian vitalism and any simple conception of progress on evolutionary grounds. "Degeneration," he wrote, "is a far commoner phenomenon than progress. . . . Certainly the study of evolution does not point to any general tendency of a species to progress." In a work that was to become a classic of evolutionary theory and the neo-Darwinian synthesis, Haldane did not hesitate to mention Marx along with Darwin on the first page, or to quote Lenin, H. G. Wells, and George Bernard Shaw (the last of which he chided for his rejection of evolutionary theory). Haldane's interest in Marxism and dialectical thinking was already evident.[88]

In his early daring work *Daedalus: Science and the Future* (1924) Haldane had reflected on the eventual exhaustion of coal and oil fields and of an economy based on fossil fuels. He did not perceive this as a tragedy, however, since the pollution from fossil fuels was very great. Instead, he looked forward to an energy economy based on solar, wind, and hydrogen energy. Demonstrating enormous foresight and ecological concern, he wrote:

> Ultimately, we shall have to tap those intermittent but inexhaustible sources of power, the wind and the sunlight. The problem is simply one of storing their energy in a form as convenient as coal or petrol. If a windmill in one's back garden could produce a hundredweight of coal directly (and it can produce its equivalent in energy), our coal mines would shut down to-morrow. Even to-morrow a cheap, foolproof, and durable storage battery may be invented, which will enable us to transform the intermittent energy of the wind into continuous electric power.

> Personally, I think that four hundred years hence the power question in England may be solved somewhat as follows: The country will be covered with rows of metallic windmills working with electric motors which in their turn supply current at a very high voltage to great electric mains. At suitable distances, there will be great power stations where during windy weather the surplus power will be used for the electrolytic decomposition of water into oxygen and hydrogen. These gases will be liquefied, and stored in vast vacuum jacketed reservoirs, probably sunk in the ground. . . . Liquid hydrogen is weight for weight the most efficient known method of storing energy, as it gives about three times as much heat per pound as petrol. . . . These huge reservoirs of liquefied gases will enable wind energy to be stored, so that it can be expended for industry, transportation, heating and light, as desired. The initial costs will be very considerable, but the running expenses less than those of our present system. Among its more obvious advantages will be the fact that energy will be as cheap in one part of the country as another, so that industry will be greatly decentralized; and that no smoke or ash will be produced.[89]

Haldane's vision in *Daedalus* was so broad that Vernadsky in the early 1920s listed it as one of three crucial books (along with works of Alfred North Whitehead and Alfred J. Lotka) that were central to the development of his conception of *The Biosphere* (1926).[90]

In 1928 Haldane made his first trip to the Soviet Union. The following year, possibly influenced by the kind of thinking he had been exposed to there, he published his famous 1929 article in the *Rational Press Annual* on "The Origin of Life," in which he introduced (parallel to Oparin in the USSR) the modern theory of the origins of life via chemical action from non-living inorganic molecules, known as abiogenesis or the "primordial soup theory." In this theory, the origins of life were made possible by a reducing (oxygenless) atmosphere and the accumulation in the oceans of a vast quantity of materials from which organic substances are made—until, in Haldane's words, "the primitive oceans reached the consistency of hot dilute soup." The spontaneous generation of newly formed organisms, such as cyanobacteria, out of this soup, were, in turn, to alter the conditions that had made this generation of life *de novo* possible.[91] The general approach was consistent with Vernadsky's theory of the biosphere, in which the planetary influence of living matter became more pronounced over time.[92]

Rachel Carson was later to characterize the Haldane-Oparin theory of the origin of life as constituting the core of an integrated ecological view of life on the planet: "From all this we may generalize that, since the beginning of biological time, there has been the closest possible interdependence between the physical environment and the life it sustains. The conditions on the young earth produced life; life then at once modified the conditions of the earth, so that this single extraordinary act of spontaneous generation could not be repeated. In one form or another, action and interaction between life and its surroundings has been going on ever since."[93]

In the early 1930s, when he took up his appointment at the University of London, Haldane, now a Fellow of the Royal Society, was already a materialist and a socialist, and had begun the serious study of Marx, Engels, and Lenin, but was not yet a historical materialist. The change in his outlook was to follow the rise of Hitler in Germany and the onset of the Spanish Civil War. In March 1936, Germany remilitarized the Rhineland and four months later the Spanish Civil War began. Within a few months, Haldane was offering his help. He made three journeys to Spain to advise the Republican government on gas attacks and on aerial bombardment. In support of Franco, the Nazis dropped millions of bombs on Spain in 1936–39. This was the first major experience of massive aerial bombing in Europe, which shook the world when Germany in 1937 used Guernica as experiment for testing a blend of high-explosive, incendiary, and splinter bombs, utterly destroying the city. Haldane visited the front lines to see the fighting. At one point he was sitting next to a woman on a bench in a park in Madrid when an air raid began, and a splinter from a bomb swiftly killed her.

Haldane's stepson, Ronald Burgess (changed from Burghes), joined the international brigades fighting in defense of the Spanish Republic. Soon after Haldane's wife, Charlotte Haldane, joined the Communist Party of Great Britain (CPGB), and Haldane, though not a member of the Party, began writing for the *Daily Worker*.[94] He gave frequent lectures on the Spanish Civil War to working-class groups as the Communist Party urged aid to the Spanish Republic. By the late 1930s, Haldane had become a convinced Marxist, and rapidly turned himself into a major theorist of the role of dialectics in science.[95]

In the Second World War, based on his experiences of aerial bombardment as well as gas warfare, Haldane emerged as Britain's leading scientific adviser to the war ministry on civil defense. He also aided in determining escape and rescue techniques for sailors in the military use of submarines.

Haldane's most famous discussion of the dialectic of science was his 1939 book on *Marxist Philosophy and the Sciences*, based on a group of lectures that he delivered in Birmingham the year before. The main influences on his thought in this respect were Engels's three works, *Anti-Dühring*, *Ludwig Feuerbach*, and the *Dialectics of Nature* and Lenin's *Materialism and Empirico-Criticism*. His goal was to elucidate how the materialist and dialectical philosophy provided in such works bore on problems in natural science, particularly biology.[96]

Marxism, Haldane stated, directly challenging the view of Georgi Plekhanov in his *Fundamental Problems of Marxism*, was "not a system" in the sense of a closed and all-encompassing framework and was "only in the second place theoretical. It is not complete because it is alive and growing, and above all because it lays no claim to finality." All of which was not to deny that Marxism included "a great deal of systematic content." Nevertheless, it was primarily an outlook and a guide to investigation. Marx, like Descartes, "regarded his philosophy as primarily a method," and although theory is essential to Marxism, Marx proclaimed the primacy of practice over theory. Marxist theory, like natural science, derived the details of its analysis from "applying the method to concrete situations."[97]

With respect to the application of the Marxian method to the investigation of the natural-material world, Engels was the chief guide. "In discussing the relation of Marxism to science," Haldane wrote, "we shall mainly be concerned with the views of Engels." Lenin's work was crucial, but Engels, Haldane stated, was "the chief source." Nevertheless, Engels himself had indicated that "most of the leading principles in his work derived from Marx."[98]

In self-consciously developing his ideas almost exclusively on the basis of Engels, although drawing on Lenin and Marx as well, Haldane was careful to distinguish his approach to dialectical materialism from crude interpretations that had often characterized Soviet thought. Employing the term "dialectical materialism" (first introduced by Joseph Dietzgen and popularized by Georgi Plekhanov), he nonetheless interpreted this in terms of a line of inquiry emanating almost exclusively from Engels and Marx. The Marxian dialectic was no universal key but was a method that could "only tell a scientist what to look for. It will rarely, if ever, tell him what he is going to find, and if it is going to be made a dogma, it is worse than useless." He emphasized the "utter nonsense" of much of what had been written in the name of dialectical materialism in the USSR in the first two decades. Moreover, "the worse a scientific paper was, the more likely it was to be laced with irrelevant quotations from Marx, Engels, and Lenin. Good science needs no such justification, and an experienced Marxist will notice evidence of dialectical thinking without any need to draw attention to it." There were plenty of examples, he pointed out, of "bogus dialectical materialism" in the USSR, which did not, however, disprove the importance of materialist dialectical analysis in general. He indicated that he was "the last to suggest that all biologists in the Soviet Union are thinking as dialectically as they might." Haldane was critical of the "mechanical view of Lamarck" in which changes in organisms in response to changes in the environment were directly inherited. He contended that the renewed emphasis on Lamarckianism in the USSR was to be faulted not so much in absolute terms, since important questions were being raised, but rather in its practical consequences, since it had led to the proliferation of views that appear "to be untrue in the light of actual biological research." Engels himself, Haldane pointed out, had adopted some Lamarckian views but only in "about the same degree as Darwin." It was not until the 1890s that Lamarckianism had come under strong attack in England, principally through the agency of E. Ray Lankester, who promoted the research of August Weismann and had himself presented a devastating logical critique of Lamarck's laws on evolution.[99]

As early as 1938, in his lectures that made up *Marxist Philosophy and the Sciences*, Haldane took pains to separate himself from what he called "the violent discussions which have taken place on this question in the Soviet Union." He preferred to develop his own approach to the dialectic of nature, based straightforwardly on Engels and a few other sources, rather than drawing on Soviet thought, outside of Lenin.[100] He claimed that Soviet scientists, though subject to criticism in some areas, were taking the lead in exploring "the dialectical opposition of mutation and selection," raising issues, with respect to the internal and external causes of evolution, which were also being addressed in a different way in his own laboratory.[101] Nevertheless, he was clear about the distinctiveness of his individual research into material conditions, which he pursued on his own, with no direct connection to research being conducted in the USSR.

Where the convergence between Haldane's work and Soviet science in the 1930s was the greatest was in a shared philosophical commitment to dialectical materialism in the broadest sense of the term. Haldane's approach to dialectics was sometimes philosophically crude. He made references to mind mirroring nature rather than nature mirroring mind, as if this was a one-dimensional, one-way process. He thus had a tendency to speak in terms of a non-nuanced correspondence theory of knowledge. Yet, his actual scientific applications were marked by considerations of dialectical reflectivity, interpenetration, and contradiction. He was, in general, little interested in epistemology and content with simple metaphors in that respect. But he was much more interested than were the epistemologists themselves in the endless complexity and dynamism of the material world.

Haldane presented Engels's three "principles" (rather than laws) of dialectic—unity of opposites, quantitative change leading to qualitative transformation, and the negation of the negation—as constituting useful forms of inquiry into a complex, contradictory, changing reality. At the same time, he noted that such principles, taken by themselves, had the appearance of mere "rules of thumb" approaches to dialectical thinking, which was, in truth, far more complicated. Downplaying his own presentation, he said that it necessarily bordered on a kind of "caricature" and was open to "severe criticism" from a philosophical viewpoint.[102] Nevertheless, his grasp of these principles was acute in the sense that he was able to use them to elucidate scientific practice and to extend that practice. More important, he excelled at demonstrating how these principles could generate crucial insights within both natural and social science. His greatest successes in this regard had to do with those areas with which he was most familiar: biology, genetics, and ecology.

In exploring the identity or unity (and interpenetration) of opposites, Haldane followed Lenin in contending that this reflected the contradictory and contingent nature of reality, in which any given state was conditional, and subject to change through interaction with opposites, and forces of attraction and repulsion. Metabolism, he emphasized, consisted of both "anabolism and catabolism—that is to say, the building up of complicated organic compounds, and their breaking down. . . . This particular unity of opposites is part of the very nature of the higher animals." Life and development could thus be seen as "a unity of opposites and their reciprocal correlation." At another point, he observed, similarly, that "the living organism is a union of anabolism and catabolism," which together constitute metabolism, while "the end of this unity of opposites is death."[103]

In addressing the transformation of quantity into quality, Haldane referred to Democritus's (and after him Descartes's and Locke's) mechanistic contention that only quantity was real, while quality, was ephemeral. As he put it: "Now according to the view of matter which was first clearly formulated by Locke, though it goes back to Descartes and Democritus, the quantitative aspect of matter is real, whilst many of its qualities are illusory. Thus what we call colours and tones are 'really' only vibration frequencies." Yet, for Marxian dialectics, "both quantity and quality are properties of the real world."[104] Hyman Levy stressed in *A Philosophy for a Modern Man* that such qualitative transformations related to quantitative changes could be seen in the various phase changes, for example, from solid to liquid to gas, in physics.[105]

The negation of the negation expressed how development was neither a matter of increase nor decrease, much less repetition of the same forms in different quantities, but the emergence of qualitative transformations as a result of the reciprocal correlation of mutually exclusive opposites. This led, as in C. Lloyd Morgan's theory of emergence, to novel entities, which nonetheless reflected early phases of development. The expropriation of the means of production (land and tools) of the peasants resulted in the development of both the capitalist class and the modern working class. Within biology, as in nature altogether, there were no fixed lines; rather, species shaded into each other, producing various "hybrid" species, such as amphibians, that negated their earlier forms.[106] Similarly, in *The Causes of Evolution*, Haldane emphasized the importance of understanding nature as giving rise to new integrative levels of existence that in some ways negated other levels of organization, though this needed to be understood in strictly materialist terms.[107]

Haldane and Levy emphasized that there were both internal relations (of isolates or systems) and external relations, and that these gave rise to both internal and external contradictions.[108] The fact that nature consisted of processes rather than things meant that many of the lines drawn between distinct entities (and even between the inorganic and organic) were fluid and changing. Haldane argued in dialectical fashion that, although an organism is defined in relation to its environment, "there is no sharp line between an organism and its environment." This is because of the complex dynamism of both the organism and its environment both separately and together. "It is part of the very nature of an organism to interact with its environment, but to some degree it adapts the environment to itself."[109] Hence, it was possible under certain circumstances for an organism to negate, that is, transform its environment, which would, in the process transform the organism, and vice versa. None of this, of course, occurred in a linear or symmetrical way. "There is a law of uneven development in animal and plant evolution as in the social evolution of capitalism."[110]

Levy emphasized that a dialectical understanding allowed one to surmount the crude notion of humanity and nature as separate entities, and to capture the unity in opposition. Hence, the notion of "Man *as opposed* to Nature" is "progressively broken down and re-erected in a new way, Man *and* Nature."[111]

"The dialectical method in science," Haldane stressed, "is to push theory to its logical point of conclusion, and show that it negates itself."[112] Marxism found in creative antagonism reasons for hope and struggle, and the negation of the negation, in which the expropriators would eventually be expropriated and a more egalitarian society would triumph. Charles Dickens in works such as *Bleak House*, *Hard Times*, and *Our Mutual Friend* and Engels in *The Condition of the Working Class in England* had both recognized the deep poverty and pervasive pollution that characterized proletarian life in the industrial cities. But their responses were different. "Dickens had a first-hand knowledge of these conditions. He described them with burning indignation and in great detail. But his attitude to them was one of pity rather than hope. Engels saw the misery and degradation of the workers, but he saw through it. Dickens never suggested that if the workers were to be saved they must save themselves. Engels saw that this was not only desirable but inevitable."[113]

An analogous emphasis on creative antagonisms, even where divorced from conscious social action, was evident in Haldane's evolutionary ecology. A strong defender of Darwinism, Haldane nonetheless argued that "a good Marxist would expect the Darwinian theory of natural selection to contain its own contradictions." Darwin had taken "variation for granted and thought they were all inheritable." Modern genetics had uncovered a far greater complexity of inheritance, including such elements as mutations and recessive genes. This, coupled with the leaps in the paleontological record (later to be explained by Gould and Niles Eldridge in terms of "punctuated equilibrium"), raised questions about Darwin's exclusive emphasis on the slow process of natural selection. Not only was it untrue that "nature makes no leaps," but Darwin's tendency to place almost exclusive emphasis on the adaptation of species to their environment was called into question. All of this raised larger, dialectical questions.[114]

As Richard Lewontin explained much later in *The Triple Helix*:

> In Darwin's theory variation among organisms results from an internal process, what is now known as gene mutation and recombination, that is not responsive to the demands of the environment. The variants that are produced are then tested for acceptability in an environment which has come into being independent of that variation. The process of variation is causally independent of the conditions of selection. . . . Darwin's alienation of the outside from the inside was an absolutely essential step in the development of modern biology. Without it, we would still be wallowing in the mire of an obscurantist holism that merged the organic and the inorganic into an unanalyzable whole. But the conditions that are necessary for the progress at one stage of history become bars to further progress in another. The time has come when further progress in our understanding of nature requires that we reconsider the relationship between the outside and the inside, between organism and environment.[115]

In contrast to the simple story of the adaptation of species to a changing environment, Lewontin has argued, it is necessary to recognize the constructionist role of organisms in altering their environments, and the role of genes as transforming filters and transmitters in this complex process of evolution, governed by both internal and external change. Lewontin has called this the "triple helix" of "gene, organism, and environment."[116]

It was this dialectical relation between gene, organism, and environment that Haldane, more than a half-century earlier, was aiming at in much of his work on genetics, population dynamics, and evolution, which questioned the simple Darwinian adaptationist framework, focusing rather on the complex, dynamic interactions. Evolutionary theory, in the "modern synthesis" (or Neo-Darwinism) as developed by Haldane and others, suggested that the extent to which internal or external factors dominated in the evolution of a given species at a given time might be governed primarily by the population density, which could dramatically alter the chances of survival of an individual organism and a species—either in relation to competition with other species in its environment or competition to members of its own species. For example:

> So long as a species is sparse, the fitness of an individual will depend almost wholly on its success in coping with inorganic nature and other species. But if it exists in dense populations, and occasionally under other circumstances, fitness comes to depend largely on defeating other members of the same

> species. Thus in the case of animals where each individual or pair lives in a restricted territory, a gene favouring the habit of devouring young members of the same species will diminish fitness. For its possessors will eat their own young. But where they live in large aggregates that will not be so. The first few cannibal fish in a school of many thousands will rarely eat their own young. They will generally eat those of others, and will thus have more food to turn into eggs and spermatozoa. Thus a gene favouring cannibalism will tend to spread. And in so far as it becomes common it will depress the fitness of the species as a whole.
>
> Exactly the same argument applies to polygamous species where the males fight for females. Such males commonly develop special weapons and instincts (or modes of behavior, if a more neutral word is preferred) which fit them for mutual combat, but not necessarily for the struggle for food and against enemies of other species. They also tend to be much larger than the females, and it is probable that some of this increase in size is transferred to the females (i.e. that not all the size-genes selected are sex-limited). Thus the size, behavior, and so on are shifted from the optimum configuration needed for the struggle with "external nature," and the species become less fit.[117]

An obvious example, no doubt on Haldane's mind with respect to "special weapons," was the famous case of the Irish elk (the largest deer—not elk—species that ever lived, now extinct), with its extraordinary twelve-foot span of antlers. Gould was to argue in *Ever Since Darwin* that the Irish elk's antlers can be seen as adaptive in Darwinian terms, but that, like so many species, though well-equipped for its environmental conditions, the Irish elk was ill-equipped for climatic changes that radically altered those conditions. It flourished in the warmer Allerød interstadial phase, lasting for about a thousand years at the end of the last glaciation, but could not adapt to "the subarctic tundra that followed in the next cold epoch or to the heavy forestation that developed after the final retreat of the ice sheet."[118]

In this complex process of evolution, Haldane insisted, the simple notion of the "survival of the fittest" was not very meaningful. A species could become "overspecialized" by means of natural selection, either with respect to their relations to inorganic nature, or in their competition with members of their own species. This could lead to evolutionary paths that were "blind alleys."[119]

It was the growth of such interconnected analysis that focused on genes, organisms, and environment that led to what Charles Elton, the leading British animal ecologist, called the "convergence between genetics and ecology." Here, Elton referred in particular to Haldane's work. "The older idea of a constant balance of nature, keeping numbers at a steady rate," he observed, "has been completely abandoned by biologists." Instead, the concern was with complex interactions and a kind of "moving equilibrium."[120] Elton was particularly concerned with the relation between population dynamics and community metabolism, and how genetic variation played a role in a natural selection process that was much more complex on all sides than Darwin had envisioned.[121]

Much of Elton's early research, using Hudson's Bay Company data, had focused on the hunting of caribou populations by indigenous peoples in Labrador. He demonstrated that the efficiency of the hunters had increased with the change in technology from bows and arrows to rifles, yet due to the ability of the last remaining caribou to find hideaways and cover, which led to decreases in killing, the deer populations had been able to recover, while the hunters were prevented from destroying this part of their food supply. From this, Elton theorized that only moderate efficiency or fitness in relation to the environment might be an evolutionary survival trait, guaranteeing a moving equilibrium and preventing an extinction that would undermine the existence of both populations.[122]

Summarizing part of Elton's argument in an article titled "Beyond Darwin," Haldane stated, "The Oxford biologist Elton has given many examples of this principle." That is, that "too great efficiency may cause a species to destroy its food and starve itself to death." Hence, only a moderate level of efficiency may be optimal.

> For example, the Red Indians in Labrador used to hunt caribou with spears and other primitive weapons. When they got guns they killed off so many deer that they starved or were compelled to buy imported food and live in settlements, where they caught European diseases.
>
> Elton takes the view that it does not always pay a species to be too well adapted. A variation making for too great efficiency may cause a species to destroy its food and starve itself to death. This very important principle may explain a good deal of diversity in Nature, and the fact that most species have some characters which cannot be accounted for on orthodox Darwinian lines.
>
> Elton is not, so far as I know, a Marxist. But I am sure that Marx would have approved of his dialectical thinking, and that it is on such lines that Darwinian theory will develop. I do not think that Darwinism will be disproved. But it will certainly be transformed.[123]

Elton influenced Haldane's connection of genetics to ecology via population dynamics, as well as his explorations of ecology, which were also influenced to a lesser extent by what Haldane called "the beautiful work" of Alfred Lotka on "mathematical ecology." Haldane returned to Elton's work again and again, particularly Elton's early works, *Animal Ecology* (1927) and *Ecology and Evolution* (1930). He was impressed by Elton's insistence on the active role played by animals with respect to their environments; for example, the contention that "every animal has at least a motile period in its life cycle during which it chooses its environment." At the same time, Haldane believed that Elton sometimes gave too little a role to natural selection. Elton was right in pointing out that species were at times prey to their environment in ways that were largely independent of Darwinian fitness, such as the appearance of major epidemics or large natural catastrophes, which introduced an element of "random extinction." But such events, Haldane argued, only played a "subordinate part in evolution."[124]

As a theorist of genetics, population dynamics, and evolution, Haldane's concerns regarding crises of natural ecosystems focused especially on questions of extinction. Here he did not employ the concept of ecosystem, which, though introduced by Arthur Tansley in 1935, had little influence prior to Raymond Lindeman's analysis of trophic dynamics of lakes in the 1940s, and did not come into general usage until the 1950s when Eugene Odum made it a core concept in his *Fundamentals of Ecology* in 1953. Instead, Haldane employed the term "bioeconomic" (related to E. Ray Lankester's "bionomics") to refer to plant and animal communities. Nikolaevich Sukachev in the USSR was to expand the concept of bioeconomic in the early 1940s to one of "biogeocoenosis," integrating the inorganic part of the environment, creating a concept that was the functional equivalent of ecosystem (and more developed in spatial terms) but linked to the Soviet frame of analysis associated with Vernadsky's biosphere.[125]

The "scientific study of plant and animal species is called ecology," Haldane observed in 1940 in "A World Biological Survey." The greater part of our knowledge in this respect, and the main reason for concern, he insisted, was a result of imperialism. It was colonialism and imperialism that not only opened up knowledge of species worldwide, for figures like "the great Swedish biologist Linnaeus," but also how these same colonial and imperial expansions across the globe had devastated the world's ecology, by disrupting natural systems, driving may species into extinction. Often this was due to the human introduction of invasive species, such as the importation of rabbits into Australia, which was a "national calamity." Other ecological destruction was due to a rapacious relation to the earth promoted by capitalism. "Large tracts of the earth's surface," he wrote,

> have been devastated. Wild animal species such as the American and European bison and . . . others, like the American passenger pigeon, and the tarpan, one of the wild horse species, are dead. Many forests have been cut down, leaving bare rocky hillsides. Large areas of the central United States have turned into a dust bowl. . . . Today whales are being exterminated, and many areas grossly over-fished. . . . The extinction of a species is far worse than the killing of an individual. The individual is replaced in one generation. It may take a million years to make a new species.[126]

The only answer to such ecological devastation was ecological and social planning. Hence, a world biological survey "inspired by Socialism" was essential. Attention had to be given to the protection of "climax" plant and animal associations, which, though subject to change, were normally characterized by relative stability over long periods of time. Hence, human activities in relation to the environment needed to be assessed for their long-term, often unintended, ecological effects. Irrigation, for example, though leading to a big cotton crop, could also lead to unintended ecological disasters. "In a planned world community," Haldane insisted, "the probable results of any change in agricultural methods, or of clearing forests, would be investigated before this was done on any scale. . . . In the same way the exploitation of the sea would be controlled." Significant efforts needed to be made with regard to "the preservation of valuable species."[127]

Haldane was unusual for his time in the degree to which he recognized affinities between humans and animals, something that developed out of his materialism and Darwinism, and was later extended due to the influence of Hinduism on his thought. He argued that mammals (besides *Homo sapiens*) and birds not only learned but communicated, transmitted culture, and had traditions. There was no definite line between the higher animals and the human species.[128] Haldane thus demonstrated considerable sympathy for other species and deplored their treatment under capitalism. On the topic of "Overcrowding in the Zoo" he contended that the way in which animals "were kept was a reflexion of imperialism." This allowed for the diversity of life-forms that were brought home from the Empire, many of which were not taken adequate care of in the overcrowded zoos. It was important to recognize, he asserted, "the right of animals to freedom." He deplored the class-based customs that "until recently in England" had led to "the ritual killing of foxes, grouse, salmon, and so on, at appropriate times of year" as "the hall-mark of respectability."[129]

Ecology of course extended to human ecology. In the urban-industrial environment, one of the central issues was air pollution. Building on an interest that went back to his childhood investigation of gases in coal mines with his father, and his later studies of gas warfare, Haldane explored issues of "bad air" or air pollution, particularly as it related to occupational health conditions. He singled out the seven occupations with the highest death rate for respiratory disease—"cutlery grinders, tin-miners, china and earthware kiln and oven men, cotton strippers and grinders, potters, cotton blow-room operatives and stevedores"—and proposed various ways in which trade unions could fight for compensation cost to be forced on employers in order to push for improvements. A big concern, he argued, was "lead tetra-ethyl, which is used as an anti-knock in petro." In industry, lead tetra-ethyl had killed large numbers of workers and subjected others to brain injury. Industry in the 1930s was claiming that the problem was solved and that workers were protected, but he argued that "as lead may accumulate in the human body over long periods, this may only mean that they are not now being killed so quickly."[130]

Haldane made explicit reference in the late 1930s to "the theory that great weather changes are due to change in the [levels of] carbon dioxide" in the atmosphere. His father was one of the pioneers in this area, having measured carbon dioxide concentration in the atmosphere in 1935 (coming up with a figure of 324+ parts per million) based on instrumentation he had developed. (John Scott Haldane died in March 1936 and his results were published the following month in *Nature* by J. B. S. in an article entitled "Carbon Dioxide Content of the Atmosphere" in April 1936.) Like most scientists at the time, J. B. S. Haldane continued to believe that another ice age, still thousands of years in the future, was the main challenge that humanity could expect from changes in the climate. Such climate change would affect the population of the world unevenly and would, he believed, be most detrimental to the northern climes. Although humanity might find itself able by then to reverse the glaciation process by melting the ice, this would require economic sacrifices that would likely be thuoght impractical and would be detrimental to other parts of the globe.[131]

Haldane was a strong advocate of a switch from fossil fuels to alternative forms of energy. In the 1940s, he insisted that countering pollution even more than resource scarcity constituted the key reason for shifting away from coal and petroleum. Extending the argument he had made in *Daedalus* in the 1920s, he argued that a shift should be made to hydrogen power, tidal power, wind power, and "liquid methane from underground natural gas," while also relying more on water (hydroelectric) power. "Power would be available in vast quantities, but it would not be based on the yearly sacrifice of thousands of coal-miners, and the spoiling of vast areas of what was once beautiful countryside. The nearest approach to this idea is found today in countries such as Switzerland, where water power is very abundant. In a properly organized world it will be the normal human environment."[132]

Haldane also made a strong case for afforestation in Britain, arguing that absentee ownership had led to poorer woodland management.[133] Another critical issue, he recognized, was the maintenance of the soil metabolism, and particularly the prevention of the loss of soil nutrients such as nitrogen, phosphorus, and potassium. In line with ecological modernization, he insisted that there were possibilities for "farming the sea," which would also require that efforts be devoted to the conservation of aquatic resources.[134]

This general ecological perspective led Haldane to take seriously the question "Back to Nature?" in a 1938 *Daily Worker* article with that title. He argued that just as it was impossible politically to go all the way back to primitive communism, it was necessary to start from humanity's current historical conditions. Still, he suggested, "We have got much farther from Nature than was necessary." An indication was the fact that "even well-to-do people in the towns have shorter lives on average than agricultural labourers." The same point was made in an article titled "The Disorder of Nature," published about the same time, where he stated: "It is no good saying that we should go back to Nature. . . . We have certainly gone too far from Nature in some respects. But we can't go all the way back."

In "Back to Nature?" Haldane pointed out that many of the chemicals that entered into our food and drink were not adequately tested. Disease resistance of the population had decreased. Numerous recently introduced foods were less nutritious than the ones they replaced. "If every new invention which takes us farther from Nature were judged on a basis of social utility rather than individual profit or prestige," Haldane wrote, "I do not doubt we should reject a great many artificialities, including stiff colours, bombing aeroplanes and high-speed motor cars. But we should realize that a complete return to Nature would mean living without clothes, houses, cookery or literature." Instead, society should be oriented to changing its "economic system" in order to enhance human life and the natural conditions of human existence. The rational reconstruction of the human relation to nature, along socialist lines, would constitute not a backward turn to an earlier, irretrievable era, but a kind of negation of the negation, and a moving forward.[135]

The general humanistic value system that Haldane, as a socialist theorist and scientist, promoted made him a strong opponent of social Darwinism, eugenics, and theories of racial superiority, as well as a critic of most biological race conceptions generally. He insisted on the fundamental equality of the major racial groupings of humanity, and argued that perceived differences, beyond those of the most superficial kind, were due to varying social environments. While not all individual human beings were entirely equal in their individual capacities, there were no systematic inequalities attributable to race or gender—or class.[136]

"Everything has a history."[137] Indeed, "at bottom," Haldane suggested, the natural world consisted of "processes, not things." Marxian theorists were concerned with how these processes interacted with human processes, and with the creation of a better society. Vavilov's great discovery of the point of origin of the world's major crops, and of the areas of greatest diversity in the germplasm leading to these crops, was based on a notion of human-nature coevolution that was a reflection of historical-materialist dialectical thinking. In the end, as Haldane emphasized, it was the rational organization of this coevolution of nature and society that was most important.[138]

NEEDHAM: INTEGRATIVE LEVELS

When Joseph Needham died at ninety-four, on March 26, 1995, an obituary in *The Independent* in the UK referred to him as "one of the greatest scholars of this or any country, of this or any century. For more than thirty years Needham had been the greatest Sinologist in the West, having previously achieved an international status as a research biochemist and as an historian of more than science. Intellectually a bridge-builder between science, religion and Marxist socialism, and supremely so between East and West, he has been called the Erasmus of the 20th century."[139]

Noel Joseph Terence Montgomery Needham was born in London on December 9, 1900, an only child, to Dr. Joseph Needham, a physician and pioneer in anesthesiology, and Mrs. Alicia Needham, known to the wider public as Alicia Adelaide Montgomery. A flamboyant, Irish-born composer of popular songs, she instilled in her son a love of music. More than two hundred of her published compositions are to be found in the British Library. The marriage was, in Needham's own account, a misalliance, between a sober scientific father and a stormy artist mother, helping account for his lifelong role as a bridge-builder between different spheres of thought. Needham's mother was a romantic lover of nature, writing of the environs of their house in South London, "Each spring there was a glorious show of chestnut, lilac, laburnum, and hawthorn and one of the last windmills was nearby."

Dr. Joseph Needham was a strong supporter of Darwin and a rationalist, a disbeliever in miracles, who opposed the Church of England's fundamental beliefs regarding the sacraments. Although coming out of Anglo-Catholicism, he subscribed to a kind of philosophical theology that he passed on to his son. He would take the ten-year old Needham each Sunday to Temple Church in central London where they listened to the sermons of its master, mathematician E. W. Barnes, FRS, and later Bishop of Birmingham. Mixed into the sermons were lectures on the pre-Socratic philosophers and a wide variety (including Eastern) religious doctrines. Needham was to adhere for the rest of his life to devout Christianity, though of a highly individualized, philosophical, and compartmentalized kind, which did not conflict significantly with his strong commitment to materialism in science and history or his recognition of the value of other religious traditions. For Needham the Kingdom of God on earth would come to be, but it would be as a result of human struggles for social betterment. Late in life, he described himself as "an honorary Taoist."[140]

At the time of the outbreak of the First World War in 1914, Needham was sent off to Oundle School in Northamptonshire, which was one of the oldest English schools, having been founded in 1485. Its headmaster during Needham's time there was the modernizing, F. W. Sanderson, who incorporated physical science and engineering into the curriculum. Sanderson's good friend H. G. Wells lauded the headmaster's "vision of the school as a centre for the complete reorganization of civilized life." In addition to the usual classical education and modern languages, students were all required to work in the metals shop and were given the fundamentals of engineering. In the classics, students were not only educated in the Greek and Latin grammars but were also encouraged to read classical thinkers such as Plato and Aristotle in English in order to better absorb their philosophical ideas. Wells sent his sons to Sanderson's school, and was eventually to write a biography of Sanderson. The young Needham encountered Wells there and became enamored with his socialist views and progressive outlook on science. At an early age, Needham had already devoured many of Wells's science-fiction novels, viewing Wells as "a great hero," and preferring his works to the writings of Jane Austen and the Brontës.[141]

In 1918 Needham was accepted to study at Cambridge University at Gonville and Caius College (usually known simply as Caius). Needham had originally intended to pursue medicine but became interested in biological studies more generally, beyond physiology and zoology. In the electrifying atmosphere in Cambridge immediately after the First World War, he was soon to be caught up in dramatic changes occurring in science, in which biological phenomena were increasingly discovered to follow physical, especially chemical, laws. As a result, he was "pitchforked," as he put it, into areas such as biochemistry. He was also busy exploring Freudian views. At around the time he received his B.A. at Caius in 1921 (the year after the death of his father), "We talked about nothing else . . . but psychology, and especially Freudian psychology, then being introduced widely to European readers through the explanatory books of A. G. Tansley." After receiving his degree, Needham spent a year doing research in Breisgau in Germany under the physiological chemist Franz Knoop, becoming fluent in German.[142]

In 1922 Needham was admitted as a postgraduate student at the Cambridge Biochemical Laboratory, directed by Frederick Gowland Hopkins. For the next twenty years, he made the Biochemical Lab at Cambridge the center of his activities, first as a student, then a researcher, demonstrator, and finally a William Dunn Reader in Biochemistry, beginning in 1932. Under the inspiration of Hopkins Needham made the biochemistry of embryonic development his main specialty, researching the borders of biochemistry and morphology (the structure and forms of organized beings).

Haldane described "the ultimate aim of biochemistry" as an attempt to provide a "complete account of intermediary metabolism, that is to say, of the transformations undergone by matter in passing through organisms." Needham sought to combine biochemistry with embryology in order to take on "the enormous problem of seeing the connections between the chemical level and the morphological form, the atoms and molecules on the one hand and the organism and tissues of the body on the other, indeed the whole structure of the developed human organisms." He carried out one experiment after another on the metabolism of the developing egg for all kinds of invertebrates. His crowning achievement was to be his three-volume *Chemical Embryology*, published in 1931. It consisted of more than two-thousand pages and almost a million words, including a history of embryology that drew on original sources in German, French, Italian, Spanish, Greek, Latin, and Arabic.[143]

In 1924, the year before he received his doctorate, Needham married Dorothy Moyle. She was a researcher in the Cambridge Biochemistry Lab, specializing in the biochemical processes occurring in muscular contraction and in carbohydrate metabolism. Theirs was from the beginning an open marriage, reflecting the changing sexual mores of the time, with each pursuing (and in Joseph Needham's case numerous) extramarital relationships. The Needhams were the first practicing scientists, husband-and-wife team, to be elected Fellows of the Royal Society. Joseph Needham receiving his FRS in 1941, around the time of his completion of his *Biochemistry and Morphogenesis*; Dorothy Moyle Needham received the same honor in 1948.[144]

In 1937, Needham met Lu Gwei-djen, a brilliant biochemical researcher, who had traveled from China to Cambridge to work with Dorothy Needham. Lu and Needham soon became lovers. Dorothy Needham and Lu Gwei-djen were also close friends, and the intimate relationship between Joseph and Gwei-djen was seemingly not a problem in Dorothy and Joseph's marriage. It was from Lu that Needham learned Chinese, which was to lead later to his second career as a Sinologist. Lu joined Needham in the writing and editing of the multi-volume *Science and Civilization in China*. In 1987 Dorothy Needham died, at age ninety-two. Two years later Needham and Lu married.[145]

Needham always emphasized that he had sought "liberation from the bondage of conventional ideas" on "race and class" and also "sex." On sexuality, he had been strongly influenced by writers such as Edward Carpenter, Havelock Ellis, and D. H. Lawrence.[146] On race he drew upon historical-materialist scientists like Hogben, Haldane, and U.S. geneticist H. J. Muller who attacked scientific racism.[147] But it was on class issues, related to Marxism, that Needham devoted the greatest attention in the sphere of social science (and in the understanding of how social science impinged on natural science) over the course of his life. Here his source of inspiration was the Marxian classics. In 1925 Joseph and Dorothy visited the Marine Biological Station in Roscoff in Brittany where they met Louis Rapkine, a biologist and a Marxist. Rapkine came from a Jewish-Lithuanian family that had settled in Canada to escape the pogroms. Much of his life had been spent in France, where he also did his scientific work.

Rapkine introduced the Needhams to the Marxist classics, including Marx's *Capital*. But Needham's favorite was Engels's *Dialectics of Nature*, which had been published in German only that year, and around which there was undoubtedly much excitement. This work was to be crucial to his subsequent work. Although Needham had prior to this been well versed in Fabian tracts, such as the works of Wells and George Bernard Shaw, it was from this date that his serious study of Marxism began.[148]

Needham's introduction to Marxian theory was interrupted by the Great Rail Strike of 1926. Needham had a long-standing hands-on interest in trains. While still at Oundle he had convinced a train driver to take him into the cab and together with the fireman teach him the principles and practical aspects of driving a steam locomotive, which extended to his taking over (illegally) the regulator and the brake and getting some practical experience. Needham's eagerness to have a chance to drive trains partly explains how he participated in the General Strike of 1926 "on the wrong side." He joined the group of volunteers who jumped in to help run the railways, thereby playing the role of a strikebreaker. But when the General Strike had ended, and the private company he was working for wanted to keep on the volunteers and victimize the workers, Needham spoke against it and led an exodus. From then on, he was ever more firmly on the side of the workers in every struggle, concluding, "The people are *never* wrong."[149]

Another crucial development in Needham's life, around this time, was his and Dorothy's first acquaintance with the church at the parish of Thaxted in North Essex and its revolutionary socialist vicar, Conrad Noel. Noel had been a member of H. M. Hyndman's Social Democratic Federation in the late 1880s and 1890s when it was avowedly Marxist, and his approach to society continued strongly to reflect Marxian views. Frances Brook, the Countess of Warwick, herself of strong socialist convictions, had appointed Noel to Thaxted, the largest of the churches under her patronage. Noel was a founding member of the British Socialist Party in 1911. He hung in his church the tricolor of Sinn Féin, after the Irish Uprising in 1916, and the red flag after the Russian Revolution. Noel's militant Christian socialism, which earned him the nickname of the Red Vicar of Thaxted, had a strong impact on Needham, who dedicated his *Time: The Refreshing River* "To CONRAD NOELS/Priest of Thaxted/and/Prophet of Christ's Kingdom on Earth."[150] It was under the influence of Noel in particular that Needham was to adopt something like an early version of liberation theory. As Needham later recalled about the personal transformation that occurred in his thinking at this time, he adopted

> the conviction, never afterwards abandoned, that it [the Kingdom of God] should be regarded as a realm of justice and comradeship on earth, to be

> brought about by the efforts of men throughout the centuries, not primarily as some mystical body already existing, or some spiritual state to be expected somewhere in the future. Gradually this became linked up . . . with a conviction of the essential unity of cosmological, organic, and social evolution, in which the idea of human progress, with all due reservations, would take place. Parallel with this was the conviction that the Christian must take Marxism extremely seriously, such doctrines as historical materialism and the class struggle being perhaps recognition of the ways in which God had worked during the evolution of society.[151]

In the late 1920s and early 1930s, Needham, like his comrades Bernal, Haldane, and biologist and geneticist C. H. Waddington, became increasingly involved in socialist groups and political actions of all kinds. He was a member of zoologist Solly Zuckerman's dining club Tots and Quots, which was a kind of meeting point of the socialist scientific left, also including Bernal, Blackett, and Waddington. He was a member of the National Council for Civil Liberties founded in 1934, where he rubbed shoulders with leading left figures such as Clement Attlee, Havelock Ellis, Julian Huxley, Harold Laski, R. H. Tawney, H. G. Wells, and Rebecca West. In the 1931 General Election, the Needhams took an active role in supporting the Labor Party. Needham also helped in these years with the building of the Association for Scientific Workers. In 1935 he was elected Cambridge branch chair of the Socialist League. The Needhams were early on involved in the Cambridge Anti-War Group, which took to carrying out studies on bomb shelters and protections against gas and chemical warfare as the likelihood of war increased. As with many others on the left, he saw the Spanish Civil War as a historical turning point, and his attitudes toward war changed with the growing fascist threat. Needham put considerable effort into providing political, financial, and even scientific (though his design of a new kind of ambulance was a failure) support for the Republican cause.[152]

Intellectually, the 1931 Second International Congress on the History of Science and Technology was to constitute the greatest turning point in Needham's thought, propelling him in the direction of dialectical materialism.[153] For Needham it came just as he had completed his *Chemical Embryology* in which he had delved into the history of science. Hessen's reinterpretation of Newton's discoveries within the context of an externalist history of science thus had a big effect on him. Yet, more important than that for Needham, at least initially, were the papers of Bukharin, and especially Zavadovksky. The latter's presentation of dialectical materialism as an answer to the controversy between mechanism and materialism (as well as between materialism and vitalism) helped inspire Needham's later work on integrative levels.[154] In his key concept of integrative levels, Needham's central contribution to dialectical thought, he sought to bring together a complex synthesis of the overlapping ideas to be found "in the dialectical materialism of Marx and Engels, the organic mechanism of [Alfred North] Whitehead, the axiomatic biology of [J. H.] Woodger, the evolutionary naturalism of [Roy Wood] Sellars, the emergent evolutionism of [C.] Lloyd Morgan and Samuel Alexander, the holism of [Jan Christiaan] Smuts."[155] Materialist dialectics, as "a general world view," he indicated, was "another way of expressing the fact of emergent evolution, i.e., the principle that social evolution should be understood as the continuation of biological evolution, part of the rise in organizational level that has happened throughout the development of our world."[156]

Needham's general approach to materialism can be broadly defined as Epicurean-Marxist. He emphasized, as had Engels in *Ludwig Feuerbach,* materialism's fundamental character as a non-teleological view, whereby nature was explicable in and of itself without recourse to final causes in evolutionary terms. He traced this outlook within Western thought particularly to Epicurus (and within Eastern thought to Taoism), declaring at one point, "Today we are all Taoists and Epicureans."[157] Epicurus's and Lucretius's attempts to transcend any merely mechanical materialism or rigid determinism via the famous concept of the swerve were crucially important in defining Needham's basic view.[158] Finally, he saw in Epicurean materialism the beginnings of an analysis of emergence or integrative levels that represented a dialectical perspective on reality.[159] Drawing on the research of Farrington on Epicurus, Needham viewed Epicureanism as a social and political as well as materialist philosophy, one that had resisted the idealism of the ancient world.[160]

It was the kind of non-mechanical materialism that ancient Epicureanism had sought to promote, and which was developed more fully within critical realism (for example, Sellars) and Marxian-influenced materialist dialectics, that represented for Needham the most advanced philosophical view. "A realist metaphysics," he wrote, "joined with a clear understanding of the successive stages of evolutionary levels of organisation, in which mind is seen as originating, like any other natural phenomenon, at a definite point in the history of the world, proved in the end to be a far better philosophy than either mechanical materialism or metaphysical idealism."[161]

Although materialism of any sort was, Needham believed, superior to idealism, a vitalistic view (of the kind represented by John Scott Haldane), had the virtue of pointing to the complexity of life and the universe, and its active form.[162] A critical-dialectical materialism was thus the key to transcending both vitalism and mechanical materialism, and the sterility of the debate between the two.[163] Yet, in developing dialectical materialism, he sought to synthesize it (and to give it an English idiom) via Whitehead's organic philosophy and the emergent evolution of Alexander, Morgan, and Sellars.

As a materialist Needham was not concerned simply with the *materialist conception of nature* but also with the *materialist conception of history*. His most original contribution to the latter was his little 1939 book *The Levellers and the English Revolution*, written under the pen name of Henry Holorenshaw, chosen because Needham did not want to jeopardize his chance to be elected a Fellow of the Royal Society, an honor he did not receive until two years later.[164] In this brilliant and accessible book, Needham characteristically saw the Levellers and Diggers as prefiguring a higher level of society still to come, though in a form that could not then have been imagined: a future cooperative social commonwealth, now known as socialism. In this respect history was a weapon, and English socialists were too ignorant of their own history. The notion of society reaching a higher level based on a process of revolutionary historical transformation, drawing on emancipatory traditions of the past, was one that Needham consciously took from Marx and Engels. Marx and Engels, Needham declared, "adumbrated the idea of levels of organisation in setting the Hegelian dialectic actually within evolving nature."[165] Moreover, Marx, he said, went further than previous thinkers and

> showed that the evolution of social systems continued from that of biological systems, and urged the optimistic but tolerably convincing view that human misery is essentially connected with a low and inferior stage of social organisation. . . . If history is the history of class-struggles (and to some extent it undeniably is), there is room for hope that when mankind has united in a world co-operative commonwealth unmarked by social classes, a good many of the more unpleasant features of life in a semi-barbarous state will have ceased to exist.[166]

Needham first took up the issue of emergence, or what he called "Integrative Levels: A Reevaluation of the Idea of Progress," in his Herbert Spencer Lecture at Oxford University in 1937. The Spencer Lecture series was extraordinarily prestigious. Lecturers in the first decade of the lecture series (1905–1914) had included figures such as Francis Galton, C. Lloyd Morgan, and Bertrand Russell. Only a few years before, in 1933, Albert Einstein had presented "On the Method of Theoretical Physics" as a Spencer Lecture.[167] Recognizing its importance, Needham delved deeply into the works of Darwin, Spencer, Marx, Engels, Lenin, Blaise Pascal, Lloyd Morgan, Samuel Taylor Coleridge, and many others, taking down extensive notes on the organization of the material and ideas. On a page in his notes, he prepared a parallel chronology of published works divided into three parts: Spencer, Marx, and Darwin.[168]

Boldly taking up the issue of integrative levels or emergence in his lecture, Needham suggested that the first formal use of "levels" in this sense, probably came from Samuel Alexander, although Sellars and Lloyd Morgan had had large roles to play in its development.[169] The original idea, however, went back to the ancient Greek and Roman materialists, particularly Epicurus and Lucretius, and was advanced by Marx and Engels among others.

The whole idea was a dialectical one. Referring to emergence in *Order and Life*, Needham stated, "Translated into terms of Marxist philosophy, it is a new dialectical level."[170] "We cannot consider Nature," he observed much later in his notes for his Spencer Lecture, "otherwise than as a series of levels of organisation, a series of dialectical syntheses."[171] This reflected the arrow of time; as he wrote in his unpublished preparatory notes for his *Integrative Levels*: "Science can hope to *grasp* and to *control* higher levels, but not to *reduce* them to the lower levels."[172]

Such a view, Needham suggested, was consistent with Whitehead's non-obscurantist (non-vitalistic) organic philosophy, which took as its "immortal dictum" that "physics is the study of the simpler organisms and biology is the study of the more complicated ones."[173] In such an organic-dialectical view, the world could be conceived as consisting of *succession* in time and *envelopes* in space, with higher, more complex levels of organization in a sense governing both. In what was to be his most powerful statement in this respect he wrote: "The syntheses at all the successive levels of being, resolving the successive contradictions, form a series of envelopes, for they each include the elements of the contradictions on the levels below them as a series of parts. Like so many things in nature, the successive syntheses form a dendritic continuum or hierarchy of wholes."[174] Needham therefore declared in his essay on Whitehead, "The fundamental thread that seems to run through the history of our world is a *continuous rise in level of organisation*."[175]

Although believing in progress in this broad sense (a view he never entirely abandoned), Needham was critical of Victorian optimism and disdained the Whig interpretation of history.[176] Influenced by Engels, he did not discount the prospect of ecological degradation and social disorganization coming to dominate the world for long periods of time, and even the likelihood of an end at some point of human advancement. Decades later he was to declare: "It seems that abundance, unless controlled by ethics, brings deep evil with it; more washing machines, more television sets, more private cars, more large flats for small families, may mean . . . 'hire-purchase debauchery' and the selfish passion for the acquisition of things" at the expense of real-life conditions and connections.[177]

For Needham the dialectical perspective offered by the theory of integrative levels or emergence offered not just a more complex, evolutionary picture of development, but, more important, demonstrated that one level of reality was irreducible to another, thus providing an answer to reductionism in science. The question of "irreducibility" was given a central place in Needham's understanding of dialectics. Not only was there an "'irreducibility' of biological categories" to physico-chemical or biological laws, it was also to be understood as a general principle that higher levels, representing succession in time and envelopes in space, were not reducible to lower levels, since they constituted qualitatively new organizational relations, giving rise to emergent properties. The search for organizing relations, Needham noted, was more and more the aim of science. In his *Order and Life* in 1936 Needham quoted Zavadovsky on dialectical hierarchy and irreducibility: "The true task of scientific research," Zavadovsky had stated in his 1931 Second International Congress on the History of Science and Technology,

> is not the violent identification of the biological and the physical, but the discovery of the qualitatively specific controlling principles which characterise the principal features of every given phenomenon, and the finding of methods of research appropriate to the phenomenon studied. . . . Affirming the unity of the universe and the qualitative multiformity of its expression in different forms of motion of matter, it is necessary to renounce both the simplified reduction of some sciences to others, and the sharp demarcation between the physical, biological, and socio-historical sciences.

What this meant, according to Needham, was that the "biological order is both comprehensible and different from inorganic order."[178] He saw understanding this as one of the major contributions of dialectical materialism. Indeed, just as he wrote of the "irreducibility of the biological" to the physical, so he emphasized the irreducibility of the social to the biological. "Denial of the sociological level" led to a crude "biologism" or even a cruder "physicalism."[179] The critical standpoint of integrative levels was thus utilized by Needham to combat eugenics, social Darwinism, and the Nazi philosophy, and later on, in the 1970s, the kind of biological reductionism associated with Desmond Morris's popular *The Naked Ape*. Citing the work of Hogben, Haldane, and Muller, Needham strongly opposed eugenics proposals in the 1930s—often emanating from prestigious scientists—for sterilization of the most "inferior" elements of "lower" classes and races. In the struggle against all forms of biological reductionism, Needham believed, dialectical materialism was the most important weapon.[180] It was "neglect" of the analysis of integrative levels, the significance of which was most fully developed within Marxian dialectics, Needham was to argue, that led to "notable sociological heresies such as the Nazi-fascist determination to apply purely biological standards to human societies, or the use of physico-chemical concepts for . . . high organisms, which is associated with the name of Pareto."[181]

The analysis of integrative levels or emergence of new organizational forms resulted in "the entire liquidation," in Needham's words, "of all controversies of the vitalism-mechanism type."[182] Descartes had compared the body to a machine, which led others to argue that there was an inscrutable anima or vital principle that set it working. For mechanists in science, all could be explained by physico-chemical and mechanistic properties of matter. With the rise of dialectical materialism, theories of emergent evolution, and non-obscurantist organicism, as in Whitehead, it was recognized that it was no longer necessary to assert some vital principle to explain different levels of material existence.[183] As Bukharin put it, "Every new form of moving matter . . . has its own special laws. But this enriched form and these new laws are not cut off by a Chinese wall from those historically preceding them. The latter exist in these in 'sublated form.'"[184]

With the transcendence of the distinction between mechanism and vitalism, the latter was essentially obliterated (while the role of the former was only circumscribed) because it postulated properties outside the realm of scientific investigation. Here Needham turned to J. H. Woodger's *Biological Principles*. According to Woodger's criteria, Needham wrote, "the term 'vitalism' must henceforward be restricted to all propositions of the type: 'The living being consists of an X *in addition* to carbon, hydrogen, oxygen, nitrogen, etc . . . *plus organizing relations*.'" But this destroyed the whole notion of vitalism. By refusing to allow such an inscrutable and mystical concept as anima to account for organizational relations, which were themselves to be the object of biological science, vitalism was left with nothing but a redundant and obscurantist X.[185]

Nevertheless, Needham, in his usual fairness of mind, did not underestimate the service that vitalism had contributed to the advancement of thought in safeguarding complexity and creativity.[186] However, these concepts were the proper domain of materialist dialectics rather than a mystical vitalism or idealism. Dialectics in its widest sense, Needham argued, was concerned with the emergence of the qualitatively new.

Needham's analysis of integrative levels and emergent evolution led to his wider insights into dialectical synthesis. In a section titled "The Creativeness of Contradictions" in "Metamorphoses of Scepticism," the introductory chapter of *Time: The Refreshing River*, Needham based his analysis of dialectic contradictions on the notion that, rather than violations of formal logic (the principle of contradiction), they constituted real contradictory oppositions, the transcendence and synthesis of which occurred on a higher level.[187] Such contradictions within nature and society were thus real and reflected shifting organizational relations and the emergence of new levels, thus embodying the heterogeneity and complexity, as well as syntheses (or relatively stable organizational relations and laws pertaining to a given level), within existence itself. Dialectical ways of thinking were thus rational and scientific insofar as they captured complex evolutionary movements and integrative levels—a material process of which human beings themselves were a part. In what ranks as one of the most direct and powerful statements on materialist dialectics ever written, worth quoting at length, Needham stated:

> But it was left to Karl Marx and Frederick Engels in the last century, building on the dialectic process of the idealist philosopher Hegel, but profoundly influenced through Darwin by the new understanding of evolution which was then dawning on men, to take the revolutionary step of placing the resolution of contradictions within the historical and pre-historical process itself. Contradictions are not resolved only in heaven; they are resolved right here, some in the past, some now, and some in time to come. This is the dialectical materialist way of expounding cosmic development, biological evolution, and social evolution, including all history. . . .
>
> Marx and Engels were bold enough to assert that it [the dialectical process] happens actually in evolving nature itself, and that the undoubted fact that it happens in our thought about nature is because we and our thought are a part of nature. We cannot consider nature otherwise than as a series of levels of organisation, a series of dialectical syntheses. From the ultimate particle to atom, from atom to molecule, from molecule to colloidal aggregate, from aggregate to living cell, from cell to organ, from organ to body, from animal body to social association, the series of organisational levels is complete. Nothing but energy (as we now call matter and motion) and the levels of organisation (or the stabilised dialectical syntheses) at different levels have been required for the building of our world.[188]

In Needham's view, materialist dialectics, rather than obscurantist or irrational, constituted the only entirely rational way of understanding a world and a universe characterized by heterogeneity, evolution, complexity, and integrative levels; one that made possible the understanding of change, that is, the emergence of the qualitatively new by way of contradictions/mediations that eventually arose within any given level of evolving material reality. The fact that humans were capable of thinking dialectically, that is, in ways that captured a world of Heraclitan movement and change, was itself no mystery, since we were ourselves part of this complex, dialectical process of evolution that characterized the universe.[189] Idealist thinkers like Kant and Hegel claimed that the world was mind-like.[190] Dialectical materialists, in contrast, claimed that the mind was, in a sense, world-like, as a result of the whole process of human-social evolution and the human practical relation to the world. Yet, the complexity was such that the material relations of nature and society could not be comprehensively grasped except by means of dialectical reason.

Dialectical materialism, for Needham, was far removed from the mechanical materialism that dominated nineteenth and early twentieth-century science. He listed three "limitations" of mechanical materialism indicated by Engels: (1) the notion that chemical and organic processes could be reduced to the logic of mechanics; (2) the anti-dialectical character of mechanism, which did not allow for ever-shifting boundaries in natural processes; and that (3) mechanism permitted the existence of idealism "up above in the realm of the social sciences."[191]

In opposing mechanism, Needham supported the view presented by M. J. Adler in his 1927 *Dialectic* that there was, in Needham's words, a natural affinity "between dialectical and organicistic thought." Both Needham and Adler argued that "entities in opposition are likely to be parts (on one level) of which the whole, the synthesis, occupies the next higher level."[192] Indeed, Needham saw his own understanding of dialectical materialism, based on Marx and Engels, as congruent with Whitehead's organic philosophy. "It may be," he wrote, referring to Whitehead's *Science and the Modern World*, "that we are on the threshold of a long period, lasting perhaps for several centuries, in which the organic conception of the world will transform society. . . . In Alfred North Whitehead we surely have to recognise the greatest living philosopher of the organic movement in philosophy and science." If Whitehead in some places spoke in terms of Lloyd Morgan's emergent evolution, in other places he spoke "like Marx. Little though the philosophers of organic evolutionary naturalism may have borrowed from one another, they march in the same ranks."[193]

What Marxian materialist dialectics offered that was truly distinctive, Needham suggested like Bernal and Haldane, was a conscious focus on the origins of the qualitatively new in an evolving material reality. However, "Dialectical materialism," he claimed, "has been perhaps more successful in emphasizing the existence of the levels of organisation and in showing the dialectical character of human thought and discovery than in elucidating the dialectical character of the transitions between the natural levels." An exception to this was Oparin's *The Origin of Life* (1936).[194] Moreover, there had been useful suggestions. In Needham's organic-dialectical view, the successive envelopes of space that represented syntheses of what had gone before were introduced by processes that contained within themselves their own negation. Here he relied on the argument in Bernal's essay, "Dialectical Materialism," with its emphasis on residuals. As Needham put it:

> J. D. Bernal has pointed out that natural processes are never 100 per cent efficient. Besides the main process or reaction, there are always residual processes or side-reactions, which, if cyclic or if adjuvant to the main reaction, will not matter very much. But they may be opposing and cumulative, so that after some time a new situation will arise in which such opposing processes may make an antithesis to the main reaction's thesis. This situation may be unstable, and wherever instability occurs, one of the possible

> resulting syntheses may be a level of higher organisation. Such a scheme can be worked out for the aggregation of particles in planets, the formation of hydrosphere and atmosphere, and the development of economic processes since the renaissance.[195]

A key aspect of such a dialectical perspective was an emphasis on reciprocal forces, which informed Needham's approach to ecological issues. Needham viewed Lawrence J. Henderson's 1913 *The Fitness of the Environment* as the "classic" account "of the reciprocal fitness of the environment" and the fitness of the organism, in Darwinian evolution. Henderson's book had started off with the words: "Darwinian fitness is compounded of a mutual relationship between the organism and the environment. Of this, fitness of environment is quite as essential a component as the fitness which arises in the process of organic evolution," that is, of the organism.[196] Through this reciprocity and the resulting synthesis arose the particular organizational relations; they generated a specific "physico-chemical [and ecological] niche in the external and internal environment."[197] From this Needham concluded: "In the case of an animal occupying a known oecologial niche, there is but one possible environment, and the dominant species may be said to be well fitted for it. But the environment of man is not given *a priori*."[198] Human beings were especially adept at transforming environments to meet their needs through their social production. For this reason, human beings had to be seen as *social beings* living in a *social environment*, at a higher, more organized level than other animals, but not free from ecological influences. Although all life-forms—for example, an amoeba—took part in metabolism, there was something qualitatively different and more varied about the human social metabolism.[199]

Needham followed Marx in believing that ecology essentially began with the critical science of Liebig, which, for all its shortcomings, was not afraid to attack the capitalist robbery system, rather than the closed political economy of Malthus, with its narrow class-determined logic. Liebig had shown that the issue was one of the metabolism of the human relation to nature, not simply a static set of natural limitations in relation to the soil.[200]

In this same vein, Needham explored the issue of "metabolism and irreversibility," that is, the thermodynamic basis of life, incorporating the thermodynamic analyses of physicist Erwin Schrödinger and mathematical biologist/ecologist Alfred Lotka. "The 'metabolic' theory," he wrote, "asserts that biological order and thermodynamic order are identical, but that the former is overcompensated" as a dissipative structure. Yet, Needham wanted to emphasize the distinctiveness as well of biological order. That is, biotic relations were not reducible to energetics, though conforming to thermodynamic laws. According to Schrödinger in *Science and the Human Temperament*, as quoted by Needham:

> The radiation of heat from the sun, of which a small proportion reaches us, is the compensating process making possible the manifold forms of life and movement on earth, which frequently present the features of increasing order. A small fraction of this tremendous dissipation suffices to maintain life on the earth by supplying the necessary amount of "order," but of course only so long as the prodigal parent, in its own frantically uneconomic way, is still able to afford the luxury of a planet which is decked out with cloud and wind, rushing rivers and foaming seas, and the gorgeous finery of flora and fauna and the striving millions of mankind.[201]

For Needham such thermodynamic conditions pointed to the ecological limits of the organic world, and the need for conservation, and restraints on the wasting of physical energy and human effort. At the same time, it did not preclude progress and a more ordered world if regulated by science and human reason.[202]

It was his theory of integrative levels that pointed most dramatically to the unifying role of ecology in Needham's thought. Hence, in his 1932 "Thoughts on the Problem of Biological Organisation," he captured in the briefest possible form the newly emerging understanding of the time: "The hierarchy of relationships, from the molecular structure of the carbon compounds at one end to the equilibrium between species in oecological wholes at the other, will probably be the guiding idea of the future."[203]

THE RETURN OF ENGELS'S *DIALECTICS OF NATURE*

The publication in 1940 of the English translation of Engels's *Dialectics of Nature* was a major event for English-speaking Marxists.[204] Even in Germany it had taken over forty years from its date of composition before the *Dialectics of Nature* first appeared in print, and in the case of the English edition it had taken another decade and a half.[205] A work that had been written by Engels in London in the late Victorian Age, when the horse and buggy was the most common form of local transportation, was now available for the first time to English readers in the year of the Blitz, when Germany was massively bombing London from the air. In the six decades that had gone by, science had advanced enormously. Some things that Engels had written, though perfectly in accord with the science of his time, were clearly no longer viewed as valid, but the dialectical method of inquiry he had promoted had lost none of its significance.

Haldane wrote an extensive preface for the English edition of the *Dialectics of Nature*, coupled with detailed annotations throughout the book, in which he related Engels's analysis to science as it had developed over the succeeding sixty years. "While we can everywhere study Engels's method of thinking to advantage," he said, "I believe that the sections of the book which deal with biology are the most immediately valuable to scientists to-day. . . . Had his remarks on Darwinism been generally known, I for one would have been saved a certain amount of muddled thinking." Most remarkable was Engels's "insistence," in Haldane's words, "that life is the characteristic mode of behavior of proteins." This "appeared to be very one-sided to most biochemists, since every cell contains many other complicated organic substances besides proteins. Only in the last four years has it turned out that certain pure proteins do exhibit one of the most essential features of living things, reproducing themselves in a variety of environments."[206]

In Haldane's view, *Anti-Dühring*, which covered "the whole field of human knowledge" was possibly "a greater book than *Dialectics of Nature*." The main weakness of the *Dialectics of Nature* was that it was never finished and indeed could be seen as never fully having been written. Much of it would have been altered as Engels completed the work. What Engels left were extensive drafts and a large series of rough notes. If the originally planned book "had been written it would have been of immense importance for the development of science." But Engels had been forced by circumstances to consign it to the gnawing of the mice following Marx's death in 1883, faced as he was with the immense task of editing the second and third volumes of *Capital* for publication.[207]

Yet, this was not to deny the importance of the four files constituting the drafts and notes to the *Dialectics of Nature* that Engels left behind. The modern reader could everywhere gain from Engels's manner of thinking and his attempts to apply dialectical inquiry to nature and natural science, drawing, as we know, on the first two subdivisions of Hegel's *Logic* (the Doctrine of Being and the Doctrine of Essence).[208] Haldane wrote in his preface to Engels's *Dialectics of Nature*: "Marx and Engels were not content to analyse the changes in society. In dialectics they saw the science of the general laws of change, not only in society and in human thought, but in the external world which is mirrored by human thought. That is to say it can be applied to problems of 'pure' science as well as the social relations of science."[209]

Here Haldane, with his reference to "mirroring," showed his lack of epistemological sophistication.[210] But the idea that dialectical inquiry was as Haldane emphasized and as Marx and Engels clearly believed, a much more sophisticated form of human reason, able to address the complexity of relations both in the social (reflexive) and external natural-physical (intransitive) realms was certainly correct.[211] Following the lead of Lenin (and Bukharin), Haldane contrasted Engels's dialectical approach to such issues as the idealist views propounded by Pearson in his *Grammar of Science*. Engels's attempts in the *Dialectics of Nature* to explore the "dialectical laws of movement" were aimed at nothing less than grasping the quantitative dynamics and qualitative breaks—the continuities and emerging discontinuities—of change in a world in which the human species and human society co-evolved with nature.[212]

Indeed, in his discussions of life, proteins, and metabolism Engels most fully demonstrated the superiority of his thinking in his time. "Life," Engels wrote, as noted in chapter 6, "is the mode of existence of protein bodies, the essential element of which consists in *continual, metabolic interchange with the natural environment outside them*, and which ceases with the cessation of this metabolism." (This is a definition of life similar to that offered more than two-thirds of a century later by Nobel Prize–winning Austrian physicist Schrödinger in his famous *What Is Life?*) "Such metabolism," Engels noted, "can also occur in the case of inorganic bodies and in the long run it occurs everywhere, since chemical reactions take place, even if extremely slowly, everywhere. The difference, however, is that inorganic bodies are destroyed by this metabolism, while in organic bodies it is the necessary condition of their existence."[213] Like Marx, and like much of modern systems theory, Engels, as we have seen, employed a concept of the "universal metabolism of nature" in order to explain the complex, dialectical interchanges that constitute life as a whole.[214]

For Bernal, who discussed the *Dialectics of Nature* in 1940 in a review of the English-language edition, Engels's erudition and insight, given that the work was sixty years old, was breathtaking. "He saw more clearly," Bernal wrote of Engels, "than most distinguished physicists of his time the importance of energy and its inseparability from matter. No change in matter, he declared could occur without a change in energy, and vice versa. In many ways his questioning of fundamentals was of the kind that many years later led to the formulation of the quantum theory and the relativity theory." Indeed, Engels's "general physical standpoint," Bernal pointed out, "was based on the dialectical relation of attraction and repulsion; though it is clear from the way he uses these terms that they are not to be understood as merely mechanical forces drawing bodies together or pushing them apart, but essentially as motions, the one tending to bring everything in the universe together and the other to keep them apart, the first associated with potential and the second with kinetic energy. This substitution of motion for force which Engels battles for throughout was the starting-point of Einstein's own criticism of mechanics."[215]

For Bernal, however, it was the broad perspective on ecology emanating from Engels's dialectics that constituted the most important insight of the *Dialectics of Nature*, and the reason why a return to Engels's way of reasoning was so important. A crucial contribution on Engels's part, he argued, was his critique of notions of the human mastery of nature from which Bernal quoted at length. Engels had powerfully diagnosed the failure of human society to foresee the ecological consequences of its actions, including, in Bernal's words, "the effects of undesired physical consequences of human interference with nature such as cutting down forests and the spreading of deserts."[216] Human progress under the present system could by no means be assumed.

For Needham too, Engels's analysis raised the question of the ecological limits to human expansion. He observed that "Engels, whom nothing escaped," wrote in *Ludwig Feuerbach*:

> It is not necessary here to go into the question of whether this mode of outlook [evolutionary dialectical materialism] is thoroughly in accord with the present position of natural science which predicts a possible end for the earth, and for its habitability a fairly certain one; which therefore recognises that for the history of humanity also there is not only an ascending but also a descending curve. At any rate we will still find ourselves a considerable distance from the turning point at which the historical course of society becomes one of descent.[217]

Commenting on this passage, Needham observes: "By this he [Engels] would seem to have meant that a time may some day come when the struggle of mankind against the adverse conditions of life on our planet will have become so severe that further social evolution will become impossible."[218]

Indeed, there was a fundamental ecological issue here, Needham insisted, related to the second law of thermodynamics: "The most highly organised social communities should also be the least wasteful," raising the question of the wastefulness of the present order of society, which could be characterized as "wasteful of human effort, when infinite care is devoted to the growing of a crop of coffee, only for it to be shoveled into locomotive fireboxes. Wasteful of energy, when heavy goods, the transport of which is not urgent, are transported by air or rail, while for purely financial reasons canals lie unused or derelict. Is there not a thermodynamic interpretation of justice? Is not injustice wasteful? Is not the failure to utilise to the maximum the available talent and genius of men a wasteful thing?"[219] Here Needham questioned the disorganizing and dissipative nature of the capitalist system, which wasted energy and human creativity along with the gifts of nature, in accordance with purely financial (or commodity value) relations. When placed against both the real, human possibilities, still unrealized in the present, and alongside Engels's point on natural-ecological limits to human society, the present system based on waste and class domination must give way to another, more sustainable path of human development. The object was to create a society in which the alienation of nature and the alienation of labor no longer fed upon the other: a condition that if allowed to continue could only result in humanity rapidly moving from its ascending to its descending phase.[220]

Forward movement in history, for thinkers such as Bernal, Haldane, and Needham, echoing the Engels of an earlier century, required a struggle over the social relations of science—and the social relations of what we now call ecology. Above all it required an understanding of "the freedom of necessity."

CHAPTER TEN

Dialectics of Art and Science

Social relations must be changed so that love returns to the earth.
—CHRISTOPHER CAUDWELL

In December 1936 and January 1937, J. B. S. Haldane gave some military training in Madrigueras, Spain, to the British Battalion of the International Brigades fighting on behalf of the Spanish Republic.[1] A photograph at the Imperial War Museum in London shows Haldane giving gas-mask instruction along with his assistant against the background of a bombed-out, devastated area.[2] Haldane was responsible for helping to train the British volunteers not only with respect to how to protect themselves in the event of gas warfare, but also in the handling of Mills grenades, a type of fragmentation hand grenade that had been used by the British army in the First World War. As it turned out, neither form of training proved to be of practical value in the conflict. Gas did not play a significant part, if any, in the Spanish Civil War, and the British Battalion never acquired more than the half-dozen defused Mills grenades used for training purposes.[3]

Yet, even though the training that Haldane gave in 1936 was of little direct consequence for the fighting that followed, it can be seen as of symbolic significance, since it constituted the only moment of contact between two of Britain's leading Marxist thinkers of the 1930s. For among the few hundred British volunteers that constituted Haldane's audience was one Christopher St. John Sprigg, better known to the world today by his pen name Christopher Caudwell, the author of such posthumously published works as *Illusion and Reality*, *Studies in a Dying Culture*, *Further Studies in a Dying Culture*, *Romance and Realism*, *The Crisis of Physics*, and *Heredity and Development*. Caudwell's identity as a writer and Marxist theorist was entirely unknown to his comrades in Spain and to the British left as a whole. His only published works at the time (mostly under his real name) were in the areas of aeronautics and detective novels. Within the British Battalion he was seen simply as a particularly modest and likeable person (affectionately referred to as Spriggy), but otherwise an ordinary private infantryman, largely indistinguishable from the rest of the British volunteers, all of whom had crossed the sea to commit their lives to the Republican cause.[4]

On February 12, 1937, on the first day of the Battle of Jarama, the British Battalion was forced to pull back in the face of an onslaught by Francisco Franco's fascist forces. In Company 3, Caudwell and Clem Beckett, who had achieved notoriety in England as a motorcycle rider, had been operating a Chauchat light machine gun (one of the most undependable weapons of its class ever manufactured) all that day on Casa Blanca Hill. Disobeying the call to withdraw, they stayed behind to cover the retreat of their comrades, buying them some extra time. Their gun jammed and the enemy charged, killing them both. Caudwell was then a few months past his twenty-ninth birthday.[5]

Caudwell's death in the Spanish Civil War at such a young age, before his major works had been published—and before most of those works had achieved what would have been their final form—has contributed to an enduring controversy on the long-term historical significance of a figure who constituted the most brilliant and agile mind among the British Marxists of his generation. Caudwell has often been praised and then dismissed, as E. P. Thompson observed, as "an extraordinary shooting star crossing England's empirical night," a forerunner of the more sophisticated cultural Marxism of the 1960s. Yet such a view, with its neat closure, Thompson argued, is a grave error. For Caudwell's dialectics, though uneven, allowed him to cross the various chasms of thought, from art to science, giving his work a boldness and complexity all its own, and demanding that his work be interrogated again and again.[6] In his famous foreword to *Studies in a Dying Culture*, Caudwell wrote: "Either the devil has come amongst us having great power, or there is a causal explanation for a disease common to economics, science, and art."[7]

In essence, Caudwell can be understood as a thinker who sought to give new life and meaning to William Morris's view that art and science were the two "inexhaustible" forms of human knowledge.[8] The intellectual failures of bourgeois modernism, he argued, were all traceable to the fact that these two inexhaustible fountains of knowledge were alienated in capitalist society. "It is the special achievement of later bourgeois civilization," Caudwell contended, "to have robbed science of desirability and art of reality."[9] The cultural chasms this created, extending to every aspect of the human consciousness, arose from the estrangement of the human metabolism with nature, and thus the alienation of human labor itself, attributable in most developed form to the rise of the commodity-based economy.

Caudwell's work was deeply ecological in structure in aesthetic and historical as well as scientific terms, at a time when this form of materialist analysis was still largely undeveloped within the left. It was this unifying element of his thought that allowed him to develop, in just a few years, surprisingly sophisticated philosophical critiques of bourgeois aesthetics and science, although sometimes displaying signs of the enormous haste and the considerable pressures in which his works were written.

THE CAUDWELL PHENOMENON

Christopher St. John Sprigg (Christopher Caudwell) was born on October 20, 1907, in Putney, England. Christopher's father, William Stanhope Sprigg, a journalist, was literary editor for the *Daily Express* and the provincial *Yorkshire Observer* and was founder-editor of *Windsor Magazine* and *Cassell's Magazine*. He wrote books about world affairs and several novels. Christopher's mother, Jessica Mary Caudwell, was a graphic artist and a miniaturist, who died when he was only eight. His older brother Theodore Stanhope Sprigg, with whom he was close, became a journalist, and wrote some twelve books on aviation. His father was a convert to Catholicism, and his sister, Paula Sprigg, became a nun. Christopher received his initial education at a Roman Catholic preparatory school in Bognor Regis in Sussex. From there he went to Ealing Priory School (later called St. Benet's) near London. The Benedictine curriculum to which he was exposed at Ealing as a member of the Roman Catholic middle class was crucial to his later development. At Ealing he was taught some Greek and considerable Latin. He left school, ending his formal education, before his fifteenth birthday due to family financial difficulties when his father lost his job as the literary editor of the *Daily Express*.

In November 1922, upon turning fifteen, Caudwell obtained a job as an apprentice reporter on the *Yorkshire Observer* in Bradford, where his father was then employed. In May 1926 he returned to London to take up an editorial position (first as sub-editor and then editor) in the trade journal *British Malaya* in London, a publication of the Association for British Malaya. The following year, he and his brother Theodore received a legacy from an aunt, which allowed them to establish an aeronautical publishing company, Airways Publications, and its monthly publication *Airways*. Caudwell wrote advertising copy and became manager of Aeromarine Advertising Ltd. He also became a director alongside his brother of another company, the Air Press Agency. In 1929, he published theoretical notes on improvements of the automobile gear in *Automotive Engineer*. The following year, he was to patent a design for a variable speed gear that attracted some interest in the industry but was never adopted. Airways Publications went bankrupt at the end of 1933, ending this phase of Caudwell's career.[10]

Prior to the work for which he is best remembered, Caudwell wrote five books on aviation, seven crime novels, a serious novel *(This My Hand)*, numerous short stories and 150 pages of poetry. Most of this, aside from the poetry (he only published one poem in his lifetime), was mainly to earn a living. In one three-month period in 1934, while working in an office part-time four days a week, he wrote a detective novel, an aviation textbook, thirty articles on flying, six short stories, and various poems. In late 1934, he took up an interest in Marxism, and during the two years that followed, while continuing to support himself through his commercial writing, he composed all of the major works for which he was to become famous, working at the furious pace of up to 5,000 words a day on these manuscripts alone. All of these works were written in two years, under his new pen name of Christopher Caudwell (using his mother's maiden name), first adopted in May 1935 for his novel, *This My Hand*.[11]

Much of Caudwell's immense creative output in this period was carried out during the summer and early fall of 1935, which he spent in relative isolation in Porthleven, Cornwall, where he immersed himself in the works of Karl Marx, Frederick Engels, and V. I. Lenin, and completed *Illusion and Reality*. Later that fall he moved to Poplar in the dockside district of London in order to become more acquainted with working-class life and experience the atmosphere of the times. He had three different mailing addresses during his year in Poplar, suggesting that he had no stable residence. He soon joined the Communist Party of Great Britain (CPGB) and took part in various street rallies, particularly against fascists. He visited Paris briefly to experience the Popular Front firsthand and came back with renewed energy and enthusiasm. He also took a course on Marxism and literature with Alick West and Douglas Garman, who knew him as Christopher Sprigg. He told them nothing of his writings, however, of which his comrades in the CPGB were also unaware. He would write until 5 p.m. every day and then go to the CPGB branch and participate in open-air meetings or sell the *Daily Worker* on the streets. On June 7, 1936, he was arrested as a result of a fight with Oswald Mosley's Blackshirts, and was accused falsely of assaulting the police.[12]

Very little is known about Caudwell's personal relationships. His closest friends were his school friend Paul Beard from Ealing Priory, who had become a literary critic and editor, and Paul Beard's wife, Elizabeth Beard, a writer. Both took great interest in Caudwell's work. Those who knew Caudwell best referred to him as quiet, reserved, and sincere, but not without humor, a good companion able to entertain others. He had various romantic relationships, without making any lasting commitments. Interestingly, Celia Harrison, Caudwell's protagonist in the first part of *This My Hand*, has been described as "a fictionalized female version of his younger self," learning Greek and Latin at an early age, along with geometry, French, history, geography, and literature. Moving with her father at age fourteen to Yorkshire, she attends University Extension courses and the Mechanics Institute, loves poetry and writes book reviews for the local paper. This manifests in part Caudwell's own ideals with respect to women and life.[13]

Caudwell was supportive in his writings of the early feminist movement and its intellectual aspirations, but argued that figures such as the Brontes, George Eliot, George Sand, and Virginia Woolf were not at that time fighting for substantive equality, but rather for equality in a male bourgeois world. Thus the "woman revolts *within* the categories of bourgeois culture. . . . Of course this revolt is bound to fail, because it asserts woman's right to be man, in other words to enslave herself to masculine values. It is like those pseudo-socialisms in which the proletariat is given bourgeois rights." The problem was that "none of these revolutions [including the vote for women] gain real equality because they are ultimately parasitic on male values." Real, substantive equality was essential to any genuine conception of socialism.[14] As Helena Sheehan has commented:

> His [Caudwell's] sensitivity to the life experience of women as "aliens" within the bourgeois world view was particularly extraordinary. With uncanny perceptiveness, he showed how the dominant world view was based on the male experience of life and how the first stages of rebellion took the form demanding women's rights in male terms and in a male world. He traced the stages of development of women's consciousness as at first partial, inchoate, noncognitive, as a result of exclusion from control of the economy and the cognitive and cultural apparatus of society and he expressed his expectation that a fusion of male and female experience would occur in the course of the revolutionary process and would result in the transformation of both in a new and higher synthesis.[15]

Caudwell's love of poetry is full of earthly passion, and longing for the fulsomeness of love foregone:

> When I could bite my tongue out in desire,
> To have your body, local now to me,
> You were a woman and your proper image
> Unvarying on the black screen of night,
> What are you now? A thigh, a smile, an odour:
> A cloud of anecdotes and fed desires
> Bubblingly unfolds inside my brain
> To vex its vision with a monstrous beast.[16]

Caudwell soon became the secretary of his branch of the CPGB. Late in 1936, he was chosen to drive an ambulance purchased by the members to aid the Republican cause in Spain. In December 1936, rather than returning from Spain, he enlisted in the British Battalion of the International Brigade and was trained as a machine gunner. He also became the political representative of his group and the joint editor of the battalion's newspaper.[17] It was there that

Caudwell gave up his life, covering the retreat of his comrades on the first day of the Battle of Jarama fought in defense of Madrid and the Spanish Republic.

In his final letter to his friend Paul Beard, on December 9, 1936, shortly before he left for Spain, Caudwell wrote: "There is always the possibility that I may not come back from Spain, in which case I shall leave behind me a mass of manuscript[s] some of which may be worth publishing." The letter contained a list of these manuscripts and his opinion of the state in which he had left them. *Studies in a Dying Culture*, he said, "was only drafts with some good ideas," and *The Crisis in Physics* was "half written"— half ready for the press, the other half needed to be redone "for grammar and sense." His plays and novels, he claimed, were "all completely worthless," and his short stories were a product of his earlier sentimental period—"partly worth publishing."[18] Caudwell's failure to mention other manuscripts, such as *Romance and Realism* and *Heredity and Development* was no doubt due to his seeing them as part of his *Studies in a Dying Culture,* which was itself later published, more than a decade apart, in two separate collections: *Studies in a Dying Culture* and *Further Studies in a Dying Culture*. *Illusion and Reality* was already in press when he left for Spain. All the manuscripts were left with his brother Theodore, with the stipulation that decisions on publication would be "guided entirely" by Beard, and presumably his wife, Elizabeth Beard, Caudwell's closest friends, critics, and advisers. Within three years of his death *Illusion and Reality*, *Studies in a Dying Culture,* and *The Crisis of Physics* all appeared. With the publication of *Further Studies in a Dying Culture*, the main corpus of Caudwell's work had been published. Nevertheless, such important works as *Romance and Realism* and *Heredity and Development*, and much of his poetry and correspondence did not appear until the 1970s and 1980s.

THE CAUDWELL CONTROVERSY

The controversies that Caudwell's work generated in left circles were so great that it would be naïve to attempt to approach his work directly, without first taking a look at the debates his work stirred. Caudwell's *Illusion and Reality*, *The Crisis in Physics*, and *Studies in a Dying Culture* created a sensation in left circles in the late 1930s. As Maynard Solomon has written, "Marxist criticism [had] virtually disappeared from English letters after William Morris's lectures of the 1890s."[19] Caudwell was the first to fill this as well as other gaps, and his work was initially greeted enthusiastically on the left. The Marxist classicist George Thomson wrote in his opening "Biographical Note" to *Illusion and Reality* that Caudwell's work marked "an entirely new departure in literary criticism. It is the first comprehensive attempt to work out a Marxist theory of art."[20]

Haldane declared: "No one who has read *Illusion and Reality* can doubt" that Caudwell "was one of the ablest men of his generation." Of Caudwell's *The Crisis in Physics*, he said, "I know of no writer of our time whose analysis of the problem of freedom goes so deep." Haldane added that Caudwell's book would be "a quarry of ideas" for future generations of philosophers, and that he would "be surprised if some at least of his ideas are not accepted by physicists. In its final form it might have been one of the most important books of our time."[21]

Hyman Levy, in his preface to *The Crisis of Physics*, observed that Caudwell provided "a combined social and scientific understanding that would be rare in a scientist of mature experience; to find them in this man is almost phenomenal."[22]

But it was Caudwell as the aesthetic theorist that stood out most at the time. In a review of *Illusion and Reality*, the celebrated poet W. H. Auden wrote:

> We have waited a long time for a Marxist book on the aesthetics of poetry. . . . Now at last Mr. Caudwell has given us such a book.
>
> *Illusion and Reality* is a long essay on the evolution of freedom in Man's struggle with nature . . . and of the essentially social nature of words, art and science, an approach which enables Mr. Caudwell to make the clearest and most cogent criticism of Freud and Jung, while using their discoveries which I have ever read. . . . This is the most important book on poetry since the books of Dr. [I. A.] Richards, and in my opinion provides a more satisfactory answer to the many problems which poetry raises.[23]

Georg Lukács referred respectfully to Caudwell numerous times in his own writings on aesthetics, calling him a "highly gifted English aesthetician," a "discerning philosopher," and "spirited and progressive." Although Lukács criticized Caudwell for going too far in the direction of Romantic subjectivism, he nonetheless praised him for the acuteness of his theoretical observations.[24]

Nevertheless, Caudwell's work, which was initially looked upon so favorably on the left, was to spark a fierce debate within the Old Left in the late 1940s, involving such figures as Maurice Cornforth, J. D. Bernal, and Thomson, followed shortly after by an intervention by Raymond Williams, a New Left figure. A second debate on Caudwell's work, no less fierce than the first, took place in the 1970s, between the First and Second New Lefts, involving such celebrated theorists as Terry Eagleton, Francis Mulhern, Thompson, and Williams. In general, the Second New Left, representing younger theorists who were more dismissive of Caudwell, triumphed over the First New Left on this issue, despite the power of Thompson's and Williams's responses. The result of these cumulative critiques was that Caudwell's reputation was severely marred, especially in relation to the New Leftists of the 1960s, influenced by the Althusserian tradition. Interest in his work therefore waned.

A number of sophisticated works on Caudwell's literary and cultural theories were written in the late 1980s, and some of his still unpublished work was released at that time, including *Heredity and Development* (published in a 1986 collection called *Scenes and Actions: Unpublished Manuscripts*, edited by Jean Duparc and David Margolies).[25] None of this work, seeking to rehabilitate Caudwell in the eyes of cultural theorists, seems to have attracted the attention of the more prominent left cultural theorists, who by that time had moved on, and thus interest in his work continued to wane. Nevertheless, the publication of *Heredity and Development* was to lead to renewed appreciation of his dialectics of art and science, and the relation of this to the human interaction with nature through production, emanating this time not so much from Marxist literary theorists but from Marxian ecologists, who were linked with the older Romantic socialist tradition, associated with thinkers like Morris and Caudwell.[26]

Caudwell's reputation originally took a beating in the Cold War era when Cornforth, a philosopher known for his writings on dialectical materialism and a leading figure within the CPGB, launched a major attack on Caudwell's work in an article titled "Caudwell and Marxism" in the Winter 1950–1951 issue of *Modern Quarterly*. This was to result in a larger debate within the CPGB in particular. Most of the criticisms were directed at Caudwell's *Illusion and Reality*, although they extended to his other works as well.

Cornforth argued that Caudwell, despite the prestige his work had attained, had not developed a Marxist aesthetics. Rather, his approach was contaminated from the start with Sigmund Freud's theory of instincts as well as bourgeois genetics, specifically the work of August Weismann and his notions of germplasm (a criticism designed to place Caudwell outside the Lysenko camp and thus opposed to the then Soviet orthodoxy). In Cornforth's interpretation, Caudwell's whole "conception of the changeless 'instincts' and their contradictory relation with 'cultural environment' and 'environmental reality' is borrowed from bourgeois ideologists and is foreign to and hostile to Marxism. . . . Applied to human affairs, this is a singularly reactionary theory. It teaches that human nature never changes, but remains at bottom always the same." It was precisely this that undermined Caudwell's theory of poetry and aesthetics in general. Caudwell had declared that "all art is emotional and therefore concerned with the instincts whose adaptation to social life produces emotional consciousness."[27] Caudwell's theory of poetry thus, Cornforth charged, derived "from his Freudian, idealist premises" and from his overall "Weismann-Freud metaphysics" that led him dualistically to write of both the "inner world" of the unconscious self and the "outer world" of external reality—both of which were seen as affecting poetic imagery. Rejecting Caudwell's purported idealism,

Cornforth faithfully quoted Stalin: "'Poets,' as Stalin said, 'are engineers of the human soul.'"

Cornforth condemned Caudwell especially for contending that poetry and art are based on "illusion"—a concept that Caudwell used in the sense of the theory of *mimesis* (art as creative imitation) in Aristotle's *Poetics. Mimesis* here referred to the ideal-potential as well as the actual, and was seen as having a (cognitive) reality all its own.[28] It was Caudwell's claim, following Aristotle, that poetic images in his sense represented a secondary, but in many ways higher, and more complex, interaction with the world that Cornforth rejected as inherently anti-Marxist. Likewise, Caudwell's notion of the "genotype," which stood for the human biological and psychological inheritance as constantly transformed in human social life but still existent, was condemned as the crude, emotional "underworld" that supported Caudwell's concept of "illusion." For Cornforth, this was to be categorically rejected, as denying the full malleability of human beings. This despite the fact that the concept of genotype was fundamental to biology at the time and has remained so. Most objectionable, Cornforth insisted, was Caudwell's notion of the "inner energy" flowing out from the individual human being, which was characterized as idealist in nature, stemming from sources that were not social. All of this was taken as evidence that Caudwell's aesthetics and his thought in general had been initially embraced by the left with "uncritical enthusiasm" and now had to be rejected as idealist and un-Marxist. Reflecting the different atmosphere of the 1950s from the 1930s, Cornforth's charges clearly emanated from an official Marxism, which had become much narrower in its overall conception and less open to critical synthesis with other perspectives than ever before.[29]

Among those who strongly backed Cornforth's criticisms of Caudwell was Bernal. The attraction of Caudwell's thinking and its major flaw, he contended, was its introduction of concepts derived from the sciences to explore issues primarily in the realms of aesthetics and philosophy. Caudwell's ideas were largely those of "contemporary bourgeois scientific philosophy, Einsteinian—Morganist—Freudian, and not those of Marxism. . . . No attentive reader can escape an uneasy feeling on reading Caudwell, as if written in two languages at once, Freud, Einstein and Marx are uncomfortable bedfellows." Quite untypical of his thought in general, Bernal here seemed to narrow Marxism down to a dogmatic doctrine, walled off from all other traditions of thought, and Caudwell had dangerously ventured outside this walled-off discourse. More meaningfully, Caudwell was accused of a kind of biological determinism. "For all the emphasis on society and labour," Bernal wrote, "Caudwell cannot escape from biologism, the introduction into human social affairs of concepts derived from the lower levels of non-social organic evolution." Caudwell's dialectic was "far more Hegelian than Marxist. The material unity is not objective matter in any sense but much more like the matter-mind stuff of Russell's neutral monism." Bernal concluded: "Though Caudwell's work contains many original and suggestive ideas, and much closely woven argumentation, it cannot be considered as a Marxist classic. To read it with profit and without danger of confusion requires an already matured grasp of the principles of Marxism." Yet, as if contradicting his own argument, he acknowledged that Caudwell "criticised, brilliantly and destructively, the philosophical conclusions of bourgeois scientists."[30]

Thomson defended Caudwell against such attacks in an article for the Spring 1951 issue of the *Modern Quarterly*, titled "In Defense of Poetry."[31] He contended that his own *Aeschylus and Athens*, his most influential book (and destined to be recognized as a classic), "could not have been written" without the basis that Caudwell had provided in *Illusion and Reality*. The two leading ideas in *Illusion and Reality*, Thomson argued, were:

> First, science and art are complementary and mutually indispensable activities of the human mind, both concerned with the extension of man's understanding and control of nature and himself, the one directly, through the reason, by changing the external world, the other indirectly, through the emotions, by changing the subjective attitude to it. Secondly, neither can be understood without reference to their origin and development, and the origin of both is to be sought in the emergence of those interdependent characteristics which distinguish man from animals—tools and speech.[32]

For Thomson, it was Caudwell's larger dialectics of art and science, and his tracing of these issues, particularly art, to their anthropological and historical origins in the long path of human evolutionary and social development that captured the brilliance of Caudwell's work, and which he applied to his own investigations. Overall Caudwell, in Thomson's interpretation, was engaged in "a long argument in which he is trying to define the complementary functions of art and science in associated men's struggle with nature." As with Marx, Caudwell "begins with man acting on nature," and his position is like that of "Marx, who describes the labour process as one 'in which man *of his own accord* starts, regulates and controls the material relations [metabolism] between himself and nature.'"[33] It was from this that he develops his understanding of the origins of art and science, which can only be seen in relation to the human interrelationship with nature through labor and production.

The extraordinary range of Caudwell's analysis and the synthesis at which he aimed, Thomson contended, made his work difficult. "Æsthetics, anthropology, linguistics, psychology, philosophy, history, economics—all these disciplines are harnessed to the argument of *Illusion and Reality*: and in his other books he explores, physics, mathematics, and neurology."[34] (Thomson was not aware of

Caudwell's unpublished *Heredity and Development*, and his treatment of biological evolution.)

Thomson adamantly rejected the notion that Caudwell's concept of genotype reduced human beings, as Cornforth said, simply to a "pack of genes," or that it denied the social and historical development of human nature, and he provided passages in Caudwell to demonstrate that this was not the case. He pointed out that Caudwell's analysis was always dialectical, relating the organism to its environment, or, as Caudwell put it, "its ecology," but invariably connecting this to the distinctly human role in mediating this relation through the organization of production.[35] Although Caudwell drew on Freud's theory of instincts, he did so in a critical fashion, transforming it in relation to historical materialism through a focus on human labor. Caudwell's treatment of poetry as arising out of the process of mimesis (in Aristotle's sense), and having its anthropological origins in the mimetic dance (as described by Jane Harrison and the Cambridge Ritualists), opened up whole new vistas for historical materialist analysis, which had inspired Thomson's own investigations. To give all this up for a mechanical dogmatism represented a threat to historical materialism itself. "Appeals to Stalin," Thomson dryly remarked, in response to Cornforth, "can never be a substitute for a serious study of one's subject."[36]

A different response, more distant, came from Williams in his *Culture and Society, 1780–1950*. Looking at the Caudwell debate from the standpoint of "one who is not a Marxist," Williams noted the "extraordinary difference of opinion" on Caudwell and Marxism that separated thinkers like Bernal and Thomson. Williams indicated some doubts about Caudwell as a literary theorist, since he seemed to display little subtlety in the knowledge of "actual literature." Indeed, "For the most part his discussion is not specific enough even to be wrong."[37]

Nevertheless, Williams conceded that Caudwell was "immensely prolific of ideas, over an unusually wide field of interest." What was of interest to Williams was that Caudwell did not approach issues of culture through a rigid superstructure model, but rather focused on the relationship between science and art, and the role of illusion, the imaginary, of mimesis, in the treatment of the latter. As Caudwell had written, "Just as the scientist is the explorer of new realms of outer reality, the artist continually discovered new realms of the heart."[38] The case of Caudwell, Williams observed, raised the issue in this respect of "an improvement of Marx," one in which the English Romantic tradition of culture came together with Marxism, reminiscent of Thompson's interpretation of Morris. "In fact, as we look at the English attempt at a Marxist theory of culture, what we see is an interaction between Romanticism and Marx, between the idea of culture which is the major English tradition and Marx's brilliant reevaluation of it. We have to conclude that the interaction is as yet far from complete." This was of course to define Williams's own later work as well as Thompson's as leading figures of the First New Left. As John Higgins writes, "What Williams finds in at least some of the English Marxists, and most explicitly in Caudwell, is a significant debt to Romanticism in their conception of the value of art as an active force in social change."[39]

In *Culture and Society*, Williams, as he later observed, was still "reading against" Caudwell.[40] However, this had changed three years later, in *The Long Revolution*, where Williams, in his opening chapter on the "creative process," drew on Caudwell's essay on "Consciousness" as representing a sophisticated, dialectical epistemology. It was at this time that Williams began a serious reassessment of Caudwell's contribution, focusing not on *Illusion and Reality*, but rather on Caudwell's later (though not much later) *Studies in a Dying Culture*, and more significantly, his *Further Studies in a Dying Culture*.[41] Nevertheless, Williams's reconsideration of Caudwell was left largely implicit and undeveloped, and its significance was not widely recognized. Williams, as he was at pains to indicate at the time, was not a Marxist. The Caudwell controversy of the 1950s seemed to have put Caudwell beyond the pale. As E. P. Thompson later observed, "By the time the dust had settled, his work had fallen into general disrepute."[42]

But it was in the 1970s rather than the 1950s that Caudwell was subject to the harshest criticism, when he came under criticism emanating from the emerging Second New Left. In "The Marxist Aesthetics of Christopher Caudwell" in *New Left Review* in 1974, Francis Mulhern, in criticizing Caudwell, charged that his whole theoretical structure was, "in [Louis] Althusser's sense of the term, *historicist*," lacking in all theoretical determination. Caudwell was mainly concerned, Mulhern's readers were told, with "freedom from the forces of nature," that is, an abstract bourgeois conception of freedom. Moreover, besides being historicist, Caudwell was said to have propounded a "*timelessness*" and a "fixed human nature." Poetry itself was supposedly defined by Caudwell in "supra-historical" terms, minus the theoretical foundations later provided by Althusserian structuralism. According to Mulhern, the "regression" in Caudwell's analysis, from which his historicism derived, was "at heart, a *psychologism*." Caudwell saw art simply as emotion, and thus as mere "expression," the poetic counterpoint of the reflection of crude materialism.[43]

Mulhern alleged that Caudwell's analysis was aimed at the Promethean goal of "freedom from nature" through the mastery of nature as society's objective, whereas, in truth, Caudwell, in the cited passages, had argued for a much more dialectical view, seeing the growth of "freedom and individuality" as occurring reflexively "through organisation imposed by nature, [and] in his [the human actor's] interaction with it."[44]

Terry Eagleton's dismissal of Caudwell in his 1976 *Criticism and Ideology: A Study of Marxist Literary Theory*, was even more severe. Here, in a well-known passage, Eagleton remarked:

> Who is the major English Marxist critic? Christopher Caudwell, *hélas*. It is in such pat question and answer that the problem of a Marxist criticism in contemporary Britain is most deftly posed. For though Caudwell is the major forebear—"major," at least, in the sheer undaunted ambitiousness of his project—it is equally true that there is little, except negatively, to be learnt from him. Not that we can learn only from the English, or that Caudwell's limitations were just his own. Insulated from much of Europe, intellectually isolated even within his own society, permeated by Stalinism and idealism, bereft of a "theory of superstructures," Caudwell nonetheless persevered in the historically hopeless task of producing from these unpropitious conditions a fully-fledged Marxist aesthetic. His work bears all the scars of that self-contradictory enterprise: speculative and erratic, studded with random insights, punctuated by hectic forays into and out of alien territories and strewn with hair-raising theoretical vulgarities. If Caudwell lacked a tradition of Marxist aesthetics, it is a measure of that absence that we, coming after him, lack one too.[45]

These unrelenting attacks on Caudwell by figures from the Second New Left, represented by Mulhern and Eagleton, were to generate powerful critical rejoinders from those identified with the First New Left, such as Thompson, and to some extent Williams.[46] Responding to Eagleton and Mulhern's criticisms of Caudwell, but also to those emanating from Cornforth and Bernal two decades before, Thompson wrote a long, passionate essay on "Christopher Caudwell," for the *Socialist Register* in 1977, in which he defended Caudwell and emphasized his importance—but not without some sharp criticisms of his own, directed at Caudwell's work. Key to Thompson's response was a devaluing of Caudwell's *Illusion and Reality*, which Mulhern and others had characterized as Caudwell's "major work." *Illusion and Reality* was, in Thompson's words, "a bad book" if seen as a single, coherent argument. It was an "ill-organized, involuted, and repetitive book," and some of its concepts were unsatisfactory or undeveloped. It was "beyond the repair of close criticism."[47] But *Illusion and Reality* was also a misunderstood work, to which many of the criticisms directed at it did not apply. And though its faults were apparent, it contained elements of originality and brilliance, making it a source of considerable critical inspiration for later thinkers.

These seemingly contradictory appraisals arose from the circumstances in which *Illusion and Reality* was composed. Caudwell had started writing it at his usual breakneck pace early in 1934, but by the summer of 1934 he had become engaged in Marxist theory. The book thus had the character of an analysis that had been started under one set of preconceptions and then shifted to another, with considerable rewriting along the way, giving it an inconsistent and even contradictory shape. It was best seen as an incomplete, hasty synthesis, and a radical but partial breaking away from earlier forms of thinking. It read neither like a Marxist work (particularly in terms of the orthodoxy of the time) or a non-Marxist one, but a kind of unsettled amalgamation of the two, which nonetheless revealed much of Caudwell's creative process and the heretical nature of his analysis. On top of this, the book's argument was interrupted by four misconceived chapters on the development of English poetry that were universally seen as an embarrassment, indicating Caudwell's lack of "any real sense of history" and its relation to literary forms, or even the particulars of the poetry to which he referred. This tended to highlight, especially for those interested in literary criticism, Caudwell's specific weaknesses, including his lack of knowledge of particular art forms, rather than his theoretical strengths. Thompson noted that his later *Romance and Realism*, which was spun off from *Studies*, partly altered this verdict: "*Romance and Realism* reveals a quite new specificity of judgement, a more watchful eye and a more attentive ear, notably in its treatment of Meredith, Hardy, Kipling, Moore and Virginia Woolf. This suggests reserves of critical power only casually drawn upon in Caudwell's earlier writings."[48]

In Thompson's view, it was not *Illusion and Reality* that represented the best in Caudwell, but rather the essays that Caudwell had written in his *Studies* series: *Studies in a Dying Culture*, *Further Studies in a Dying Culture*, *The Crisis in Physics,* and *Romance and Realism* (*Heredity and Development* had not yet been published). Although these works were all written only a year or so after *Illusion and Reality*, they represented "not the mature Caudwell, but as mature as Caudwell became." Astonishingly, "In the transition from *Illusion and Reality* to the *Studies*," Thompson noted, "more had changed in Caudwell than could be expected in the passage of one year."[49] Of particular importance were the five essays published in the late 1940s in *Further Studies:* "The Breath of Discontent: A Study of Bourgeois Religion," "Beauty: A Study in Bourgeois Aesthetics," "Men and Nature: A Study in Bourgeois History," "Consciousness: A Study in Bourgeois Psychology," and "Reality: A Study in Bourgeois Philosophy." Of the five essays, only the one on history, in Thompson's judgment, had little to recommend it. Together these works plus parts of the *Crisis in Physics*, and no doubt a few of the elements of *Illusion and Reality*, were what Thompson wanted considered of lasting significance.

"Perhaps ninety percent" of Caudwell's work, he wrote, "no longer affords any point of entry" into the present. Yet, the remaining "ten percent" displayed "an extraordinary, searching vitality." It offered a heretical and synthetic approach to historical materialism that brought the *subjective* back into the argument, in many ways linking up with the Romantic tradition of Marxism going back to

Morris. For Thompson, Caudwell's "unfinished manuscripts . . . represent the most heroic effort of any British Marxist to think his own intellectual time."[50]

Caudwell's virtue lay in his deep insights, promising a more critical, heretical, and constructive historical materialism. Yet, his entire intellectual corpus did not extend beyond his *early writings* (there were no later ones), written in a few years in his late twenties. Although undoubtedly the most powerful and precocious Marxist theorist in Britain of his generation, his enormous promise was cut short by an early death. "Nothing he wrote," Thompson stated (perhaps conceding too much), "is of a maturity or a consistency to merit election as a Marxist or any other kind of 'classic.'"[51] Yet, what was interesting in Caudwell was what he attempted and how far he got in his bold attempts, which caused thinkers in his generation to return to him again and again. His dialectical imagination was daunting. The consensus on Caudwell, Thompson believed, was correct, that he presented an immense "quarry of ideas," in Haldane's words. Indeed, what was surprising was the sheer productiveness of this quarry in providing much of the stone necessary to reconstruct historical materialism on new foundations.

Illusion and Reality, although containing flaws, was, in Thompson's view, grossly misunderstood by most of his critics, including Cornforth, Eagleton, and Mulhern. Caudwell had never perceived it as providing a Marxian aesthetics. Instead, its subtitle was "A Study of the Sources of Poetry." It was primarily anthropological in its emphasis, seeking to understand the role of the imagination, in the form of art (and also science) in human evolution and the evolution of human society. One of the difficulties faced by English literary theorists in reading Caudwell's book is that it extended far beyond their bounds. Caudwell's *Illusion and Reality* had started out as a much larger manuscript called *Verse and Mathematics*. The published book had a bibliography of over 500 titles: "A rough-and-ready breakdown into categories gives us: Linguistics, 14; Philosophy, 33; General science (including genetics, physics), 37; Ancient civilizations (Egypt, Greece, Rome), 39; Marxism, 39; History, economics, general politics, 64; Literary criticism and the arts, 75; Psychology and neurology, 78; Anthropology and archaeology, 122. A few titles evade even these classifications. And there are two or three volumes of poetry."[52]

Although Eagleton had described Caudwell's book as an excursion in literary analysis that included "hectic forays into and out of alien territories" such as anthropology and psychology, it was rather the other way around: with the anthropological origins of art, as the *imaginative correlate* of the mediation between human beings and nature through labor, constituting the principal emphasis of Caudwell's theoretical endeavor. The fact that there was so little poetry contained in his bibliography reflected that literary exegesis was not his principal concern.[53]

Caudwell's focus on the anthropological origins of art was an area in which Thompson declined to tread. But there was no doubt, as later thinkers were to discover, that the most important work in the development of Caudwell's Marxian theory of the origins of art was the anthropology of Jane Harrison and the Cambridge ritualists, or that Caudwell's Marxian analysis of the sources of poetry had opened up a whole new realm for historical materialism.[54] This, as Thompson contended, was "realised, less in Caudwell's own work than in that of those most directly influenced by him: notably in George Thomson's *Aeschylus and Athens* (1941) and in his lucid *Marxism and Poetry* (1945)."[55]

More important than this, for Thompson, was Caudwell's dialectical and materialist approach to issues of art and science, and to the whole question of culture, one that provided a kind of prologue—never followed up due to Caudwell's early death—to an alternative, heretical historical-materialist approach to culture. Attempts to dismiss Caudwell's approach as a crude psychologism were wrong. His concept of the formation of myth, ritual, and poetry, accompanying production and language—both seen (following Marx and Engels) as mediations between human beings and nature—relied on a broad psychological construct that Caudwell called the "genotype"—that is, a notion of prehuman, instinctual characteristics that persisted in a timeless though transformed way throughout human culture. But Caudwell's insistence that humanity was a product of society and particular cultures saved him from an "essentialist paradigm" that constantly threatened to take over in his work.[56]

The concept of genotype was transformed in Caudwell's treatment from a purely genetic-physiological basis into something that was more socio-psychological, owing as much to Emile Durkheim as to Freud. This gave to Caudwell's work a sense of the perennial human conflict between those "primitive" aspects of human evolution and existence that were, in his analysis, prehuman, and the social-cultural developments that defined humanity in society. Such ideas did not arise from Marxism; rather they emanated from Caudwell's pre-Marxian phase. But he sought to integrate it in complex ways with the Marxian theory of human nature as something that was made in history through the development of society in the context of human labor and production.

Moreover, Caudwell's tendency to an essentialism of sorts almost completely fell away in his *Studies* as he got further into Marxism. What was important for Thompson was Caudwell's refusal (though this was never worked out consistently) simply to consign culture to the superstructure, seeing it rather as integral to production and the imaginative counterpart of human labor.[57] Here Caudwell's dialectics came into play. It is true that he often paraded binaries as if this was in itself dialectics, but this was only to express the extent of the antagonisms within bourgeois society itself, particularly in the struggle between human beings and nature, which could only be traversed by various mediations—at root labor and language, and manifested imaginatively in art and science. In *Romance and Realism*, Caudwell counterposed the liberal "diet of dualisms," which could not "conceive that subject and object are not mutually exhaustive opposites," to a conception of the unity of opposites, arising through various mediations.[58]

Indeed, Thompson stressed, Caudwell strongly condemned the crude reflection or correspondence theory that dominated Marxian epistemology at the time. At all times, he conveyed "a complexity of relationship which cannot be sustained by the image of 'reflection.'" In his *Studies* manuscripts, he was openly antagonistic to any idea of simple reflection or mirroring as a valid epistemological view: "Social consciousness," he wrote, "is not a mirror-image of social being. If it were, it would be useless, a mere fantasy."[59] Caudwell's "way of seeing coincident and opposed potentialities within a single 'moment' and of following through the contradictory logic of the ideological progress," Thompson argued, was a rare gift, attained fully only in his final year. "After Blake and Marx, this faculty of dialectical vision has been rare enough for us to regard it with special respect."[60]

This dialectical character of Caudwell's thought could be seen in his treatment of the notion of "the struggle of man with nature" that was a constant trope, particularly common in the natural sciences and in Marxism, in his day. At times, he seemed himself to have fallen prey to this trope. But Caudwell, as Thompson said, was not at all "Promethean," and indeed it was this struggle in the human transformation of nature—and the transformation at the same time of the human relation to nature and of human beings themselves—that he sought above all to understand, particularly through kaleidoscopic reflection in the main repositories of human knowledge: art and science. For Caudwell, even the notion of production needed to be broken down and removed from dualistic conceptions. In his essay on "Love," he wrote: "Just as human life is being mingled with knowing, society is economic production mingled with love." It was this alienation of love and community through an alienated system of production that was in fact his guiding concern.[61]

Thompson's defense of Caudwell was complemented by Williams's insistence on a need for a reassessment of Caudwell's contribution to cultural theory. In the "Introduction" to his important *Marxism and Literature* in 1977, the same year as Thompson's essay, Williams insisted on the need to read Caudwell differently, as part of a much wider Marxian tradition, of which the stale official Marxism of the Stalin era that Caudwell rejected was merely a part. Williams did not there, however, disclose his own new appreciation of Caudwell. Two years later, though, Williams addressed the problem of Caudwell again in his *Politics and Letters*, indicating that it was much more useful to read "with him," recognizing the partial breakthroughs he represented, rather than "against him," and that Caudwell's work had reached another level with his various works associated with *Studies*, which transcended *Illusion and Reality*. Williams was most critical of Caudwell's reliance on anthropology and psychology, reaching back to the concept of genotype, which had largely disappeared form Caudwell's writing after *Illusion and Reality*.[62]

In the late 1970s and in the '80s, a number of significant studies dedicated to reclaiming Caudwell as a literary theorist were written in the academy.[63] None of these served to revive Caudwell as a thinker within the broader literature. However, one crucial development was a reemphasis on the deep anthropological origins of art so central to Caudwell's aesthetics. This was to dovetail with the interest in Caudwell as an ecologically oriented theorist, which arose with the publication in 1986 of his *Heredity and Development*. A whole new conception of his work began to emerge, in which his contributions were seen as directed at both an aesthetic materialism and an ecological materialism, providing a long coevolutionary view of the rise of art and science rooted in the changing human metabolism with nature as a whole.

Caudwell declared in a letter to Paul and Elizabeth Beard in November 1935 that his "weakness" hitherto had "been the lack of an integrated *Weltanschauung*," allowing him to link art and science in human development. He by then had found his worldview in historical materialism. But Caudwell was not tied to some rigid orthodoxy. "My approach," he wrote to Elizabeth Beard later that month—contemplating his work on *Studies*, and already achieving some distance from his *Illusion and Reality* as a milestone, but one not without limitation—"will of course be that of historical materialism, but I hope to avoid thrusting the richness of our heritage of knowledge of art into sterile forumulae." Rather, he sought to confront the question: "How can we think of the future without holding it to our own barrenness?"[64]

Historical materialism was for Caudwell a creative form of inquiry allowing him to explore the complex and contradictory developments of culture in contemporary capitalism. As Paul and Elizabeth Beard were to note, Caudwell was fully aware that his thought was "heretical" from the standpoint of the Marxism of his day, which he saw as somewhat "outmoded" and requiring development.[65] Although he adhered to classical historical materialism in its fundamentals, the wider connections related to human consciousness, the dialectic of subject-object, and the relation of art and science, were all approached anew. The final stage of Caudwell's thought, as Paul Beard remarked, was that of "the Marxist who believed he had at last discovered a world-view to which both . . . [science and art] had to be adjusted to become fully intelligible and purposeful. . . . Fundamentally, every way of understanding the world is shown to be a form of art or science. Illusion and reality are the names he gives to these two fields of feeling and knowing, subject and object, which together—polarized yet interpenetrating—symbolize the complete universe."[66]

DIALECTICS OF ART

Even as strong a defender of Caudwell as Thompson, as we have seen, was to decry Caudwell's *Illusion and Reality* as a "bad book." Yet the brilliance and complexity of that frequently misunderstood work have continued to fascinate subsequent thinkers, despite the overall decline that Caudwell's reputation suffered. If *Illusion and Reality* was criticized in the 1950s by thinkers like Cornforth and Bernal for having given in to psychologism, and if it was rejected in the 1970s for having huge inadequacies in its treatment of modern literature, both criticisms can be seen as having largely missed the point of Caudwell's book, resulting from narrower concerns than those that Caudwell exhibited. To regard Caudwell "as a literary critic," Robert Sullivan wrote, "is to look for his weaknesses rather than his strengths."[67]

Trained in the Greek and Latin classics from an early age, Caudwell was inspired primarily by the revolution in the understanding of the classics that emerged in the interwar years. The works of Jane Harrison, Francis Cornford, Gilbert Murray, and the Cambridge ritualists in general sought to reinterpret the classics based on new anthropological and archaeological studies as well as new developments in psychology. It was also in this period that Marxist interpretations of the classics emerged in the work of figures like Benjamin Farrington, Thomson (who was heavily influenced by Caudwell), W. K. C. Guthrie, and Jack Lindsay. A contemporary of Caudwell's and later a leading Marxist classicist, G. M. E. de Ste Croix, whose major writings were to come later, was also a product of the Marxist classicist research of the time. Additionally, this period saw the emergence of social archaeology in the work of the influential Australian Marxist V. Gordon Childe, who resided in London in the 1920s and published *The Dawn of European Civilisation* (1926), which influenced Caudwell.

Decades of scholarship have established, in the words of Henry Stead and Edith Hall, that "Caudwell's fundamental thesis in *Illusion and Reality* is inspired by the argument between Plato and Aristotle on the topic of the relationship between the empirically discernible world (reality) and the worlds conjured up in art (mimesis)."[68] For Plato, the mimesis (imitation, representation) that characterized poetry or imaginative art was harmful, to be banned from the utopia depicted in *The Republic*.[69] In Aristotle's *Poetics*, in contrast, mimetic art played a crucial constructive role in the life of the polis. Caudwell's analysis of the sources of poetry/art in *Illusion and Reality* derives its inner logic from the attempt to unite a historical materialist aesthetics with Aristotle's *Poetics*.[70] "Aristotle's theory of mimesis . . . so far from being superficial," Caudwell writes in *Illusion and Reality*, "is fundamental for an understanding of the function and method of art."[71]

Aristotle had distinguished rhetoric, which was devoted to persuasion, from poetics (including more generally drama and art), which had its basis in mimesis. Yet mimesis was not mere imitation in today's sense, but was directed at activating the emotions, bringing to the fore what was merely potential, and doing so precisely by virtue of the forms of mimesis evoked. "Poetics," in the Aristotelian view, Caudwell wrote, is "a mimesis whose success in imitating reality can be judged by the poignancy of the emotions roused."[72] In this sense, mimesis, for Caudwell, following Aristotle, was be understood as an imaginary *re*-presentation, itself creative, an illusion aimed at emotional affect.

Caudwell's emphasis on Aristotle's theory of mimesis, his conception of the anthropology of art, and his entire aesthetic view were deeply affected by the work of Harrison in her *Art and Ritual.* Indeed, this is so much the case that Caudwell's own aesthetics is most usefully seen as a synthesis of Aristotle and Marx's historical materialism, mediated by the Cambridge ritualists and the anthropological and archaeological (as well as psychological) discoveries of his day.

Jane Ellen Harrison was born in 1850 to a wealthy family and was educated by a series of governesses from whom she learned German, ancient Greek, Latin, and Hebrew, eventually extending her knowledge to sixteen languages. She studied at Cheltenham's Ladies College and then went on to the study of Classics at Newnham College, Cambridge University, where she was to spend most of her professional life. Building on recent archaeological and anthropological discoveries, she pioneered the view that classical mythology and ritual are interlinked, seeing this as the key to unlocking the origins of classical art and literature.

In the early 1880s, a set of private theatricals were set up in conjunction with a King's College Lecture for Ladies. Harrison played the part of Penelope in a production of the "Tale of Troy," dramatizing the *Iliad* and the *Odyssey*. In preparing for the role, she had as her coach the classicist and archaeologist, Charles Waldstein (later Sir Charles Walston), a friend of Karl Marx. Harrison, through her books and lectures, was to emerge as one of the most successful women of her day, helping to inspire figures like Eliot and Woolf. Woolf classified Harrison as one of the pantheon of English women who had contributed to the world of letters, alongside Jane Austen, the Brontës, and George Eliot.[73]

In 1888 both Harrison and Waldstein were considered for the Yates Chair of Classical Archaeology at University College, London, for which both were eminently qualified—Waldstein at this time was a Lecturer in Archaeology at Cambridge; Harrison had already written four major books on the archaeology, mythology, and art of Ancient Greece. Neither was offered the chair, with the extant evidence suggesting that anti-Semitism played strongly against Waldstein, and sexism against Harrison. One of those who opposed Harrison on sexist grounds was Edward Spencer Beesly, Professor of Ancient and Modern History at University College. Beesly was a socialist and had played an instrumental role in the formation of the International Working Men's Association, chairing the meeting in which it was founded.[74]

Harrison's most important works, in which she developed her interpretation of ancient ritual as a medium for the understanding of ancient mythology and art, were written when she was in her fifties and sixties. Her best-known presentation of her ideas was in *Ancient Art and Ritual* (1913), which was to have a strong impact on Caudwell. For Harrison, the conceptualizations of mimesis underlying art in Plato and Aristotle were absolutely crucial. Focusing on ritual, however, she emphasized that mimesis was not mere imitation, but an imagined thing desired, which is either *re*-presented or *pre*-presented, and thus a call to the emotions and tied to future actions. Ancient rituals were designed to promote "the habit of this mimesis of the thing desired," and thus served a practical end. In this sense, "*mimesis*," in line with Aristotle, is "the very source and essence of all art." In ritual, such as the Dionysian festival, "*representation repeated*," helps generate "*abstraction* which helps the transition from ritual to art," explaining, for example, the roots of Greek tragedy. For Harrison, "The origin of art is not *mimesis*, but *mimesis* springs up out of art, out of emotional expression, and constantly and closely neighbours it. Art and ritual are at the outset alike in this, that they do not seek to copy a fact, but to reproduce, to re-enact an emotion." Greek statues, she remarked, in a manner similar to Marx (but unaware of Marx's observation in this respect), were "like the gods of Epicurus, cut loose alike from the affairs of men, and even the ordered ways of Nature," resembling some distant ideal brought out in epic literature, testimony to the powers of imagination.[75]

Harrison's notions of the emotional function of art and mimesis were partly a product of an age in which an emphasis on vitalism, irrationalism, emotion, and the psyche partly displaced the Enlightenment emphasis on reason. Yet the rooting of art in material reality and social relations, via discoveries in archaeology and anthropology, constituted a break with the more idealist character of classical studies before, and to a considerable sense since, so much so that the Cambridge ritualists continue to stand out in the history of classicism. Harrison and the other Cambridge realists saw art as taking a collective-social form. In this sense, the work of the Cambridge ritualists was influenced by the work on the collective consciousness of Durkheim. As Harrison put it, in almost philosophy-of-praxis terms, in art "the life of the imagination, cut off from practical reaction as it is, becomes in turn a motor-force, causing new emotions, and so pervading the general life, and thus ultimately becoming 'practical.'"[76] Caudwell was to draw on all of Harrison's views, along with, more critically, the psychoanalysis of Freud and Carl Jung. For Caudwell, Lindsay, Thomson, and other

Marxian theorists in the 1930s–1950s, "Harrison's neo-Romantic conviction that the origins of art lay in ritual praxis helped prepare . . . a labour theory of culture."[77]

Caudwell's discovery of Marxism in the midst of writing *Illusion and Reality*, however, gave real coherence to his ideas. In Caudwell's conception, Harrison's work, and that of Cornford and Murray, fit with an understanding of art or culture as inextricably connected to production, and in that sense economic. The theory of art as mimetic, emotional, and connected to the inner world could be seen as part of a dialectical unity, only when viewed within the context of production and the human material interaction with nature. For Caudwell, art, via mimesis, was a product of the necessity "to harness man's instincts to the mill of labour, to collect his emotions and direct them into the useful, the economic channel. Just because it is economic [social-productive], *i.e.* non-instinctive, this instinct must be *directed*. The instrument which directs them is therefore economic [productive] in origin."[78]

Caudwell's own term for this process of creative mimesis, emphasizing its imaginative, emotional, and practical characteristics, and its dialectical connection to the human productive interaction with nature-environment, was *phantasy* or *illusion*. But artistic illusion is not in Harrison's or Caudwell's view the same thing as religious illusion, since art has illusion as its emotive object, while the inverted world of religion seeks to translate illusion in the form of myth into actuality.[79] In line with historical materialism, Caudwell argued that with the division of labor and class, art became increasingly alienated from work, undermining its creative-productive role, and creating new forms more related to ideology. Yet the evolutionary social origins of art were not, in Caudwell's view, superstructural, but rather related to essential human needs and production relations directly, and his general analysis thus had an emphasis quite distinct from the dominant Marxian orthodoxy of the time, more closely related to the earlier views of Morris. "Art," Caudwell wrote in a manner akin to Morris, "ultimately is completely separated from work" in capitalist class society, "with disastrous results to both."[80]

Caudwell's whole materialist and dialectical approach, his focus on human freedom, and his emphasis on how human relations with the world of nature (of which humanity was a part) were mediated by production and language, pushed his analysis beyond that of Harrison, which had placed so much emphasis on the social role of emotion in the formation of the inner world of art. The dialectic of subject and object, however, required for Caudwell some way of conceptualizing the subject in bodily terms, both physiological and psychological—if necessarily abstract—in order to understand how that struggle of human subject was in permanent contradiction with an alienated class society, in the struggle for freedom as necessity. For this reason. Caudwell, rather than adopting a strict biological view, introduced the genotype as a stand-in for all that was not merely social and cultural, and in that sense the prehuman aspects of the individual. In his original manuscript, *Verse and Mathematics*, Caudwell had been careful to indicate that "the genotype is a pure abstraction . . . one of [Hans] Vaihinger's 'as-ifs.'" As Sullivan says, "The genotype and the instincts are, in Caudwell's system, something like Kant's 'thing-in-itself,' unknowable, but a necessary postulation, a necessary thesis in contradistinction to the antithesis of the social environment."[81] Caudwell's concept of the genotype was a kind of useful fiction that stood for the whole question of the body, or corporeal existence, and of innate, inherited characteristics, instincts, and emotions, underlying human subjectivity. The genotype, while interwoven with and inseparable from the social, nonetheless contained elements that were not explainable simply in terms of the social. In later works, he was to refer more simply to the body in this respect.

If there was an essentialism here, it was the essentialism of freedom as necessity, a kind of summation of human drives in relation to the environment. It was here that Caudwell referred abstractly to "inner energy" and the realm of desire and the possible, which together served to constitute the human subject through society but also antecedent to all known society, related at most to its more "primitive" communal forms. Although Caudwell studied the psychological theories of his time, besides Freud and Jung, Jean Piaget and Ivan Pavlov, he opted in the end not for specific psychological postulates, but for an abstract concept of the genotype, as an unknowable thing-in-itself that allowed one to recognize, without being able to explain, the continuing role of innate instincts or genetic predispositions at some level in the determination of the subject.[82] The genotype stood abstractly for the fact that human beings are a complex product of prehistory and history or the long coevolution of hominins with the environment, stretching all the way back to the prehuman. The evolution of the genotype was most visible in the social origins of art, which drew upon this inner necessity and inner energy, manifesting a realm of desire and possibility that was not strictly historical, and certainly could not be explained in terms of mechanical materialism, and was only to be viewed in terms of historical effects in the human relation to the environment, the dialectic of subject and object.

The concept of the genotype was thus a kind of conceptual marker for Caudwell, a necessary abstraction (or as-if) in constituting an idea of the human subject, but representing at the same time his rejection of Freud's theory of instincts, or any of the dominant psychological theories of his time, all of which no doubt appeared to him as too reductionist, not allowing sufficiently for human coevolution with the environment. He seems to have been influenced, in this respect, by K. N. Kornilov's "Psychology in the Light of Dialectical Materialism," which rejected both Freudian psychology and the mechanical materialist views of physiological reflexology. Kornilov insisted on the imaginative faculty of the human mind; he followed Marx and Engels in arguing: "*My* relationship to *my* environment—this is *my* consciousness." Caudwell would have agreed with Kornilov that instincts or drives were transient forms, with material development "organically wedging them into the formation of habits of man." For Marx and Engels in *The German Ideology*, as Caudwell seems to have been aware, consciousness was a historical product, while instinctual drives had preceded consciousness. These drives were not simply displaced, they had rather increasingly become *conscious drives* resulting from the social relations of human beings to one another and their environment. The question of the innate, pre-conscious inheritances of human evolution thus remained, mediated by historical-cultural developments.[83]

For Caudwell, the genotype, in its current form in society, therefore stands for the whole complex anthropological development of human beings in their concrete bodily forms, but also as transformed by the social ego in the context of the struggle with and through the environment. Art is only one part of this, the other is science. At the center of the unity of opposites that constitutes human corporeal development is the mind-body of the historical actor. It is the alienated character of class society, with what Caudwell called its alienated "cultural capital," that splits the world apart and creates the "mock world," where science is connected to the "external reality" and art to the "social ego." In truth, art and science are inherently connected, and this splitting them apart is a sundering of the human being, which reaches its apex in bourgeois society.[84] Art is necessary to science, just as science is to art. "Science and art," Caudwell writes, "are like the two halves produced by cutting the original human hermaphrodite in half, according to the story of Aristophanes in Plato's *Symposium*, so that each half evermore seeks its counterpart. But science and art do not when fitted together make a complete concrete world: they make a complete hollow world—an abstract world only made solid and living by the inclusion of the concrete living of concrete men, from which they are generated."[85]

Humanity's struggle with nature, that is, the increasingly complex interpenetration of human society with the natural conditions of its existence, that generated both art and science as the two principal organized forms of human consciousness. Both were indispensable to the two primary forms of mediation between human beings and nature—labor and language. "Art is the science of feeling, science the art of knowing. We must know to be able to do, but we must feel to know what to do. . . . The value of poetry's illusions in securing catharsis, as compared to religion's, is that they are known for illusion, and as compared to dream, that they are social." Poetry and art can therefore be seen as a kind of social "dream-work."[86]

"Art," for Caudwell, "is born in struggle, because there is in society a conflict between phantasy and reality. It is not a neurotic conflict because it is a social problem and is solved by the artist for society."[87] Thus "the primitive who would lose interest in the exhausting labour necessary to plough an arid abstract collection of soil, will find heart when the earth is charged with the affective colouring of 'Mother Nature,' for now, by the magic of poetry, it glows with the appetitive tints of sexuality or filial love."[88] The very existence of a "genotype," in Caudwell's conception, which stood for the human body and its reservoir of hidden emotive needs, potentials, and drives, which were subject to historical development, guaranteed an unending conflict with class-property relations that went against such emotions, needs, and potentials. In these circumstances, art was able to play a truly revolutionary role in history through the creation of whole new social structures of feeling, to be realized in a society of associated producers.

In Caudwell's materialist aesthetic, mechanical materialism, which rejected the realms of imagination and emotion, needed to be replaced by a broader, richer conception; one that Marx and Engels had aspired to when they referred in *The Holy Family* to an earlier materialism in which "matter, surrounded by a sensuous poetic glamour, seems to attract man's whole entity by winning smiles."[89]

Caudwell's aesthetics were carried forward in the later essays that constituted his *Studies* series. There the analysis was more developed and elegant. Yet the short-essay format of *Studies* (and *Further Studies*) aimed at wider audiences lacked the more integrated, systematic approach displayed in *Illusion and Reality*. Nor were the anthropological-historical roots of his analysis, particularly as pertaining to the classical era of Greece and Rome, as apparent. For these and other reasons, *Illusion and Reality* remains crucial to understanding Caudwell's aesthetics as a whole.

In "D. H. Lawrence: A Study of the Bourgeois Artist," Caudwell once again emphasized the mimetic nature of art, its form as illusion, and that it necessarily contained "a measure of reality." Art was a mimetic "social representation." Indeed, "It is the property of art that it makes mimic pictures of reality which we accept as illusory. We do not suppose the events of a novel really happen, that a landscape shown in a painting can be walked upon—yet it has a measure of reality. The mimic representation, by the technique appropriate to the art in question, causes the social representation to sweat out of its pores an affective emanation. The emanation is *in* us, *in* our affective reaction with the elements of representation. Given in the representation are not only the affects, but, simultaneously, their organisation in an affective *attitude* towards the piece of reality symbolised in the mimicry."[90]

The nature of the aesthetic mediation is most fully explained in Caudwell's essay on "Beauty," in which he sought to give concrete meaning to John Keats's famous lines, so important to the Romantic movement:

Beauty is truth, truth beauty—that is all
Ye know on earth, and all ye need to know.

The conception of beauty and the whole realm of the aesthetic, Caudwell argued, could only be understood "if in addition to naked subject and naked environment, we had a third mediating term" to account for changing relations.[91] That third term was social production, or the labor process, which entailed affective forms as well as practical action. This labor process, in this sense, is to be seen as cultural in its inception:

> From the very start the labour process gives rise to material capital. Simple enough at first, taking the form of mere tools, customs, magico-scientific objects, seeds, huts, these were yet all-important at the beginnings of culture. ... Once established the labour process, extending as remotely as observation of the stars, as widely as organization of all human relations, and as abstractly as the invention of numbers, gathers and accumulates truth. ... Truth is the past relation of society to the environment accumulated in ages of experience. It is actually created by the conflict of social organisms with new situations in the course of the labour process. ... Truth, then, is in my environment, that is, in my culture, in the enduring products of the labour process. ... But I do not regard myself as bound to the social criteria of truth; on the contrary it is my task to change their formulations, where my experience contradicts them.[92]

In Caudwell's conception, both science and art, like social consciousness, are products of the active interrelationship of the human being and the physical environment, enacted through the labor and production process. Here he used the concept of "the body" to refer to the physical subject in this dialectic, replacing his earlier notion of the genotype.[93] Both art and science as elements of social cognition partake of truth, one the felt truth of the subject, the other reasoned truths with respect to objects, but neither is usefully separated from the other (and indeed mathematics is a bridge between the inner and the outer). "Just as the scientist is the explorer of new realms of outer reality, the artist continually discovers new kingdoms of the heart." Beauty, for Caudwell, is the product of the social organization of things within the affective domain. "It arises from the labour process, because there must not only be agreement about the nature of outer reality, but also agreement about the nature of desire." For Caudwell, "the artist takes bits of reality, socially known, to which affective associations adhere, and creates a mock world, which calls into being a new affective attitude, a new emotional experience. New beauty is thus born as the result of his social labour."[94]

Presenting a historical-materialist conception of art and culture that seems to have been inspired by Morris, whose *Hopes and Fears for Art* he knew well, Caudwell refused to see art or beauty as something removed (except in the context of alienation) from the labor process, and from all forms of labor. "Our own proposition about beauty is this: whenever the affective elements in socially known things show social ordering, there we have beauty, there alone we have beauty. The business of such ordering is art, and this applies to all socially known things, to houses, gestures, narratives, descriptions, lessons, songs and labour."[95] It is no wonder that Williams in *Marxism and Literature*, where he systematically reordered the Marxian theory of culture, rejecting a primarily base-superstructure approach in favor of one that saw cultural production as material, prefaced his book by noting, as if in a debt unfulfilled, that he had learned to "read even the English Marxists of the thirties differently, and especially Christopher Caudwell." Caudwell, if taken seriously, had opened Marxism to wholly different forms of inquiry, playing into Williams's own later cultural materialism—and that of others like Lindsay.[96]

The notion of beauty as the result of the labor process, that is, the metabolism between human beings and nature, however, appears to make beauty simply artificial, separating it from nature. This causes Caudwell to write, "But if art workers were artificial, and beauty is a social product, how do we find beauty in the natural thing, in seas, skies, a mountain, and daffodils?" His answer is:

> Society itself is a part of nature, and hence all artificial products are natural. But nature itself, as seen, is a product of society. The primitive does not see seas, but the river Oceanus; he does not see mammals, but edible beasts. He does not see, in the night sky, blazing worlds in the limitless void, but a roof inlaid with patines of bright gold. Hence all natural things are artificial. Does that mean that we can make no distinction between nature and art? On the contrary, we can clearly distinguish two opposites, although we must recognize their interpenetration. . . .
>
> We may oppose the art-work just made to the enduring mountain as an artificial to a natural beauty, but the difference is one of degree. In both cases beauty emerges as a quality due to a man, in the course of social process, gazing at a piece of his environment. The ancient town, with weathered walls, full of history and character, is a part of nature, and is yet a completely artificial product; the sun lights it and the wind weathers it. There is no dichotomy between nature and art, only the difference between pioneers and settled inhabitants.[97]

The distortion and alienation of the labor process, the fetishism of commodities in the interest of capital accumulation, and the distorted mediation between the human subject (body) and the environment, thus combine to create the alienation of art and the alienation of science. The everyday alienated art of bourgeois society is indifferent to affective form (except insofar as it serves the cash nexus), and hence the production of "the unbeautiful." In contrast, the highest form of art takes the form of the completely imaginary, no longer connected to active life, but providing an alternative escapist world of the aesthetic as personal distraction devoid of truth. "The bourgeois floods the world with art projects of a baseness hitherto unimaginable. Then, reacting against such an evident degradation of the artist's task, art withdraws from the market and becomes non-social, that is, *personal*. It becomes 'highbrow' art, culminating in personal fantasy. The art work ends as a fetish because it was a commodity. Both are equally signs of the decay of bourgeois civilisation due to the contradictions in its foundation. . . . Money becomes the god of society. Thus the complete disintegration of a culture on the affective side is achieved."[98]

These contradictions, however, create their social antagonists. In *Illusion and Reality* Caudwell praised the aesthetic movement in England in the late nineteenth century, led by the Pre-Raphaelites, including "Morris before he became a socialist," as revealing the aesthetic contradictions of capitalist society, engendering a revolt which took the form of the struggle for "art for art's sake." This eventually spurred all sorts of revolutionary movements among artists, evident in the 1930s. The contradiction between art and society, however, could only be resolved by the reconstitution of society at large, so that labor was no longer alienated art, and art was no longer alienated labor. Concluding his essay on "Beauty," Caudwell wrote, in a manner reminiscent of Morris: "In a society which is based on co-operation, not on compulsion . . . beauty will then return again, to enter consciously into every part of the social process. It is not a dream that labour will no longer be ugly, and the products of labour once again beautiful."[99]

DIALECTICS OF SCIENCE

For Caudwell, the dialectical reconstruction of science was as essential to the critique of capitalist society as the dialectical reconstruction of art. Both had been severed within contemporary culture from their ultimate ground in the labor process, that is, from the social-metabolic relation between human beings and their environment. The analysis of these contradictions as they played out in the present as history was to lead him in the direction of a broad ecological metaphysic.

Caudwell's best-known work on science is *The Crisis in Physics*, which grew out of his *Studies* manuscripts and developed into a full-sized book in its own right, the second half of which only existed in a rough, incomplete draft. The *Crisis in Physics* was directed at the disarticulation of philosophical-conceptual basis of physics due to the displacement of Newtonian physics in the early decades of the century, and the successive impacts of relativity theory, quantum mechanics, and Heisenberg's Uncertainty Principle. The paradigm shifts represented by these new scientific conceptions had given rise, in the work of figures like James Jeans and Arthur Eddington, to indeterminateness and idealism supplementing a more basic mechanism, along with various forms of positivism. This was widely viewed as constituting a crisis, related to the general crisis of the economy and culture that characterized the 1930s.

The Crisis in Physics was thus primarily about how a subtler, and at the same time more complex dialectical view allowed a transcendence of the ontological and epistemological problems plaguing bourgeois science. It was a dialectical and materialist perspective centered in the human metabolism with nature, and relying on such conceptions as relation, contradiction, qualitative change, emergence, and unity of opposites, which offered the essential solution to this crisis; a solution, however, that could only fully manifest in the new society of the associated producers. In the process of developing this view, Caudwell referred to the entire philosophical history of physics from the Enlightenment on, beginning with such early modern figures as Isaac Newton and Gottfried Wilhelm Leibniz. He argued that the mechanistic materialism of Newton and the idealist teleology of Leibniz simply reinforced each other forming the overall bourgeois outlook. The dominant mechanism had stripped nature of all qualities and conceived nature as passive and essentially timeless—an outlook that was breeched but not fundamentally altered with the introduction of evolutionary theory.

Caudwell focused considerable attention on Leibniz's notion that the universe consisted of extensionless, figureless, and "windowless" *monads* (a term based on the Greek word *Monas* meaning unity or that which is one). Monads were simple substances without parts, analogous to souls, mirroring a predetermined totality constituted by God. They represented Leibniz's teleological answer to the atoms of the ancient materialists like Epicurus and Lucretius, and to that of most seventeenth-century materialist science. In Leibniz's *Monadology* the weaknesses of the reigning mechanism, with its exclusively external relations, reductionism, and dualism were highlighted, but only by wedding seventeenth-century concepts of substance to the most illusory forms of idealism that were based on notions of harmonious final causes in a perfect universe consecrated by God.[100]

In Caudwell's words: "How impossible it is for bourgeois man to escape at that period [the seventeenth century] from this [rigid, deterministic] conception of objectivity is shown by the contemporary conception of Leibniz, superficially different from Newtonianism but in fact the same in essence. The self-moving particles are monads. The regulating principle of the market is the God to which all the monads open their windows."[101] Leibniz's monads were thus soul-like, reflecting nothing so much as God:

> Leibniz, in spite of his idealist approach, equally bases his system on absolute determinism. Although his monads are windowless, they appear to act and react on each other according to causal laws, because all has been arranged by God beforehand according to a pre-established harmony. This harmony is therefore an overriding necessity; it is absolute determinism. It is true that Leibniz attempts to introduce "pure possibles" and a distinction between hypothetical necessity and absolute necessity. . . . At each stage the monad has before it various "pure possibles" in the form of a choice of acts, of which it chooses one. Thus it is free. God however foresaw that it would choose this "pure possible" and therefore there is a pre-established harmony.[102]

These same dilemmas, in terms of a mechanistic and deterministic worldview, of which idealism itself was a part, were reflected in the metaphysical system of René Descartes, with its mechanism and dualism, and that of Baruch Spinoza, with its "resolute monism."[103] Immanuel Kant's critical idealism with his concept of the "thing in itself" did not reject determinism but set limits to it by establishing the importance of *a priori* knowledge. Kant, however, in Caudwell's view, was supplanted by George Wilhelm Friedrich Hegel, who gave centrality to dialectics:

> It remained for Hegel to point out the non-existence of the unknowable and delete the thing in itself. This did not however lead to positivism, for he substituted for the necessity of objective reality or mechanism the necessity of subjective reality, or logic. Phenomena unfolded themselves with the determinism of logic. But in doing so, the mind dissolved into Ideas which began to lead an existence independent of the subject. They were absolute ideas and unfolded themselves according to their own necessity. They had therefore become objective reality, and Logic had become equivalent to the God of Malebranche, the substance of Spinoza, the spirit of Newton and the matter of Diderot. There were two important differences. These Ideas, just because they had sprung from the loins of the human subject, changed—they unfolded themselves. Cartesian and Newtonian objective reality, being grounded on God, had always been eternal and changeless. Thus objectivity for the first time had been given the quality of self-evolution and change, because of its former history attached to the subject. It had become dialectic—or, as Malebranche would put it—pagan. It had returned to the live matter of Epicurus, but containing within itself all the subjective complexity developed in the interim.[104]

Hegelian dialectics grasped "the emerging of the unlike, the birth of quality, the movement of evolution, the passing of history, the process of real Time."[105] It was thus the dialectical opposite of mechanism. But the difficulty of this supreme idealist dialectic in Hegel was, though it recognized change, a closed speculative universe of pure logic; hence it could no longer incorporate change as experienced by the concrete subject. "It could not drag into itself any fresh knowledge from outside (as man does by practice on objects) because there was no 'outside.' Hence Hegelianism could not be a physicist's creed, for it denied the need for physics. It could only be a speculator's creed."[106]

In developing these views, Caudwell returned again and again to Epicurus (and Lucretius). In his notebooks, he translated extracts from the ancient materialists, including Diogenes Laertius on Epicurus's death, and Lucretius's Epicurean account of time.[107] Like Marx, Caudwell placed key importance on Epicurus's notion that time was not an absolute category in and of itself, but rather represented qualitative change, as exhibited particularly in the human bodily relation to the world. He pointedly quoted the Epicurean axiom "Time . . . exists, not by itself but simply from the things that happen." Caudwell wrote: "As long ago as Lucretius, philosophers have advanced theories as to the relativity of motion and the secondary and dependent character of abstract Time," but they did so metaphysically without all the advances of modern science.[108]

For Epicurus, Marx observed, time is "the abstract form of sensation," of experience and change, in relation to the material world. "Human sensuousness is therefore embodied time, the existing reflection of the sensuous world in itself." Thus, time becomes "*the absolute form of appearance*. . . . Epicurus was the first to grasp appearance as appearance, that is, as alienation of the essence, activating itself in its reality as such an alienation." What time represented abstractly was change itself, the activation of irreversible qualitative differences experienced through the bodily senses. This constituted the real essence: the coming to be and the passing away: "death the immortal."[109]

In a similar fashion, Caudwell, following Epicurus, argued, "These [transitory] qualities do not come into being in time. Time does not flow on while they emerge. The emergence of such qualities is what time is. Time is then an aspect of, or abstraction from, change. . . . Time is not something in which things change, but the change itself," experienced in bodily form, through the senses, in interaction with the world.[110] It was this materialist conception, via Epicurus, that led Caudwell to his wider conception of the dialectics of historical materialism, in a manner that was to replicate aspects of Marx's early development and his struggle with the Hegelian system.[111] Here it is significant that Caudwell, like Marx, saw Epicurus (as rendered by Lucretius) as the leading ancient philosopher of the Hellenistic period, following Plato and Aristotle.[112]

Central to Caudwell's *Crisis in Physics* was the rejection of the predeterminism and "strict determinism" that characterized mainstream mechanistic science, along with the rejection of indeterminism. Instead, he defended determinism in terms of causality, but seeing this as related to open systems and emergent form, going against the "closed world" of bourgeois physics.[113] As the contemporary classicist A. A. Long has noted, Epicurean materialism introduced the idea that "life and mind are not basic to the world, but emergent properties of particular types of atomic conglomerates."[114]

With his deep knowledge of Epicurean philosophy, Caudwell readily grasped the materialist approach to emergence, developed in J. H. Woodger's *Biological Principles*, which he studied, together with Joseph Needham's *The Sceptical Biologist*. In Caudwell's materialist and dialectical concept of emergence, any two terms, representing the identity of opposites, both repulse and attract each other in the relation, constituting the real realm of material interaction and creating the "synthetic quality that 'emerges'"—the unity of opposites. He strongly opposed, while recognizing the value of, the idealist theories of emergence associated with Samuel Alexander, C. Lloyd Morgan, and Henri Bergson, arguing that they saw the qualitative leaps as arbitrarily imposed and thus having a "Jack-in-the-box appearance" rather than arising out of genuine material development.[115] The "critical realist" approach to emergence, extending back to Epicurus, introduced into the modern discussion by Roy Sellars, and further developed by figures like Woodger and Needham, offered, in Caudwell's terms, a materialist and dialectical approach to life and to the existence of different levels within reality, emanating from the evolutionary process itself.

In the bourgeois outlook, Caudwell believed, the world was inherently deterministic and mechanistic, insofar as it was materialist, and disembodied and teleological insofar as it was idealist. Mechanistic materialism and idealism reinforced each other. All of this had to do with the denial of the social and the attempt to root reality entirely in the individual. Since human society could only control its relation to nature through social action, and this was denied to each individual, a world conceived in atomistic terms was necessary, strictly determined, and freedom was conceived as merely the denial of determinism, including the denial of the social. Alienation, in the bourgeois view, then became freedom. The characteristics of the dominant approach to the philosophy of nature and modern physics all carried these characteristics based in a reified society of possessive individualism. Only a society of associated producers, *acting socially* in all of its relations, could conceive that freedom was, as Engels had said, the consciousness of necessity. Such a conception allowed for the successive emergence of new qualitative forms of the human interaction with nature, and the changing consciousness of these relations, which were themselves the result of the historical process, of the active metabolism of socialized humanity and nature.[116]

In Caudwell's words, "The new organization, once it emerges as the *conscious* (that is, controlled) organization of society, generates a new view of the world as a whole, as the integration of all the rich parts uncovered by the separate descriptions. This emergence represents the uncovering of a whole new body of knowledge about Nature—Nature in its interconnectence—Nature as dialectic. . . . The crisis of physics is solved by the emergence of a new worldview, as the condition of the shattering of the old."[117]

It was, however, in *Heredity and Development: A Study of Bourgeois Biology*, rather than his more famous *Crisis in Physics*, where Caudwell's dialectical approach to science was most fully developed. *Heredity and Development* was a little more than forty pages in length in print, and had a somewhat unfinished quality, perhaps lacking a conclusion. A product of the Studies series, it had evolved like *The Crisis in Physics* and *Romance and Realism* into a monograph (in this case, a short one). Caudwell's plan was no doubt to extend it and publish it as a short book. When literary theorists Duparc and Margolies finally published it in 1986 (around a half-century after Caudwell's death) in the edited collection *Scenes and Actions: Unpublished Manuscripts*, it was myopically treated as a minor and faulty manuscript, though in reality it represented an extraordinary achievement for its time.[118] As evolutionary biologist Rob Wallace, author of *Big Farms Make Big Flu*, wrote, it is "as perspicacious a meditation on biology as I have read," one that prefigured many of the conceptual breakthroughs in dialectical biology associated with figures such as Richard Levins, Richard Lewontin, and Stephen Jay Gould.[119]

The explanation given by Edgell Rickword, the editor of *Further Studies*, as to why *Heredity and Development* was not included in that volume was that it was "quite long." But the real reason, as Helena Sheehan indicates, was that the publication of *Further Studies* occurred during the "high tide of Lysenkoism in the world communist movement in 1948–1949."[120] Hence, Caudwell's heretical approach, which constituted a repudiation of Lysenkoist (and certainly Lamarckian) views, went against the official Communist Party ideology. In reality, Caudwell's analysis transcended the whole debate by offering a dialectical alternative to the simplistic controversies between neo-Darwinianism and neo-Larmarckianism (and Lysenkoism).

The central theme of Caudwell's *Heredity and Development* was that the dualisms that continually tore at bourgeois biology, and that seemingly forced it to choose between environment and organism, evolution and genetics, mechanism and vitalism, and innate and acquired characteristics, were the products of the alienation that characterized bourgeois thought itself. Applying a dialectical view to these questions, and exploring the mediations and qualitative transformations, Caudwell again and again pointed to a broader ecological and evolutionary view and dynamic systems perspective. There was in this work no mention of the concept of "genotype" that has played such a fundamental role (as a stand-in for biological inheritances of the human species) in *Illusion and Reality*. Rather, Caudwell focused on the more dialectical relations between environment, gene (or genetic predispositions), and organism.

Caudwell's approach was evolutionary and broadly Darwinian. "Darwinism as found in Darwin's writings," he stated, "is still fresh from the contact with the multitude of biological facts then being discovered. It does not as yet pose organism aridly against environment, but the web of life is still seen fluidly interpenetrating with the rest of reality. . . . The extraordinary richness of the pageant of change, history and conflict in life which Darwin unfolds, gives an insurgent revolutionary power to his writings and those of such immediate followers as Huxley. Biology is still unified."[121]

Nevertheless, Caudwell was critical of Darwin's natural selection. He argued that the problem with Darwinian natural selection was "not that it explains too little, but that it explains too much." What was needed was an understanding of the complex relations and mediations between organism and environment rather than the abstract concept of "fitness." Viewing things ecologically, or in terms of developmental systems theory, he declared: "It is not possible to separate organism from environment as mutually distant opposites. Life is the relation between opposed poles which have separated themselves out of reality, but remain in relation throughout the web of becoming. This relation is mutually determining. It is a relation of antagonism, but just because it is a relation, the poles remain a unity."[122] He continues:

> The laws of the environment, in so far as they constrain the operations of life, are not given in the environment, but given in the relation between environment and life. The laws of the human environment are therefore different from those of the amoebic environment. There is no universal "law of supply and demand" ruling nature. Hence we can never postulate as primary a system of external laws governing the interaction between environment and organism, for any such laws emerge from the relation between the two, and this is a developing relation.[123]

In Caudwell's conception, the treatment of the environment—what he called the whole question of "ecology,' as "solely inimical" to the organism—as in crude versions of Darwinism, was a gross misconception. Like Engels in *Anti-Dühring*, he emphasized that both competition and cooperation belonged to nature.[124] Within the environment of one species lived other species, all of which were mutually dependent, forming a system of environmental interaction: "the emergence, as discontinuities, of new material qualities," reflecting the developing relations of organism and environment. Hence, "The environment, by interaction with the incipient organism, produces in history a multiplication and elaboration of life. Its effect on life is therefore such as to increase its domain and complexity. How can it be conceived as solely inimical?"[125]

Most remarkable was his anticipation of the broad contours of Lewontin's argument in *The Triple Helix*, arguing that gene, organism, and environment always had to be seen in their interrelationships, that none could be seen in isolation or as inherently dominant, and that all one-way cause-and-effect relationships had to be abandoned. In Caudwell's version of the triple helix: "The gene is discontinuous. We can locate and separate genes. But its expression is continuous. The genes can only be expressed as an interpenetrating relation between the whole organism and the whole environment."[126]

In this way, as Wallace argues,

> Caudwell sketches out many of the core themes and precepts of modern dialectical biology. It is quite a shock to see so boldly analyzed, eighty years ago, such staples as the idea of the gene as a Platonic abstraction, the alienation of gene and environment, causal interpenetration, the preformationist trap, norms of reaction, genetic canalization, niche construction, a refutation of Lysenko from the left, and, as [E. P.] Thompson noted, the myopia of the bourgeois scientist. All of this is a full fifty years before Richard Levins and Richard Lewontin's *The Dialectical Biologist*, which developed many of the same ideas.[127]

Ecology, viewed in relation to society and economy, stands for the whole domain of the interpenetration of humans (or organisms) and their environment—"the interaction of men and the environment *together*."[128] "Human body, mind, and human environment," Caudwell observed, "cannot exist separately, they are all parts of the one set."[129] His dialectical biology thus gravitated toward evolutionary ecology. In the young Caudwell's analysis (and there was no older Caudwell), there is no sign of a generalized ecological concern in the sense of a critique of the concept of progress—which, however, he seldom referred to except in terms of the broad trope of the conquest of nature, standing for the advance of science and production. Nor is there any concrete discussion of environmental waste or destruction. Yet, his thought was thoroughly anti-mechanist (despite his fascination with technology in relation to automobiles and aircraft) and pointed toward a wider ecological ontology. The environment, he argued, was always changing partly as a result of human activity; for example, through anthropogenic "forest denudation." The human relation to the natural environment is one of constant change and mutual interaction, in which human beings play an active role by transforming their environment and their relation to nature through production. History constitutes in its most general terms the creation of new ecological syntheses between human beings and nature. This takes the form of the "'humanisation' of nature" and "'naturalisation' of humanity." The environment consequently is never the same. Such transformations in the relation between human beings and their natural (and social) environment do not occur on an individual basis but are the product of societal production.[130]

Yet, in class society, and particularly capitalist class society, control of human production and of the human relation to the natural and social conditions of production underlies the entire system of exploitation, which comes to serve the interests of capital rather than society as a whole. Hence, the human-social relation to nature and to society as a whole is alienated. The "owner and master of social capital" stands in a "dominating relation to 'Nature,' his environment," and to all of humanity. For the first time in history, bourgeois culture produces a "science of the environment of nature," but it is an estranged science, put in service of the "manipulation of nature" for purely exploitative ends aimed at the domination of the rest of humanity.[131]

In Caudwell's romantic communist view, "Social relations must be changed so that love returns to the earth."[132] Economic production, "in its primary individual form of metabolism, necessarily appears before love, for it is the essence of life. . . . But because metabolism in the very dawn of life's history precedes the relation of love, it does not follow that love is a chance iridescence on life's surface." Rather, "We love with our bodies and we eat and labour with our bodies, and deep love between two persons is generally distinguished from more transient forms of it by this test, that the two want to live together and thereafter function as one economic unit of society."[133] Love is thus connected to the subject-object relation of organism to environment, humanity to ecology, human being to human being, lovers to each other. For Caudwell, love is a mediation in the creative process, linked to production in its broadest sense, encompassing all of our material and affective relations, our connections to the earth and to the stars, our knowledge of ourselves and what is outside ourselves. Love thus stood for the unity in difference at its highest level.[134] The deepest fissures in bourgeois society are apparent in the breakdown (or as Morris would have said, sundering) of the institutions of love, that is, of our human-metabolic relations in their most earthly, passionate, and at the same time most socially developed, forms. In present-day circumstances, Caudwell, wrote,

> love could prepare an appalling indictment of the wrongs and privations that bourgeois social relations have inflicted upon it. . . . It is as if love and economic relations have gathered at two opposite poles. All the unused tenderness of man's instincts gather at one pole and at the other are economic relations, reduced to bare coercive right to commodities. This polar segregation is the source of a terrific tension, and will give rise to a vast transformation of bourgeois society. They [love and production] must, in a revolutionary destruction

and construction, return in on each other and fuse in a new synthesis. This is communism.[135]

Caudwell saw the human metabolism with nature in its most complete manifestation as "economic production mingled with love," since it had its roots in associated labor.[136]The alienation of humanity and the earth, the estrangement of human beings from each other via class, and the commodification of art and science all propelled the world in a revolutionary direction, toward the reunification of humanity on a higher level. Writing in his notebook, Caudwell penned the formula: "Class = the night of the thing-in-itself."[137] His outlook was both dialectical and ecological, Marxist and Romantic, as manifested in his call for a synthesis of art and science, of human sense and sensibility.

At the core of Caudwell's analysis of the world was dialectics. "Thought," he declared, "is naturally dialectical."[138] The usual way of thinking about dialectics focused too much on the terms, subject and object, mind and matter, humanity and environment, and not the *relation* itself. Human beings were a part of nature as a lived relation; dialectics was the metabolizing in thought of this lived relation. "The external world," he wrote, "does not impose dialectic on thought, nor does thought impose it on the external world. The relation between subject and object, ego and Universe, is itself dialectic. Man, when he attempts to think metaphysically, merely contradicts himself, and meanwhile continues to live and experience reality *dialectically*."[139]

It was the lived, material relation of human beings, in which freedom was an outcome of the continual struggle with necessity, requiring the constant transformation of the human relation to the world and of human-social relations themselves, that gave rise to dialectic as a mode of thought expressing this complex material relation. "A relation to a thing," Caudwell wrote, "is a mutually determining relation, whether it be a relation of knowing or fabricating. In learning about or acting upon outer reality, man is himself altered, and this forms the basis for new action."[140] For Marx, Caudwell contended, "the active subject-object relation was nothing but man's living in nature."[141] Our knowledge of change in the universe arises from our own interactions with the world. These, though, can be distorted through the cleavage in our social relations that arises with class society. With the development of class, "theory and practice were sundered in consciousness because they were divided in social reality." The dialectical unification of consciousness and of reality could only be achieved together through revolutionary praxis.[142]

Although materialism was the key to dialectics, Caudwell's approach was at odds with any approach that discounted the role of consciousness and *a priori* knowledge. His critical apprehension of the world was that of a dialectical-critical realism.[143] "Nature," he wrote, "is prior to mind and this is the vital sense for science. . . . Nature therefore produced mind. But the nature which produced mind was not nature 'as seen by us,' for this is importing into it the late subject-object relationship called 'mind.' It is nature as known by us, that is, as having indirect not direct relations with us. It is nature in determining relation with, but not part of, our contemporary universe. Yet, by sublation, this nature that produced mind is contained in the universe of which the mind relation is now a feature; and that is why it is known to us."[144]

Caudwell was extremely critical of attempts to replicate within dialectical materialism "the closed world" of bourgeois consciousness. Rather the world, and the universe, needed to be seen as open, and thus not a circle (Hegel's good infinity). It was also necessary to reject thought as a mere "mirroring" of reality and thus so-called reflection theory in this crude sense. Attempts to overcome the inherent difficulties of the classical materialist dialectics of Marx, Engels, and Lenin, which had entailed a view of the universe as open, by simply "dissolving it into the [pre-Marxian outlooks of] Hegelianism or mechanical materialism," were bound to fail.[145] This pointed to the limits of the dialectical perspective itself. Taking a strong stand on such limits, Caudwell declared: "Dialectics is not therefore—as the Scholastics imagined formal logic to be—a machine for extracting the nature of reality from thought. It is the denial of the possibility of the existence of such a machine. It is a recognition of mutually determining relations between knowing and being. It is a creed of action, a constant goad forcing the thinker into reality. Thought is knowing; the experience is being, and at each new step new experience negates old thought. Yet their tension causes an advance to a new hypothesis more inclusive than the old."[146] Bending Descartes's "I think therefore I am" in a more materialist and dialectical direction, Caudwell concluded: "I live, therefore I think I am."[147] For Caudwell, like Marx, it is only when theory detaches itself from the abstractly concrete and becomes practice that theory becomes truly revolutionary.

All of this was related to what could be called Caudwell's broader, ecological dialectic. "The real factors in history," he argued, "are *environmentalised* men and *humanised* environment. [But] what is meant by environmentalised men? How can a human being be said to be conditioned by the environment?" Whereas the "organic adaptions" of the otter or the whale to their environments, Caudwell contended, are primarily individual (although he would surely have modified this had he known more about the social actions of these and other creatures), with human beings the adaptation is always social, as organized social production mediates between humanity and its natural surroundings. "The otter is adapted to the water through his innate corporeal transformations. Man is still better adapted to the water, but only through society, because society has built ships, created ports, developed navigation, and so can master the water."[148]

For Caudwell, "History is the study of the object-subject relation of men-nature, and not of either separately. It is the study of the products of men acting on nature and being acted on by it" in a coevolutionary process. "Nature never finds itself faced by individual men, but always by men working co-operatively in economic production; and man never finds himself faced by nature directly, but always by society organized by nature. . . . History occurs not only on the human side," but on the side of a changed nature as well. What lies between humanity and nature is the social metabolism of the labor process, mediating between the two and establishing at the same time the basis of all social relations. But this metabolism means that as human beings socially transform nature through their production they also transform themselves and their natural needs, creating new dependencies on nature, which imposes new social requirements: "The ancient Britons lived over coal seams, but for them the coal did not exist, and could not therefore determine their existence."[149]

The development of ecology, Caudwell suggested, like genetics and embryology, each transforming our notions of evolution, had broken through the dualism, mechanism, and idealism of the bourgeois standpoint, requiring more complex, integrated, dialectical visions, recognizing the contradiction-laden nature of change, and the necessity of a coevolutionary outlook, breaking through "the circle of bourgeois categories" into a more open universe, and the recognition of qualitatively new forms and levels of existence. The interpenetration of reality went against any notion of the fixity of relations.[150]

This complex process of coevolution and emergence could be best conceived "if we [were to] picture life diagrammatically as a series of steps, then at each step the environment has become different—there are different problems, different laws, different obstacles at each step even though any series of steps besides its differences has certain general problems, laws and obstacles in common. Each new step of evolution is itself a new quality, and this involves a newness, which affects both terms—organism and environment. The environment 'lives' as well as life, because both affect each other through and through."[151]

Caudwell's dialectic exuded ecology and his ecology exuded dialectic. Already in *Illusion and Reality*, he wrote:

> But men cannot change Nature without changing themselves. The full understanding of this mutual interpenetration or reflexive movement of men and Nature, mediated by the necessary and developing relations known as society, is the *recognition* of necessity, not only in Nature but in ourselves and therefore also in society. Viewed objectively this active subject-relation is science, viewed subjectively it is art; but as consciousness emerging in active union with practice it is simply concrete living—the whole process of working, feeling, thinking and behaving like a human individual in one world of individuals and Nature.[152]

Caudwell's attempt to develop a dialectic of art and science, led him in the course of his investigations to a dialectic of nature and society, and a deeper, more ecological conception of socialism. Still in his twenties when he died, he had achieved much.

R. F. Willetts in his 1962 "Homage to Christopher Caudwell," wrote:

> I see a man
> Last heard of alive on a hill-crest
> In Spain, expecting to die at his gun,
> Alone, his youth and work all over,
> His stars and planets
> Reduced to yards of ground,
> Hoping others will harvest his crop.[153]

CHAPTER ELEVEN

A Science for the People

The years of the Second World War marked the peak of the influence of the scientific left in Britain, followed by its decline and eventual defeat in the Cold War period that followed. Yet, even in an era of political descent, the major red scientists sought out new forms of struggle devoted to anti-racism, anti-imperialism, peace, and the promotion of a global human ecology.

The year that the Second World War commenced in Europe, 1939, saw the publication of J. D. Bernal's influential *The Social Function of Science*, the foundational work in what became known as the "social relations of science" movement. It was under this banner that the scientific left, at the height of its influence, argued for increased funding of science by government, the development of scientific teams to address society's problems, and the conscious redirection of science to the social needs of the population in a class-divided society. The Soviet Union's greater support for science and its early achievements in this respect were seen as indications of what might be accomplished.

Other key works in the social relations of science movement, beyond Bernal's book, included Patrick Blackett's "The Frustration of Science" (1935), Lancelot Hogben's *Science and the Citizen* (1938), C. H. Waddington's *The Scientific Attitude* (1941), and J. G. Crowther's *The Social Relations of Science* (1941).[1]

The social relations of science movement had a broad backing in British science, which was dominated by leftists, with three-quarters of British scientists in this period supporting the Labour Party.[2] Under the editorship of Richard Gregory, the leading scientific journal, *Nature*, promoted the idea of the social responsibility of science, providing a forum for ideas on the radical reconstruction of science to give it a larger role in the reconstitution of society.

Nevertheless, despite considerable successes, the scientific left was soon confronted with oppositional movements. In the fall of 1940, John R. Baker, an Oxford zoologist, eugenicist, and virulent anti-Communist, wrote a letter to forty-nine prominent British scientists on the threat of Bernalism. Two of the scientists to which his letter was sent were Baker's Oxford colleague, the ecologist Arthur Tansley, and the physical chemist Michael Polanyi, a Jewish-Hungarian refugee (the brother of the no less famous economic anthropologist Karl Polanyi). Baker, Polanyi, and Tansley proceeded to draft a circular in 1941, which became the basis of the formation of the Society for Freedom in Science (SFS). Referring to their opponents as "gangsters" and "Bernalists," they argued against planning in science and condemned the Soviet Union.[3]

Polanyi published *The Contempt of Freedom* in 1940, and Baker wrote *The Scientific Life* in 1942, both of which attacked the red scientists, focusing primarily on Bernal. Similarly, Tansley's 1942 Herbert Spencer Lecture, *The Values of Science to Humanity*, sought to promote the ideal of pure science removed from practical concerns such as those voiced by the social relations of science movement.[4] In 1941, Polanyi launched a polemic in *Nature* directed at Bernal and Hogben for their advocacy of a planned society and socialized science.

It was not, however, until after the Second World War ended and the Cold War had begun that this struggle became acute. Finding themselves increasingly beleaguered and isolated, and faced with the deep contradictions of the actually existing socialist societies, the Marxian scientists in these years nonetheless stuck to their radical principles: opposing racism, imperialism, nuclear contamination, and ecological destruction in the context of a widening struggle for socialism and world peace.

THE SOCIAL RELATIONS OF SCIENCE

Bernal's *The Social Function of Science*, which was highly acclaimed when it first appeared, was an extraordinary treatise for the comprehensiveness and clarity of the vision it propounded. The book was divided into two parts: "What Science Does" and "What Science Could Do." It began by referring to "The Revolt from Reason," represented by the development of fascism, and went on to discuss the more general problem of science in capitalist class society, including its distorted ideological and religious forms and the corruption of science by profit.[5] Given all of this, Bernal asked, what was the future for science and society? This led to an extended discussion of science as it had developed historically since ancient times, followed by science in the modern world in its various forms.

The first part of *The Social Function of Science* posed the question of "theory and practice in science" in the past and present, displaying the virtues of Bernal's historical, holistic, and dialectical thinking. In his historical discussion, he highlighted the role of Francis Bacon in the seventeenth-century scientific revolution in emphasizing science as power, and in presenting the views that then led to the formation of the Royal Society. In the twentieth century, however, new institutions of science that were more socialist in character were required.[6]

An important element in Bernal's discussion of the current organization and reorganization of science was his consideration of "the new sciences, like ecology and social psychology."[7] With respect to the emerging field of ecology, he declared:

> The study of the relations between organisms is as important as that of the organism in artificial isolation. The animal and plant world form between them a beautifully balanced system of chemical and physical interchanges, but this system is not invariant; it changes both in place and time, and particularly it has been altered by human interference. Agriculture implies the imposition of a new ecology and produces, besides its immediate objects of humanly valued goods, many other results, some of them highly undesirable from the human point of view.[8]

The integration of the lessons of ecological science was vitally necessary for contemporary agriculture, which tended to impair the soil, due to such complexities as "the relations between crops and domestic animals, soil bacteria and insect pests." Ecology was also essential for the understanding of the problem of parasitism and the relations of organisms, as well as infectious disease. Closely related to this were issues of animal behavior and "animal societies." Just as history had proven crucial to understanding the evolution of human society, so it was crucial, Bernal argued, to focus on the evolution of animal societies more generally, where issues of biology, geology (paleontology), and history came together.[9]

Bernal's early approach to ecological issues was in many ways a contradictory one, reflecting the discordant trends of the time and the difficult emergence of the ecological worldview in a context dominated by economic growth and planning. This led at times to his exaggeration of the degree to which a rational society, if once freed from capitalism, could dictate to nature. Still, characteristic of Bernal's thought from the beginning was an emphasis on the dialectical relation of organism (including the human organism) and the environment, breaking with the one-sided adaptationist perspective characteristic of Darwinism.

This inner struggle in Bernal's thought around environmental issues, growth, and planning was to continue into his later years, during which increasing ecological concerns with respect to the misuse of technology—particularly in relation to the development of nuclear weapons—drove him toward more critical environmental insights. Nevertheless, even in his most ecomodernist phase, he stood out in his recognition of the developing dangers both for humanity and other species arising from widening ecological depredations. "Smokes and noxious dusts and gases," he explained, were responsible for the degradation of life and ill-health in urban centers attributable mainly to industry. New sources of energy and "prohibition of smoke and dust and gas emission" in populated areas could help solve these problems. In line with what Justus von Liebig, Karl Marx, and Frederick Engels had argued in the nineteenth century, Bernal wrote: "We are throwing away, and polluting rivers and sea in the process, essential elements such as phosphorus and complex and valuable chemicals."[10] Emphasizing the frequent failure of modern society to anticipate the destructive consequences of its own actions, he observed: "The tragedy of man has too often lain in his very success in achieving what he imagined to be his objects."[11]

Bernal's concerns with respect to ecology and the retrogressive features of so-called progress were to be even more evident later in his 1954 *Science in History*, where he wrote at length on "Organisms and Their Environment: Ecology." He noted that Darwin had made the first steps toward an ecological view "in his work on the fertilization of flowers and on the earthworm. But the work that has been done up till now only emphasizes the extreme complexity of the relations between organisms and our practically total ignorance of their significance." For example, soil science had previously been treated as "largely inorganic, based on geology and mineralogy. We are only now beginning to realize that the soil itself is a whole complex of organisms, not one of which can be changed without affecting all the rest. The interrelated complex of organisms—of animals, plants, and bacteria—wherever they are found, is the subject of the study of *ecology*: the analysis of the total effect of all organisms in a specific locality on each other." Bernal emphasized that "the *association* of organisms in, for example, a field or a pond is found to have a coherence and permanency of its own greater than those of any individual organism. The old crude concept of the struggle for existence is giving place to one of the evolved co-operation of different organisms." Ecology raised issues of complexity and irreversibility, "once there has been a breakthrough on to a new level of complexity." However, qualitative changes create definite pathways in evolutionary development, such that "the possibility of similar jumps occurring elsewhere rapidly vanishes. Once, for instance, the green plants had spread on to the land, there was no more room for plant-forms with any other metabolic basis to do the same."[12]

Science in History stressed that "Man's interference with the balance of Nature" had become a major threat to ecological systems, introducing a whole new history of organic systems. "Large-scale intensive [ecological] devastation . . . is simply due to the essentially predatory nature of capitalism, now spread as imperialism over so large an area of the world."

Recognizing the systematic role of capitalism and colonialism in the degradation of the soil, Bernal avoided the dominant ideological tendency to blame some of the worst forms of ecological destruction on the poor, placing such destruction rather in its wider social and ecological context. Thus, he wrote:

> The success of modern mechanical agriculture and lumbering has been at the expense of ruining a dangerously large proportion of the soil of the planet and of changing its climate unfavourably to almost all forms of life.... The destruction of the soil has been enormously accelerated in the last fifty years by the methods characteristic of ruthless capitalist exploitation for immediate profit. The actual destroyers of the soil need not themselves be the capitalists, they may be poor share-cropping farmers who have to secure a large harvest of cash crops in order to prevent themselves from being evicted; or Africans driven on to reserves by Europeans who take all the best land. The different causes lead to the same result, and the process is continually accelerating. The less there is in the land, the more it has to be exploited and the worse its condition gets.[13]

Because of this, the destruction of the soil had expanded enormously over the last half-century, calling for an emphasis on conservation in response. Conservation, though, could not be left to private industry. It required state planning.[14]

Yet, at this point Bernal undermined his argument by characteristically adopting an uncritical attitude toward the USSR. Although the Soviet Union had clearly played a pioneering role with respect to forest preservation and nature reserves, and was to be rightly congratulated in that respect, Bernal also praised it uncritically for its role in promoting mega-dams and vast irrigation (including river-diversion) schemes. These were commonly seen at the time, in the United States as well as the Soviet Union, as great boons to food production, and even as examples of good environmental management, but were later to be recognized as ecological disasters.[15]

On population, Bernal was stridently anti-Malthusian. He opposed on ethical as well as scientific grounds the Malthusian-racial position presented by physiologist A. V. Hill in his presidential address to the British Association of Science. Hill insisted that medicine and hygiene not be promoted in those countries where "men . . . breed like rabbits." As Bernal disparagingly said of Hill's views: "The whole of the work of medical science is to be thrown away rather than face the full implications of economic freedom for 'backward' peoples. The sanctity of human life, one of the highest professions of Western civilization, is discarded in the ultimate cause of the protection of private property." Only by raising the standard of living, particularly the development of industry and agriculture in poorer countries, and thus leading peoples through the demographic transition, was it possible to rise above the "vicious circle" of population growth and the struggle for subsistence. For that, however, underdeveloped nations needed to be free of the chains of imperialism.[16]

Such arguments reflected genuine concerns for the wretched of the earth and a recognition of the social (as opposed to purely demographic) causes of overpopulation. Nevertheless, in the late 1930s and early 1940s, Bernal's anti-Malthusianism, coupled with his faith in science and technology if coupled with planning, took exaggerated forms, leading him in this period to spout extreme productivist claims about the carrying capacity of the earth, undermining his more careful arguments. He rashly wrote in *The Social Function of Science* that not only could deserts be turned into greenhouses, but "if we used our reserves of coal, or even limestone, as basic food materials we should have enough for a population thousands or millions of times that which exists at present on our globe."[17]

The approach to environmental issues adopted in *The Social Function of Science* and, later (but to a lesser extent), in *Science in History* thus displayed at times the modernizing (and ecomodernizing) vision almost universal at the time, the age of mega-projects in the United States, the Soviet Union, and elsewhere. Here, problems of overpopulation were seen as solved through the development of new hybrid crops and new technological methods, including greater irrigation that required big dams and diversion of rivers. In a more grating and shortsighted observation from today's perspective, Bernal in 1939 in *The Social Function of Science* pointed to the possibility of planned climate change, based on Soviet attempts to tame the Arctic. As he put it, in terms that cannot but strike today's reader, some eighty years later, as naïve (the dialectics of unintended consequences seems to have failed him here): "By an intelligent diversion of warm ocean-currents together with some means of colouring snow so that the sun could melt it, it might be possible to keep the Arctic ice-free for one summer, and that one year might tip the balance and permanently change the climate of the northern hemisphere."[18]

Bernal presented this view decades before the post–Second World War development of modern climate science and Earth System science. Ironically, it was the Soviet promotion of climatology, as a science in the context of the attempt to alter the climate of the Arctic, that led to the first discoveries of the heat balance of the Earth System by M. I. Budyko and the first warnings on accelerated global warming as a threat to humanity.[19]

Still, an indication of the often contradictory, Janus-faced character of Bernal's thought at this time can be seen in the juxtaposition of ecological concerns that pervade much of *Science in History* with extreme Promethean and ecomodernist notions, particularly where issues of overcoming famine were concerned—often reflecting his susceptibility to Soviet ideology. Thus, he wrote in an ecologically tone-deaf manner near the end of *Science in History* in a section titled "The Transformation of Nature":

> The transformation of Nature, along lines indicated by the biological and geological sciences, will be undertaken with the use of heavy machinery, including possibly atomic energy. In this way all the river basins of the world can be brought under control, abolishing floods, droughts, and destructive soil erosion, and widely extending the areas of cultivation and stock raising.... The transformation should establish a new level of human control over its total environment.[20]

Such views did not entirely obliterate the ecological insights that pervaded *Science in History*. Nevertheless, they did suggest that Bernal still believed, in line with most other scientists and industry in his time, that the solutions to problems such as famines, drought, and loss of soil fertility could be addressed by mega-projects such as large dams and diverting rivers.

Most telling is his reference here to the use of atomic power. Yet, Bernal's ecological views in this respect were to change dramatically, and to take on a far more critical perspective following the Bikini Atoll test and the revelations about radioactive fallout. In the end, his growing integration into the world peace movement was to affect his ecological views in this and other areas.[21]

Despite his major missteps in this period, Bernal's deep concern for ecological problems, in areas such as the degradation of the soil and deforestation, frequently gave his work a critical edge well ahead of his times, as did his recognition that the severe ecological problems of much of the globe emanated largely from imperialism. One work that was to influence him immensely in the latter respect was Josué de Castro's *The Geography of Hunger* (1952), a classic study of poverty, population, and hunger.[22] In this vein, Bernal strongly criticized monocultures in agriculture, writing in *Science in History*: "The soil is exhausted by single-crop agriculture, often on foreign-owned plantations."[23] However, more significant in the development of his ecological views, as we shall see, were his deep concerns about the development of nuclear weapons.

Bernal's expansive view of science, and the wider, dynamic (though not yet Earth System) perspective presented in both *The Social Function of Science* and *Science in History* were to attract much less attention than his proposals for the reorganization of science, as suggested in the second part of *The Social Function of Science*. Looking at the major proposals with respect to the future of science, very little would seem controversial today. Indeed, Bernal was to remark in his 1964 essay "After Twenty-Five Years," in which he looked back at *The Social Function of Science* a quarter-century after its publication, that almost everything he argued for on practical grounds had already been accomplished, though unfortunately often under the domination of the military-industrial complex.[24]

In *The Social Function of Science* Bernal was particularly concerned with the funding of science and the need for the state to increase its direct role in this respect, since the only other sources of financing scientific research were from universities, whose main purpose was education, and from private industry or philanthropy. He strongly emphasized the importance of state involvement in funding research (including through universities) on the grounds of the practical importance of science with respect to human welfare.[25] Indeed, many of his proposals on the need for state funding of science and for promotion of the sciences in the university curriculum resembled those that E. Ray Lankester had put before the British Association for the Advancement of Science more than three decades before in his 1906 presidential address.[26]

A "science for the people" in a more democratic and egalitarian society would be a necessary complement to a state for the people. Although freedom in science should be at all times maintained, this did not conflict with the notion of the organization of science to place greater stress on practical, social goals, since "freedom," as Engels had famously said, "is the insight into necessity."[27]

Such a stance, however, necessarily involved a critique of the hegemonic "ideal of pure science." For Bernal, "pure science," conceived as an isolated "ideal," was often "a form of snobbery, a sign of the scientist aping the don and the gentleman. An applied scientist must needs appear somewhat of a tradesman. . . . By insisting on science for its own sake the pure scientist repudiated the sordid material foundation on which his work was based." The ideal of pure science had arisen historically in accompaniment with the development of capitalist machine industry. Scientific results were increasingly exploited for material means, while scientists were portrayed, not least among themselves, as independent of and oblivious to the practical purposes to which their research was put. "The scientist's responsibility," in this hegemonic, pure-science view, was "limited to carrying out his own work," while "leaving the results to an ideal economic system, ideal because natural and open to the free play of economic forces." Hill had argued in 1933 in a letter to *Nature* that science should see itself completely independent of social and political needs, and *neutral in the face of the rise of fascism*—a view that Bernal considered both ideologically naïve and ethically reprehensible.[28]

There was no getting around the fact that science had become a power in the world and could be used in ways that served the needs of humanity, or that, alternately, it could undermine those pressing needs, in some cases promoting actual destruction. The notion of pure scientific detachment under these circumstances was naïve. Freedom in this realm, as in others, could not simply be a case of absolute individuality and detachment. Rather, freedom could only exist, in science, as in all other domains as well, if accompanied with struggle. Freedom in science, Bernal insisted, required not only the absence of outside control, but also funding, since science required a material basis. To leave such funding to private sources and class-based philanthropy was likely to impede the freedom and independence of science.[29]

Bernal was personally aware through his own career of the deplorable funding of scientific research in Britain. He had been forced to carry out his early experiments in x-ray crystallography—one of his ex-students recalled—in "a few ill-lit and dirty rooms on the ground floor of a stark, dilapidated grey brick building." The difficulties of producing critical research under these impoverished conditions were worsened by a lack of technicians and poor support for student researchers.[30] In documenting in his book the paucity of scientific funding in Britain compared to other advanced capitalist countries, Bernal must have recalled these poor laboratory conditions.

The reality of the late 1930s was that science was being organized primarily by capitalist class forces, limiting the actual *self-organization of science* by scientists themselves, as well as attention to the genuine needs of society as a whole. Moreover, under monopoly capitalism, there was the danger that science would simply become subject to corporations and the military. Thus, Bernal pointed to "the increasing tendency to national monopoly of science in the interest of State power, economic and military."[31] In confirmation of this, a quarter-century later he was to note that though science was now more than adequately funded, it was dominated by military spending and military priorities. This was the effect of the Second World War followed by the Cold War and the rise of a permanent military-industrial complex. As a result, the freedom of science was compromised in a climate where "military science was sacrosanct."[32] Secrecy motivated by national security had displaced the freedom of scientific communication.

What gave a radical, even revolutionary character to *The Social Function of Science* was the focus on the movement toward socialism as a necessary complement to the advancement of science. This was most evident in his final chapter, "The Social Function of Science." There Bernal presented his thesis that though the bourgeois revolution had been "essential" for the development of science, "giving it, for the first time, a practical value, the human importance of science transcends in every way that of capitalism, and, indeed, the full development of science in the service of humanity is incompatible with the continuance of capitalism."[33] Not only the physical sciences were impaired under capitalism by the class nature of the society, but social science was made virtually impossible by the dominance of bourgeois ideology and the ignoring (or indeed active marginalization) of all social science research that pointed to the need for fundamental social change. He was later to devote a quarter of his *Science in History* to a devastating critique of the ideological role of the social sciences in capitalist society.[34]

The stress on the importance of Marxism to science revolved around its emphasis on *origins* and thus its concern with qualitative change and contradiction. Socialism emphasized the "co-operative and popular character" of science, making it a "popular possession," an organic "science for the people." Rather than pretend to a false detachment, historical materialism looked squarely at how science was affected by the structuring of social and economic development, leading to a more rational, reasoned, and critical scientific inquiry, and thus to the laws of discovery. As an example of this, Bernal pointed to Nikolai Vavilov's discovery of the main centers of the origin of agriculture around the globe and thus the world's reservoirs of germplasm.[35]

Yet, Bernal's approach to socialism and science was pragmatic as well as radical, tied to the Communist Party–dominated and trade-union sections of the Labour Party. An appendix to his book included the policy statement and principles of the British Association of Scientific Workers, which was a principal force in the social relations of science movement. Bernal believed in working generally with governments—whether capitalist or socialist—on the promotion of science. Adhering to a notion of "complete socialism" that required the transcendence of capitalism rather than social democracy, he nonetheless was actively engaged in transforming the relations of science and society in the context of the present system: a philosophy of reform *and* revolution. Nevertheless, "it would be absurd," he noted, "to imagine that a rationalization of scientific application to industry would be easy to adapt to the conditions of Monopoly Capitalism."[36]

Opposed to any system like those proposed by Plato and H. G. Wells, in which philosophers or scientists were the rulers of society, Bernal stated: "We may dismiss as fantasy the prospect of the scientist ruler." He also rejected mechanical utopias, particularly scientific utopias, such as those associated with Wells, or earlier figures like Edward Bellamy in *Looking Backward*. The reactionary dystopias of Aldous Huxley's *Brave New World* or E. M. Forster's *The Machine Stops* simply carried forward the worst aspects of the Wellsian-type utopias that they were meant to criticize. With the notable exception of William Morris's remarkable *News from Nowhere*, which, as a utopian romance, concerned with the "emotional detail" of a complete communist society, all utopias, he suggested, had "two repulsive features":

> a lack of freedom consequent on perfect organization, and a corresponding lack of effort. To be a citizen of a modern Utopia, the critics feel, is to be well-cared for, regulated from birth to death, and never needing to do anything difficult or painful. The Utopian seems, notwithstanding his health, beauty, and affability, to partake too much of the robot and the prig. Fairly envisaged, it seems hardly worth while sacrificing much in the present if this is all the future has to offer.

In contrast, the Marxian outlook was quite different, that of open-ended historical development, of "freedom and struggle." What was needed was "faith in humanity."[37]

The last paragraph of *The Social Function of Science*, however, was to be most widely quoted by friend and foe alike. There he audaciously wrote:

> *Science as Communism.*—Already we have in the practice of science the prototype of all human common action. The task which the scientists have undertaken—the understanding and control of nature and of man himself—is merely the conscious expression of the task of human society. The methods by which this task is attempted, however imperfectly they are realized, are the methods by which humanity is most likely to secure its own future. In its endeavor, science is communism. In science men have learned consciously to subordinate themselves to a common purpose without losing the individuality of their achievements. Each one knows that this work depends on that of his predecessors and colleagues, and that it can only reach its fruition through the work of his successors. In science men collaborate not because they are forced to by superior authority or because they blindly follow some chosen leader, but because they realize that only in this willing collaboration can each man find his goal. . . . Facts cannot be forced to our desires, and freedom comes by admitting this necessity and not by pretending to ignore it.[38]

For humanity as a whole, the difficult but urgent task was one of "welding a really organic society."[39]

Waddington's *Scientific Attitude* and Crowther's *The Social Relations of Science* adopted similar stances on the natural communism of science. Like Bernal, Waddington insisted that in their free sharing of information and ideas, their consciousness of working toward collective ends, and their general interest in the promotion of social betterment, scientists could be said to behave "like communists" in the broadest sense of the term.[40] The prestigious sociologist of science Robert K. Merton adopted the notion that "communism," along with universalism, disinterestedness, and organized skepticism, constituted the four key scientific norms. However, he later changed "communism" to "communalism." Science, in this view, was a collective enterprise based ideally on the free and collaborative exchange of ideas and aimed at general human welfare.[41]

ANTI-COMMUNIST INTELLECTUALS AND THE CIA

The social relations of science movement of the scientific left generated an immediate reactionary response from conservative scientists, which would have little real effect until it merged later with the wider Cold War attacks on these same scientists. From the start, Polanyi and Baker, who, together with Tansley, founded the SFS, were the main critics of Bernal's *The Social Function of Science* and the social relations of science movement. In his book *The Contempt of Freedom*, Polanyi objected to Marxism's attack on pure science as an unrealizable ideal in a class society. For Polanyi, Bernal's approach was simply the "propagandist attitude to which Marxist thinkers" commonly deferred, and it was hypocritical in its advocacy of freedom since it constituted in reality the denial of freedom in science. Polanyi complained that Epicurus and Charles Darwin were beyond criticism, requiring "compulsory acceptance" in Marxist circles, simply because Marx had praised them. "Marxism," Polanyi went so far as to contend in his book, was "a more complete philosophy of oppression than . . . either Italian or German Fascism."[42]

In *The Scientific Life*, Baker charged that Bernal's *The Social of Function of Science* preached the "doctrine of the reduction of freedom for research workers." Waddington and Crowther were likewise accused of advocating the "ushering in the totalitarian régime for scientists." Alarmed by plans for postwar reconstruction in Britain under the Labour Party, in which Marxian scientists were influential, Baker warned: "Another and a vastly different prospect looms ahead. An ugly new god called the state demands worship. Nourishment, shelter, health and leisure are falsely regarded as ends in themselves. Culture is looked down on with contempt. Science is equated with technology and both decay. Individualism and free enquiry are ridiculed. Everything is planned from 'above.' A dreary uniformity descends. Each person is a cog in a vast machine, grinding towards ends lacking all higher human values."[43]

Both Baker and Polanyi were animated by reactionary views, with Baker an arch-conservative, avid eugenicist, and believer in racial inequality, and Polanyi an early neoliberal thinker and virulent anti-Communist. In a friendly response to Baker's initial letter in 1940, which was to lead to the formation of the SFS, Polanyi declared outright: "We cannot defend the freedom of science unless we attack collectivism." It was the socialist outlook of the scientific left rather than their alleged "contempt of freedom" in science that was the real issue for him from the start.[44]

Tansley's role in the SFS was that of a moderate left or social democratic figure. He insisted, in contrast to Baker, that the SFS did not oppose scientists working at times in teams. Tansley supported social planning in science, while rejecting centralized planning of science by the state. His most important statement, as a representative of the SFS, was his 1942 Herbert Spencer Lecture on *The Values of Science to Humanity*. He stressed, in opposition both to Baker and Polanyi, that if the Association of Scientific Workers and the Bernalists were actually supportive of freedom in science then there was indeed no quarrel, that is, the battle was not a general political-ideological one.[45]

In sharp contrast to Tansley, Baker and Polanyi saw the SFS as a key part of the anti-communist struggle, in which so-called Bernalism became the primary ideological target. Baker's extreme polemical approach was evident in his piece "Counterblast to Bernalism," published in the *New Statesman and Nation* in 1939. It started out with the sentence: "Bernalism is the doctrine of those who profess that the only proper objects of scientific research are to feed people and protect them from the elements, that research workers should be organised in gangs and told what to discover, and that the pursuit of knowledge for its own sake has the same value as the solution of crossword puzzles. Professor Bernal will no doubt permit the immortalisation of his name by the introduction of this new word [Bernalism] into the English language." Baker went so far as to charge that a socialist scientist would stop for lunch in the countryside with "Tansley's 'Types of British Vegetation' in [his] haversack," without pausing to think of the extent of "his debt" to Tansley in allowing him to perceive the ecology around him.

Baker's fantastic criticisms were completely off the mark here, since Bernal and other figures on the scientific left—for example, Hogben, J. B. S. Haldane, Joseph Needham, and Julian Huxley—had indicated many times over their interest in the nascent field of ecological science. Nor was their argument on science as praxis and its role in the promotion of human welfare to be confused with mere bourgeois utilitarianism rooted in possessive individualism. Still, in the virulence of his condemnation of these leading figures in British science in his day, Baker knew few bounds and went so far as to refer to "the Bernalist rut" and explicitly calling Britain's leading socialist scientists "gangsters."[46]

Science for the aristocratic Baker was an elite, gentleman's endeavor, beyond the ordinary individual. What he objected to most in Bernal, then, was the idea of a science for the people. Baker believed strongly not only in the inherently low level of culture of the common people, but also in the deep inferiority of non-white races. Hence, he was also concerned "to keep Eugenics alive," characterizing those "opposed to it" as "communists." This reflected the fact that Hogben, Haldane, and Bernal were all leading opponents of eugenics.[47] In a 1933 BBC broadcast debate with Haldane, Baker openly declared: "The people who were inferior we would encourage to have few children."[48] In November 1942, during the Battle of Stalingrad, Baker wrote to Carlos Blacker: "I do not at all appreciate our alliance with the USSR. I should have preferred to have nothing to do with her, *whatever the consequences*. The regime seems to me more evil . . . than . . . [Hitler's] Germany."[49]

Polanyi was not overtly racist in his outlook, but highly elitist, attracted to classical liberalism with its possessive individualist ideology and class bias.

He was to form a view of science as a personal endeavor based on tacit knowledge. However, it was not the supposed centralism of the scientific left that so disturbed Baker and Polanyi, as the wider, public character insisted on by the Bernalists, who believed in enlisting the state for social betterment. The SFS's criticisms of the red scientists in the midst of the Second World War had little effect initially, and it was only later, as it merged such criticisms with a broader anti-communism and Cold War "anti-totalitarian" ideology, that the condemnations began to tell.

In the Cold War era, it was not altogether surprising that a left figure like political theorist Neal Wood, in his 1959 *Communism and British Intellectuals*, would take his cue from Polanyi, whose help he acknowledged in the book. The stances of Baker and Polanyi along with that of the SFS were dutifully presented, while Wood harshly criticized the British Marxist scientists, who he presented as enemies of scientific freedom and critical thought. As Edwin Roberts has noted, Wood simply adopted "the criticisms used by Baker and Polanyi, for the most part, without any qualification."[50]

The main vulnerability of the Marxist scientists was not in their immediate ideas or proposals with respect to British science, but rather their close identification with the Soviet Union and the Communist Party of Great Britain (CPGB), in which they were hostage to events beyond their control—and frequently beyond their knowledge, as in the case of Stalin's wider purges. This was particularly the case with Lysenkoism, which arose around the work of Trofim Denisovich Lysenko, a dominant figure in Soviet biology from the mid-1930s to the late 1950s, who attained enormous power and influence, particularly after 1948, through his directorship of the Lenin All-Union Academy of Agricultural Sciences and the Institute of Genetics of the USSR Academy of Sciences. Lysenko introduced exaggerated claims with respect to vernalization and hybridization that went against traditional genetics, but which were attractive to the Soviet state because the implementation of these methods promised to speed plant growth and produce greater productivity in agriculture in a harsh environment. Lysenko and his associates raised some important questions about the relation of genetics to the environment that fed the controversy. However, their scientific methods were defective.[51]

The British red scientists, most notably Haldane, as one of the world's leading geneticists, but also Bernal, were under pressure to respond by taking one side or the other in the controversy generated by Lysenkoism. Instead, they mostly sought to respond rationally, presenting the controversy as an important scientific debate to be decided on its merits on scientific grounds. In Bernal's words, "There is nothing like controversy to stimulate theory and experiment." He stressed that there were genuine Marxist biologists (here he singled out B. M. Zavadovsky whom he had first met at the Second International Congress of the History of Science and Technology in 1931 and who was strongly opposed to Lysenko) on both sides of the controversy.[52] Haldane, for his part, made it clear in 1949 that he did not share all of Lysenko's views, which "had gone a great deal too far and rejected a lot of sound biology" and that he was himself a "Mendel-Morganist." Nevertheless, he was unwilling to condemn the developments in Soviet biology altogether.[53]

At the center of the controversy, and close to the British red scientists, was Nikolai Vavilov, Lysenko's chief opponent and the Soviet Union's leading geneticist, who, like Zavadovsky, had been a member of the Soviet delegation under Bukharin that visited Britain for the Second International Congress of the History of Science and Technology in 1931. Vavilov was a pioneer in the study of the centers of origin of the germplasm associated with world's principal crops. Haldane, Bernal, Needham, and Hogben, also had close connections with H. J. Muller, the U.S. Marxist geneticist and later winner of the 1948 Nobel Prize in Physiology of Medicine, who had worked closely with Vavilov at the Institute of Genetics in Leningrad. The very nature of these close connections and the clear recognition on the part of the British socialist scientists that Lysenko and his associates had often gone too far in their rejection of Western genetics meant that they avoided any straightforward adoption of Lysenkoist ideas, which were portrayed, at best, as at the experimental stage, and thus as mere hypotheses, some of which were doubtless worth investigation.

In the end, the real problem with Lysenkoism, as Richard Levins and Richard Lewontin argued in *The Dialectical Biologist* in 1985, was not so much its promulgation of ideas that were to prove to be of negligible scientific value, but rather the political backing given to Lysenko by Stalin.[54] This had the effect, as Waddington put it, of placing the full power of the state behind "Lysenko and [his close colleague Isaak] Prezent, a pair of able charlatans who did much to corrupt the growth of Soviet genetics." The result was the purging of scientific opponents, including Vavilov, who was arrested and died in prison of malnutrition during the war—facts that were not known for many years.[55]

In the developing Cold War context, Lysenkoism was presented by figures like Baker and Polanyi as representing the absolute rejection in the Soviet Union of modern genetics. All attempts of Haldane and others to bring some degree of critical rationality to bear on the question failed to take hold in the deepening political divide. Meanwhile, the Communist Party of Great Britain (CPGB) adhered slavishly to the dominant Soviet view, undermining the British left scientists, who sought to chart an independent course. "More than anything else," Werskey wrote, "it was Stalin's sudden decision in July 1948 to put T. D. Lysenko in charge of Soviet biology that served to catalyse the decline of the scientific Left" in Britain.[56]

One member of the SFS with whom Polanyi and Baker developed a strong alliance in their attempt to undermine the Marxist scientists was Friedrich Hayek, the arch-conservative, neoliberal professor of economics at the London School of Economics and author of the leading anti-Communist tract, *The Road to Serfdom* (1944).[57] Hayek approached Polanyi in 1941, asking him to enter into combat against "the Propaganda of the Haldanes, Hogbens, Needhams etc."[58] He encouraged Polanyi to write a vitriolic review essay titled "The Growth of Thought in Society," attacking Crowther's *Social Relations of Science* and the scientific left in general. The review essay was published in 1941 in *Economica*, which Hayek edited. Polanyi's 28-page calumny for Hayek's journal was one of the most rabid attacks on Marxian scientists. Taking on the whole social relations of science movement, dating back to the Soviet delegation led by Bukharin to the 1931 Second International Congress on the History of Science and Technology, and encompassing Hogben, Bernal, and Crowther, Polanyi charged that any criticism whatsoever of "pure science" amounted to a criticism of "scientific ideals" and was a form of "totalitarian doctrine." The views of the British Marxian scientists, "concerning the position of science," he contended, were "identical in principle with those of Fascist Totalitarianism" as enunciated by Adolf Hitler.

Polanyi based these allegations on a grossly distorted treatment of the argument in Crowther's *Social Relations of Science* in which Polanyi claimed (falsely) that Crowther was defending "the methods of the Spanish Inquisition." Crowther, as one would expect, had in fact taken the side of Galileo, which represented the rising bourgeoisie, against the Inquisition, seeing the repression of the heliocentric view as a sin against science and the new revolutionary class. Yet, Crowther also observed that during the rule of Cromwell, who had introduced repressive measures to defend the revolutionary Parliamentary forces in the midst of the English Revolution, science had advanced rapidly—a fact impossible to deny. If Crowther's historical argument raised questions from a moral standpoint, it could hardly be seen as a defense of inquisitions. Instead, he was seriously grappling with the complex relation of scientific advancement to historical change, as opposed to the usual Whig history. Rather than confront Crowther's historically based argument directly, Polanyi, with Hayek's support, simply lifted phrases out of context, suggesting, inaccurately, that Crowther was defending inquisitional methods. Readers were led to believe that these criticisms of Crowther, a well-known socialist science writer, sufficed to dispatch the scientific left in general, including leading scientists such as Bernal and Hogben.[59]

Baker and Polanyi were both enthusiastic readers of Hayek's *Road to Serfdom* (part of which had been devoted to polemics against the scientific left, focusing on Waddington). Baker in private correspondence emphasized its enormous propagandistic value in relation to their cause. Hayek, in recognition of Polanyi's role in the SFS and their shared values, invited Polanyi to the original organizational meeting of the Mont Pelerin Society in Switzerland—the birthplace of neoliberalism. Not only was Polanyi one of the original thirty-eight organizers, he was also one of the sixty-four founding members.[60]

In 1950, the anti-Communist Congress for Cultural Freedom was founded. Based in Paris, it aimed to fund and facilitate a larger number of cultural publications. Acknowledged funding for the CCF came from recognized foundations, including the Rockefeller Foundation, which the CIA regarded as providing excellent funding cover. What was undoubtedly the greater part of the CCF's funding, though, was channeled through a number of dummy fronts, such as the Fairfield Foundation, the Price Foundation, and Vernon Foundation, all with false boards of directors, which served as CIA conduits. The journal *Encounter* was directly connected to the CCF (and thus the CIA), while sociologist of science Edward Shils's journal *Minerva* (Polanyi wrote "The Republic of Science" for the first issue) received covert CIA funds.

In this way, the CCF served as a clearing house for a wide array of journals, including *Daedalus*, the *Journal of the History of Ideas*, and *Partisan Review*. Its Secretariat, responsible for running the organization and obtaining funding, was headed by Michael Josselson, a CIA operative. Josselson's second in command, John Hunt, an Oklahoman novelist and a direct descendant of Davy Crockett, was handpicked by the CIA in 1956, after Josselson had a heart attack in 1955—lest the CIA lose control of the organization.

Hayek, Polanyi, and Baker were all directly involved with the CCF with Polanyi playing a leading role throughout. Polanyi was soon enlisted to chair the CCF's Committee on Science and Freedom. He was also president of the Organizing Committee for a 1953 CCF meeting in Hamburg, under the theme of Science and Freedom, the first large meeting of the CCF following its founding. In Hamburg, 120 scholars and scientists were to gather, including Polanyi, Baker, and Hayek, along with such dedicated Cold Warriors as French philosopher Raymond Aron, the American philosopher Sidney Hook, and the American sociologist Shils.[61] The scientific left was to be the major target. Baker commented in his correspondence on the free flow of money and the "lavish expenditure" at the conference, beyond anything he had ever seen at a scientific-cultural gathering.[62]

Polanyi, who joined the Executive Committee of the CCF in 1953, went on to organize its Milan meeting in 1955. The CIA's role in the CCF, as one participant indicated, was an open secret to those deeply involved in the organization. After the CIA's central role in the organization was exposed in 1967 by *Ramparts* magazine, among those who admitted to knowing or strongly suspecting CIA involvement were Daniel Bell, Willy Brandt, James Burnham,

Louis Fischer, Hook, George Kennan, Mary McCarthy, Dwight Macdonald, Robert Oppenheimer, Arthur Schlesinger Jr., Shils, and Lionel Trilling. Polanyi, though not admitting having known of CIA's role in the organization (a position that was hardly credible given his membership on the executive committee and the numbers of others with lesser roles who knew), nonetheless strongly supported Josselson once it all came into the open. In his words, "I would have served the CIA (had I known of its existence) in the years following the war, with pleasure."[63]

In the United States, the earlier Committee for Cultural Freedom had been started in 1939 largely at the instigation of Hook, but also with the help of John Dewey. Hook was to dissolve the CCF in 1951 and replace it with the new American Committee for Cultural Freedom (ACCF) in order to secure funding from the Congress for Cultural Freedom. The American Committee under Hook was even more openly anti-Communist than the much larger European-based CCF of which it was then an affiliate. Whittaker Chambers, who testified against Alger Hiss in the McCarthy era, was a member of the Executive Committee of the ACCF. Many of the European intellectuals associated with the CCF, such as Aron and Polanyi, believed that Communism had been largely defeated in the West by the mid-1950s and wanted to give the CCF a wider focus. The ACCF was thus seen as a liability given its visible participation in the vigilantism of the McCarthy era. The Paris-based CCF therefore decided to rein in the American Committee, particularly in the wake of the demise of McCarthyism—a dispute that was described by historian Frances Saunders as a "conflict between the gunslingers in New York and the sophisticates of the Paris operation." In 1954, Josselson cut off the funds to the ACCF, depriving it of its indirect access to the financing from the CIA. In response, Hook went directly both to the CIA operative Cord Meyer, who worked with the CCF, and then to CIA director Allen Dulles, and managed to obtain direct CIA funding for the ACCF. However, the ACCF was to find itself in growing financial difficulties in subsequent years, due to its conflict with the CCF, and its inability to continue obtaining CIA support. It disbanded in early 1957.[64]

Hook's enmity toward the British red scientists and their avowed commitment to dialectical naturalism was deep-seated and unending. He had early earned a reputation as a leading American Marxist philosopher with the publication of his *Towards the Understanding of Karl Marx* (1933).[65] By 1939, however, when he played the leading role in founding the original Committee for Cultural Freedom in the United States, he had already shifted his views considerably, making the scientific left his main target. Hook was early in adopting the position, to become widespread among Western Marxists, that Engels had distorted Marxism by introducing the notion of the dialectics of nature. Refusing to address the complex issues of epistemology and science associated with dialectical realism/materialism, he claimed that "the only sense in which the dialectic is applicable to nature is the sense in which it is an abbreviated synonym for scientific method." In these terms, he sought systematically to undermine all of Engels's discussions with respect to the dialectics of nature, as well as that of the entire scientific left, characterizing any attempt to see dialectics as applicable to nature as either a form of "metaphysical idealism" or else merely a stand-in for the scientific method and thus redundant.

On this shallow basis, Hook proceeded to throw scorn on Needham's notion of integrative levels; Haldane's discussions on how dialectical-evolutionary thinking could help one understand hemophilia; and Hyman Levy's use in *A Philosophy for a Modern Man* of the concept of phase change to explain the material significance of dialectics. At times, Hook highlighted the real philosophical difficulties in the analyses of some of these natural scientists. More generally, he sought to throw utter scorn on their analyses by focusing on what he viewed as particular weak points, such as Levy's claim that fascist thinking was prone to mechanism. Engels was said to have fallen prey to Aristotelian essentialism. For Hooks, the pragmatist philosopher, there was nothing to be gained by applying dialectical thinking to nature—that is, nothing that was not already comprehended by science apart from dialectics. Dialectics in relation to science represented nothing more than "a new obscurantism." Hook was somewhat less severe with respect to the application of dialectics to history, but here too he claimed it was of little true value.[66]

Hook's enmity toward the Marxist left was further on exhibit in 1969 in the support he offered to the Regents of the University of California system and Governor Ronald Reagan on the firing of Angela Davis. Davis was a newly appointed philosophy professor with a two-year contract at the University of California at Los Angeles, but Reagan and the UC Regents sought to fire her before she had even taught a course based on political grounds. Hook, in his *Heresy Yes—But Conspiracy, No!*, a pamphlet version of which was published in 1952 by the ACCF, and later in his 1970 *Academic Freedom and Academic Anarchy*, argued that a Communist should never be allowed to teach in the United States because Marxists were politically opposed to principles of academic freedom. For Hook, Reagan, and the California Regents, mere membership in the Communist Party was evidence of Davis's "incompetence" (despite her being a student of Herbert Marcuse at Brandeis, where she graduated *magna cum laude*, followed by her year of study in France, her two years in Germany at the University of Frankfurt, and her PhD candidacy at the University of California at San Diego). The attempt to fire Davis in 1969 was stopped by the courts, but Reagan and the California Regents managed to fire her at the end of the 1969–70 academic year on trumped up-charges based on the "inflammatory language" she had used in a number of speeches.

The American Association of University Professors censured the University of California Regents for their actions. Hook was to end his career at the right-wing Hoover Institution.[67]

THE RACE CONTROVERSY

The SFS was to persist until May 1963 when it was brought to a rather ignominious end at the hands of Baker. Its demise is often seen as due to its task being completed, through the defeat of the scientific left. However, the SFS's decline was precipitated by internal disputes that broke out in its last decade, particularly in relation to Baker's criticisms of the role of the scientific left in developing UNESCO's famous statements on race (discussed below). For Baker and his closest allies, it was the war of the scientific left on eugenics, which was their greatest crime—leading to criticisms on their part that were to split the SFS.

There were several years of discussions in the early 1950s over whether the SFS should merge into CCF's Committee for Scientific Freedom, now chaired by Polanyi and occupying the greater part of his time, with Baker also a member. The incentive for such a merger was that considerable funding would flow from the CCF and its Committee on Science and Freedom to the SFS. Yet Baker continually raised the question of the "apparently illimitable funds, and the absence of any explanation" where the CCF was concerned.[68] The secrecy around the CIA's funding of the CCF, which Baker was not party to, leading to his persistent questioning, therefore became a significant issue blocking the SFS's direct affiliation with the Paris-based organization.

A bigger conflict in the SFS arose in 1955 when strikes and protests broke out at Göttingen University over the appointment of a former Nazi and neo-Nazi publisher, Leonhard Schlüter, as Minister of Education and Culture for Lower Saxony. The CCF came out in favor of the protests. This outraged Baker, who wrote a circular for the CCF leadership indicating that they should not take sides in the dispute. Baker's action was strongly opposed by Polanyi, who refused to have Baker's circular distributed, arguing that the CCF could neither take the side of Nazis, nor remain neutral. Baker resigned from the Committee on Science and Freedom in defiance, and the relations between the two turned cold, although they continued to work together for a time.[69] Baker was also an adamant opponent in these years of non-white immigration into Britain and openly supported continued white rule in South Africa and Rhodesia.[70]

Baker had been a member of the Eugenics Society since the 1920s and was encouraged in this respect initially by his supervisor and mentor, Julian Huxley. But by 1936, Huxley, a scientific humanist closely connected to the British socialist scientists, had moved to a position that was strongly critical of the biological concept of race. In 1931, Hogben, having returned from a position in South

Africa where he had opposed Jan Christian Smuts and the developing apartheid movement, had published his pioneering *Genetic Principles in Medicine and Social Science* with its famous chapter on race, where he had shown the fallacy of the genetic concept of race. Hogben's book created a great stir and was strongly attacked by figures like the psychiatrist and eugenicist Carlos Blacker, general secretary of the Eugenics Society, author of *Voluntary Sterilisation* (1934), and Baker's closest friend. In *Voluntary Sterilisation*, Blacker explicitly defended Nazi Germany's 1934 Sterilization Act.[71] He later criticized Haldane for his general rejection of eugenics and for his position in favor of remodeling society as a means of human improvement.[72]

Hogben's sophisticated critique of biological race theories was soon taken up by Haldane, Huxley, and the scientific left in general and was to gain widespread support throughout the scientific community.[73] The work of Hogben and Huxley in this regard inspired Ashley Montagu to write his famous *Man's Most Dangerous Myth: The Fallacy of Race* in 1942, in the midst of the Second World War. The rejection of eugenics was given further impetus by the effects of Nazism.[74] In his 1950 piece "They Want to Geld the Poor," Haldane wrote a scathing attack on sterilization aimed at the poor and racial minorities in the United States. He pointed to a book by R. L. Dickinson and C. J. Gamble called *Human Sterilization: Techniques of Human Conception Control* (distributed by the Planned Parenthood Federation in the United States), in which the authors, in Haldane's words, sought "to alter one of the [Christian] beatitudes, to 'Blessed are the poor, for they shall be sterilized.' " He strongly criticized this book for its apologetics with regard to sterilizations conducted in Nazi Germany, along the lines of Blacker's argument in Britain.[75]

The criticisms of eugenics by the scientific left sparked a major cultural and scientific assault on biological racism immediately after the war in the context of the formation of the United Nations Educational, Scientific and Cultural Organization (UNESCO). UNESCO was to issue a series of landmark, authoritative statements on race between 1950 and 1967, in which figures in the British scientific left played central roles. Responding to UNESCO and left scientists, Baker sought to enlist the SFS in a counterattack on the influential UNESCO statements on race equality.

As early as 1943, the Council of Allied Ministers on Education, which was in the process of forming a United Nations cultural organization, eventually to become UNESCO, created a Science Commission, in which Crowther was secretary. This was followed by the appointment of Huxley in 1946 as the first Director-General of UNESCO. Huxley was the grandson of Thomas Huxley and had been a close friend of E. Ray Lankester.[76] He was also co-author of *The Science of Life* (1929) with H. G. Wells and G. P. Wells, which had promoted the concept of ecology and its crucial relation to human society via human ecology. At the time when the *Science of Life* was written, as Huxley was to note in his memoirs, "Ecology was a new subject, not fully approved of by 'classical' zoologists."[77]

From 1926 to 1929, Huxley was president of the National Union of Scientific Workers that preceded the Association of Scientific Workers, and around which the scientific left was organized. He was close friends with Needham, Haldane, and Hogben. Animal ecologist Charles Elton and Tansley were former colleagues of Huxley, and Huxley worked with Tansley in the early stages of the creation of the Nature Conservancy (a British government conservation agency established in 1949).[78]

In 1947, Huxley wrote an essay on "Ethics and the Dialectics of Evolution" that provided a materialist and ecological perspective as the basis of a general ethical stance, reflecting a scientific humanism. Here he quoted Marx's statement on religion as the "opium of the people" in line with his own secular humanist views. In the same essay he raised, via a commentary on his brother Aldous Huxley's *The Perennial Philosophy*, the question of how human beings were to view their control of nature, and whether society was inherently Promethean in this respect. Looking back to William Blake, Julian Huxley declared, "We must build [the new] Jerusalem in the green and pleasant lands of the physical world."[79]

On March 5, 1946, soon after he was made director-general of UNESCO, Huxley sent an urgent telegram to his friend Needham in China, where the latter was then a Scientific Counselor in Chungking, asking him to become a member of the Preparatory Commission of UNESCO, in charge of creating a Division for the Natural Sciences. Needham immediately traveled in great haste from Chungking to London. Needham's role in bringing science into the new organization during its first few years was so significant that he became known as the person who was "largely responsible for the 'S' in UNESCO." He stepped down in 1948 to return to Cambridge, but in 1949 the Executive Board of UNESCO conferred on him the title of Honorary Counsellor and he continued to play a key role.[80]

For UNESCO, a crucial challenge in seeking to provide a unified cultural and scientific outlook after the Second World War was addressing the question of race. In 1950, UNESCO provided its first "Statement on Race," which emphasized the equality of races, authored by a group of eight, mainly sociologists. Natural scientists entered into the final version, however, and the text was revised by Montagu in response to criticism by a number of important figures, including Huxley, Muller, and Needham. Still, some biologists thought that the 1950 statement did not reflect fully the shift in the understanding of racial traits toward statistical conceptions. In 1951, a second statement on race, titled "Statement on the Nature of Race and Race Differences," was issued by UNESCO, this time by a group of fourteen authorities, including natural scientists (zoologists and geneticists) and anthropologists, with the weight this time on the natural scientists. Haldane, Huxley, Montagu, and Solly Zuckerman were among the authors. Ninety-six other geneticists and physical anthropologists were asked to provide comments on the 1951 statement, including Hogben, Muller, Huxley, Needham, and Waddington. UNESCO then published a booklet in 1952 that contained the statement and the responses, including those of Needham.

The 1951 statement, like the statement from the year before, was adamant that "available scientific knowledge provides no basis for believing that the groups of mankind differ in their innate capacity for intellectual and emotional development." UNESCO's final statement on race was issued in 1967, titled "Statement on Race and Racial Prejudice." Here the goal was to go beyond the biological and anthropological aspects of the race concept to address the philosophical and moral issues. This statement was authored by sociologists, anthropologists, lawyers, a social psychologist, a historian, and two geneticists, of which one was Waddington. This report went beyond statements on racial equality to examine racism. "Racial prejudice and discrimination in the world today arise from historical and social phenomena and falsely claim the sanction of science."[81]

Baker was enraged by UNESCO's publication of the 1951 statement on race, particularly by its statement that all races were equal with respect to innate intelligence, a claim he believed had no scientific basis. UNESCO, he complained to the SFS, was inappropriately setting itself up as a scientific authority led by the scientific left, including Huxley. He therefore proposed to the SFS that it devote itself to a struggle to reform UNESCO, attacking the influence that socialist scientists had played in the process. Others within the leadership of the SFS rejected the idea of confronting UNESCO. Frustrated, Baker declared to his SFS colleagues that he would take the issue up with the CCF in Hamburg in 1953, where there would be no committee to silence him. He followed up this threat and got in a public row with the German geneticist Hans Nachtsheim over racial equality.[82]

Baker, who considered himself a physical anthropologist as well as a zoologist, subsequently devoted his efforts primarily to disproving the innate equality of races, leading to the research for what he considered to be his life work, his book, *Race*, published by Oxford University Press in 1974. Baker was an admirer of the eugenicist Karl Pearson (formerly of the Men and Women's Club of the late 1880s), who, in Baker's words, was to be praised not only for his commitment to eugenics but also for his view that "the advancement of man could only come about by natural selection between races." He dedicated *Race* to Blacker as a "lifelong friend," in recognition of their common lifelong promotion of racial eugenics.[83]

In *Race*, Baker did not so much present original research as compile all the information he could, much of it merely anecdotal, that pointed to the inequality of races. Much of his book was concerned with historic anthropological observations attached to European colonialism on various indigenous peoples. His thesis was that only the races he designated as "Europids" and "Mongolids" (together constituting Eurasians) had been successful at building civilizations, whereas "Indianids" (the Indians of the Americas) had only done so to a small extent—in specific "subraces." In contrast, "Negrids" and "Australasids" (a category he used for Australian Aborigines) had not done so at all. For Baker, these results with regard to racial inequality were confirmed by genetic speech characteristics, craniometry, and IQ testing. His supposedly "scientific" conclusion was that the races were innately unequal.[84] He wanted to incorporate into his book attacks on UNESCO and the American Anthropological Association, as well as diatribes on the dangers of miscegenation, but his Oxford Press editors dissuaded him.

Oxford published Baker's *Race* largely at the recommendation of Peter Medawar, who had won a Nobel Prize in 1960 for his work on immunological research directed at tissue transplantation. Medawar, however, had not read the final draft of the book. The critical reception to Baker's book, outside the eugenics community, was cold, an expected response that his friend Blacker attributed in advance to "communists and other ill-disposed people." Oxford University Press quickly let the book go out of print. Baker eventually had his book reprinted in the United States by the right-wing Foundation for Human Understanding, financed by the openly racist Pioneer Fund. His work was to influence later proponents of biological race inequality, such as Arthur Jensen.[85]

Baker's single-minded dedication to attacking UNESCO and the scientific left on race, and to promoting the notion of innate racial inequality while advancing eugenics, divided the SFS. After Tansley's death in 1955, the SFS membership waned.

THE DEFEAT OF THE SCIENTIFIC LEFT

The British Marxian scientists, not at all adverse to debate, responded to the attacks of the SFS with reasoned arguments. It was Needham who first provided a powerful rejoinder in a major 1941 address, "Pure Science and the Idea of the Holy," given to the annual conference of the National Union of Students. Here he criticized Polanyi's notion that "pure science," removed from all social relations, was in some sense more "holy" than socially connected science, and to Tansley's contention that a sharp distinction could be made between "pure" and "applied" science. In response to such claims, Needham pointed to the seventeenth-century formation of the Royal Society of London, highlighting the obvious fact that the scientists in the Baconian tradition who saw science as power and who were behind the establishment of the Royal Society were anything but socially uninvolved; nor were their scientific discoveries "detached" from the reality around them. "Science," Needham stressed, "does not exist in a vacuum. It is essentially a product of society, and the communism of its co-operating observers is but a prefiguration of that economic and social solidarity which humanity is destined to achieve." Replying specifically to Polanyi's association of science with the "holy," Needham indicated that the notion of the "holy" as something pure and above the people and a means of class oppression had been challenged on genuine scientific grounds as far back as the Epicureans in antiquity. The freedom of science required a free society, but this was to be achieved at its highest level not in a society of possessive individualism and class rule but in "the World Co-operative Commonwealth."[86]

Bernal, in responding to Baker, wrote: "I protest against the addition of this barbarous perversion of the language [in the use of the term 'Bernalism']. I do not know where Dr. Baker has met the Bernalists; I have never seen one myself and I don't believe they exist." For Bernal, there was absolutely "no contradiction between considering the practical use of science to a community as a justification for encouraging it and considering that the scientist carries on his work for what he thinks is a sheer love of truth and beauty." Nor was there any conflict between the organization of science, which was already taking place, and freedom, since "the keys to the successful organisation of science are freedom and democracy."[87] Replying to still further attacks on another occasion, he observed that the only way to ensure that science served humanity as a whole, was for scientists to develop "a much closer, more personal, day-to-day and working contact between them and the rest of the population, particularly the organised working class. . . . In this way science can become such an integral part of society that science will never be in danger of destroying society."[88]

Hogben not only defended planning in science, but went after his arch-conservative economics colleagues at the London School of Economics, including Hayek (an SFS member) and Lionel Robbins, whom he depicted as "astrologists of the machine age" and "professional apologists for social paralysis."[89] He wrote: "Professor Polanyi, who opposes scientific planning in the name of freedom, has suggested that we should compile a complete code of moral behaviour. I only wonder he didn't suggest a world conference on Mount Sinai to draw up a code. How easily one is led into spiritual planning if one rejects economic planning."[90]

Avoiding direct confrontation with the SFS critics, Haldane simply declared: "I agree with Spinoza, Hegel, Engels, and Caudwell, to whose analysis of freedom in *Illusion and Reality* I am profoundly indebted, in defining freedom as the recognition of necessity." Science divorced from either freedom or necessity was a contradiction in terms.[91]

Such attempts on the part of the scientific left to ward off the attacks of the SFS were fairly successful at first, but then the Cold War set in and changed the balance. As William McGucken notes, Wood could not have been more wrong in his claim that the decline of the social relations of science movement "was largely due to the growth of a small but extremely articulate and hard-hitting opposition among the scientists"—that is, the Society for Freedom in Science, a view he probably got directly from Polanyi. Rather, the successes of the social relations of science movement in forging a growing role between science and government were palpable in the late 1930s and in the '40s. The declining influence of the Marxian scientists, particularly by the mid-1950s, was to be attributed to wider social causes associated with the Cold War. Only then did the ideological attacks directed at them begin to tell.

The barrage of attacks that Marxian scientists faced seemed to come from every direction, not only from the SFS and the Polanyi-led Committee on Science and Freedom within the CCF, but also from the other side—the humanities as distinct from the sciences—of what Bernal's friend and supporter C. P. Snow famously called the "two cultures."[92] The leading representatives of the humanities and the arts in the British Isles at this time were mainly on the other side of the political divide. Some figures like D. H. Lawrence and William Butler Yeats even exhibited sympathies with fascism, while others were often virulently anti-Communist. George Orwell, not ill-disposed to playing the Cold War game, savagely declared that "Bernal's writing is at once pompous and slovenly, for like all apologists for totalitarianism, he is unable to say what he means."[93] Forster went so far as to compare scientists as a group unfavorably to "intellectuals," whom he treated as an entirely different breed. The scientist—Bernal was presented as the leading example—"patronises the past, over-simplifies the present, and envisages a future where his leadership will be accepted. . . . He is subsidised by the terrified governments who need his aid, pampered and sheltered as long as he is obedient, and prosecuted under Official Secrets Acts when he has been naughty." In contrast, the intellectuals, largely associated with the humanities and encompassing creative artists, were the Platonic guardians of humanity itself.[94]

The main precipitating factor in the fall from grace of the red scientists was not the hostility of anti-Communist intellectuals, however, but the Cold War itself, which came to dominate all aspects of capitalist society in the postwar years. Left scientists were essentially given a choice between co-optation, on the one hand, or isolation, on the other.[95] Those who refused to join the anti-Communist crusade, and indeed continued to characterize themselves as unreconstructed Marxists, were considered "fair game" in the repression of these years. In some cases, such as Bernal, the most intransigent positions taken by figures on the scientific left were products of the fact that they were in a sense already isolated and backed into a corner. As Gary Werskey put it, "Leading Communist scientists like Bernal and Haldane were naturally singled out in the ensuing onslaught." Others within the scientific left, such as Patrick Blackett and Solly Zuckerman, became part of the state planning apparatus, advancing left-liberal or social democratic views in some areas (focusing, for example on economic development issues and the need to limit nuclear weapons), while increasingly distancing themselves from the class-based critique. Huxley, who had been close to the red scientists, was to distance himself from them by the end of the 1940s. The Association of Scientific Workers lost thousands of members beginning in the late 1940s. Bernal was stripped of his various positions as a scientific adviser to the government and was not reelected to the council of the British Association in 1949, partly in response to a pro-Soviet speech he had delivered.[96]

The British Marxian scientists, particularly Bernal and Haldane, because of their political affiliations, were held hostage in the late 1940s to the actions of the Soviet Union, with which they had somewhat uncritically identified themselves. Lysenko's 1948 speech denouncing Mendelian genetics placed the British Marxian scientists in an untenable position, followed less than a decade later by Khrushchev's revelations on Stalin and the Soviet invasion of Hungary in 1956, which together split the British left. Fully a fifth of the CPGB would resign or let their membership lapse in the immediate aftermath.[97] Major intellectuals within the British Communist movement left the party and created (together with independent socialists, who had not been members of the party) what is known as the First New Left. This was followed by the emergence of a new, younger intellectual left (the Second New Left) in the 1960s, mainly in philosophy, history, and cultural studies, within what was understood as "Western Marxism," largely defined by its rejection of the dialectics of nature and thus dialectical materialism.[98] Both groups, and particularly the Second New Left, were virulently critical of "Stalinists," a term that was often applied indiscriminately to nearly all members of the CPGB. Bernal, "the most influential British Marxist of his generation," was suddenly rejected not only on the right but by much of the left as well.[99] Cultural theorist and historian, Perry Anderson, writing in the *New Left Review* in 1968, dismissed Bernal and a whole generation of British Marxists with such phrases as "false science . . . and the fantasies of Bernal," citing Wood's *Communism and the British Intellectuals* as his sole source.[100]

THE ECOLOGY OF PEACE

For the besieged scientists of the Old Left who were caught in the Cold War onslaught coupled with attacks from the New Left, there seemed to be no simple and easy response to the multiple forces buffeting them, none consistent with their past beliefs. After 1956, the major British Marxist thinkers of the 1930s were all compelled to carry out their individual metamorphoses as best they could. Levy entered into a fierce struggle with the CPGB from within and then became an important figure in the origin of the First New left. Hogben sought to advance his own conception of scientific humanism, while seeking to help Third World states. Haldane left for India, forging a more holistic, ecological, organic worldview. Bernal turned to the struggle for world peace, unifying this with a wider ecological perspective that also encompassed the origins of life and the growing threats to organic existence. Needham focused on Chinese science and civilization, ultimately finding in it (particularly in Taoism) a humanistic, organic, ecological, and dialectical outlook akin to Epicureanism, a viewpoint compatible with historical materialism. Each of these thinkers was to exhibit a widening engagement with what can be called an ecology of peace.

Hogben's course in the late 1950s and '60s reflected the Romantic Morrisean-socialist values that had shaped his outlook. He and Enid Charles finally parted company after forty years, when she took a position as director of statistics for the South East Asia branch of the World Health Organization. Hogben settled in the panoramic Ceiriog Valley in North Wales, where he had a riverside cottage that he later shared with his second wife, Sarah Jane Evans. Nevertheless, his withdrawal into North Wales was far from complete, since he found himself drawn to the decolonization movement in the Third World, and to the new postcolonial states breaking from the British Empire. In the late 1950s, he served as educational adviser to Kwame Nkrumah's government in the Gold Coast (Ghana), with its philosophy of African socialism. Beginning in 1963, at the request of the socialist Premier Cheddi Jagan, he took up a position for two years as vice chancellor of a new university in British Guiana, soon to become Guyana. He later relinquished his post there during the political instability of the period, which he attributed to a considerable extent to Washington's attempt to bring down the "quasi-Marxist government," conditions that Hogben, who was under no illusions, later compared to the role the United States played in the coup in Chile.[101]

Hogben's opposition to biological race conceptions and his advocacy of human ecology continued to guide his actions. In a 1959 address to the Institute of Race Relations in honor of the Darwin Centenary, he spoke out strongly against the biological race concept and genetic determinism, and presented an outlook aimed at bringing together biology, anthropology, as well as historical and cultural studies to address "human ecological systems." Drawing on anthropologist Daryll Forde's *Habitat, Economy and Society*, Hogben argued that racist accounts as to why, for example, indigenous peoples in the Americas had not perfected the wheel, had to give way to wider, human-ecological explanations that recognized the absence of horses and other large draft animals in their environments (an issue raised long before by Lewis Henry Morgan and

Engels). He launched excoriating attacks on eugenics and biological racism. Social responsibility in science, he insisted, required a rejection of the new secrecy in science, promoted by corporations and the state. What was emerging in the context of the new military-industrial complex was a "new authoritarianism" that was destroying the community of knowledge essential to freely developing science. He argued for a "radical reform of human communication" in face of the dangerous degradation of political discourse in the Cold War era. "For *Nuclear Deterrence*," he insisted, "we must learn to say *Incentive to Annihilation*, for *Civil Defense*, we must learn to say *There Is No Hide-Out*, for *Massive Retaliation*, we must learn to say *Universal Suicide*."[102]

Hogben's consistent ecological perspective made him an adamant critic after 1945 not only of nuclear weapons but of nuclear energy generally. As he explained, in the closing pages of his unfinished autobiography, written in 1974–75:

> That we can use this new source of energy for peaceful purposes, if we sidestep the suicide of our species, is of little comfort to me. On a long view, disposal of radioactive waste material has formidable dangers to add to the pollution of our atmosphere and its degradation through denudation of forests which contribute to the maintenance of a viable balance between oxygen, carbon dioxide and water vapour. Unless we can devise some not as yet foreseeable way of disposing harmlessly of atomic waste, peaceful use of atomic power has no long-term future.[103]

Conscious of his Jewish heritage and shocked by Nikita Khrushchev's revelations about the Stalin period, Levy entered into an intense struggle within the CPGB after 1956, focusing principally on the issue of anti-Semitism in the USSR under Stalin. Levy was closely allied with historians E. P. Thompson and John Saville, and novelist Doris Lessing at *The Reasoner*, during a brief period in which they sought to change the CPGB from within. Dismayed by reports of widespread persecution of Jews in the USSR between 1948 and 1952, Levy led a fact-finding mission to the Soviet Union in fall 1956 and published a report in January 1957. The report dealt with the "Black Years" when numerous Jews were dismissed from their posts, and when many Jewish writers had their works suppressed, were arrested, accused of treason, and purged. A summary of the report, complete with Levy's signature, was published in the CPGB's weekly *World News and Views*. But at the CPGB's congress in spring 1957, during which Levy criticized the leadership for having misled Party members for so long about the reality in the Soviet Union, he was met with a vituperative response. As the official Party organ, the *Daily Worker*, reported afterward: "Revisionist Views Smashed."[104]

Rather than retreating, Levy responded by waging a virtual one-man oppositional struggle within the Party that lasted from 1956 until his expulsion in 1958. Lessing, who was close to Levy and deeply involved in these events, wrote in her novel *The Golden Notebook* (her most important work, which earned her the Nobel Prize in Literature):

> About three weeks ago I went to a political meeting. This one was informal at Molly's house. Comrade Harry, one of the top academics in the C.P., recently went to Russia to find out, as a Jew, what happened to the Jews in the "black years" before Stalin died. He fought the communist brass to go at all; they tried to stop him. He used threats, saying if they would not let him go, would not help him, he would publicise the fact. He went; came back with terrible information; they did not want any of it made known. His argument the usual one from the "intellectuals" of this time: just for once the Communist Party should admit and explain what everyone knew to be true. Their argument, the old argument of the Communist bureaucracy—solidarity with the Soviet Union at all costs, which means admitting as little as possible. They agreed to publish a limited report, leaving out the worst of the horrors. He has been conducting a series of meetings for Communists and ex-Communists in which he had been speaking about what he discovered. Now the brass are furious, and are threatening him with expulsion; threatening members who go to his meetings with expulsion. He is going to resign.[105]

But rather than resigning in 1956, as the above suggests, Levy joined with Thompson (who had only recently published his biography of William Morris), Saville, Lessing, and others in supporting the cyclostyle (similar to mimeograph) publication *The Reasoner*, edited by Thompson and Saville. For a very short time—three issues—*The Reasoner* sought to transform the Party from within, under the banner of a new socialist humanism. By the fall of 1956, however, it was clear that the CPGB was not going to accept the new dissident publication within its midst. In August and September of 1956, Thompson and Saville wrote several times to Levy and Lessing explaining that though the original plan in the face of the Party's orders had been for Thompson and Saville to resign, they had decided to bring out one last issue of *The Reasoner*, and then cease publication. Soon afterward they were suspended from the Party for three months. But at this point, following the Soviet invasion of Hungary in October–November 1956 and the refusal of the CPGB to protest, they both resigned, having given up on any attempt to change the Party from within.[106]

Thompson and Saville, along with others, including Lessing and the Marxist economist Ronald Meek, founded *The New Reasoner* in 1957, the goal of which was to ensure the continuity of the Marxist movement from outside the Party.

The members of the editorial board of *The New Reasoner* all sought to convince Levy to join with them. Both Thompson and Saville wrote letters to him separately strongly urging him to agree to be on the board of the new publication. However, at the time, Levy was still deeply engaged in his own struggle within the Party, seeking to get it to acknowledge and criticize Soviet anti-Semitism and related crimes committed under Stalin. He was therefore not yet ready to break with the Party, a step that joining the editorial board of *The New Reasoner* would have required.[107]

Levy continued to battle the CPGB leadership, writing a letter to John Gollan of the Party's Political Committee, pointing to the hypocrisy and apologetics of Andrew Rothstein's *The Soviet Union and Socialism* that was published by the Party in 1957, calling the book a "howling failure."[108] In a fateful step, he took his struggle over the Stalinist persecution of Jews to the public realm in 1958 in his book *Jews and the National Question*, arguing that self-criticism was essential to the future of Marxism. The result, however, was his expulsion from the Party.

In his later years, though alienated from much of the Old Left, Levy continued to support Marxian analysis, if now as an independent socialist. Significantly, he was to become a subscriber in 1959 to *Monthly Review: An Independent Socialist Magazine* in the United States, then edited by Leo Huberman and Paul M. Sweezy, and to which various figures of the British New Left were to contribute, including Thompson and Williams.[109] Levy increasingly gravitated toward socialist humanism, but his active political contributions were much reduced in his later years. Still, he was a strong opponent of the escalating nuclear arms race and an avid supporter of the World Council of Peace led by Bernal. In 1968, at age eighty, he was still fighting racism and drawing new hope from the revolutions in China and Africa.[110]

Haldane went through a more complete metamorphosis. Faced with the events of 1956, he chose to leave England altogether. In 1957, with Helen Spurway, his second wife and former research assistant, he left for a position at the Indian Statistical Institute in Calcutta. There he inserted himself into the culture of the newly independent state, then under the leadership of Jawaharlal Nehru. Ever since 1917, when he was sent to a British Army hospital in India while recovering from a wound in Mesopotamia (now Iraq), Haldane had wanted to return. He was excited by the prospects of the new, independent, non-aligned India with its emphasis on socialist-inspired planning and economic and scientific development, along with its Third Worldist stance. Haldane quickly embraced aspects of Hindu cosmology and ethics, including vegetarianism and animal rights. He became an opponent of all violence in the scientific study of animals. As his colleague, Krishna Dronamraju, later recalled, he "enjoyed returning to nature as was evident in his participation . . . in bird watching, observing wasp and fish behavior, and other studies of an ecological nature."[111]

In two places—first at the Indian Statistical Institute in Calcutta from 1957 to 1961, and then in Bhubaneswar in the state of Orissa (now Odisha) in 1962–63, where the chief minister was building an Institute for Genetics and Biometrics for him—Haldane trained younger Indian scientists and directed experiments in genetics, botany, biometrics, and ecology. He stressed the need for the development of tropical plant varieties and agriculture aimed at food self-sufficiency, breaking with the monocultures of Western agribusiness. He also explored problems of animal behavior including the nest-building of wasps and the selective visits of butterflies to flowers.

In all of this, Haldane sought to bring "Darwin to India." He took the position that Darwin's most unique contributions to science lay not in his theory of evolution, an area in which many others had made contributions, but rather in his research in experimental botany together with his later study of earthworms. Most important were Darwin's experiments with respect to insectivorous plants, climbing plants, sexuality in plants, and inbreeding in plants. Carefully replicating some of Darwin's experiments, Haldane concluded that the greater density of the tropical flora generated interdependencies among plant (and animal) species, involving both competition and cooperation among species. This pointed in a direction directly opposed to Western-capitalist monocultures in agriculture. He also developed quantifiable studies to test his hypotheses with respect to symbiotic relations. This great project came to an end abruptly in 1963, when he was diagnosed with cancer; he died the following year.[112]

Haldane's most distinguished student and younger colleague at University College, London, the leading evolutionary geneticist and ecological theorist, John Maynard Smith, was, like Haldane, heavily influenced by Marxism, joining the CPGB in 1938, and like so many others leaving the Party in 1956. He remained sympathetic with socialism throughout his life. His classic *The Theory of Evolution,* first published in 1958 with the object of presenting the neo-Darwinian synthesis, incorporated a theory of human evolution focused on the development of the hands and tools giving rise to language and a more developed brain, that was closely related to Engels's argument in "The Part Played by Labour in the Transition from Ape to Man."[113]

As an evolutionary geneticist, Maynard Smith generally eschewed dialectics (though strongly supporting Engels's law of the transformation of quantity into quality, which he saw as subject to mathematical presentation). Nevertheless, he was fascinated by developments in dialectical biology and was part ally, part critic of thinkers like Lewontin, Levins, and Stephen Jay Gould, writing pieces like "Reconciling Marx and Darwin" on Lewontin-inspired research, "Molecules Are Not Enough" on Levins and Lewontin's *The Dialectical Biologist*, and "Tinkering" on Gould's *The Panda's Thumb*.[114] Maynard Smith was highly critical of genetic determinism and its use "to justify the enslavement of blacks, the confinement of women to a reproductive role, and the poverty of the laboring class," along with similar arguments directed against "gays and lesbians, and the handicapped."[115] All human beings, he argued, were unique products of the "interaction between genes and the environment." Haldane's influence on Maynard Smith, as well as that of Levins and Lewontin, could be seen in such works as Maynard Smith's seminal 1974 *Models in Ecology*.[116]

Bernal metamorphosed in the post–Second World War years from his role as a war adviser into a leading exponent of an ecology of peace, representing the overall tendency of the radical scientists in response to the growing dangers of the Cold War years. What we see is the emergence—albeit not without contradictions—of a wider ecological worldview that increasingly embraced planetary issues. Bernal devoted himself almost completely in the late 1950s and early 1960s to the struggle for world peace. But in the meaning he gave this, it encompassed not only resistance to nuclear armaments but also a growing focus on the effects of imperialism and the need for independent and sustainable development in the Third World. Moreover, ecological considerations came more and more to the forefront in his attempt to develop a more critical social relations of science analysis, and to address the new concerns that arose with the nuclear age. In Bernal's later work, peace and ecology were thus merged. This reflected that the first great ecological movement of the post–Second World War years was the struggle against nuclear testing in the atmosphere and the oceans. It was this that laid the foundations for all the ecological movements that were to follow.[117]

Bernal's immediate response to the atomic bombing of Hiroshima and Nagasaki was that "the world will never be the same"; a qualitative change that would affect the entire future of humanity had occurred. Like many, before increasing concerns about radiation arose, he initially saw immense possibilities with respect to the peaceful use of the atom. Yet this gave way soon to concern over nuclear radiation and the growing threat of nuclear war, all of which effaced the peaceful uses of nuclear energy. Within a year, he had written an article explaining that the nuclear arms race was only just the beginning, and that there would soon be a proliferation of nuclear weapons with hundreds of times the explosive power of the bombs dropped on Hiroshima and Nagasaki. Galvanized into action, he became involved around the clock in every major peace effort dedicated to addressing the problem, beginning with the Conference of Intellectuals for Peace in Wroclaw in August 1948.

Bernal's speech at the Soviet Peace Committee in August 1949—in which he explained that the majority of expenditures in science in Britain and the United States were going into war preparations, and that this had a direct effect on scientific freedom with the growth of "national security" secrets, thus limiting the dissemination of knowledge in vital areas—led to his suspension from the council of the British Association. Nonetheless, he persisted. He was appointed vice president of the World Peace Council (WPC), and in 1958 president, succeeding the eminent French physicist Frédéric Joliot-Curie. The WPC was dedicated to banning nuclear weapons and other weapons of mass destruction and to ending the Cold War, though it relied on Soviet state funding for its operations. Bernal threw himself fully into these efforts with his usual indomitable energy; a struggle for world peace that put him in direct contact with figures such as Nehru, Mao Zedong, Ho Chi Minh, Khrushchev, Linus Pauling, Georg Lukács, and many others.[118]

At the center of Bernal's concerns, following the Castle Bravo test on Bikini Atoll on March 1, 1954, was the question of radiation from nuclear testing and nuclear war. On that date, the United States set off a thermonuclear bomb with an explosive power a thousand times greater than the fission bomb on Hiroshima and Nagasaki. The blast was two and a half times greater than what the scientists conducting the test had predicted, since they had overlooked an important nuclear fusion reaction. Much of the atoll where the test took place was vaporized by the underwater explosion, while a Japanese fishing boat, the *Lucky Dragon*, eighty miles outside the exclusion zone, was covered in radioactive fallout. More than a hundred Marshall Islanders were exposed to radioactive fallout.[119] Only in February 1955, due to enormous public pressure, did the Atomic Energy Commission reveal its results on the enormous range of nuclear fallout.

The USSR tested its first partial thermonuclear weapon in August 1953, and dropped a hydrogen bomb from a plane in 1955, demonstrating that they not only had the H-bomb, but could also deliver it. This was followed by the first British H-bomb tests in 1956. Meanwhile, scientists in the United States such as Pauling, Ralph Lapp, Muller, and Barry Commoner pressed the fallout issue. In 1958, a test-ban moratorium was initiated that lasted until 1961, when the Soviets were the first among the three signatories to resume testing, in response to the threats represented by the U.S. U-2 spy flight over the Soviet Union and French nuclear tests. In 1963, the Partial Nuclear Test Ban Treaty was signed, banning nuclear tests in the atmosphere, underwater, and in outer space.[120]

Throughout this process, as the vice president and the president of the World Peace Council, Bernal played a leading role in pushing for limits on nuclear weapons. In 1961, he wrote to President Kennedy: "The world cannot live indefinitely under a balance of terror. The powers of destruction are already only too ample. To attempt to guard against their use by increasing them is a proved way to disaster." At the same time, he opposed Khrushchev's decision to resume nuclear weapons testing in 1961, telling him, with the backing of the WPC: "Lovers of Peace throughout the world will deeply regret that the Soviet

Government has however reluctantly found it necessary to resume the testing of nuclear weapons."[121]

Some figures on the left saw Bernal's stance as too ideologically chained to the USSR to be truly effective in promoting peace. Philip Morrison, a U.S. physicist who had been part of the Manhattan Project in Los Alamos during the war, and was then a regular columnist for *Monthly Review*, wrote to Bernal in 1962, stating emphatically that his treatment of the confrontation between the United States and the Soviet Union over Cuba was ultra-leftist and "too tendentious to be sober politics." Morrison added that he would like to see the WPC "play a role" that was "not necessarily more neutral, but at least more objective," in a coming rapprochement between the superpowers. Bertrand Russell, then president of the Committee for Nuclear Disarmament (CND), took the stance that it was necessary to challenge both superpowers, which the WPC had failed to do. For Russell the problem encompassed the "militaristic imperialism by Russia and China," in addition to the economic imperialism and warmongering of the United States and its Western allies.[122]

Despite the inevitable Cold War contradictions, there was no doubting Bernal's commitment to peace. He continually reached out to all peace movements and peace activists worldwide. Of nuclear weapons he stated: "We must find ways to make it clear . . . that the mere existence of such weapons is a permanent threat to peace and inevitably creates international tension. . . . The central case is that these weapons are inhuman in themselves and that their use cannot be tolerated whatever the excuse. . . . Atomic bombs are evil things, whatever government makes them—American, Soviet, or British."[123]

Bernal was horrified by the level of fallout from thermonuclear devices, the longtime effects of radiation, and by what had happened to the Pacific Islanders and the Japanese fishermen on the *Lucky Dragon*. In *World Without War*, he raised the issue of Strontium-90 and the massive incidence of leukemia arising from nuclear tests and the increase in background radiation.[124]

In November 1958, Bernal sent his newly published *World Without War* to his friend Pauling, who had sent him his own book, *No More War*. Pauling was playing a leading role in international peace efforts in relation to nuclear weapons. He was to receive the Nobel Peace Prize for his efforts in 1962. Bernal told Pauling he was "horrified" by what he had learned from a brief article by Danish biochemist Herman M. Kalckar in *Nature* in August 1958, showing an autoradiograph of a tooth. Kalckar indicated in the article that this would be the best way of measuring radioactive isotopes, using the teeth of babies. It was this technique that was to be used by Commoner and the Committee for Nuclear Information, in close cooperation with Pauling, in the famous St. Louis baby tooth survey (published in *Science* in November 1961), which showed the prevalence of Strontium-90 in the teeth of children in the United States, providing conclusive proof in the most powerful way imaginable (300,000 baby teeth) of the effects of nuclear radiation.[125]

World Without War became Bernal's major work on world peace. It advanced a new "world approach" emphasizing national development, peace, and economic and environmental planning, seeking to transcend the Cold War ideology of the time by placing greater emphasis on the third world within a global perspective. He criticized the new imperialism of the world of monopoly capitalism and argued for the necessity of socialism. His was a picture of socialism as embracing progress for the entire world, with a focus on the solving of the world's most urgent problems. Although he placed his emphasis on how the scientific and technical revolution then taking place in the world could promote modernization, and therefore once again supported many of the big ecological modernization schemes that captured the imagination of the time (such as big dams and irrigation), he demonstrated growing ecological concerns.

Both in *World Without War* and his shorter 1960 work, *A Prospect of Peace*, Bernal raised issues of pollution and ecological destruction, arguing for example for the displacement of coal as an energy source because of its inefficiency and the pollution it generated. As early as 1947, he had pointed out that "of the coal we burn in our houses, only about 5 percent goes to heat them." Looking back to the problem of fertilizer, he addressed the structural problem (or metabolic rift)—raised in the nineteenth century by Liebig and Marx—of the loss of natural soil nutrients from the land with the shipment of food and fiber to the towns. In this context, he highlighted the various proposals of "conservation agriculturalists," relying on intensive agriculture as in China, to address this. Ultimately, however, he suggested that, given urban density, there was no alternative to the reliance on mineral fertilizers combined with the most advanced forms of soil conservation in many countries. He raised issues of the detrimental effects of urban heat islands (cities with temperatures significantly higher than the surrounding rural areas) and remarked more generally that "the climate itself is not a fixed thing." Much of his analysis criticized Malthusian gloom with respect to the population-food ratio. An important point was that meat eating and other dietary tendencies of the industrialized countries were inherently inefficient even in providing protein, and that movement back to a more vegetarian diet was desirable. Bernal put his hope, in this as in other areas, in world economic development, cooperation in science, and peace.[126]

Central to his thinking was the waste of resources led by the United States. In "Science Against War," written in the early 1950s, Bernal pointed to the excesses in the U.S. per capita consumption of oil, which, according to United Nations statistics, was six times that of Britain, ten to fifty times that of most countries in Europe, and as much as a hundred times that of many less developed countries. "The wastefulness of the American economy," he wrote, "is due primarily to the capitalist nature of its exploitation. It is not an intrinsic feature of the scientific transformation of industry. . . . A fully scientific economy would be much more economical in the use of materials by reducing the amounts required for any purpose and by a planned system of recovery and re-use."[127]

Building on similar stances taken by Bertrand Russell and Jean-Paul Sartre, Bernal argued that the Cold War had become an international political order in itself, conducted in military terms, and needed to be set aside if the whole world was to advance. "The Cold War" had "become a large and vested interest," generating untold profits. Indeed, "One fundamental reason for condemning the state of the Cold War," he stated,

> is its hopelessness, a hopelessness shared by its most fervent advocates. The best hope they can offer is a negative one—the destruction of communist states and communism throughout the world. If this cannot be done by nuclear war, then it will be by internal dissension produced by the strains of the Cold War itself. But having done this and restored the rule of capitalism throughout the world, what is there for most of the world to look forward to. Even for the United States and a few other favoured countries, the only prospect held out is of carrying on as before 1917, without the fear that their system may be upset by military force, as they often claim but do not really believe, or by foreign subversion. But this world-wide capitalist system was precisely that which broke down in the first world war and gave rise in 1917 to the first socialist government. Nothing has happened since to alter it so fundamentally as to remove the internal strains that led to these events. . . .
>
> The prospect for the underdeveloped countries is likely to be far worse. With the destruction of the only socialist governments of the world, there would be no longer the restraint on imperialist exploitation and oppression which their presence exercised particularly during the last fifteen years.[128]

Bernal's concern over the plight of underdeveloped countries was a continuing theme in his writings throughout the 1950s and '60s. This was evident in an extraordinary article on "Science and Natural Resources" that he wrote in 1953 for *The Indian Student*, a journal published in Britain. Here he presented perhaps his most critical analysis of science, viewed from the standpoint of Third World countries. Although most poor countries had abundant natural resources, they were unable to make use of them in ways that fulfilled their own needs: "Not only is the poverty in most parts of the world not alleviated by the use of science but in certain places it may have actually increased" as a result of the misuse of science. This arises because "no account is taken of conditions, economic, social, and political, that determine the application of science to any country. Science is not a thing which can be given or bought and then used. It is an activity with a history and its development and utilization are determined by factors outside its own disciplines. The use of science to release natural resources must be considered not as a static thing but as an operation."[129]

Most important here was the imperialist structure of science. Science in the capitalist world was concentrated in a small number of countries, in the highly industrialized centers of "England, Germany, and certain parts of America." This led Bernal to formulate his important thesis that "the pattern of scientific research is even more centralised than that of capitalist investment." This helped create a condition where "the hard work is done by 'natives' and the profits and the scientific knowledge acquired" in their exploitation "flow back to the centres of world capitalism." It was important to recognize that "much of the science of so-called Western civilization is in fact of Indian origin, including the mathematics which is the distinguishing mark of modern science." Development in underdeveloped, postcolonial countries required a revolt against the profit system, so that the actual needs of the people could be addressed, along with a revolt against the empire of capital and its exploitative use of science. "How best to use science in India," he contended, "is something that only the Indian scientists themselves can find. It is for them to assess the problems and to determine the solutions. The one thing they must not do is to accept the opinions of foreign experts. . . . Their minds work in an atmosphere of company flotation, profits and dividends." Instead, the practical object should be "how to create in the shortest possible time the basic elements of a planned industrial and agricultural civilization in India and to do it almost entirely from the resources of the soil of India and the labour of her people."

Here Bernal encouraged creative ecological responses. Large dams, he now concluded, were not necessarily the answer. Rather, the rivers of India could be channeled through millions of ponds in little tributaries and gullies, a method that constituted the secret of Chinese river control. He also argued that India could free itself from energy limitations by making widespread use of solar power. "Much," he wrote, "can be learned by scientists on the spot, of the traditional ways of peasants and craftsmen so as to make small and cheap modifications and additions, blending new with old knowledge. . . . But it is not for us, the scientists of the old industrial countries, who are not in India, to prescribe such remedies. . . . The real lesson of modern science is that it is not something that is taken from outside and given to people for their good, but something they must learn and want to use for themselves."[130]

It was this new thinking that underpinned Bernal's analysis of Third World conditions in *World Without War*, and that guided his efforts in this period. In an attempt to ensure the advancement of all of humanity, Bernal argued, the World Council of Peace sought to act "as a kind of Parliament of Man, attempting, and with some success, to influence governments to halt their conflicts, to negotiate, to disarm, and to ban all nuclear weapons."[131]

Bernal's own attempts in the late 1950s and in the 1960s to promote this Parliament of Man, while also continuing with his efforts in science, involved him in what were superhuman commitments. This can be seen in his extensive activities in 1962. In January Bernal, at age sixty-one, presented a lecture in Paris on "The Theory of Liquids." This was followed by a lecture tour in South America in January–February. In March, he delivered two lectures in Berlin. In April–May, he delivered seven lectures in the New York area, including at Yale. Topics in these lectures included the origin of life, molecular structure, the order of disorder, crystal synthesis and solid state, fossils and meteorites—and were accompanied by private talks with U.S. peace leaders. In May, he was in Stockholm for the World Peace Council preparatory. In June, he presented the Bakerian Lecture to the Royal Society on "The World Without the Bomb" and lectures in Accra and New York. In July, he participated in a meeting in Munich to commemorate the fiftieth anniversary of the discovery of x-ray diffraction. In September, he attended a World Peace Council general assembly in Moscow, and a Pugwash Conference peace meeting in London. In October, an urgent World Peace Council meeting in Finland on the Cuban Missile Crisis was called, at which he was present. In the same month, he also delivered scientific talks in Amsterdam and Groeningen. In November, he participated in a meeting in Brussels on the problems of divided Germany. A similar hectic pace continued into 1963. In June of that year, he suffered his first stroke on the day he returned from a trip to the United States.

With his health deteriorating, Bernal was forced to resign as president of the World Peace Council. He made the announcement in his opening address to the delegates at the eighth WPC Congress in Helsinki in July 1965—an address that was devoted primarily to the Vietnam War. He condemned the use of military force by the United States to prop up governments it favored and to carry out destructive regime change throughout the globe, thereby seeking "world dominion." At the final session of the Congress, as Bernal was about to step down officially as president of the World Peace Council, Chilean Pablo Neruda (who was to receive the Nobel Prize in Literature in 1971) read a poem he had written just moments before as a tribute to him, ending with the stanza, "Bernal! Bernal! And doves will fly!" Neruda's voice caressed "the Spanish syllables: 'Bernal . . . Bernal . . . ' as the thousands present rose cheering and Bernal, himself presiding, this time indeed blinking—and unable to rise."[132]

Bernal continued to work as before, but he suffered a second, disabling stroke in September 1965.[133] Unable to use his right arm, consigned to a wheelchair, his ability to communicate impaired, but his mind still clear, Bernal persisted with his efforts right up to his death in 1971. His remarkable work *The Origin of Life*, which presented an extraordinarily rich, analysis of the materialist conception of life, arising from the earlier work of Haldane and Alexander Oparin, integrating Vernadsky's biosphere and contemporary ecological analysis, was published in 1967. In explaining the basis of this book, he wrote:

> Biology is a particular field of the behaviour of certain common chemical systems occurring on this Earth which have differentiated into a number of different kinds of organisms and yet have an underlying unity. I had a very interesting discussion on this point with Einstein in Princeton in 1946, from which it appeared to me that the essential clue was that life involved another element, logically different from those occurring in physics at that time, by no means a mystical one, but an element of *history*. The phenomena of biology must be, as we say, contingent on events. In consequence, the unity of life is part of the history of life and, consequently, is involved in its origin.[134]

In *The Origin of Life*, Bernal strongly emphasized *history* and *ecology* as governing our understanding of life, pointing to the essential *self-creativity* of life itself. "The great liberation of the human mind, of the realization first stressed by Vico and then put into practice by Marx and his followers that *man makes himself*" had been "enlarged with the essential philosophical content of the new knowledge of life and the realization of its self-creative character." Yet, this new ecological understanding came also with the realization that the destruction of the environmental conditions of life, extending to the entire biosphere, was now emerging as a product of industrial civilization. "The destruction of the environment . . . in the unintentional or intentional slaughter of wild life, from butterflies to whales," Bernal emphasized, was a major concern. Our growing scientific knowledge of ecology and the biosphere had to be measured against the reality of increasing threats of destruction. In the nuclear age, ecological considerations were applicable to humanity itself. "The pursuit of old ends by modern means is already going far to destroy civilization and threatens the complete destruction of humanity." Life on earth as currently known, the product of a long evolution, was in danger. "If life is not to die, we have to see to it that we stop now the forces threatening its existence."[135]

Bernal's mature ecological views were rooted in his understanding of the physical basis of life. Here he emphasized the role of "the processes of metabolism," the "biochemical character of life as a process," and the "thermodynamics of living organisms." Presenting a view associated with Vernadsky, which was to play into his later work on *The Origins of Life*, he declared in *Science in History*: "In the fully developed *biosphere*, as it has existed at least for the last 1,000 million years, relatively few organic molecules are permanently set aside; but those that are, such as coal and oil, are of the greatest value to man. Most go round in endless cycles of transformation through plant, animal, and bacterium, back to plant again. The whole biosphere can be considered as one evolving biochemical system."[136]

Responding to the work of Paul Ehrlich and others, Bernal wrote an editorial for the *Morning Star* (London) in 1968 titled "Can Humanity Be Saved from World Starvation?" Here he took on the population and food questions, and the application of science to these issues, arguing that neither the capitalist nor the socialist world had sufficiently addressed these problems facing the Third World. He analyzed, in terms similar to Paul Baran's *The Political Economy of Growth* (1957), the siphoning of economic surplus from underdeveloped countries as a result of the class structure, and the role of international capital in robbing poor countries of needed capital resources. The answer was not foreign aid or the application of science by foreign powers, but "a real use of science and technology directed not so much to profit as to the service of the people in agriculture and medicine." Bernal believed that the natural resources of almost all countries were sufficient to feed and provide the necessities for their populations, and that the key was that "it should be done by the activity and initiative of the people themselves—by them and not for them—which implies not only social revolution but a great development of education, especially scientific and technical education"—a path for which Cuba was to be a model.[137]

Ernesto "Che" Guevara, then head of the Banco Nacional de Cuba, wrote to Bernal on April 12, 1960, at the suggestion of *Monthly Review* editors Huberman and Sweezy. In his letter, Che invited Bernal to Cuba "for the length of time as you may wish." In his response, Bernal declined visiting Cuba then, but indicated he would like to acquaint himself more fully with Cuba and its problems, for which he asked Che's help, with the expectation that he would visit Cuba in the not too distant future. He explained that he was "most encouraged by the resurgence of popular liberties in Cuba and by the way in which the Cuban people, together with their leader, are determined to redress the economic misery of their country."[138] His arduous schedule in 1961–62, followed by his two strokes, however, precluded his following up on Che's personal invitation to visit Cuba.

Even more than Bernal, Needham was to transform himself in the post–Second World War decades, becoming the leading Western expert on Chinese science, history, and culture. On February 24, 1943, a C-47 military transport and cargo plane of the Army Corps Ferrying Command flew over the Himalayas into China carrying the forty-two-year-old Needham. He had been sent by the British government to aid the Chinese nationalist government, as a scientific envoy and representative of the Royal Society. Looking out of the windows of the plane, he saw the mountain peaks clearly, as the plane, seeking to reach a safe altitude, rose by spirals to 17,000 feet. With the shortage of oxygen in the cabin, he was unable to execute his plan to write a poem to celebrate his first entry into China. So, he turned instead to Lucretius's *De rerum natura*, soothing his nerves with Epicurean philosophy and poetry.

Upon his arrival at Kunming in Yunan, Needham startled the British Consul-General with his ability to converse freely with the Chinese people. This was to be the beginning of what Needham referred to as his "second half life." To the end of his life, with the exception of his role in UNESCO at its inception, Needham's efforts were devoted primarily to his magisterial, multi-volume encyclopedic project on *Science and Civilization in China*. This, however, was consistent with his earlier intellectual and political commitments, since it allowed him to deepen his materialism, humanism, socialism, and dialectical ecology. He became the principal force behind the British-Chinese Friendship Association and the Society for Anglo-Chinese Understanding, and strongly supported the revolution in Mao's China. He also courageously took a stand against the use of bacteriological warfare by the United States against North Korea in the Korean War. Needham headed the International Scientific Commission for the Investigation of the Facts Concerning Bacterial Warfare in Korea and China, the report of which was published by the Chinese government in 1952, and which condemned the United States for its use of bacterial warfare. This underscored Needham's strong opposition to weapons of mass destruction. Beyond this, Needham openly deplored Washington's massive bombing and near complete destruction of North Korea's nascent industrial infrastructure in the Korean War.[139] Bertrand Russell was later to follow the lead of Needham in documenting the war crimes of the United States with his 1967 *War Crimes in Vietnam*.[140]

The writing of *Science and Civilization in China* propelled Needham toward what he called "correlative thinking" of a more synchronic, relational kind, derived from Chinese culture. This gave rise to a deeper ecological perspective, in which he emphasized the Taoist concept of *wu wei* or nonaction. Rather than referring to passivity, Needham explained, this had to do with refraining from activity that was "contrary to nature" or that went "against the grain." It emphasized interdependence and interpenetration and the need to respect the harmony of natural processes.[141]

Needham believed there was a natural affinity between "dialectical materialism" and traditional Chinese thought, such that Chinese scholars might well see it as resembling their "own *philosophia perennis* integrated with modern science," which had "at last come home." Needham's admiration of the Taoist conception of nature, which he saw as a form of scientific humanism that resembled Epicureanism, was rooted in the Taoist sentiments of "production without possession, action without self-assertion, development without domination."[142]

In the 1970s, following the rise of the environmental movement, Needham considered the social causes of ecological problem, the growing ecological movement in the West, and the relation of this to the misuse of science under capitalism, in two articles: "An Eastern Perspective on Western Anti-Science" (1974) and "Light from the Orient" (1978). In these two essays, he contemplated the "anti-science" tendencies that were then emerging in the West in response to the misuse of science—contrasting Western to Chinese views in these areas. In describing the "'disenchantment' with science" that had emerged in the "counter-culture" in response to Hiroshima, the Vietnam War, industrial pollution, the alienation of nature, and the technological domination of human beings, he relied especially on Theodore Roszak's books *The Making of a Counter-Culture* and *Where the Wasteland Ends*.[143] Summarizing these views, which he took as representing the ecological dissent of a new generation, Needham explained:

> He [Roszak] and the young are against modern science because they feel that it has had evil, totalitarian and inhuman social consequences. They are not content to put this down merely to misapplied technology; their criticism of science itself goes deep. They attack "the myth of objective consciousness," detesting that "alienated dichotomy" which separates the observing self from the phenomena in Nature, and sets up what they call an "invidious hierarchy" which raises the observer to an inquisitorial level, free to torment Nature, living or dead, in whatever way will bring intellectual light. They feel too that science encourages a "mechanistic imperative," that is to say, an urge to apply every piece of knowledge, in every possible way, whether or not its application is health-giving for human beings, or preservative of the non-human world in which they have to live. The scientific world-view is thus accused of a cerebral and ego-centric mode of consciousness, completely heartless in its activity. It is not as if scientific methods of control were applied only to non-human nature; the "scientization of culture" is calculated to enslave man himself. There are many techniques of human control, such as the behavioral and managerial sciences, systems analysis, control of information, administration of personnel, market and motivational research, and the mathematization of human persons and human society. In a word, technocracy is rampant, and the more complete the domination of Nature, the more fully does it become possible for ruling elites to increase their control of individual human behavior.[144]

Characteristically, Needham took this critique of the "scientization of culture" and its effects seriously, while bringing to bear the insights of Marxism and the more holistic cultural view, less alienated from nature, of China. Turning to the Marxian analysis provided in William Leiss's *The Domination of Nature*, Needham commented on how the domination of nature was tied to the domination of humanity in Western capitalist culture. What was needed, he argued, was not the rejection of science, but new social structures and new social relations of science, allowing for "a stage in human consciousness so advanced that intelligence can regulate its relationship to Nature, minimizing the self-destructive aspects of human desires and maximizing the freedom of the human individual within a classless and egalitarian society." He endorsed Marcuse's view that the distinctive aspects of non-Western cultures, where capitalism had *not* triumphed, when combined with the critical viewpoint of historical materialism, could be, in Needham's words, the key to "avoiding the repressive and destructive uses of advanced technologies." The traditional culture of China held out most hope, he argued, for transcending both the alienation of nature and the "scientization of culture," through which other realms of human experience were discarded. China, he stressed, had avoided some of the worst aspects of the metabolic rift in soil fertility, pointed out by figures such as Liebig and Marx through the continued "use of human excreta as fertilizer," preventing "the losses of phosphorus, nitrogen and other soil nutrients which happened in the West."[145]

As Needham emphasized in the first volume of *Science and Civilization in China*, a distinctive feature of Chinese science, despite its backwardness in some respects, was "an organic philosophy of Nature . . . closely resembling that which modern science has been forced to adopt after three centuries of mechanical materialism."[146] "To its credit, Chinese culture," he observed, "has never been really tempted to regard the natural sciences as the sole vehicle of human understanding." Nor did Chinese culture offer the extreme alienation characteristic of Christianity with its supreme deity. Rather, the equation of naturalism with humanism was much more central to Chinese culture. In the traditional Chinese view:

> The universe did not exist specifically to satisfy man. His role in the universe was "to assist in the transforming and nourishing process of heaven and earth," and this was why it was so often said that man formed a triad with heaven and earth (*Thien, ti, jen*). . . . It was as if there were three levels each with its own organization, as in the famous statement, "Heaven has its seasons, man his government, and the earth its natural wealth.". . .
>
> Thus, for the Chinese the natural world was not something hostile or evil, which had to be perpetually subdued by will-power and brute force, but something much more like the greatest of all living organisms, governing principles of which had to be understood so that life could be lived in harmony with it.
>
> Man is central, but he is not the centre for which the universe was created. Nevertheless, he has a definite function within it, a role to fulfill, i.e. the

> assistance of Nature, action in conjunction with, not in disregard of, the spontaneous and interrelated processes of the natural world.[147]

The "Order of Nature," according to Taoism, Needham explained, "was a principle of ceaseless motion, change, and return.... This was a concept not of non-action, but of no action contrary to Nature." In this outlook, deeply embedded in ancient Chinese thought, "Matter disperses and reassembles in forms ever new."[148]

If these were the traditional views of Chinese culture, in Needham's view, they coincided with where his own *Weltanschauung* had finally led him: the transcendence of the alienation of nature and humanity, and the reunification of science and culture.

For the Marxian scientists of the 1930s generation, one thing was clear: capitalism and science were ultimately incompatible. Socialism derived much of its necessity in the twentieth century, they believed, from this very fact. For an *ecology of peace* to be promoted, what was needed, as Bernal had recognized in *Marx and Science*, was nothing less than a *science for the people*.[149]

Epilogue

By dialectics I mean a Logic capable of dealing with life and the world as process.

—JACK LINDSAY

The Age of Ecology is often said to have arisen in 1962, with the publication of Rachel Carson's *Silent Spring*.[1] It is more accurate, however, to see it as having its origin in the public response to the disastrous thermonuclear weapons test under the code name "Castle Bravo" carried out at Bikini Atoll in the Marshall Islands on March 1, 1954. The dire ramifications of the Bravo test were to ignite a worldwide struggle against atmospheric nuclear testing. At its initial stage, with the U.S. left disorganized by McCarthyism, the movement was heavily dependent on scientists and a relatively small number of concerned citizens. Nevertheless, the nascent protest was to lay the foundations for the larger mass movement that followed. The rise of the ecology movement was thus in many ways the product of the nuclear age, and of the first indications that it was now within the power of humanity to destroy its own global habitat.[2]

Sixty-seven nuclear weapons tests were carried out by the United States in the Marshall Islands between 1946 and 1958. The first thermonuclear device detonation, code name Ivy Mike, yielding an explosive power of ten megatons (a million tons of TNT), took place on November 1, 1952, on Enewetak Atoll. In contrast, the Castle Bravo test was intended to have a yield of no more than six megatons. But it turned out to be the largest nuclear explosion ever detonated by the United States, amounting to fifteen megatons. This was two and half times greater than what the nuclear scientists involved expected, and one thousand times the explosive power of the bombs the United States dropped on Hiroshima and Nagasaki. In a colossal error, the scientists conducting the test failed to recognize that the "'dry' source of fusion fuel, lithium deuteride with 40 percent content of lithium-6 isotope," would lead to a vast increase in the explosive yield, creating a fireball nearly four miles in diameter.[3]

The Castle Bravo bomb released an enormous, unexpected level of radiation, with fallout extending over 11,000 square kilometers and traces of radioactive material being detected not only in Japan, India, and Australia, but also in the United States and Europe. Populations of the inhabited atolls in the Marshall Islands, including Rongelap and Utrik, were covered with a fine white-powdered substance (calcium precipitated from vaporized coral) containing radioactive fallout. Decades after the incident, most of the Rongelap children as well as many adults developed thyroid nodules, some of which proved malignant. The crew of a Japanese fishing boat, the *Lucky Dragon*, which at the time of the test was some eighty-two nautical miles from Bikini, outside the official danger zone, were unlucky victims of the explosion. When the boat reached Japan two weeks later, some of the twenty-three members of the crew were already exhibiting signs of substantial radiation exposure. This had a galvanizing effect in a society that knew all too well the symptoms of radiation sickness, and an international controversy was immediately ignited. The Japanese population boycotted fish markets and marched against nuclear testing, leading to the development of a mass-based movement. Soon after Castle Bravo, Japanese scientists and officials announced that the bomb's fallout contained Strontium-90.[4]

The Eisenhower administration attempted to downplay the disaster and to avoid releasing information on the Bikini Atoll test and on the radiation effects of nuclear testing. But the world at large was alarmed by the information that seeped out with respect to Castle Bravo. Scientists began asking questions and presenting their own analyses based on the data they had available. In February 1955, almost a year after the disastrous Castle Bravo test, the government, under enormous pressure, finally issued a statement on the full dimensions of the radioactive threat, with more and more information released over the subsequent year. The alarm this set off in the international scientific community was enormous, as the incalculable threats to life posed by human-made radionuclides released into the environment—Iodine-131, which attacked thyroid glands; Caesium-137, which concentrated in muscles; Strontium-90, which built up in children's bones and teeth; and Carbon-14, which lodged in all the tissues of the body—began to emerge over the next few years.[5] The public soon learned that the fallout from nuclear weapons was even more dangerous than the blast and the heat, and might kill millions of additional people. In 1957, Nevil Shute's novel *On the Beach*, a story about a world population extinguished by radiation, became a bestseller (followed in 1959 by a film), suggesting "that the American public now understood the strategic implications of the *Castle-Bravo* test." In 1957, activists associated with Nonviolent Action Against Nuclear Weapons attempted to occupy a Nevada nuclear test site in order to halt nuclear tests. The radiation scare would feed into the struggle of scientists and citizens over the following years to enact the 1963 Nuclear Test Ban Treaty.[6]

THE SCIENTISTS' MOVEMENT

In its attempts to control the public relations damage associated with Castle Bravo and the growing fear of radioactive fallout, the U.S. Atomic Energy Commission (AEC) tried to suppress the views of the noted U.S. biologist and geneticist Hermann Joseph Muller, winner of the 1946 Nobel Prize in Physiology or Medicine, for his work on the mutagenetic effects of radiation. Muller was a friend of British left scientists, such as J. D. Bernal, J. B. S. Haldane, Lancelot Hogben, and Julian Huxley.[7] Born in New York in 1890, Muller attended Columbia. At the invitation of Huxley, Muller took up a position as an instructor at Rice University in Houston, Texas, in 1914–18, and then, after a stint at Columbia, returned to Texas as an associate professor at the University of Texas in Austin from 1920 to 1932. In 1927, he startled the world scientific community with his publication of a paper on genetic mutations arising from radiation, based on his studies of *Drosophila*.

Along with his research on genetics, Muller was an active Marxian thinker, and first visited the Soviet Union in 1922. In the early 1930s, he was the sponsor and editor of the Texas branch of the National Student League's publication *Spark*, named after Lenin's *Iskra*—with the result that he was under constant FBI surveillance. In 1933, after a year in Germany on a Guggenheim Fellowship, he moved to the Soviet Union, where as a foreign member of the USSR Academy of Sciences he carried out research as a Senior Geneticist at the famous Institute of Genetics of the Academy of Sciences of the USSR headed by N. I. Vavilov. One of his more philosophical contributions in this period was a noteworthy 1934 essay on V. I. Lenin, dialectics, and genetics in which he described "the complicated processes ('movements' in the Marxian sense) whereby . . . objects are interrelated to one another and undergo their development." Such a dialectical approach, he contended, was crucial to the "realization of the complex realities of matter, especially of living matter, of its inter-connectedness."[8]

By the mid-1930s, with growing pressure on Vavilov from Trofim Lysenko (associated with the notorious Lysenko controversy), Muller's own resolute opposition to Lysenko, whom he had openly accused in a conference of "quackery," and the enmity directed at him by Joseph Stalin due to his 1935 book on eugenics, *Out of the Night*, Muller's position in the Soviet Union was in jeopardy. In 1937, he attached himself to the Canadian International Brigade in the Spanish Civil War, working with Norman Bethune on blood transfusion for eight weeks, before returning briefly to the Soviet Union, and then moving on to the Institute of Animal Genetics at the University of Edinburgh, from 1937 to 1940. He returned to the United States in 1940 and took up positions at Amherst College and Indiana University, also working (although without full knowledge) as adviser to the Manhattan Project. Although a strong critic of Stalinism and totalitarianism, Muller retained his fundamental left convictions. In 1956–58 he was president of the American Humanist Association. In 1958, on the centennial of the presentation by Charles Darwin and Alfred Russel Wallace of their papers on evolution, Muller was one of twenty recipients awarded the Linnean Society's Darwin-Wallace Medal (others included Haldane and Huxley).[9]

Though initially supporting U.S. nuclear testing on the theory that deterrence would reduce the chances of nuclear war, Muller in the 1950s issued repeated warnings on the dangers of nuclear radiation, particularly from the standpoint of genetic effects, arguing that all radiation exposure was harmful and cumulative and that there was no safety threshold in exposure to radiation. "No exposure is so tiny," he declared, "that it does not carry its corresponding mutational risk."[10] In the context of the international controversy generated by the Castle Bravo test, Muller delivered a talk at the National Academy of Sciences in April 1955 on "The Genetic Damage Caused by Radiation," in which he directly related genetic damage to the use of nuclear weapons in war (in the cases of Hiroshima and Nagasaki) and nuclear testing. He proceeded to publish his talk in the *Bulletin of the Atomic Scientists*.[11]

Muller's presentation to the National Academy created panic in U.S. government circles. He had been invited to speak as a technical adviser to the American delegation of the United Nations conference in Geneva on atomic energy. The AEC, however, quickly intervened to prevent Muller from speaking, requesting that the United Nations refuse to accept his paper for oral presentation, even though it had been printed in the conference proceedings. He was, however, permitted to attend the conference at his own expense. He sat silently when it would have been his turn to speak while the assembled scientists acting in solidarity gave him a standing ovation. The AEC later declared that Muller was prevented from speaking at the Geneva conference because the text of his speech had referred in this respect to the U.S. nuclear bombing of Hiroshima and Nagasaki. What was objected to was Muller's willingness to address openly the dangers of nuclear fallout.[12]

Muller was one of the eleven prominent intellectuals who signed the Russell-Einstein letter leading to the Pugwash Conference in 1957 that addressed the control of nuclear weapons. He was one of the twenty-seven initial signatories of the 1957 petition, an "Appeal by American Scientists to the Government and Peoples of the World," initiated by the Nobel Prize–winning chemist Linus Pauling, calling for an end to nuclear weapons testing.[13]

Another central figure in the fight against radioactive fallout from nuclear weapons testing was the cellular biologist and socialist ecologist Barry Commoner, who played a key role in initiating and drafting the Pauling petition. "The Atomic Energy Commission," Commoner was to declare, "made me an environmentalist." Born in 1917, Commoner was a "child of the Depression" and of the left movements at that time. He was strongly influenced by the numerous rallies to support the Spanish Loyalists in the Spanish Civil War, by Socialist and Communist meetings defending the labor movement, and by protests against lynchings in the U.S. South. Drawn early on to both science and socialism, he was a close reader of the work of Frederick Engels, and he saw J. D. Bernal's *The Social Function of Science*, aspects of which were later to resonate in his own *Science and Survival*, as a guide to how scientists might operate in more socially responsible ways.[14]

Commoner attended Columbia where he received his B.A. in zoology in 1937, and then went on to Harvard where he obtained his PhD in 1941. In 1942, during the Second World War, he helped to develop an apparatus that would allow torpedo bombers to spray DDT on beachheads to reduce insect-induced diseases affecting U.S. soldiers. At the time, he noticed the large numbers of dead fish appearing as a result of the spraying, giving him an ominous sense of the damage it did to the environment.[15] He took up a position of professor of plant physiology at Washington University in St. Louis in 1947, where he was to remain for most of his career.

Commoner's deep concern over radioactive fallout had arisen in 1953, the year before the Castle Bravo test, and was only to intensify in the face of the latter. On April 26, 1953, Troy, New York, experienced a sudden cloudburst, and as the rain fell, scientists in university laboratories nearby who were experimenting with radiation registered a sharp increase in background radiation. They discovered that the rain was highly radioactive as a result of what was later revealed to be the Upshot-Knothole Simon nuclear test in Nevada. Although their discoveries were not publicly announced due to the secrecy of the times, these scientists communicated with their counterparts in other areas of the country, and it became evident that the radioactive fallout was everywhere across the country: in the rain, water, soil, and food.[16]

Commoner's alarm over nuclear weapons testing was heightened by the information on radioactive fallout reluctantly released by the AEC following Castle Bravo. On a Sunday evening in the fall of 1956, Commoner was discussing the nuclear fallout question with his close personal friend Virginia Warner Brodine, a Marxist and labor and civil rights activist in the Communist Party in the 1930s, who had worked as editor for a medical publishing house. At the time of her discussion with Commoner, she was the public relations director for the International Ladies Garment Workers Union (ILGWU). In their discussion, Commoner referred to Edna Gellhorn's famous campaign for the sanitary regulation of milk and suggested that milk be tested for Strontium-90. Soon after, Brodine approached Gellhorn and other women activists in the St. Louis area. Gellhorn was a founder of the League of Women Voters and a friend of Eleanor Roosevelt. Gellhorn, Brodine, and Gertrude Faust, a local activist associated with the St. Louis Metropolitan Church Federation, and including more than twenty-seven women altogether, some associated with the ILGWU, wrote a letter in 1956 to the St. Louis City Health Commissioner asking them to test the St. Louis milk supply for Strontium-90. Though their efforts were not immediately successful, they turned to exerting pressure on politicians at the national level, including Adlai Stevenson. As a result, the Senate Foreign Relations Committee's Subcommittee on Disarmament, headed by Hubert Humphrey, met in St. Louis in December 1956 to hear public testimony. Gellhorn, in her testimony, declared: "I am here today because many of us feel that the information already available so strongly indicates increasing danger and points to the fact that each H-bomb exploded increases the danger to such an extent that we cannot afford to wait." She went on to ask, "Do H-bomb tests add so greatly to our security that we are justified in risking the health of our children?"[17]

The struggles of these women activists in St. Louis led to the formation of the Greater St. Louis Citizens' Committee for Nuclear Information (CNI) in 1958. (After 1963 it was to be known as the Committee for Environmental Information, CEI.) CNI/CEI was a science and citizens' organization, led by Commoner, focusing on providing citizens with the critical scientific information for the political issues of the nuclear age. Brodine, Gellner, and Faust were all directly involved. Brodine was on the board of CNI and was for several years its secretary. More important, she served as editor of its main publication, originally called *Nuclear Information*, the title of which was changed in August 1964 to *Scientist and Citizen*, and then later *Environment*. Until her retirement in mid-1969 (after which she remained a consulting editor), the publication in all of its phases was edited by Brodine, but its content was subject to approval by the Technical Division of the CNI/CEI, made up of scientists.[18] The CNI became famous, beginning in 1959, for its spearheading of the famous baby tooth survey, headed by Louise Reiss, a medical doctor in St. Louis, and a member, along with her husband, Eric Reiss, also a physician, of CNI. Over twelve years, more than 300,000 baby teeth collected in the St. Louis region were tested for Strontium-90. The results of the testing showed that babies born in 1950, before most of the bomb testing (and before thermonuclear testing), contained about 50 percent less Strontium-90 than those born in 1963. In 1963, Eric Reiss presented the results of the baby tooth survey to a Senate Committee. CNI/CEI also demonstrated that civil defense programs and fallout shelters were practically useless in the face of the thermonuclear threat.[19]

A later CNI campaign was directed in 1961 against Project Chariot, in which the AEC proposed the "peaceful" use of nuclear explosives to create a harbor in Alaska, as well as a host of similar proposals, involving nuclear tests up through the early 1970s that went under the name of Project Plowshare. The Storax Sedan test in Nevada on July 6, 1962, as part of Project Plowshare, was the second most fallout-intensive test to take place in the continental United States, after the "Dirty Harry" (Upshot-Knothole Harry) nuclear weapons test in Nevada in May 1953. The United States National Cancer Institute determined that Sedan had released around 880,000 curies of Iodine-131. The Sedan test displaced more than 12 million tons of soil and created the largest human-made crater in the United States, 100 meters deep and almost 400 meters in diameter. Worldwide nuclear tests, both weapons tests and so-called peaceful nuclear tests, reached an all-time height of 178 in 1962.[20]

In May 1957, Pauling, who had won the Nobel Prize in Chemistry in 1954, the nuclear physicist Edward Condon, and Commoner drafted the bomb test petition in Commoner's office at Washington University in St. Louis. It was printed, with Commoner's insistence, in a union shop, carrying a union label and signed initially by Pauling, Commoner, and Condon and twenty-four other notable scientists, including Muller and the former Manhattan Project physicist Philip Morrison (then a columnist for *Monthly Review: An Independent Socialist Magazine* edited by Leo Huberman and Paul M. Sweezy). Within a few weeks, two thousand U.S. scientists had put their names to the petition and Pauling presented it to President Eisenhower on June 6, 1957. Later, a total of nine thousand scientists from forty-nine countries signed it, and it was presented to the United Nations. It was this petition that generated the momentum that was to result in the August 1963 Partial Test Ban Treaty prohibiting above-ground nuclear weapons testing. Pauling received the Nobel Peace Prize in 1962, making him the only individual to obtain two undivided Nobel Prizes.[21]

Beginning in the 1960s, Commoner emerged as an intellectual leader of the burgeoning ecological movement in the United States and the world. Commoner's 1966 *Science and Survival*, written only a decade after McCarthyism, read in many ways like Bernal's *The Social Function of Science*, although it was more cautious, given that it was published in the much more conservative era of the nuclear age in the United States. In this work, Commoner insisted on the importance of the dissemination of scientific information to the public, and the dangers of nuclear technology, synthetic chemicals, and global warming.[22]

In his bestselling 1971 book *The Closing Circle*, Commoner captured both the dangers and the possibilities of the Age of Ecology. Influenced by K. William Kapp's famous work *The Social Costs of Private Enterprise*, which had pointed to Karl Marx's analysis of the metabolic rift, based on the work of the German chemist Justus von Liebig, Commoner observed: "Marx in *Das Kapital* does point out that agricultural exploitation in the capitalist system is, in part, based on its destructive effects on the cyclical ecological processes that link man to the soil."[23] In its February 1970 issue, *Time* magazine, in pointing to "the emerging science of survival," placed a portrait of "Ecologist Barry Commoner" on its cover. In April 1970, at the time of the first Earth Day, *Scientific American* published a special issue with the Biosphere on the cover. The author of the article featured on the cover was the prominent ecologist G. Evelyn Hutchinson, formerly a student of Haldane and Needham, who had been introduced to limnological research and ecology by Hogben.[24]

With Commoner's support, Brodine went on to expand her own ecological critique, aimed at mainstream audiences but with clear radical intent. She wrote two major informative books, *Air Pollution* (1972) and *Radioactive Contamination* (1975), both part of an Environmental Issues Series published by Harcourt Brace Jovanovich and edited by Commoner. In the latter book, she discussed Castle Bravo; in the former she took on the issue of global warming.[25]

THE *SILENT SPRING* REVOLUTION

The radical upsurge in ecology as both a science and a mass movement, however, was made possible by Rachel Carson's 1962 book, *Silent Spring*. Carson's deep sense of ecological disruption, which was to inspire a generation of environmental activists, had its origins in her concern over the effects of radiation from nuclear tests on ocean life, following the Castle Bravo disaster.[26] As a marine biologist she was deeply affected by the revelations in the mid-1950s with respect to radioactive fallout as well as information that surfaced on government dumping of radioactive wastes in the ocean. In the 1961 edition of *The Sea Around Us,* after noting that the "concentration and distribution of radioisotopes by marine life" was sometimes a million times their abundance in the surrounding water, Carson asked the pregnant question: "What happens then to the careful calculation of a 'maximum permissible level' [of radioactivity]? For the tiny organisms are eaten by larger ones and so on up the food chain to man. By such a process tuna over an area of a million square miles surrounding the Bikini bomb [Castle Bravo] test developed a degree of radioactivity enormously higher than that of the sea water."[27]

When the cloud of secrecy surrounding the fallout problem lifted in the mid-1950s, the scientific community was able to study the extent of environmental degradation and contamination caused by nuclear weapons tests. Such work required the expertise of biologists, geneticists, ecologists, pathologists, and meteorologists, who explored the effects of radiation on plants and animals, as well as the movement of radioactive materials through the atmosphere, ecosystems, and food chains. Nuclear testing had joined the world's population in a common environmental fate, as radioactive fallout was distributed globally by wind, water, and living creatures.

Research on the effects of radioactive substances on food chains led to the development of the concepts of bioaccumulation and biological magnification. Bioaccumulation refers to a process whereby a toxic substance is absorbed by the body at a rate faster than it is lost. Biological magnification occurs when a substance increases in concentration along the food chain. Several variables influence biological magnification, such as the length of the food chain, the rate of bioaccumulation within an organism, the half-life of the nuclide (in the case of radioactive substances), and the concentration of the toxic substance in the immediate environment. Ecologist Eugene Odum noted that due to biological magnification, it was possible to release an "innocuous amount of radioactivity and have her [nature] give it back to us in a lethal package!"[28]

Carson pointed to how biological magnification resulted in dangerously high burdens of Strontium-90 and Caesium-137 in the bodies of Alaskan Eskimos (Inuit and Yupik) and Scandinavian Lapps (Sámi) at the terminal end of the food chain that included lichens and caribou. In her 1963 speech on "Our Polluted Environment," she emphasized the importance of CNI's investigation into radioactive contamination, pointing to Muller's most recent calculations on the hereditary damage inflicted by radiation on posterity, in addition to the physical effects on present generations. "Environmental contamination by radioactive materials," she observed, "is apparently an inevitable part of the atomic age. It is an accompaniment of the so-called 'peaceful' uses of the atom as well as of the testing of weapons."[29]

It was hardly an accident, therefore, that when Carson wrote *Silent Spring*—with its emphasis on bioaccumulation and biomagnification of synthetic chemicals, resembling radioactive isotopes in this respect—that her biggest scientific supporter was Muller, whom she had cited several times in her book, and who underscored the credibility of her analysis in a review for the *New York Herald Tribune*.[30] Muller wrote that Carson's book was "a smashing indictment that faces up to the disastrous consequences, for both nature and man of the chemical mass-warfare that is being waged today indiscriminately against noxious insects weeds and fungi. It argues that these widely heralded—and sold—triumphs of modern chemistry are being applied with only the crudest foreknowledge of the intricate biological hazards entailed." Carson's ecological perspective was "indispensable," bringing enlightenment to "the public regarding the high complexity and interrelatedness of the web of life in which we have our being."[31]

As Carson explained to the National Council of Women of the United States, in October 1962, two weeks after the publication of *Silent Spring*:

> When I was a graduate student at Johns Hopkins University, studying under the great geneticist H. S. Jennings, the whole biological community was stirring with excitement over the recent discovery of another distinguished geneticist, Professor H. J. Muller, then at the University of Texas. Professor Muller had found that by exposing organisms to radiation he could produce those sudden changes in heredity characteristics that biologists call mutations.

> Before this it had been assumed that the germ cells were immutable—immune to influences in the environment. Muller's discovery meant that it was possible for many, by accident or design, to change the course of heredity, although the nature of the changes could not be controlled.
>
> It was much later that two Scottish investigators discovered that certain chemicals have a similar power to produce mutations and in other ways to imitate radiation. This was before the days of modern synthetic pesticides, and the chemical used in these experiments was mustard gas. But over the years it has been learned that one after another of the chemicals used as insecticides or as weedkillers has power to produce mutations in the organisms tested or to change or damage the chromosome structure in some other way.[32]

It was these revelations about the closely related genetic effects of radiation and synthetic chemicals, made enormously more lethal as a result of bioaccumulation and biomagnification, that were to underlie Carson's powerful critique in *Silent Spring* of the widespread application of DDT and other "biocides," as she called them.[33]

What made Carson's analysis so compelling was her ability to place this critique in a larger ecosystem frame. In this respect she was deeply affected by the work of British ecologist Charles Elton, the founder of animal ecology, and particularly by his 1958 work, *The Ecology of Invasions by Animals and Plants*. In this work, Elton had combined an ecosystem perspective with a critique of the "chemical warfare" against animals and plants being waged by industry and reductionist science. For Elton it was crucial to challenge the "astonishing rain of death," now being systematically inflicted on life on so much of the earth's surface without any understanding of the threat to biological diversity and the stability of ecosystems that this represented. Such "mass destruction," he wrote, "may some day be looked back upon as we do upon the mistakes of the industrial age, the excesses of colonial exploitation or the indiscriminate felling of climax forests."[34] Carson quoted Elton's statement on the "rain of death" in an April 1959 letter to the *Washington Post* in which she opened her attack on pesticides.[35] She referred to his book a number of times in *Silent Spring*.[36]

Elton's analysis had also provided the foundation for the work of Carson's friend and associate, Robert Rudd, a professor of zoology at the University of California at Davis. Carson first contacted Rudd in April 1958 to get help with her pesticide research and to obtain some publications on the subject. He visited her with his children at her Maine cottage in July of that year, and the two struck up a strong friendship and working relationship. Rudd was a sophisticated left thinker with a deep sense of the ecology, sociology, and political economy of the pesticide issue. When he met Carson, he had already started his own book on the subject funded by the Conservation Foundation. In 1959, he wrote two articles for *The Nation*: "The Irresponsible Poisoners" and "Pesticides: The *Real* Peril." The only real answer to the pest/pesticide problem, he argued, was to oppose the extreme simplification of monoculture and the reductionism of pesticides as a solution. It was necessary to "cultivate ecological diversity." Carson drew extensively on Rudd's research in two chapters of *Silent Spring*: "And No Birds Sang" and "Rivers of Death." Rudd's *Nation* articles also helped inspire Murray Bookchin's first work on ecology, *Our Synthetic Environment*, published in 1962 (the same year as *Silent Spring*) under the pseudonym of Lewis Herber.[37]

What angered the chemical industry more than anything else about Carson's book was that she chose to begin *Silent Spring* with a literary device, "A Fable for Tomorrow," the tale of "a town . . . where all life seemed in harmony with its surroundings"; and yet a town which unthinkingly, almost unbeknownst to itself, had introduced chemicals of destruction into its midst. A "grim specter," she suggested, was haunting modern industrial society, threatening to silence its spring. Her fable was clearly "for tomorrow" in two senses: it represented both an unprecedented threat to all life, and the possibility of overcoming it. Coupled with the devastating facts on the dangers of pesticides, laid out in page after page of her book, this approach struck a nerve, resonating with a vast public, and igniting a new level of environmental struggle.[38]

But it was her willingness to confront the system, in the form of sharp attacks on industry and capitalism itself, in a society that thought it had vanquished the left only a few years before in the McCarthy era, that gave Carson's work its sharp critical edge. In *Silent Spring* and after, in the two years that remained of her life, Carson was explicit, condemning "the gods of profit and production" and "an era dominated by industry in which the right to make a dollar at whatever cost is seldom challenged." The economic system, "blinded by the dollar sign," was geared to "overproduction" and "intensivism." Indeed, "the modern world," she declared, "worships the gods of speed and quantity, and of the quick and easy profit, and out of this idolatry monstrous evils have arisen." She added: "The struggle against the massed might of industry is too big for one or two individuals . . . to handle," a view that clearly called for the formation of an environmental movement to counter the power of capital and its "enormous stream of propaganda."[39]

It was Carson, above all, who introduced the broad public of her day to the concept of ecology as a new basis for the critique of industrial capitalism. Providing an overall coherence to her ecological worldview was her unified Earth System perspective. *The Sea Around Us* commenced with the ocean as the setting "of the creation of life from non-life."[40] One of the fundamental conceptions of the materialist conception of the origin of life that had emerged in the early twentieth century—going back to the work of the Soviet biologist A. I. Oparin and Haldane—was the notion that life had altered the atmosphere as well as consuming the complex organic compounds upon which the origin of life had depended, making such spontaneous creation of new life from non-life in what came to be called the "primordial soup" no longer possible.[41] Carson in her talk on "The Pollution of Our Environment" placed enormous emphasis on this point and its significance for an ecological critique, arguing:

> From all of this we may generalize that, since the beginning of biological time, there has been the closest possible interdependence between the physical environment and the life it sustains. The conditions on the young earth produced life; life then at once modified the conditions of the earth, so that this single extraordinary act of spontaneous generation could not be repeated. In one form or another, action and interaction between life and its surroundings has been going on ever since.
>
> This historic fact has, I think, more than academic significance. Once we accept it we see why we cannot with impunity make repeated assaults upon the environment as we do now. The serious student of earth history knows that neither life nor the physical world that supports it exists in little isolated compartments. On the contrary, he recognizes that extraordinary unity between organisms and the environment. For this reason, he knows that harmful substances released into the environment return in time to create problems for mankind.
>
> The branch of science that deals with these interrelations is Ecology. . . . We cannot think of the living organism alone; nor can we think of the physical environment as a separate entity. The two exist together, each acting on the other to form an ecological complex or an ecosystem.[42]

Such complex ecosystems, Carson argued, were conceived as highly dynamic and at the same time delicate entities, as were the biosphere and the Earth System. Consequently, the alterations they were undergoing and their ramifications in terms of the creation of entire phase changes were frequently unforeseen until it was too late. An activist human response was thus necessary.

Behind all of Carson's analysis, as Mary McCay noted in her biography of Carson, was the fundamental materialist principle, derived from Epicurus/Lucretius, of "material immortality" (*mors immortalis*—death the immortal). This was introduced early on in Carson's thought, dating back to her article "Undersea" in 1937, and pervaded her thinking as a whole. As a scientist, Carson approached the natural world from a materialist standpoint, rejecting all non-naturalistic explanations.[43]

THE NEW LEFT AND SCIENCE FOR THE PEOPLE

It was the Vietnam War that led to the formation in 1969 of what has been called "the most important radical science movement in U.S. history," namely Science for the People.[44] It arose out of the rebellion of numerous scientists against the militarization of science and the deadly consequences in Indochina. The movement initially took the name Scientists for Social and Political Action. This was later changed to Scientists and Engineers for Social and Political Action. But it came to be commonly known as Science for the People after the name of its magazine. A total of 109 issues of *Science for the People* were published between 1969 and 1989, when it ceased to exist.[45] (A new Science for the People and accompanying magazine with the same title was launched by a new generation in 2018.)

Science for the People, as Donna Haraway and others have argued, was in many ways an outgrowth of the earlier movement of Marxist scientists centered in Britain in the 1930s, and associated with such figures as Bernal, Haldane, Needham, Hogben, Hyman Levy, and C. H. Waddington. The works of some of these earlier Marxian thinkers, including Bernal's *Marx and Science* and *The Social Function of Science*, were listed as recommended readings in *Science for the People*.[46] Like their Old Left predecessors, the New Left scientists associated with Science for the People rejected the division between "pure" and "applied" research, emphasizing the social relations of science.[47] The very term "Science for the People" was taken from Bernal's *Marx and Science*, while the struggles of the British left scientists in the 1930s were known as "the social relations of science" movement.[48] But unlike the earlier Marxist scientists, who advocated a larger role for state funding of science to meet social needs, those linked to Science for the People faced an entirely different situation in the post–Second World War period, particularly in the United States, where "big science" under the control of the military-industrial complex and monopolistic corporations was now dominant. Here it was the misuse rather than the use of science that was the major issue.[49]

Science for the People thus did far more than publish a magazine. Members of the organization formed chapters around the country, and these included physicists, engineers, biologists, geneticists, ecologists, as well as numerous representatives of other scientific groupings and social movements. It became well known in the later years of the Vietnam War, from 1969 to 1973, for its role in principled disruptions of the conventions of mainstream scientific organizations and for its active promotion of its central themes—as one FBI report indicated, of (1) anti-imperialism, (2) social control of science, and (3) science for survival.[50]

As an organization, Science for the People was known for the intellectual stars with which it was associated, including such giants in their fields as Rita Arditti,

Anne Fausto-Sterling, Stephen Jay Gould, Ruth Hubbard, Richard Levins, and Richard Lewontin. In particular, Levins, Lewontin, and Gould, all of whom took up positions at Harvard, then the leading center for evolutionary biology, were to become known for the creative ways in which they drew on the dialectical, historical, and materialist views of Marxism (as well as other influences such as Darwinism) to develop their evolutionary and ecological critiques. In many ways, this constituted a further iteration, but in startlingly new ways, of the dialectic of nature and society, symbolized by the Marx-Darwin relation, that had so engaged Engels and the British Marxist scientists of the 1930s. It manifested itself practically in strong research-based repudiations of crude mechanism, idealism (teleology), and racialism in science, along with exposing the inherent misuse of science in a capitalist society.

Levins (1930–2016) in his early years had grown up with both Marxism and science, and assumed early on that he would end up as "both a scientist and a red." One of the earliest books he read was "Bad Bishop Brown's" (William Henry Brown) 1932 radical *Science and History for Girls and Boys*, which was inspired by the rise of the Soviet Union. In his teens he studied the works of Haldane, Bernal, and Needham, and from there went on to Marx and Engels. As he emerged as a biologist, ecologist, population geneticist, and biomathematician, he rebelled against the reductionism that prevailed within science. Later he was to have considerable experience working with the developing Cuban ecological movement, where ecological destruction from the start was recognized as an internality, not an externality.[51]

In *Humanity and Nature: Ecology, Science, and Society*, written together with the Finnish ecologist Yrjö Haila, Levins set out a broad analysis of ecology that incorporated the "social history of nature" as seen from a Marxist perspective. They introduced the critical concept of "ecohistorical periods" to explain the complex, changing specificity of the human coevolutionary relation to nature—not within a static framework, but seen within a larger perspective that focused on the processes of change inherent in both nature and society—recognizing always that society was an emergent part of nature. Ecology, in this view, raised complex problems that were both social and ecological, problems that from a socialist ecological perspective had to be addressed as both "red and green." Haila and Levins argued, "The idea of nature lies in shambles. Unified nature has been dismembered, the privileged position accorded to humans in nature has disappeared, the foundation of the idea of linear progress has collapsed. This also of course implies that Romantic ideals of the inherent harmony of nature adopted as the other side of rationalistic exploitation, are no longer viable. The era of ecological risks calls forth a fundamental revision in our cultural view of nature."[52] Only a dialectical understanding of the interpenetration of nature and society and the pervasiveness of the ecological crisis of society would now suffice.

Lewontin, born in 1929, a lifelong friend and collaborator with Levins, became a radical activist initially as a result of the civil rights movement and its protests against police brutality toward African Americans. Both Levins and Lewontin were strong supporters of the Black Panther Party.[53] To this was added a deep revulsion toward the Vietnam War, and an attraction to materialist dialectics. Lewontin is known for his pioneering work on the mathematical basis of population genetics and as a major contributor to evolutionary biology. He has played a leading role in combatting notions of the genetic basis of race and the racial use of IQ tests.[54] His article on "Are the Races Different?" for a special 1982 issue of *Science for the People* on "Racism in Science" famously stated: "Human racial differentiation is, indeed, only skin deep."[55] This view was also advanced in Gould's great critical study, *The Mismeasure of Man* (1981).[56] Later, in works such as *Biology as Ideology* (1991) and *The Triple Helix: Genes, Organism and Environment* (2000), Lewontin was to present an elegant dialectical perspective on the interconnections of genetics, evolution, and ecology.[57]

Levins and Lewontin teamed up in writing their now classic work *The Dialectical Biologist* (1985), and later their *Biology Under the Influence: Dialectical Essays on Ecology, Agriculture, and Health* (2007).[58] The hallmark of *The Dialectical Biologist*, which they dedicated to none other than Frederick Engels—"who got it wrong a lot of the time but who got it right where it counted"—is its complex, non-teleological, coevolutionary perspective rooted in Marxian dialectics. Criticizing traditional Darwinian theory, they approach "the organism as the subject and object of evolution," both responding to its environment and changing it. Organism and environment are co-determinant: "The organism cannot be regarded as simply the passive object of autonomous internal and external forces; it is also the subject of its own evolution." A dialectical ecology rests on the five "principles of materialist dialectics": (1) historicity, (2) universal connection, (3) heterogeneity, (4) interpenetration of opposites, (5) and integrative levels.[59]

"The tradition of dialectics," in this sense,

> goes back to Engels (1880) who wrote, in *Dialectics of Nature* that, "to me there could be no question of building the laws of dialectics of nature, but of discovering them in it and evolving from it." Engels's understanding of the physical world was, of course, a nineteenth-century understanding, and much of what he wrote about it seems quaint. Moreover, dialecticians have repeatedly attempted to make the identification of contradictions in nature a central feature of science, as if all scientific problems are solved when the contradictions have been revealed. Yet neither Engels' factual errors nor the rigidity of idealist dialectics changes the fact that opposing forces lie at the base of the evolving physical and biological world.

> Things change because of the actions of the opposing forces on them, and things are the way they are because of the temporary balance of opposing forces. . . . The dialectical view insists that persistence and equilibrium are not the natural state of things but require explanation, which must be sought in the actions of the opposing forces.[60]

Gould (1941–2002) was not only one of the world's leading paleontologists and evolutionary theorists, but also, in the words of Lewontin and Levins, "by far, the most widely known and influential expositor of science who has ever written for a lay public," able to unravel many of the complexities of the natural world and reveling in dialectical relations of complexity and change.[61] He was best known for the theory of punctuated equilibrium (with Niles Eldridge), which questioned a crude Darwinian gradualism, suggesting major discontinuities in evolution. This was often criticized as a Marxian theory, though Gould denied any direct relationship, while admitting that a dialectical way of thinking had been a significant source of inspiration. Rather, he stressed that his "intellectual ontogeny" with respect to Marxism was much deeper and less direct, stating he had "learned his Marxism, literally at his daddy's knee."[62]

In a wider sense, however, there was no doubt about Gould's commitment to socialism and to radical causes in general. He identified himself as a Marxist, recognizing that Marxism was a very rich world.[63] One of his last essays was "The Darwinian Gentleman at Marx's Funeral" on the relationship between Marx and E. Ray Lankester.[64] As Lewontin and Levins observe:

> [Gould] was a consistent political activist in support of socialism and in opposition to all forms of colonialism and oppression. The figure he most closely resembled in these respects was the British biologist of the 1930s, J. B. S. Haldane, a founder of the modern genetical theory of evolution, a wonderful essayist on science for the general public, and an idiosyncratic Marxist and columnist for the *Daily Worker* who finally split with the Communist Party over its demand that scientific claims follow Party doctrine. What characterizes Steve Gould's work is its consistent radicalism.[65]

Gould's intellectual corpus was full of dialectical accounts of the evolution of organisms in relation to the environment, considering numerous factors, including structural change and the pathways they generated, and contingent historical developments. It was contingency that destroyed all teleological accounts and made evolution a *historical* phenomenon.

Gould's singular contribution to ecological analysis was his critique of the crude concept of progress—a critique that pervaded all of his thought and was a product of his dialectical-evolutionary view. The most serious fallacy associated with Western norms, he argued, was "the idea of progress, the idea that we can see ourselves as predictably and properly on top of this biological heap," and that evolution can be depicted "as moving upward from single-celled creatures predictably toward the eventual appearance of some self-conscious form, like human beings." Far from advancing human progress as an inherent teleological trait, he pointed to the fact that "no other species has ever had the capacity to destroy itself and drag large parts of the earth down with it." Speaking as a paleontologist, he noted that the earth itself was not threatened by global warming any more than by a general thermonuclear exchange. It would recover in hundreds of millions of years from the worst conceivable disaster. But humanity might not. In the case of climate change, "most of our major cities, built at sea level as ports and harbors, will founder, and changing agricultural patterns will uproot our populations." In this respect, he fancifully suggested that humanity should make a sustainability pact with our planet to live and let live: the problem lay entirely on the side of humanity and its defective notions of progress.[66]

Figures like Levins, Lewontin, and Gould were not alone. In the early 1970s, *Science for the People* already was presenting a powerful ecological vision, accompanying the rapid development of Marxian and neo-Marxian political economy during that period, which abated somewhat in the more conservative 1980s. In January 1973, the magazine published an unsigned editorial titled "Ecology for the People," which argued against both Paul Ehrlich's populationism and Garrett Hardin's "tragedy of the commons conception"—the dominant liberal environmental ideas. Instead, drawing on Paul A. Baran and Paul M. Sweezy's *Monopoly Capital* and Barbara and John Ehrenreich's *The American Health Empire*, the problem was seen as lying in the "mechanisms basic to the [capitalist] system which produce *both* economic inequalities and ecological disruptions." Hence, a "sound ecology" was "incompatible" with the capitalist economic system. Rather than attribute environmental problems to population or to the "commons," *Science for the People* declared, "ecologists must struggle with the people for fundamental social change. When the life of the biosphere is at stake, ecological principle points in the direction of nothing less than revolution. Let us begin by creating an Ecology for the People!"[67]

This call for a revolutionary ecology for the people was echoed in a number of major Marxian and neo-Marxian works that poured out at the time, including Barry Weisberg, *Beyond Repair: The Ecology of Capitalism* (1971), Charles H. Anderson, *The Sociology of Survival: The Social Problems of Growth* (1976), and Alan Schnaiberg, *The Environment: From Surplus to Scarcity* (1980).[68] All three of these thinkers drew heavily in their analyses on the tradition of Marxian political economy in the United States presented in *Monthly Review* and Monthly Review Press (including authors such as Baran, Sweezy, Magdoff,

Harry Braverman, Harvey O'Connor, Barbara Ehrenreich, Edward Herman, Richard Du Boff, Michael Tanzer, Frank Ackerman, Stephen Hymer, Mahmood Mamdani, and Andre Gunder Frank), which formed the basis of the wider critique of capitalism. Anderson's *Sociology of Survival* stands out today in that it incorporated an early critique of capitalism's role in generating global warming and employed the concept of "ecological debt," as well as addressing the question of a steady state economy.[69] Weisberg wrote of "the structure of social and ecological responsibility,"[70] and Schnaiberg introduced the notion of the treadmill of production, as both a metaphor for capitalism and a way of explaining the inherent conflict between capitalism and the environment.[71]

In this same period, Herbert Marcuse's *Counter-Revolution and Revolt* (1972) included a chapter titled "Nature and Revolution," and Murray Bookchin's *Post-Scarcity Anarchism* introduced the perspective of anarchist social ecology.[72] Sweezy's 1973 article "Cars and Cities" presented a dialectical ecological critique of urbanism under monopoly capital.[73] In the late 1970s, Brodine began writing essays on Marxism and ecology, including "Rediscovering the Dialectics of Nature," for *Political Affairs,* under the pseudonym Grace Fredricks.[74] However, liberal environmental reforms in the 1970s, followed by the Reagan reaction, and the dire revelations about Soviet management of the environment, were all to weaken the influence of radical, anti-capitalist ecology, which would only regain lost ground a generation later, as a result of the cumulative global catastrophes unleashed by the capitalist system.

ECOLOGY AND BRITAIN'S FIRST NEW LEFT

The development of a radical ecological movement in Britain, as in the United States, can be seen as arising initially out of the anti-nuclear movement. It was intertwined with the rise of the First New Left in 1956, following the revelations on Stalin and the Soviet invasion of Hungary. An important figure in both the First New Left and the Committee for Nuclear Disarmament (CND) was the historian Edward Palmer Thompson. Born in 1924, E. P. Thompson was intellectually influenced by the Popular Front outlook of the Second World War. After the war, in which he had served as an officer in a tank unit in the Italian campaign, he continued his studies in history at Cambridge and participated in the famous Communist Party of Great Britain (CPGB) Historians' Group, which included such luminaries as Maurice Dobb, Christopher Hill, Rodney Hilton, Eric Hobsbawm, Victor Kiernan, George Rudé, Ralph Samuel, John Saville, Dorothy Thompson (Edward Thompson's wife and a distinguished historian of Chartism), and Dona Torr. In 1948, E. P. Thompson took a position at the University of Leeds and wrote his first major work, *William Morris* (1955).

Thompson's book on Morris was an attempt to resurrect his contribution to socialism and to provide a crucial moral compass to complement Marx's political economy. In this respect, Thompson was already seeking both to extend Marxism and to change it from within. This was followed in 1956 by the attempt on the part of Thompson, Saville, Levy, and Doris Lessing to publish a new journal within the Communist Party movement, *The Reasoner*, which would chart an independent Communist path based on British history and realities. Only three issues of *The Reasoner* were published. After Thompson and Saville had left the Party on the threat of being expelled near the end of the year (following the Soviet invasion of Hungary), *The Reasoner* was succeeded by *The New Reasoner.*

The New Reasoner was an outspokenly New Left publication, focusing on socialist humanism, largely inspired by Thompson. Here Thompson had free rein to generate a historical materialist critique open to a wider set of historical values rooted in the ideas of thinkers like William Morris and Christopher Caudwell, both of whom had raised humanist and ecological issues. In 1959, *The New Reasoner* and *Universities and Left Review* merged to form the *New Left Review*, but the new publication soon came to be dominated by a Second New Left, younger socialists who did not come out of the Popular Front movement. The leading thinkers of the Second New Left drew their main sources of inspiration from the work of Continental Marxist theorists, including the French Marxist philosopher Louis Althusser, and were less directly inspired by the historical currents of British radicalism and the endeavor to build a movement based on the "peculiarities of the English." As a result, Thompson and others associated with *New Reasoner* and the First New Left pulled away from the *New Left Review*.[75]

These political shifts associated with the rise of the First New Left in Britain corresponded to the heightening of the Cold War and the growing nuclear scare. The rapid development of thermonuclear weapons and the fallout question of the mid-1950s were heightened in Britain by the detonation of the country's first nuclear device in 1952, followed by its first hydrogen bomb test in 1957. Thompson believed that a peace movement responding to these developments would need to be nonaligned, refusing to side with either of the two superpowers, charting an independent course. This stance placed him at odds with the World Peace Council, in which Bernal was then a leading figure. Thompson was attracted to the Campaign for Nuclear Disarmament, which strove for unilateral nuclear disarmament. He was a part of a small group of notable figures at the first meeting of the CND, which also included Marxian sociologists Ralph Miliband and Stuart Hall. Bertrand Russell was elected as president of the new organization, and Julian Huxley was among the founders. Thompson himself became one of the foremost supporters of the CND. In 1957, even prior to the launch of the CND, he had approached the National Council for the Abolition of Nuclear Weapons Tests (NCANWT), a movement that had begun in West Yorkshire, with hopes that it could be expanded into a truly national movement. In 1958, the NCANWT merged with CND.[76]

CND in its inception was a New Left organization, particularly characterized by its relation to the nonaligned movement and strongly anti-imperialist. It drew widely from left youth. There was no doubt about the depth of its concern over nuclear warfare and fallout from nuclear testing. In Easter 1958, the Aldermaston march, in which the CND as well as other peace groups took part, saw thousands (including Bernal) marching for four days to the Atomic Weapons Research Establishment at Aldermaston in Berkshire. In 1960, 100,000 people gathered in Trafalgar Square as a part of the Easter demonstrations sponsored by the CND.[77]

Thompson and other New Leftists sought, seemingly with considerable success at first, but in the long run unsuccessfully, to transform the CND from a single-issue movement into one with a broader internationalist orientation, representing both neutrality in the Cold War and socialism. In the end, the failure to achieve these goals was marked by CND's incorporation into the dominant Labour Party politics, which were neither nonaligned nor socialist. The movement, which had been constructed in single-issue terms—despite the best efforts of Thompson and other New Left activists—declined after the 1963 Nuclear Test Ban Treaty. As he later observed, "There was some hope, at one time, that the New Left might, in an embryonic way, do exactly this"—that is, turn in an independent socialist direction in its political practice— "and the 'miracle' of C.N.D. was a related phenomenon, when the moral bankruptcy of the C.P. after 1956 actually gave rise to the resurgence of an *independent* Left. It was a precious historical moment, and, in so far as we have lost it, it is an unqualified defeat."[78]

For Thompson, the late 1960s and 1970s were periods of a relative diminishment of political activity on his part, during which he concentrated on radical scholarship. His most influential historical work, *The Making the English Working Class*, appeared in 1963, followed later by such major historical works as *Whigs and Hunters* (1975) and *Customs in Common* (1991), along with a prodigious number of essays on figures in English Romantic and working-class history, and works concerned with Marxian theory, such as *The Poverty of Theory* (1978).[79] *The Making of the English Working Class* established a tradition of working-class history from below. Rather than seeing the working class simply as the objective by-product of capitalism, Thompson stressed agency and self-making. He thus delved into working-class culture and the development of class consciousness on the ground. In *The Making of the English Working Class*, Thompson made frequent favorable reference to Engels's *The Condition of the Working Class in England*, anticipating his later defense of Engels against his detractors in *The Poverty of Theory*, containing his great critique of Althusserian structuralism.[80]

Like Giambattista Vico, Thompson insisted that we can understand history because we have made it.[81] As a thinker who emphasized human agency, he was critical of any one-sided objectivist conception of the dialectics of nature. "The attempt to see a logic inscribed within 'natural' process itself," he wrote in *The Poverty of Theory,* "has been disabling and misleading." But the dialectic was nonetheless necessary to epistemology and to our apprehension of nature, since it offered "a description, within the terms of logic, of the ways in which we apprehend this process. . . . In my own work as a historian I have repeatedly observed this kind of process, and have, in consequence, come to bring 'dialectics,' not as this or that 'law' but as a habit of thinking (in co-existing opposites or 'contraries') and as an expectation as to the logic of process, into my own analysis."[82]

Both *William Morris* and *The Making of the English Working Class* had focused primarily on the nineteenth century. In his subsequent works, Thompson was to shift his emphasis to the eighteenth century. Here he emphasized the struggle over the commons as the key not only to understanding traditions of popular resistance to the development of capitalism, but also in terms of what was lost in the relation to the land. Like Morris, Peter Linebaugh observes, "Thompson . . . possessed strong attachments to what I can only call 'the commons.'"[83] As a historian, confining himself to the language of the eras he was studying, Thompson seldom referred explicitly to *ecology*. Nevertheless, an ecological perspective was deeply embedded in his writing from *William Morris* to his final posthumous book on William Blake.[84] In *Customs in Common* he provided a brief but devastating historical critique of Garrett Hardin's notion of the "tragedy of the commons" as an explanation of "ecological crisis," which had been based on late eighteenth and early nineteenth century Malthusian myths.[85] In *Whigs and Hunters*, he explored how a free peasantry pursuing its customary rights on the land was turned into a body of "poachers" persecuted by the law.

Thompson made clear his position with respect to ecology in one of his very last writings, "Ecology and History," a 1993 review of *This Fissured Land: An Ecological History of India* by Madhav Gadgil and Ramachandra Guha, which he considered an important contribution to the understanding of "large portions of the ecological history of the globe" and "a vindication of the ecological approach to human history." Here he declared that "ecology matters," while calling for a more revolutionary ecology: "Is it absolutely necessary," he asked, "that so much ecological writing should be so deeply depressing? Maybe it is, and should be. Yet despite all exploitation and abuses, that vast area of fissured land, from the Himalayas to the tip of the peninsula, is so rich still in so many resources and species that one wonders if one might be permitted a glimmer of utopian encouragement. Might the downward drift not yet be turned around?"[86]

Thompson's fascination with the English Romantic tradition, was the result of his being attracted to its revolutionary rather than its conservative tendencies, as indicated in the subtitle he gave to *William Morris: Romantic to Revolutionary*. Pervading his work was a strong critique of the concept of progress. As he wrote in "The Long Revolution," his review of Raymond Williams's book by that title: "'Growth' can be a misleading term. Suffering is not just a wastage in the margin of growth: for those who suffer it is absolute."[87]

Williams himself, beginning with his *Culture and Society* (1958), was to follow this same path from Romanticism to socialism, seeing modern ecology as the emergence of a kind of common ground.[88] In 1973, the Socialist Environment and Resources Association, a small left ecological movement organization, was founded with Williams as its vice president. In 1981 he gave his pathbreaking talk, "Socialism and Ecology," to the organization, insisting on the need to refashion socialism into an ecosocialism along lines best represented by Morris, but also in line with Engels's critique of the conquest of nature.[89]

But if the late 1950s and early 1960s saw the rise of the New Left in Britain and the beginnings of an ecological critique arising initially out of the anti-nuclear struggle, building on "the long revolution" represented by radical Romantic cultural movements, this was not accompanied at first by a revival of left science or the social relations of science movement. The British Marxist scientists had lost their influence in the domestic context in the Cold War period. Consequently, some of its major figures, like Bernal, Needham, Hogben, and Haldane, had turned mainly to internationalist, anti-imperialist, antiwar, and ecological struggles. Although Levy was closely allied with Thompson and Saville in *The Reasoner*, and brought a science-based critique to that publication, he decided to continue his dissent within rather than without the CPGB, until his inevitable expulsion. He thus declined Thompson and Saville's repeated invitations to join them on the editorial board of *The New Reasoner* and never played a very active role in the New Left movement that followed. So divorced was the new Marxism in Britain from science in this period that Perry Anderson, at the helm of *New Left Review*, summarily denied any relationship between Marxism and natural science—not only in Britain in the 1960s, but even earlier.[90] Natural science was generally depicted as outside the dialectic (viewed as the realm of the identical subject-object). In the criticisms made famous by the Frankfurt School, those who had subscribed to the dialectics of nature, following Engels, were seen as inherently leading, if by a more circuitous path, to the very positivism that characterized bourgeois science.[91]

Both the Cold War atmosphere and the new critiques of science and technology on the left thus militated against the further development of a Marxian dialectics of science in this period. In Britain, as in the United States, a new radical science arose only in response to the Vietnam War in the late 1960s, associated with figures such as Hilary Rose and Steven Rose, and the emergence of the British Society for Social Responsibility in Science (BSSRS). Among the founding members, when the organization was launched in a one-day meeting at the Royal Society in 1969, were Bernal, Hogben, Levy, and Needham.[92] Beginning in October 1972, the BSSRS's publication was titled *Science for the People*, not to be confused with the U.S. publication, which had commenced three years earlier. Both the U.S. and UK organizations took the term "science for the people" from Bernal's 1952 *Marxism and Science*. The BSSRS was concerned initially with the use of chemical and biological weapons by the West in the Vietnam War, as well as wider environmental questions and issues of women's rights, including control over reproduction. It strongly emphasized the class component in the analysis of ecological problems. It also focused on pointing to the dangers of the new technologies of crowd control (for example, plastic bullets) being used by the police in Northern Ireland. In the 1980s, the BSSRS concentrated its energies on protesting the "Strategic Defense Initiative" and the New Cold War. The organization was disbanded in the early 1990s.[93]

Two of the leading figures in the radical science movement coming out of the historical materialist tradition were Hilary Rose, who specialized in the sociology of science, and Steven Rose, a neuroscientist. The Roses were founding members of the BSSRS. More than any other thinkers in Britain, they sought to bridge the gap in theory and practice that separated the social relations of science movement of the red scientists of the 1930s and the radical science movement of the New Left of the late 1960s and '70s. In the 1970s, they wrote and edited a number of books that sought to promote a critical-socialist-materialist approach to science, including their seminal work, *Science and Society* (1969), and an edited collection, *Ideology of/in the Natural Sciences* (1976), published in two edited volumes as *The Political Economy of Science* and *The Radicalisation of Science*.[94] *The Political Economy of Science* contained Hans Magnus Enzensberger's "A Critique of Political Ecology," which deserves to be recognized as one of the classic expressions of the whole ecological problem from a Marxist perspective. In their work, the Roses sought to renew the critique of the social (and ideological) relation of science. Much of their analysis was aimed at a complex negotiation between the views of the red scientists of the 1930s and the new science-based critique within the New Left.

To a greater extent than Science for the People in the United States, representatives of the British radical science movement were haunted by the ghostly battles of the past. For the Roses the dialectics of nature as presented by Engels "pushes ephemeral humanity from the centre of the stage to be replaced by the metaphysic of nature."[95] The disagreement, however, was more a matter of form than substance, since the issue for them as well as for Engels, was ultimately the relation of humanity to nature through social metabolism/production, that is, the question of the dialectics of nature and society. *The Radicalisation of Science* contained essays by Needham and Levins and Lewontin, representing the perspective of dialectical biology.

In November 1979, Thompson learned from an article in the *Guardian* that Britain would be procuring sixty cruise missiles from the Pentagon to be armed with nuclear warheads in a major NATO nuclear buildup against the USSR. Rather than turning simply to CND, which was reviving in this context, Thompson began to envisage the creation of an entirely new organization, an autonomous, nonaligned left movement aimed at combatting the growing nuclear threat. The new organization would be called European Nuclear Disarmament (END) and had as its objective a nuclear-free Europe. The immediate goal was to create an alliance between independent anti-nuclear movements that crossed the Cold War divide separating Western and Eastern Europe. As Thompson put it: "Only an alliance which takes in churches, Eurocommunists, Labourists, East European dissidents (and not only 'dissidents'), Soviet citizens unmediated by Party structures, trade unionists, ecologists—only this can possibly muster the force and the internationalist élan to throw the cruise missiles and the SS-20s back."[96] The object was to "arouse everywhere a new kind of peace consciousness, founded upon the human ecological imperative of neighbourly survival."[97]

In establishing END, Thompson drafted the *European Nuclear Disarmament Appeal*, which, in the words of Mary Kaldor, "became the mobilising document for literally millions of people all over Europe."[98] He also wrote the enormously successful pamphlet *Protest and Survive*, accompanied by his landmark article "Notes on Exterminism and the Last Stage of Civilisation."[99] Speaking to rallies of as many as a quarter of a million people, Thompson showed himself able to fire up audiences. As END's unofficial spokesperson, he was "the leading theoretician of the disarmament movement."[100] He provided devastating critiques of the fine details of deterrence doctrine, exploring both the technology and budgets. In this he was aided in his efforts by the new critical trends within science emerging by that time.[101] END played significantly in the massive popular mobilization in Europe and in the United States, where the grassroots Nuclear Weapons Freeze Campaign emerged, and brought the world back from the nuclear brink in the 1980s. Ronald Reagan introduced the Strategic Defense Initiative (SDI—better known as "Star Wars") in 1983, but the world pulled back from the madness—for a time.[102]

Thompson's powerful "Notes on Exterminism" was directed at the seemingly inexorable Cold War logic that pointed toward nuclear annihilation arising from competing blocs, a danger that remains today, not only in the continuing nuclear danger, but also in our accelerating planetary crisis.[103] Yet, exterminism as a concept was at the same time the product of a deep socialist ecological critique rooted in Blake, Marx, Morris, and Caudwell of the destructive tendencies embedded in the underlying alienated logic of capital as a system of power. Thus, Thompson defined *exterminism* as embodying "these characteristics of a society—expressed, in differing degrees, within its economy, its polity and its ideology—which thrust it in a direction whose outcome must be the extermination of multitudes."[104] It referred to the historical growth of social formations so alienated that they posed the question of "the common ruin of the contending classes." Indeed, "to express the exterminism-thesis in Marxian terms," Rudolf Bahro wrote in *Avoiding Social and Ecological Disaster*, "one could say that the relationship between productive and destructive forces is turned upside down. Like others who looked at civilisation as a whole, Marx had seen the trail of blood running through it, and that 'civilisation leaves deserts behind it.'"[105] To reverse this destructive relation to nature thus required the revolutionary reconstitution of society at large. Thompson penned:

> Throw the forbidden places open.
> Let the dragons and the lions play.
> Let us swallow the worm of power
> And the name pass away.[106]

THE EPICUREAN SWERVE

For the 1930s generation of Marxian theorists in Britain, it was the classicists who can be said in many ways to have had the last word with respect to the contradictions of the human social metabolism with nature, drawing on the "immanent dialectics" that Marx (and Engels) had discovered in Epicurean philosophy.[107] Benjamin Farrington's masterwork, *The Faith of Epicurus*, a study that can be said to have been the product of decades of research, appeared in 1967, and had a significant impact on Epicurean studies. Farrington had played a central role in introducing the British scientists of his day, such as Hogben, Needham, Haldane, and Bernal to Marx's doctoral thesis on Epicurus and to Epicurean materialism in general.[108] In *The Faith of Epicurus* he had two signal accomplishments. First, he convincingly demonstrated that Epicurus's materialist arguments were not directed primarily against his contemporaries among the Stoics, but rather against Plato and his followers in the Academy (and to a lesser extent Aristotle's Lyceum) and particularly Plato's proposal to establish a state religion.[109] Second, he was able to prove that Epicureanism was not a depoliticized philosophy, as previously argued, but one that had been associated, in the seven centuries in which it was an organized movement, with rebellious political attitudes, and at times mass actions, aimed at both the state and religion.[110] As Farrington had written in 1939 in *Science and Politics in the*

Ancient World, "It is the specific originality of Epicurus that he is the first man known to history to have organized a movement for the liberation of mankind at large from superstition."[111] For Jean-Paul Sartre, writing in a similar vein in his "Materialism and Revolution" essay, "The first man who made a deliberate attempt to rid men of their fears and bonds, the first man who attempted to abolish slavery in his domain, Epicurus, was a materialist."[112]

In accord with the great British Epicurean scholar Cyril Bailey, Farrington emphasized that Marx in his doctoral dissertation had been the first to point to the importance of Epicurus's concept of the swerve, that is, the role of contingency in nature and history, breaking down any notion of mechanistic determinism.[113] In thus combatting both idealism and mechanism, Farrington argued that Epicurus held the key to the development of a more critical Marxism. As he noted in his conclusion to *The Faith of Epicurus*: "The searching Epicurean critique of the inherent injustice of state power set Karl Marx dreaming of the day when the state would wither away, when the freedom of each individual would be the condition of the freedom of all, and the truly human period of history would begin."[114]

Other classicists—such as the analyst of Greek poetry and drama (and follower of Caudwell), George Thomson, and Jack Lindsay, translator of Latin works, novelist, historian, and poet—also turned to Epicureanism as a key to a more consistently materialist and dialectical Marxism. A similar stance was adopted by the German utopian Marxist, Ernst Bloch. For Thomson, writing in 1955 in his *Studies in Ancient Greek Society*, "The philosophy of Epicurus is the culmination of ancient philosophical materialism. His sense of dialectics, revealed in his conception of the interdependence of necessity and chance, of the relation between man and nature, and of the uneven development of human progress, invites comparison with the intuitive dialectics of Ionian materialism, which culminated in Herakleitos."[115] Bloch's chapter on "Epicurus and Karl Marx" in his 1959 book *On Karl Marx*, explained that it was Marx who first understood the full implications of "Epicurus' cuckoo egg, which he alone had laid in the nest of rigid mechanistics." Epicureanism thus presented a materialist approach to nature and history that allowed for both subjective and objective factors, freedom and determinacy—"and, O Epicurus, vice versa, in mutuality."[116]

But it was the Australian-born classicist and writer Lindsay—a key figure in the 1930s *Left Review*, and a friend of Thompson, who saw him as "a premature socialist humanist"—who reached back to Epicureanism as the basis for an ecological critique of class society.[117] Born in 1900, son of the acclaimed Australian artist Norman Lindsay, Jack Lindsay emigrated to England in the 1920s and became involved in Marxism in the 1930s, working with CPGB's Historians' Group. Hobsbawm praised him for his "encyclopedic erudition and constantly simmering kettle of ideas." A translator of Homer, Sophocles,

Catullus, Petronius, and other classical authors, Lindsay became a master of the communist historical novel, writing and editing around 170 books.[118]

In his extraordinary 1949 work, *Marxism and Contemporary Science*, Lindsay sought to build on the ideas of Bernal, Haldane, Hogben, Levy, Needham, Waddington, and others in an analysis of the dialectics of nature, unifying this with Alfred North Whitehead's process philosophy. Close attention was given to Needham's integrative levels and its framework of "succession in time" and "envelopes in space," pointing to a unity of process that encompassed the relation of organism and environment, humanity and nature.[119] "The view that dialectics apply only to human beings and not nature as well, logically applied," Lindsay contended in his *Decay and Renewal*, "leads to an atrophy of Marxism, turning it into a mystique of praxis. Lukács later rejected it."[120]

Lindsay's criticisms of the rigidity of the base-superstructure model, however, antagonized the CPGB, and he was forced to issue a retraction, in what he later saw as a "loss of nerve." His chief supporter at the time being a young E. P. Thompson.[121] Refusing nevertheless simply to follow the party doctrine, Lindsay chose in his later works to internalize his critical views within his classical studies of the ancient world, as well as in his novels, histories, and biographies. This was evident in such works as: *The Song of a Falling World* (1948), *Civil War in England: The Cromwellian Revolution* (1954), *Thunder Underground* (1965), *The Origins of Alchemy in Graeco-Roman Egypt* (1970), *Blast-Power and Ballistics: Concepts of Force and Energy in the Ancient World* (1974), *William Morris* (1978), *The Monster City: Defoe's London* (1978), *William Blake* (1978), and *The Crisis of Marxism* (1981).[122] These works reflected his central concern with alienation (of both nature and labor), and his critique of progress, evident in his conviction, expressed in *Marxism and Contemporary Science*, that "the enormous expansion of the control of nature" in the 1930s and '40s "has not led to any immediate actualisation of world-harmony."[123]

In *Crisis in Marxism*, written in his eighties, Lindsay was among the first to focus on Marx's concept of metabolism as the key to a contemporary ecological critique. He highlighted Marx's treatment of *use values* in *Capital* as constituting, in Marx's words, "a necessary condition independent of forms of society, for the existence of man; an eternal natural necessity, which mediates the metabolism between man and nature, and hence makes possible human life in general."[124] According to John T. Connor in "Jack Lindsay, Socialist Humanism and the Communist Historical Novel," Lindsay envisioned a "transformed ecology" derived "from Marx's early research into the 'metabolism' between nature and man."[125] The ecological crisis demanded that critical thought be "freed from the concept of progress" viewed as merely quantitative growth.[126]

But it was in *Blast-Power and Ballistics*, written in the early 1970s, that Lindsay sought to demonstrate through a study of classical sources how an emphasis on the technology of destruction was implicit in the development of alienated class society. His ultimate concern was to lay bare the deep cultural and historical roots leading to the twofold contemporary reality of nuclear weaponry and environmental destructiveness. "The modern world," he wrote, "took the reductive line and, because this line is essentially dehumanised and alienated in its outlook, the result was a science leading into ever more devastating weapons, into nuclear fission, and into universal pollution and destruction of the environment."[127]

The most devastating classical critique of this tendency toward creative destruction in Western civilization, in Lindsay's view, was introduced by Lucretius, at the time of the beginning of the civil wars that were to destroy the Roman Republic, the gathering storm of which was already evident in the years leading up to his death (ca. 55 BCE). In the powerful Book 6 to *De rerum natura*, Lucretius pointed to how the Epicurean notion that "the world is our friend" was being ruptured, a rift symbolically portrayed in the earthly destruction of the world, from thunderbolts to earthquakes to fire and floods, to pollution and plagues.[128] In the Epicurean view, the physical world as a whole was subject to death and revitalization just like everything in life, presenting what Marx was to refer to, in his comments on Book 6 of *De rerum natura*, as a "negative dialectic."[129] Only atoms, the void, and infinite space were permanent. Yet, this reinforced the Epicurean view that nothing came from nothing and nothing being destroyed is ever reduced to nothing. Even in decay there was hope of renewal.[130]

In Lindsay's interpretation, this materialist worldview was symbolically employed in Book 6 of Lucretius's poem to highlight the accelerated destruction brought on human alienation from nature, together with human self-alienation. Emblematic of this was the great Athenian plague in the fifth century BCE, which was the subject of the closing stanzas of Lucretius's poem.[131] In Lucretius's *De Rerum Natura*, however, as distinct from Thucydides's account of the plague in *The History of the Peloponnesian War* on which Lucretius relied, there is a strong congruity between the physical disaster and mental terror arising from the destruction of reason, such that they are seen as mutually interconnected, and the social is even given primacy: "Lucretius wants to show the infection of man pervading nature and to make the disease not a chance biological misfortune but the inescapable result of man's inner unbalance. . . . Society breaks down under pressures of fear and greed generated or brought to a head by plague."[132]

Lucretius's Book 6, then, Lindsay argued, can be read as a symbolic portrayal of the human destructiveness arising from the alienation of nature:

> We may claim then that here is a picture of the pollution of the earth by man's inability to find a living and harmonious relation with nature. The destructive

> forces are fear (fear of the unknown, fear of death, fear of the truth), together with the greed and powerlust thus created. The society that destroys itself and pollutes nature is one crazed with unresolved conflicts that issue in war and greed. The meaning here in Book VI [of *De rerum natura*] is brought out by comparison with Book I. The end of the poem stands in complete contrast with the opening.
>
> Book I opened with the glorification of Venus, the positive life-spirit, whose advent clears away the winds and clouds of heaven, bringing into action all the healthy and creative forces. The goddess is heralded by the birds; in the last book birds are killed off by noxious fumes and effluences, then by the lethal contagion that man has spread in nature. Now they flee before man as the winds and clouds fled from Venus. . . .
>
> He [Lucretius] was . . . condemning with every fibre of his being those elements in human culture which were already implicating the destructive and polluting forces that we in our world lament and seek to dethrone.[133]

Two millennia after Lucretius's *De rerum natura*, Rachel Carson in *Silent Spring* evoked the killing off of birds by noxious fumes and effluvia as the symbol of a new, more lethal age of destruction brought on by "the gods of profit and production."[134] What we must dethrone today is the idol of capital itself, the concentrated power of class-based avarice, which now imperils the ecology of the earth. It is this that constitutes the entire meaning of *freedom as necessity* and the return of nature in our time.

Notes

PREFACE

1. Epicurus, *The Epicurus Reader* (Indianapolis: Hackett Publishing, 1994), 35.

INTRODUCTION

1. Epigraph: Karl Marx, *Early Writings* (London: Penguin, 1974), 397.
2. John Bellamy Foster, *Marx's Ecology: Materialism and Nature* (New York: Monthly Review Press, 2000).
3. Sean Creaven, *Emergentist Marxism* (London: Routledge, 2007).
4. Raymond Williams, *Culture and Society* (New York: Columbia University Press, 1983), xii.
5. E. P. Thompson, *The Making of the English Working Class* (New York: Vintage, 1963), 12.
6. Quentin Skinner, "Meaning and Understanding in the History of Ideas," *History and Theory* 8/1 (1969): 53.
7. Virginia Woolf, *A Room of One's Own* (New York: Harcourt Brace, 1929).
8. Raymond Williams, *Keywords* (New York: Oxford University Press, 1976), 286–91.
9. "Œcology," *Oxford English Dictionary* (Oxford: Oxford University Press, 1971), 1:1975; "Ecology," Oxford English Dictionary Online; Ernst Haeckel, *The History of Creation* (London: Henry S. King, 1876), translation supervised by E. Ray Lankester, 2:354. If Haeckel coined the word *ecology* based on the ancient notion of *oikos* (the same Greek word that gave rise to the concept of "economics"), this is not to say that scientific analyses related to what we now call ecology did not exist prior to that. For a history of science and ecology since antiquity see Frank N. Egerton, *The Roots of Ecology* (Berkeley: University of California Press, 2012).
10. Williams, *Keywords*, 110–11.
11. Karl Marx and Frederick Engels, *Collected Works* (New York: International Publishers, 1975), 1: 413; Foster, *Marx's Ecology*, 21–65. See also the useful treatment in Michael Heinrich, *Karl Marx and the Birth of Modern Society* (New York: Monthly Review Press, 2019), 292–312.
12. Marx and Engels, *Collected Works*, 1:458.
13. Ibid., 1:64–65.
14. Karl Marx, *Early Writings* (London: Penguin, 1974), 328; James G. Fox, *Marx, the Body, and Human Nature* (London: Palgrave Macmillan, 2015), 123–52.
15. John Bellamy Foster and Brett Clark, "The Robbery System," *Monthly Review* 70/3 (July–August 2018): 1–21; Justus von Liebig, "1862 Preface to *Agricultural*

Chemistry," *Monthly Review* 70/3 (July–August 2018): 146–50; Kohei Saito, *Karl Marx's Ecosocialism* (New York: Monthly Review Press, 2017).

16. Marx and Engels, *Collected Works*, 4:295–96.
17. The *Dialectics of Nature* and *Anti-Dühring* together make up the contents of vol. 25 of Marx and Engels's *Collected Works*.
18. Marx and Engels, *Collected Works*, 25:460–61.
19. Ted Benton, "Engels and the Politics of Nature," in *Engels Today*, ed. Christopher J. Arthur (New York: St. Martin's Press, 1996), 88.
20. Alexei Mikhailovich Voden, "Talks with Engels," in Institute of Marxism-Leninism, *Reminiscences from Marx and Engels* (Moscow: Foreign Languages Publishing House, n.d.), 332–33.
21. Thomas S. Hall, *Ideas of Life and Matter* (Chicago: University of Chicago Press, 1969), 19–20.
22. Frederick Engels, *Ludwig Feuerbach and the Outcome of Classical German Philosophy* (New York: International Publishers, 1941), 59.
23. Marx and Engels, *Collected Works*, 25:23.
24. Ibid., 25:105, 460–62.
25. The landmark work that best captures the dialectic of the Marxian scientists of the 1930s, particularly in Britain, is Helena Sheehan, *Marxism and the Philosophy of Science* (Atlantic Highlands, NJ: Humanities Press, 1985). However, Sheehan's work is not concerned directly with ecology.
26. Russell Jacoby, "Western Marxism," in *A Dictionary of Marxist Thought*, ed. Tom Bottomore (Oxford: Blackwell, 1983); Fredric Jameson, *Valences of the Dialectic* (London; Verso, 2009), 6–7.
27. Georg Lukács, *History and Class Consciousness* (Cambridge, MA: MIT Press, 1971), 24.
28. Giambattista Vico, *The New Science* (Ithaca, NY: Cornell University Press, 1976), 493.
29. Lucio Colletti, *Marxism and Hegel* (London: Verso, 1973), 191–92.
30. Herbert Marcuse, *Reason and Revolution* (Boston: Beacon Press, 196), 314.
31. Jean-Paul Sartre, *Critique of Dialectical Reason*, vol. 1 (London: Verso, 2004), 32.
32. Marx and Engels, *Collected Works*, 25:492; Lukács, *History and Class Consciousness*, 24, 207; Z.A. Jordan, *The Evolution of Dialectical Materialism* (New York: St. Martin's Press, 1967), 169–75.
33. Antonio Gramsci, *Selections from the Prison Notebooks* (New York: International Publishers, 1971), 448.
34. Lukács, *History and Class Consciousness*, 207.
35. Ibid.; Georg Lukács, *Hegel's False and His Genuine Ontology* (*Ontology of Social Being. 1. Hegel*) (London: Merlin Press, 1978), 31.
36. Georg Lukács, *A Defence of History and Class Consciousness: Tailism and the Dialectic* (London: Verso, 2000), 102–7.
37. Georg Lukács, *Conversations with Lukács* (Cambridge, MA: MIT Press, 1967), 43. See also Lukács, *History and Class Consciousness*, xvii; Georg Lukács, *Marx's Basic Ontological Principles* (London: Merlin Press, 1978), 95.
38. Benjamin Farrington, *Head and Hand in Ancient Greece* (London: Watts, 1947), 1–9, 28–29.
39. Roy Bhaskar, *Dialectic: The Pulse of Freedom* (London: Verso, 1993), 399–400.
40. Lukács, *Conversations with Lukács*, 21.
41. Lukács, *History and Class Consciousness*, xix–xx. Lukács's early contention that Engels had simply taken over Hegel's view on the dialectic of nature was one that he would later reject on another ground. In *The Young Hegel*, Lukács was to emphasize

that Hegel's conception of nature lacked all historicity or evolution—something that certainly could not be laid at the door of Engels. See Georg Lukács, *The Young Hegel* (Cambridge, MA: MIT Press, 1975), 543.

42. Ibid., 280; Lukács, *Conversations with Lukács*, 73–74; Lukács, *Hegel's False and His Genuine Ontology*, 87.
43. Lukács, *History and Class Consciousness*, 207; Lukács, *Hegel's False and His Genuine Ontology*, 62–95; Georg Lukács, *Labour* (London: Merlin Press, 1980).
44. Lukács, *Hegel's False and His Genuine Ontology*, 113.
45. J. D. Bernal, *The Freedom of Necessity* (London: Routledge and Kegan Paul, 1949).
46. On *mors immortalis* see Karl Marx, *The Poverty of Philosophy* (New York: International Publishers, 1963), 110; Lucretius, *On the Nature of the Universe* (Oxford: Oxford University Press, 1999), 93 [Lucretius, *De rerum natura* III, 869].
47. Joseph Needham, *Time: The Refreshing River* (London: George Allen and Unwin, 1943), 14–15.
48. Christopher Caudwell, *Scenes and Actions* (London; Routledge and Kegan Paul, 1983), 186; Christopher Caudwell, *Studies and Further Studies in a Dying Culture* (New York: Monthly Review Presss, 1971) (*Further Studies*), 227.
49. Caudwell, *Studies and Further Studies in a Dying Culture*, xix.
50. Caudwell's later pieces, all meant as part of his "Studies and Further Studies" series, included not only *Further Studies,* which is contained in the consolidated collection, but also *The Crisis in Physics* and *Heredity and Development*, which were viewed as separate monographs—the latter not published until almost a half-century after his death.
51. Barry Commoner, *The Closing Circle* (New York: Alfred A. Knopf, 1971).
52. J. D. Bernal, *The Origin of Life* (New York: World Publishing Co., 1967), xvi, 176–82.

CHAPTER ONE: ECOLOGICAL MATERIALISM

1. "The Funeral of Mr. Darwin," *The Times* (London), April 27, 1882, http://en.wikisource.org/wiki/The_Times/1882/News/Funeral_of_Charles_Darwin.
2. Yvonne Kapp, *Eleanor Marx*, vol. 1 (New York: Pantheon, 1972), 247.
3. On the weather: "The Weekly Weather," *Times* (London), March 16, 1883, 3; "Meteorological Reports, Weather Chart, Friday, March 16, 6 P.M.," *Times* (London), March 17, 1883, 12; "Readings of the Jordan Glycerine Barometer," *Times* (London), March 17, 1883, 12. The March 17, 1883, paper contained the weather forecast. On the time of day: see Frederick Engels to Friedrich Lessner, March 15, 1883, in Philip S. Foner, ed., *Karl Marx Remembered* (San Francisco: Synthesis Publications, 1983), 29. On the cemetery see Felix Barker, *Highgate Cemetery: Victorian Valhalla* (Salem, NH: Salem House, 1984), 7–9, 41–42; Roger Gaess, "The Shades of Highgate Cemetery," *Counterpunch*, July 10, 2009, https://www.counterpunch.org/2009/07/10/the-shades-of-highgate-cemetery/.
4. Frederick Engels, "The Funeral of Karl Marx," in Foner, *Karl Marx Remembered*, 38–45; "By His Death the Progress of Humanity Is Retarded," *Progress*, April 1883, in Foner, ed., *Karl Marx Remembered*, 127; Saul Padover, *Karl Marx: An Intimate Biography* (New York: McGraw Hill, 1978), 590; Rachel Holmes, *Eleanor Marx: A Life* (New York: Bloomsbury, 2014), 178.

   The report in *Progress,* edited by Aveling, which placed Aveling and Radford at the funeral, has been questioned by some, given Aveling's doubtful veracity; see Foner, *Karl Marx Remembered*, 283. However, it seems unlikely that Aveling would have put this into print, in a publication that was well known to Eleanor and undoubtedly Engels as well, or that his co-editor, Radford, who was a friend of the Marx family would have allowed him to do so if it had been false. Engels's list of people at the funeral for *Der Sozialdemokrat* included figures that were all notable from the standpoint of social democracy: longtime associates of Marx (and family members in the cases of Lafargue and Longuet), each of whom had an important political or scientific role (with the exception of G. Lemke who laid the wreaths). The list was clearly not meant to be inclusive of all who were present on the occasion. Indeed, Engels's list included the words "among others." It is significant in this respect that Engels did not mention Eleanor's own presence at the funeral, which was simply left unsaid. Nor was Helena Demuth mentioned. Another figure present but not referred to by Engels was Donkin, Marx's physician, and a close friend to Lankester and the Marx family. J. V. Weber of the German Workers' Educational Society attended as well. Heinrich Gemkow, et. al., ed. (Institute für Marxismus-Leninismus) *Ihre Namen leben durch die Jahrhunderte fort* (Berlin: Dietz Verlag Berlin, 1983), 92.

The reported presence of Radford and Aveling, despite the non-inclusion of their names in Engels's report to *Der Sozialdemokrat,* should not be looked on as altogether surprising. Radford, along with his wife, Dollie Radford, one of Eleanor's closest friends, had been a visitor at the Marx home and was an associate of Aveling's at *Progress*. Eleanor also came to be connected with *Progress* at around this time. Eleanor was in charge of the invitations to the funeral (no doubt with Engels's advice). Radford and Aveling were comparatively young figures, not particularly notable then from the standpoint of socialist politics. Engels would therefore have had no reason to have mentioned them in his report. Also likely present and not mentioned by Engels was Dollie Radford.

In 1925, David Riazanov, the great Marxist scholar in the Soviet Union, responsible for the publication of Marx and Engels's *Collected Works*, wrote to Lankester, referring to him as one of "the choice friends who accompanied Karl Marx to his grave." Joseph Lester, *E. Ray Lankester and the Making of Modern British Biology* (Oxford: British Society for the History of Science), 192.

5. Engels, "The Funeral of Karl Marx," 39–40.
6. Foner, *Karl Marx Remembered*, 28.
7. Karl Marx, *The Poverty of Philosophy* (New York: International Publishers, 1963), 110.
8. Olive Schreiner to Havelock Ellis, October 26, 1885, Olive Schreiner Letters Online, http://www.oliveschreiner.org/vre?view=collections&colid=137&letterid=128; Lester, *E. Ray Lankester*, 61.
9. Lester, *E. Ray Lankester*, 53; Sir Francis Galton and Edgar Schuster, *Noteworthy Families (Modern Science)* (London: John Murray, 1906), 39; Stephen Jay Gould, *The Structure of Evolutionary Theory* (Cambridge, MA: Harvard University Press, 2002), 25; Stephen Jay Gould, *I Have Landed* (New York: Three Rivers Press, 2003), 117; Richard Milner, "Huxley's Bulldog: The Battles of E. Ray Lankester," *Anatomical Record* 257/3 (1999): 90. See also John Bellamy Foster, "E. Ray Lankester, Ecological Materialist," *Organization & Environment* 13/2 (June 2000): 233–35.
10. Edwin Lankester's father was a Congregationalist, and he too practiced Congregationalism most of his life. He married Phebe Pope, whose background was Baptist, which posed no obstacles for a religious dissenter. He was buried in the graveyard of a parish church. Mary English, *Victorian Values: The Life and Times of Dr. Edwin Lankester, M.D., F.R.S.* (Bristol: Biopress Ltd., 1990), 3–5,10, 37, 49; Lester, *E. Ray Lankester*, 5–6.
11. Lester, *E. Ray Lankester*, 6–10; English, *Victorian Values*, 1–5; "Lankester, Edwin

(1814–1874)," *Oxford Dictionary of National Biography* (Oxford: Oxford University Press, 2004), http://www.oxfordnb.com/view/article/16054,; Peter J. Bowler, "Lankester, Sir (Edwin) Ray (1847–1929)," *Dictionary of National Biography* (Oxford: Oxford University Press, 2004); Edwin Lankester, *The Aquavivarium: An Account of the Principles and Objects Involved in the Domestic Culture of Water Plants and Animals* (London: Robert Hardwicke, 1856).

12. English, *Victorian Values*, 45–49.
13. Edwin Lankester, *Cholera: What It Is and How to Prevent It* (London: George Routledge and Sons, 1866), 33.
14. Steven Johnson, *The Ghost Map: The Story of London's Most Terrifying Epidemic—and How It Changed Science, Cities, and the Modern World* (New York: Riverhead Books, 2006), 213–14; English, *Victorian Values*, 59; "Who First Discovered Vibrio Cholera?" UCLA Department of Epidemiology, http://www.ph.ucla.edu/epi/snow/firstdiscoveredcholera.html. On the failure of the medical profession at the time to perceive of water as a means of transmission of disease see the discussion in Lankester, *Cholera*, 35.
15. Edwin Lankester later observed that depsite the fact that there was no doctor (and indeed no other individual) in the parish at the time that Snow made his appeal to the Board of Governors who entirely supported Snow's theory on the transmission of the disease agent through water, nonetheless the pump handle was removed. It was only later in the investigation that followed the epidemic that Lankester and Whitehead came to the same conclusion as Snow. See Lankester, *Cholera*, 34–35.
16. Marx and Engels, *Collected Works* (New York: International Publishers, 1975), 39:481; Johnson, *The Ghost Map*, 68–77, 159–62. Edwin Lankester estimated the deaths somewhat lower, at around five hundred. See Lankester, *Cholera*, 35.
17. Johnson, *The Ghost Map*, 181–82; English, *Victorian Values*, 63–70; Cholera Inquiry Committee, Vestry of St James Parish, Westminster, *Report on the Cholera Outbreak in the Parish of St. James, Westminster during the Autumn of 1854* (London: J. Churchill, 1855), http://johnsnow.matrix.msu.edu/work.php?id=15-78-AA.
18. English, *Victorian Values*, 89, 91, Cholera Inquiry Committee, *Report on the Cholera Outbreak*; Edwin Lankester, "On the Presence of Microscopic Fungi in Water Deleterious to Health," *Quarterly Journal of Microscopical Science* 4 (1856): 270–72: Lankester, *Cholera*, 28–36: Edwin Lankester, *Sanitary Defects and Medical Shortcomings* (London: Jarrold and Sons, 1860), 27.
19. English, *Victorian Values*, 59–75, 95–112, 136–55, "Lankester, Edwin (1814–1874)," *Oxford Dictionary of National Biography*; Marx to Engels, September 13, 1854, Marx and Engels, *Collected Works*,39:481; Johnson, *The Ghost Map*, 84.
20. John Simon, *Report on the Last Two Cholera-Epidemics of London, as Affected by the Consumption of Impure Water*, General Board of Health, May 13, 1856, http://johnsnow.matrix.msu.edu/work.php?id=15-78-7F; "Sir John Simon (1816–1904)," *Oxford Dictionary of National Biography*, http://www.oxforddnb.com/templates/article.jsp?articleid=36097&back=; English, *Victorian Values*, 86, 95, 103, 113–14; Royston Lambert, *Sir John Simon (1816–1904)* (London: MacGibbon and Kee, 1963), 49–55, 247–49.
21. Edwin Lankester, "President's Address in the Public Health Department of the Social Science Association," *British Medical Journal* 2/252 (October 28, 1865): 438.
22. Lester, *E. Ray Lankester*, 9, 204; English, *Victorian Values*, 21, 36–39, 42–44, 93–94, 164–65; Phebe Lankester (obituary), *Times* (London), April 14, 1900; Ann B. Shteir, "Finding Phebe: A Literary History of Women's Science Writing," in *Women and*

Literary History, ed. Katherine Binhammer and Jeanne Wod (London: Associated University Presses, 2003), 152–66, "Lankester, Phebe (1825–1900)," *Oxford Dictionary of National Biography* (Oxford: Oxford University Press, 2004), http://www.oxforddnb.com/view/article/58526.

23. Lester, *E. Ray Lankester*, 10–14, 80; Sir J. Arthur Thomson, *Great Biologists* (New York: Books for Libraries Press, 1932), 162; Richard Milner, "Huxley's Bulldog: The Battles of E. Ray Lankester," *The Anatomical Record* (NEW ANAT.) 257 (1999): 90–95.
24. E. Ray Lankester, "Appendix A: Remarks on the 'Blue Mist' Observed by Mr. Glaisher," in Lankester, *Cholera*, 90–92.
25. Ernst Haeckel, *The History of Creation*, 2 vols. (London: Henry S. King, 1876), translation supervised by E. Ray Lankester.
26. Darwin quoted in Lester, *E. Ray Lankester*, 51.
27. Ibid., 52; E. Ray Lankester, *Zoological Articles Contributed to the "Encyclopedia Britannica"* (New York: Charles Scribner's Sons, 1890).
28. Lester, *E. Ray* Lankester, 64, 166; Gould, *I Have Landed*, 116.
29. Lester, *E. Ray Lankester*, 93–104; ; Richard Milner, "Charles Darwin and Associates, Ghostbusters," *Scientific American*, February 11, 2009, http://www.scientificamerican.com/article.cfm?id=charles-darwin-and-assoc&print=true; Milner, "Huxley's Bulldog."
30. E. Ray Lankester, *Degeneration* (London: Macmillan, 1880); Thomson, *Great Biologists*, 165–66.
31. Lankester, *Degeneration*, 28–33.
32. Ibid., 59–60.
33. Ibid., 33, 59.
34. Ibid., 60–61.
35. Quoted from unpublished notes in Lankester family papers by Lester in *E. Ray Lankester*, 186.
36. H. G. Wells, "Zoological Retrogression," in *The Fin de Siècle: A Reader in Cultural History, c. 1880–1900*, ed. Sally Ledger and Roger Luckhurst (Oxford: Oxford University Press, 2000), 5–12; H. G. Wells, *The Time Machine* (New York: Ace Books, 1957). Wells wrote to Thomas Huxley that "the central idea" of the book was "degeneration following security," obviously referring to Lankester's work. H.G. Wells to Thomas Huxley, May 1895, in H.G. Wells, *Correspondence*, vol. 1 (London: Pickering and Chatto, 1998), 238.
37. There are four extant letters from Lankester to Marx, all of which are reprinted in an appendix to Feuer, "The Friendship of Edwin Ray Lankester and Karl Marx," 647–48. There also exist a few extant documents in which Marx or members of Marx's family and close associates mention Lankester. It appears that no letters of Marx to Lankester, though they must have existed, have survived, as there is nothing by Marx that has been preserved in the Lankester family papers. Lester, *E. Ray Lankester*, 187.
38. Feuer, "The Friendship of Edwin Ray Lankester and Karl Marx," 644–47. On Waldstein's relation to Marx see Sir Charles Waldstein, *Aristodemocracy* (London: John Murray, 1916), 251–54.
39. Lester, *E. Ray Lankester*, 185; Hal Draper, *The Marx-Engels Glossary* (New York: Schocken Books, 1986), 17. Eleanor Marx would have had a great affinity for the views of Ray Lankester. When she was working in the British Library, her interests included Alfred Russel Wallace's reversion from being an advocate of a pure materialist evolutionary theory to being a proponent of spiritualistic beliefs with respect to humanity and the evolution of its mental capacities—a view on which

Lankester had already come out as Wallace's chief opponent. See Kapp, *Eleanor Marx*, vol. 1, 187.

40. The walking distances are determined by Google Maps. Also "Walking with Communists in Hampstead," Timeout.com, no date. (Note original Timeout.com url to "Walking with Communists in Hampstead" removed from the web. It can be accessed in Spanish: http://www.forocomunista.com/t25662-las-caminatas-de-marx-y-engels-un-itinerario-londinense-texto-publicado-en-agosto-de-2012-en-el-blog-critica-marxista-leninista). Sometime after Edwin Lankester's death in 1874, Phebe Lankester moved closer to central London (5 Upper Wimpole Street). It is not clear, however, when. English, *Victorian Values*, 119, 158–59, 164; Phebe Lankester (obituary), *Times* (London), April 14, 1900.
41. On the Society of Arts see English, *Victorian Values*, 119; D. G. C. Allan and Arnold Whittick, "The Red Doctor Amongst the Virtuosi: Karl Marx and the Society," Part 1, *Journal of the Royal Society of Arts* 129/5296 (March 1981): 259–61, and "The Red Doctor," Part 2, 129/5297 (April 1981): 309–10; Walt Contreras Sheasby, "Karl Marx and the Victorians' Nature: The Evolution of a Deeper View—The Age of Aquaria," *Capitalism Nature Socialism* 15/3 (September 2004): 66. The role of Simmonds in relation to the waste issue and his close connections to Edwin Lankester on this issue (which also interested Marx) can be found in Pierre Desrochers, "Promoting Corporate Environmental Sustainability in the Victorian Era: The Bethnel Green Permanent Waste Exhibit (1875–1928)," *V&A Online Journal* (Victoria and Albert Museum) 3 (Spring 2011), http://www.vam.ac.uk/content/journals/research-journal/issue-03/promoting-corporate-environmental-sustainability-in-the-victorian-era-the-bethnal-green-museum-permanent-waste-exhibit-1875-1928/; Ann Christie, "'Nothing of Intrinsic Value': The Scientific Collections at the Bethnal Green Museum," *V&A Online Journal* 3 (Spring 2011), http://www.vam.ac.uk/content/journals/research-journal/issue-03/nothing-of-intrinsic-value-the-scientific-collections-at-the-bethnal-green-museum/; P. L. Simmonds, *Waste Products and Undeveloped Substances* (London: Robert Hardwicke, 1862).
42. Lester, *E. Ray Lankester*, 185; Kapp, *Eleanor Marx*, vol. 1, 236; Lankester to Wells, Saturday, September 9, 1926, Wells Papers archive, University of Illinois, Urbana.
43. On Donkin's continued treatment of Eleanor after the death of her parents see Yvonne Kapp, *Eleanor Marx*, vol. 2 (New York: Pantheon, 1976), 25, 32. He also treated Olive Schreiner.
44. H. Donkin, "Thoughts on Ignorance and Quackery," Address at Westminster Hospital Medical School, 1880–81 session, published in the *British Medical Journal*, October 9, 1880, reprinted for the author by the British Medical Association; included in E. Ray Lankester Scientific Papers Collection, Marine Biological Association Library, Marine Biological Association, Plymouth, Devon.
45. H. Donkin, "Suggestions as to the Aetiology of Some of the So-Called System Diseases of the Spinal Cord," *Brain* 5 (January 1883): 438–39. Copy included in E. Ray Lankester Scientific Papers Collection, Marine Biological Association Library.
46. G. Bidder, E. Ray Lankester (obituary), *Nature* 124 (1929): 345–46; Lester, *E. Ray Lankester*, 69.
47. Lester, *E. Ray Lankester*, 185.
48. Marx and Engels, *Collected Works*, 35:261, 780; Marx, *Capital*, vol. 1 (London: Penguin, 1976), 364–67; *Marx-Engels Gesamtausgabe* (MEGA) II/6, 259, 1137. The working conditions that Edwin Lankester reported on were part of the investigations of the Children's Employment Commission, *Reports of the Commission* presented to

both houses of Parliament (London, 1864), *Appendix to the Second Report*, 118–19, *Appendix to the Third Report*, 53, 95–96. Edwin Lankester is quoted here, including the very statement on the amount of physical space needed by each human being that Marx drew on in *Capital*. This statement is also quoted in Edwin Lankester's letter to the *Times* (London), June 29, 1863, to which Marx refers. See also English, *Victorian Values*, 95–112, esp. 107; M.D. (pseudonym), *Times*, June 22, 1863; Edwin Lankester, letter to *Times*, December 22, 1860. Marx's concern for the issues raised by Lankester can be seen in the fact that the Children's Employment Commission is referred to on some sixty pages of *Capital*, vol. 1.

49. Edwin Lankester, "President's Address in the Public Health Department of the Social Science Association," 443. On Dr. Lankester's insistence on the need for 500 cubic feet of living space per person, see Lankester, *Cholera*, 65.
50. The elder Lankester addressed some of these horrendous working-class conditions at the end of his book on *Cholera* to which E. Ray Lankester contributed an appendix.
51. Lester, *E. Ray Lankester*, 184–86.
52. Ibid., 185; Feuer, "The Friendship of Edwin Ray Lankester and Karl Marx," 647.
53. Stephen Jay Gould's essay, "A Darwinian Gentleman at Marx's Funeral," was uncharacteristically full of factual errors: placing Jenny, Marx's deceased wife at his funeral, and confusing a letter of Lankester's to H. G. Wells with one to Arthur Conan Doyle. He argued that Marx and Lankester had little in common with respect to either science or politics, characterizing Lankester as a conservative, simply on the basis of his position in his sixties on women's suffrage, and that Marx's interest in Lankester was therefore that of an older scholar who wished to encourage a younger, rising one. The facts of the matter, however, were quite different. Lankester was strongly attracted to political radicalism, particularly at this stage in his life, while Marx had a deep interest in physical science and materialism. Both engaged with ecological issues. See Gould, *I Have Landed* (New York: Three Rivers Press, 2003), 113–29.
54. Grant Allen, "Geology and History," *Popular Science Monthly* 17 (August 1880): 495–507; E. Colman, "Short Communication on the Unpublished Writings of Karl Marx Dealing with Mathematics, the Natural Sciences, Technology, and the History of these Subjects," in *Science at the Cross Roads*, ed. Nikolai Bukharin et al. (London: Frank Cass, 1971), 233; Lester, *E. Ray Lankester*, 155.
55. Sheasby, "Karl Marx and the Victorian's Nature," 60–61, 66; Marx and Engels, *Collected Works*, 19:132–33; "History of the Aquarium and Dolphinarium" My Brighton and Hove, https://www.mybrightonandhove.org.uk/places/placeland/brighton_aquarium/sea-life-centre-4, Lankester, *The Aquavivarium*.
56. Karl Marx, *Capital*, vol. 1, 493.
57. J. Reid Moir, *Prehistoric Archaeology and Sir Ray Lankester* (Ipswich: Northern Adlard and Co., 1935); Milner, "Huxley's Bulldog," 91.
58. On Marx's ecological critique see John Bellamy Foster, *Marx's Ecology* (New York: Monthly Review Press, 2000); Paul Burkett, *Marx and Nature* (New York: St. Martin's Press, 1999).
59. Lewis S. Feuer, "The Friendship of Edwin Ray Lankester and Karl Marx," *Journal of the History of Ideas* 40 (1979): 640–43.
60. Ibid., 640–43; Lankester to Wells, Friday, September 3, 1926; Lankester to Wells; Saturday, September 9, 1926, Wells Papers, University of Illinois, Urbana; Lester, *E. Ray Lankester*, 187; H. G. Wells, *The World of William Clissold* (New York: George H. Doran Co., 1926), 166–73.
61. This report was supplied by Lankester's former housekeeper, interviewed by Joseph

Lester. See Lester, *E. Ray Lankester*, 192. In his biography, Lester, who had access to the Lankester family papers, indicated that were no extant material on Marx to be found in the papers.

62. "Eugenic Society Members, A–Z" (2012), http://www.scribd.com/doc/97123506/Eugenics-Society-Members-A-Z-2012; Wikipedia, "The Galton Institute," http://en.wikipedia.org/wiki/Galton_Institute.
63. Gould, *I Have Landed*, 119.
64. Unfortunately, Gould also drew on the Cold War scholarship of Lewis Feuer, which was based on various unfounded suppositions, such as the false view, shown to be factually incorrect, that Wells had based his vehement description of Marx on information provided to him by Lankester. In general, Feuer sought by such means to draw a political (and scientific) wedge between Marx and Lankester. See Lewis S. Feuer, "The Friendship of Edwin Ray Lankester and Karl Marx: The Last Episode in Marx's Intellectual Evolution," *Journal of the History of Ideas* 10/4 (October–December 1979): 636–48.
65. Peter J. Bowler, *Science for All* (Chicago: University of Chicago Press, 2009), 219. Elsewhere Bowler claimed, in discussing Lankester's friendship with Marx, that Lankester's "own views were meritocratic rather than socialist." The point is not argued in any way, however, and is in sharp conflict with both the tenor and the evidence of Lester's biography of Lankester (which Bowler edited after Lester's death). Given the variety of British socialisms of the time, the evidence that we have on Lankester's critical views with respect to capitalism, and his various close associations, it is more appropriate to refer to him as a moderate socialist (or social democrat) of the Fabian variety, one with close affiliations to "rationalism" or secular humanism.
66. "London Talk," *The Advertiser* (Adelaide, South Africa), November 25, 1895, http://trove.nla.gov.au/ndp/del/article/34529897; Lester, *E. Ray Lankester*, 124–26.
67. Eleanor Marx-Aveling to Horatio Bryan Donkin, February 8, 1886, in Marx and Engels, *Collected Works*, 547–48 (also editors' notes, 637); Ruth First and Ann Scott, *Olive Schreiner* (New York: Schocken Books, 1980), 145–70; Ruth Livesey, *Socialism, Sex, and the Culture of Asceticism in Britain, 1880–1914*, 49–85; Kapp, *Eleanor Marx*, vol. 1, 192–94; Olive Schreiner and Havelock Ellis, *My Other Self: The Letters of Olive Schreiner and Havelock Ellis, 1884–1920* (New York: Peter Lang, 1992), 404–5; Judith R.Walkowitz, "Science, Feminism and Romance: The Men and Women's Club of 1885–1889," *History Workshop* 21 (Spring 1986): 39–42, and *City of Dreadful Delight* (Chicago: University of Chicago Press, 1992), 140; Olive Schreiner to Maria Sharpe, Tuesday. December 1886, http://www.oliveschreiner.org/vre?view=collections&colid=75&letterid=5; Olive Schreiner to Karl Pearson, October 18, 1886, http://www.oliveschreiner.org/vre?view=collections&colid=74&letterid=101; Olive Schreiner, *The Story of an African Farm* (Oxford: Oxford University Press, 1992).
68. Such a statement on Lankester's part might have been attributed to the fact that he was well aware that Schreiner was enamored of Pearson.
69. Olive Schreiner to Karl Pearson, October 18, 1886, http://www.oliveschreiner.org/vre?view=collections&colid=74&letterid=101.
70. Lucy Bland, *Banishing the Beast: Sexuality and the Early Feminists* (New York: New Press, 1995), 5, 40; Walkowitz, "Science, Feminism, and Humanism," 39–42, and *City of Dreadful Delight*, 141–42; Olive Schreiner to Karl Pearson, October 11, 1885, in *Olive Schreiner, Letters*, ed. Richard Rive (Oxford: Oxford University Press, 1988), 67–68. In this letter, Schreiner indicated that Lankester, presumably also Donkin,

and some others were making fun of Pearson's role in starting the Men and Women's Club at the Saville Club (to which Lankester, Donkin, and Pearson all belonged). This, however, did not prevent Schreiner, as she indicated, from urging Donkin to join the Men and Women's Club and his agreeing to do so.

71. The term "The Woman Question" (in relation to Pearson, "The Woman's Question") already had a long history but Pearson's articulation of it in the context of the Men and Women's Club in 1884 was undoubtedly influential in early British socialist and feminist discussions—particularly in the case of figures like Schreiner and Eleanor Marx-Aveling who had some relation to the club (direct in the case of the former, indirect in case of the latter).
72. Karl Pearson, *The Ethics of Freethought* (London: Adam and Charles Black, 1901), vii, 301–78. In his essay on "The Woman's Question," Pearson mingled such views with positive references to Marx's theory of surplus value. Such an eclectic joining of ideas could not persist, and he ultimately dropped the more radical aspects of his analysis in favor of an approach developing out of Galton's eugenics.
73. Pearson, *The Ethics of Freethought*, 411–31; Walkowitz, *City of Dreadful Delight*, 154. As indicated in a letter from Schreiner to Pearson, Lankester was probably invited to participate in the session of the Men and Women's Club in which Pearson's "Socialism and Sex" was presented. See Oliver Schreiner to Karl Pearson, June 11, 1886, http://www.oliveschreiner.org/vre?view=collections&colid=74&letterid=68.
74. Bland, *Banishing the Beast*, 28–29; Walkowitz, "Science, Feminism, and Romance," 45–48.
75. Edward Aveling and Eleanor Marx-Aveling, "The Woman Question," in Eleanor Marx-Aveling and Edward Aveling, *Thoughts on Women and Society* (New York: International Publishers, 1987), 13–15; August Bebel, *Woman in the Past, Present, and Future* (London: The Modern Press, 1885). It is often assumed by scholars that Eleanor Marx-Aveling had the primary role in writing "The Woman Question," which grew out of an earlier review of Bebel's book. Nevertheless, the article that grew out of the review was considerably extended and more theoretically developed. Edward Aveling's name was listed first in the article, so there is no real justification for the common practice of reversing their names, or excluding his altogether. They worked at this time as a political–literary team, and he was by far the more accomplished writer. Various commentators have, of course, noted that the powerful sentiments expressed in this article were undermined by Aveling's numerous sexual betrayals, which led to Eleanor Marx-Aveling's suicide. However, the *argument* of "The Woman Question" loses none of its importance as a result of this further example of gender oppression propagated by one of its authors against the other.

    The Contagious Diseases Act introduced in 1864 and extended in 1866 and 1869 gave the police the authority to regulate "common prostitutes" ostensibly in order to stem the spread of sexually transmitted diseases to the British army and navy. It required women suspected by the police of prostitution to register with the police and to submit to invasive medical examinations. If the woman was found to have a venereal disease she would be confined in a "lock hospital" until she was pronounced "clean."
76. Aveling and Marx-Aveling, *Thoughts on Women and Society*, 27–28.
77. In 1899, Schreiner, then back in South Africa, wrote her own piece, "The Woman Question," published in two parts in *The Cosmopolitan* (New York), Olive Schreiner, *The Olive Schreiner Reader* (London: Pandora, 1987), 63–100. These ideas were developed further in Olive Schreiner, *Woman and Labor* (New York: Frederick A. Stokes, 1911). Schreiner's main emphasis was to describe women's role in present

society as "parasitic"—a parasitism that had been forced onto them by patriarchal conditions, and that needed to be surmounted for the good of society. See Stack, *The First Darwinian Left*, 94–95.

78. Olive Schreiner to Ray Lankester, January 31, 1886, http://www.oliveschreiner.org/vre?view=collections&colid=40&letterid=22; Olive Schreiner to Havelock Ellis, January 17, 1886, http://www.oliveschreiner.org/vre?view=collections&colid=137&letterid=152. See also Olive Schreiner to Karl Pearson, January 18, 1886, http://www.oliveschreiner.org/vre?view=collections&colid=74&letterid=43; Olive Schreiner to Havelock Ellis, February 2, 1886, http://www.oliveschreiner.org/vre?view=collections&colid=137&letterid=156. Lankester's long January 1886 letter to Schreiner on the woman question appears to have been lost even though it was copied, together with Schreiner's letter, by Havelock Ellis. The fact that its whereabouts (or whether it still exits) is unknown was confirmed in personal correspondence on August 12, 2013, from Liz Stanley, the Principal Investigator of the Olive Schreiner Letters Project. Schreiner, it appears, received more than one letter from Lankester, but none have survived. She circulated correspondence with Lankester on one or more occasions in confidence to Ellis and Pearson.

79. Olive Schreiner to Karl Pearson, March 10, 1886, http://www.oliveschreiner.org/vre?view=collections&colid=74&letterid=53; Olive Schreiner to Karl Pearson July 4, 1886, http://www.oliveschreiner.org/vre?view=collections&colid=74&letterid=78.

80. E. Ray Lankester to Phebe Lankester, early 1875, quoted in Lester, *E. Ray Lankester*, 72.

81. Ibid., 72, 121. Lankester used to say, perhaps not seriously, that he came close to marrying a young woman, Marie Baranowska, who nursed him when he was seriously ill from the typhus fever, but was stopped by the arrival of his mother in the household in which he was staying. Marie soon married Lankester's good friend, the Italian marine biologist Anton Dohrn. She remained Lankester's close, lifelong friend (ibid., 44, 47).

82. Gould, *I Have Landed*, 121–22. The mystery surrounding the personal details of Lankester's controversial life have to do with his private papers remaining in the custody of his family. The papers, preserved by his niece Mrs. N. Pain, were made available to Joseph Lester on the condition that he would write an "approved" biography. Paul Bower, "Editor's Preface," in Lester, *E. Ray Lankester*. Interestingly, Lankester, who, in not marrying and having a family displayed a behavior unusual in Victorian times, was not thereby unusual in the context of his own family. Of the seven children of Edwin and Phebe Lankester who lived to adulthood, only one was to have children, and in that case not in Victorian Britain, but in Java. See English, *Victorian Values*, 165–67; Phebe Lankester (obituary), *Times*, April 14, 1900.

83. Charles Darwin, *The Descent of Man, and Selection in Relation to Sex* (Princeton: Princeton University Press, 1981), ii, 272–79, 326–28, 371; Russett, *Sexual Science*, 1–2; John Stuart Mill, "The Subjugation of Women," in John Stuart Mill and Harriet Taylor Mill, *Essays on Sex Equality* (Chicago: University of Chicago Press, 1970).

84. W. K. Brooks, "The Condition of Women from a Zoölogical Point of View," *Popular Science Monthly* 15/10 (June 1879), 145, 154–55; in part 2 of his article (July 1879, 350–53), Brooks argued that John Stuart Mill's "The Subjection of Women" could be interpreted as supporting the idea that there were profound differences between the sexes similar to those designated by Brooks—though Mill contended that these were primarily sociological, not biological, in origin. A reprint of the Brooks article is included in Lankester's library of scientific papers retained in the E. Ray Lankester

Scientific Papers Collection, Marine Biological Association Library. Brooks was a leading figure in the early construction of marine biological laboratories in the United States and undoubtedly corresponded with Lankester in that respect. See E. A. Andrews, "William Keith Brooks (1848–1908)," in David Starr Jordan, *Leading American Men of Science* (New York: Henry Holt, 1910), 427–55. See also W. K. Brooks, *The Law of Heredity* (Baltimore: John Murphy, 1883), 242–74, 325–26.

85. Virginia Woolf, *A Room of One's Own* (New York: Harcourt, Brace, Jovanovich, 1981).
86. On Ellis's relationship to Schreiner and Eleanor Marx see Rachel Holmes, *Eleanor Marx: A Life* (New York: Bloomsbury, 2014), 204–7, 218; Joyce Avrech Berkman, *The Healing Imagination of Olive Schreiner* (Amherst: University of Massachusetts Press, 1989), 28, 152; Carolyn Burdet, *Olive Schreiner and the Progress of Feminism* (New York: Palgrave, 2001), 47–49.
87. Sheila Rowbotham, *Edward Carpenter* (London: Verso, 2008), 89–95.
88. Russett, *Sexual Science*, 28.
89. Havelock Ellis, *Man and Woman* (London: A. & C. Black, 1926), 492.
90. Ibid., vi–ix, 262–63, 429–39, 478, 491–97, 514–21, 527–46.
91. Carolyn Merchant, *The Death of Nature* (New York: Harper and Row, 1980).
92. Ellis, *Man and Woman*, 522–23.
93. Holmes, *Eleanor Marx*, 207–08.
94. Quoted in Russett, *Sexual Science*, 124.
95. Ibid. With respect to Ellis, even Stephen Jay Gould was taken in, saying that Havelock Ellis in *Man and Woman* pointed to the "superiority of women," while Ellis in his book—and more adamantly with each new edition—argued the opposite: insisting that genius was far rarer in women than men. Stephen Jay Gould, *The Mismeasure of Man* (New York: W. W. Norton, 1996), 149.
96. Patrick Geddes and J. Arthur Thomson, *The Evolution of Sex* (New York: Humboldt, 1889), 19, 247–50; Russett, *Sexual Science*, 89–92.
97. Lankester, 1873 note on "Development of Human Character and Beliefs," Lankester family papers, quoted in Lester, *E. Ray Lankester*, 60–61.
98. Ibid., 67, 73, 124–26; Ray Lankester, *The Kingdom of Man* ((New York: Henry Holt, 1911), 151; "Philippa Garrett Fawcett," http://www-history.mcs.st-and.ac.uk/Biographies/Fawcett.html. Engels, who was interested in both science and the progress of women, and who no doubt retained an interest in Lankester as a thinker, observed in a June 1888 letter that Lankester's lectures were not open to women. He was doubtless unaware of the nature of the controversy in which the latter was embroiled. Marx and Engels, *Collected Works*, 48:189.
99. "London Talk," *The Advertiser* (Adelaide, South Africa), November 25, 1895, http://trove.nla.gov.au/ndp/del/article/34529897; Lester, *E. Ray Lankester*, 124–26.
100. Lankester, *From an Easy Chair* (London: Archibald Constable and Co., 1909), 117–23: Gould, *The Mismeasure of Man*, 135–39.
101. Lankester to Mrs. Wells, July 8 (year uncertain, probably 1910–1913), H. G. Wells Archives, University of Illinois, Urbana. Lankester in his later years seems to have echoed the much more conservative John Ruskin, who had written with respect to women's suffrage: "So far from wishing to extend parliamentary suffrage, I would take it from most of those who possess it." James Fuchs, ed., *Ruskin's Views of Social Justice* (New York: Vanguard Press, 1926), 8–11.
102. Hunt, *Equivocal Feminists*, 46–50, 62–63, 153–55.
103. H. G. Wells, *Ann Veronica* (Toronto: Copp Clark Co., 1909), 229–32; 302–04; H. G. Wells, *Experiment in Biography* (New York: Macmillan, 1934), 396; Vincent Brome,

H. G. Wells (New York: Longman, Green, 1951), 112; Lester, *E. Ray Lankester*, 200. Wells's book *Ann Veronica* was caught up in the real-life scandal that Wells, a married man, had with the young, single, feminist writer Amber Reeves. The character Ann Veronica was partly modeled on Reeves, who had a child with Wells. However, it was not this that shocked Edwardian England so much as that Ann Veronica proposed sexual intercourse with a married man with whom she had fallen in love. For Lankester, who always supported free love, backing Wells in this area presented no problem. This resembled in some ways the position of a Social Democratic figure like Ernest Belfort Bax, whose views were much more hostile to women than Lankester's—which did not, however, prevent Bax from taking a more radical position than many socialist women in supporting free love as a principle. Hunt, *Equivocal Feminists*, 101–02.

104. Karl Pearson, *The Grammar of Science* (London: Adam and Charles Black, 1911), viii.
105. V. I. Lenin, *Materialism and Empirico-Criticism* (New York: International Publishers, 1927), 45.
106. Helen Meller, *Patrick Geddes: Social Evolutionist and City Planner* (New York: Routledge, 1990), 141–42.
107. E. Ray Lankester, "Darwinism and Statescraft," *Nature* 63/1638 (March 21, 1901); supp., iii–v; Lester, *E. Ray Lankester*, 174–76; Karl Pearson, *National Life from the Standpoint of Science* (London: Adam and Charles Black, 1905).
108. H. M. Hyndman, "The Socialist Victory," *Times*, January 24, 1908; E. Ray Lankester, "Physical Degeneration and Socialism," *Times*, January 27, 1908; H. M. Hyndman, "Physical Degeneration and Socialism," *Times*, January 29, 1908; E. Ray Lankester, "Physical Degeneration and Socialism," *Times*, February 3, 1908. Donkin became a member of the "Eugenics Society" while Wells promoted "voluntary sterilization" and isolation as eugenics strategies in his *Modern Utopia*, which Lankester read. Lester, *E. Ray Lankester*, 176–77.
109. E. Ray Lankester, *From an Easy Chair*, 107–8.
110. Karl Pearson, "Heredity and Crime," *Times*, November 8, 1910, "Heredity and Crime," *Times*, November 14, 1910 (letters to the editor); H.B. Donkin, "Heredity and Crime, *Times*, November 10, 1914 (letter to the editor); Havelock Ellis, *The Criminal* (New York: Charles Scribner's Sons, 1910).

Daniel Pick, referring to the version of Lankester's "Zoology" article in the 11th (1910–1911) edition of the *Encyclopedia Britannica*, claims that Lankester in his survey mentioned Galton's eugenics, and that, though not actually supporting it outright, nonetheless did so by implication. Pick's aim is to draw a connection between Lankester's notion of degeneration and the advancement of eugenics in his work—part of the larger case he wishes to build in his book. However, Pick's claims have no basis in the text he cites. Lankester only mentioned "eugenics" in the concluding sentence of his 17-page article surveying the development of biological ideas in the 1910–1911 *Britannica*—and he did so only in the context of indicating in an entirely noncommittal way that these issues have come to "public attention" and "are of an exceedingly difficult and delicate nature." He does not mention Galton at all and does not relate eugenics to degeneration (as an evolutionary process), which is dealt with elsewhere in his article. Moreover, as we have seen, Lankester in those very same years was engaged in numerous public criticisms of Galton, Pearson, and others for their eugenics theories—which appears to have escaped Pick entirely. Daniel Pick, *Faces of Degeneration* (Cambridge: Cambridge University Press, 1995), 173–74, 216–18, 224; E. Ray Lankester, "Zoology," *Encyclopedia Britannica,* 11th ed. (1919–1911), 1039; Lankester, *The Advancement of Science*, 349–51.

111. H. B. Donkin, *On Inheritance of Mental Characters: The Harveian Oration for 1910* (London: Adlard and Son, Bartholomew Press, 1910), 17, 20, 25–28, 32–34, 45–46; Gould, *The Mismeasure of Man*, 156–57.
112. Sir Martin Gilbert, "Churchill and Eugenics," The Churchill Centre, May 31, 2009, http://www.winstonchurchill.org/support/the-churchill-centre/publications/finest-hour-online/594-churchill-and-eugenics.
113. E. Ray Lankester, "Heredity and the Direct Action of the Natural Environment," in *The Nineteenth Century and After* (1920): 482–91, esp. note 20; Lankester "Physical Degeneration and Socialism," *Times*, February 3, 1908.
114. Lester, *E. Ray Lankester*, 177.
115. See David Stack, *The First Darwinian Left* (Gretton, Cheltenham: New Clarion Press, 2003), 90.
116. Lankester, preparatory notes to "Nature and Man," quoted in Lester, *E. Ray Lankester*, 190.
117. Gould, *I Have Landed*, 117–18; Peter Ayres, *Shaping Ecology: The Life of Arthur Tansley* (Oxford: John Wiley and Sons, 2012), 41; Sir J. Arthur Thomson, *The Great Biologists*, 163–66; Charles Darwin, *The Descent of Man* (Princeton: Princeton University Press, 1981) 168, 171–73; Lester, *E. Ray Lankester*, 171; Bowler, "Lankester, Sir (Edwin) Ray"; E. Ray Lankester, "Limulus an Arachnid," *Quarterly Journal of Microscopical Science* 21 (1881): 504–649; "Study Confirms Horseshoe Crabs are Really Relatives of Spiders, Scorpions," EurekaAlert.org, March 8, 2019.
118. Ayres, *Shaping Ecology*, 42.
119. See "Œcology," *Oxford English Dictionary*, vol. 1 (Oxford: Oxford University Press, 1975), 1975; "Ecology," *Oxford English Dictionary* Online.
120. Haeckel, *The History of Creation*, translation supervised by E. Ray Lankester, vol. 2, 354.
121. Lankester's *Encyclopedia Britannica* article was reprinted as "The History and Scope of Zoology," in Lankester, *The Advancement of Science*, 287–387. There is some question about the date of the original version of the article since articles from the 9th edition of the *Britannica* appeared over the years 1878 and 1888. However, the "Bionomics" article of the *Oxford English Dictionary* Online (2013) dates the article as 1888. See also Mark A. Largent, "Bionomics: Vernon Lyman Kellogg and the Defense of Darwinism," *Journal of the History of Biology* 32 (1999): 468; letter from John T. Gulick, "Like to Like—A Fundamental Principle in Bionomics," *Nature* 41 (April 10, 1890): 536–37.
122. Jan Freedman, "The First President," in Marine Biological Association, *The Laboratory on the Hoe* (Plymouth: Marine Biological Association, n.d.), 20.
123. Lankester, *The Advancement of Science*, 193–222; Thomas H. Huxley, "Opening Fisheries Exhibition (1882)," http://aleph0.clarku.edu/huxley/SM5/fish.html.
124. Lankester, *The Advancement of Science*, 61–117; E. Ray Lankester, "The Value of a Marine Laboratory to the Development and Regulation of Our Sea Fisheries," *Nature* (May 21, 1885): 65–67; Lester, *E. Ray Lankester*, 105–13; Freedman, "The First President," 20–24; Ian Cooper, "The Origins of the Laboratory," and Marine Biological Association, "Introduction," *The Laboratory on the Hoe*, 1–12.
125. Lankester, *Advancement of Science*, 369–70.
126. E. Ray Lankester, "Memorandum for Members of the M.B.A. Council Only" (exact date unknown, 1887–88), Archives, Marine Biological Association, Plymouth, Devon.
127. E. Ray Lankester, "Darwinism," *Nature* (October 10, 1889), 567.
128. Lankester, *Advancement of Science*, 304–11, 367–71; "Bionomics" and "Ecology" articles in *Oxford English Dictionary* Online (2013).

129. Lankester, *The Advancement of Science*, 368; Largent, "Bionomics," 469; David A. West, *Fritz Müller: A Naturalist in Brazil* (Blacksburg, VA: Pocahontas Press, 2003), 1, 33–53, 116–29; J. Arthur Thomson, *The Science of Life* (London: Blackie and Son, n.d.), 185–98. See the numerous references to Müller in Darwin, *The Descent of Man*.
130. Patrick Geddes, *Chapters in Modern Botany* (New York: Charles Scribner's Sons, 1893), 22–26, 194; Largent, "Bionomics," 471; Thomson, *Science of Life*, 194; Charles Darwin, *The Various Contrivances by which Orchids Are Fertilised by Insects* (New York: D. Appleton and Co., 1877).
131. Thomson, *Science of Life*, 72–73, 190, 193; J. Arthur Thomson, *The System of Animate Nature* (New York: Henry Holt, 1920), 58–59. Thomson, in his discussion of bionomics, brought in the issue of how changes in the environment of an organism interact with its metabolism, but in the specific context of Lamarckian inheritance of acquired characteristics. Lamarck's views were rejected outright by Lankester. However, the issue of metabolic processes of an organism, involving an exchange between the organism and the environment, was increasingly central to ecological thought.
132. Thomson, *Science of Life*, 186–87, 189–90; Charles Darwin, *The Formation of Vegetable Mould, Through the Actions of Worms, With Observations on Their Habits* (London: John Murray, 1881); Brett Clark, Richard York, and John Bellamy Foster, "Darwin's Worms and the Skin of the Earth," *Organization & Environment* 22/3 (September 2009): 345–48. Haeckel had introduced the concept of ecology in 1866, treating it as equivalent to Darwin's "economy of nature." See Franklin Benjamin Golley, *A History of the Ecosystem Concept in Ecology: More Than the Sum of the Parts* (New Haven: Yale University Press, 1993), 2, 207; Charles Darwin, *The Origin of Species* (Cambridge, MA: Harvard University Press, 1964; facsimile of 1859 edition), 62, 207.
133. V. M. Spalding, "The Rise and Progress of Ecology," *Science* 17/423 (February 6, 1903): 201–10.
134. Bowler, *Science for All*, 68.
135. Lankester, *Kingdom of Man*, 1–4. 26; Lester, *E. Ray Lankester*, 163.
136. Lankester, *Kingdom of Man*, 31–33.
137. Ibid., 184–85, 189.
138. Ibid., 11, 41, 187.
139. Ibid., 31–32.
140. Ibid., 30, 41.
141. Lankester, "Nature and Man Notes," quoted in Lester, *E. Ray Lankester*, 164-65.
142. Lankester, *Kingdom of Man*, 190.
143. E. Ray Lankester, "The Significance of the Increased Size of the Cerebrum in Recent as Compared with Extinct Animals," *Nature* 61 (April 26, 1900): 624–25; Lankester, *Kingdom of Man*, 123; Lester, *E. Ray Lankester*, 172; E. Ray Lankester, *Great and Small Things* (London: Methuen and Co., 1923), 77–81, 87–88; E. Ray Lankester, *Diversions of a Naturalist* (New York: Macmillan Co., 1915), 213. Lankester's views in this regard were treated by the American psychologist James Mark Baldwin as a new emphasis on "plasticity" in human psychology arising from Lankester's (and Darwin's) evolutionary theory. See James Mark Baldwin, *Darwin and the Humanities* (Baltimore: Review Publishing, 1909), 23.
144. Upton Sinclair, *The Profits of Religion* (Pasadena, CA: Sinclair, 1918), 306–7.
145. Lester, *E. Ray Lankester*, 60, 154–156; Arthur Conan Doyle, *The Lost World* (Oxford: Oxford University Press, 1998). Doyle also drew on Lankester's book for the description of extinct animals in his novel.

146. E. Ray Lankester, *Extinct Animals* (New York: Henry Holt, 1906), 28–29.
147. E. Ray Lankester, "Nature Reserves," *Nature* 93 (March 12, 1914): 33.
148. E. Ray Lankester, *Science from an Easy Chair* (New York: Henry Holt, 1913), 365–69.
149. Charles Darwin, *Journal of Researches into the Geology of the Various Countries Visited During the Voyage of the H.M.S. Beagle* (New York: E. Dutton, 1906), 470–71; Charles Darwin, *Beagle Diary* (New York: Cambridge University Press, 1988), 428–29; Richard Grove, *Green Imperialism* (Cambridge: Cambridge University Press, 1995), 42–44, 95–109, 121–25, 343–45; Marx and Engels, *Collected Works*, 25:459.
150. E. Ray Lankester, *Science from an Easy Chair*, 369–71.
151. M. J. Schleiden, *The Plant: A Biography* (London: H. Baillere, 1853), 295, 303–7; on Fraas see the quotations by Engels, in Karl Marx and Friedrich Engels, *Gesamtausgabe* (MEGA), IV, 31 (Amsterdam: Akadamie Verlag, 1999), 512–15; Marx and Engels, *Collected Works*,42:558–59.
152. Lankester, *Science from an Easy Chair*, 371; E. Ray Lankester, "Was It Necessary?" *Times*, April 19, 1912; Lester, *E. Ray Lankester*, 190.
153. Lankester, *Science from an Easy Chair*, 373–79.
154. Ibid., 366.
155. Lankester, *Diversions of a Naturalist*, 13–22; Lankester, "Nature Reserves," 33–35; Lester, *E. Ray Lankester*.
156. Lester, *E. Ray Lankester*, 123.
157. Lankester, *Diversions of a Naturalist*, 243–44; Lester, *E. Ray Lankester*, 178; Stephen Jay Gould, *Ever Since Darwin* (New York: W. W. Norton, 1977), 207–13; Karl Marx and Frederick Engels, *Collected Works*, 25:452–64; Peter J. Bowler, *Theories of Human Evolution* (Baltimore: Johns Hopkins University Press, 1986), 151, 159–60. Like many of his contemporary scientists, Lankester fell for the infamous Piltdown Hoax, in which a human skull was cleverly combined with a cleverly altered jaw of an ape. The hoax put anthropology back many years and was not exposed until 1955. Lester, *E. Ray Lankester*, 181–82.
158. Lankester, *Great and Small Things*, 74–82; Lankester, *From an Easy Chair*, 97–116; Lankester, *Diversions of a Naturalist*, 213; E. Ray Lankester, "Progress!," *Nature* 105 (August 12, 1920): 733–35.
159. E. Ray Lankester, "The Making of New Knowledge," in H. G. Wells et al.. *The Great State* (New York: Harper and Brothers, 1912), 127. In the preface to *The Great State*, Wells and two others insisted that the book did not simply consist of socialist contributions and singled Lankester out as someone "who would not dream of calling himself a socialist," but who would also, Wells suggested, not call himself an individualist. It is undoubtedly true that Lankester did not generally refer to himself as a socialist in a political party sense. Yet, his sympathies with socialism were evident in his published statements (and even more in some of his unpublished ones). His willingness to associate himself with largely socialist views in the volume on *The Great State* and his criticism of the dominant classes in his contribution stand as cases in point. See E.W., G.R.ST., and H.G.W., "Prefatory Note," *The Great State*, vi.
160. Lester, *E. Ray Lankester*, 189.
161. Lankester, "The Making of New Knowledge," 129.
162. Lankester, *The Kingdom of Man*, 159.
163. Lankester, *Degeneration*, 59.
164. Lankester quoted in Lester, *E. Ray Lankester*, 174.
165. Lester, *E. Ray Lankester*, 190, 195–97; Margaret A. Rose, *Marx's Lost Aesthetic* (Cambridge: Cambridge University Press, 1984).

166. E. Ray Lankester, "Draft of 'Easy Chair' Article," Lankester family papers, quoted in Lester, *E. Ray Lankester*, 190.
167. Lankester, "The Making of New Knowledge," 127.
168. Lester, *E. Ray Lankester*, 191.
169. Lankester quoted in *R.P.A. Annual, 1925* (Rational Press Association, 1925), frontispiece; A. Gowan Whyte, *The Story of the R.P.A., 1899–1949* (London: Watts and Co., 1949), 95–97. Notable Honorary Associates of the Rationalist Press Association in the twenty years after Lankester's death included John Dewey, H. S. Salt, Albert Einstein, Sigmund Freud, Hyman Levy, V. Gordon Childe, Joseph Needham, and J. D. Bernal.
170. E. Ray Lankester to H. G. Wells, October 28, 1925, Wells Papers, University of Illinois, Urbana; Lester, *E. Ray Lankester*, 212; Ronald W. Clark, *JBS: The Life and Work of J. B. S. Haldane* (New York: Coward-McCann, 1968), 66. The Wells Papers archivists considered this letter from Lankester to Wells to have been written in October 1925, although the year is not included in Lankester's dating of the article. Presumably the *R. P. A. Annual, 1926* was actually published (or made available to Lankester) in the fall of 1925.
171. J. B. S. Haldane, "The Causes of Evolution," *R.P.A. Annual, 1926* (Rationalist Press Association, 1926), 54–64.
172. Gould, *I Have Landed*, 119; Charlotte Haldane, *Truth Will Out* (New York: Vanguard Press, 1950), 21; Lester, *E. Ray Lankester*, 159. Gould's statement that Lankester never told Haldane of his connection to Marx, though most likely true, was probably a mere supposition on his part as he offers no evidence.

CHAPTER TWO: THE ART OF LABOR

1. Walter Crane, *An Artist's Reminiscences* (London: Methuen, 1907), 103–4; William Morris to Jane Morris, March 18, 1884, in William Morris, *Collected Letters* (Princeton: Princeton University Press, 1987), vol. 2, part 1, 270–71. The description of Morris is mainly taken from the socialist artist Walter Crane, reflecting Crane's dramatic memory of his first sight, while looking out a window, of Morris walking, in the 1870s. It is employed here (although in a different context around a decade later) not only because it reflects an artist's eye, but also because it conveys how Morris carried himself when walking in the streets of London. Crane has Morris clad in snuff brown, but I have changed it here to blue, since descriptions of him in the 1880s and '90s invariably refer to his trademark blue serge suit and artisanal-blue shirt without a collar. See also Henry James's description of Morris quoted in E. P. Thompson, *William Morris: Romantic to Revolutionary* (New York: Pantheon Books, 1976), 89.
2. Morris, *Collected Letters*, vol. 2, 270–71; Eleanor Marx to Laura Lafargue, in *The Daughters of Karl Marx*, ed. Olga Meier and Faith Evans (New York: Harcourt Brace Jovanovich, 1979), 176; Mary Gabriel, *Love and Capital* (New York: Little, Brown, 2011), 517.
3. Fiona McCarthy, *William Morris: A Life for Our Time* (London: Faber and Faber, 1994), 22; Linda Parry, "Introduction," in *William Morris* (New York: Harry N. Abrams, Inc., 1996), 12–13. Thompson, *William Morris: Romantic to Revolutionary*, 3, 22.
4. Paul Thompson, *The Work of William Morris* (London: Quartet Books, 1977), 10; George P. Landow, "Wages, the Cost of Living, Contemporary Equivalents to Victorian Money," Victorian Web, http://www.victorianweb.org/economics/wages.html. Of

the annual income that Morris received at this time, more than £700 per annum came from his Devon Great Consol shares. See "William Morris Internet Archive: Chronology," https://www.britannica.com/art/Pre-Raphaelite-Brotherhood.

5. "The Pre-Raphaelite Brotherhood," http://www.pre-raphaelite-brotherhood.org/biography.html.
6. Jack Lindsay, *William Morris: His Life and Work* (New York: Taplinger Publishing, 1975), 92–93, 107, 132–33, 138–39, 162–69.
7. William Morris, *Collected Works*, vol. 1 (London: Longmans, Green and Co., 1910), 1.
8. Anna Marie Attwell, "Sexual Politics, Pomegranates and Production: William Morris's *Defense of Guenevere* and *La Belle Iseult* in Dialogue," Open Educational Resources, University of Oxford, March 5, 2013, https://open.conted.ox.ac.uk/resources/documents/sexual-politics-pomegranates-and-production-william-morris's-defence-guenevere; Florence S. Boos, "Sexual Polarities in *The Defence of Guenevere*," *Browning Institute Studies* 13 (1985): 181–200; "The William Morris Internet Archive: Chronology"; Morris, *Collected Works*, 1:1–11.
9. R. Page Arnot, *William Morris: The Man and the Myth* (New York: Monthly Review Press, 1964), 19; McCarthy, *William Morris: A Life for Our Time*, 166–85. Morris has been criticized recently for his skepticism with regard to the poisonous effects of arsenic contained in the wallpaper produced, in accordance with the established artistic practices of the time, by the firm Morris, Marshall, Faulkner and Co. In 1875, however, once he had bought out the other members and established Morris and Co. under his sole ownership, he ceased using arsenic, replacing it with old fashioned vegetable dyes to obtain his colors. In the same year he resigned from his position as a director of the Devon Great Consols, then the world's leading arsenic producer, and soon sold off his shares inherited from his father. These actions were to precede his commitment to socialism and his growing environmental awareness. Nevertheless, this has not kept certain critics from condemning him for having ostensibly put his business affairs for a number of years before public health. See Lucinda Hawksley, *Bitten by Witch Fever* (London: Thames and Hudson, 2016), 59–61,164–65, 225–26. Here it should be noted that Morris had some basis, as a result of extensive experience with wallpapers in homes (including his own), to be skeptical of the widespread claims of the mass poisoning of Victorians by the arsenic contained in wallpapers, via the action of fungi. Today's scientific research has indeed found that the widespread Victorian belief in arsenic poisoning from wallpaper was nothing more than an "urban myth" with no basis in modern toxicology. See Patrick Sullivan, "William Morris and Arsenic and Old Lace," *The Guardian*, May 29, 2015; William R. Cullen and Ronald Bentley, "The Toxicity of Trimethylarsine: An Urban Myth," *Journal of Environmental Monitoring* 7 (2005): 11–15.
10. Oliver Lovell Triggs, *Chapters in the History of the Arts and Crafts Movement* (Chicago: Industrial Arts League, 1902).
11. *Times* quoted in Paul Greenhalgh, "Morris After Morris," in Parry, *William Morris*, 363.
12. Arnot, *William Morris: The Man and the Myth*, 22. *Sigurd the Volsung* was part of a collaboration between Morris and Eiríkr Magnusson. Magnusson provided literal translations from the Icelandic, and Morris refined and developed it in English verse. Nancy Marie Brown, *Song of the Vikings* (New York: Palgrave Macmillan, 2012), 197–98.
13. Thomas Carlyle, *Past and Present* (New York: E. P. Dutton, 1960), 182.
14. Ibid., 147, 179–81.

15. Thompson, *William Morris: Romantic to Revolutionary*, 29–31; Raymond Williams, *Culture and Society* (New York: Columbia University Press, 1983), 140.
16. William Morris, *William Morris: Artist, Writer, Socialist*, ed. May Morris (Cambridge: Cambridge University Press, 1936), 2:584; Thompson, *William Morris: Romantic to Revolutionary*, 245.
17. William Morris, "How I Became a Socialist," in Morris, *News from Nowhere and Selected Writings and Designs*, ed. Asa Briggs (London: Penguin, 1962), 35–36.
18. John Ruskin, *The Works of John Ruskin* (London: George Allen, 1903), vol. 27, 167.
19. Williams, *Culture and Society*, 139–40.
20. John Ruskin, *The Stones of Venice*, vol. 2 (New York: Peter Fenelon Collier and Son, 1900), 163–65 ("Nature of the Gothic," paragraphs 13–15); Thompson, *William Morris: Romantic to Revolutionary*, 37–38.
21. Ruskin, *The Stones of Venice*, vol. 2, 163–65 ("Nature of the Gothic," paragraphs 13–15).
22. Thompson, *William Morris: Romantic to Revolutionary*, 35–37; Ruskin, *The Stones of Venice*, vol. 2, 164 ("Nature of the Gothic," paragraph 15).
23. Although Coketown in Dickens's *Hard Times* is a generic nineteenth-century mill town, it has been generally associated in the public mind with Manchester viewed as the quintessential mill town. See Charles Dickens, *Hard Times* (New York: Knopf, 1992).
24. John Ruskin, *Sesame and Lilies; The Two Paths; and the King of the Golden River* (New York: E. P. Dutton, 1907), 158–59, italics added. See also Shigeto Tsuru, *Economic Theory and Capitalist Society*, vol. 1 (Brookfield, VT: Edward Elgar, 1994), 380.
25. John Bryson, "Introduction," in John Ruskin, *Unto this Last/The Political Economy of Art/Essays on Political Economy* (New York: E.P. Dutton, 1968), vii–xii; Seth Koven, "How the Victorians Read *Sesame and Lilies*," in John Ruskin, *Sesame and Lilies*, ed. Deborah Epstein Nord (New Haven: Yale University Press, 2002), 168–75; Ruskin, *Sesame and Lilies*, 63.
26. Ruskin, *Unto This Last*, 96.
27. Ibid., 171, 185, 189–90, 216.
28. Ibid., 205–6, 212–13; Williams, *Culture and Society*, 142.
29. Williams, *Culture and Society*, 140.
30. Ruskin, *Sesame and Lilies*, 49–54.
31. John Ruskin, *The Works of John Ruskin* (London: George Allen, 1903), vol. 27, 91–93.
32. John Ruskin, *The Crown of Wild Olive: Four Lectures on Work, Traffic, War, and the Future of England* (Thomas Y. Crowell and Co., n.d.), 6–7.
33. Morris, *Collected Works*, 22:131–32; Thompson, *William Morris: Romantic to Revolutionary*, 244. The crossing of the "river of fire" metaphor is frequently employed by Thompson to refer to Morris's conversion to socialism in the late 1870s and early 1880s.
34. Ruskin, *Works*, vol. 27, 111, 113, 116, 126–27; Thompson, *William Morris: Romantic to Revolutionary*, 196–97.
35. William Morris, "Address at the Twelfth Annual Meeting (Anti-Scrape), July 3, 1889, in Morris, *William Morris: Artist, Writer, Socialist*, 1:148; Thompson, *William Morris: Romantic to Revolutionary*, 235.
36. Morris emphasized that his political transitional period was short, as his development in this direction was already extensive by the time he turned to political action. He moved quickly from political radicalism to socialism. See Morris, "How I Became a Socialist," 34.
37. Snorri Sturluson, *The Prose Edda* (London: Penguin Books, 2005).

38. Thompson, *William Morris: Romantic to Revolutionary*, 192; William Morris, *Journalism: Contributions to* Commonweal, *1885–1890* (Bristol: Thoemmes Press, 1996), 458–59.
39. Burne-Jones and Scheu quoted in Thompson, *William Morris: Romantic to Revolutionary*, 250–51.
40. Thompson, *The Work of William Morris*, 210–12; Thompson, *William Morris: Romantic to Revolutionary*, 193, 202–25.
41. William Morris, *Letters* (Longmans, Green and Co., 1950), 388–89; Thompson, *William Morris: Romantic to Revolutionary*, 193.
42. See H. C. G. Matthew, *Gladstone, 1809–1898* (Oxford: Oxford University Press, 1997), 307–8, 374–410.
43. Morris, "Architecture and History," 301–2; Morris, *Collected Works* 22:301; Morris, *William Morris: Artist, Writer, Socialist*, 1:129–30, 142; Thompson, *William Morris: Romantic to Revolutionary*, 228.
44. Morris, *William Morris: Artist, Writer, Socialist*, I:152; Thompson, *William Morris: From Romantic to Revolutionary*, 239.
45. Morris, *William Morris: Artist, Writer, Socialist*, I:126; Thompson, *William Morris: From Romantic to Revolutionary*, 236–37.
46. William Morris, "The History of Pattern Designing," in Morris, *Collected Works*, 22:232–33.
47. Morris, "How I Became a Socialist," 34, Paul Meier, *William Morris: The Marxist Dreamer* (Sussex: Harvester Press, 1978), vol. 1, 172–73; John Stuart Mill, *Collected Works* (Toronto: University of Toronto Press, 1967), vol. 5, 705–63.
48. Thompson, *William Morris, Romantic to Revolutionary*, 270; Nick Salmon, *The William Morris Chronology* (Bristol: Thoemmes Press, 1996), 192.
49. Thompson, *William Morris: From Romantic to Revolutionary*, 37–39; Alan K. Bacon, "Morris's View of the History of Industrialism," *Journal of the William Morris Society* 5/1 (Summer 1982): 2–3.
50. Karl Marx, *Capital*, vol. 1 (London: Penguin, 1976), 480–91.
51. Thompson, *William Morris: From Romantic to Revolutionary*, 38; Karl Marx, *Capital*, vol. 1 (London: Penguin, 1976), 481.
52. William Morris, *Signs of Change* (London: Reeves and Turner, 1888), 152.
53. William Morris, "Art and Its Producers" (1888), in Morris, *Art and Its Producers and The Arts and Crafts To-day: Two Addresses Delivered Before the National Association for the Advancement of Art* (London: Longmans and Co., 1901), 9–10. The suspension points here are Morris's own, used as a pause, and do not constitute an ellipsis.
54. A. L. Morton, "Morris, Marx, and Engels," *Journal of William Morris Studies* 7/1 (Autumn 1986): 47. See also A. L. Morton, "Introduction," in William Morris, *Three Works* (London: Lawrence and Wishart, 1986), 22.
55. Thompson, *The Work of William Morris*, 1–2.
56. Morton, "Morris, Marx, and Engels," 45.
57. William Morris, "How I Became a Socialist," 34; Thompson, *William Morris: Romantic to Revolutionary*, 619.
58. William Morris and E. Belfort Bax, *Socialism: Its Growth and Outcome* (London: Swan Sonnenschein, 1893); "Socialism from the Root Up" articles in their original form are available in William Morris, *Political Writings* (Bristol: Thoemmes Press, 1994), 497–622.
59. Karl Marx and Frederick Engels, *Collected Works* (New York: International Publishers, 1975), 50:277–78, 299.

60. Morris and Bax, *Socialism: Its Growth and Influence*, 267.
61. Morris, *Collected Letters*, vol. 2, part 2, 393–94.
62. Salmon, *The William Morris Chronology*, 174–75.
63. Morris, *Collected Letters*, vol. 2, part 2, 729.
64. Ruth Kinna, *William Morris: The Art of Socialism* (Cardiff: University of Wales Press, 2000), 123–25. As further evidence of Morris's resistance to the Fabian, presumably Jevons-based, criticisms of Marx, Annie Besant, who was preparing a pamphlet on *Modern Socialism*, based on articles that had previously appeared in serial form in *Our Corner*, sent the proposed pamphlet to Morris in October 1886 for comments. Morris replied that a footnote criticizing Marx's economics as "pseudo-scientific" (which E. P. Thompson surmised was actually inspired by Shaw, then engaged in a "secret *amour*" with Besant) be dropped. Thompson, *William Morris, Romantic to Revolutionary*, 761–62.
65. Morris, *Political Writings*, 457; George Bernard Shaw, ed., *Fabian Essays in Socialism* (Gloucester, MA: Peter Smith, 1967).
66. William Morris, *We Met Morris: Interviews with William Morris* (Reading: Spire Books, n.d.), 48; Morris, *Collected Letters*, vol. 2, 393–94; Florence Boos, ed., *William Morris's Socialist Diary* (London: Journeyman Press, 1982), 32; Thompson, *William Morris: From Romantic to Revolutionary*, 748.
67. Thompson, *William Morris: From Romantic to Revolutionary*, 37–39, 305–6, 749–51; Morton, "Morris, Marx, and Engels," 45; Meier, *William Morris: The Marxist Dreamer*, vol. 1, 212.
68. William Morris, *Collected Works*, 23:153; Thompson, *The Work of William Morris*, 218–19.
69. E. Belfort Bax, "Leaders of Modern Thought XXIII," *Modern Thought* 3/12 (December 1881): 349–54, http://www.marxists.org/archive/bax/1881/12/marx.htm; "E Belfort Bax" in H. Hyndman et al., *How I Became a Socialist* (London: Twentieth Century Press, n.d.), 9–16; Thompson, *William Morris: Romantic to Revolutionary*, 287–88; MacCarthy, *William Morris: A Life for Our Time* (London: Faber and Faber, 1994), 506–07; Tsuzuki, *H.M. Hyndman and British Socialism,* 49.
70. Hal Draper, *The Marx-Engels Glossary* (New York: Schocken Books, 1986), 125.
71. Thompson, *William Morris: Romantic to Revolutionary*, 306–7; Salmon, *The William Morris Chronology*, 122.
72. MacCarthy, *William Morris: A Life for Our Time*, 507–8.
73. George Bernard Shaw, "Morris as I Knew Him," in William Morris, *William Morris: Artist, Writer, Socialist,* ed. May Morris (Cambridge: Cambridge University Press, 1936), 2:ix.
74. Henry Mayers Hyndman, *England for All* (London: Gilbert and Rivington, 1881), 32–87. The original 1850 translation of *The Communist Manifesto* by Helen MacFarlane and the 1888 authorized English translation are published side by side in Hal Draper, *The Adventures of the Communist Manifesto* (Berkeley: Center for Socialist History, 1998).
75. Engels quoted in Chushichi Tsuzuki, *H. M. Hyndman and British Socialism* (Oxford: Oxford University Press, 1961), 42.
76. Ibid.
77. Ibid.
78. Thompson, *William Morris: Romantic to Revolutionary*, 292–95, 313; David McLellan, *Karl Marx: His Life and Thought* (New York: Harper and Row, 1973), 445–46.
79. H. M. Hyndman, *The Historical Basis of Socialism in England* (London: Kegan, Paul,

Trench, and Co., 1883), 119, 476; Morris, *Collected Letters*, vol. 2, 393–94; Thompson, *William Morris: Romantic to Revolutionary*, 295, 333–35. Typical of Hyndman's eclecticism in *Historical Basis* was his contention that Marx's surplus value theory had been anticipated by English socialists and Rodbertus, even though Marx was the first to put it on a truly scientific basis (126). Another negative feature of Hyndman's *Historical Basis*, which no doubt disturbed Morris, was the jingoistic tone in which he declared that socialism would need to be based for the time being on "Celto-Teutonic peoples in America, in Australia, in these islands, and possibly Germany" rather than "semi-Asiatic" Russia and other regions around the globe. For Morris, the determined anti-imperialist, this would have raised serious objections (433). Tsuzuki, *H. M Hyndman and British Socialism,* 51.

80. H. M. Hyndman and William Morris, *A Summary of the Principles of Socialism* (London: The Modern Press, 1884), 16–18, 38, 42, 48, 62.
81. Morris, *Collected Letters*, vol. 2, part 2, 393–94. In 1887, with the English translation of volume 1 of Marx's *Capital* available, Morris in 1885 recommended it to an unknown recipient. Next to that the only book he recommended (though sending three pamphlets) was Gronlund's *Co-operative Commonwealth*. At that point, two years after his original recommendation of Gronlund in a letter, Morris's view of it had changed sufficiently for him to characterize it as "a weakish book." Nevertheless, he still commended it has having "much information in it." Morris, *Collected Letters*, vol. 2, part 2, 695. He no longer recommended Hyndman at all.
82. Laurence Gronlund, *The Co-operative Commonwealth in Its Outlines: An Exposition of Modern Socialism* (Boston: Lee and Shepard, 1884), 50; Laurence Gronlund, *The Co-operative Commonwealth in Its Outlines: An Exposition of Socialism* (Boston: Lee and Shephard, 1890), 46; Morris, *Collected Letters*, vol. 2, 445; Chushichi Tsuzuki, "Lawrence Gronlund and American Socialism," *Hitotsubashi Journal of Social Studies* (January 1968): 18–25; Hal Draper, *The Two Souls of Socialism*, *New Politics* 5/1 (Winter 1966): 57–84; Mark Pittenger, *American Socialists and Evolutionary Thought, 1870–1920* (Madison: University of Wisconsin Press, 1993), 43–63; "Gronlund, Laurence," *The Encyclopedia of Social Reform* (New York: Funk and Wagnalls Co., 1897), 674.
83. Marx and Engels, *Collected Works,* 47:295; Tsuzuki, "Lawrence Gronlund and American Socialism," 18–25; Pittenger, *American Socialists and Evolutionary Thought*, 56–60; Hal Draper, *The Marx-Engels Glossary* (New York: Schocken Books, 1986), 83; Laurence Gronlund, "The Work Before Us," *Commonweal* 1/6 (July 1885): 61–62; "First General Meeting of the Socialist League," *Commonweal,* 1/7 (August 1885): 75.
84. Karl Marx and Frederick Engels, *Letters to Americans, 1848–1895* (New York: International Publishers, 1953), 146–47; Dorothy Rose Blumber, *Florence Kelley* (New York: Augustus M. Kelley, 1966), 48–49, 55, 115; Florence Kelley, "The Need for Theoretical Preparation for Philanthropic Work," in Florence Kelley, *Autobiography*, ed. Kathryn Kish Sklar (Chicago: Charles H. Kerr, 1986), 102.
85. Meier, *William Morris: The Marxist Dreamer*, vol. 1, 166–70, 212–13, vol. 2, 503; Morris, "How I Became a Socialist," 34; MacCarthy, *William Morris: A Life for Our Time*, 469; Salmon, *A Morris Chronology*, 143, 148–49; Morris and Bax, *Socialism: Its Growth and Outcome*, 214; Blumberg, *Florence Kelley*, 82; Eleanor Marx-Aveling and Edward Aveling, *Thoughts on Women and Society* (New York: International Publishers, 1987). The first edition of Edward Aveling and Eleanor Marx-Aveling's pamphlet, *The Factory Hell*, was advertised on the back of the second (July 1885) edition of the *Manifesto of the Socialist League*; a second edition appeared in 1891. Morris was also

no doubt familiar with their *Shelley's Socialism* (1888), which was printed in a private edition of only twenty-five copies. Edward Aveling and Eleanor Marx-Aveling, *Shelley's Socialism* (London: Journeyman Press, 1975). Aveling's weekly lectures became the basis for his later work on Marx, which was a kind of textbook to volume 1 of *Capital*: Edward Aveling, *The Student's Marx* (London: Swan Sonnenschein and Co., 1891); E. Belfort Bax, *The Religion of Socialism* (Freeport, NY: Books for Libraries Press, 1886, repr. 1972).

86. Thompson, *William Morris, Romantic to Revolutionary*, 792. Thompson added in a footnote: "I write 'Communist Utopian' when I refuse the term 'Marxist Utopian'. . . since the term 'Communist' may appertain to value-systems as well as to theoretical systems in a way which 'Marxist' has ceased to do. By 'Communist' I mean especially those values which Morris himself attributed to the society of the future" (815).
87. Thompson, *The Work of William Morris*, 240.
88. Morris, *Collected Works*, 22:323.
89. On the importance of revolutionary vernaculars, see Teodor Shanin, "Marxism and the Vernacular Revolutionary Traditions," in Shanin, ed., *Late Marx and the Russian Road* (New York: Monthly Review Press, 1983), 243–75.
90. Thompson, *William Morris, Romantic to Revolutionary*, 270.
91. Morris, *Collected Works*, 23:165–66.
92. Ibid., 23:166.
93. Ibid., 23:170–75, 168.
94. Ibid., 23:176–77, 180–83; Morris, *Political Writings*, 459–60; Marx, *Capital*, vol. 1, 492.
95. Morris, *Signs of Change*, 169, 187; Salmon, *The William Morris Chronology*, 127; William Morris, *Unpublished Lectures* (Detroit: Wayne State University Press, 1969), 232; David Leopold, "Introduction," in William Morris, *News from Nowhere* (Oxford: Oxford University Press, 2003), xvi; Marx, *Capital*, vol. 1, 798.
96. Morris, *Collected Works*, 23:167, 176–77, 180.
97. Ibid., 23:170–71, 173–74.
98. Ibid., 23:172, 189.
99. *Times*, quoted in Thompson, *William Morris, From Romantic to Revolutionary*, 271; J. W. MacKail, *The Life of William Morris* (2 vols. bound as one) (New York: Dover, 1995), vol. 2, 117–20; MacCarthy, *William Morris: A Life for Our Time*, 476–79.
100. Perry Anderson, *Arguments Within English Marxism* (London: Verso, 1980), 172.
101. Thompson, *William Morris, Romantic to Revolutionary*, 540–41.
102. Eugene D. Lemire, "Appendix 1: A Calendar of William Morris's Platform Career," in Morris, *Unpublished Lectures*, 303, 305.
103. Morris, *Signs of Change*, vii–viii.
104. Ibid., v–vii.
105. Morris, *Signs of Change*, 1–2.
106. Ibid., 33–36.
107. Ibid., 37–54.
108. Anderson, *Arguments Within English Marxism*, 176.
109. Morris, *Signs of Change*, 46.
110. William Morris, *On History* (Sheffield, UK: Sheffield Academic Press, 1996), 120.
111. Ibid., 122–23.
112. Morris, *Signs of Change*, 56–80.
113. Ibid., 81–99, 130.
114. Ibid., 101–16.

115. Ibid., 119; Morris, *News from Nowhere and Selected Writings and Designs*, 140–43.
116. Georg Wilhelm Friedrich Hegel, *Introductory Lectures on Aesthetics* (London: Penguin Books, 1993), 34–36, 40, 52–53.
117. Marx and Engels, *Collected Works*, 5:393; also see Mikhail Lifshitz, *The Philosophy of Art of Karl Marx* (New York: Critics Group, 1938), 90–92.
118. Marx and Engels, *Collected Works*, 5:394.
119. Caroline Arscott, *Interlacings: William Morris and Edward Byrne Jones* (New Haven: Yale University Press, 2008), 134–35.
120. Oscar Wilde, *Essays and Lectures* (London: Knickerbocker Press, 1894), 121–23.
121. Morris, *Political Writings*, 277.
122. Morris, *Unpublished Lectures*, 86–88.
123. Morris quoted in MacCarthy, *William Morris: A Life for Our Times*, 562.
124. Marx and Engels, *Collected Works*, 5:391–93; Lifshitz, *The Philosophy of Art of Karl Marx*, 90–93.
125. Morris, *Signs of Change*, 122, 128.
126. Ibid., 125–40; Morris, "Art and Its Producers," 15.
127. Morris, *Signs of Change*, 166–69.
128. Ibid., 151, 167–69, 184.
129. Ibid., 148–49.
130. Ibid., 158–62.
131. Ibid., 174–202.
132. William Morris, "'Socialism' and 'What We Have to Look For': Two Unpublished Lectures," ed. Florence S. Boos, *Journal of the William Morris Society* (Winter 2010): 22, 29, 31.
133. Morris, *We Met Morris*, 77.
134. Morris, quoted in Thompson, *William Morris: Romantic to Revolutionary*, 550.
135. William Morris, *Collected Works*, 22:311. The Society for the Protection of Ancient Buildings, also known as Anti-Scrape, was founded by Morris, Phillip Webb and others in 1877, in order to combat the destructive "restoration" of ancient buildings in Victorian times. Morris argued that ancient buildings should be repaired not restored, in order to protect their entire cultural heritage.
136. Morris, *William Morris: Artist, Writer, Socialist*, 1:128.
137. William Morris, *News from Nowhere or an Epoch of Rest: Being Some Chapters from a Utopian Romance* (Oxford: Oxford University Press, 2003), 89–111.
138. William Morris, *Three Works* (London: Lawrence and Wishart, 1986), 53.

CHAPTER THREE: THE MOVEMENT TOWARD SOCIALISM

1. Workers striking in Chicago's Haymarket Square on May 4, 1884, for the eight-hour day (as well as protesting the killing of several workers in a police crackdown the previous day) were blamed for a bomb that went off and ensuing gunfire in which seven police and four civilians were killed, and many more wounded. The "Haymarket riot" led to the hanging in November 1887 of four labor activists on trumped up charges. See "The Haymarket Affair," Illinois Labor History Society, http://www.illinoislaborhistory.org/the-haymarket-affair; "The Haymarket Execustions," *The Nation*, November 17, 1887.
2. E. P. Thompson, *William Morris: Romantic to Revolutionary* (New York: Pantheon, 1976), 482–88.
3. The phrase "in the greyness of the chilly November afternoon" is taken from *News from Nowhere*, in which Morris alluded to Bloody Sunday. See William Morris, *News from Nowhere or an Epoch of Rest: Being Some Chapters from A Utopian Romance*

(Oxford: Oxford University Press, 2003), 35–36. "Thickset and short, and dressed in shabby blue" is Morris's own self-description in *The Pilgrims of Hope*. See William Morris, *Three Works* (London: Lawrence and Wishart, 1986), 137. See also Thompson, *William Morris: Romantic to Revolutionary*, 488–89; and *Writing by Candlelight* (London: Merlin, 1980), 155; Fiona MacCarthy, *William Morris: A Life for Our Time* (London: Faber and Faber, 1994), 566–67.

4. Walter Crane, *An Artist's Reminiscences* (London: Methuen and Co., 1907), 266–68; Morris, *Political* Writings, 302–06; Thompson, *William Morris: Romantic to Revolutionary*, 486–93; MacCarthy, *William Morris: A Life for Our Time*, 567–70; Lisa Keller, "Bloody Sunday Demonstration, 1887," *International Encyclopedia of Revolution and Protest* (London: Blackwell, 2009), http://www.blackwellreference.com/public/tocnode?id=g9781405184649_yr2012_chunk_g9781405184649217#citation; Yvonne Kapp, *Eleanor Marx*, vol. 2 (New York: Pantheon, 1976), 226–29; Rachel Holmes, *Eleanor Marx* (London: Bloomsbury, 2014), 298–300.
5. William Morris, "Death Song," quoted in Kapp, *Eleanor Marx*, 2:241–47.
6. Thompson, *William Morris: Romantic to Revolutionary*, 492–96; MacCarthy, *William Morris: A Life for Our Time*, 570–73; Nicholas Salmon, *The William Morris Chronology* (Bristol: Thoemmes Press, 1996), 192.
7. Thompson, *William Morris: Romantic to Revolutionary*, 344–50, 357–66; MacCarthy, *William Morris: A Life for Our Time*, 493–503; Holmes, *Eleanor Marx*, 233.
8. Thompson, *William Morris: Romantic to Revolutionary*, 370–71; MacCarthy, *William Morris: A Life for Our Time*, 509; Karl Marx and Frederick Engels, *Collected Works* (New York: International Publishers, 1975), 47:224; William Morris, *Collected Works* (London: Longmans, Green, 1910), vol. 12; *The Poetic Edda* (Austin: University of Texas Press, 1990); Snorri Sturluson, *The Prose Edda* (London: Penguin, 2005).
9. Edward B. Aveling, *The Student's Darwin* (London: Freethought Publishing Co., 1881), *The Student's Marx* (London: Swan Sonnenschein, 1897).
10. Thompson, *William Morris: Romantic to Revolutionary*, 366–75; MacCarthy, *William Morris: A Life for Our Time*, 506–09; Edward Aveling, *Charles Darwin and Karl Marx: A Comparison* (London: Twentieth Century Press, n.d.), 12–13.
11. Bax, E. Belfort Bax, *Religion of Socialism* (Freeport, NY: Books for Libraries Press, 1886), 117.
12. May Morris, Introduction, in William Morris, *William Morris: Artist, Writer, Socialist*, ed. May Morris, vol. 2 (Cambridge: Cambridge University Press, 1936), 174.
13. E. Belfort Bax, *Essays in Socialism: New and Old* (London: E. Grant Richards, 1906), 301, 305–8; Karen Hunt, *Equivocal Feminists* (Cambridge: Cambridge University Press, 1996), 60–61. In support of his later contention on women's "organic inferiority," Bax cited the early twentieth-century Italian "socialist" and social Darwinist Enrico Ferri, who insisted on the inferiority of women, making various pseudo-scientific claims to that effect. Although initially claiming to be a follower of Marx, who, he insisted, "completes Darwin and Spencer," Ferri was to become a vocal supporter of Mussolini's fascism. See Enrico Ferri, *Socialism and Modern Science* (Chicago: Charles H. Kerr, 1912), 20, 159. On Eleanor Marx-Aveling's dispute with Bax over his anti-feminism see Eleanor Marx-Aveling, "Exchange with Bax," Marxists.org, https://www.marxists.org/archive/eleanor-marx/1895/11/bax-exchange.htm.
14. Thompson, *William Morris: Romantic to Revolutionary*, 333. MacCarthy, *William Morris: A Life for Our Time*, 553; Salmon, *William Morris Chronology*, 142.
15. Thompson, *William Morris: Romantic to Revolutionary*, 382–85; Bax, *Religion of Socialism*, 124.

16. William Morris and E. Belfort Bax, "Manifesto of the Socialist League," 1st ed. (from *Commonweal*, February 1885) in William Morris, *Journalism* (Bristol: Thoemmes Press, 1996), 2–8.
17. William Morris and E. Belfort Bax, *Manifesto of the Socialist League*, 2nd ed. (annotated) (London: Socialist League Office, October 1885), 10.
18. Karl Marx, *Critique of the Gotha Programme* (New York: International Publishers, 1938), 10.
19. See, for example, David Graeber, *The Democracy Project* (New York: Spiegel and Grau, 2013), 293–94; Gregory Titelman, "From each according to his ability, to each according to his needs," *Random House Dictionary of Popular Proverbs and Sayings* (New York: Random House, 1996), 108.
20. Paul Meier, *William Morris: Marxist Dreamer*, vol. 1 (Sussex: Harvester Press, 1978), 186.
21. Karl Marx and Frederick Engels, *Collected Works*, 11:555; Frank E. Manuel, *A Requiem for Karl Marx* (Cambridge, MA: Harvard University Press 1995), 164, 171–72, 238.
22. Marx and Engels, *Collected Works*, 11:555.
23. Ibid., 5:537.
24. Philippe Buonarroti, *Conspiration pour l'égalité dite de Babeuf* (1828), quoted in István Mészáros, *Beyond Capital* (New York: Monthly Review Press, 1995), 221. See also Meier, *William Morris: Marxist Dreamer*, 1:170.
25. Morris, *Collected Works*, 22:341; 23:267–70; William Morris and E. Belfort Bax, *Socialism: Its Growth and Outcome* (London: Swan Sonnenschein, 1893), 227; Meier, *William Morris: Marxist Dreamer*, 1:166–70.
26. See the passages from Lenin's *State and Revolution* included in Marx, *Critique of the Gotha Programme*, 81–88.
27. Morris and Bax, *Manifesto of the Socialist League*, 2nd ed., 11; William Morris, "Equality," *Journal of Pre-Raphaelite Studies* 19 (Spring 2011): 60–61. Morris quoted in Meier, *William Morris: Marxist Dreamer*, 1:285–86. Meier believed that Morris and Bax's use of "from each according to their ability, to each according to their need" was evidence of their having seen Marx's unpublished *Critique of the Gotha Programme*, which was in Engels's hands. However, this was based on the false presumption that the phrase had not appeared earlier in Blanc. Meier, *William Morris: Marxist Dreamer*, vol. 1, 186, 28–83.
28. Laurence Gronlund, *The Co-operative Commonwealth it Its Outlines: An Exposition of Modern Socialism* (Boston: Lee and Shepard Publishers, 1884), 107–8.
29. Morris and Bax, *Manifesto of the Socialist League*, 2nd ed., 11.
30. E. Belfort Bax, *The Religion of Socialism* (New York: Books for Libraries Press, 1972; repr. of 1886 edition), 2–5.
31. William Morris, "The Arts and Crafts of To-day" (1889), in Morris, *Art and Its Producers and the Arts and Crafts of To-day: Two Addresses Delivered Before the National Association for the Advancement of Art* (London: Longman and Co., 1901), 42–44. See also Morris, *Three Works*, 53; Meier, *William Morris: Marxist Dreamer*, 2:479–80.
32. Morris, *Three Works*, 103; Morris and Bax, *Socialism: Its Growth and Outcome*, 267.
33. Jack Lindsay, *Decay and Renewal* (London: Lawrence and Wishart, 1976), 413.
34. Marx and Engels, *Collected Works*, 26:295–301.
35. Ibid., 26:300.
36. Thompson, *William Morris: Romantic to Revolutionary*, 387; Salmon, *William Morris Chronology*, 144; Provisional Council of the Socialist League, *Manifesto of the So-*

cialist League on the Soudan War, March 2, 1885, repr. in *Labour Monthly* 34 (July 1952): 303–6. In the reprint the nineteenth-century spelling "Soudan" is given the modern spelling. In its uncompromising critique of imperialism, the Socialist League distinguished itself from much of the socialist movement of the period, including Shaw and the Fabians. See Bernard Semmel, *Imperialism and Social Reform: English Social Imperial Thought, 1895–1914* (Garden City, NY: Doubleday, 1960). Morris's critique of Gordon was ahead of its time. It was not until the Edwardian Era that Lytton Strachey revealed for all and sundry the sordid reality behind the myth. See Lytton Strachey, *Eminent Victorians* (London: G. P. Putnam's Sons, 1918), 245–350.

37. On the issue of unity and diversity in the First International, see Samir Amin, "Popular Movements Toward Socialism," *Monthly Review* 66/2 (June 2014): 5–6.
38. Thompson, *The Work of William Morris*, 226–27; Shaw quoted in MacCarthy, *William Morris: A Life for Our Time*, 506; Thompson, *William Morris: Romantic to Revolutionary*, 423.
39. Thompson, *William Morris: Romantic to Revolutionary*, 395–97 (correction made in Thompson quote: "inequal" changed to "unequal"); Edward Aveling, "The Police and Mr. Saunders," *Commonweal* 1/9 (October 1885): 91–92; Phillip Henderson, *The Letters of William Morris to His Family and Friends* (London: Longmans, Green, 1950), 390–91.
40. Thompson, *The Work of William Morris*, 229–30.
41. Thompson, *William Morris: Romantic to Revolutionary*, 455.
42. Quoted in Thompson, ibid., 380–81.
43. Morris, *Political Writings*, 98–100; Thompson, *William Morris: Romantic to Revolutionary*, 381–82
44. R. Page Arnot, *William Morris: The Man and the Myth* (New York: Monthly Review Press, 1964), 36–37.
45. Marx and Engels, *Collected Works*, 47:484; Thompson, *William Morris: Romantic to Revolutionary*, 405, 422, 448–49, 470, 780–88. Arnot, *William Morris: The Man and the Myth*, 37, 40; MacCarthy, *William Morris: A Life for Our Time*, 553; Marx and Engels, *Collected Works*, 48:51, 360.
46. Morris, *Political Writings*, 336–42; Thompson, *The Work of William Morris*, 227–29.
47. Morris, *William Morris: Artist, Writer, Socialist*, 2:434–53.
48. Morris, *Political Writings*, 222–27, 460; William Morris, *Journalism* (Bristol: Thoemmes Press, 1996), 440–41.
49. Morris, *Political Writings*, 460.
50. Thompson, *William Morris: Romantic to Revolutionary*, 508–9.
51. Letter to John Glasse, May 23, 1887, in William Morris, *Collected Letters* (Princeton: Princeton University Press, 1987), vol. 2, part 2, 658, 669; Morris, *Political Writings*, 414–18; William Morris, "Interviews with William Mooris: I. From *Justice* 27th January 1894," *Journal of William Morris Society* (Autumn 1993), 4; http://www.morrissociety.org/JWMS/10.3Autumn1993/AU93.10.3.Interviews.pdf; William Morris, "'Socialism' and 'What We Have to Look For': Two Unpublished Lectures by William Morris," edited by Florence S. Boos in *Journal of the William Morris Society* (Winter 2010): 42; Morris quoted in Florence and William Boos, "The Utopian Communism of William Morris," *History of Political Theory* 7/3 (Winter 1986): 494; Ruth Kinna, "Morris, Anti-Statism, and Anarchy," in *William Morris: Centenary Essays*, ed. Peter Faulkner and Peter Preston (Exeter: University of Exeter Press, 1999), 217–20. See also the compilation of numerous quotes in which Morris presents his critique of anarchism in Meier, *William Morris: Marxist Dreamer*, 2:319–27.

52. Morris, *Collected Works*, 235; Thompson, *William Morris: Romantic to Revolutionary*, 504–8. Kinna, "Morris, Anti-Statism, and Anarchy," 220; Peter Kropotkin, *The Coming Revival of Socialism* (London: Freedom Press, 1903), 21–22. In his *Socialist Diary* Morris treats the Anarchists and their doctrines (including Kropotkin) at considerable distance. See *Socialist Diary,* edited and annotated by Florence S. Boos (London: London History Workshop Centre, 1982), 28–29.
53. Morris quoted in Thompson, *William Morris: Romantic to Revolutionary*, 509.
54. Morris, *We Met Morris*, 81–88; Nicholas Salmon, "Introduction," in Morris, *Political Writings*, xliii; MacCarthy, *William Morris: A Life for Our Time*, 583, 641–42; Thompson, *The Work of William Morris*, 231; Bernard Porter, "M: MI5's First Spymaster," *English Historical Review* 120/489 (2005): 21459-60.
55. William Morris, *News from Nowhere and Selected Writings and Designs*, ed. Asa Briggs (London: Penguin 1962), 34–35.
56. Morris, *Socialist Diary*, 50–54; MacCarthy, *William Morris: A Life For Our Time*, 559–61.
57. See Kapp, *Eleanor Marx*, 328–63.
58. Morris quoted in John Tully, *Silvertown: The Lost Story of a Strike that Shook London and Helped Launch the Modern Labor Movement* (New York: Monthly Review Press, 2014), 29, 111; Rosemary Taylor, "'The City of Dreadful Delight': William Morris in the East End of London," *Journal of the William Morris Society* 18/3 (Winter 2009): 9–28.
59. MacCarthy, *William Morris: A Life for Our Time*, 579–80; 534–37; 818; Morris, *Political Writings*, 431–40; Thompson, *William Morris: Romantic to Revolutionary*, 818.
60. Thompson, *William Morris: Romantic to Revolutionary*, 569–70.
61. Ibid., 514.
62. H. D. Lloyd, "The Story of a Great Monopoly," *Atlantic Monthly* 67 (March 1881): 328; Gronlund, *The Co-operative Commonwealth*, 20, 48–54, 60–62,100–103, 127–28.
63. Erich Fromm, "Introduction," in Edward Bellamy, *Looking Backward* (New York: New American Library, 1960), v.
64. Bellamy, *Looking Backward*, 51–55.
65. William Morris, *Signs of Change* (London: Reeves and Turner, 1888), 114.
66. William Morris, "Commercial War: A Critical Edition," edited by Florence S. Boos in *Journal of Pre-Raphaelite Studies* 19 (Fall 2010): 55.
67. David A. Wells, "The Great Depression of Trade," *Contemporary Review*, 52 (August and September 1887): 391–94; William Morris, *Journalism*, 286–89.
68. William Morris, "Equality," *Journal of Pre-Raphaelite Studies* 19 (Spring 2011): 67.
69. Morris, *Collected Works*, 23:247, 251; Ruth Kinna, *William Morris: The Art of Socialism* (Cardiff: University of Wales Press, 2000), 122–23; Salmon, *The William Morris Chronology*, 188. Kinna's often insightful discussion of Morris and monopoly capitalism suffers, unfortunately, from a lack of familiarity with the economic analysis of monopoly (and emerging monopoly capitalism) among socialists and others in the period, including not only Morris's discussions in this respect, but also that of other thinkers with whom he was connected or influenced in this regard, such as Marx, Engels, Gronlund, Bellamy, and David A. Wells. Consequently, she approaches monopoly in Morris's argument as reflecting a new kind of slavery, related to ancient slavery, rather than as new phase of capitalist production.
70. Morris, *Journalism*, 462–63, 472–73.

71. Florence S. Boos, "An Aesthetic Ecocommunist: Morris the Red and Morris the Green," in Faulkner and Preston, *William Morris: Centenary Essays*, 41; Rick Tilman, *Thorstein Veblen, John Dewey, and C. Wright Mills and the Generic Ends of Life* (New York: Rowman and Littlefield, 2004), 140.
72. Thompson, *William Morris: Romantic to Revolutionary*, 514; Morris, *Journalism*, 412; Salmon, *The William Morris Chronology*, 216.
73. Morris, *Political Writings*, 422–24.
74. Morris, *Collected Works*, 22:318–30, 334–35, and 23:176; Wells, "The Great Depression of Trade," 286–87, 392.
75. Kinna, *William Morris: The Art of Socialism*, 125–26. A similar treatment of the epochs of production is to be found in Morris and Bax, *Socialism: Its Growth and Outcome*, 243–47.
76. Morris, *Collected Works*, 23:272–73; Morris, *Political Writings*, 32.
77. Morris, *William Morris: Artist, Writer, Socialist*, 2:478–79. The ellipsis in the first paragraph removes a "not" that was clearly a typographical error.
78. William Morris, "Equality," *Journal of PreRaphaelite Studies* 19 (Spring 2011): 58, 60.
79. Morris, *William Morris: Artist, Writer, Socialist*, 479–50; Morris, *Political Writings*, 40; Morris, *Signs of Change*, 141–73.
80. Morris, *William Morris: Artist, Writer, Socialist*, 525. See also J. W. Mackail, *The Life of William Morris* (2 vols. bound as one) (New York: Dover, 1995), 2:292. On the concept of "specifically capitalist use values" see John Bellamy Foster, *The Theory of Monopoly Capitalism* (New York: Monthly Review Press, 2014), iv–xx, 39–41; and Foster, "The Ecology of Marxian Political Economy," *Monthly Review* 63/4 (September 2011): 1–16.
81. Morris, *William Morris: Artist, Writer, Socialist*, 469–70.
82. Ibid., 470.
83. Salmon, *The William Morris Chronology*, 277; Morris, *Collected Works*, 22:72; Morris, "Commercial War": 53–54.
84. Morris, "How I Became a Socialist," 34; John Stuart Mill, *Collected Works*, vol. 5 (Toronto: University of Toronto Press, 1967), 719–24; Jonathan Beecher, *Victor Considerant* (Berkeley: University of California Press, 2001), 262–63, 499.
85. Morris and Bax, *Manifesto of the Socialist League*, 5.
86. Morris, *Collected Works*, 23:194–95.
87. Morris, *Art and Its Producers and the Arts and Crafts of To-day*, 22; William Morris, *News from Nowhere* (Oxford: Oxford University Press, 2003), 82. On the truth behind the smallpox incident, see John Bellamy Foster, "Multiculturalism and the American Revolution of 1776," *Monthly Review* 45/11 (April 1994): 32.
88. Morris, *Signs of Change*, 185–86.
89. Morris and Bax, *Manifesto of the Socialist League*, 9.
90. Morris, *Political Writings*, 421.
91. Morris, *News from Nowhere and Selected Writings and Designs*, 305–6.
92. E. J. Hobsbawm, *Industry and Empire* (London: Penguin, 1969), 131; and *The Age of Empire* (New York: Vintage, 1987), 43–45, 59–62. See also Harry Magdoff, *Imperialism: From the Colonial Age to the Present* (New York: Monthly Review Press, 1978), 34–44.
93. Morris, *Political Writings*, 440–41, 446–47, 455, 470–71.
94. Morris, "Commercial War": 61–62; Thompson, *William Morris: Romantic to Revolutionary*, 272.

95. Morris, *News from Nowhere and Selected Writings and Designs*, 306.

CHAPTER FOUR: AN EARTHLY PARADISE

1. J. Bruce Glasier, *William Morris and the Early Days of the Socialist Movement* (London: Longmans, Green, 1921), 76, 81–82; Alan B. Campbell, *The Lanarkshire Miners* (Edinburgh: John Donald Publishing, 1979), 181; Carolyn Baylies, *The History of the Yorkshire Miners, 1881–1918* (London: Routledge, 1993), 15. Glasier's recollections of Morris, written decades after Morris's death while Glasier was on his own deathbed, have been questioned on some points, especially with respect to his memory of alleged fine theoretical comments by Morris on Marx for which there is no corroboration and that contradict everything else we know—and which E. P. Thompson and others have seen as colored by Glasier's own prejudices. Nevertheless, since Glasier knew Morris well, and was one of his most important correspondents in the 1880s, his memoir is viewed by historians as a valuable supplementary source in other, more general respects, where its reliability is less suspect. The story told with respect to Morris's trip to Coatbridge seems quite authentic in style and content, and closely in line with Morris's views. Still, unless Glasier took notes on the occasion, it has to be seen as having all the limitations of a reconstruction from memory years later. See E. P. Thompson, *William Morris: Romantic to Revolutionary* (New York: Pantheon, 1976), 745–50.
2. See William Morris, *News from Nowhere* (Oxford: Oxford University Press, 2003), 59.
3. Thomas Gradgrind is the schoolteacher and advocate of utilitarian philosophy in Charles Dickens's *Hard Times*.
4. William Morris, *Collected Works* (London: Longmans Green, 1910), 22:335; Ruth Kinna, "Time and Utopia: The Gap Between Morris and Bax," *Journal of the William Morris Society* 18/4 (Summer 2010): 41–42; William Morris, *Three Works* (London: Lawrence and Wishart, 1986), 91–111.
5. Morris, *Collected Works*, vols. 14, 15, and 21.
6. Ibid., 23:255–59.
7. Morris, *News from Nowhere and Other Writings* (London: Penguin, 1962), 141.
8. Morris, "'Socialism' and 'What We Have to Look For: Two Unpublished Lectures by William Morris," edited by Florence S. Boos, in *Journal of the William Morris Society* (Winter 2010): 49.
9. J. W. Mackail, *The Life of William Morris* (2 vols. bound as one) (New York: Dover, 1995; repr. of 1899 edition), vol. 2, 301–4; Morris, *News from Nowhere and Other Writings*, 160, 364.
10. Mackail, *The Life of William Morris*, 305.
11. Karl Marx and Frederick Engels, *The Communist Manifesto* (Chicago: Haymarket, 2005), 46. Marx and Engels's famous passage was mistakenly translated as "idiocy of rural life" rather than "isolation of rural life" in the Samuel Moore translation. In the classical Greek sense, *idiotes* meant isolation from the polis, the center of cultural life. On this see John Bellamy Foster, *The Ecological Revolution* (New York: Monthly Review Press, 2000), 136–37. Morris's frequent use of this comparison in his work is usually seen as stemming from *The Communist Manifesto*, although he could have been influenced by Marx's *Capital* as well in this respect. See the notes by Clive Wilmer in Morris, *News from Nowhere and Other Writings*, 415, 423.
12. Karl Marx, *Capital*, vol. 1 (London: Penguin, 1976), 637.
13. Laurence Gronlund, *The Co-operative Commonwealth in Its Outlines: An Exposition of Modern Socialism* (Boston: Lee and Shepard Publishers, 1884), 119; Marx and Engels, *The Communist Manifesto*, 40.

14. William Morris and E. Belfort Bax, *Socialism: Its Growth and Outlook* (London: Swan Sonnenschein, 1893), 313–16. It should be noted that although *Socialism: Its Growth and Outlook* was based on the Morris and Bax articles "Socialism from the Root Up," in *Commonweal*, which preceded *News from Nowhere*, the final chapter of their book was greatly expanded from the final article in that series, and none of the discussion of the arrangement of cities was included in the former. This treatment thus postdated rather than antedated *News from Nowhere*. See William Morris, *Political Writings* (Bristol: Thoemmes Press, 1994), 611–22.
15. Karl Marx, *Capital*, vol. 1 (London: Penguin, 1976), 636–39.
16. Gronlund, *The Co-operative Commonwealth*, 119–20, 124.
17. August Bebel, *Woman in the Past, Present, and Future* (London: The Modern Press, 1885), 207–8.
18. Ibid., 209–11. On nineteenth-century sewage problems in London see Ian Angus, "Cesspools, Sewage, and Social Murder," *Monthly Review* 70/3 (July–August 2018): 32–68.
19. William Morris, *The Unpublished Lectures* (Detroit: Wayne State University Press, 1969), 121. Its should be clear that Morris's observations here closely resemble those of Marx, and what can be viewed as the derivative outlooks of Gronlund of Bebel. Related observations (though lacking a clear articulation of the metabolic rift [see John Bellamy Foster, *Marx's Ecology* [New York: Monthly Review Press, 2000], 141–77]) were to be found in Kropotkin's *Fields, Factories, and Workers*, written in the late 1880s, and especially in *The Conquest of Bread*, written as a series of articles and published in Paris in 1892. However, though Morris's 1885 observations here came after those of Marx, Gronlund, and Bebel, they preceded those of Kropotkin. See Peter Kropotkin, *Fields, Factories, and Workshops* (London: G. P. Putnam's Sons, 1913).
20. Edward Aveling and Eleanor Marx-Aveling, *The Factory Hell* (London: James Leatham, 1891), 17. The Avelings referred in their pamphlet to information that Morris had given them that were rooted in his experiences at Merton Abbey and his knowledge of exploitative working conditions elsewhere, on how an unscrupulous employer could use the division of parts of an establishment into factory or workshop to get around factory regulations. Some of this was based on an article by Aveling titled "The Factory Inferno," *Commonweal* 1/6 (July 1885): 54–55.
21. William Morris, *News from Nowhere and Selected Writings and Designs* (London: Penguin, 1962), 156.
22. Morris, *Political Writings*, 33–34.
23. Ibid., 50.
24. Morris, *Collected Works*, 23:185.
25. Morris, *Political Writings*, 25–26.
26. William Morris, *Signs of Change* (London: Reeves and Turner, 1888), 29–30.
27. Morris, *Collected Works*, 3:3.
28. Morris, *News from Nowhere and Other Writings*, 361–64.
29. Morris, *Signs of Change*, 151.
30. William Morris, *Journalism* (Bristol: Thoemmes Press, 1996), 584.
31. William Morris, *William Morris: Artist, Writer, Socialist*, ed. May Morris (Cambridge: Cambridge University Press, 1936), 1:290.
32. William Morris, "Three Letters on Epping Forest," *Organization and Environment* 11/1 (March 1998): 93–97; John Bellamy Foster, "William Morris's Letters on Epping Forest," *Organization and Environment* 11/1 (March 1998): 90–92.
33. Morris, *Political Writings*, 416; *Collected Works*, 23:235.

34. Peter C. Gould, *Early Green Politics* (Sussex: Harvester Press, 1988), 29, 32–34; William Morris, *Collected Letters*, vol. 2 (Princeton: Princeton University Press, 1987), 353; Sheila Rowbotham, *Edward Carpenter* (London: Verso, 2008), 83–84; Morris, *Collected Works*, 23:227; Morris, *William Morris: Artist, Writer, Socialist*, 2:462.
35. Morris, *Collected Letters*, 2:353; Thompson, *William Morris: Romantic to Revolutionary*, 361–62.
36. Richard Jefferies, *After London, or, Wild England* (London: Cassell and Co., 1886), 26- 33, 50–51, 68; J. R. Ebbatson, "Visions of Wild England: William Morris and Richard Jefferies," *Journal of the William Morris Society* 3/3 (Spring 1977): 12–29.
37. Morris, *Collected Letters*, 2:426–27, 435–36; Mackail, *The Life of William Morris*, 2:144–45.
38. William Morris, *On History* (Sheffield, UK: Sheffield Academic Press, 1996), 130; Arnold J. Toynbee, *A Study of History*, vol. 1 (abridgement of vols. 1–6) (Oxford: Oxford University Press, 1946), 11–13, 375–79.
39. Morris, "Equality," *Journal of Pre-Raphaelite Studies* 19 (Spring 2011): 64.
40. William Morris and E. Belfort Bax, *Manifesto of the Socialist League*, 2nd ed., annotated (London: Socialist League Office, October 1885), 11.
41. On the nineteenth-century Romantic "return to nature" sentiment as it was played out, particularly in the literary realm in the United States but also affecting figures like Carpenter in England, see Lewis Mumford, *The Golden Day* (Boston: Beacon Hill, 1926), 20–39.
42. Morris, *Collected Letters*, vol. 2, part 1, 306.
43. Morris, *Signs of Change*, 192; Marx and Engels, *Collected Works*, 5:141.
44. William Morris, *The Unpublished Lectures*, 51.
45. Morris, *William Morris: Artist, Writer, Socialist*, 2:466.
46. Paul Meier, *William Morris: The Marxist Dreamer*, vol. 1 (Sussex: Harveser Press, 1978), 27–74.
47. An earlier version of this section was published as John Bellamy Foster, "William Morris's Romantic Revolutionary Ideal: Nature, Labour and Gender in *News from Nowhere*," *Journal of William Morris Studies* 22/2 (2017): 17–35.
48. The dates provided in the text leave matters somewhat uncertain. Morris changed some of the dates from the serialized version in *Commonweal*, pushing events further into the future. For example, the bridge, mentioned in chapter 2, is said to have been built in 1971 in the *Commonweal* version, while in the book edition this is changed to 2003. Following the dates in the 1891 book edition, the Great Change occurs during the early 1950s. The civil war begins in 1952 and appears to be over by the time of the "clearing of houses" in 1955. William Guest is informed early in the text that the bridge built in 2003 was "not very old" by historical standards. Hammond later refers to the new epoch as having lasted for around 150 years, which would place it in the early 2100s. A more oblique reference to two hundred years ago would appear to have referred to the time since the end of the nineteenth or the beginning of the twentieth century. Morris, *News from Nowhere* (Oxford: Oxford University Press, 2003), 8, 14, 46, 69, 94, 184.
49. William Morris, *News from Nowhere* (Oxford), 182.
50. Edward Bellamy, *Looking Backward* (New York: New American Library, 1960).
51. William Morris, *Political Writings*, 420.
52. Ibid., 419–25.
53. Morris provides a scornful assessment of anarchism as he understood it in *News from Nowhere*, making it clear that he did not see it as a viable way forward. Morris, *News from Nowhere* (Oxford), 77.

54. Morris, *News from Nowhere* (Oxford), 3.
55. Krishan Kumar, "A Pilgrimage of Hope: William Morris's Journey to Utopia," *Utopian Studies* 5 (1994): 97.
56. Morris, *News from Nowhere* (Oxford), 12–14.
57. Ibid., 29, 56.
58. Kumar, "A Pilgrimage of Hope," *Utopian Studies* 5 (1994): 96; Morris, *News from Nowhere* (Oxford): 20–44; Ruth Levitas, *Morris, Hammersmith and Utopia* (London: William Morris Society, 2005), 21–22, 9.
59. Thompson, *William Morris: Romantic to Revolutionary* , 482–96.
60. Morris, *News from Nowhere* (Oxford), 89–111; Perry Anderson, *Arguments Within English Marxism* (London: Verso, 1980), 180–82.
61. Morris, *News from Nowhere* (Oxford), 90.
62. The notions of a "structure of feeling" and of a "long revolution" are of course associated with Raymond Williams, but reflect his own lifelong study of the Romantic revolutionary tradition, including the work of Morris. See Raymond Williams, *Politics and Letters* ((London: New Left Books, 1979), 155–59.
63. On Morris's two-stage view see Meier, *William Morris: Marxist Dreamer*, 2:288–327.
64. Morris and Bax, *Socialism: Its Growth and Outcome*, 278.
65. Morris, *Collected Works*, 23:160; Jack Lindsay, *William Morris: His Life and Work* (London: Constable, 1975), 257–58.
66. Morris, *News from Nowhere* (Oxford), 176; On the contrast between the views of work to be found in Morris and Bellamy see Harry Magdoff, "The Meaning of Work," *Monthly Review* 34/5 (October 1982): 1–15.
67. Morris, *News from Nowhere* (Oxford), 162.
68. Ibid., 84, 153.
69. Morris and Bax, *Socialism: Its Growth and Outcome*, 215; Morris, *News from Nowhere* (Oxford), 79.
70. Morris, *Collected Works*, 22:331–41; *News from Nowhere* (Oxford), 40, 78–85, 140, 153–55.
71. Morris, *News from Nowhere* (Oxford), 84, 145–46; Morris, "How I Became a Socialist," *News from Nowhere and Selected Writings and Designs* (London: Penguin, 1962), 36; William Morris, *We Met Morris: Interviews with William Morris, 1885–96* (Downton, Wiltshire: Spire Books, 2005), 76; Christopher Kendrick, *Union, Carnival, and Commonwealth in Renaissance England* (Toronto: University of Toronto Press, 2004), 7–9. Huxley used a physiological argument to defend the notion that capital, not labor, was the preeminent source of economic value. T. H. Huxley, "Capital—The Mother of Labour," http://aleph0.clarku.edu/huxley/CE9/CaML.html. The pseudo-mathematical nature of the argument caused Morris to refer scornfully to "the Huxleymathematical sort of thing." Morris, *We Met Morris*, 76.
72. Morris, *News from Nowhere* (Oxford), 83–84.
73. Ibid., 56–64.
74. Morris, *Political Writings*, 32–35, 39–46.
75. Morris, *News from Nowhere* (Oxford), 60, 76–77; Morris, *Political Writings*, 32–35; Hassan Mahamdallie, *Crossing the 'River of Fire': The Socialism of William Morris* (London: Redwords, 2008), 87–89.
76. Morris, *News from Nowhere* (Oxford), 154.
77. Ibid., 128, 137, 155.
78. Ibid., 136, 173, 176.
79. Ibid., 176.

80. Ibid., 174.
81. Charles Fourier, *The Theory of the Four Movements* (Cambridge: Cambridge University Press, 1996), 132; Frederick Engels, *Socialism, Utopian or Scientific* (New York: International Publishers, 1978), 39.
82. Morris, *Collected Letters*, vol. 2, part 2, 404–05.
83. Morris, *Collected Letters*, vol. 2, part 2, 584.
84. Morris, *News from Nowhere* (Oxford), 31, 45–54, 142–43.
85. Ibid., 31; Ady Mineo, "Beyond the Law of the Father: The 'New Woman' in *News from Nowhere*," in *William Morris: Centenary Essays*, ed. Peter Faulkner and Peter Preston (Exeter: University of Exeter Press, 1999), 203.
86. Morris, *News from Nowhere* (Oxford), 51–52.
87. Ibid., 52. On the wider discussion see Florence S. Boos, "An (Almost) Egalitarian Sage: William Morris and Nineteenth-Century Socialist Feminism," in *Victorian Sages and Cultural Discourse*, ed. M. Thais (New Brunswick, NJ: Rutgers University Press, 1990), 187–206; Jan Marsh, "Concerning Love: News from Nowhere and Gender," in *William Morris and* News from Nowhere: *A Vision for Our Time*, ed. Stephen Coleman and Paddy O'Sullivan (Bideford, Devon: Green Books, 1990), http://www.morrissociety.org/worldwide/agregation.marsh.html.
88. Morris, *We Met Morris*, 91–93.
89. Morris, *Collected Letters*, vol. 1, 545.
90. Gronlund, *The Co-operative Commonwealth in Its Outlines: An Exposition of Modern Socialism*, 201–14.
91. Bebel, *Women in the Past, Present and Future*, 113.
92. Morris, *We Met Morris*, 93–95; William Morris, "A Morris Speech on Women's Trade Unions," *William Morris Society in the United States, Newsletter* (Summer 2008): 21–23, http://williammorrissociety.org; Morris, *Collected Letters*, vol. 2, part 2, 545; E. Ray Lankester, *Secrets of Earth and Sea* (London: Methuen,1920), 122–23.
93. Fiona MacCarthy, *William Morris: A Life for Our Time* (New York: Knopf, 1995), 637–38.
94. William Morris, "An Unpublished Lecture of William Morris" ("How Shall We Live Then?"), ed. and introduced by Paul Meier, *International Review of Social History* 16 (1971): part 2, 217.
95. Paul Meier in Morris, *An Unpublished Lecture of William Morris*, part 2, 217.
96. Mineo, "Beyond the Law of the Father," 206.
97. Morris, *News from Nowhere* (Oxford), 148–51.
98. Morris, *We Met Morris*, 93–95; Jan Marsh, "Concerning Love": Mike Dash, "The Woman Who Bested the Men at Math," Smithsonian.com, October 28, 2011, http://www.smithsonianmag.com/history/the-woman-who-bested-the-men-at-math-120480965/.
99. Zetkin quoted in Vijay Singh, "Clara Zetkin Remembered," http://www.revolutionarydemocracy.org/rdv13n2/zetkin.htm; Meier, *William Morris: Marxist Dreamer*, 2:503.
100. Morris, *News from Nowhere* (Oxford), 13, 128–37, 157, 237. Morris and Bax, *Socialism: Its Growth and Outcome*, 311.
101. See MacCarthy, *William Morris: A Life for Our Time*, 635–36.
102. Morris, *Collected Works*, 15:143–44, 178, 245, 324–25, 334–35, 339, 350; Lindsay, *William Morris*, 335.
103. Mineo, "Beyond the Law of the Father," 201–5.
104. For the concept of substantive equality and the necessary revolution in women's place

in society see István Mészáros, *Beyond Capital* (New York: Monthly Review Press, 2005), 203–7.

105. See Clive Wilmar, "Introduction," in Morris, *News from Nowhere and Other Writings*, xxxvii–xxxviii.
106. Morris, *News from Nowhere* (Oxford), 165–67. A figure closely resembling Morris's wife, Jane Burden, who was famously beautiful, a "stunner"—the subject of Rossetti's paintings, and of Morris's only known oil-based painting—appears momentarily at the very end of *News from Nowhere* as a gaunt figure, completely overshadowed by the active, vivacious Ellen. Morris's romances, it is often believed, were colored by his unhappy marriage (171); MacCarthy, *William Morris: A Life for Our Time*, 135–37, 140–41; "William Morris Show Explores Artist's Ideals, Visions," *Guardian*, May 28, 2014, http://www.theguardian.com/artanddesign/2014/may/28/william-morris-national-portrait-gallery-100-years-influences/print.
107. Morris, *News from Nowhere* (Oxford), 181–82.
108. William Morris, *A Note by William Morris on His Aims in Founding the Kelmscott Press, Together with a Short Description of the press by S. C. Cockerell, and an Annotated List of the Books Printed Thereat* (London: Kelmscott Press, 1898), 1.
109. Morris, *We Met Morris*, 114–15.
110. Morris, *William Morris: Artist, Writer, Socialist*, 1:321.
111. Ibid., 1:311.
112. Ibid., 1:311–13, S. C. Cockerell, in Morris, *A Note By William Morris*, 1–20; H. Haliday Sparling, *The Kelmscott Press and William Morris Master-Craftsman* (London: Macmillan, 1924).
113. Sparling, *The Kelmscott Press*, 165–69; "Kelmscott Chaucer," British Library Online, https://www.bl.uk/collection-items/the-kelmscott-chaucer.
114. Sparling, *The Kelmscott Press,* 148–72; Morris, *A Note by William Morris*, 21–59; Morris, *News from Nowhere* (Oxford), 14; Florence S. Boos, "The Critique of the Empty Page," in *Victorian Sages and Cultural Discourse,* ed. Thaïs E. Morgan (New Brunswick, NJ: Rutgers University Press, 2010), 74.
115. Morris, *We Met Morris*, 71.
116. Ibid., 56.
117. Morris, *Collected Works*, 3:1; Joseph Dorfman, *Thorstein Veblen and His America* (New York: Viking Press, 1934), 30, 67–68, 119, 133, 272; Elizabeth Watkins Jorgensen and Henry Irvin Jorgensen, *Thorstein Veblen: Victorian Firebrand* (Armonk, NY: M. E. Sharpe, 1999), 65–66, 152. On Veblen and monopoly capitalism see Paul M. Sweezy, *Four Lectures on Marxism* (New York: Monthly Review Press, 1981), 60–61.
118. See David Riesman, *Thorstein Veblen: A Critical Interpretation* (New York: Charles Scribners' Sons, 1953), 58–59; Charles B. Friday, "Veblen on the Future of American Capitalism," in *Thorstein Veblen*, ed. Charles C. Qualey (New York: Columbia University Press, 1968), 16–29; John Bellamy Foster, *The Theory of Monopoly Capitalism* (New York: Monthly Review Press, 2014), 38, 65, 107–9, 218.
119. See Morris, *We Met Morris*, 133–38.
120. Thorstein Veblen, *The Theory of the Leisure Class* (New York: New American Library, 1953), 115–18.
121. Thorstein Veblen, *Essays in Our Changing Oder* (New York: Viking Press, 1943), 194–99; Olivier Lovell Triggs, *Chapters in the History of the Arts and Crafts Movement* (Chicago: Bohemia Guild, Industrial Art League, 1902).
122. Veblen, *The Theory of the Leisure Class*, 118.
123. Morris, *Three Works*, 103.

124. Morris, *News from Nowhere* (Oxford), 174.
125. Lindsay, *William Morris*, 382.
126. Morris quoted in Thompson, *William Morris: Romantic to Revolutionary*, 631–32. Thompson attributes the authorship of this statement to Morris, indicating that this remains the judgment of other scholars as well. It was included in part by May Morris in her edition of Morris, *William Morris: Artist, Writer, Socialist*, 361–63.
127. Morris, *Signs of Change*, 138–39.
128. Morris, "Equality," 64; Morris, *Signs of Change*, 139.
129. Morris, *Signs of Change*, 139–40.
130. William Morris, "A Death Song," in Yvonne Kapp, *Eleanor Marx*, vol. 2 (New York: Pantheon Books, 1976), 241–42.

CHAPTER FIVE: ENVIRONMENTAL CONDITIONS OF THE WORKING CLASS

1. Although Engels had coauthored *The Holy Family* with Marx, the work had fallen into obscurity; *The German Ideology*, which they also coauthored, was not published in their lifetimes.
2. Franz Mehring, "Frederick Engels," in Institute of Marxism-Leninism, ed., *Reminiscences of Marx and Engels* (Moscow: Foreign Languages Press, n.d.), 361–64.
3. Raymond Williams, *Culture and Society, 1780–1950* (New York: Columbia University Press, 1983), 161–62. What Williams calls the "Interregnum," reflecting a change in mood in art (and science), corresponds of course to what Marxian political economists, basing themselves on Marx, Engels, and Lenin, have called the era of the rise of monopoly capitalism/imperialism.
4. John Bellamy Foster, "Marx's Open-Ended Critique," *Monthly Review* 70/1 (May 2018): 1–16.
5. In criticizing Marx's *Capital*, Eugen Dühring referred to its "dialectical frills and mazes and conceptual arabesques." Engels responded in *Anti-Dühring* by repeating this criticism in a way that did not reject the term "arabesque" but insisted that dialectical categories in Marx's analysis were not ideal (much less idle) constructs but had real, material significance. See Karl Marx and Frederick Engels, *Collected Works* (New York: International Publishers, 1975), 113, 134. It was from this that Nikolai Bukharin clearly took the title for *Philosophical Arabesques* (New York: Monthly Review Press, 2005).
6. Frederick Engels visited England for a short stay with his father in 1837 at the time the firm was being established. John Green, *Engels: A Revolutionary Life* (London: Artery Publications, 2008), 55.
7. George Julian Harney, "On Engels," in Institute of Marxism-Leninism, *Reminiscences of Marx and Engels*, 192–93.
8. Steven Marcus, *Engels, Manchester, and the Working Class* (New York: Vintage, 1974), 98–100; Green, *Engels*, 69–71, 101–03; Belinda Webb, "Who Was Mary Burns?," May 2, 2010, http://belindawebb.blogspot.com/2010/05/who-was-mary-burns.html; Edmund and Ruth Frow, *Frederick Engels in Manchester* (Salford: Working Class Movement Library, 1995), 11–14; Sarah Irving, "Frederick Engels and Mary and Lizzy Burns," Manchester's Radical History, March 15, 20110, https://radicalmanchester.wordpress.com/2010/03/15/frederick-engels-and-mary-and-lizzy-burns/; Tristram Hunt, *Marx's General* (New York: Henry Holt, 2009), 94–96, 201–2; Belinda Webb, "Mary Burns" (PhD diss., Kingston University, 2012), http://ethos.bl.uk/OrderDetails.do?uin=uk.bl.ethos.554317. Many of the details about Engels in this

period are unclear since he destroyed most of his personal correspondence, including letters to Marx that contained private information. In 1851, when they were worried about prosecution in England as in Cologne, Marx suggested to Engels that he burn some of his letters, keeping only the important ones. More important, undoubtedly, was the culling of his letters that Engels carried out at the time of his death. Roy Whitfield, "The Double Life of Friedrich Engels," *Manchester Region History Review* 2/1 (1988), 13–19.

9. In order to avoid arrest in Cologne for his role together with Marx in the *Neue Rheinische Zeitung* Engels had fled in early October 1848 to Brussels where he was arrested, jailed overnight, and expelled across the French border. He then went to Paris where the June Days uprising had been defeated, repression had set in, and a new bourgeois constitutionalism was the order of the day. Engels thus sets out on the long journey by foot from Paris to Berne. Hal Draper, *The Marx-Engels Chronicle* (New York: Schocken Books, 1985), 36–37.
10. Marx and Engels, *Collected Works,* 507–29.
11. Green, *Engels*, 146–55; Marx and Engels, *Collected Works*, 24:336; Draper, *The Marx-Engels Chronicle*, 45.
12. Mick Jenkins, *Frederick Engels in Manchester* (Leicester, UK: Lancashire and Cheshire Communist Party, 1951), 10.
13. Irving, "Frederick Engels and Mary and Lizzy Burns," https://radicalmanchester.wordpress.com/2010/03/15/frederick-engels-and-mary-and-lizzy-burns/; Belinda Webb, "Who Was Mary Burns?"; Jenkins, *Frederick Engels in Manchester*, 17-18; Whitfield, "The Double Life of Friedrich Engels"; Karl Marx and Frederick Engels, *The Marx-Engels Correspondence: The Personal Letters, 1844–1877* (London: Weidenfeld and Nicolson, 1981), 22, 104; Irving, "Frederick Engels and Mary and Lizzy Burns"; Tristram Hunt, "Introduction," in Frederick Engels, *The Origin of the Family, Private Property, and the State* (London: Penguin, 2010), 21–22; Marx and Engels, *Collected Works*, 41:441. Hunt makes a point of referring to Mary Burns as "illiterate" (along with her sister). But there is no basis for this with respect to Mary Burns, and there is evidence to the contrary. Indeed, Hunt himself on the page of his book just prior to this statement quotes Eleanor Marx as saying that Mary could "read and write a little." Hunt, *Marx's General*, 94–95. This for the highly literate Marx family probably meant that she had no book knowledge. Hunt no doubt confused Mary with her younger sister Lizzy, later also Engels's partner, who was illiterate, and could neither read nor write, according to Eleanor Marx.
14. Marx and Engels, *Collected Works* 41:441. Draper, *The Marx-Engels Chronicle*, 115. Marx wrote to Engels that he had been "shattered" by hearing of Mary's passing "as if my nearest and dearest had died." Marx and Engels, *Collected Works* 41: 444-45.
15. Karl Marx and Frederick Engels, *Ireland and the Irish Question* (Moscow: Progress Publishers, 1971), 83–85; "Ireland's History in Maps (1841 AD)," http://www.rootsweb.ancestry.com/~irlkik/ihm/ire1841.htm; Marx and Engels, *Collected Works*, 41:441.
16. Marx and Engels, *Collected Works*, 41:441, 446-47.
17. Marx and Engels, *Ireland and the Irish Question*, 184.
18. Hunt, *Marx's General*, 203–5, "Engels, the Red Who Rode to Hounds," *The Telegraph*, May 2, 2009; Paul Lafargue, "Reminiscences of Engels," in Institute of Marxism-Leninism, *Reminiscences of Marx and Engels*, 88. Engels later used his experience in fox hunting to argue in "The Part Played by Labour in the Transition from Ape to

Man" that animals had a creative intelligence akin to that of humans. Marx and Engels, *Collected Works*, 25:460.

19. Gustav Mayer, *Friedrich Engels* (New York: Alfred A. Knopf, 1936), 201–09. Lizzy died in September 1878, Engels married her at her request in a legal ceremony as she lay on her deathbed. Hunt, *Marx's General*, 227–28, 310–11; Whitfield, "The Double Life of Friedrich Engels."
20. Eleanor Marx-Aveling, "Frederick Engels," in Institute of Marxism-Leninism, *Reminiscences of Marx and Engels*, 186.
21. The way in which ecological conceptions were dialectically incorporated in all of Marx's and also Engels's writings is discussed in John Bellamy Foster, *Marx's Ecology* (New York: Monthly Review Press, 2000). But this wider understanding of the relation of the materialist conception of history to the materialist conception of nature, although embedded in Engels's *Condition of the Working Class in England* and Marx's *Capital*, was developed in large part in in a series of extraordinary works that remained unpublished in their lifetimes, principally, Marx's doctoral dissertation, the *Economic and Philosophic Manuscripts*, the *German Ideology*, the *Grundrisse*, *Theories of Surplus Value,* and Engels's own manuscripts on the *Dialectics of Nature* and the Marx-Engels correspondence. Engels's *Anti-Dühring* and his *Ludwig Feuerbach and the Outcome of Classical German Philosophy* exerted an extraordinary effect on those figures, like Karl Kautsky and Georgi Plekhanov, who were to become Marxists in the late 1870s and early 1880s, precisely because it gave a sense of this larger philosophical foundation, connecting Marxism to science and nature in their eyes for the first time. This, then, had all the appearance of a "return of nature" in the sense of a reemphasis on the natural-material foundations, which were conceived of as dialectically connected to political-economic relations.
22. See Kohei Saito, *Karl Marx's Ecosocialism* (New York: Monthly Review Press, 2017).
23. David R. Keller and Frank B. Golley, "Introduction," in Keller and Golley, eds., *The Philosophy of Ecology* (Athens: University of Georgia Press, 2000), 2–3.
24. William Cronon's *Nature's Metropolis* (New York: W.W. Norton, 1991) revives this nineteenth- and early twentieth-century sense of urban ecology, drawing on the early history of Chicago.
25. Marx and Engels, *Collected Works*, 30:54–66.
26. Charles Dickens, *Bleak House* (London: Penguin, 1996), 165.
27. Lafargue, "Reminiscences of Engels," 90–92.
28. Marx and Engels, *Collected Works*, 2:9–10.
29. Marx and Engels, *Collected Works*, 3:428–29, 432.
30. Marx and Engels, *Collected Works*, 2:95–101.
31. Marx and Engels, *Collected Works*, 4:528.
32. Marx and Engels, *Collected Works*, 4:326.
33. Eric Hobsbawm, "Introduction" in Frederick Engels, *The Condition of the Working Class in England* (Chicago: Academy Chicago Publishers, 1984), 9–10.
34. Howard Waitzkin, *The Second Sickness* (New York: Free Press, 1983), 66.
35. Vaclav Smil, *Energy in Nature and Society* (Cambridge, MA: MIT Press, 2008), 191.
36. For the Malthusian interpretation see R. G. Wilkinson, *Poverty and Progress: An Ecological Model of Economic Development* (London: Methuen, 1973), 112–18.
37. Marx and Engels, *Collected Works*, 3:483–84.
38. Max Weber, *General Economic History* (Mineola, NY: Dover, 2003), 191, 304–5; John Bellamy Foster and Hannah Holleman, "Weber and the Environment," *American Journal of Sociology* 117/6 (May 2012): 1644–50.

39. Engels thought that Paine had constructed the first iron bridge. Paine, however, never erected his bridge, but his components and design went into the construction of the second iron bridge over the river Weir in 1796. Marx and Engels, *Collected Works*, 4:704.
40. Marx and Engels, *Collected Works*, 4:317–8.
41. William Stanley Jevons, *The Coal Question* (New York: Augustus M. Kelley, 1965), 138–39; Eric Hobsbawm, *Industry and Empire* (London: Penguin, 1969), 70–71.
42. Marx and Engels, *Collected Works*, 4:325; 384; Karl Marx, *Capital*, vol. 1 (London: Penguin, 1976), 799.
43. Marx and Engels, *Collected Works*, 4:327.
44. Marx and Engels, *Collected Works*, 4:351, 365; Frederick Engels, *The Condition of the Working Class in England* (Stanford, CA: Stanford University Press, 1958), 372–74; Edwin Chadwick, *Report on the Sanitary Condition of the Labouring Population of Great Britain*, edited with an introduction by M. W. Flinn (Edinburgh: Edinburgh University Press, 1965).
45. E. P. Thompson, *The Making of the English Working Class* (New York: Vintage, 1963); Frow, *Frederick Engels in Manchester*, 4–5.
46. Jenkins, *Frederick Engels in Manchester*, 17; Ruth Frow, *Frederick Engels in Manchester*, 7–9; Irving, "Frederick Engels and Mary and Lizzy Burns."
47. James Leach (written anonymously and designated as "a Manchester Operative"; "dedicated to THE WORKING CLASSES"), *Stubborn Facts from the Factories* (London: John Ollivier, 1844), 73–74; Marx and Engels, *Collected Works*, 4:429–32, 468–70, 485–88; Engels, "Postscript of 1846: An English Strike," in Engels, *The Condition of the Working Class in England* (Stanford edition), 342; E. Frow and J. Saville, "Leach, James," *Dictionary of Labour Biography* (London: Macmillan, 1972), 9, 171–75; Paul A. Pickering, *Chartism and the Chartists in Manchester and Salford* (New York: St. Martin's Press, 1995), 30, 198–99; Edmund and Ruth Frow, *Frederick Engels in Manchester*, 12–13.
48. Pickering, *Chartism and the Chartists in Manchester and Salford*, 30.
49. Marx and Engels, *Collected Works*, 4, 330; Ernst Jones, "The London Doorstep (A True Story" (1848), in *The Literature of Struggle*, ed. Ian Haywood (New York: Ashgate, 1995), 170–72; Gregory Vargo, *An Underground History of Early Victorian Fiction* (Cambridge: Cambridge University Press, 2018), 68–96. Engels's use of the concept of social murder can be compared to Rob Nixon's recent use of the category of "slow violence." See Rob Nixon, *Slow Violence and the Environmentalism of the Poor* (Cambridge, MA: Harvard University Press, 2011).
50. Marx and Engels, *Collected Works*, 4:347–48.
51. Marx and Engels, *Collected Works*, 4:345, 355.
52. Marx and Engels, *Collected Works*, 4:347, 355 (for Engels's drawings see 350, 356–69); Robert H. Kargon, *Science in Victorian Lankester* (Baltimore: Johns Hopkins University Press, 1977), 109. On the historical accuracy of Engels's firsthand descriptions (backed up by contemporary reports) on the conditions of the working class in 1844 see E. J. Hobsbawm, *Labouring Men* (New York: Doubleday, 1967), 123–47. Engels elsewhere indicates that the numbers of the actual working class in Manchester and its environs was about 350,000. Marx and Engels, *Collected Works*, 4:364.
53. Marcus, *Engels, Manchester, and the Working Class*, 195.
54. Marx and Engels, *Collected Works*, 4:viii; Marcus, *Engels, Manchester, and the Working Class*, 180–81; Peter Maw, Terry Wyke, and Alan Kidd, "Canals, Rivers, and the

Industrial City: Manchester's Industrial Waterfront, 1790–1850," *Economic History Review* (2011): 24. For a map of industrial Manchester in Engels's day see Engels, *The Condition of the Working Class* (Stanford edition), 59.

55. Hobsbawm, *Labouring Men*, 132.
56. Marx and Engels, *Collected Works*, 4:351–52; Marcus, *Engels, Manchester, and the Working Class*, 185–86.
57. Marx and Engels, *Collected Works*, 4, 361–62. For a map of Little Ireland and its relation to the Medlock see Engels, *The Condition of the Working Class* (Stanford edition), 195.
58. Marx and Engels, *Collected Works*, 4:363–66; Marcus, *Engels, Manchester, and the Working Class*, 185, 190–91.
59. Marx and Engels, *Collected Works*, 4:353.
60. Chadwick, *Report on the Sanitary Condition*, 116, 365, 375, 422–24. Chadwick used Liebig to justify using water carriage as a means of dealing with waste, arguing that it could by that means more effectively be used to irrigate surrounding areas (121–22). See also Michelle Elizabeth Allen, *Cleansing the City: Sanitary Geographies in Victorian London* (Athens: Ohio University Press, 2008), 14–18; Charles-Edward Amory Winslow, *The Conquest of Epidemic Disease* (New York: Haftner Publishing 1967), 242–49; Royston Lambert, *Sir John Simon, 1816–1904* (London: MacGibbon and Kee, 1963), 49–50.
61. Louis Pasteur, "Experiments Related to Spontaneous Generation," in A. S. Weber, ed., *Nineteenth-Century Science: A Selection of Original Texts* (Peterborough, Ont: Broadview Press, 2000), 249–51.
62. W. Luckin, "The Final Catastrophe—Cholera in London, 1866," *Medical History* 21/1 (January 1977): 32–42.
63. Winslow, *The Conquest of Epidemic Disease*, 236.
64. Marx and Engels, *Collected Works*, 4:395.
65. Marx and Engels, *Collected Works*, 4:394–95.
66. Faucher quoted in Anthony S. Wohl, *Endangered Lives: Public Health in Victorian Britain* (Cambridge, MA: Harvard University Press, 1983), 208.
67. Marx and Engels, *Collected Works*, 4:395.
68. Wohl, *Endangered Lives*, 129.
69. Marx and Engels, *Collected Works*, 4:396–98; M. W Flinn, "Introduction," in Chadwick, *Report on the Sanitary Condition*, 10; Ann Hardy, "Urban Famine or Urban Crisis: Typhus in Victorian Cities," in *The Victorian City*, ed. R. J. Morris and Richard Rodger (London: Longman, 1993), 209–40; Wohl, *Endangered Lives*, 125.
70. Flinn, "Introduction," *Report on the Sanitary Condition*, 10; Wohl, *Endangered Lives*, 118; Marx and Engels, *Collected Works*, 4:365.
71. Nassau Senior, *Letters on the Factory Act as It Affects the Cotton Manufacturer* (London: B. Fellowes, 1837): 24, emphasis Engels; Marx and Engels, *Collected Works*, 4:364.
72. Marx and Engels, *Collected Works*, 4:364; Marcus, *Engels, Manchester, and the Working Class*, 207
73. Marx and Engels, *Collected Works*, 4:395, 405; R. H. Mottram, "Town Life," in *Early Victorian* England, ed. G. M. Young (London: Oxford University Press, 1934), 1, 167; Marcus, *Engels, Manchester, and the Working Class*, 207.
74. Wohl, *Endangered Lives*, 298–99.
75. Waitzkin, *The Second Sickness*, 67; Marx and Engels, *Collected Works*, 4:399–400.
76. Marx and Engels, *Collected Works*, 4:370.
77. Wohl, *Endangered Lives*, 52–53.

78. Marx and Engels, *Collected Works*, 4:401.
79. Marx and Engels, *Collected Works*, 4:401–3.
80. Marx and Engels, *Collected Works*, 4:445; Waitzkin, *The Second Sickness*, 68–69.
81. Marx and Engels, *Collected Works*, 4:445–47, 491.
82. Marx and Engels, *Collected Works*, 4:454.
83. Marx and Engels, *Collected Works*, 4:492–93. On grinder's asthma see Wohl, *Endangered Lives*, 264, 271.
84. Marx and Engels, *Collected Works*, 4:495–96.
85. Waitzkin, *The Second Sickness*, 69–70. On lead poisoning in the Victorian workplace see Wohl, 270–71.
86. Marx and Engels, *Collected Works*, 4:481–84, 498–500.
87. Marx and Engels, *Collected Works*, 4:535–37. Waitzkin, *The Second Sickness*, 70.
88. Marx and Engels, *Collected Works*, 4, 436–37, 455–56, 466.
89. Marx and Engels, *Collected Works*, 4:450.
90. Marx and Engels, *Collected Works*, 4:403–07, 532; Waitzkin, *The Second Sickness*, 68. See also Melanie Reynolds, *Infant Mortality and Working-Class Child Care* (London: Palgrave Macmillan, 2016), 2–3, 74, 146.
91. Marx and Engels, *Collected Works*, 4:394; Marcus, *Engels, Manchester, and the Working Class*, 204–5.
92. Marx and Engels, *Collected Works*, 4:407. See also Ian Angus, "Cesspools, Sewage, and Social Murder," *Monthly Review* 70/3 (July–August 2018): 38; Robert Chernomas and Ian Hudson, *Social Murder* (Winnipeg: Arbeiter Ring Publishing, 2007), 2–3; Gregory Vargo, *An Underground History of Victorian Fiction* (Cambridge: Cambridge University Press, 2017).
93. Marcus, *Engels, Manchester, and the Working Class*, 133.
94. Marx and Engels, *Collected Works*, 4:466;
95. Marx and Engels, *Collected Works*, 4:474–77.
96. Marx and Engels, *Collected Works*, 4:527.
97. Waitzkin, *The Second Sickness*, v, 70; Sydney Gordon and Ted Allen, *The Scalpel, the Sword: The Story of Doctor Norman Bethune* (New York: Monthly Review Press, 1952), 250.
98. Marx and Engels, *Collected Works*, 41:468–9. Ludwig Kugelmann had written to Marx on March 18, 1863, indicating that there were rumors in the German movement that Engels had disowned his book as "infantile juvenilia" and whether it was not time to reprint it. Engels indicated to Marx in a letter on April 8, 1863, how much he adhered to his original views, but that given the quiescence of the English workers, reprinting it at that time would not be appropriate. It was to this that Marx was replying. But Marx was also, as he indicated, using Engels's book continually in his own work on *Capital* (465, 646).
99. Karl Marx, *Capital* (London: Penguin, 1976), 348.
100. Ibid., 349.
101. Marx and Engels, *Collected Works*, 46:140–41. Engels was not aware in writing this that Simon had by then retired as chief medical officer to the Privy Council, partly because Simon continued to be active in these years in a semi-official capacity.
102. John Simon, *Report on the Last Two Cholera-Epidemics of London, as Affected by the Consumption of Impure Water*, General Board of Health, May 13, 1856, http://johnsnow.matrix.msu.edu/work.php?id=15-78-7F.
103. John Simon, *Public Health Reports*, ed. Edward Seaton (London: Offices of the Sanitary Institute, 1887), 1:145.

104. "Sir John Simon (1816-1904)," *Oxford Dictionary of National Biography*, http://www.oxforddnb.com/templates/article.jsp?articleid=36097&back=; Lambert, *Sir John Simon*, 41, 47–55, 247–49, 485–50; Mary P. English, *Victorian Values: The Life and Times of Dr. Edwin Lankester* (Bristol: Biopress Ltd., 1990), 86, 95, 103, 113–14; Eileen Janes Yeo, *The Contest for Social Science* (London: Rivers Oram Press, 1996), 97.
105. Marx, *Capital*, vol. 1, 812; Simon, *Public Health Reports*, 2:206.
106. Marx, *Capital*, vol. 1, 595; Karl Marx, *Capital*, vol. 3 (London: Penguin, 1981), 188; Simon, *Public Health Reports*, 2:118.
107. Marx, *Capital*, vol. 1, 594; Simon, *Public Health Reports*, 2:117–20. This passage, which, in addition to vol. 1, is also quoted in Marx, *Capital*, vol. 3 (London: Penguin, 1981), 190, is full of misquotes (though differing in the two volumes) in all English-language editions of *Capital*. (It is likely that it was translated back into English from the German without consulting Simon's original English text.) I have therefore quoted Simon's own words here.
108. Simon quoted in Marx, *Capital*, vol. 1, 811; Simon, *Public Health Reports*, 2:96–97; William Aitkin, *The Science and Practice of Medicine* (London: Charles Griffin and Co., 1868), vol. 1, 801–02. Simon's punctuation has been restored here (using also the slightly altered version quoted in Aitken in which semicolons replace dashes in the original).
109. Simon, *Public Health Reports*, 2:408–09.
110. John Simon, *Ninth Report of the Medical Officer of the Privy Council* (London: Her Majesty's Stationary Office, 1866), 38; William Farr, *Report on the Cholera Epidemic of 1866 in England* (London: Her Majesty's Stationery Office, 1868), see esp. xxi, xxxix– xlvi, lvii–lviii; Luckin, "The Final Catastrophe"; "Rise and Fall of Cholera in London,' *British Medical Journal* 2/2999 (September 22, 1866), 337–39; Edwin Lankester, *Cholera: What It Is and How to Prevent It* (London: George Routledge and Sons, 1866).
111. Marx and Engels, *Ireland and the Irish Question*, 273–74; Mary Gabriel, *Love and Capital* (New York: Little, Brown, 2011), 379.
112. Eamonn Slater, "Engels on Ireland's Dialectics of Nature," *Capitalism Nature Socialism* 29/4 (2018): 46.
113. Marx and Engels, *Ireland and the Irish Question*, 171–90.
114. Ibid., 190.
115. Ibid., 190–91.
116. Frederick Engels, *Engels on Capital* (New York: International Publishers, 1937), 95.
117. Frederick Engels, *The Housing Question* (Moscow: Progress Publishers, 1975); Thomas Angotti, "The Housing Question: Engels and After," *Monthly Review* 29/5 (October 1977): 39–51; Stuart Hodkinson, "The Return of the Housing Question," *Ephemera*, http://www.ephemerajournal.org/contribution/return-housing-question.
118. Frederick Engels, *The Housing Question* (Moscow: Progress Publishers, 1975); Thomas Angotti, "The Housing Question: Engels and After," *Monthly Review* 29/5 (October 1977): 39–51; Hodkinson, "The Return of the Housing Question."
119. Engels, *The Housing Question*, 40–41.
120. Ibid., 66. On the smallpox epidemic in Manchester and Salford in 1871 see "Manchester," *Lancet* (June 8, 1871): 71.
121. The extent to which the germ theory of disease was still not part of the scientific consensus, although the notion of waterborne poisons causing disease had gained ground, was indicated by Simon's *Filth—Diseases and Their Prevention*, first published in 1874, two years after Engels's *Housing Question*. Although Simon

had moved away considerably from the miasma concept and had referred in his introduction to the sixth (1863) *Public Health Report* to "germs of parasites" as a factor in the spread of disease, there was not yet any emphasis on the germ theory, which he undoubtedly thought had not been sufficiently scientifically established. John Simon, *Filth—Diseases and Their Prevention* (Boston: James Campbell, 1876), *Public Health Reports*, vol, 2, 150, 563–85.

122. Simon quoted in Winslow, *The Conquest of Epidemic Disease*, 265; John Simon, "Contagion," in Richard Quain, *A Dictionary of Medicine* (New York: D. Appleton and Co., 1890), 286–94. Simon's use of "metabolic contagia" in the etiology of disease in an early edition of Quain's *Dictionary of Medicine* may partly have been aimed at getting around the non-acceptance of the germ theory of disease.
123. Engels, *The Housing Question*, 71.
124. Ibid., 72–74.
125. On the metabolic rift see John Bellamy Foster, "Marx's Theory of the Metabolic Rift," *American Journal of Sociology* 105/2 (September 1999): 366–405; *Marx's Ecology* (New York: Monthly Review Press, 2000), 141–77.
126. Engels, *The Housing Question*, 92.
127. Marx and Engels, *Collected Works*, 27:312. Engels's argument, introduced in 1845, and repeated in 1872 and 1892, that the advent of cholera and other epidemics, and particularly the spread of disease from poor to rich areas, led to sanitary reform is generally validated by Simon's history of these developments. See John Simon, *Filth—Diseases and Their Prevention*, 2nd ed. (London: Smith, Elder, Co., 1897), 166–245.
128. Marx and Engels, *Collected Works*, 27:547.
129. Hobsbawm, "Introduction" to Engels, *Condition of the Working Class* (Chicago: Academy Chicago), 8.
130. The 1887 American edition of *The Condition of the Working Class in England* had a very limited distribution in England. Extracts were published in *Commonweal* under the editorship of William Morris. See Dorothy Rose Blumberg, *Florence Kelley: The Making of a Social Pioneer* (New York: Augustus M. Kelley, 1966), 82.
131. Sir John Simon, *English Sanitary Institutions*, 2nd ed. (London: Smith, Elder, Co., 1897), 437–39, 443–45, 455–58, 480–491. Simon's biographer, Lambert, although not able to avoid a vague allusion to Simon and Fabianism, constantly seeks to put him firmly in the liberal fold, complaining of the tendency of some historians to present Simon as "more radical" than he was. He contends that Simon did not directly promote centralized state and social welfare solutions. Lambert, however, characteristically solves the problem of Simon's references in *English Sanitary Institutions* to the proletariat, socialism, socialistic taxation, etc., for his own interpretation, *by not mentioning them at all*—though they are central to the conclusion to what he calls "the most important literary achievement of Simon's retirement." Simon placed so much importance on this that the Table of Contents for the Conclusion to his book refers pointedly to the "self-helpfulness of the proletariat" and "the growing sense of socialistic duty." Lambert, *Sir John Simon*, 583–84, 614–15. Although Simon cited the article on "The Dock Life of East London" recently published by Beatrice Potter (later Webb), what is remarkable is the more radical conclusions that he drew from this, more directly critical of the logic of capital. Beatrice Potter, "The Dock Life of East London," *The Nineteenth Century* (October 22, 1887): 483–99.
132. Waitzkin, *The Second Sickness*, 71–72; Erwin H. Ackerknecht, *Rudolf Virchow: Doctor, Statesman, Anthropologist* (Madison: University of Wisconsin, 1953), 199–202; Rudolf Virchow, *Letters to His Parents, 1839 to 1864* (Canton, MA: Science History

Publications, 1990), 33, 77, 82–84, 153; August Bebel, *Women Under Socialism* (New York: New York Labor News Co., 1904), 191. This edition of Bebel's book, translated from the 33rd German edition, has a more extensive discussion of Virchow's statement on Darwin and Socialism and its significance. For Engels, Virchow's absurd position on Darwin served as an example of the common failures of mechanistic science whenever it strayed beyond its own narrow realm, or attempted to develop a more integrative approach while lacking a fully developed dialectical perspective. Marx and Engels, *Collected Works*, 25:7.

133. Waitzkin, *The Second Sickness*, 72; Ackerknecht, *Rudolf Virchow*, 52, 128–31, 166; Rudolf Virchow, *Disease, Life, and Man* (New York: Collier Books, 1962), 102, 146–47.
134. Waitkzin, *The Second Sickness*, 72–75; Virchow, *Disease, Life, and Man*, 80; Ian F. McNeely, *"Medicine on a Grand Scale": Rudolf Virchow, Liberalism, and Public Health* (London: Wellcome Trust, University College London, 2002), 32–49; Ackerknecht, *Rudolf Virchow*, 133–35.
135. Kelley married Lazare Wischnewetzky in 1884, and they separated (soon followed by a divorce) in 1891. For most of her life, apart from these few years, she was known as Florence Kelley. The words "*in 1844*" were added to the title of the translated book by Engels to emphasize the historical nature of the work. Subsequent editors were to revert to the original title without this addition.
136. Felix Frankfurter, "Foreword," in Josephine Goldmark, *Impatient Crusader: Florence Kelley's Life Story* (Urbana: University of Illinois Press, 1953), v.
137. On Kelley's relation to Engels, the best treatments, providing the closest looks at the extensive ten-year Engels-Kelley correspondence, are Dorothy Rose Blumberg, "'Dear Mr. Engels': Unpublished Letters, 1884–1894 of Florence Kelley (-Wischnewetzky) to Friedrich Engels," *Labor History* (Spring 1964): 103–33; Blumberg, *Florence Kelley*. See also Engels's letters to Kelley in Karl Marx and Frederick Engels, *Letters to Americans, 1848–1895* (New York: International Publishers, 1953), 144, 148–50, 152, 157–59, 165–74, 187, 189, 193, 196–97, 198–200, 205, 207–08.
138. Blumberg, *Florence Kelley*, 43–45; Kathryn Kish Sklar, "Introduction" in Kelley, *Autobiography* (Chicago: Charles H. Kerr, 1986), 9.
139. Florence Kelley, "The Need of Theoretical Preparation for Philanthropic Work," in Kelley, *Autobiography*, 93–103. In 1889 Kelley also translated Marx's "Speech on Free Trade."
140. Kathryn Kish Sklar, *Florence Kelley and the Nation's Work* (New Haven: Yale, 1995), 15; Brett Clark and John Bellamy Foster, "Florence Kelley and the Struggle Against the Degradation of Life," *Organization and Environment* 19/2 (June 2006): 253; Marx and Engels, *Letters to Americans*, 251–52; John L. Thomas, *Alternative America* (Cambridge, MA: Harvard University Press, 1983), 279.
141. Blumberg, *Florence Kelley*, 123–25, 143; Sklar, *Florence Kelley and the Nation's Work*, 225–28, "Introduction," in Kelley, *Autobiography*, 10.
142. Blumberg, *Florence Kelley*, 135; Sklar, *Florence Kelley and the Nation's Work*, 278; Florence Kelley, *Some Ethical Gains Through Legislation* (London: Macmillan, 1905), vii: Residents of Hull House, *Hull House Maps and Papers* (New York: Thomas Y. Crowell, 1895); Charles Booth, *Life and Labour of the People of London* (London: Macmillan, 1902); Hal Draper, *The Marx-Engels Glossary* (New York: Schocken Books, 1986), 128.
143. Florence Kelley, State Factory Inspector, *First Special Report of the Factory Inspectors of Illinois on Small-Pox in the Tenement House Sweat–Shops of Chicago*, July 1, 1894

(Springfield, IL: Hw. Rokker, State Printer and Binder, 1894), 6; Blumberg, *Florence Kelley*, 141–45, Kelley, *Autobiography*, 87–88; Sklar, *Florence Kelley and the Nation's Work*, 265–68.

144. Florence Kelley and A. P. Stevens, "Wage-Earning Children," in Residence of Hull House, *Hull House Maps and Papers*, 70. Florence Kelley, *Selected Letters* (Urbana: University of Illinois Press, 2009), 223: Clark and Foster, "Florence Kelley and the Struggle Against the Degradation of Life," 259; Florence Kelley, "The Factory Laws in Illinois," in Kathryn Kish Sklar, Anja Schüller, and Susan Strasser, eds., *Social Justice Feminists in the United States* (Ithaca, NY: Cornell University Press, 1998), 91–94.

145. Blumberg, *Florence Kelley*, 146–48, 161; Sklar, *Florence Kelley and the Nation's Work*, 223.

146. Blumberg, *Florence Kelley*, 129; Florence Kelley, *Selected Letters*, 58, 63–64, 69; Green, *Engels*, 286; Hunt, *Marx's General*, 349. Engels's gratitude and respect for Kelley can be seen in the fact that he once referred to her English translation of his book as "our book." Marx and Engels, *Letters to Americans*, 190.

CHAPTER SIX: THE DIALECTICS OF NATURE

1. Karl Marx and Frederick Engels, *Collected Works* (New York: International Publishers, 1975), 40:323–24; James D. Ciherry, "Historical Review of Pertussis and the Classical Vaccine," *Journal of Infectious Diseases* 174 (supplement 3) (1996): 259–60; American Society for Microbiology, "Historical Perspectives on Pertussis and Use of Vaccines to Prevent It," http://forms.asm.org/microbe/index.asp?bid=48816. On mortality rates of pertussis in the eighteenth and nineteenth centuries see Robert Weston, "Whooping Cough: A Brief History to the Nineteenth Century," *Canadian Bulletin of Medical History* 29/2 (2012): 329–49.

2. Marx and Engels, *Collected Works*, 40:325–26; Mary Louise Goudge, *A History of the Clinical Hospital for the Diseases of Children (Northern Hospital) and Its Founders Drs. August Schoepf Merei and James Whitehead* (1996), http://www.goudges.com/mary/history-of-the-clinical-hospital-for-the-diseases-of-children/chapter-2-james-whitehead/; W. O. Henderson, *The Life of Friedrich Engels* (London: Frank Cass, 1976), 271–72; Charles Edward Amory Winslow, *The Conquest of Epidemic Disease* (New York: Hafner Publishing, 1967), 257–58. Engels's statement that he now had an opportunity to write "at greater length" in response to Marx's previous letter suggests that he sent a quick note on hearing of Eleanor's illness, on which he proceeded to comment and to supplement with the forthcoming hospital/medical reports. The reports from the Clinical Hospital for the Diseases of Children confirmed his statement that whooping cough was generally not fatal, though highly contagious and endemic, hence resulting in a certain proportion of deaths in the population.

3. Marx and Engels, *Collected Works*, 40:325–26; August Schoepf Merei and James Whitehead, *First Report of the Clinical Hospital for Diseases of Children* (Manchester, UK: Bradshaw and Blacklock, 1856), 35, *Second Report of the Clinical Hospital for Diseases of Children* (Manchester, UK: Bradshaw and Blacklock, 1857), 5; Goudge, *A History of the Clinical Hospital for the Diseases of Children*. Marx either had met Merei or Engels had discussed him before as he wrote as if Marx were well acquainted with his character.

4. Schoepf Merei and Whitehead, *First Report of the Clinical Hospital for Diseases of Children*, 39–40, 49–51, *Second Report of the Clinical Hospital for Diseases of Children*, 9, 13, 20, 29–31.

5. Marx and Engels, *Collected Works*, 40:326–27.

6. Adrian Desmond and James Moore, *Darwin: The Life of a Tormented Evolutionist* (New York: W. W. Norton, 1991), 469–70.
7. J. D. Bernal, *Engels and Science* (London: Labor Monthly Pamphlet, n.d. [1935]), 2.
8. Marx and Engels, *Collected Works*, 40:249.
9. Marx and Engels, *Collected Works*, 16:475.
10. Marx and Engels, *Collected Works*, 16:472–73.
11. Marx and Engels, *Collected Works*, 16:473; Christian Wolff, *Preliminary Discourse on Philosophy in General* (Indianapolis: Bobbs-Merrill, 1963); Immanuel Kant, *The Critique of Pure Reason* (Cambridge: Cambridge University Press, 1997), 119; "Christian Wolff," *Stanford Encyclopedia of Philosophy*, http://plato.stanford.edu/entries/wolff-christian/.
12. Ludwig Büchner, *Force and Matter: Principles of the Natural Order of the Universe* (London: Asher and Co., 1884) (4th English edition of Buchner's *Force and Matter* based on the 15th German edition); Frederick C. Beiser, *After Hegel: German Philosophy, 1840–1900* (Princeton: Princeton University Press, 2014), 70; Frederick Gregory, *Scientific Materialism in the Nineteenth Century* (Boston: D. Reidel, 1977), ix–x.
13. Marx and Engels, *Collected Works*, 16:475–76.
14. Marx and Engels, *Collected Works*, 16:475.
15. Marx and Engels, *Collected Works*, 25:578.
16. G. W. F. Hegel, *The Phenomenology of Spirit* (Oxford: Oxford University Press, 1977), 11.
17. Terence W. Deacon, *Incomplete Nature* (New York: W. W. Norton, 2013), 157.
18. Ted Benton, "Engels and the Politics of Nature," in *Engels Today*, ed. C. J. Arthur (New York: St. Martin's Press, 1996), 88.
19. "On the Origin of Species," Darwin Online, http://darwin-online.org.uk/EditorialIntroductions/Freeman_OntheOriginofSpecies.html.
20. Marx and Engels, *Collected Works*, 40:551.
21. Ilya Prigogine and Isabelle Stengers, *Order Out of Chaos* (New York: Bantam Books, 1984), 252–53; Marx and Engels, *Collected Works*, 25:476–80.
22. Marx and Engels, *Collected Works*, 25, 482–87, 660, 673, 695; Terrell Carver, *Marx and Engels* (Bloomington: Indiana University Press, 1983), 126.
23. Vogt quoted in Franz Mehring, *Karl Marx* (Ann Arbor: University of Michigan Press, 1979), 280; Beiser, *After Hegel*, 73.
24. David Riazanov, *Karl Marx and Friedrich Engels* (New York: Monthly Review Press, 1973), 207; Ted Benton, "Natural Science and Cultural Struggle: Engels on Philosophy and the Natural Sciences," in *Issues in Marxist Philosophy*, ed. John Mepham and David-Hillel Ruben (Brighton, Sussex: Harvester Press, 1979), 118–19.
25. Hal Draper, *The Marx-Engels Glossary* (New York: Schocken Books, 1986), 33, 216; Gregory, *Scientific Materialism in Nineteenth-Century Germany*, 99, 103, 192, 204–7; Mark Wartofsky, *Feuerbach* (Cambridge: Cambridge University Press, 1977), 413–15: Ludwig Büchner, *Man in the Past, Present and Future: A Popular Account of the Results of Recent Scientific Research as Regards the Origin, Position and Prospects of the Human Race* (London: Asher and Co., 1872), 187–91; Mehring, *Karl Marx*, 280–97, 388: Karl Marx, *Herr Vogt* (London: New Park Publications, 1982). Lassalle also betrayed the workers, as evident in his secret correspondence with Bismarck. István Mészaros, *The Power of Ideology* (New York: New York University Press, 1989), 296–97.
26. Gregory, *Scientific Materialism in Nineteenth-Century Germany*, ix–x, 2, 83, 156.
27. David Stack, *The First Darwinian Left* (Cheltenham, Gloucestershire: New Clarion Press, 2003), 2.

28. Büchner, *Force and Matter*, 216.
29. Ibid., 9, 18, 33, 151–52, 225, 233, 255; Marx and Engels, *Collected Works*, 25:720.
30. Benton, "Natural Science and Cultural Struggle," 112.
31. Beiser, *After Hegel*, 71–72.
32. Büchner, *Man in the Past, Present and Future*, 223.
33. Ibid., 341–42.
34. Büchner, *Force and Matter*, ix–xxii, 244.
35. Büchner, *Man in the Past, Present and Future*, 115, 138, 144, 151, 156–60, 163, 172, 175–76, 350.
36. Ibid., 183–91.
37. Ibid., 126, 131, 154–57, 307, Büchner put heavy emphasis on the environmental determinism of the French scientist Pierre Trémaux, who contended that geological formations and the soil determined the physical and mental character of the nations and races that arose therein, with those living in new soils, rather than ancient ones, having a natural advantage. Büchner, *Force and Matter*, 466–67. In correspondence with Marx, Engels sharply criticized Trémaux for his geological determinism and racism. See Marx and Engels, *Collected Works* 42:320, 323–24.
38. Büchner, *Man in the Past, Present and Future*, 354.
39. Marx and Engels, *Collected Works*, 25:340, 476.
40. Marx and Engels, *Collected Works*, 25:482.
41. Lezek Kołakowski, *Main Currents on Marxism* (Oxford: Oxford University Press, 2005), 310, 315.
42. Marx and Engels, *Collected Works*, 25:482.
43. Marx and Engels, *Collected Works*, 25:679.
44. Engels to Marx, May 30, 1873, in Marx and Frederick Engels, *Collected Works*, 44:500–04. Engels's decision not to outline the forms of motion characterizing organic life was due to his belief that such analysis was still at a rudimentary state. Although mechanics was revealing the physical nature of human motion related to work, although J. R. Mayer had developed an analysis of the relation of the conservation of energy to metabolism as early as 1845, and while chemistry was laying the foundations for an analysis of organic motion, relatively little was known concretely in this area. As Engels wrote in *Dialectics of Nature*: "While mechanics has for a fairly long time already been able adequately to refer the effects in the animal body of the bony levers set in motion by muscular contraction to the laws that are valid also in non-living nature, the physic-chemical substantiation of the other phenomena of life is still pretty much at the beginning of its course. Hence, in investigating here the nature of motion, we are compelled to leave the organic forms of motion out of account." Marx and Engels, *Collected Works*, 25:362.
45. Marx and Engels, *Selected Correspondence*, 265.
46. On Marx and Dakyns see Marx and Engels, *Collected Works,* 43:291–92; Draper, *The Marx-Engels Glossary*, 51.
47. See Ian Angus, *A Redder Shade of Green* (New York: Monthly Review Press), 15–26.
48. Marx and Engels, *Collected Works*, 44:503–4.
49. Carl Schorlemmer, marginal notes, Marx and Engels, *Collected Works*, 44:500, 503, 506.
50. Marx and Engels, *Collected Works*, 25:485–486, 491, 674; Michael Inwood, *A Hegel Dictionary* (Oxford: Blackwell, 1992), 141.
51. "Friedrich Albert Lange," *Stanford Encyclopedia of Philosophy*, November 14, 2016, https://plato.stanford.edu/entries/friedrich-lange/.

52. Beiser, *After Hegel*, 24–25, 36–44, 56, 89–104, 112–32; Marx and Engels, *Collected Works*, 25:297–300, 340–43, 314, 373, 512–16; Frederick Albert Lange, *The History of Materialism* (New York: Humanities Press, 1950), 153–62, 308–25; A. Voden, "Talks with Engels," in Institute of Marxism-Leninism, ed., *Reminiscences of Marx and Engels* (Moscow: Foreign Languages Publishing House, n.d.), 330–31; Enrico Ferri, *Socialism and Modern Science* (Chicago: Charles H. Kerr, 1912), 13–19.
53. Marx and Engels, *Collected Works*, 25:313. This of course also meant a critical return to Hegel in which both Marx and Engels were engaged. See S. H. Rigby, *Engels and the Formation of Marxism* (Manchester, UK: University of Manchester Press, 1992), 97.
54. Frederick Engels, *Dialectics of Nature* (Moscow: Progress Publishers, 1954), 14.
55. Marx and Engels, *Collected Works*, 25:11, 648. As Engels noted, the moulting metaphor was taken from Liebig, who used it in this way in his great book on agricultural chemistry. Büchner used the same metaphor, mistakenly attributing its origin to Huxley. Büchner, *Man in the Past, Present, and Future*, 1.
56. Engels, *Dialectics of Nature*, 14, 359. The chronological listing of manuscripts in the *Collected Works* edition (25) mistakenly referred to the six-page chapter/section on "Dialectics" as having been written in 1878. This was contradicted elsewhere in the same volume where it was definitively demonstrated that the date of composition was 1879. Marx and Engels, *Collected Works*, 25:667, 699. The error in the chronology was later corrected in the separate edition of *Dialectics of Nature* published by Progress Publishers. This section on "Dialectics," unlike the nine chapters/sections included in the main text of the published work, was not included in the second and third folders that indicated material definitely meant to be incorporated into the book. Rather, it was in the fourth folder of miscellaneous materials. The section on "Dialectics" was only about a third drafted, as only the first of the three dialectical laws around which it was organized was discussed (itself only in part).
57. Marx and Engels, *Collected Works*, 25:13.
58. In 1940, Einstein confirmed this statement that he had made sixteen years prior with regard to Engels's work in his report to Bernstein, and the fact that he had seen the entire manuscript. Sidney Hook, *Out of Step* (New York: Harper and Row, 1987), 466–67; J. B. S. Haldane, "Preface," in Frederick Engels, *Dialectics of Nature* (New York: International Publishers, 1940), xiv.
59. The first printing of the English edition of *Dialectics of Nature*, translated by Clemens Dutt, is listed as 1934 in the Progress Publisher's edition. It seems not to have been widely available, however, until the International Publisher's edition with Haldane's preface was brought out in 1940. The English edition was revised in 1954 based on the definitive 1941 Russian edition. Engels, *Dialectics of Nature* (Progress) 15. The *Collected Works* version of *Dialectics of Nature* is generally used here, except where improvements were made in the scholarly apparatus, such as correcting the error in the "Chronology" to the *Collected Works* edition, with respect to the writing of the "Dialectics" manuscript.
60. Engels, *Dialectics of Nature* (Progress), 328–29.
61. "Natural Science and the Spirit World" was found in the third folder, in which a number of manuscripts clearly intended to be included in some form or another in the final work were located. It was not mentioned in the 1878 general plan, but was added to the folders later, probably indicating it was written later that year. Marx and Engels, *Collected Works*, 25:313–14, 588, 666.
62. Marx and Engels, *Collected Works*, 25, 588.
63. See, for example, Richard Levins and Richard Lewontin, *The Dialectical Biologist*

(Cambridge, MA: Harvard University Press, 1985), 279–83; Stephen Jay Gould, *Ever Since Darwin* (New York: W. W. Norton, 1977), 207–13.

64. Marx and Engels, *Collected Works*, 25:313.
65. Marx and Engels, *Collected Works*, 25:318–23.
66. Marx and Engels, *Collected Works*, 25:323–27.
67. Marx and Engels, *Collected Works*, 25:327–28, 333–35. For a treatment of the ecological conceptions of the ancient Greeks see Clarence E. Glacken, *Traces on the Rhodian Shore* (Berkeley: University of California Press, 1967), 3–168.
68. Marx and Engels, *Collected Works*, 25:331.
69. Marx and Engels, *Collected Works*, 25:330–31.
70. Marx and Engels, *Collected Works*, 25:313.
71. Marx and Engels, *Collected Works*, 25:339–40.
72. Marx and Engels, *Collected Works*, 25:492–93. Engels preferred the term "conscious dialectics" to subjective dialectics.
73. Marx and Engels, *Collected Works*, 25:476–80.
74. As Slavoj Žižek writes, "one topic where even the crudest dialectical materialism has advantage over Western Marxism" is in allowing "us to think humanity as part of nature, while Western Marxism considers socio-historical dialectics" to be "the ultimate horizon of reference." One need merely add that Engels's dialectical naturalism was far from being the "crudest dialectical materialism." Slavoj Žižek, "Where is the Rift?: Marx, Lacan, Capitalism and Ecology," The Philosophical Salon, January 20, 2020, https://thephilosophicalsalon.com/where-is-the-rift-marx-lacan-capitalism-and-ecology/.
75. Marx and Engels, *Collected Works*, 25:545.
76. Marx and Engels, *Collected Works*, 25:356. The significance of Engels's statement is best understood if it is recognized, as Evald Ilyenkov argued, that dialectics in both his and Marx's perspectives (and later that of Lenin as well), arising out of a critical engagement with Hegel, represented the essence of an *all-encompassing conception of logic*, which, rather than being relegated to being simply a subcategory of epistemology, as in neo-Kantian and most later philosophy, was integrated with history and practice and formed the overall context, out of which our human conceptual apparatus and our conceptions of knowledge took form. E. V. Ilyenkov, *Dialectical Logic* (Delhi: Aakar Books, 2008), 297–319.
77. Marx and Engels, *Collected Works*, 25:356.
78. Marx and Engels, *Collected Works*, 25:313.
79. Z. A. Jordan, *The Evolution of Dialectical Materialism* (New York: St. Martin's Press, 1967), 167–77.
80. Marx and Engels, *Collected Works*, 25:356–57.
81. Marx and Engels, *Collected Works*, 25:359–60, 571; Benton, "Natural Science and Cultural Struggle," 122.
82. Marx and Engels, *Selected Correspondence*, 175, 177–78; Karl Marx, *Capital*, vol. 1 (London: Penguin, 1976), 423–24; Carl Schorlemmer, *The Rise and Development of Organic Chemistry*, rev. ed. (London: Macmillan, 1894), 6, 75, 81–96; Marx and Engels, *Collected Works*, 25:21, 359–61. John L. Stanley provides a critical response to anti-Engels thinkers who, in attempting to separate Engels's dialectics of nature conceptions from Marx's views, have tried to play down, distort, or otherwise sideline Marx's use of Hegel's law of the transformation from quantity to quality in relation in precisely the same sense (and the same application to chemistry) as Engels. However, Stanley and the thinkers he criticizes seem to have overlooked the explicit discussion

of this (and a further confirmation of Marx's as well as Engels's usage of this notion) in their correspondence. See John L. Stanley, *Mainlining Marx* (New Brunswick, NJ: Transaction Publishers, 2002), 123–26, 134.

83. Marx and Engels, *Collected Works*, 25:115–19; Schorlemmer, *The Rise and Development of Organic Chemistry*, 142, 183–84.
84. Marx and Engels, *Collected Works*, 25:119.
85. The fact is that even the "law of the transformation of quantity and quality" was not complete in Engels's six-page draft of the unfinished chapter on "Dialectics." Hence, chapter 2 of *Anti-Dühring* on "Dialectics. Quantity and Quality" had a wider scope than the discussion of this law in *Dialectics of Nature*.
86. On the concept of unity in difference or "unity of opposites," as a more developed way of addressing the interpenetration of opposites in classical Marxian theory, see Sean Creaven, "The Pulse of Freedom?: Bhaskar's Dialectic and Marxism," *Historical Materialism* 10/2 (2002): 112–13.
87. Marx and Engels, *Collected Works*, 25, 84.
88. Marx, *Capital*, 1, 929.
89. Marx and Engels, *Collected Works*, 25:128–29.
90. Marx and Engels, *Collected Works*, 25:129.
91. See John Bellamy Foster and Brett Clark, "The Empire of Barbarism," *Monthly Review* 56/4 (December 2004): 1–15.
92. Marx and Engels, *Collected Works*, 25:129–31.
93. Marx and Engels, *Collected Works*, 25:514.
94. For examples of such criticisms, see Z. A. Jordan, *The Evolution of Dialectical Materialism*, 8–15; Terrell Carver, *Marx and Engels: The Intellectual Relationship* (Bloomington: Indiana University Press, 1983), 139–52; Terence Ball, "Marxian Science and Positivist Politics," in *After Marx*, ed. Terence Ball and James Farr (Cambridge: Cambridge University Press, 1984), 251–54; George Lichtheim, *From Marx to Hegel* (New York: Herder and Herder, 1971), 70–71. Responding to such criticisms, Rigby rightly says, "Given Engels's repeated emphasis on the active role of mind in the creation of knowledge, the criticisms of him as *simply* an empiricist or an advocate of a passive 'reflectionist' theory of knowledge become virtually incomprehensible except as the result of a mania to see Marx and Engels in terms of a binary opposition constructed by means of selective quotation." Rigby, *Engels and the Formation of Marxism*, 120. For systematic critiques of such tendencies to separate Marx and Engels, see Stanley, *Mainlining Marx*, 31–62, 117–47; and J. D. Hunley, *The Life and Thought of Frederick Engels* (New Haven: Yale University Press, 1991).
95. Marx and Engels, *Collected Works*, 25:34–35.
96. Marx and Engels, *Collected Works*, 25:131–32.
97. Roy Bhaskar, *Dialectic: The Pulse of Freedom* (London: Verso, 1993), 150–52.
98. See Ilyenkov, *Dialectical Logic*, 289–319.
99. Kołakowski attributes to Engels—with no evidence whatsoever to support this interpretation, apart from a misreading of Engels's use of "reflection" (in fact what evidence that Kołakowski presents flatly contradicts his interpretation and is attributed to Engels's inconsistencies)—the crude belief that our knowledge is "a perfect reflection of the worlds as it exists independently of man's cognitive and practical activity," and the related notion that, in Kołakowski's words, "thought is a copy of the real world." The whole strategy here is to suggest that the "general lines" of Engels's thought pointed to the crude reflection or copy theory later adopted by (some) Marxist thinkers in the Stalin period. Kołakowski, *Main Currents on Marxism*, 324–25. For a similar

unfounded attack on Engels, see Shlomo Avineri, *The Social and Political Thought of Karl Marx* (Cambridge: Cambridge University Press, 1968), 67, 86.

100. Kołakowski, *Main Currents on Marxism*, 325.
101. Rigby, *Engels and the Formation of Marxism*, 138; Marx and Engels, *Collected Works*, 25:596; Allen W. Wood, *Karl Marx* (New York: Routledge, 2004), 193.
102. John Hoffman, *Marxism and the Philosophy of Praxis* (New York: International Publishers, 1975), 73–77, 94.
103. G.W. F. Hegel, *Hegel's Philosophy of Nature: Part Two of the Encyclopaedia of the Philosophical Sciences* (Oxford: Oxford University Press, 2004), 87; *The Encyclopaedia Logic* (Indianapolis: Hackett, 1991), 179; Christopher Yeomans, *Freedom and Reflection: Hegel and the Logic of Agency* (Oxford: Oxford University Press, 2004), 45; Inwood, *A Hegel Dictionary*, 247–50; Sean Sayers, "Materialism, Realism, and the Reflection Theory," *Radical Philosophy* 33 (1983): 16–26.
104. Hegel, *The Phenomenology of Spirit*, 12, 106; Walter Kaufmann, ed., *Hegel: Texts and Commentary* (New York: Doubleday, 1965), 32–33; Inwood, *A Hegel Dictionary*, 250.
105. Marx and Engels, *Collected Works*, 25:43; Engels, *Dialectics of Nature*, 213; G. W. F. Hegel, *The Science of Logic* (New York: Humanities Press, 1969), 490–91; *The Encyclopaedia Logic*, 161. Engels saw Hegel's "Doctrine of Essence" as having its basis in the notion of "reciprocal action," which had its roots in Spinoza's "*substance is causa sui*" (cause of itself). Marx and Engels, *Collected Works*, 25:511; Georg Lukács, *Hegel's False and His Genuine Ontology* (London: Merlin Press, 1978), 28–29. Actuality, for Hegel, was the interpenetration of a double reflection: "reflection-into-otherness and reflection-into-self." Hegel, *Science of Logic*, 480, 529.
106. Hegel, *The Science of Logic*, 399, 405–12, 536; Lukács, *Hegel's False and His Genuine Ontology*, 74–82; Marx and Engels, *Collected Works*, 25:131; Inwood, *A Hegel Dictionary*, 250; Daniel O. Dahlstrom, "Between Being and Essence," in *Essays on Hegel's Logic*, ed. George D. Giovanni (Albany: State University of New York Press, 1990), 107; Norman Levine, *Dialogue Within the Dialectic* (London: George Allen and Unwin, 1984), 132–33.
107. Georg Lukács, *The Young Hegel* (Cambridge, MA: MIT Press, 1966), 280. Marx wrote, "There is something special about such reflection-determinations. This man here is (e.g.) only King, because other men behave towards him like subjects. They believe, however, that they are subjects because he is king." Marx, chap. 1, "The Commodity," in the first German edition of *Capital*, trans. Albert Dragstedt, https://www.marxists.org/archive/marx/works/1867-c1/commodity.htm, 17–18, 33.
108. Raymond Williams, *Marxism and Literature* (Oxford: Oxford University Press, 1977), 95–100.
109. Hegel, *Phenomenology of Spirit*, 11.
110. Marx and Engels, *Collected Works*, 25:66; Engels, *Dialectics of Nature,* 211.
111. Lukács, "Introduction to Hegel's *Aesthetics*," trans. David S. Taffel, 87_124, 40, https://www.academia.edu/28711650/HEGEL_S_AESTHETICS_BY_GEORG_LUKÁCS_by_GFPJ_on_July_29_2014_in_23_2_Georg_Lukács_Hegel_s_Aesthetics_trans._David_Taffel_Graduate_Faculty_Philosophy_Journal_23_2_2002._
112. See, for example, David McLellan, *Friedrich Engels* (London: Penguin Books, 1977), 87. For more nuanced criticisms of "reflection theory," see Williams, *Marxism and Literature*, 33-34, 95; E. P. Thompson, *Making History* (New York: New Press, 1994), 95–98. It is true that in the Introduction of volume 25 of Marx and Engels's *Collected Works*, written by the editors of the volume, we find statements like: "Thinking is a reflection of the material world." But this crude, one-dimensional view is not to

be found in Engels, who always emphasized motion and contradiction, and frequently the constitutive role of knowledge. See Tatyana Chikileva, Valentina Smirnova, and Yuri Vasin, "Preface," Marx and Engels, *Collected Works*, 25:xv, xxi.

113. V. I. Lenin, *Collected Works*, 38 (Moscow: Progress Publishers, 1961), 195. The translation here follows George Thomson, "In Defense of Poetry," *The Modern Quarterly* 6/2 (Spring 1951): 131.
114. Henri Lefebvre, *Key Writings* (London: Bloomsbury, 2017), 193.
115. Bhaskar, *Dialectic: The Pulse of Freedom*, 216–17. Bhaskar's recognition that the simple reflection criticism did not apply to Engels contrasts with his own earlier partial criticisms of Engels in this respect. See Roy Bhaskar, *Philosophy and the Idea of Freedom* (Oxford: Blackwell, 1991), 170. Here Bhaskar says that Marx and Engels's metaphors, such as "images" and "reflections" sometimes encouraged the collapse of their deep reflection theory into a crude notion of reflection as mere copying or one-dimensional mirroring—a distortion, however, for which they themselves were not responsible.
116. Hegel, *Hegel's Philosophy of Nature*, 8–9.
117. Marx and Engels, *Collected Works*, 25:34.
118. Engels gave a prominent place to the critique of Nägeli's crude epistemology in his plan of *Dialectics of Nature*. Marx and Engels, *Collected Works*, 25:314.
119. Marx and Engels, *Collected Works*, 25:33–43; Alfred North Whitehead, *Science and the Modern World* (New York: Free Press, 1925), 51.
120. Marx and Engels, *Collected Works*, 25:30, 35.
121. Marx and Engels, *Collected Works*, 25:511.
122. Marx and Engels, *Collected Works*, 25:353.
123. Marx and Engels, *Collected Works*, 25:512–14; Beiser, *After Hegel*, 117–20.
124. Hegel, *Hegel's Philosophy of Nature*, 8.
125. Marx and Engels, *Collected Works*, 25:314, 322, 341, 501. Engels regarded Kant's thing-in-itself (*noumena*) as the "last form of this outlook"—"of formal science," after which dialectics via Hegel comes into play (520) Engels's epistemological critique of Nägeli demonstrates the complete fallacy of Alfred Schmidt's crude dismissal of Engels's *Dialectics of Nature* for developing "three hypostatized 'fundamental laws' . . . which stand over against reality," converting the dialectic into "a positive principle," and thus open to criticism as "metaphysics." Schmidt goes on to denounce Engels for introducing an "ontological trait" into his "understanding of nature," with the implication that dialectical epistemology does not permit such ontological conceptions with respect to the natural world. Yet, such rejection of all ontological naturalism is only "valid" insofar as there is no need in abstract philosophy, divorced from material existence, to address science, nature, or material reality at all, as if the hermeneutic circle were sufficient. See Alfred Schmidt, *The Concept of Nature in Marx* (London: New Left Books, 1971), 57. In contradiction to Schmidt's argument here, it is important to note that Engels's commitment to ontology is fully consistent with Roy Bhaskar's later rejection of the "epistemic fallacy," that is, the notion that ontological questions can always be subsumed within epistemological ones. Roy Bhaskar, *A Realist Theory of Science* (London: Verso, 1975), 36–55.
126. Marx and Engels, *Collected Works*, 25:326, 507; Haldane footnote in Engels, *Dialectics of Nature* (International Press edition), 226; E. Ray Lankester, "Limulus an Arachnid," *Quarterly Journal of Microscopical Science* 2 (1881): 504–48, 609–49; Joseph Lester, *E. Ray Lankester and the Making of Modern British Biology* (Oxford: British Society of the History of Science/Alden Press, 1995), 81–82. Engels's comments on

the classification of species here were probably written in 1882, along with the section "On the Classification of Judgments" (which it follows in the published work), since Lankester's article did not appear until 1881. However, it is possible that Engels may have learned of the significance of the reclassification of Limulus and the importance of this for evolutionary theory from Lankester, in conjunction with Marx, given that H. A. Nicholson, *A Manual of Zoology,* which Engels cites here, was written three years before Lankester wrote his breakthrough "Limulus an Arachnid" essay and could not have been the source for Engels's observations.

127. Marx and Engels, *Selected Correspondence*, 459; Engels, *Ludwig Feuerbach and the Outcome of Classical German Philosophy*, 59.
128. Marx and Engels, *Collected Works*, 25: 364–77.
129. J. B. S Haldane, "Preface" and "Notes" in Engels, *Dialectics of Nature* (International Press edition), 11, 28, 56, 80, 135.
130. Marx and Engels, *Collected Works*, 25:362.
131. Marx and Engels, *Collected Works*, 25:363–65.
132. Marx and Engels, *Collected Works*, 25:518.
133. Benton, "Natural Science and Cultural Struggle," 122–23. Benton's insightful discussion of Engels's dialectical insights and generally sympathetic account here are peppered with all sorts of unsubstantiated criticisms pointing to Engels's obvious crudity that contradict Benton's actual results, and have to be seen as qualifications and defensive bulwarks erected in order to stave off criticism given the very harsh view of Engels's work in this area by numerous Marxists, who have sought to "purify" Marx of Engels's influence. Thus Benton unnecessarily, and in a way discordant with his overall approach, accompanies such treatments of Engels's dialectical historicizing of emergence with a constant flow of strong qualifying references to Engels's "defective philosophical instrument which yielded the dialectic of Nature"; "indifferent application of the dialectical laws"; his "dubious quasi-teleological notion of history"; "the looseness of his appropriation of the dialectic," etc. (103, 124–25).
134. Ibid., 124.
135. Jordan, *The Evolution of Dialectical Materialism*, 167–68.
136. Paul Crook, "Social Darwinism: The Concept," *History of European Ideas*, 22/4 (1996): 261; Robert C. Bannister, *Social Darwinism: Science and Myth in Anglo-American Thought* (Philadelphia: Temple University Press, 1979), 252; Oscar Schmidt, "Science and Socialism," *Popular Science Monthly* 14 (1879): 557–91.
137. Marx and Engels, *Collected Works*, 45:122.
138. Marx and Engels, *Collected Works*, 25:XII.
139. Frederick Engels, *Socialism: Utopian and Scientific* (New York: International Publishers, 1978), 7; Rigby, *Engels and the Formation of Marxism*, 102; Marx and Engels, *Collected Works*, 25, 5, 645–47; Richard Adamiak, "Marx, Engels, and Dühring," *Journal of the History of Ideas* 35/1 (January-March 1974): 104–08.
140. Marx and Engels, *Collected Works*, 25:xii–xiii.
141. Dühring quoted by Engels in Marx and Engels, *Collected Works*, 25:30–32, 198; Richard Adamiak, "Marx, Engels, and Dühring," 100–102; Beiser, *After Hegel*, 174.
142. Marx and Engels, *Collected Works*, 25:39–42.
143. Adamiak, "Marx, Engels, and Dühring," 102; Marx and Engels, *Collected Works*, 25, 171–83.
144. Marx and Engels, *Collected Works*, 45:119.
145. Marx and Engels, *Collected Works*, 25:339–40, 470–71, 672.

146. Marx and Engels, *Collected Works,* 24:339. Terrell Carver disputes Engels's claim that he read *Anti-Dühring* to Marx, saying that Engels only indicated this after Marx's death, and that Engels falsified this point. He goes so far as to say that there is no reason why Marx would have "had to *listen* to it being read aloud." In this, Carver goes one step further in his criticisms of Engels, insinuating that he deliberately lied about aspects of his relationship with Marx, for which there is not a shred of evidence anywhere and which is contradicted by everything we know about his character. Carver, *Marx and Engels*, 125. For similar, extreme attacks on Engels and on "Marxism" as the invention of Engels, who is thus seen as betraying Marx, see Tom Rockmore, *Marx's Dream* (Chicago: University of Chicago Press, 2018).
147. In *The German Ideology* Marx and Engels had used the term *anti-critique* to describe Bruno Bauer's responses to their criticisms of him in *The Holy Family*. Marx and Engels, *Collected Works*, 5:15.
148. Marx and Engels, *Collected Works*, 25:5–8, 39.
149. Marx and Engels, *Collected Works*, 25:23.
150. Karl Marx, *Early Writings* (London: Penguin, 1974), 389.
151. Henri Lefebvre, *Metaphilosophy* (London: Verso, 2016), 135.
152. Marx and Engels, *Collected Works*, 25:22.
153. Marx and Engels, *Collected Works,* 25:23–24, 30, 54–66, 578. In his references to metaphysics, Engels follows Hegel in associating it with the older metaphysics of Wolff that Kant and Hegel had challenged. See Hegel, *The Encyclopaedia Logic*, 65–68, 299, 314; Inwood, *A Hegel Dictionary*, 273.
154. In *Capital* Marx had applied "the law of the transformation of quantity to quality" to chemistry, while he applied the "negation of the negation" to the realm of social science/history in the form of the "expropriation of the expropriators" and the socialist transcendence of capitalism. See Marx, *Capital*, vol. 1, 423–24, 929. It is ironic that it has become widely believed that Engels introduced these "dialectical laws" into Marxian theory in *Anti-Dühring*, while Engels expressly defended Marx's use of these Hegelian laws against Dühring's criticism of Marx for having employed them. That is, the exact opposite of what is usually supposed. On Dühring's attacks on Marx in this respect, see Marx and Engels, *Collected Works*, 25:163–80.
155. Frederick Engels, *Anti-Dühring* (*Herr Eugen Dühring's Revolution in Science*), 2nd ed. (Moscow: Foreign Languages House, 1959), 36–37. This edition of Engels's *Anti-Dühring* is superior to the *Collected Works* version in that it incorporates in square brackets passages that were added in his revisions in *Socialism: Utopian and Scientific*. For that reason, it is quoted here. Volume 25 of the *Collected Works* includes those passages in a special appendix of volume 25 called "Additions to the Text of *Anti-Dühring Made by Engels* in the Pamphlet *Socialism: Utopian and Scientific*."
156. Marx and Engels, *Collected Works*, 25:63, 65–69.
157. Marx and Engels, *Collected Works*, 25:63–65; John Bellamy Foster, *Marx's Ecology* (New York: Monthly Review Press, 2000), 185–89, 198, 205.
158. Marx and Engels, *Collected Works*, 25:69–70, 501.
159. Marx and Engels, *Collected Works*, 45:107.
160. Marx and Engels, *Collected Works*, 25:64–65.
161. Marx and Engels, *Collected Works*, 25:501, 582.
162. Marx and Engels, *Collected Works*, 25:64.
163. Marx and Engels, *Collected Works*, 25:71–78.
164. Rudolf Virchow, *The Freedom of Science in the Modern State* (London: John Murray, 1878), 19–20.

165. Thomas Huxley, "Prefatory Note," in Ernst Haeckel, *Freedom in Science and Teaching* (New York: D. Appleton and Co., 1879), xviii–xx.
166. Ernst Haeckel, *Freedom in Science and Teaching* (New York: D. Appleton and Co., 1879), 91–93; Enrico Ferri, *Socialism and Modern Science* (Chicago: Charles H. Kerr and Co., 1912), 13–17.
167. "Notes," *Nature*, 18/455 (July 18, 1878): 316.
168. Marx and Engels, *Collected Works*, 45:313–14, 316–17, 501.
169. On Schmidt's role in originating the notion of social Darwinism, see Stuart K. Hayashi, *Hunting Down Social Darwinism* (Lanham, MD: Lexington Books, 2015), 27; Paul Crook, "Social Darwinism: The Concept," 261; Bannister, *Social Darwinism: Science and Myth in Anglo-American Thought*, 252.
170. Oscar Schmidt, "Science and Socialism," *Popular Science* 14 (1879): 580.
171. Ibid., 583.
172. Ibid., 583, 587–88.
173. Ibid., 579, 588.
174. Ibid., 583, 590.
175. Oscar Schmidt, *The Doctrine of Descent and Darwinism* (London: Henry S. King and Co., 1875), 143–44, 297–98.
176. Schmidt, "Science and Socialism," 587.
177. Marx and Engels, *Collected Works*, 25:314.
178. Marx and Engels, *Collected Works*, 46:376–77.
179. See John Bellamy Foster, Brett Clark, and Richard York, *The Ecological Rift* (New York: Monthly Review Press, 2010), 308–15.
180. See, for example, Marx and Engels, *Collected Works*, 25:587.
181. Marx and Engels, *Collected Works*, 25:498–501, 582; Hegel, *The Encyclopaedia Logic.*, 215–25.
182. On Malthus see Foster, *Marx's Ecology*, 81–104.
183. Marx and Engels, *Collected Works*, 25:331, 584, 46, 108.
184. Alfred Kelly, *The Descent of Darwin: The Popularization of Darwin in Germany* (Chapel Hill: University of North Carolina Press, 1981), 101.
185. Marx and Engels, *Collected Works*, 25:582–85.
186. E. Ray Lankester, *Degeneration* (London: Macmillan, 1880). The similarity in argument here is likely fortuitous, however, since it is presumed that these pages in Engels's notes for the *Dialectics of Nature* were written in 1875, five years before the publication of Lankester's book.
187. Marx and Engels, *Collected Works*, 25:583–84, 45, 107.
188. Marx and Engels, *Collected Works*, 50:349. See also Ferri, *Socialism and Modern Science* (the English translation of *Darwin, Spencer, Marx*).
189. Marx and Engels, *Collected Works*, 25:501.
190. Schmidt, *The Doctrine of Descent and Darwinism*, 296–98; Büchner quoted in Richard Weikart, *From Darwin to Hitler: Evolutionary Ethics, Eugenics, and Racism in Germany* (New York: Palgrave Macmillan, 2004), 191. See also Haeckel, *The Evolution of Man* (New York: D. Appleton and Co., 1896), 180–81 (and Plate xiv); Kelly, *The Descent of Darwin*, 116–22; Beiser, *After Hegel*, 174; Vogt was a leading proponent of racial polygenesis. Ferri became a follower of Mussolini.
191. Klaus Christian Köhnke, *The Rise of Neo-Kantianism* (Cambridge: Cambridge University Press, 1991), ix, xii, 160.
192. Ilyenkov, *Dialectical Logic*, 293–95.
193. Ibid., 285–96.

194. Ibid., 297.
195. Roy Bhaskar, *The Possibility of Naturalism* (New York: Routledge, 2015).
196. Engels, *Ludwig Feuerbach and the Outcome of Classical German Philosophy*, 22–23; A. Voden, "Talks with Engels," 330–31; Köhnke, *The Rise of Neo-Kantianism*, 227, 244–46.
197. Marx and Engels, *Collected Works*, 25:512–18.
198. Beiser, *After Hegel*, 97–104, 108–16.
199. Ibid., 116–20; Marx and Engels, *Collected Works*, 25:513–14.
200. Marx and Engels, *Collected Works*, 25:512–16.
201. Marx and Engels, *Collected Works*, 25:46–48, 516–18; Inwood, *A Hegel Dictionary*, 139–42.
202. Marx and Engels, *Collected Works*, 25:514–18; Joseph Fracchia and Cheyney Ryan, "Historical Materialist Science, Crisis and Commitment," in *Open Marxism*, vol. 2, ed. Werner Bonefeld, Richard Gunn, and Kosmas Psychopedis (London: Pluto, 1992), 59, 65.
203. Marx and Engels, *Collected Works*, 25:517.
204. Engels, *Socialism: Utopian and Scientific*, 40.
205. Marx and Engels, *Collected Works*, 25:331–32.
206. Marx and Engels, *Collected Works*, 25:335.

CHAPTER SEVEN: THE ECOLOGY OF HUMAN LABOR AND SOCIAL REPRODUCTION

1. Karl Marx and Frederick Engels, *Collected Works* (New York: International Publishers, 1975), 25:314.
2. Fredrick Engels, *Dialectics of Nature* (Moscow: Progress Press, 1954), 328–29; Marx and Engels, *Collected Works*, 25:314.
3. Marx and Engels, *Collected Works*, 45:122.
4. Frederick Engels, *The Origin of the Family, Private Property, and the State* (Moscow: Progress Publishers, 1948), 172. (All references to *The Origin of the Family*, unless otherwise indicated, are for this edition.)
5. Engels, *The Origin of the Family, Private Property, and the State*, 172–74.
6. Marx and Engels, *Collected Works*, 25:461–62.
7. In the opening paragraph of "The Part Played by Labour," Engels provides a description of the earliest hominins taken from Darwin's *The Descent of Man*. Marx and Engels, *Collected Works*, 25:452; Charles Darwin, *The Descent of Man* (Princeton: Princeton University Press, 1981, facsimile of 1871 edition—two vols. bound together, 1:206. (All references to *The Descent of Man*, unless otherwise indicated, are for this edition.)
8. Eleanor Burke Leacock, "Editor's Introduction" to Frederick Engels, "The Part Played by Labor in the Transition from Ape to Man," in Frederick Engels, *The Origin of the Family, Private Property, and the State* (New York: International Publishers, 1973, 247. (Hereafter referred to as Leacock edition.)
9. Darwin, *The Descent of Man*, 1:94, 201, 238–40; Adrian Desmond and James Moore, *Darwin's Sacred Cause* (Boston: Houghton Mifflin, 2009): "Introduction" in Charles Darwin, *The Descent of Man and Selection in Relation to Sex* (London: Penguin, 2004), xxvii–xxx. On just how deeply the notion of the extirpation of "savage" races was in the general European consciousness at the time, see Sven Lindqvist, *Exterminate All the Brutes* (New York: New Press, 1996).
10. Desmond and Moore, "Introduction" to Darwin, *The Descent of Man* (Penguin edi-

tion), xlvii–xlix; Darwin, *The Descent of Man*, 1:328. Here, in order to make the case with respect to male superiority, Darwin relied partly on Lamarckism, which argued for the inheritance of acquired characteristics, rather than natural selection.

11. Leacock, "Editor's Introduction" to Engels, "The Part Played by Labor in the Transition from Ape to Man," in *Origin of the Family* (Leacock edition), 245.
12. In this respect, the editors of Engels's *Dialectics of Nature* were clearly wrong in removing his fragment on slavery on the basis that it was "obviously unconnected with the *Dialectics of Nature*," despite his inclusion of it in the first folder for that work.
13. Marx and Engels, *Collected Works*, 25:452.
14. As Leacock noted, Engels's "The Part Played by Labour," though for the most part remarkably insightful in its argument given the knowledge of his day, contained two passing observations tangential to his argument, each developed in a single sentence, which would seem bizarre today, if noticed, but that reflected the scientific discussions of his time. In the first of these, he claimed near the beginning of his essay that human beings had their origin in a single location in the Tertiary period (early Pleistocene) "in the tropical zone—probably on a great continent that has now sunk to the bottom of the Indian Ocean." This was the hypothesis commonly presented by zoologists at the time, such as the ornithologist Philip Lutley Sclater, and above all Ernst Haeckel, Germany's leading Darwinian biologist, who devoted a considerable part of his *History of Creation* to defending the idea, including a map in which he hypothesized the location and the relation to the migration of early humans. See Ernst Haeckel, *The History of Creation*, two volumes (translated under the supervision of E. Ray Lankester) (New York: D. Appleton and Co., 1901), 2, frontispiece, and map of "Hypothetical Sketch of the Monophyletic Origin," 325–326. The other passage referred in a single phrase to some tribes of savages that had experienced "regression to a more animal-like condition with a simultaneous physical degeneration." Such assumptions of physical degeneration among some populations, which were tied to Western racial theories, were universal at the time. This is the only oblique reference to race in Engels's analysis in this work. His work overall stands out among the discussions of human evolution at the time, in giving a wide berth to racial distinctions. Eleanor Burke Leacock, "Introduction" to "The Part Played by Labour," in Engels, *The Origin of the Family, Private Property, and the State* (Leacock edition), 246.
15. Paul Heyer, *Nature, Human Nature, and Society* (Westport, CT: Greenwood Press, 1982), 209.
16. Darwin, *The Descent of Man*, 1:141–48, 206, 2:389; Ernst Haeckel, *The History of Creation*, two vols., trans. under the supervision of E. Ray Lankester (New York: D. Appleton and Co., 1901), 2, 293–94, 298–300; Richard Leakey, *The Origin of Humankind* (New York: Basic Books, 1994), 3, 10.
17. Marx and Engels, *Collected Works*, 25:453–54. Translation altered in accordance with Engels, *The Origin of the Family, Private Property and the State* (Leacock edition), 252–53. Engels's argument in "The Part Played by Labour" pointed in places to Lamarckian inheritance of acquired characteristics, but within a general context that emphasized Darwinian natural selection. In this, his work was not at all unusual for his day. Reliance on inheritance of acquired characteristics as a supplementary principle to natural selection was almost universal in evolutionary theory in the 1870s, as exemplified by Darwin himself, who had introduced Lamarckian assumptions into *The Descent of Man* (1871) and later editions of *The Origin of Species*, particularly the sixth edition (1872). Rather than Lamarckian in his tendencies, Engels was exceptional in his time in the degree to which he adhered almost exclusively to natural

selection in *Anti-Dühring*, and in his strong criticism of Lamarckism. Nevertheless, in some of his unpublished writings and notes, including "The Part Played by Labour," he gave credence to the inheritance of acquired characteristics as envisioned by the "modern science" of his day, and in ways closely resembling Darwin, who for example, suggested in *The Descent of Man*, that laborers inherited larger hands than the gentry due to the cumulative effects of social habits of use/disuse. As Helen P. Liepman notes in a careful study of the various editions of *The Origin of Species*, "The inherited effects of the use and disuse of parts, habit, direct and indirect action of external conditions, correlation and compensation and spontaneous variations which initially merely provided the raw material on which natural selection could work were, in later editions, capable of giving modification independent of natural selection." Marx and Engels, *Collected Works*, 25;545; Charles Darwin, *The Descent of Man* (Princeton edition), 1:117–8, 157, 160–61; Helen P. Liepman, "The Six Editions of the 'Origin of Species': A Comparative Study," *Acta Biotheoretica* 30 (1981): 211; John Bellamy Foster, *Marx's Ecology* (New York: Monthly Review Press, 2000), 193–94, 205–6.

Today biologists are once again exploring the inheritance of acquired characteristics with the development of epigenetics, a term first introduced by C. H. Waddington. On this see Peter Ward, *Lamarck's Revenge: How Epigenetics Is Revolutionizing Our Understanding of Evolution's Past and Present* (New York: Bloomsbury, 2018); Eva Jablonka and Mario J. Lamb, *Epigenetic Inheritance and Evolution: The Lamarckian Dimension* (Oxford: Oxford University Press, 1995).

18. Marx and Engels, *Collected Works*, 25:330.
19. Marx and Engels, *Collected Works,* 25:453; Stephen Jay Gould, *Ever Since Darwin* ((New York: W.W. Norton, 1977), 209–11.
20. Marx and Engels, *Collected Works*, 25:453–54; Charles Darwin, *The Origin of Species.*
21. Marx and Engels, *Collected Works*, 25:454–56.
22. Stephen Jay Gould, *An Urchin in the Storm* (New York: W. W. Norton, 1987), 111–12: Charles Woolfson, *The Labour Theory of Culture* (London: Routledge and Kegan Paul, 1982), 7–8. It should be noted that Gould's interpretation of Engels's "The Part Played by Labour in the Transition from Ape to Man" evolved over time. In his first essay on this subject, "Posture Maketh the Man," included in his collection *Ever Since Darwin*, Gould assumed that Engels had taken his analysis from Haeckel's outline of human evolution in *The History of Creation*. Yet, Haeckel in that work, though stressing erect posture, had come nowhere near to emphasizing the evolution of the hand along the lines that were to be developed by Engels. Moreover, in this early essay Gould believed that Engels's contribution was not in its "substantive conclusions" with respect to evolution but rather centered simply on his critique of "cerebral primacy" in evolutionary theory. By the time he wrote "Genes on the Brain" in 1983 (included in *An Urchin in the Storm*), Gould indicated that Engels had drawn on both Darwin and Haeckel, no doubt recognizing by this time the importance for Engels of Darwin's discussion in *The Descent of Man* of the evolution of the hand with respect to weapons. By then Gould had concluded that the real significance of Engels's essay was that it was the best account of "gene-culture coevolution" in the nineteenth century, placing Engels's substantive achievements in this particular respect not only above Haeckel's but Darwin's own. On the contrast between Haeckel's and Darwin's arguments see Misia Landau, *Narratives of Human Evolution* (New Haven: Yale University Press, 1991), 19, 31–60.
23. Thomas C. Patterson, *Karl Marx, Anthropologist* (New York: Berg, 2009), 75–81.

24. Marx and Engels, *Collected Works*, 25:459.
25. Adam Kuper refers to "the Darwinian view that human evolution was brain-led," while referring to the extreme views of Grafton Elliot Smith, one of the principal figures in the Piltdown affair, as evidence of this. Yet Darwin and other Darwinian materialists, like Thomas Huxley and E. Ray Lankester, leaned the other way. If cerebral primacy nevertheless remained the dominant conception in treatments of human evolution, it was therefore not primarily due to the strong Darwinians. In his argument, Engels merely claimed that idealist social biases partly clouded the issue, impeding a consistent materialist interpretation in this area. See Adam Kuper, *The Chosen Primate* (Cambridge, MA: Harvard University, 1994), 32; Leakey, *Origin of Humankind*, 2–3, 11–12; Gould, *Ever Since Darwin*, 208.
26. Roger Lewin, *The Origin of Modern Humans* (New York: Scientific American Library, 1993), 49–5, 54–57; John Evangelist Walsh, *Unraveling Piltdown* (New York: Random House, 1996), 10–11, 64–73; Stephen Jay Gould, *The Panda's Thumb* (New York: W. W. Norton, 1980), 108–24; Stephen Jay Gould, *Hen's Teeth and Horse's Shoes* (New York; W.W. Norton, 1983), 201–26; Kenneth P. Oakley, *Man the Toolmaker* (London: British Museum, 1950), 6–8, 69–70, 92; John Reader, *Missing Links* (Oxford: Oxford University Press, 2011),179–80. Stephen Jay Gould made a strong case that the young French priest and paleontologist Pierre Teilhard de Chardin, later involved in the discovery of Peking Man, and the author of the posthumously published *The Phenomenon of Man* was a co-conspirator of Dawson in the Piltdown fraud. It seems likely from the evidence that Gould presents that Teilhard had come to suspect that a fraud had taken place. Recent discoveries, though, have tended to point to Dawson as a forger working alone.
27. Grafton Elliot Smith, *The Evolution of Man* (London: Oxford University Press, 1924), 67–68.
28. There is no doubt that there was a cultural bias as well, in which the seeming inability to detect the Piltdown fraud may have derived in some case from racial and nationalistic prejudices. Richard G. Delise, *Debating Humanity in Nature, 1860–2000* (Upper Saddle River, NJ: Pearson, 2007), 143.
29. Walsh, *Unraveling Piltdown*, 50.
30. Miles Russell, *The Piltdown Man Hoax* (Stroud, Gloucestershire: History Press, 2012), 117–18.
31. E. Ray Lankester, *Diversions of a Naturalist* (London: Methuen and Co., 1919), 243–44. Lankester would of course have been familiar with what Darwin and Haeckel had said about the role of the development of the hand in human evolution.
32. Lankester quoted in Walsh, *Unraveling Piltdown*, 21.
33. Lankester, *Diversions of a Naturalist*, 275–91.
34. S. L. Washburn and Ruth Moore, *Ape Into Man* (Boston: Little, Brown. 1974), 85–89, 102–6, 156–57.
35. As late as 1951, the historical materialist V. Gordon Childe, whose argument was generally materialist through and through, was so confused by the supposed existence of *Eoanthropus* that elements of cerebral primacy entered into his argument. See V. Gordon Childe, *Man Makes Himself* (New York: Mentor, 1951), 21–29.
36. Delisle, *Debating Humankind's Place in Nature*, 132, 178, 250.
37. Oakley, *Man the Tool-Maker*, 1; Gould, *Ever Since Darwin*, 207–13; Washburn and Moore, *Ape Into Man*, 61–82, 186; Delisle, *Debating Humankind's Place in Nature*, 257–58.
38. V. Jakimov, "Basic Trends in the Adaptive Radiation of the Apes at the End of the

Tertiary and the Beginning of the Quaternary Periods," in *Soviet Ethnology and Anthropology Today*, ed. Yu Bromley (The Hague: Mouton, 1974), 270–72.

39. Shannon P. McPherron et al., "Evidence for Stone-Tool-Assisted Consumption of Animal Tissues Before 3.39 Million Years Ago at Dikika, Ethiopia," *Nature* 466/12 (August 2010): 857–60; Leakey, *The Origin of Humankind*, 1–20, 36–41; Ian Tattersall, *The Monkey in the Mirror* (New York: Harcourt, Inc., 2002), 83, 97–99; Reader, *Missing Links*, 432, 436; Ann Gibbons, "Deep Roosts for the Genus Homo," *Science* 347/6226 (March 6, 2015): 1056–57.
40. California Academy of Sciences, "Oldest Evidence of Stone Tools Use and Meat-Eating Among Human Ancestors Discovered: Lucy's Species Butchered Meat," August 11, 2010, https://www.sciencedaily.com/releases/2010/08/100811135039.htm.
41. "Early Pleistocene Third Metacarpal from Kenya and the Evolution of Modern Human–Like Hand Morphology," *Proceedings of the National Academy of Sciences* 111/1 (January 7, 2014): 121–24; BBC News, "Oldest Stone Tools Pre-Date Earlies Humans," May 2015; https://www.bbc.com/news/science-environment-32804177; California Academy of Sciences, "Scientists Discover Oldest Evidence of Stone Tool Use and Meat-Eating Among Human Ancestors," August 11, 2010, http://www.calacademy.org/press/releases/scientists-discover-oldest-evidence-of-stone-tool-use-and-meat-eating-among-human; Carol V. Ward et al., Reader, *Missing Links*, 381–82; Leakey, *The Origin of Humankind*, 40; Tattersall, *Monkey in the Mirror*, 93. As Tattersall says, there is evidence that these early hominins relied on tools in butchering carcasses of animals, but this does not constitute evidence that they hunted and killed the animals as opposed to scavenging. Recent discoveries have found stone tools in China, dated 2.1 million years ago. "Archaeologists in China Discover the Oldest Stone Tools Outside Africa," *New York Times*, July 11, 2018.
42. Marx and Engels, *Collected Works*, 25:457–58.
43. "Humans Shaped Stone Axes 1.8 Million Years Ago Study Says," Lamont-Doherty Earth Laboratory, August 31, 2011, http://www.ldeo.columbia.edu/news-events/humans-shaped-stone-axes-18-million-years-ago-study-says.
44. Leakey, *The Origin of Humankind*, 123.
45. Ibid.
46. Ibid., 123–24.
47. Marx and Engels, *Collected Works*, 25:460, 503. Engels's reference to his dog Dido in the context of developing more fully the argument on developed animal consciousness points to the unfinished character of the manuscript. Engels was in the habit of referring to his "black and white dog Dido" in letters to Marx. See Marx and Engels, *Collected Works*, 42:306.
48. Marx and Engels, *Collected Works*, 25:459–60.
49. Charles Darwin, *Journal of Researches into the Geology of the Various Countries Visited During the Voyage of the HMS Beagle* (New York: E. P. Dutton, 1906), 470–71; Charles Darwin, *Beagle Diary* (New York: Cambridge University Press, 1988), 428–29; Richard Grove, *Green Imperialism* (Cambridge: Cambridge University Press, 1995), 42–44, 95–109, 121–25, 343–45; John Bellamy Foster, "Capitalism and the Accumulation of Catastrophe," *Monthly Review* 63/7 (December 2011): 5; Marx and Engels, *Collected Works*, 25:459.
50. Marx and Engels, *Collected Works*, 25:459–60.
51. Marx and Engels, *Collected Works*, 25:461. This, and the following paragraph, draw on Foster, "Capitalism and the Accumulation of Catastrophe," 3–4.

52. Fraas quoted by Frederick Engels in Karl Marx and Friedrich Engels, *Gesamtausgabe* (*MEGA*), IV, 31, 512–15. Translation into English by Joseph Fracchia.
53. Ibid.
54. Marx and Engels, *Collected Works*, 25:671, 40, 314.
55. M. J. Schleiden, *The Plant: A Biography* (London: H. Balliere, 1853), 295, 303–7.
56. Karl Marx, *Capital*, vol. 3 (London: Penguin, 1981), 754.
57. Marx and Engels, *Collected Works*, 42:558–59; Karl Marx, *Capital*, vol. 1 (London: Penguin, 1976), 381.
58. Marx and Engels, *Collected Works*, 25:403–04.
59. Francis Bacon, *Novum Organum* (Chicago: Open Court, 1994), 29, 43.
60. Marx and Engels, *Collected Works*, 25:461. On Marx's critique of capitalism in this respect, see Karl Marx, *Grundrisse* (London: Penguin, 1973), 409–10. Bacon's complex notion of the domination and subjugation of nature, though frequently expounded in the form of metaphors drawn from the domination of society, was compatible with notions of sustainability insofar as it demanded that society genuinely follow "nature's laws" and on a long-term basis. The Baconian ruse was that nature could be mastered through its own laws. But nature's laws *if followed completely*, Marx (and Engels) suggested, went against this narrow exploitation of nature's laws, demanding attention to issues of reproduction and sustainability in relation to the chain of human generations. It should be noted that some of the earlier Baconians were at the same time some of the first modern conservationists, most notably John Evelyn. For a discussion of the full complexity of Bacon's maxim in this respect see William Leiss, *The Domination of Nature* (Boston: Beacon Press, 1974).
61. Marx and Engels, *Collected Works*, 25:460–62, 583.
62. Marx and Engels, *Collected Works*, 25:167. On the wider background here see Mike Davis, *Victorian Holocausts* (London: Verso, 2000).
63. Marx and Engels, *Collected Works*, 25:516–17.
64. Marx and Engels, *Collected Works*, 25:460–64.
65. Leacock, "Introduction" to Engels, "The Part Played by Labour," in Engels, *The Origin of the Family, Private Property and the State* (Leacock edition), 245.
66. Frederick Engels, "The Mark," in Frederick Engels, *Socialism: Utopian and Scientific* (New York: International Publishers, 1978), 77–93. It is worth noting that a similar treatment of the institution of the Mark as reflecting the original genetic constitution was to be found in William Morris's writings on the early German commune, and in his Romantic historical novel *House of the Wolfings*. See William Morris, *On History* (Sheffield: Sheffield Academic Press, 1996), 107–9, and *Collected Writings*, 14, 42–58; Florence Boos, "Morris's German Romances as Socialist History," *Victorian Studies* 27/3 (Spring 1984): 321–42.
67. Engels's treatment in "The Mark" dealt with prehistory only in the sense that the German tribal communities did not leave their own written records. However, the understanding of these developments at the time Engels was writing were principally based on Latin sources, such as Tacitus, and hence obviously were not prior to written history in that respect.
68. Lewis H. Morgan, *Ancient Society* (New York: World Publishing Co., 1963); Karl Marx, *The Ethnological Notebooks* (Assen, the Netherlands: Van Gorcum and Co., 1974).
69. See Sandra Bloodworth, "The Origins of Women's Oppression—A Defense of Engels and a New Departure," *Marxist Left Review* 16 (Summer 2018), http://marxistleftreview.org/index.php/no-16-summer-2018/158-the-origins-of-women-s-oppression-a-defence-of-engels-and-a-new-departure.

70. Engels, *The Origin of the Family, Private Property, and the State*, 5–6. In recent social reproduction theory Engels is often criticized, based on this quote, for having presented a "dualist" approach to production and reproduction. In his *Friedrich Engels and Modern Social and Political Theory* Paul Blackledge has strongly countered such claims that Engels was promoting a dualistic perspective as opposed to dialectical approach. At the same time, Blackledge notes that recent social reproduction theory has gone well beyond the limitations of Engels's analysis, which, although suggestive of a dialectical social reproductive approach to gender relations in capitalist society, did not actually develop such an analysis. The key work in accomplishing this was Lise Vogel's *Marxism and the Oppression of Women* (Chicago: Haymarket, 2014). See Paul Blackledge, *Friedrich Engels and Modern Social and Political Theory* (Albany: State University of New York Press, 2019), 205–8, 216–17; and Tithi Bhattacharya, "Liberating Women from 'Political Economy,'" *Monthly Review* 71/3 (January 2020): 1–14.
71. Engels, *The Origin of the Family, Private Property, and the State*, 74, 84, 100.
72. Lise Vogel, "Engels's *Origin*," in Christopher Arthur, *Engels Today* (New York: St. Martin's Press, 1996), 136.
73. Engels, *The Origin of the Family, Private Property, and the State*, 65.
74. Ibid., 65, 100.
75. Ibid., 13–18.
76. Ibid., 46–49.
77. This part of Engels's analysis has been questioned, and even designated by some as erroneous. The idea that the domestication of animals somehow preceded the domestication of plants and cultivation is rejected by most of today's anthropologists, who see these developments as simultaneous. Peter Aaby, "Engels and Women," *Critique of Anthropology* 3/9 (1977): 26. Still, there is little doubt that men, as opposed to women, dominated pastoral relations. Moreover, it is conceivable that animal husbandry and grazing were more effective than cultivation early on in generating an agricultural surplus that could be monopolized, and that this encouraged the development of private property controlled by men.
78. Engels, *Origin of the Family, Private Property, and the State*, 55–58, 68, 73, 156–57, 163.
79. Ibid., 25–26, 54. Periodization of pre-history and history, Engels explained, was based on the changing means of subsistence and the production of economic surplus rather than changing gender relations. "The evolution of the family," he wrote, "proceeds concurrently, but does not offer such exclusive criteria for determination of periods" (23).
80. Ibid., 56–58, 160.
81. Karen Hunt, *Equivocal Feminists: The Social Democratic Federation and the Woman Question, 1884–1911* (Cambridge: Cambridge University Press, 1996).
82. Lawrence Krader, "Introduction," in Marx, *The Ethnological Notebooks*, 87.
83. Marx, *Ethnological Notebooks*, "On the Measurement of Gender Equality," trans. Pradip Bakski, 20, https://www.academia.edu/5512528/Karl_Marxs_Critique_of_Political_Economy_and_Measurement_of_Gender_Inequality.
84. Engels, *The Origin of the Family, Private Property and the State*, 58, 66; Tristram Hunt, "Introduction," in Friedrich Engels, *The Origin of the Family, Private Property and the State* (London: Penguin, 2010), 11. Tristram Hunt provides important insights into Engels's *Origin of the Family, Private Property and the State* in his Introduction to the 2010 Penguin edition. Yet he follows this up by defending the notion of universal patriarchy and dismissing altogether as "erroneous" Engels's claim regard-

ing the decline of women's status with the *historical rise* of patriarchy and class society. For Hunt, Engels's argument simply contradicts "modern anthropology," though he does not seriously attempt to support this assertion and fails to recognize the continuing debate and differing evidence (as in the Leacock and Reiter books referenced below in this note).

Worse still, Hunt's deeply marred biography accuses Engels of "misogyny," providing as his sole basis for this serious allegation that Engels gave some women activists, such as Annie Besant, the title "Mother," hence referring to Besant as "Mother Besant" (although he refrains from providing any concrete evidence of this). For Hunt this constituted "misogynist abuse," disregarding the fact that Besant was to be widely known internationally, especially in India, as "Mother Besant," where the title was viewed, as with other activist women of the time, such as Mother Jones in the United States, as a sign of approbation. It is true that Engels also referred to Florence Kelley (Wischnewetzky), a woman for whom he had considerable esteem, as "Mother Wischnewetzky," in an 1889 private letter to Friederich Albert Sorge. Engels at the time of that writing was perturbed by Kelley's irritation with him for not staying with her during his visit to the United States, when he was ill with what her husband had diagnosed as bronchitis. This, however, was hardly an indication of "misogynist abuse" on his part. Marx and Engels, *Collected Works* 48: 253–54. Engels continued to be supportive of Kelley and included her in his will (leaving her all the royalties to the English edition of *The Condition of the Working Class in England*, which she had translated). John Green, *Engels: A Revolutionary Life* (London; Artery Publications, 2008), 286.

Likewise Engels is faulted by Hunt for allegedly rejecting women's suffrage, without noting that his stance here was the same as that of all other socialists at the time, particularly within Hyndman's Social Democratic Federation and Morris's Socialist League, of rejecting the extension of the vote simply to women who were property owners (middle class and above)—rather demanding instead universal suffrage for women and men.

At other points Hunt refers to Engels in his twenties as a "sexual predator" and a "shameless philanderer." Yet, other than one affair in his twenties with the wife of Moses Hess, and the conflicts that arose with Hess as a result—along with vague suppositions that Engels may have slept around for a short time in Paris and elsewhere during the 1848 Revolution before settling down completely with Mary Burns—Hunt's sole evidence appears to be that Engels indicated in one letter that he enjoyed the company of French and Belgian *grisettes*, young working-class women in the garment industry who were active in bohemian and radical circles. Hunt simply translates *grisettes* in his biography as "prostitutes" and uses Engels's attraction to *grisettes* with their radical lifestyle as the alleged grounds for pronouncing again and again in his various writings that Engels frequented brothels. Such scurrilous claims aimed at sullying Engels's support of women's rights may add spice to Hunt's biography of Engels, and no doubt made it more successful in mass media and book publishing industry terms, but they mar what might possibly have been a valuable work. See Tristram Hunt, "Feminist Friend or Foe," *The Guardian*, April 28, 2009; Hunt, "Introduction," in Engels, *Origin of the Family, Private Property and the State* (Penguin) 20–22, Hunt, *Marx's General*, 139–41, 160, 310–12; Hannah Manchin, "The Grisette as the Female Bohemian," Brown University, 2000, https://www.mtholyoke.edu/courses/rschwart/hist255s13/grisette/manchin.htm; Eleanor Burke Leacock, *The Myth of Male Dominance* (New York: Monthly Review Press, 1981); Rayna Reiter, ed., *Toward an Anthropology of Women* (New York: Monthly Review Press, 1975).

85. Engels, *The Origin of the Family, Private Property and the State*, 72–73.
86. Ibid., 73–74.
87. Ibid., 74, 158.
88. Ibid., 48, 65, 69, 76–77.
89. Eleanor Leacock, "Introduction," in Engels, *Origin of the Family, Private Property, and the State* (Leacock edition), 44–45; Eleanor Leacock, *Myths of Male Dominance* (New York: Monthly Review Press, 1981), 193.
90. Aaby, "Engels and Women," 36.
91. Robin Fox, *Kinship and Nature: An Anthropological Perspective* (Cambridge: Cambridge University Press, 1984), 31-32. Quoted in Aaby, "Engels and Women," 28. In defense of the hypothesis of "universal patriarchy," mainstream academics like Cynthia Eller have polemically promoted the straw person of a "matriarchal myth" in order to attack Engels along with certain late twentieth-century socialist feminist anthropologists, all of whom are erroneously criticized for postulating a primordial "matriarchy." Yet, Eller cannot avoid acknowledging between the lines (as well as through the absence of any concrete evidence) that the idea of an original matriarchy was never part of the argument of Engels or today's socialist feminists. The matrilineal argument promoted by Morgan, Engels, and others is quite different from matriarchy. Historical materialists simply pointed to the fact that relative equality of women characteristic of early social forms had declined over the course of history, along with the development of class societies and more entrenched patriarchal social formations. See Cynthia Eller, *The Myth of Matriarchal Prehistory* (Boston: Beacon Press, 2000), 30–35.
92. Aaby, "Engels and Women," 28–37; Leacock, *The Myth of Male Dominance*, 13–29, 37, 141; Reiter, *Toward an Anthropology of Women*, 36–76, 211-51.
93. Engels, *The Origin of the Family, Private Property and the State*, 71, 174; Engels, *Socialism: Utopian and Scientific*, 39.
94. Stephanie Coontz and Peta Henderson, "Property Forms, Political Power, and Female Labour in the Origins of Class and State Societies," in *Women's Work, Men's Property* (London: Verso, 1986), 108. Numerous radical ecological thinkers subscribe to such views, arguing that the decline of women's status in society, the degradation of nature, and the rise of private property and patriarchy were all historically intertwined. As Murray Bookchin was to write in the 1990s in *Towards an Ecological Society*, "The breakup of these [early] unified organic communities, based on a sexual division of labor and kinship ties, into hierarchical and finally class societies gradually subverted the unity of society with the natural world," leading to "the objectification of nature" and its instrumentalist manipulation, finally in the interest of class society. Murray Bookchin, *Towards an Ecological Society* (Montreal: Black Rose, 1980), 62–63.
95. Engels, *Origin of the Family, Private Property, and the State*, 96–97. In contrast to Engels's views see the racist Victorian perspective on Africa critically depicted in Lindqvist, *Exterminate All the Brutes*.
96. Heyer, *Nature, Human Nature, and Society*, 205.
97. On the varying racial views of Lyell, Agassiz, Darwin, and Wallace see Desmond and Moore, *Darwin's Sacred Cause*, 171, 180–81, 195, 199, 264–65, 311–12, 343–44. In one famous instance, Engels was known to warn Marx off from a race-based interpretation. Marx and Engels, *Collected Works*, 42:304–5, 320–24, 327.
98. Stephen Jay Gould, *The Flamingo's Smile* (New York: W.W. Norton, 1985), 185–98.
99. Engels, *The Origin of the Family, Private Property, and the State*, 5–6.
100. Marx and Engels, *Collected Works*, 48: 503–5, 613; Marx and Engels, *Collected Works*,

27: 80–85; Lee Baxandall and Stefan Morawski, ed., *Karl Marx and Frederick Engels on Literature and Art* (New York: International General, 1973), 86–89. Ernst later moved to the extreme right and the defense of Hitler. Hal Draper, *The Marx-Engels Glossary* (New York: Schocken Books, 1986), 66.

101. Yvonne Kapp, *Eleanor Marx* (New York: Pantheon Books, 1976), 99–103, 248–49.
102. Mayer, *Friedrich Engels*, 245.
103. Marx and Engels, *Collected Works*, 49:378. Mayer's free translation into English of Engels's letter, including English terminology, perhaps better captures the sense of Engels's statement here for the English reader. Here the above quotation is rendered: "She came of real Irish proletarian stock, and her passionate feeling for her class, which was instinctive in her, was worth more to me than all the blue-stockinged elegances of 'educated' and 'sensitive' bourgeois girls could have been." Mayer, *Friedrich Engels*, 245.
104. Engels, *Ludwig Feuerbach and the Outcome of Classical German Philosophy*, 18.
105. Ibid., 21.
106. Ibid., 21–25.
107. Ibid., 28–29, 46–47.
108. Significantly, it was in *Ludwig Feuerbach and the Close of His System* that Engels published for the first time both Marx's 1846 "Theses on Feuerbach" and Marx's section "On the History of French Materialism" from Marx and Engels's *Holy Family*. The result was to lay bare the original Marxian conception of the new materialism.

CHAPTER EIGHT: ECOLOGY AS A SYSTEM

1. Joseph Lester, *E. Ray Lankester and the Making of Modern British Biology* (London: British Society for the History of Science, 1995), 67–69.
2. G. P. Bidder, "Obituary of E. Ray Lankester," *Nature* 124 (192): 345–46.
3. H. Goodwin, "Arthur George Tansley, 1871–1955," *Biographical Memoirs of Fellows of the Royal Society* 3 (November 1957): 227–28; Peter Ayres, *Shaping Ecology: The Life of Arthur Tansley* (Oxford: Wiley-Blackwell, 2012), 42; Lester, *E. Ray Lankester and the Making of Modern British Biology*, 67–69.
4. It was coming across Beesly's *Catiline, Clodius, and Tiberius* (1878) when he was living in Cornwall and researching his first historical novel on classical Rome (*Rome for Sale*, 1934) that gave the young Jack Lindsay the notion that it was possible to develop a historical-materialist approach in novels on ancient Rome, leading to his classical novel series. Paul Gillen, "Lindsay, John (Jack) (1900–1990)," *Australian Dictionary of Biography,* vol. 18 (Melbourne: Melbourne University Press, 2012), http://adb.anu.edu.au/biography/lindsay-john-jack-14177; David Movrin and Elżbietta Olechowska, ed., *Classics and Class* (Warsaw: Ljubljana, 2016), 22.
5. Godwin, "Arthur George Tansley," 227; Ayres, *Shaping Ecology*, 20–36; William Morris, *Collected Letters* (Princeton: Princeton University Press, 1987), vol. 2, 482; J. C. Harrison, *A History of the Working Men's College, 1854–1954* (London: Routledge and Kegan Paul, 1954), 43–45, 65–69, 147–48, 112–36, 192; Rev. J. Llewelyn Davies, ed., *The Working Men's College, 1854–1904* (London: Macmillan and Co., 1904), 106, 129–80; ; G. E. M. de Ste Croix, *The Class Struggle in the Ancient Greek World* (London: Duckworth, 1981), 621–22; Rosemary Ashton, *Victorian Bloomsbury* (New Haven: Yale University Press, 2012), 202–9, 251–52, 258–65; Peder Anker, *Imperial Ecology* (Cambridge, MA: Harvard University Press, 2001), 8: Hal Draper, *The Marx-Engels Glossary* (New York: Schocken Books, 1986), 159. Although the interpretation in this chapter differs on some points from that of Anker's *Imperial Ecology*,

particularly the direct significance of Tansley's psychological work for his ecosystem ecology, Anker's important research remains indispensable for any treatment of the subject, and influences much of the following discussion.

6. H. Goodwin, "Sir Arthur Tansley: The Man and the Subject," *Journal of Ecology* 65/1 (March 1977): 2; Ayres, *Shaping Ecology*, 23–24; C .P. Lucas, "George Tansley," in Davies, *The Working Men's College*, 143.
7. Ayres, *Shaping Ecology*, 35–36.
8. Ibid., 41–42, 50; Ashton, *Victorian Bloomsbury*, 14–15.
9. Lester, *E. Ray Lankester and the Making of British Biology*, 65–68, 105–13; Ayres, *Shaping Ecology*, 42–43; Arthur G. Tansley, "Review of Charles Elton," *Animal Ecology*, 16/1 (February 1928): 163.
10. E. Ray Lankester, *The Advancement of Science* (London: Macmillan, 1890), 108.
11. Laura Cameron and John Forrester, "'A Nice Type of the English Scientist': Tansley and Freud," *History Workshop Journal* 48/1 (Autumn 1999): 66–67; Ayres, *Shaping Ecology*, 48.
12. F. W. Oliver, "On the Effects of Urban Fog Upon Cultivated Plants," *Journal of the Royal Horticultural Society* 13 (1891): 139–40; Ayres, *Shaping Ecology*, 39, 63–65; Anker, *Imperial Ecology*, 9–10.
13. Ayres, *Shaping Ecology*, 17, 39; Anker, *Imperial Ecology*, *13;* Godwin, "Sir Arthur Tansley," 1-26; Cameron, "'A Nice Type of the English Scientist,'" 66.
14. Ayres, *Shaping Ecology*, 70–74, 80–83; Cameron and Forrester, "'A Nice Type of the English Scientist,'" 66–67.
15. A. G. Tansley, "Introduction," in Tansley, ed., *Types of British Vegetation* (Cambridge: Cambridge University Press, 1911), 1–2.
16. F. F. Blackman, V. H. Blackman, Frederick Keeble, F. W. Oliver, and A. G. Tansley, "The Reconstruction of Elementary Botanical Teaching," *New Phytologist* 16/10 (December 1917): 241–52.
17. Anker, *Imperial Ecology*, 20–22; A. D. Boney, "The 'Tansley Manifesto' Affair," *New Phytologist* 118/1 (May 1991): 250; Blackman et al., "The Reconstruction of Elementary Botanical Thinking," 242, 251–52; Ayres, *Shaping Ecology*, 110; Anonymous (Tansley), "The National Union of Scientific Workers," *New Phytologist* 17/1–2 (January–February 1918): 1–2; Gary Werskey, *The Visible College* (London: Allen Lane, 1978), 39–41, 52.
18. Blackman et al., "The Reconstruction of Elementary Botanical Thinking," 242.
19. Ibid., 243, 251.
20. Ibid., 246–47; Boney, "The 'Tansley Manifesto' Affair," 7.
21. Blackman et al., "The Reconstruction of Elementary Botanical Thinking," 243–44, 245–46.
22. F. O. Bower, "Botanical Bolshevism," *New Phytologist* 17 (1918): 105–7.
23. Balfour to Bower, April 17, 1918, quoted in Boney, "The 'Tansley Manifesto' Affair," 10.
24. Boney, "The 'Tansley Manifesto' Affair," 17–18; Anker, *Imperial Ecology*, 22; Ayres, *Shaping Ecology,* 110.
25. Balfour to Bower, October 29, 1921, quoted in Boney, "The 'Tansley Manifesto' Affair," 17; Ayres, *Shaping Ecology*, 107–9.
26. Ayres, *Shaping Ecology*, 110–16; Cameron and Forrester, "'A Nice Type of English Scientist,'" 65–100; Laura Cameron, "Histories of Disturbance," *Radical History Review* 74 (1999): 4–24; Laura Cameron "Arthur Tansley and Psychoanalysis," New Phytologist Trust, https://www.newphytologist.org/trust/tansley/psychoanalysis; Anker, *Imperial Ecology*, 23.

27. A. G. Tansley, *The New Psychology and Its Relation to Life* (London: George Allen and Unwin, 1920), 5–6; William McDougall, *An Introduction to Social Psychology* (Boston: John W. Luce, 1909); Wilfred Trotter, *The Herd Instinct in Peace and War* (New York: Macmillan, 1917) (includes Trotter's 1908 article). Freud's chapter on "The Herd Instinct" in chapter 9 of his 1922 *Group Psychology and the Analysis of the Ego* (New York: W. W. Norton, 1999), 62–68, comments extensively on Trotter's work, and presumably reflects Tansley's discussion. On Freud's materialism see John Bellamy Foster, Brett Clark, and Richard York, *Critique of Intelligent Design* (New York: Monthly Review Press, 2008), 131–51.
28. Tansley, *The New Psychology*, 213.
29. Ibid., 213–17.
30. Ibid., 268.
31. Ibid., 227–35; Cicely Hamilton, *Marriage as a Trade* (London: The Women's Press, 1981). Tansley's reference to feminist claims regarding the "man made world," suggests that he may have been familiar with Charlotte Perkins Gilman's 1898, *The Man Made World* (London: T. Fischer Unwin, 1911).
32. Elaine Showalter, "Hysteria, Feminism and Gender," in *Hysteria Beyond Freud*, ed. Sandra L. Gilman et al. (Berkeley: University of California Press, 1993), 302–5, 316–17, *The Female Malady* (London: Penguin Books, 1985), 131–34; Mikkel Borsch-Jacobsen, *The Freud Files* (Cambridge: Cambridge University Press, 1012), 109. Sally Ledger and Roger Luckhurst indicate that Donkin's article contained "the enlightened realization that social and sexual restrictions on women produce mental illness." Sally Ledger and Roger Lockhurst, "Psychology" (introduction) in Ledger and Lockhurst, ed., *The Fin de Siècle: A Reader in Cultural History c. 1880–1900* (Oxford: Oxford University Press, 2000), 244. Horatio Bryan Donkin, "Hysteria" in *A Dictionary of Psychological Medicine*, ed. Daniel Hack Tuke (London: J. and A. Churchill, 1892), vol. 1, 619–20.
33. A. G. Tansley, "Psycho-analysis," *Nation and New Athenaeum*, June 13, 1925, and October 3, 1925; H. B. Donkin, "Freudian Psycho-analysis," *Nation and New Athenaeum*, August 22, 1925, October 3, 1925.
34. Anker, *Imperial Ecology*, 3, 23–35.
35. A. G. Tansley, *Practical Plant Ecology,* 5–7, 15–20, 47, 177; Jack Morrell, *Science at Oxford, 1914–1939* (Oxford: Oxford University Press, 1997), 241. Ayres describes *Practical Plant Ecology* as a "work for schoolchildren," but it was much more than that. See Ayres, *Shaping Ecology*, 117–19.
36. Morrell, *Science at Oxford, 1914–1939,* 248, 275–93; Anker, *Imperial Ecology*, 87, 98–102; Lester, *E. Ray Lankester*, 210.
37. Charles Elton, *Animal Ecology and Evolution* (Oxford: Oxford University Press, 1930), 16–17, 76.
38. Tansley, "Review of Charles Elton, *Animal Ecology*," 163; Morrell, *Science at Oxford*, 298.
39. Ayres, *Shaping Ecology*, 132.
40. R. G. Collingwood, *The Idea of Nature* (Oxford: Oxford University Press, 1945), 159, 173; Anker, *Imperial Ecology*, 137.
41. In personal correspondence, replying to my research assistant Jordan Fox Besek, on July 7, 2015, Peder Anker wrote: "Neither Lewis nor Tolkien gave papers at the club. They may or may not have been in the audience. They certainly knew what was going on at Magdalen as they participated in local activities such as dinners etc."
42. Anker, *Imperial Ecology*, 137–38; Meredith Veldman, *Fantasy, the Bomb, and*

the Greening of Britain (Cambridge: Cambridge University Press, 1994), 52–53; Kevin Lee Massey, "The Roots of Middle Earth: William Morris's Influence upon J. R.R. Tolkien" (PhD diss., University of Tennessee, Knoxville, December 2007); Walt Sheasby, "J. R .R. Tolkien: Saving the Ecosystems of Middle Earth," *MRzine*, March 10, 2007, http://mrzine.monthlyreview.org/2007/sheasby311007.html; J.R.R. Tolkien, *The Letters of J. R. R. Tolkien: A Selection* (Boston: Houghton Mifflin, 1981), 7, 303.

43. Anker, *Imperial Ecology*, 138.
44. Arthur George Tansley, "The Temporal Genetic Series as a Means of Approach to Philosophy," *Ecosystems* 5/7 (November 2002): 614–24.
45. C. Lloyd Morgan, *Emergent Evolution* (New York: Henry Holt, 1926), 9–11.
46. Samuel Alexander, *Space, Time, Deity*, vol. 1 (London: Macmillan, 1920), vi; Lloyd Morgan, *Emergent Evolution*, 18.
47. David Blitz, *Emergent Evolution: Qualitative Novelty and the Levels of Reality* (Boston: Kluwer Academic Publishers, 1992), 1.
48. Lloyd Morgan, *Emergent Evolution*, 64.
49. John Stuart Mill, *A System of Logic* (London: Longmans Green and Co., 1889, People's Edition), 243–45.
50. Mill, *A System of Logic*, 245.
51. George Henry Lewes, *Problems of Life and Mind* (Boston: Houghton Mifflin, 1891), vol. 2, 412; Blitz, *Emergent Evolution: Qualitative Novelty and the Levels of Reality*, 85.
52. Lloyd Morgan, *Emergent Evolution*, 16; Blitz, *Emergent Evolution: Qualitative Novelty and the Levels of Reality*, 99.
53. Lloyd Morgan, *Emergent Evolution*, 301.
54. Alexander, *Space, Time, Deity*, vol. 1, 47; Lloyd Morgan, *Life, Mind and Spirit* (New York: Henry Holt, 1925), ix, 287; and *Emergent Evolution*, 12, 303.
55. In Lloyd Morgan's case, this recourse to God as representing the ultimately unifying forces in an outlook that was naturalistic at its base was frequently justified as having "the ring of Spinoza." Lloyd Morgan, *Emergent Evolution*, 34.
56. Roy Sellars, *Critical Realism* (Chicago: Rand McNally, 1916), *Evolutionary Naturalism* (Chicago: Open Court Publishing, 1922), and *The Principles and Problems of Philosophy* (New York: Macmillan, 1926). For Sellars's socialism and his relation to Marx, see Roy Sellars, *The Next Step in Democracy* (New York: Macmillan, 1916). For his critical materialism see Roy Sellars, "Materialism and Human Knowing," in Roy Sellars et al., *Philosophy for the Future: The Quest of Modern Materialism* (New York: Macmillan, 1949), 75–106. It is significant that other contributors to Sellars's edition of *The Philosophy of the Future* included J. D. Bernal, Maurice Cornforth, Auguste Cornu, Maurice Dobb, Benjamin Farrington, J. B. S. Haldane, Christopher Hill, Georg Lukács, and Dirk Struik, among others.
57. Sellars, *Evolutionary Naturalism*, 27.
58. Lloyd Morgan, *Emergent Evolution*, 303. Some of Lloyd Morgan's more conservative tendencies with respect to society were evident in his writings on eugenics. In *Eugenics and Environment*, a work he dedicated to Francis Galton, he raised the "moral" issue of eugenics, giving seeming support for eugenics as a means of improving the human "stock," while placing emphasis in the end on education as the surest guide to human progress. C. Lloyd Morgan, *Eugenics and Environment* (London: John Bale, Sons, and Danielson Ltd., 1919).
59. Sellars, *The Principles and Problems of Philosophy*, 363; Blitz, *Emergent Evolution: Qualitative Novelty and the Levels of Reality*, 124.

60. Joseph Needham, "Integrative Levels," in Needham, *Time: The Refreshing River* (London: George Allen and Unwin, 1943), 185, 233–72; and *The Grand Titration: Science and Society in East and West* (Toronto: University of Toronto Press. 1969), 123–24.
61. Roy Bhaskar, *Dialectics: The Pulse of Freedom* (London: Verso, 1993), 49–56, *Plato Etc.* (London: Verso, 1994), 73–77.
62. Terence W. Deacon, *Incomplete Nature* (New York: W. W. Norton, 2013), 157–59.
63. Tansley, "Temporal Genetic Sequence," 614–17, 624.
64. Ibid., 617–20.
65. Ibid., 619–24.
66. Needham, *Time: The Refreshing River*, 233–72.
67. Ayres, *Shaping Ecology*, 134.
68. Peder Anker, "The Politics of Ecology in South Africa on the Radical Left," *Journal of the History of Biology* 37 (2004): 307.
69. Anker, *Imperial Ecology*, 119–23. The following discussion of Jan Christian Smuts is adapted from John Bellamy Foster, Brett Clark, and Richard York, *The Ecological Rift* (New York: Monthly Review Press, 2010), 315–22, and reflects research conducted with Brett Clark in particular, an earlier version of which appeared in John Bellamy Foster and Brett Clark, "The Sociology of Ecology," *Organization and Environment* 21/3 (2008): 311–52.
70. Robert Harvey, *The Fall of Apartheid: The Insider Story from Smuts to Mbeki* (Hampshire, UK: Palgrave, 2001), 36–38; Heinz L. Ansbacher, "On the Origin of Holism," *Individual Psychology* 50/4 (1994): 486–92.
71. Jan Christian Smuts, *Greater South Africa: Plans for a Better World* (Johannesburg: The Truth Legion, 1940), 2–3.
72. Anker, *Imperial Ecology*, 45–47; T. R. H. Davenport and Christopher Saunders, *South Africa: A Modern History* (New York: St. Martin's Press, 2000), 244–45; W. K. Hancock, *Smuts: The Sanguine Years, 1870–1919* (Cambridge: Cambridge University Press, 1962), 325–47.
73. Edward Roux, *Time Longer than Rope: A History of the Black Man's Struggle for Freedom in South Africa* (Madison: University of Wisconsin Press, 1964), 141–42; Anker, *Imperial Ecology*, 46–51; "A History of the Bull Hoek Massacre," available at South African History Online: Towards a People's History, http://www.sahistory.org.za/topic/history-bulhoek-massacre; Davenport and Saunders, *South Africa*, 292–93; Sven Lindquist, *A History of Bombing* (London: Granta, 2000), sec. 107.
74. Roy Campbell, *Adamastor* (London: Faber and Faber, 1930), 103.
75. Foster, Clark, and York, *The Ecological Rift*, 308–12.
76. Jan Christian Smuts, *Holism and Evolution* (New York: Macmillan, 1926), 21, 80–82, 340. See also Frank Benjamin Golley, *A History of the Ecosystem Concept in Ecology* (New Haven: Yale University Press, 1993), 25–26.
77. Smuts, *Holism and Evolution*, 99.
78. Ibid., 323–26.
79. Ibid., 213.
80. Anker, *Imperial Ecology*, 72, 191–92.
81. Jan Christian Smuts, "The Scientific World-Picture of Today," Presidential Address to the British Association for the Advancement of Science, in *Report of the Centenary Meeting* (London: British Association for the Advancement of Sciences, 1932), 17–18.
82. Alfred Adler, *Social Interest* (New York: Capricorn Books, 1964), 68; Ansbacher, "On the Origins of Holism," 491.

83. Smuts, *Holism and Evolution*, 297–313.
84. Anker, *Imperial Ecology*, 124–25.
85. Eddie and Win Roux, *Rebel Pity: The Life of Eddie Roux* (London: Rex Collings, 1970), 190; Anker, *Imperial Ecology*, 191.
86. W. E. B. Du Bois, *The World and Africa* (New York: Viking Press, 1947), 43.
87. Jan Christian Smuts, *Africa and Some World Problems* (Oxford: Oxford University Press, 1930), 30–32, 43.
88. Jan Christian Smuts, "Climate and Man in Africa," *South African Journal of Science* 29 (1932): 129, quoted in Anker, *Imperial Ecology*, 163.
89. Smuts, *Africa and Some World Problems*, 75–76.
90. In *Holism and Evolution*, Smuts used the ontogeny recapitulates phylogeny theory in support of his concept of holism. See Smuts, *Holism and Evolution*, 74, 115.
91. Stephen Jay Gould, *Ontogeny and Phylogeny* (Cambridge, MA: Harvard University Press, 1977), 126. See also Stephen Jay Gould, *The Mismeasure of Man* (New York: W. W. Norton, 1996), 142–51.
92. Smuts, *Africa and Some World Problems*, 92–93.
93. W. E. B. Du Bois, "Behold the Land" (1946), Blackpast.org, http://www.blackpast.org/1946-w-e-b-dubois-behold-land; Anker, *Imperial Ecology*, 194.
94. Oliver Schreiner to Jan Christian Smuts, April 16, 1911, Saturday 1918, and October 28, 1920; and "Jan Christian Smuts," Olive Schreiner Letters Online, https://www.oliveschreiner.org; Baruch Hirson, "Ruth Schecter: Friend to Olive Schreiner," *Searchlight South Africa* 3/1 (August 1992): 47–71.
95. Lancelot Hogben, *Dangerous Thoughts* (New York: W. W. Norton, 1940), Preface, 16, 24, 268–74; Hogben, *Science for the Citizen* (New York: Alfred A. Knopf, 1938), 1065; Helena Sheehan, *Marxism and the Philosophy of Science* (Atlantic Highlands, NJ: Humanities Press, 1985), 329–30; G. P. Wells, "Lancelot Thomas Hogben," *Biographical Memoirs of the Royal Society*, vol. 24 (November 1978), 185–88.
96. Roux and Roux, *Rebel Pity*, 76–77.
97. Unusual for the day, even among feminists, Charles was to retain her maiden name.
98. Nancy G. Slack, *G. Evelyn Hutchinson, and the Invention of Modern Ecology* (New Haven: Yale University, 2010), xi, 77–88.
99. Farrington was romantically attached to Oliver Schreiner's close friend and follower, and Marxian activist, Ruth Schecter. She divorced her husband Morris Alexander in 1933 and married Farrington, after moving to Britain in 1935. Both were closely associated with Hogben. See John Atkinson, "Benjamin Farrington: Cape Town and the Shaping of a Public Intellectual," *South African Historical Journal* 62/4 (2010): 671–92. See also the excellent treatment of Schecter, Schreiner, Farrington, and Hogben in Hirson, "Ruth Schecter: Friend of Olive Schreiner." Hirson's otherwise informative piece is marred at the end, however, by excessive anti-Sovietism, which he refers to as the "greatest tyranny" of the twentieth century, no doubt forgetting about Nazi Germany.
100. Anker, "The Politics of Ecology in South Africa on the Radical Left," 303–26; Ayers, *Shaping Ecology*, 107–8; Roux and Roux, *Rebel Pity*, 245; Roux, *Time Longer than Rope*; Edward Roux, *Grass: A Story of Frankenwald* (Cape Town: Oxford University Press, 1969), 195–96; Edward Roux, *The Veld and the Future: A Book on Soil Erosion for South Africans* (Cape Town: The African Bookman, 1946), 59.
101. Lancelot Hogben, *Lancelot Hogben, Scientific Humanist: An Unauthorized Autobiography*, ed. Adrian and Anne Hogben (London: Merlin Press, 1998), 105, 109, 113–14; G. P. Wells, "Lancelot Thomas Hogben," 189, 194–97; Anker, *Imperial Ecology*, 122–23.

102. Hogben, *Lancelot Hogben, Scientific Humanist*, 114.
103. Ibid., 114–15. The whole horrendous journey is recounted in somewhat different, and even more dramatic, terms by Roux and Roux, *Rebel Pity: The Life of Eddie* Roux. 75, 88–89.
104. Roux and Roux, *Rebel Pity*, 75.
105. Anker, *Imperial Ecology*, 290.
106. Kenneth Calvin Page (pseudonym for Lancelot Hogben), *A Journey to Nineveh and Other Poems* (London: Noel Douglas, 1932), 11–12.
107. Smuts quoted on the subject of his presentation in the Nature of Life debate in Anker, *Imperial Ecology*, 123; Smuts, *Holism and Evolution*.
108. In the foreword to his book, Hogben indicated that his presentation to the British Association was the fourth essay. It is assumed here that he was referring to chapter 3, titled "The Nature of Life," and counting the Introduction as the first essay. The title plus the contents of that chapter and the following one on adaptation seem to leave no other interpretation possible. Lancelot Hogben, *The Nature of Living Matter* (London: Kegan Paul, Trench, Trubner and Co., Ltd., 1930), vii–viii.
109. Ibid., 96–98, 294–95.
110. Ibid., 290–91, 295–96.
111. Ibid., 224.
112. Lancelot Hogben, "Contemporary Philosophy in Soviet Russia," *Psyche* 12/1–4 (1931–1932): 3, 9–11, 14; Hogben, *Dangerous Thoughts*, 9–10, 262–79; Needham, *Time: The Refreshing River*, 244.
113. Needham, *Time: The Refreshing River*, 244. The seriousness with which Hogben approached questions of dialectics in his *Psyche* article on the Soviet philosophy of science, and the affinity he displayed toward many of those ideas, casts considerable doubt on Edwin Roberts's all too assertive claim that Hogben had "a violent aversion to dialectics." Hogben's views in this respect were far more complex and clearly changed over the course of his career. To say, as Roberts does, that Hogben's article "Our Social Heritage" maintained that "it was perverse for English Marxists to insist on using dialectics" simply because it objected to certain Hegelianisms is to make a significant category mistake. Roberts, *The Anglo-Marxists*, 148; Lancelot Hogben, "Our Social Heritage," *Science and Society* 1/2 (1936): 137–51.
114. Hogben, "Contemporary Philosophy in Soviet Russia," 14.
115. Lancelot Hogben, *Author in Transit* (New York: W. W. Norton, 1940), 158–59; Hogben, *Science for the Citizen*, 1072.
116. Hogben, *Science for the Citizen*, 1072.
117. Lancelot Hogben, "Planning for Human Survival," in G. D. H. Cole et al., *What Is Ahead of Us?* (London: Macmillan, 1937)185–87, *Science for the Citizen*, 1072. Hogben's focus in "Planning for Human Survival" was on the decline in fertility in Britain and the widely perceived population problem—problem of survival—associated with it. His wife, Enid Charles, had just completed a book on the subject, titled *The Menace of Underpopulation: A Biological Study of the Declining Population Growth* (London: Watts and Co., 1936). This was followed up by a work on *Political Arithmetic*, edited by Hogben and including essays on declining fertility by Charles. Yet, Hogben's ecological views, although loosely integrated with this argument, were in many ways logically independent of the proposition on declining fertility, and were promoted on other grounds as well, not only in the essay in the "Planning for Human Survival," but also in his sharp criticisms of the Malthusian doctrine in *Political Arithmetic* and his argument for the construction of a rational relation between human beings and their

environment. See Lancelot Hogben, "Introduction: to Part 1: Prolegomena to Political Arithmetic," in Hogben, ed., *Political Arithmetic* (New York: Macmillan, 1938), 30–32.

118. Hogben, "Planning for Human Survival," 189–192.
119. Ibid.
120. Lancelot Hogben, *The Retreat from Nature* (New York: Random House, 1938), 42–49. At the time Hogben was concerned with the issue, raised most famously by his wife Enid Charles, regarding the decline in population growth (which proved temporary). His answer to this was a rational one applicable to our times, that the equilibrium of population and the environment depended on the quality of life, not just in terms of the social environment, but in the human relation to nature in general.
121. Hogben, *Dangerous Thoughts*, 14–15.
122. Hogben, *The Retreat from Reason*, 38–39.
123. Lancelot Hogben, *Science in Authority* (New York: W. W. Norton, 1963), 18–21.
124. Pauline M. H. Mazumdar, *Eugenics, Human Genetics and Human Failings* (London: Routledge, 1992), 146–50, 161, 166.
125. Bruce Baum, *The Rise and Fall of the Caucasian Race* (New York: New York University Press, 2006), 175.
126. Ashley Montagu, *Man's Most Dangerous Myth: The Fallacy of Race* (London: Almira, 1997), 36.
127. Mazumdar, *Eugenics, Human Genetics and Human Failings*, 170–72, 184–85, 194–95, 214–15; Lancelot Hogben, *Nature and Nurture* (London: George Allen and Unwin, Ltd., 1933), 33, 114–16. Marx explicitly quoted Marx on praxis in *Nature and Nurture*, 114.
128. Hogben, *Lancelot Hogben, Scientific Humanist*, 126–27.
129. Hogben, *Nature and Nurture*, 91–121; Hogben, *Lancelot Hogben: Scientific Humanist*, 127. Tabery writes that "the legacy" of Hogben's pioneering analysis of the genotype–environment interaction in works such as *Genetic Principles in Medicine and Social Science* and *Nature and Nurture* was to inspire "the developmental tradition" that included later figures such as Richard Lewontin. See James Tabery, "R. A. Fisher, Lancelot Hogben, and the Origin(s) of Genotype–Environment Interaction," *Journal of the History of Biology* 41/4 (Winter 2008): 757.
130. Werskey, *The Visible College*, 67; Hogben, *Author in Transit*, 54–55.
131. Hogben, *Science for the Citizen*, 959, 1071–72.
132. This was not confined to South Africa, of course. See, for example, Franz-Joseph Brüggemeir, Mark Cioc, and Thomas Zeller, eds., *How Green Were the Nazis* (Athens: Ohio University Press, 2005).
133. Anker, *Imperial Ecology*, 131–33.
134. Jan Smuts, "The Scientific World-Picture of Today," Presidential Address to the British Association of the Advancement of Science, in its *Report to the Centenary Meeting* (London: British Association for the Advancement of Science, 1932), 17–18; Karl Marx and Frederick Engels, *Collected Works* (New York: International Publishers, 1975), vol. 45, 50; John Tyndall, *Fragments of Science* (New York: D. Appleton and Co., 1899), vol. 2, 135–201; Anker, *Imperial Ecology*, 158–59.
135. Smuts, "The Scientific World Picture of Today," 10–18.
136. Anker, *Imperial Ecology*, 159.
137. The following two paragraphs on Phillips's and Bews's ecological–racist holism are adapted from Foster, Clark, and York, *The Ecological Rift*, 323–24.
138. John Phillips, "A Tribute to Frederick E. Clements and His Concepts in Ecology,"

Ecology 35/2 (1954):114–15; "Man at the Cross-Roads," in Jan Christian Smuts, ed., *Our Changing World-View* (Johannesburg: University of Witwatersrand Press, 1932), 51–52; Anker, *Imperial Ecology*, 148, 192.

139. John William Bews, *Human Ecology* (Oxford: Oxford University Press, 1935), 18–20, 54, 155, 256; Bews, "The Ecological Viewpoint," *South African Journal of Science* 28 (1931): 1–15; Anker, *Imperial Ecology*, 166–67, 171–75.
140. Bews, *Human Ecology*, 159.
141. Julian Huxley, *Africa View* (New York: Harper and Brothers, 1931), 442–49.
142. H. G. Wells, *The Fate of Man* (New York: Longmans, Green and Co., 1939), 191–92.
143. H. G. Wells, *The Outline of History* (London: Newness, 1920); Wells, *Experiment in Autobiography* (Boston: Little, Brown, 1934), 552, 616–17; Lester, *E. Ray Lankester*, 87, 176–77, 198–202; Peter J. Bowler, *Science for All* (Chicago: University of Chicago Press, 2009), 47–48, 104. Lankester indicated in a letter to Wells that he thought that *The Outline of History* was too Eurocentric, as it should consider the Byzantine and Islamic civilizations. Lester, *E. Ray Lankester*, 178.
144. H. G. Wells, *Men Like Gods* (New York: Macmillan, 1923), 107–8.
145. Lester, *E. Ray Lankester*, 176.
146. Julian Huxley, *Essays in Popular Science* (London: Chatto and Windus, 1926), 67–74.
147. Bowler, *Science for All*, 105–7; Anker, *Imperial Ecology*, 110–17; H. G. Wells, Julian Huxley, and G. P. Wells, *The Science of Life* (New York: Literary Guild, 1934), 976, 987, 1009–11, 1022. The overall structure of *The Science of Life* was determined by its materialist depiction of life as metabolism and interaction, both at the beginning and by the closing section of the book.
148. Wells, Huxley, and Wells, *The Science of Life*, 4–5.
149. Ibid., 961–62.
150. Ibid., 961–66, 989.
151. Ibid., 1012, 1025. See also H. G. Wells, *The Work, Wealth and Happiness of Mankind* (Garden City, NY: Doubleday, 1931), 180–81. On Marx's theory of metabolic rift see John Bellamy Foster, *Marx's Ecology* (New York: Monthly Review Press, 2000), 141–77.
152. Wells, Huxley, and Wells, *The Science of Life*, 966.
153. Ibid., 1029–30.
154. Ibid., 1027.
155. Ibid., 1028.
156. Ibid., 1029.
157. Ibid., 1029–31.
158. Ibid., 1031–32.
159. Ibid., 1030.
160. A. G. Tansley, "The Use and Abuse of Vegetational Concepts and Terms," *Ecology* 16/3 (July 1935): 284–307.
161. Anker, *Imperial Ecology*, 119.
162. Ibid., 131–33.
163. Tansley, who recognized the importance of his Magdalen "Temporal Genetic Series" paper with respect to the debate on holism, sent a copy of it to Phillips, whose views he opposed, but no doubt with the intention of generating a constructive debate. Phillips saw Tansley's essay as "an onslaught on holism" by "a good old mechanist of the conservative type" and sent a copy on to Smuts, who was occupied elsewhere at the time and did not reply. Phillips quoted in Anker, *Imperial Ecology*, 152.
164. J. J. O'Connor and E .F. Robertson, "Hyman Levy," MacTutor History of Mathematics

Archive, School of Mathematics and Statistics, University of St. Andrews, Scotland, http://www-groups.dcs.st-and.ac.uk/~history/Biographies/Levy_Hyman.html; Werskey, *The Visible College*, 44–52, 115–27; Hogben, *Lancelot Hogben: Scientific Humanist*, 128 Biographical Description of Levy, in Hyman Levy Collection, Charles Deering McCormick Library of Special Collections, Northwestern University Library, Evanston, Illinois.

165. Hyman Levy, *The Universe of Science* (London: Watts and Co., 1932), vi.
166. Ibid., 53–54.
167. Ibid., 51–52.
168. Ibid., 19, 77–80.
169. Ibid., 79.
170. Ibid., 74–75; Lucretius, *On the Nature of the Universe* (London: Penguin, 1951), 30 (I: 817–22). Smuts rejected Morgan's emergent evolution for laying stress on "emergence" rather than "the tendency to wholes, ever more intensive and effective wholes, which," according to Smuts, "is basic to the universe." Smuts, *Holism and Evolution*, 321.
171. Levy, *The Universe of Science*, 78, 80.
172. Hyman Levy, *A Philosophy for a Modern Man* (New York: Alfred A. Knopf, 1938).
173. John Phillips, "Succession, Development, the Climax, and the Complex Organism: An Analysis of Concepts," *Journal of Ecology*, Part 1, vol. 22 (1934): 565; Part 2, vol. 23 (1935): 216; Part 3, vol. 23 (1935): 488; 504; Anker, *Imperial Ecology*, 150–51; Golley, *A History of the Ecosystem Concept in Ecology*, 22–26.
174. Frederick Clements, "Experimental Ecology in Public Service," *Ecology* 16 (1935): 342; Anker, *Imperial Ecology*, 153, 165; Robert McIntosh, *The Background of Ecology* (Cambridge: Cambridge University Press, 1985), 303.
175. Tansley, "The Use and Abuse of Vegetational Concepts and Terms," 285–86.
176. For a related argument to the one that follows see Foster, Clark, and York, *The Ecological Rift*, 327–31.
177. Tansley, "The Use and Abuse," 286–90.
178. Ibid., 289, 293, 295–97, 306.
179. Ibid., 299; Phillips, "Succession, Development, the Climax, and the Complex Organism," Part 3, 500; Anker, *Imperial Ecology*, 153.
180. Ayres writes: "Introduced to the world of ecology by Tansley who, in view of his detailed explanation and justification of it, has received credit for it, the term 'ecosystem' was actually suggested to Tansley in the early 1930s by his young colleague, [A. Roy] Clapham. This happened when Tansley asked him if he could think of a suitable word to denote the physical and biological components of an environment considered in relation to each other as a unit." Ayres, *Shaping Ecology*, 138. Nicholas Polunin, Tansley's student at the time that he introduced the notion of ecosystem, recalls that Tansley extensively discussed "the theme of vegetation as a 'quasi-organism,' but concluded that more should be considered together with it, and so came out with what he was apt to write on the blackboard in two words as 'eco system.' This was composed of both the inorganic and dead parts of the system and the various organisms which live together in it and comprise the *biota*." Nicholas Polunin, "Preface," in Polunin, *Ecosystem Theory and Application* (New York: John Wiley and Sons, 1986), xiv.
181. Tansley, "The Use and Abuse," 299–300; Levy, *The Universe of Science*.
182. Tansley, "The Use and Abuse," 300; Lucretius, *On the Nature of the Universe*, 4 (II: 215–30).

183. Tansley, "The Use and Abuse," 300–302.
184. Ibid., 303–4.
185. A. G. Tansley, "British Ecology During the Past Quarter-Century: The Plant Community and the Ecosystem," *Journal of Ecology* 27/2 (August 1939): 518, 524; Tansley, *The British Islands and their Vegetation* (Cambridge: Cambridge University Press, 1939), vi.
186. Tansley, *The British Islands and Their Vegetation*, 128.
187. Arthur G. Tansley, "What Is Ecology?," *Biological Journal of the Linnaean Society* 32 (1987): 9–14.
188. On the later history of the ecosystem concept, see Golley, *A History of the Ecosystem Concept in Ecology*.
189. E. P. Odum, "Introductory Review: Perspective of Ecosystem Theory and Application," in Polunin, *Ecosystem Theory and Application*, 1–4, *Fundamentals of Ecology* (Philadelphia: W. B. Saunders, 1953).
190. Polunin, "Preface," *Ecosystem Theory and Application*, xiv; Nicholas Polunin and Jacques Grinevald, "Vernadsky and Biospheral Ecology," *Environmental Conservation* 15/2 (Summer 1988): 117–22; Jacques Grinevald, "Introduction," in Vernadsky, *The Biosphere*, 22.

CHAPTER NINE: THE RETURN OF ENGELS

1. J. G. Crowther, *Fifty Years with Science* (London: Barrie and Jenkins, 1970), 76–80; Gary Werskey, *The Visible College* (London: Penguin, 1978), 138–49; "New Introduction: On the Reception of *Science at the Cross Roads* in England," in Nikolai Bukharin et al., *Science at the Cross Roads* (London: Frank Cass, 1971), xi–xxix; Neal Wood, *Communism and the British Intellectuals* (New York: Columbia University Press, 1959), 123–26; Helena Sheehan, *Marxism and the Philosophy of Science: A Critical History* (Atlantic Highlands, NJ: Humanities Press, 1985), 206–9; Edwin A. Roberts, *The Anglo-Marxists* (New York: Rowman and Littlefield, 1997), 149–53.
2. Karl Marx, *Texts on Method* (Oxford: Basil Blackwell, 1975), 190; N. I. Bukharin, "Theory and Practice from the Standpoint of Dialectical Materialism," in Bukharin et al., *Science at the Cross Roads*, 12–13.
3. Bukharin, "Theory and Practice," 12.
4. Ibid., 13, 17.
5. Ibid., 17; Vladimir I. Vernadsky, *The Biosphere* (New York: Springer-Verlag, 1998); Karl Pearson, *The Grammar of Science* (London: Adam and Charles Black, 1911), 60–63. In 1930, Bukharin replaced Vernadsky as the head of the Institute of the History of Sciences and Technology, previously known as the Commission on the History of Sciences. See Jacques Grinevald, "Vladimir Ivanovich Vernadsky (1863–1945): A Biographical Chronology," in Vernadsky, *The Biosphere*, 156.
6. Bukharin, "Theory and Practice," 16, 19–20.
7. Ibid., 14; Nikolai Bukharin, *Historical Materialism* (New York: International Publishers, 1925), 108; Nikolai I. Bukharin, *Philosophical Arabesques* (New York: Monthly Review Press, 2005), 114.
8. Bukharin, "Theory and Practice," 22, 33; Bukharin, *Historical Materialism*, 108–12. It should be noted that Marx's use of social and ecological metabolism was taken from the work *Mikrokosmos* by his good friend Roland Daniels, who died as a result of an illness contracted while he was imprisoned during the Cologne Communist Trials, and to whom Marx dedicated *The Poverty of Philosophy*. Daniels wrote extensively in *Mikrokosmos* on *Stoffwechsel* (metabolism), depicting that the entire plant and animal

community mutually condition each other, a reality he captured with the concept of metabolism. This, then, constituted the root of Marx's conception, and anticipated later systems ecology. See Roland Daniels, *Mikrokosmos* (New York: Verlag Peter Lang, 1988), 49.

9. Karl Marx and Frederick Engels, *Collected Works* (New York: International Publishers, 1975), vol. 25, 113.
10. Bukharin, *Philosophical Arabesques*, 60, 198.
11. Ibid., 101–02.
12. Ibid., 259, 350; Marx and Engels, *Collected Works,* 4:83, 25:331–32, 350; Nikolai Bukharin et al., *Marxism and Modern Thought* (New York: Harcourt Brace and Co., 1935), 35, 37, 83; Karl Marx, *Capital*, vol. 3 (London: Penguin, 1981), 959.
13. B. Zavadovsky, "The 'Physical' and the 'Biological' in the Process of Organic Evolution," in Bukharin et al., *Science at the Cross Roads*, 69–80.
14. Zavadovsky, "The 'Physical' and the 'Biological,'" 70–71.
15. Ibid., 75–77.
16. Ibid., 74–77. It was this last point on integrative levels that Needham stressed again and again, in referring to Zavadovsky's analysis. See Joseph Needham, *Time: The Refreshing River* (London: George Allen and Unwin, 1943), 188–89, 244.
17. Crowther, *Fifty Years with Science*, 79.
18. Hessen, "The Social and Economic Roots of Newton's 'Principia,'" in Bukharin et al., *Science at the Cross Roads*, 188.
19. Ibid., 203.
20. Joseph Needham, "Foreword," in Bukharin et al., *Science at the Cross Roads*, vii–x; Crowther, *Fifty Years with Science*, 76–80, 330; Hyman Levy, *Modern Science* (New York: Alfred A. Knopf, 1939), 97; J. D. Bernal, *The Social Function of Science* (New York: Macmillan, 1939), 406; Bernal, "Dialectical Materialism," in Hyman Levy et al., *Aspects of Dialectical Materialism* (London: Watts and Co., 1934), 110–11; Eric Hobsbawm, "Preface," in Brenda Swann and Francis Aprahamian, *J. D. Bernal: A Life in Science and Politics* (London: Verso, 1999), xvii; W. Adams, "The International Congress of the History of Science and Technology," *History* 16/63 (October 1931): 212–13; Crowther, *Fifty Years with Science*, 86–87, 142–43.
21. Stephen F. Cohen, "Introduction," in Nikolai Bukharin, *How It All Began* (New York: Columbia University Press, 1998), vii–xxviii; Léon Rosenfeld, *Physics, Philosophy and Politics in the Twentieth Century* (Hackensack, NJ: World Scientific Publishing, 2012), 143; Peter Pringle, *The Murder of Nikolai Vavilov* (New York: Simon and Schuster, 2008), 310; Vadim J. Birstein, *The Perversion of Knowledge* (Boulder, CO: Westview Press, 2001), 252, 255. Lysenkoism, it should be noted, involved genuine scientific issues, and the debates in that respect in the Soviet Union in this period, could, notwithstanding the weaknesses of Lysenko's own work, have pushed scientific discussions forward. Unfortunately, it was coupled with political denunciations and purges that violated all standards of scientific ethics, leading to the imprisonment and death of leading scientific figures. See Richard Levins and Richard Lewontin, *The Dialectical Biologist* (Cambridge, MA: Harvard University Press, 1985), 163–96.
22. Even in 1971, when Needham wrote his Foreword to the 1971 edition of *Science at the Cross Roads*, the fate of Hessen was unknown, and presumably that of Zavadovsky as well, and the full story on Vavilov came out only slowly.
23. Stalin's purging of major ecological thinkers as well as many of the core political and intellectual figures of the Russian Revolution in general put a huge damper on Soviet development in this area and encouraged the reduction of official dialectical materialism

into a kind of rigid dogmatism antagonistic to any meaningful dialectical perspective. Nevertheless, critical dialectical views persisted in the margins and in important pockets in Soviet science. An example is the importance of biospheric thought following Vernadsky, Sukachev's introduction of the concept of biogeocoenosis, and advances in climate science. See John Bellamy Foster, "Late Soviet Ecology and the Planetary Crisis," *Monthly Review* 67/2 (June 2015): 1–20.

24. J. B. S. Haldane, "Darwinism and Its Perversions" (1948), Haldane Papers, University College London, Reference HALDANE/2/1/2/203.
25. Roberts, *The Anglo-Marxists*, 144; Helena Sheehan, "J. D. Bernal: Philosophy, Politics and the Science of Science," *Journal of Physics: Conference Series* 57 (2007): 38.
26. Eric Hobsbawm, "Era of Wonders," *London Review of Books* 31/4 (February 2009): 19–20.
27. Wood, *Communism and British Intellectuals*, 144–45; H. B. Acton, *The Illusion of the Epoch* (Boston: Beacon Press, 1955), 254. For a strong critique of Wood's views, see Roberts, *The Anglo-Marxists*. Wood later identified with the British New Left and with historical materialism but, as I learned in conversations with him, never altered his views on the British scientists of the 1930s and 1940s.
28. John Bellamy Foster, *Marx's Ecology* (New York: Monthly Review Press, 2000), 5–6, 21–65. On Epicurus, materialism, and modernity, see Stephen Greenblatt, *The Swerve: How the World Became Modern* (New York: W. W. Norton, 2011).
29. Benjamin Farrington, *Francis Bacon: Philosopher of Industrial Science* (New York: Collier, 1949). Farrington's book, though useful, was less political and far-reaching in its analysis than most of his work. He wrote in a letter to Bernal on November 25, 1950: "The book was written for Schuman's Life of Science series. It had to be popular and fit to publish in the USA. It therefore suffers from limitations other than my own ignorance." Bernal Papers, Cambridge University Library, Farrington Correspondence file.
30. Benjamin Farrington, *Science and Politics in the Ancient World* (London: George Allen and Unwin, 1939); *Head and Hand in Ancient Greece* (London: Watts and Co., 1947); *The Faith of Epicurus* (London: Weidenfeld and Nicolson, 1967).
31. George Thomson, *The First Philosophers* (London: Lawrence and Wishart, 1955), 311–14.
32. Joseph Needham, *The Great Amphibium* (New York: Charles Scribner's Sons, 1932), 35.
33. Needham, *Time: The Refreshing River*, 20, 124. See also Joseph Needham, "Mechanistic Biology and the Religious Consciousness," in Needham, ed., *Science, Religion, and Reality* (New York: George Braziller, 1955; original ed. 1925), 230–31.
34. J. D. Bernal, *The Extension of Man* (Cambridge, MA: MIT Press, 1972), 85–88. On the recognition of Epicurus's importance see J. D. Bernal, *The Origin of Life* (New York: World Publishing Company, 1967), 11, 20; and Bernal, *Marx and Science* (London: Lawrence and Wishart, 1952), 11–12.
35. J. B. S. Haldane, "Eighty Years of Darwinism," December 7, 1939, Haldane Papers, University College London, handwritten document, Reference HALDANE/2/1/3/47.
36. Lancelot Hogben, *Lancelot Hogben: Socialist Humanist* (London: Merlin Press, 1998), 105.
37. Bacon was of course greatly admired by these thinkers, along with most British scientists, for his role in the promotion of the institution of science itself, and particularly the inspiration that his work gave to the creation of the Royal Society. As Bernal put it, "The ideal of Bacon—the use of science for the welfare of human

beings—was indeed a guiding thread of the constructive side of Marxism." J. D. Bernal, *The Social Function of Science* (New York: Macmillan, 1939), 33. But this would hardly suffice to label these thinkers as "Baconian" or "Baconian Marxists."

38. Marx and Engels, *Collected Works*, 4:126–28.
39. Wood, *Communism and British Intellectuals*, 138–44, 150.
40. J. B. S. Haldane, *The Marxist Philosophy and the Sciences* (New York: Random House, 1939), 13–14, 43.
41. For a polemical and distorted attack on these thinkers, reflecting what came to be a common view, see Sidney Hook, *Reason, Social Myths, and Democracy* (New York: Cosimo, 2009), 227–49.
42. Hobsbawm, "Preface," xi–xii; Patrick Blackett, "The Frustration of Science," in Sir Daniel Hall et al., *The Frustration of Science* (New York: Books for Libraries Press, 1935), 144.
43. E. P. Thompson, *Making History* (New York: New Press, 1994), 137.
44. J. B. S. Haldane, *The World, the Flesh, and the Devil* (Bloomington: Indiana University Press, 1969), 73–74; Hilary and Steven Rose, "Red Scientist," in Swann and Aprahamian, *J. D. Bernal*, 132; Wood, *Communism and British Intellectuals*, 136, 140–42. In a fourth characterization of the British Marxian scientists, inconsistent with all the rest, Wood presented them as "nihilists"(121, 143).
45. For a left perspective on the war, see Basil Davidson, *Scenes from the Anti-Nazi War* (New York: Monthly Review Press, 1980).
46. Anderson quoted in Sheehan, "J. D. Bernal: Philosophy, Politics and the Science of Science," 39.
47. Andrew Brown, *J. D. Bernal: The Sage of Science* (Oxford: Oxford University Press, 2005), 205–54.
48. Blackett, "The Frustration of Science," 140–44; Hyman Levy, *Science in an Irrational Society* (London: Watts and Co., 1934).
49. The "first printing" of the English translation by Clemens Dutt of the *Dialectics of Nature* is listed in the Progress Publishers edition (1972, fifth printing) as 1934. However, the work, which had presented immense problems for its editors, was undergoing revisions at that time in its Russian and German editions, including the clarification of certain passages, and an accessible English-language edition does not seem to have been available until the publication of the 1940 International Press edition, with the preface and notes by J.B.S. Haldane. See Frederick Engels, *Dialectics of Nature* (New York: International Publishers, 1940); Marx and Engels, *Collected Works*, 25:663.
50. This can be seen in Haldane's *The Marxist Philosophy and the Sciences*, in which the five works emphasized in the text (and for which abbreviations were provided) were the three works by Engels then available in English (*Anti-Dühring*, *The Origin of the Family*, and *Ludwig Feuerbach*), along with Marx's *Capital* and Lenin's *Materialism and Empirico-Criticism*. Almost all of the references with respect to the dialectics of science in the text are thus to Engels. Engels's *Dialectics of Nature* is also mentioned, which Haldane, who wrote the 1939 preface to the 1940 English edition translated by Clemens Dutt, had already seen by that point. The overall impression is an attempt to relate Engels's views to contemporary science, with little in the way of other Marxian influences. See J. B. S. Haldane, *The Marxist Philosophy and the Sciences* (New York: Random House, 1939).
51. See Cyril Bailey, "Karl Marx and Greek Atomism," *Classical Quarterly* 22/3–4 (July–October 1928): 205–6.

52. Werskey, *The Visible College*, 68, 74; Anne Synge, "Early Years and Influences," in Swann and Aprahamian, *J. D. Bernal: A Life*; "Calendar of Events," in Swann and Parahuman, *J. D. Bernal: A Life*, 303–4; 1–5; Brown, *J. D. Bernal: The Sage*, 1–3; C. P. Snow, "J. D. Bernal: A Personal Portrait," in Maurice Goldsmith and Alan Mackay, *The Science of Science* (Harmondsworth: Penguin, 1964), 19–21.
53. Snow, "J. D. Bernal," 25; C. P. Snow, *The Search* (New York: Charles Scribner's, 1934).
54. J. D. Bernal, "The Structure of Matter," *Modern Quarterly* 3/3 (July 1939): 272–76; Peter Trent, "The Scientist," in Swan and Aprahamian, *J. D. Bernal: A Life*, 80–92; Snow, "J. D. Bernal," 25–26; Hyman Levy, *A Philosophy for a Modern Man* (New York: Alfred A. Knopf, 1938), 40–42; Gale Rhodes, *Crystallography Made Crystal Clear* (New York: Academic Press, 2000); Ashish Lahiri, "Needham and Bernal," in Sushil Kumar Mukherjee and Amitabha Ghosh, *The Life and Works of Joseph Needham* (Calcutta: Asiatic Society, 1997), 136–39.
55. Fred Steward, "Political Formation," in Swann and Aprahamian, *J. D Bernal: A Life*, 37–45, 57–60; Brown, *J. D. Bernal: The Sage*, 70; Synge, "Early Years and Influences," 13–14.
56. J. D. Bernal, *Engels and Science* (London: Labour Monthly Pamphlets, n.d. (article version 1935, pamphlet printing 1936), 12–13.
57. Maurice Goldsmith, *Sage: A Life of J. D. Bernal* (London: Hutchinson, 1980), 223–24; Werskey, *Visible College*, 82; Steward, "Political Formation," and Hilary Rose and Steven Rose, "Red Scientist" in Swann and Aprahamian, *J. D Bernal: A Life*, 45–48, 132–35; Brown, *J. D. Bernal: The Sage*, 42–45, 56–58; Bernal, *Engels and Science*, 12–13.
58. J. D. Bernal, "Dialectical Materialism," in Hyman Levy et al., *Aspects of Dialectical Materialism* (London: Watts and Co., 1934), 89–122.
59. Bernal, "Dialectical Materialism," 89, 101, 109. The Bernal papers in the Cambridge University Library include extensive notes by Bernal on dialectics, most of them quite cryptic, made for his own use in composing his various essays on dialectics, in which he attempted to outline and diagram the main conceptual relations. They indicate the utmost seriousness with which he approached the subject.
60. Bernal, "Dialectical Materialism," 92–95, 115.
61. Ibid., 96, 107.
62. Ibid., 104–6, 112.
63. Ibid., 97–102.
64. Ibid., 115; J. D. Bernal, "Notes in Reply to Mr. Carritt's Paper," in Levy, et. al., *Aspects of Dialectical Materialism*, 148.
65. Bernal, "Dialectical Materialism," 103–4. Sociologist and philosopher Henri Lefebvre, who was a close student of dialectical materialism, developed a philosophical approach focusing on "the method of residues" that was no doubt influenced by Bernal's conception of residuals, which entered into discussion of dialectics in the 1930s and '40s, and was seen as crucial to the understanding of the emergence of novel entities and the negation of the negation. See Henri Lefebvre, *Metaphilosophy* (London: Verso, 2016), 291–304; Lefebvre, *Dialectical Materialism* (London: Jonathan Cape, 1974).
66. Bernal, *Engels and Science*, 1–2.
67. Ibid., 5.
68. Ibid., 5–7; Marx and Engels, *Collected Works*, 25:359 (translation follows Bernal).
69. Bernal, *Engels and Science*, 7.
70. Ibid., 8; Bernal, "Dialectical Materialism," 107–8.

71. Bernal, *Engels and Science*, 8–10; Frederick Engels, *Ludwig Feuerbach and the Outcome of Classical German Philosophy* (New York: International Publishers, 1941), 65–69.
72. Bernal, *Engels and Science*, 4.
73. Ibid., 10–12.
74. Richard Levins and Richard Lewontin, *The Dialectical Biologist* (Cambridge, MA: Harvard University Press, 1985), 277; A. I. Oparin, "The Origin of Life," in J. D. Bernal, *The Origin of Life* (New York: World Publishing Co., 1967), 197–234; J. B. S. Haldane, "The Origin of Life," in Bernal, *The Origin of Life*, 242–49; A. I. Oparin, *Life: Its Nature, Origin, and Development* (New York: Academic Press, 1962).
75. See Bernal, *The Origin of Life*, 237–38. Vernadsky himself, though emphasizing that life was the major geological force with respect to the earth as a whole, and thus the centrality of the biosphere, for a long time resisted the idea that life had originated from inorganic matter. Rather, he wrote: "Living organisms have never been produced by inert matter." Vernadsky, *The Biosphere*, 56.
76. Bernal, *Engels and Science*, 13–14.
77. Bernal, "Dialectical Materialism," 90, 102, 107, 112–17.
78. Benjamin Farrington, "Introduction," in J. D. Bernal, *Marx and Science* (London: Lawrence and Wishart, 1952). If *Marx and Science* was, as Farrington said, one of Bernal's most penetrating discussions of Marx and science, his piece "Stalin as a Scientist," *Modern Quarterly* 8/1 (Winter 1952–53): 133–142, was undoubtedly his worst. Despite the grand title it was not a work of scholarship but rather an obituary, with all the attendant weaknesses, including suspension of judgment, that typically accompany the latter. For another interpretation, see Goldsmith, *Sage*, 206–7.
79. Bernal, *Marx and Science*, 11–12.
80. Ibid., 27–29.
81. Ibid., 20.
82. Ibid., 6, 55; Frederick Engels, "The Funeral of Karl Marx," in *Karl Marx Remembered*, ed. Philip S. Foner (San Francisco: Synthesis Publications, 1983), 38–40.
83. Stephen Jay Gould, *Ever Since Darwin* (New York: W. W. Norton, 1977), 262.
84. Roberts, *The Anglo-Marxists*, 179; Werskey, *The Visible College*, 59–60; First World War.com, "The Battle of Loos, 1915," http://www.firstworldwar.com/battles/loos.htm; J. B. S. Haldane, *Science and Everyday Life* (New York: Macmillan, 1940), 139–42.
85. Ronald W. Clark, *JBS: The Life and Work of J. B. S. Haldane* (New York: Coward-McCann Inc., 1968), 57–73, 79–84; Werskey, *The Visible College*, 84.
86. Werskey, *The Visible College*, 83; Egbert G. Leigh, "Introduction," in J. B. S. Haldane, *The Causes of Evolution* (Princeton: Princeton University Press, 1990), ix; Julian Huxley, *Evolution: The Modern Synthesis* (London: George Allen and Unwin, 1963), 21–22, 27–34.
87. E. Ray Lankester to H. G. Wells, October 28, 1925, Wells Papers, University of Illinois, Urbana; Lester, *E. Ray Lankester*, 212; Clark, *JBS,* 66; J. B. S. Haldane, "The Causes of Evolution," *R.P.A. Annual, 1926* (London: Rationalist Press Association, 1926),. 54–64.
88. Haldane, *The Causes of Evolution*, 1, 61, 65, 78–91.
89. J. B. S. Haldane, *Daedalus: Science and the Future* (New York: E. P. Dutton, 1924), 23–26.
90. Vladimir I. Vernadsky, "Evolution of Species and Living Matter: Appendix to the Biosphere," in Jason Ross, ed., *150 Years of Vernadsky,* vol. 2: *The Noösphere* (Washington, D.C.: 21st Century Science and Technology, 2014), 48; Jacques Grinevald, "Introduction," in Vernadsky, *The Biosphere*, 30.

91. J. B. S. Haldane, *Science and Life* (London: Pemberton Publishing, 1968), 6–11; Bernal, *The Origin of Life*, 24–35; Richard Levins and Richard Lewontin, *The Dialectical Biologist* (Cambridge, MA: Harvard University Press, 1985), 277.
92. Lynn Margulis et al., "Foreword," in V. I. Vernadsky, *The Biosphere* (New York: Copernicus, 1998), 15.
93. Rachel Carson, *Lost Woods* (Boston: Beacon Press, 1998), 229–30.
94. Werskey, *Visible College*, 159. In the preface to his 1938 *Science and Everyday Life*, which republished many of his *Daily Worker* articles, Haldane compared this to the earlier set of essays written by E. Ray Lankester for the *Daily Telegraph*. Haldane, *Science and Everyday Life*, 8.
95. Clark, *JBS*, 139–45; Sven Lindqvist, *A History of Bombing*, sections 156–62; British Batallion," XV International Brigade in Spain," https://internationalbrigadesinspain.weebly.com/british-battalion.html.
96. Haldane wrote at the outset of his book that he was entering areas, such as philosophy and Marxism, with which he had limited acquaintance. Here he claimed: "I am by no means qualified to speak on Marxism. I have only been a Marxist for about a year" (*The Marxist Philosophy and the Sciences*, 3). It was clear that he was still in some ways at the beginning of his studies in this respect and was weak on the philosophy and political economy. Still, he had considered himself a socialist in some sense since the early 1920s and had been studying socialist work off and on during this period. As he indicated, he had read numerous Marxist works before actually becoming a Marxist. Moreover, he had had considerable contact with socialists in the Spanish Civil War and had given lectures to mass working audiences, as well as writing for the *Daily Worker*. His statement about his own lack of knowledge can thus not be taken as ignorance but rather as a sense of gaps in his background in this respect, natural for someone approaching Marxism mainly from the standpoint of natural science, however learned in that respect.
97. Haldane, *The Marxist Philosophy and the Sciences*, 7–8.
98. Ibid., 10–14.
99. Ibid., 43–44, 119, 132–33; Edward B. Poulton, "The History of Evolutionary Thought," *Science* 86 (September 3, 1937): 209–10; Huxley, *Evolution: The Modern Synthesis*, 458; Ernst Mayr, *The Growth of Biological Thought* (Cambridge, MA: Harvard University Press, 1982), 535.
100. Haldane, *The Marxist Philosophy and the Sciences* , 43, 133; J.B.S, Haldane, *Adventures of a Biologist* (New York: Harper and Brothers, 1940), 228–29, 255.
101. Haldane, *The Marxist Philosophy and the Sciences*, 133.
102. Ibid., 23–24.
103. Ibid., 25, 107; J. B. S. Haldane, *A Banned Broadcast and Other Essays* (London: Chatto and Windus, 1946), 241; and Haldane, "Dialectical Account of Evolution," *Science and Society* 1/4 (Summer 1934): 473.
104. Haldane, *The Marxist Philosophy and the Sciences*, 27–28.
105. Ibid., 32–40; Levy, *A Philosophy for a Modern Man*, 30–32, 117, 227–28.
106. Haldane, *The Marxist Philosophy and the Sciences*, 31, 41.
107. Haldane, *The Causes of Evolution*, 90.
108. Levy, *A Philosophy for a Modern Man.*
109. Haldane, *The Marxist Philosophy and the Sciences*, 109.
110. Haldane, *Science and Everyday Life*, 122.
111. Hyman Levy, "Ends and Means Lecture: Scientific and Mathematical Thinking," n.d., Hyman Levy Papers, Charles Deering McCormick Library of Special Collections, Northwestern University.

112. Haldane, *Science and Everyday Life*, 124.
113. Haldane, *The Marxist Philosophy and the Sciences*, 199–200.
114. Ibid., 119–20, 138; Stephen Jay Gould and Niles Eldredge, "Punctuated Equilibria: The Tempo and Mode of Evolution Reconsidered," *Paleobiology* 6 (1977): 115–51.
115. Richard Lewontin, *The Triple Helix: Gene, Organism, and Environment* (Cambridge, MA: Harvard University Press, 2000), 42, 47.
116. Ibid., title page, 64.
117. Haldane, *The Marxist Philosophy and the Sciences*, 141–42.
118. Gould, *Ever Since Darwin*, 79–90.
119. J. B. S. Haldane, "Darwinism and Its Perversions," Haldane Papers, University College London Special Collections, n.d.
120. Charles Elton, "Animal Numbers and Adaptation," in G. R. de Beer, *Evolution* (Oxford: Oxford University Press, 1938), 131.
121. Joel B. Hagen, *An Entangled Bank* (New Brunswick, NJ: Rutgers University Press, 1992), 58.
122. Elton, "Animal Numbers and Adaptation," 131–32; Haldane, *The Marxist Philosophy and the Sciences*, 141–43.
123. Haldane, *Science and Everyday Life*, 125–26. The original handwritten copy of "Beyond Darwin" in the Haldane Papers is dated August 4, 1938. Instructions are given at the end of the article to send a copy to Charles Elton at Oxford. J. B. S. Haldane, "Beyond Darwin," August 4, 1938, Haldane Papers, University College, London, Special Collections, Reference HALDANE/2/1/3/2.
124. Haldane, *Causes of Evolution*, 65, 86, 117, 126, 128.
125. Haldane, *A Banned Broadcast*, 241–42; Frank Benjamin Golley, *A History of the Ecosystem Concept in Ecology* (New Haven: Yale University Press, 1993), 48–54, 62; J. D. Ovington, "Quantitative Ecology and the Woodland Ecosystem Concept," in *Advances in Ecological Research* 1 (1962): 104–5; Foster, "The Planetary Crisis of Late Soviet Ecology," 4–5; 18–19.
126. Haldane, *A Banned Broadcast*, 192–94.
127. Ibid., 192–94.
128. J. B. S. Haldane, "The Argument from Animals to Man," *Journal of the Royal Anthropological Institute of Great Britain and Ireland* 86/2 (December 1956): 1–14.
129. J. B. S. Haldane, "Overcrowding in the Zoo," Haldane Papers, University College, London, Special Collections, n.d.; Haldane, *A Banned Broadcast*, 213, 230.
130. Haldane, *Science and Everyday Life*, 143, 150, 152.
131. Haldane, *Adventures of a Biologist*, 1–8. At the time Haldane was writing, the notion of anthropogenic global warming was still a farfetched idea. Guy Steward Callendar argued before the Royal Meteorological Society in 1938 that carbon dioxide in the atmosphere was rising as a result of climate change, drawing on evidence mostly from old and obscure publications, and contended that this was having an effect on the climate, but very few meteorologists took his claims seriously and accurate measurements were not available. Callendar saw global warming as beneficial to humanity. One of the principal sources of the data on carbon dioxide concentration in the atmosphere upon which Callendar relied was the work of J. B. S. Haldane's father, John Scott Haldane, presented in *Nature* in 1935 in an article by J. B. S. Haldane. See Spencer Weart, *The Discovery of Global Warming* (Cambridge, Massachusetts: Harvard University Press, 2003), 2, 18–19; G.S. Calllendar, "On the Amount of Carbon Dioxide in the Atmosphere," *Tellus* 10/2 (1958): 245, 248, http://www.rescuethatfrog.com/wp-content/uploads/2017/01/Callendar-1958.pdf; J. B.

S. Haldane, "Carbon Dioxide Content of Atmospheric Air," *Nature* 137 (April 4, 1936), 575 (presenting his father's research).

132. Haldane, *A Banned Broadcast*, 196–97.
133. J. B. S. Haldane, "Britain's Trees" (1940s), Haldane Papers, University College London Special Collections, Reference HALDANE/2/1/2/6.
134. J. B. S. Haldane, "Farming the Sea" (1940s), Haldane Papers, University College, London Special Collections, reference HALDANE/2/1/2/48.
135. Haldane, *Science and Everyday Life*, 236–39. The handwritten article of "Back to Nature?," originally titled "Drugs: Back to Nature?," dated August 18, 1938, is available in the Haldane Papers, University College, London, Special Collections, Box 7. "Stiff colours" refers to the attempt by painters such as George Frederic Watts to counter industrial oil paints by requesting special, stiff, dry paints replicating the textures of preindustrial paints, see Kirsty Sinclair Dootson, "The Texture of Capitalism," *British Art Studies*, November 29, 2019, https://britishartstudies.ac.uk/issues/issue-index/issue-14/texture-of-capitalism. Haldane may have had in mind the more general move to synthetic organic compounds in the paints of the early twentieth century, some of which were toxic.
136. Haldane, *Science and Everyday Life*, 262–66; J. B. S. Haldane, *Heredity and Politics* (New York: W.W. Norton, 1938), 180–89.
137. Haldane, *A Banned Broadcast*, 235.
138. Haldane, *The Marxist Philosophy and the Social Sciences*, 185–89; Haldane, *Science and Everyday Life*, 105.
139. Mansel Davies, "Obituary: Joseph Needham," *Independent*, March 26, 1995, http://www.independent.co.uk/voices/obituaryjoseph-needham-1612984.html.
140. Henry Holorenshaw (Joseph Needham), "The Making of an Honorary Taoist," in Mikuláš Teich and Robert Young, eds., *Changing Perspectives in the History of Science: Essays in Honor of Joseph Needham* (London: Heinemann, 1973), 1–20; Maurice Goldsmith, *Joseph Needham: Twentieth Century Renaissance Man* (Paris: UNESCO, 1995), 19–24, 64; Simon Winchester, *The Man Who Loved China* (New York: HarperCollins, 2008), 11–14; Werskey, *The Visible College*, 68; Sheehan, *Marxism and the Philosophy of Science*, 331; "Alicia Adelaide Montgomery," Wikipedia, https://en.wikipedia.org/wiki/Alicia_Adélaide_Needham.
141. Goldsmith, *Joseph Needham*, 25–27.
142. Joseph Needham, *Within the Four Seas* (Toronto: University of Toronto Press, 1969), 176; Goldsmith, *Joseph Needham*, 31–33.
143. J. B. S. Haldane, "The Biochemistry of the Individual," in Joseph Needham and David E. Green, eds., *Perspectives in Biochemistry* (Cambridge: Cambridge University Press, 1937), 1; Goldsmith, *Joseph Needham*, 33–38; Holorenshaw (Needham), "The Making of an Honorary Taoist," 7; Werskey, *The Visible College*, 78.
144. Goldsmith, *Joseph Needham*, 41–43; Winchester, *The Man Who Loved China*, 25–27; Joseph Needham, *Biochemistry and Morphogenesis* (Cambridge: Cambridge University Press, 1942).
145. Winchester, *The Man Who Loved China*, 6, 37–38, 193–95, 239. 246–47.
146. Holorenshaw (Needham), "The Making of an Honorary Taoist," 5.
147. Needham, *Time: The Refreshing River*, 166–71.
148. Goldsmith, *Joseph Needham*, 61–62; Holorenshaw (Needham), "The Making of an Honorary Taoist," 8.
149. Needham, *Time: The Refreshing River*, 12; Maurice Goldsmith, "Joseph Needham, Honorary Taoist," in Mukherjee and Ghosh, *The Life and Works of Joseph Needham*, 12; Goldsmith, *Joseph Needham*, 29.

150. Goldsmith, *Joseph Needham*, 64-67; Hobsbawm, "Era of Wonders"; Needham, *Time: The Refreshing River*, 6; Conrad Noel, *The Battle of Flags* (London: Labour Publishing Co., 1922).
151. Holorenshaw (Needham), "The Making of an Honorary Taoist," 9.
152. Goldsmith, *Joseph Needham*, 62–63; Winchester, *The Man Who Loved China*, 32–33.
153. Hobsbawm wrote: "The 1931 Congress and his discovery of China in 1937 have been suggested as the two events that shaped Needham's life." Hobsbawm, "Era of Wonders," 19–20.
154. Joseph Needham, "Foreword" in Bukharin et al., *Science at the Cross Roads*, vii–x; Needham, *Time: The Refreshing River*, 188–89, 244; Needham, *Order and Life* (New Haven: Yale University Press, 1936), 44–46. The importance of Zavadovksy is clear in Needham's notes for his 1937 Herbert Spencer Lecture at Oxford University, where "Zavadovksy's definition" of integrated levels occupies a prominent place at one point in his sketching out of the structure of the lecture. Joseph Needham Papers, Cambridge University Library, "Integrated Levels: A Reevaluation of the Idea of Progress" (a page outlining the Needham's plan for his Herbert Spencer Lecture).
155. Joseph Needham, *The Grand Titration* (Toronto: University of Toronto Press, 1969), 124. In listing this same group of thinkers, beginning with Marx and Engels, at another point, Needham indicated: "All these have much help to give to the scientific worker and the greatest of them is the first." Needham, *Time, the Refreshing River*, 112–13. Needham invariably included Jan Christiaan Smuts (coming up last) in his list of thinkers in this regard. He was clearly impressed by Smuts's concept of "integrated wholes." Needham, *Within the Four Seas*, 95. Indeed, in his preparatory notes for his Herbert Spencer Lecture on *Integrated Levels*, Needham went so far as to write of Smuts's *Holism and Evolution*: "Much better than LL–M [Lloyd Morgan]. Has good wide-ranging detailed account of the organisational levels, clearly sees the social evolutionary side, e.g., pp. 106, 344, 251ff, 296, but does not draw any better conclusions than Whitehead." See Joseph Needham Papers, Cambridge University Library). Given this, it is perhaps surprising that Smuts, unlike the other thinkers here, was not addressed directly in Needham's writings, beyond mere mention. This may be attributable to Needham's awareness of the sharp criticism of Smuts by Wells, Hogben, Julian Huxley, Tansley, and others for the racist and idealist aspects of his holism argument. See the discussion in chapter 7 of this book.
156. Joseph Needham, "Untitled," handwritten draft written in relation to invitation to take part in British Broadcasting Corporation series "A Centenary of *Das Kapital*," located in Science and Civilization China Files, Needham Research Institute in Cambridge. Quoted in Gregory Blue, "Joseph Needham, Heterodox Marxism and the Social Background to Chinee Science," *Science and Society* 62/2 (Summer 1998).
157. Needham, *Time: The Refreshing River*, 20, 55–56, *History Is on Our Side* (New York: Macmillan, 1947), 218; Engels, *Ludwig Feuerbach*, 21.
158. Needham, *Time: The Refreshing River*, 124.
159. Ibid., 259.
160. Ibid., 20, 113; Benjamin Farrington, *Science and Politics of the Ancient World* (London: George Allen and Unwin, 1939).
161. Needham, *History Is on Our Side*, 143.
162. Joseph Needham, "Thoughts on the Problem of Biological Organisation," *Scientia* 26 (August 1932): 87.
163. Needham also followed Lenin in rejecting the neutral monism and idealist "empirico-criticism" of thinkers like Ernst Mach and Richard Avenarius. He wrote "These

thinkers were . . . demolished by the continuator of dialectical materialism, V. I. Lenin in his *Materialism and Empirico-Criticism.* Mind is indeed the product of evolution, but an inability to grasp absolute truth is a fault of slight significance to man in his daily practical and theoretical contact with nature. Man's reason may be imperfect but it is the only tool he has." Needham, *History Is on Our Side*, 142–43.

164. Henry Holorenshaw (Joseph Needham), *The Levellers and the English Revolution* (London: Victor Gollancz Ltd., 1939).
165. Needham, *Time: The Refreshing River*, 31.
166. Ibid., 188–203. Needham argued that the notion of higher levels of social organization as a part of a process of emergent evolution (or integrative levels) was appreciated "much more boldly by Marx and Engels . . . than by Smuts, Lloyd Morgan, or Sellars" (185).
167. Frederic Harrison et al., *Herbert Spencer Lectures: Decennial Issue, 1905–1914* (Oxford: Oxford University Press, 1916); Albert Einstein, "The Method of Theoretical Physics," *Philosophy of Science* 1/2 (April 1934): 163–69. Arthur Tansley, developer of the concept of ecosystem, was to deliver the Herbert Spencer Lecture of 1942, presenting, however, an argument on the separation of pure and applied science with which Needham disagreed. Needham, *Time: The Refreshing River*, 108.
168. These notes are to be found in the Joseph Needham Papers, Cambridge University Library.
169. Of Roy Sellars, the exponent of critical realism, Needham wrote in his notes, after reading *Evolutionary Naturalism*, "Very okay but nothing about society: 'man both in nature and above it.'" Joseph Needham Papers, Cambridge University Library.
170. Needham, *Order and Life*, 45.
171. Needham, *Moulds of Understanding*, 219.
172. Needham, unpublished preparatory notes for *Integrative Levels* (page 2), Joseph Needham Papers, Cambridge University Library.
173. Needham, *Grand Titration*, 124, "Foreword," in *Science at the Cross Roads*, ix.
174. Needham, *Time: The Refreshing River*, 192.
175. Ibid., 185.
176. Needham was much impressed by H. Butterfield's *The Whig Interpretation of History* (London: G. Bell, 1931). His preparatory notes for *Integrated Levels* are critical of "Victorian optimism" as an extreme belief in progress. Joseph Needham Papers, Cambridge University Library.
177. Needham, *Moulds of Understanding*, 277.
178. Needham, *Order and Life*, 17, 46.
179. Needham, *Time: The Refreshing River*, 162–68.
180. Ibid., 166–68, and *Moulds of Understanding*, 278. In responding to eugenics arguments Needham relied heavily on the work of Hogben and Haldane, including the latter's *Human Biology and Politics* (London: The British Guild, 1934) and on an important article by the U.S. Nobel Prize–winning Marxist geneticist H. J. Muller titled "The Dominance of Economics Over Eugenics," *Science Monthly* 37/1 (July 1939): 40–47. See also H. J. Muller, *Out of the Night* (New York: Vanguard Press, 1935). Needham wrote: "It was Muller who discovered the effects of X-rays in increasing the mutation rate of animals—a discovery which, apart from being an important research tool, may still open the way to an understanding of the mechanism of evolution itself. He was for long the director of the biological departments at the University of Texas, and later he organized the famous genetics institute at the Academy of Sciences in Moscow." Needham, *Time: The Refreshing River*, 166.

181. Needham, *The Grand Titration*, 127.
182. Ibid., 126.
183. Needham commonly distinguished between obscurantist organicism, such as in the work of John Scott Haldane (obscurantist since it stipulated forces not open to scientific explanation), with non-obscurantist organicism such as Whitehead. The distinction was attributed by Needham to Nikolai Bukharin et al., *Marxism and Modern Thought* (New York: Harcourt, Brace and Co., 1935), 26. On John Scott Haldane in this respect, see Needham, *Time: The Refreshing River*, 242.
184. Bukharin, "Marx's Teaching and Its Historical Importance," in Bukharin et al., *Marxism and Modern Thought*, 31; Needham, *Time: The Refreshing River*, 243.
185. Needham, "Thoughts on the Problem of Biological Organisation," 86–89; Needham, *Time: The Refreshing River*, 182–83; J. H. Woodger, *Biological Principles: A Critical Study* (New York: Harcourt, Brace, and Co., 1929), 230.
186. Needham, *Time: The Refreshing River*, 18.
187. This argument that dialectical contradictions reflected integrative levels and that the contradictions that arose at one level could only be resolved at a higher level in this sense freed dialectical contradictions from the criticism that they represented a violation of the principle of contradiction, as argued by Karl Popper. See Karl Popper, *Conjectures and Refutations* (London: Routledge, 1963), 424–26, 433–34.
188. Needham, *Time: The Refreshing River*, 14–15. Needham's position here resembles that of Engels who wrote: "The dialectic in our minds is but a reflection of the actual development taking place in the natural world and human history in obedience to dialectical forms." Marx and Engels, *Collected Works*, 49:287.
189. The title of Needham's *Time: The Refreshing River* was inspired by a poem by W. H. Auden, but it reflected at a deeper level the emphasis on changing reality emanating from Heraclitus's ancient Greek philosophy. See Needham, *Time: The Refreshing River*, 15. The object was to point to the dialectical movement of reality and how it was reflected in complex ways in human consciousness.
190. See Popper, *Conjectures and Refutations*, 437.
191. Needham, *Time: The Refreshing River*, 19.
192. Ibid., 18, 178–206; Mortimer J. Adler, *Dialectics* (London: Kegan Paul, Trench, Trubner, and Co., 1927), 166.
193. Needham, *Time: The Refreshing River*, 186, 194.
194. See A. I. Oparin, *Life: Its Nature, Origin, and Development* (New York: Academic Press, 1962).
195. Needham, *Time: The Refreshing River*, 189–91.
196. Ibid., 258; Needham, *The Grand Titration*, 126; Needham, *History Is on Our Side*, 134; Lawrence J. Henderson, *The Fitness of the Environment* (Boston: Beacon Press, 1958), xv.
197. Needham, "Thoughts on the Problem of Biological Organisation," 86.
198. Needham, *Time: The Refreshing River*, 166.
199. Needham, *The Grand Titration*, 125.
200. Needham, *History Is on Our Side*, 129; Needham, *Time: The Refreshing River*, 38; John Bellamy Foster, *Marx's Ecology* (New York: Monthly Review Press, 2000), 149–63. Besides quoting Marx on Liebig in *History Is on Our Side*, Needham demonstrated in his little-known article "Light from the Environment" (available along with the correspondence surrounding it in the Joseph Needham Archives, Cambridge University) his awareness of the classic problem of the robbery of the soil of nutrients such as nitrogen, phosphorous, and potassium, raised by Liebig in the late

1850s and 1860s, and taken up by Marx. Joseph Needham, "Light from the Orient," *Environment* (New Zealand) 20 (Autumn 1978): 11.

201. Erwin Schrödinger, *Science and the Human Temperament* (New York: W. W. Norton, 1935), 48; Needham, *Time: The Refreshing River*, 220–21. Needham was equally impressed by Lotka's application of thermodynamics to biology in his *Elements of Physical Biology*, calling it "one of the three or four greatest contributions to biological thought in the present century" (222). See also his comments on Lotka's energeticism in Needham, *The Grand Titration*, 125–26.
202. Needham, *Time: The Refreshing River*, 231.
203. Needham, "Thoughts on the Problem of Biological Organisation," 92.
204. The Progress publisher edition of *The Dialectics of Nature* indicates that the English translation by Clements Dutt first appeared in the early 1930s, but it had at best very little circulation, and it was the 1940 edition of *The Dialectics of Nature* (including a preface and notes by Haldane) that for the first time made it widely available in English. See Frederick Engels, *Dialectics of Nature* (Moscow: Progress, 1972), 2 (copyright page), 15.
205. J. D. Bernal, *The Freedom of Necessity* (London: Routledge and Kegan Paul, 1949), 359.
206. J. B. S. Haldane, "Preface," in Engels, *Dialectics of Nature*, xii–xiv.
207. Haldane, "Preface," in Engels, *Dialectics of Nature*, viii.
208. Haldane did not seem to recognize that Engels's critical borrowings from Hegel's *Logic* were mainly confined to its first two subdivisions on the Doctrine of Being and the Doctrine of Essence, but this is crucial for understanding not only the dialectic of nature, in Engels's terms, but also its limitations. In the Doctrine of Essence in Hegel, attraction and repulsion play major roles. Although the dialectic at that point does not permit the reflexivity of the fully developed level of the Doctrine of Notion, it does point to attraction and repulsion, contradiction, transformation, etc., which were, for Hegel, part of nature as an implicate order.
209. Haldane, "Preface," in Engels, *Dialectics of Nature*, vii.
210. See Roy Bhaskar, *Philosophy and the Idea of Freedom* (Oxford: Blackwell, 1991), 170.
211. On this see ibid., 162–69.
212. Haldane, "Preface," in *Engels*, *Dialectics of Nature*, vii–viii; V. I. Lenin, *Materialism and Empirico-Criticism: Critical Comments on a Reactionary Philosophy* (New York: International Publishers, 1927), 45, 88; Pearson, *The Grammar of Science*, viii, 60–63.
213. Engels, *Dialectics of Nature*, 196–97 (Marx and Engels, *Collected Works* 25:578); Erwin Schrödinger, *What Is Life?* with *Mind and Matter* (Cambridge: Cambridge University Press, 1967), 70–71; Haldane, "A Dialectical Account of Evolution," 474.
214. Marx and Engels, *Collected Works*, 30: 54–66.
215. Bernal, *The Freedom of Necessity*, 362.
216. Ibid., 364–65. Bernal wrote these words in 1940. Unfortunately, he did not recall Engels's warnings on the unintended ecological consequences of economic action in 1952 when he wrote enthusiastically and uncritically on Soviet plans for massive river diversion. A more cautious approach, informed by the kinds of issues that Engels raised, would have indicated that there might be unintended effects on the environment, which would need to be examined. Bernal's treatment was one of celebration of Soviet plans completely devoid of any warnings or reservations and failed to foresee even the possibility of the disasters that were to ensue from such massive engineering of nature. J. D. Bernal, *The Engineer and Nature* (London: SCR, 1958). Copy in in Bernal Papers, Cambridge University Library. It was only at the end

of his life due to the struggle against nuclear armaments that his ecological critique was to become far more consistent and whole, embracing an Earth System perspective.

217. Engels, *Ludwig Feuerbach*, 12; Needham, *Time: The Refreshing River*, 214.
218. Needham, *Time: The Refreshing River*, 215.
219. Ibid., 231. During the 1930s Brazil experimented with using surplus coffee to fuel its locomotives. See Stephen C. Topik, "Coffee," in Stephen C. Topik and Allen Wells, eds., *The Second Conquest of Latin America* (Austin: University of Texas Press, 1998), 52; "Use of Coffee as Fuel in Brazil Locomotives," *Modern Mechanix* (from December 1932), http://blog.modernmechanix.com/use-coffee-as-fuel-in-brazil-locomotives/. Needham viewed this as inefficient, related to the debate over agrofuels today.
220. Needham, *Moulds of Understanding*, 301.

CHAPTER TEN: DIALECTICS OF ART AND SCIENCE

1. Epigraph: Christopher Caudwell, *Studies and Further Studies in a Dying Culture* (two separate books bound as one) (New York: Monthly Review Press, 1971), 68.
2. "The International Brigade During the Spanish Civil War; December 1936–January 1937," photo of J. B. S. Haldane, Imperial War Museum, catalogue no. 71508, http://www.iwm.org.uk_www.iwm.org.uk/collections/item/object/205020731.
3. Jason Gurney, *Crusade in Spain* (London: Faber and Faber, 1974), 77; Ben Hughes, *They Shall Not Pass: The British Battalion at Jarama—The Spanish Civil War* (Oxford: Osprey Publishing, 2011), 60.
4. Gurney, *Crusade in Spain*, 71. In a review of Caudwell's *Crisis in Physics*, in which he referred to a statement by Caudwell that "the whole consciousness of society gathers at the pole of the owning class," Haldane claimed that this was an example of a clear error that arose in a hurried draft, one that Caudwell would undoubtedly have caught and corrected prior to final publication. Nevertheless, in refuting Caudwell's careless statement, Haldane declared: "I have heard a better discussion of problems of pure science in the trenches of Jarama than any which I can remember among officers mainly drawn from the owning class in 1914–1918." The primary irony in such a statement was that he must have been acutely aware—a fact that would not have slipped by his readers—that in referring to a "discussion of problems of pure science" taking place in "the trenches of Jarama" he was recalling an exchange in which Caudwell (St. John Sprigg) might well have actively participated, though Haldane was not aware at the time of Caudwell's existence. J. B. S. Haldane, "Marxism and Science," *Labour Monthly* 8 (1939): 508.
5. Hughes, *They Shall Not Pass*, 106; James Whetter, *A British Hero—Christopher St. John Sprigg aka Christopher Caudwell* (St. Austell, Cornwall: Lyftow Trelyspen (Rosiland Institute), 2011), 225.
6. E. P. Thompson, *Making History* (New York: New Press, 1994), 77–78.
7. Christopher Caudwell, *Studies and Further Studies in a Dying Culture* (*Studies*), xix.
8. William Morris, *News from Nowhere* (Oxford: Oxford University Press, 2003), 84. Although this particular statement by Morris is not quoted by Caudwell, he was deeply influenced by Morris's early critical works on art, and was familiar with Morris's *Hopes and Fears for Art*, which was included in the bibliography to Caudwell's *Illusion and Reality*. There can be little doubt that he read Morris's *News from Nowhere*.
9. Christopher Caudwell, *Studies and Further Studies in a Dying Culture* (*Further Studies*), 106.
10. Robert Sullivan, *Christopher Caudwell* (London: Croom Helm, 1987), 24–28; Jean Duparc and David Margolies, "Introduction," in Christopher Caudwell, *Scenes and*

Actions: Unpublished Manuscripts (New York: Routledge and Kegan Paul, 1986), 2–4; Maynard Solomon, *Marxism and Art* (Detroit: Wayne State University Press, 1979), 315–16; Samuel Hynes, "Introduction," in Christopher Caudwell, *Romance and Realism: A Study in English Bourgeois Literature* (Princeton: Princeton University Press, 1970), 6; Henry Stead and Edith Hall, "Between the Party and the Ivory Tower: Classics and Communism in 1930s Britain," in *Classics and Class: Greek and Latin Classics and Communism at School*, ed. David Movrin and Elżbieta Olechowska (Warsaw: Ljubljana University Press, 2016), 12–14.

11. Hynes, "Introduction," 7–10; Solomon, *Marxism and Art*, 316.
12. Sullivan, *Christopher Caudwell*, 37–43; Thompson, *Making History*, 77–78; Solomon, *Marxism and Art*, 316; Duparc and Margolies, "Introduction," 5–6; Alan Young, "Introduction," in Christopher Caudwell, *Collected Poems* (Manchester: Carcanet Press, 1986), 13.
13. Christopher Caudwell, *This My Hand* (London: H. Hamilton, 1936), 8–9, 16; Stead and Hall, "Between Party and the Ivory Tower," 14.
14. Caudwell, *Romance and Realism*, 72–73, 113–14. On women and the whole question of substantive equality see István Mészáros, *Beyond Capital* (New York: Monthly Review Press, 1995), 216–24.
15. Sheehan, *Marxism and the Philosophy of Science*, 369.
16. Caudwell, *Collected Poems*, 135.
17. Maynard Solomon, *Marxism and Art* (Detroit: Wayne State University Press, 1979), 317.
18. Caudwell, *Scenes and Actions*, 230–32.
19. Solomon, *Marxism and Art*, 303.
20. George Thomson, "Biographical Note," in Christopher Caudwell, *Illusion and Reality* (London: Lawrence and Wishart, 1946), 5.
21. Haldane, "Marxism and Science," *Labour Monthly* 8 (1939): 507–9.
22. Hyman Levy, "Preface," in Christopher Caudwell, *The Crisis in Physics* (London: John Lane The Bodley Head, 1939), xii.
23. Auden quoted in Sullivan, *Christopher Caudwell*, 70.
24. Hynes, "Introduction," 22–23.
25. Sullivan, *Christopher Caudwell*; Christopher Pawling, *Christopher Caudwell: Toward a Dialectical Theory of Literature* (New York: St. Martin's Press, 1989).
26. See John Bellamy Foster, *Marx's Ecology* (New York: Monthly Review Press, 2000), 11, 14, 242–52; Rob Wallace, "Revolutionary Biology: The Dialectical Science of Christopher Caudwell," *Monthly Review* 68/6 (November 2016): 14–36.
27. Caudwell, *Illusion and Reality*, 206.
28. On Aristotle's concept of mimesis and its relation to critical thought, see Raymond Williams, *The Long Revolution* (London: Parthian, 2011), 20–21; Aristotle, *Poetics* (London: Penguin Books, 1996).
29. Maurice Cornforth, "Caudwell and Marxism," *The Modern Quarterly* 6/1 (Winter 1950–51): 16–33. E. P. Thompson wrote of "The Caudwell Controversy" as presented in *Modern Quarterly*: "In my view, the 'controversy' was editorially controlled throughout and directed to a foregone conclusion." Thompson, *Making History*, 137.
30. J. D. Bernal, "Contribution to Caudwell Roundtable," *The Modern Quarterly* 6/4 (Autumn 1951): 346–50.
31. George Thomson, "In Defense of Poetry," *The Modern Quarterly* 6/2 (Spring 1951): 107–34. As E. P. Thompson later reported, Thomson was only given "a few days" to prepare his defense of Caudwell, reflecting the preferential way in which the debate was handled, directed toward a predetermined end.

32. Ibid., 107–8.
33. Ibid., 112–13.
34. Ibid., 108.
35. Ibid., 118–20.
36. Ibid., 124.
37. Raymond Williams, *Culture and Society, 1780–1950* (New York: Columbia University Press, 1983), 277.
38. Caudwell, *Studies and Further Studies in a Dying Culture* (*Further Studies*), 109; Williams, *Culture and Society*, 278–80.
39. Williams, *Culture and Society*, 277–80; John Higgins, *Raymond Williams: Literature, Marxism, and Cultural Materialism* (London: Routledge, 1999),106.
40. Raymond Williams, *Politics and Letters* (London: New Left Books, 1979), 127–28.
41. Williams, *Politics and Letters*, 127–28; Williams, *The Long Revolution*, 39.
42. Thompson, *Making History*, 122.
43. Francis Mulhern, "The Marxist Aesthetics of Christopher Caudwell," *New Left Review* 85 (May–June 1974): 46, 50–58.
44. Mulhern, "The Marxist Aesthetics," 41; Christopher Caudwell, *Studies and Further Studies in a Dying Culture* (New York: Monthly Review Press, 1971), 133.
45. Terry Eagleton, *Criticism and Ideology: A Study in Marxist Literary Theory* (London: New Left Books, 1976), 21.
46. On the differences separating the First and Second New Lefts, see Christos Efstathiou, *E.P. Thompson: A Twentieth-Century Romantic* (London: Merlin, 2015), 53–115.
47. Thompson, *Making History*, 85–86, 104.
48. Ibid., 123, 136.
49. Ibid., 86, 122.
50. Ibid., 117, 133–34.
51. Ibid., 122.
52. Ibid., 80, 136.
53. Ibid., 136, 80–81.
54. Sullivan, *Cristopher Caudwell*, 98–102.
55. Thompson, *Making History*, 85.
56. Ibid., 113. On the original holist context of the concept of genotype see Nils Roll-Hansen, "The Holist Tradition in Twentieth Century Genetics: Wilhelm Johannsen's Genotype Concept," *Journal of Physiology* 592/11 (2014): 2431–38.
57. Caudwell copied into his notebook a couple of famous quotes from Engels, the most important from an 1890 letter to Joseph Bloch, on the materialist conception of history and the base-superstructure model, in which Engels indicated that Marx and he had at times placed too much emphasis on the economic. Here Engels rejected any strict determinism associated with the base-superstructure metaphor. Christopher Caudwell, *Autograph Manuscript Notebook*, Christopher St. John Sprigg Collection, Harry Ransom Center, University of Texas, Austin. Caudwell extracted these passages by Engels from Edwin R. A. Seligman, *The Economic Interpretation of History* (New York; Columbia University Press, 1924), 142–43. See Karl Marx and Frederick Engels, *Selected Correspondence* (Moscow: Progress Publishers, 1975), 394–402.
58. Caudwell, *Romance and Realism*, 56; Thompson, *Making History*, 92.
59. Caudwell, *Studies and Further Studies in a Dying Culture* (*Studies*), 25.
60. Thompson, *Making History*, 90.
61. Caudwell, *Studies and Further Studies in a Dying Culture* (*Studies*), 130–31; Thompson, *Making History*, 129.

62. Raymond Williams, *Marxism and Literature* (Oxford: Oxford University Press, 1977), 3, *Politics and Letters*, 127–28, 183. What struck Williams the most in later years was how rigid the debate about Caudwell's acceptability for Marxism had been in the Caudwell Controversy debate in the 1950s, which became a marker for him on a certain kind of official Marxism. See Williams, *Marxism and Literature, 3*; Williams, *Problems in Materialism and Culture* (London: Verso, 1980), 240.
63. Sullivan, *Christopher Caudwell*, 98–102; Pawling, *Christopher Caudwell*, 37–45, Solomon, *Marxism and Art*, 308–12. See also David Margolies, *The Function of Literature: A Study of Christopher Caudwell's Aesthetics* (London: Lawrence and Wishart, 1969).
64. Caudwell, *Scenes and Actions*, 219, 225.
65. Sheehan, *Marxism and the Philosophy of Science*, 371.
66. Paul Beard, quoted in Sullivan, *Christopher Caudwell*, 73. Bracketed words inserted by Sullivan.
67. Sullivan, *Christopher Caudwell*, 111.
68. Stead and Hall, "Between the Party and the Ivory Tower," 15–16.
69. Plato, *Republic* (Indianapolis: Hackett Publishing, 1974), 63–68, 240–52 (392a–398b, 595a–608b).
70. Aristotle, *Poetics*, 6–10, 38–41.
71. Caudwell, *Illusion and Reality*, 48–49.
72. Ibid., 53.
73. Annabel Robinson, *The Life and Work of Jane Ellen Harrison* (Oxford: Oxford University Press, 2002), 22–26, 82; Mary Beard, *The Invention of Jane Harrison* (Cambridge, MA: Harvard University Press, 2000), 51.
74. William M. Calder III, "Jane Harrison's Failed Candidacies for the Yates Professorship: What Did Her Colleagues Think of Her?" in *The Cambridge Ritualists Reconsidered*, ed. Calder (Atlanta: Scholars Press, 1991), 37–53; Hal Draper, *The Marx-Engels Glossary* (New York: Schocken Books, 1986), 17.
75. Jane Harrison, *Ancient Art and Ritual* (Bradford-on-Avon, Wilts: Moonraker Press, 1913), 19–21, 111; Karl Marx and Frederick Engels, *Collected Works* (New York: International Publishers, 1975), 1:51.
76. Harrison, *Ancient Art and Ritual*, 115.
77. John T. Connor, "Jack Lindsay, Socialist Humanism and the Communist Historical Novel," *Review of English Studies*, New Series, 66/274 (2014): 360.
78. Caudwell, *Illusion and Reality*, 27.
79. Harrison, *Ancient Art and Ritual*, 22, 124.
80. Caudwell, *Illusion and Reality*, 28.
81. Sullivan, *Christopher Caudwell*, 118. The Caudwell quote from *Verse and Mathematics* is from Sullivan.
82. For Caudwell, following Engels, the unknowable "thing-in-itself" becomes a "thing-for-us" once science has extended the boundaries of our knowledge and sensory interaction with nature, which is always changing through human historical development. Christopher Caudwell, "The Thing-For-Us," unpublished *Autograph Manuscript Notebook,* Christopher St. John Sprigg Collection, Harry Ransom Center, University of Texas, Austin.
83. K. N. Kornilov, "Psychology in the Light of Dialectical Materialism," in Alfred Adler et al., *Psychologies of 1930* (Worcester, MA: Clark University Press, 1930), 248, 257; Marx and Engels, *Collected Works*, 5:44 (translation of Marx follows Kornilov). See also Sullivan, *Christopher Caudwell,* 119–20. On Marx's use of the concept of drives in

preference to instincts (anticipating later psychology) see John Bellamy Foster and Brett Clark, "Marx and Alienated Speciesism," *Monthly Review* 70/7 (December 2018): 5–9.

84. Caudwell, *Illusion and Reality*, 268–69.
85. Ibid., 154.
86. Ibid., 111, 239–40, 265–66.
87. Ibid., 265.
88. Ibid., 218.
89. Ibid., 218; Marx and Engels, *Collected Works*, 4:128.
90. Caudwell, *Studies and Further* Studies *in a Dying Culture* (*Studies*), 49.
91. John Keats, "Ode on a Grecian Urn," *The Poems of John Keats* (London: Collins, 1955), 259. Caudwell, *Studies and Further Studies in a Dying Culture* (*Further Studies*), 86.
92. Caudwell, *Studies and Further Studies in a Dying Culture* (*Further Studies*), 96–98.
93. Ibid., 100.
94. Ibid., 108–10.
95. Ibid., 106.
96. Williams, *Marxism and Literature*, 3–4.
97. Caudwell, *Studies and Further Studies in a Dying Culture* (*Further Studies*), 111–12.
98. Ibid., 107–08.
99. Caudwell, *Illusion and Reality*, 109–17; *Studies and Further Studies in a Dying Culture* (*Further Studies*), 115.
100. Gottfried Leibniz, *Discourse on Metaphysics and Other Essays* (Indianapolis: Hackett Publishing, 1991), 68–81; Francis Copleston, *Modern Philosophy: Descartes to Leibniz*, vol. 4 of *A History of Modern Philosophy* (Garden City, NY: Doubleday, 1963), 300–13.
101. Caudwell, *Crisis in Physics*, 81.
102. Ibid., 98–99.
103. Caudwell, *Studies and Further Studies in a Dying Culture* (*Further Studies*), 217: Caudwell, Crisis *in Physics*, 103.
104. Caudwell, *Crisis in Physics*, 122–23.
105. Ibid., 58.
106. Ibid., 123.
107. Christopher Caudwell, translations of Diogenes Laertius and Lucretius, respectively, *Autograph Manuscript Notebook of Translations* and *Autograph Manuscript Notebook*, Christopher St. John Sprigg Collection, Harry Ransom Center, University of Texas, Austin. Caudwell's prose translation from Lucretius (*De rerum natura*, Book I, 459–63) in his *Autograph Manuscript Notebook* was under the heading of "An Anticipation of Einstein" and reads as follows: "Time also exists not by itself, but simply from the things which happen. The sense apprehends what has been done in time past, as well as what is present and what is to follow after. And we must admit that no one feels time by itself abstracted from the notion [of movement] and [the] calm rest of things." Caudwell in his notebooks above clearly distinguished between Epicurus and Democritus, characterizing the mere notion that all was atoms and void and that the qualities were merely illusion (as these views of ancient materialists, and particularly Democritus, were conveyed by Sextus Empiricus) as a form of "mechanical materialism."
108. Caudwell, *Crisis in Physics*, 11 (typo corrected); Lucretius, *On the Nature of the Universe* (Oxford: Oxford University Press, 1997), 16–17 (I: 455–80).
109. Marx and Engels, *Collected Works,* 1:63–65, 458; Karl Marx, *The Poverty of Philosophy*

(New York: International Publishers, 1963), 110; Lucretius, *On the Nature of the Universe*, 93 (III: 865–70).

110. Caudwell, *Studies and Further Studies in a Dying Culture* (*Further Studies*), 219–25.
111. Caudwell saw Stoicism, as opposed to Epicureanism, as a form of idealism, more closely related to Hegel than Marx. Caudwell, *Autograph Manuscript Notebook,* Christopher St. John Sprigg Collection, Harry Ransom Center, University of Texas, Austin.
112. Caudwell, *Studies and Further Studies in a Dying Culture* (*Further Studies*), 26.
113. Caudwell, *Crisis in Physics*, 47. Caudwell saw positivism (no doubt thinking of logical positivism) as characterized by the "relation" between terms "without the terms." This reflected the way he thought of dialectics in which mediation was always essential. Caudwell, *Crisis in Physics*, 73.
114. A. A. Long, "Evolution vs. Intelligent Design in Classical Antiquity," November 2006, http://townsendcenter.berkeley.edu/article2.shtml; Long, *From Epicurus to Epictetus* (Oxford: Oxford University Press, 2006), 155–77.
115. Caudwell, *Studies and Further Studies in a Dying Culture* (*Further Studies*), 233–35, *Crisis in Physics*, 240.
116. Caudwell, *Crisis in Physics*, 112–16, 124–25, 176, 214–25.
117. Ibid., 240.
118. Duparc and Margolies, "Introduction," in Caudwell, *Scenes and Actions*, 27–28.
119. Wallace, "Revolutionary Biology," 19, 23, 25.
120. Sheehan, *Marxism and the Philosophy of Science*, 367.
121. Caudwell, *Scenes and Actions*, 187–88.
122. Ibid., 167, 171; Wallace, "Revolutionary Biology," 23.
123. Caudwell, *Scenes and Actions*, 171.
124. Ibid., 170.
125. Ibid., 172–73; Caudwell, *Studies and Further Studies in a Dying Culture* (*Further Studies*), 129.
126. Caudwell, *Scenes and Actions*, 190.
127. Wallace, "Revolutionary Biology," 19–20.
128. Caudwell, *Studies and Further Studies in a Dying Culture* (*Further Studies*), 129–31.
129. Ibid., 229.
130. Ibid., 71.
131. Ibid., 167–68.
132. Ibid., 68.
133. Ibid., 131.
134. Compare Marx and Engels, *Collected Works* 49: 286.
135. Caudwell, *Studies and Further Studies in a Dying Culture* (*Studies*), 156–57.
136. Ibid., 130–31.
137. Caudwell, *Autograph Manuscript Notebook*, Christopher St. John Sprigg Collection, Harry Ransom Center, University of Texas, Austin.
138. Caudwell, *Scenes and Actions*, 186. Here Caudwell adopted an approach to dialectics similar to that which Needham was to develop. See Joseph Needham, *Time: The Refreshing River* (London: George Allen and Unwin, 1943), 14–15.
139. Caudwell, *Studies and Further Studies in a Dying Culture* (*Further Studies*), 227.
140. Caudwell, *Scenes and Actions*, 175.
141. Caudwell, *Studies and Further Studies in a Dying Culture* (*Further Studies*), 113.
142. Caudwell, *Illusion and Reality*, 8.
143. Sheehan, *Marxism and the Philosophy of Science*, 373.

144. Caudwell, *Studies and Further Studies in a Dying Culture* (*Further Studies*), 229.
145. Ibid., 238–39; Caudwell, *Illusion and Reality*, 195–96.
146. Caudwell, *Studies and Further Studies in a Dying Culture* (*Further Studies*), 254–55.
147. Ibid., 239.
148. Caudwell, *Studies and Further Studies in a Dying Culture* (*Further Studies*), 131–32.
149. Ibid., 133–36.
150. Caudwell, *Scenes and Actions*, 187.
151. Ibid., 176.
152. Caudwell, *Illusion and Reality*, 279.
153. R. F. Willets, "Homage to Christopher Caudwell," *Envo* 15 (1962), quoted in Thompson, *Making History*, 135, 140.

CHAPTER ELEVEN: A SCIENCE FOR THE PEOPLE

1. Patrick Blackett, "The Frustration of Science," in Frederick Soddy et al., *The Frustration of Science* (New York: W. W. Norton, 1935), 129–44; Lancelot Hogben, *Science and the Citizen* (New York: Alfred A. Knopf, 1938); C. H. Waddington, *The Scientific Attitude* (West Drayton, Middlesex: Penguin Books, 1941, 1948); J. G. Crowther, *The Social Relations of Science* (New York: Macmillan, 1941).
2. Gary Werskey, *The Visible College* (London: Penguin, 1978), 266–67.
3. Mary Jo Nye, *Michael Polanyi and His Generation* (Chicago: University of Chicago Press, 2011), 204–5.
4. Michael Polanyi, *The Contempt of Freedom* (New York: Arno Press, 1940); John R. Baker, *The Scientific Life* (New York: Macmillan, 1943); Arthur G. Tansley, *The Values of Science to Humanity* (London: George Allen Unwin, 1942).
5. J. D. Bernal, *The Social Function of Science* (New York: Macmillan, 1939), 2.
6. Ibid., 6, 21–23, 32.
7. Ibid., 280.
8. Ibid., 340.
9. Ibid., 340–41.
10. Ibid., 370–71.
11. Ibid., 411. Bernal made this statement in regard to the role of science in capitalism, but it applied equally to his view of human ecology.
12. J. D. Bernal, *Science in History* (London: Watts and Co., 1954), 674–75, 879.
13. Ibid., 674.
14. Ibid., 674–76.
15. Ibid., 676–79.
16. Ibid., 680–83.
17. Bernal, *The Social Function of Science*, 348. See also William B. Meyer, *The Progressive Environmental Prometheans: Left-Wing Heralds of a "Good Anthropocene"* (London: Palgrave Macmillan, 2016), 121–26.
18. Bernal, *The Social Function of Science*, 379–80.
19. John Bellamy Foster, "Late Soviet Ecology and the Planetary Crisis," *Monthly Review* 67/2 (June 2015): 7–13.
20. Bernal, *Science in History*, 925–26.
21. *Science in History* was published in 1954. The Bikini Atoll Castle Bravo test occurred in March that same year, and the implications with respect to radioactive fallout were released by the U.S. government in February 1955. The radioactive fallout from Castle Bravo more than anything else stirred scientists and citizens to organize the first great

environmental movement of the post–Second World War era. The last stage of Bernal's thought can be seen as stemming from this signal event.

22. Bernal, *Science in History*, 944.
23. Ibid., 891.
24. J. D. Bernal, "After Twenty-Five Years," in *Society and Science*, ed. Maurice Goldsmith and Alan MacKay (New York: Simon and Schuster, 1964), 209, 223.
25. Bernal, *Science in History*, 316–21.
26. E. Ray Lankester, *The Kingdom of Man* (New York: Henry Holt, 1911), xi, 151–56.
27. Bernal, *The Social Function of Science*, 242; Karl Marx and Frederick Engels, *Collected Works* (New York: International Publishers, 1975), vol. 25, 105.
28. Bernal, *The Social Function of Science*, 28–29, 95–96, 394–95. In addition see Blackett, "The Frustration of Science," in Frederick Soddy et al., *The Frustration of Science.*
29. Bernal, *The Social Function of Science*, 321–23.
30. M. Perutz quoted in Werskey, *Visible College*, 81.
31. Bernal, *The Social Function of Science*, 242, 316; Nye, *Michael Polanyi and His Generation*, 217.
32. Bernal, "After Twenty-Five Years," 223.
33. Bernal, *The Social Function of Science*, 409.
34. Ibid., 258–59; Bernal, *Science in History*, 693–702.
35. Bernal, *Marx and Science* (London: Lawrence and Wishart, 1952), 49, 53.
36. Bernal, *The Social Function of Science*, 289.
37. Ibid., 289, 381–82, 398.
38. Ibid., 415–16.
39. Ibid., 382.
40. Waddington, *The Scientific Attitude* (1948 edition), 95–99.
41. Robert K. Merton, "A Note on Science and Democracy," *Journal of Legal and Political Sociology* 1 (1942): 115–26; Nye, *Michael Polanyi and His Generation*, 220.
42. Polanyi, *The Contempt of Freedom*, 13, 20–22.
43. Baker, *The Scientific Life*, 41, 140.
44. Polanyi quoted in Reinisch, *The Society for Freedom in Science*, 13.
45. Peder Anker, *Imperial Ecology* (Cambridge, MA: Harvard University Press, 2001), 223–25; Stephen Booking, *Ecologists and Environmental Politics* (New Haven: Yale University Press, 1997), 26–27; Peter Ayres, *Shaping Ecology: The Life of Arthur Tansley* (Oxford: Wiley-Blackwell, 2012), 182–84; William McGucken, *Scientists, Society and the State: The Social Relations of Science Movement in Great Britain, 1931–1947* (Columbus: Ohio State University Press, 1984), 289, 297.
46. J. R. Baker, "Counterblast to Bernalism," *New Statesman and Nation* 29 (July 1939): 174–75; McGucken, *Scientists, Society and State*, 267–68.
47. Baker quoted in Michael G. Kenny, "Racial Science in Social Context: John R. Baker on Eugenics, Race, and the Public Role of the Scientist," *ISIS* 95/3 (September 2004): 409.
48. Baker, letter to Carlos Blacker and Baker, letter to Eugenics Society, quoted in Kenny, "Racial Science in Social Context," 404.
49. Baker to Conrad Blacker, November 25, 1942, quoted in Reinisch, *The Society for Freedom in Science*, 17–18.
50. Neal Wood, *Communism and British Intellectuals* (New York: Columbia University Press, 1959), 10, 134–35; Roberts, *The Anglo-Marxists*, 175. Wood's research was funded by a Rockefeller Foundation grant. In addition to Polanyi, Wood also thanked

such ardent Cold Warriors as Hannah Arendt, Samuel Beer, and R. N. Carew Hunt, in aiding him with his book. Some four decades after the publication of Wood's book I asked him if his views presented there with respect to the British left scientists had changed. They had not.

51. Richard Levins and Richard Lewontin, *The Dialectical Biologist* (Cambridge, MA: Harvard University Press, 1985), 163–96; Foster, "Late Soviet Ecology and the Planetary Crisis," 3–7.
52. J. D. Bernal, "The Biological Controversy in the Soviet Union," *The Modern Quarterly* 4/4 (1949): 216–17. Zavadovsky, who was directly attacked by Lysenko, was, unbeknownst to Bernal, removed from his post as director of the Timiryazev Biological Museum. He died shortly afterward. Vadim J. Birstein, *The Perversion of Knowledge* (Boulder, CO: Westview Press, 2001), 252, 255.
53. J. B. S. Haldane, "Nonsense About Lysenko," *Daily Worker*, November 9, 1949. Hogben later criticized Haldane for the degree of his scientific reticence on Lysenkoism; see *Lancelot Hogben: Scientific Humanist* (London: Merlin Press, 1998), 166. John Maynard Smith, who was working closely with Haldane at the time, suggests that Haldane had serious doubts with respect to Lysenko that he was reluctant to air publicly at first. John Maynard Smith, "Haldane's Reaction to the Lysenko Affair," https://www.webofstories.com/play/john.maynard.smith/33;jsessionid=5EE3034F75B706500950DB5368335650. However, as Helena Sheehan notes, "When Lysenkoism reached the peak of its influence in the communist movement, Haldane's opposition to the corruption of science became explicit and resolute." Helena Sheehan, *Marxism and the Philosophy of Science* (London: Humanities Press, 1985).
54. Richard Levins and Richard Lewontin, *The Dialectical Biologist* (Cambridge, MA: Harvard University Press, 1985), 163–96. On how the question of Lysenkoism got caught up with the Cold War ideologies of both East and West see William Dejong-Lambert, "On Labels and Issues: The Lysenko Controversy and the Cold War," *Journal of the History of Biology* 45 (2012): 373–88.
55. Andrew Brown, *J. D. Bernal: The Sage of Science* (Oxford: Oxford University Press, 2005), 304–5.
56. Waddington, *The Scientific Attitude* (1948 edition), 95; Werskey, *The Visible College*, 293; Edwin A. Roberts, *The Anglo-Marxists* (New York; Rowman and Littlefield), 178; J. R. Baker, *Science and the Planned State* (New York: Macmillan, 1945), 71–76.
57. On Hayek's role in the development of neoliberalism, see John Bellamy Foster, "Absolute Capitalism," *Monthly Review* 71/1 (May 2019): 1-13.
58. Nye, *Michael Polanyi and His Generation*, 206–7.
59. Michael Polanyi, "The Growth of Thought in Society," *Economica* 8/32 (November 1941): 428–29, 442–43, 450; J. G. Crowther, *The Social Relations of Science* (New York: Macmillan, 1941), 330–33.
60. Reinisch, *The Society for Freedom in Science*, 23–27.
61. Edward Shils's copy of Bukharin, et. al., *Science at the Crossroads* (in the collection of the present author) was sent to him by Michael Polanyi. The latter included a printed slip in the book (found at the beginning of the Hessen chapter) reading: "With the compliments of Michael Polanyi." Like Polanyi, Shils was directly concerned with attacking the views on the history and sociology of science associated with the British Marxist scientists and the leading early Soviet thinkers in this regard, including Hessen.
62. Peter Coleman, *The Liberal Conspiracy: The Congress for Cultural Freedom and*

the Struggle for the Mind of Postwar Europe (New York: Free Press, 1989), 104–8; Reinisch, *The Society for Freedom in Science*, 39–40; Nye, *Michael Polanyi and His Generation*, 212–13; Frances Stonor Saunders, *The Cultural Cold War: The CIA and the World of Arts and Letters* (New York: New Press, 1999), 135, 241–42; Sarah Miller Harris, *The CIA and the Congress for Cultural Freedom in the Early Cold War* (New York: Routledge, 2016), 1–3, 170–79, 143–45, 194.

63. Saunders, *The Cultural Cold War*, 391–95, 408; Coleman, *The Liberal Conspiracy*, 49.
64. Saunders, *The Cultural Cold War*, 194, 230–33; Harris, *The CIA and the Congress for Cultural Freedom*, 143–44; Hugh Wilford, *The Mighty Wurlitzer: How the CIA Played America* (Cambridge, MA: Harvard University Press, 2008), 90–92. As Wilford notes, others besides Hook, such as Norman Thomas, also approached Dulles for funds for the ACCF.
65. Sidney Hook, *Towards the Understanding of Karl Marx* (New York: John Day Co., 1933).
66. Sidney Hook, *Reason, Social Myths and Democracy* (New York: John Day Co., 1940), 213, 220–27, 233–36, 244–49, 266; Hyman Levy, *A Philosophy for a Modern Man* (New York: Alfred A. Knopf, 1938), 118–24, 131, 232–33.
67. Arnold S. Kauman, "Is a Member of the Party to Teach at UCLA?," *The New Republic,* January 3, 1970, http://newrepublic.com; "University Censured for Dismissing Angela Davis," *Jet,* May 25, 1972; Sidney Hook, *Heresy, Yes—Conspiracy, No!* (New York: American Committee for Cultural Freedom, 1952); Hook, *Academic Freedom and Academic Anarchy* (New York: Cowles Co., 1968).
68. Reinisch, *The Society for Freedom in Science*, 40, 43.
69. Ibid., 41; "Neo-Nazi Minister of Education Resigns; Other Ex-Nazis Remain," Jewish Telegraphic Agency (June 13, 1955), http://www.jta.org/1955/06/13/archive/neo-nazi-minister-of-.education-resigns-other-ex-nazis-remain.
70. Kenny, "Racial Science in Social Context," 410.
71. C. P. Blacker, *Voluntary Sterilization* (Oxford: Oxford University Press, 1934), 87–88.
72. C. P. Blacker, "J. B. S. Haldane on Eugenics," *Eugenics Review* 44/3 (1952): 146–51.
73. See the discussion with respect to Hogben and biological race theories in chapter 7.
74. Ashley Montagu, *Man's Most Dangerous Myth: The Fallacy of Race* (London: Sage, 1997), 36. In September 1939, shortly after the commencement of the Second World War, twenty-three of the world's most prominent geneticists, including Haldane, Hogben, Huxley, Muller, Needham, and Waddington, issued a statement in *Nature* entitled "Social Biology and Population Improvement," responding to a request by the Science Service, Washington, D.C., for an answer to the question: "How could the world's population be improved most effectively genetically?" The statement, while accepting the principle of "ultimate genetic improvement," nonetheless was a powerful indictment of racial eugenics and all non-voluntary measures imposed on individuals. It insisted that the key to improved human population had to start with fundamental social change and the recognition of social equality between all human beings. Sometimes misleadingly referred to as "The Eugenics Manifesto," because of its aim of ultimate genetic improvement, it nonetheless set the stage for the strong critique of racial eugenics and the notion of biological race more generally that followed the war. See F. A. E. Crew, et. al., "Social Biology and Population Improvement," *Nature* 144 (1939): 521-22.
75. J. B. S. Haldane, "They Want to Geld the Poor" (1950), 3, Haldane Papers, University College of London Special Collections, Reference HALDANE/2/1/2/78.

76. Joseph Lester, *E. Ray Lankester and the Making of Modern British Biology* (Oxford: Aldon Press, 1995), 210.
77. Julian Huxley, *Memories*, vol. 2 (London: Allen and Unwin, 1973), 241.
78. Anker, *Imperial Ecology*, 248; Peter Ayres, *Shaping Ecology: The Life of Arthur Tansley* (Oxford: Wiley-Blackwell, 2012), 165–70.
79. Julian Huxley, "Ethics and the Dialectic of Evolution," in Thomas H. Huxley and Julian Huxley, *Touchstone for Ethics, 1893–1943*, ed. Julian Huxley (New York: Harper and Brothers, 1947), 216–17, 232, 245–50; Aldous Huxley, *The Perennial Philosophy* (New York: Harper and Row, 1945), 77–80.
80. Goldsmith, *Joseph Needham*, 15, 89–97.
81. UNESCO, *Four Statements on the Race Question* (Paris: UNESCO, 1969), 18–21, 30–43, 55–56; and *The Race Concept* (Paris: UNESCO, 1952); Ashley Montagu, *Statement on Race* (New York: Henry Schuman, 1951).
82. Kenny, "Racial Science in Social Context," 410–11; Reinisch, *The Society for Freedom in Science*, 41–43.
83. John R. Baker, *Race* (New York: Oxford University Press, 1974), v, 50.
84. Ibid., 4, 117, 198–99, 485, 492–94, 533–34.
85. Kenny, "Racial Science in Social Context," 411–19; Southern Poverty Law Center, "Pioneer Fund," https://www.splcenter.org/fighting-hate/extremist-files/group/pioneer-fund.
86. Joseph Needham, *Time: The Refreshing River* (London: George Allen and Unwin, 1943), 94–113; Tansley, *The Values of Science to Humanity*, 4–5, 22.
87. J. D. Bernal, "Professor Bernal Replies," *The New Statesman and Nation* 18/441 (August 5, 1939): 210–11.
88. J. D. Bernal, "Is Science Destroying the World?," in John Lewis et al., *The Communist Answer to the Challenge of Our Time* (London: Thames Publications, 1947), 27–33.
89. Lancelot Hogben, *The Retreat from Reason*, 9, 64–65; Hogben, *Lancelot Hogben: Scientific Humanist*, 130.
90. Haldane quoted in Werskey, *The Visible College*, 291.
91. J. B. S. Haldane, *A Banned Broadcast and Other Essays* (London: Chatto and Windus, 1946), 209.
92. C. P. Snow, *The Two Cultures* (Cambridge: Cambridge University Press, 1998).
93. McGucken, *Scientists, Society and the State*, 364; Orwell quoted in Roberts, *The Anglo-Marxists*, 174; Werskey, *The Visible College*, 285–89.
94. E. M. Forster, "The Point of View of the Creative Artist," in Arthur Koestler et al., *The Challenge of Our Time* (London: Percival Marshall, 1948), 31–35.
95. Hilary and Steven Rose, "Red Scientist," in *J. D. Bernal: A Life in Science and Politics* (London: Verso, 1999), 147.
96. Werskey, *The Visible College*, 278–79; Rose and Rose, "Red Scientist," 147, 153; J. G. Crowther, "Fifty Years with the BA," *New Scientist* (September 5, 1974): 586; Peter Collins, "The Struggles that Shaped the BA," *New Scientist* (July 25, 1983): 560.
97. John T. Connor, "Jack Lindsay, Socialist Humanism and the Communist Historical Novel," *Review of English Studies,* New Series, 66/274 (2014): 342.
98. Russell Jacoby, "Western Marxism," in *A Dictionary of Marxist Thought*, ed. Tom Bottomore (Oxford: Blackwell, 1983), 523–26.
99. Roberts, *The Anglo-Marxists*, 178.
100. Alexander Cockburn, "To and From the Frontier," *The Review*16 (October 1966): 15–16.
101. Hogben, *Lancelot Hogben: Scientific Humanist*, 194–203. For a retrospective on

developments in Guyana see Cheddi Jagan, "Guyana: A Reply to Critics," *Monthly Review* 29/ 4 (September 1977): 36–46.

102. Lancelot Hogben, *Science in Authority* (New York: W. W. Norton, 1963), 9–22, 113–21, 136–51, 224; Werskey, *The Visible College*, 321–22.
103. Hogben, *Lancelot Hogben: Scientific Humanist*, 206.
104. Werskey, *The Visible College*, 309–13; Hyman Levy, *Jews and the National Question* (New York: Cameron Associates, 1958).
105. Doris Lessing, *The Golden Notebook* (London: HarperCollins, 1990), 459–61.
106. E. P. Thompson to Hyman Levy, August 1, 1956, and August 6, 1956; E. P. Thompson to Hyman Levy and Doris Lessing, September 26, 1956; E. P. Thompson to Hyman Levy, September 26, 1956, Hyman Levy Papers, Charles Deering McCormick Library of Special Collections, Northwestern University (hereafter Hyman Levy Papers); Christos Efstathiou, *E. P. Thompson: A Twentieth-Century Romantic* (London: Merlin Press, 2015), 56–69.
107. John Saville to Hyman Levy, February 21, 1957; E. P. Thompson to Hyman Levy, March 22, 1957 and May 27, 1957, Hyman Levy Papers; Efstathiou, *E. P. Thompson*, 69–90, 209, 212.
108. Hyman Levy to John Gollan, May 24, 1957, Hyman Levy Papers.
109. Correspondence on Subscriptions, *Monthly Review* (1959–1960), Hyman Levy Papers.
110. Hyman Levy to R. Bernard, November 11, 1968, Hyman Levy Papers; Werskey, *The Visible College*, 309–13.
111. Krishna Dronamraju, "J. B. S. Haldane's Last Years: His Life and Work in India," *Genetics* 185/1 (May 2010): 5–10, http://www.genetics.org/content/185/1/5; Werskey, *The Visible College*, 313–16; J. B. S. Haldane, *On Being the Right Size* (Oxford: Oxford University Press, 1985), 169–77.
112. Dronamraju, "J. B. S. Haldane's Last Years"; Werskey, *The Visible College*, 315–16; Vidyanand Nanjundiah, "A Scientist, a Marxist, a Dreamer," 1992, https://www.downtoearth.org.in/indepth/a-scientist-a-marxist-and-a-dreamer-30085.
113. John Maynard Smith, *The Theory of Evolution* (Cambridge: Cambridge University Press, 1993), 338–40.
114. John Maynard Smith, "Reconciling Marx and Darwin," *Evolution* 55/7 (2001): 1496–98, "Molecules Are Not Enough," *London Review of Books* 8/2 (February 1986): 8–9, "Tinkering," *London Review of Books* 3/17 (September 1981): 9; Richard Lewontin, "Retrospective: In Memory of John Maynard Smith (1920–2004)," *Science* 304/5673 (2004): 979; Richard Lewontin and John Maynard Smith, "Are We Robots?" *New York Review of Books*, May 31, 1990.
115. Maynard Smith, "Reconciling Marx and Darwin," 1496.
116. John Maynard Smith, *Models in Ecology* (Cambridge: Cambridge University Press, 1974).
117. John Bellamy Foster, *The Ecological Revolution* (New York: Monthly Review Press, 2009), 69–73; Joachim Radkau, *Nature and Power* (Cambridge: Cambridge University Press, 2008), 265–67.
118. Ivor Montagu, "The Peacemonger," in Brenda Swann and Francis Aprahamian, *J. D. Bernal: A Life in Science and Politics* (London: Verso, 1999), 212–34; Brown, *J. D. Bernal*, 401–2.
119. Brown, *J. D. Bernal*, 412; Comprehensive Test Ban Treaty Organization, "March 1, 1954—Castle Bravo," https://www.ctbto.org/specials/testing-times/1-march-1954-castle-bravo/.

120. Robert A. Divine, *Blowing in the Wind: The Nuclear Test Ban Debate, 1954–1960* (New York: Oxford University Press, 1978), 3–66, 78–81, 123–27; Paul M. Sweezy, "The Resumption of Nuclear Testing," *Monthly Review* 13/6 (October 1961): 244–48.
121. Brown, *J. D. Bernal*, 419–21.
122. Ibid., 422, 427.
123. Ibid., 414.
124. J. D. Bernal, *World Without War* (New York: Prometheus, 1958), 18–19.
125. J. D. Bernal to Linus Pauling, November 12, 1958, Linus Pauling Papers, Oregon State University; Barry Commoner to Linus Pauling, February 25, 1958, Linus Pauling Papers, Oregon State University; Caroline Jack and Stephanie Steinhardt, "Atomic Anxiety and the Tooth Fairy: Citizen Science in the Midcentury Midwest," *The Appendix* 2/4 (November 26, 2014), http://theappendix.net/issues/2014/10/atomic-anxiety-and-the-tooth-fairy-citizen-science-in-the-midcentury-midwest; Michael Egan, *Barry Commoner and the Science of Survival* (Cambridge, MA: MIT Press, 2007), 66–67, 87–88; The Marxist ecological thinker Virginia Brodine was a founder of the Committee for Nuclear Information along with Commoner, its first employee, editor of its publication *Nuclear Information*, and a major force in the baby tooth study. See Virginia Brodine, *Red Roots, Green Shoots* (New York: International Publishers 2007), vii, 3–11.
126. Bernal, *World Without War*, 72–81, *A Prospect of Peace* (London: Lawrence and Wishart, 1960), 13, 35, 52–53, 68, 72–76; Bernal, "Is Science Destroying the World?," 23–24.
127. J. D. Bernal, "Science Against War," in Bernal and Maurice Cornforth, *Science for Peace and Socialism* (London: Birch Books, 1950), 9–10.
128. Bernal, *World Without War*, 215, 221–22.
129. J. D. Bernal, "Science and Natural Resources," typed manuscript (November 1953), written for *Indian Student*, Bernal Papers, Cambridge University Library.
130. Bernal, "Science and Natural Resources."
131. Bernal, *World Without War*, 222.
132. Montagu, "The Peacemonger," 232–33; Brown, *J. D. Bernal*, 432.
133. Montagu, "The Peacemonger," 229–31.
134. J. D. Bernal, *The Origin of Life* (New York: World Publishing Co., 1967), xi.
135. Ibid., xvi, 176–182.
136. Bernal, *Science in History*, 630–32.
137. J. D. Bernal, "Can Humanity Be Saved from World Starvation?" *Morning Star* (London), February 17, 1968; also see draft manuscript version with edits in Bernal Papers, Cambridge University Library. Bernal sent a slightly earlier paper he had drafted on these issues to Paul Ehrlich, complimenting him on his piece "Paying the Piper" in the December 14, 1967, issue of *The New Scientist.* (Miss) A. Rimel, Secretary of Professor Bernal (letter on behalf of Bernal), to Dr. Paul Ehrlich, January 5, 1968, Bernal Papers, Cambridge University Library.
138. Com. Ernesto Che Guevara in Havana to J. D. Bernal, April 12, 1960; Bernal to Che, April 28, 1960, Bernal Papers, Cambridge University Library.
139. "A Lost Document from the Cold War: The International Scientific Commission Report on Bacterial Warfare During the Korean War," *Invictus,* September 25, 2015, https://valtinsblog.blogspot.com/2015/01/a-lost-document-from-cold-war.html; Joseph Needham, *Within Four Seas* (Toronto: University of Toronto Press, 1969), 147–50. Werskey, *The Visible College*, 316–17.

140. Bertrand Russell, *War Crimes in Vietnam* (New York: Monthly Review Press, 1967).
141. Joseph Needham, *Science and Civilization*, vol. 2 (Cambridge: Cambridge University Press, 1954), 88–89; Needham, *Moulds of Understanding*, 279-80; Fritjof Capra, *The Tao of Physics* (Boulder, CO: Shambhala, 1975), 117; Capra, *The Turning Point* (New York: Simon and Schuster, 1982), 37, 312–13.
142. Needham, *Within Four Seas*, 63, 68, 89–97; Bertrand Russell, *The Problem of China* (London: George Allen and Unwin, 1922), 194.
143. Joseph Needham, "Light from the Orient," *Environment* (New Zealand Environment) 20 (August 1978): 8–11. This little-known article is included in the Joseph Needham Papers, Cambridge University Library, together with the correspondence surrounding its composition.
144. Ibid., 9–10.
145. Needham, *Moulds of Understanding*, 300–301; Needham, "Light from the Orient," 10–11; Herbert Marcuse, *One Dimensional Man* (Boston: Beacon Press, 1964), 47.
146. Needham, *Science and Civilization*, vol. 1, 4: Needham, *Science and Civilization in China*, vol. 7, part 2, 78.
147. Needham, "Light from the Orient," 11.
148. Needham, *Science and Civilization*, vol. 4, part 1, xxvi, 61; Tu Weiming, "The Continuity of Being: Chinese Versions of Nature," in Evelyn Tucker and John Berthrong, *Confucianism and Ecology* (Cambridge, MA: Harvard University Press, 1998), 106.
149. Rose and Rose, "Red Scientist," in Swann and Aprahamian, *J. D. Bernal*, 153–55.

EPILOGUE

1. Epigraph: Jack Lindsay, *Marxism and Contemporary Science* (London: Dennis Dobson, 1949), 9.
2. Paul M. Sweezy, "Capitalism and the Environment," *Monthly Review* 41/2 (June 1989): 2–3. Michael Egan, Barry Commoner's biographer, attributes the initial rise of the Age of Ecology to two events: the Nuclear Test Ban Treaty and Carson's *Silent Spring*. But he later undermines his own argument and the significance of Commoner's early environmental efforts by tracing the ecological movement's commencement to *Silent Spring*. The actual facts of the matter, however, leave no room for doubt that the first post–Second World War environmental movement, as Commoner himself argued, was the *struggle* over atmospheric nuclear testing, whereas the Nuclear Test Ban was the first great *victory* of that struggle. Carson's critique of the pesticide industry, as we shall see, grew in large part out of that earlier environmental movement led by scientists. See Michael Egan, *Barry Commoner and the Science of Survival* (Cambridge, MA: MIT Press, 2007), 11–12, 47, 84.
3. Richard Rhodes, *Dark Sun* (New York: Simon and Schuster, 1995), 541–42; Ariana Rowberry, "Castle Bravo: The Largest U.S. Nuclear Explosion," Brookings, February 17, 2014, https://www.brookings.edu/blog/up-front/2014/02/27/castle-bravo-the-largest-u-s-nuclear-explosion/.
4. Comprehensive Nuclear-Test Ban Treaty Organization, "1 March 1954—Castle Bravo," https://www.ctbto.org/specials/testing-times/1-march-1954-castle-bravo; Rowberry, "Castle Bravo: The Largest U.S. Nuclear Explosion"; Rhodes, *Dark Sun*, 542; Richard G. Hewlett and Jack M. Holl, *Atoms for Peace and War, 1953–1961* (Berkeley: University of California Press, 1989), 175–77, 281; Jacob Robbins and William H. Adams, "Radiation Effects in the Marshall Islands," in *Radiation and the Thyroid*, ed. S. Nagataki, Proceedings of the Annual Meeting of the Japanese Nuclear

Medicine Society (Amsterdam: Excerpta Medica, 1989), 11–24, http://large.stanford.edu/courses/2017/ph241/liang2/docs/robbins.pdf; Virginia Brodine, *Radioactive Contamination* (New York: Harcourt Brace Jovanovich, 1975), 32–33, 61, 65–70; Kelly Moore, *Disrupting Science* (Princeton: Princeton University Press, 2008), 99–100; Tokue Shibata, "The H-Bomb Terror in Japan," *Monthly Review* 6/2 (June 1954): 72–76.

5. Hewlett and Holl, *Atoms for Peace and War,* 271–85; Barry Commoner, *The Closing Circle* (New York: Bantam, 1971), 45–62; Steven L. Simon, André Bouville, Charles E. Land, and Harold L. Beck, "Radiation Doses and Cancer Risks in the Marshall Islands Associated with Exposure to Radioactive Fallout from Bikini and Enewetak Nuclear Weapons Tests: Summary," *Health Physics* 99/2 (August 2010): 105–23.
6. Hewlett and Holl, *Atoms for Peace and War*, 296, 336–40, 450–59; Moore, *Disrupting Science*, 112.
7. Elof Axel Carlson, *Genes, Radiation, and Society: The Life and Work of H. J. Muller* (Ithaca, NY: Cornell University Press, 1981), 262–63; Andrew Brown, *J. D. Bernal: The Sage of Science* (Oxford: Oxford University Press, 2005), 316–17.
8. H. J. Muller, "Lenin's Doctrines in Relation to Genetics," in Loren R. Graham, *Philosophy and Science in the Soviet Union* (New York: Alfred A. Knopf, 1974), 463; "Hermann J. Muller," Nobel Prize.org, https://www.nobelprize.org/nobel_prizes/medicine/laureates/1946/muller-bio.html; Simon Ings, *Stalin and the Scientists* (New York: Grove Press, 2016), 132–33, 148–49; Carlson, *Genes, Radiation, and Society*, 129–30, 190–218; H. J. Muller, *Out of the Night* (New York: Vanguard Press, 1935).
9. Helena Sheehan, *Marxism and the Philosophy of Science* (Atlantic Highlands, NJ: Humanities Press, 1985), 409–10; Ings, *Stalin and the Scientists*, 266–67, 272–76. Carlson, *Genes, Radiation, and Society*, 235–43, 430–38. As Ings points out, Stalin's strong objection to Muller's eugenics argument was related to the development of some of the same ideas, in a quite different context and with different ends, by fascists. Although Muller's views on eugenics were questionable, he explicitly excluded racial eugenics (rejecting all notions of racial inequality) and emphasized the selective, voluntary control of human reproduction based on individual choice in a context of radical social change. Still, underlying his entire outlook, according to Lewontin, was a strong tendency toward genetic determinism in relation to human development, placing insufficient stress on social determinants. See R. C. Lewontin, *The Genetic Basis of Evolutionary Change* (New York: Columbia University Press, 1974), 31.
10. H. J. Muller, "The Genetic Damage Produced by Radiation," *Bulletin of the Atomic Scientists* 11/6 (1955): 210; Joel B. Hagen, *An Entangled Bank* (New Brunswick, NJ: Rutgers University Press, 1992), 116.
11. Muller, "The Genetic Damage Produced by Radiation," 210–12; Hewlett and Holl, *Atoms for Peace*, 266–69.
12. Hewlett and Holl, *Atoms for Peace and War*, 266–69.
13. John Bellamy Foster, *The Ecological Revolution* (New York: Monthly Review Press, 2009), 69–72; William Cuyler Sullivan Jr., *Nuclear Democracy; A History of the Greater St. Louis Citizens' Committee for Nuclear Information, 1957–1967* (St. Louis: Washington University, 1982), 11.
14. Egan, *Barry Commoner and the Science of Survival*, 19–20, 47; Barry Commoner, "What Is Yet to Be Done?," in *Barry Commoner's Contribution to the Environmental Movement*, ed. David Kriebel (Amityville, NY: Baywood Publishing, 2002), 75; Moore, *Disrupting Science*, 108.

15. Egan, *Barry Commoner and the Science of Survival*, 21–22; Commoner, "What Is Yet to Be Done?," 75.
16. Barry Commoner, *The Closing Circle* (New York: Bantam, 1971), 45–48; Egan, *Barry Commoner and the Science of Survival*, 51; Commoner, "What Is Yet to Be Done?," 75; Hugh E. Varess, et. al, *Radioactive Fallout: A Bibliography of Selected United States Atomic Energy Commission Reports* (Washington, D.C.: Atomic Energy Commission, August 1959), 304.
17. Moore, *Disrupting Science*, 105–8; Sullivan, *Nuclear Democracy*, 14–17.
18. Virginia Brodine, *Red Roots, Green Shoots* (New York: International Publishers, 2007), 3–5; Russel V. Brodine, *Fiddle and Fight* (New York: International Publishers, 2001), 144–45. Brodine was also an ardent feminist; see Brodine, *Fiddle and Fight*, 38.
19. Brodine, *Red Roots, Green Shoots*, 5–8; Pauling Blog, "The Baby Tooth Survey," June 1, 2011, https://paulingblog.wordpress.com/2011/06/01/the-baby-tooth-survey/; Paul Rubinson, *Rethinking the American Nuclear Movement* (London: Routledge, 2018), 56–57.
20. "July 1962–'Sedan'—Massive Crater, Massive Contamination," Comprehensive Nuclear Test-Ban Treaty Organization, https://www.ctbto.org/specials/testing-times/6-july-1962-sedan-massive-crater-massive-contamination; Scott Kaufman, *Project Plowshare* (Ithaca, NY: Cornell University Press, 2012).
21. Sullivan, *Nuclear Democracy*, 9–13; Egan, *Barry Commoner and the Science of Survival*, 54–55; Pauling Blog, "The Bomb Test Petition," March 11, 2008, https://paulingblog.wordpress.com/2008/03/11/the-bomb-test-petition/; Moore, *Disrupting Science*, 111.
22. The emphasis on the free dissemination of scientific information to the public, which was the core of Commoner's message at the time, was closely related (although more innocuously stated) to Bernal's famous and influential treatment in *The Social Function of Science* of "science as communism," in the sense that it required the free and collective appropriation of scientific knowledge and the application of this to society. See J. D. Bernal, *The Social Function of Science* ((New York: Macmillan, 1939), 415–16. Commoner clearly believed that science if properly used and made publicly available could enhance the struggle for human freedom and human community.
23. Commoner, *The Closing Circle*, 280; K. William Kapp, *The Social Costs of Private Enterprise* (Cambridge, MA: Harvard University Press, 1950), 34–36. Kapp's book, one of the great early works in environmental economics, was written much in the broad tradition of Bernal's *The Social Function of Science*, to which it frequently refers.
24. G. Evelyn Hutchinson, "The Biosphere," *Scientific American* 233/3 (1970): 45–53.
25. Virginia Brodine, *Air Pollution* (New York: Harcourt Brace Jovanovich, 1972), 62–64, 70, 177–78; Brodine, *Red Roots, Green Shoots*; John Bellamy Foster and Paul Burkett, *Marx and the Earth* (Chicago: Haymarket, 2016), 230–31.
26. Much of the discussion in this section draws on John Bellamy Foster and Brett Clark, "Rachel Carson's Radical Ecological Critique," *Monthly Review* 59/9 (February 2008): 1–17.
27. Rachel Carson, *The Sea Around Us* (Oxford: Oxford University Press, 1989), xi–xiii; Mary A. McCay, *Rachel Carson* (New York: Twayne Publishers, 1993), 52–53, 67, 74.
28. Eugene Odum, *Fundamentals of Ecology* (Philadelphia: Saunders, 1959), 467; Hagen, *An Entangled Bank*, 115–18; Helen Caldicott, *Nuclear Power Is Not an Answer* (New York: New Press, 2006), 64, 73.
29. Rachel Carson, *Lost Woods* (Boston: Beacon Press, 1998), 237–43.
30. Rachel Carson, *Silent Spring* (Boston: Houghton Mifflin, 1962), 187, 190, 246.

31. H. J. Muller, "In Our Battle Against Bugs, Are We Firing Blind?" *New York Herald Tribune*, September 23, 1962; Linda Lear, *Rachel Carson* (New York: Henry Holt, 1997), 437–39.
32. Carson quoted in Paul Brooks, *The House of Life* (Boston: Houghton Mifflin, 1989), 301–2. The fact that Carson chose to speak to the National Council of Women of the United States, founded in 1888 by Susan B. Anthony, only two weeks after *Silent Spring* was published, was itself significant, as an indication of her commitment to the women's movement generally.
33. Carson, *Silent Spring*, 18.
34. Charles S. Elton, *The Ecology of Invasions of Animals and Plants* (Chicago: University of Chicago Press, 2000), 142.
35. Carson, *Lost Woods*, 190.
36. Carson, *Silent Spring*, 20–21, 110, 233.
37. Carson, *Silent Spring*, 113; Robert L. Rudd, "The Irresponsible Poisoners," *The Nation*, May 30, 1959, 496–97; Carson, "Pesticides: The *Real* Peril," *The Nation*, November 28, 1959, 399–40; Lear, *Rachel Carson*, 331–32; Frank Graham Jr., *Since Silent Spring* (Boston: Houghton Mifflin, 1970), 167–69; Murray Bookchin (under the pseudonym of Lewis Herber), *Our Synthetic Environment* (New York: Alfred A. Knopf, 1962).
38. Carson, *Silent Spring*, 13–15; Carson, *Lost Woods*, 89. Socialist and environmentalist Scott Nearing wrote an important review of *Silent Spring* for the November 1962 issue of *Monthly Review,* which began with a discussion of "Poisoned Birds" and ended "Coexistence or Extermination." Scott Nearing "World Events," *Monthly Review* 14/7 (November 1962): 389–94.
39. Carson, *Silent Spring*, 23; Carson, *Lost Woods*, 162, 194–95, 210, 218–21; Mark Hamilton Lytle, *The Gentle Subversive* (Oxford: Oxford University Press, 2007), 178–79.
40. Carson, *The Sea Around Us*, 7.
41. Carson, *Lost Woods*, 228–30; J. D. Bernal, *The Origin of Life* (New York: World Publishing Co., 1967); Robert M. Hazen, *Genesis* (Washington, D.C.: John Henry Press, 2005). 86.
42. Rachel Carson, *Lost Woods,* 229–31.
43. McCay, *Rachel Carson*, 23–24, 42–43,109; Lucretius, *On the Nature of the Universe* (Oxford: Oxford University Press, 1997), 9 (III, 869). See also Karl Marx, *The Poverty of Philosophy* (New York: International Publishers, 1963), 110, 228.
44. Sigrid Schmalzer, Daniel S. Chard, and Alyssa Botelho, "Preface," in Schmalzer, Chard, and Botelho, eds., *Science for the People: Documents from America's Movement of Radical Scientists* (Amherst: University of Massachusetts Press, 2018), xi. Much of the discussion of Science for the People in the opening of this section is taken from Foster, "Notes from the Editors," *Monthly Review* 70/4 (September 2018).
45. Sigrid Schmalzer, Daniel S. Chard, and Alyssa Botelho, "Introduction," in Schmalzer, Chard, and Botelho, *Science for the People*, 3.
46. "Resources," *Science for the People* 9/6 (1977): 18.
47. Donna Jeanne Haraway, "The Transformation of the Left in Science: Radical Associations in Britain in the 30's and the U.S.A. in the 60's," *Soundings* 58/4 (1975): 441–62; Ben Allen and Sigrid Schmalzer, "Science, Power, and Ideology," in Schmalzer, Chard, and Botelho, *Science for the People*, 13.
48. J. D. Bernal, *Marx and Science* (London: Lawrence and Wishart, 1952), 49; J. G. Crowther, *The Social Relations of Science* (New York: Macmillan, 1941).

49. Peter Galison and Bruce Hevly, ed., *Big Science: The Growth of Large-Scale Research* (Stanford, CA: Stanford University Press, 1992).
50. "FBI Teletype, Boston Field Office to Acting FBI Director Patrick Gray, December 22, 1972," in Schmalzer, Chard, and Botelho, *Science for the People*, 58–59.
51. Yrjö Haila and Richard Levins, *Humanity and Nature: Ecology, Science and Society* (London: Pluto Press, 1992), 182, 190, 213, 247; Richard Lewontin and Richard Levins, *Biology Under the Influence: Dialectical Essays on Ecology, Agriculture, and Health* (New York: Monthly Review Press, 2007), 365–67; Bishop William Montgomery Brown, *Science and History for Girls and Boys* (Galion, Ohio, written 1932), posthumously published at orders of Probate Court, Crawford County, Bucyrus, Ohio.
52. Haila and Levins, *Humanity and Nature*, 190, 212–13, 245–52.
53. This was conveyed to the author in a conversation with Lewontin.
54. See Richard Lewontin, "The Concept of Race: The Confusion of Social and Biological Reality," Graduate Council Lectures, University of California, Berkeley, November 19, 2003, https://www.youtube.com/watch?v=JvG1ylKhzoo.
55. Richard C. Lewontin, "Are the Races Different?" in Schmalzer, Chard, and Botelho, *Science for the People*, 128–32.
56. Stephen Jay Gould, *The Mismeasure of Man* (New York: W. W. Norton, 1981).
57. Richard C. Lewontin, *Biology as Ideology* (New York: HarperCollins, 1991); Lewontin, *The Triple Helix; Gene, Organism, and Environment* (Cambridge, MA: Harvard University Press, 2000).
58. Richard Levins and Richard Lewontin, *The Dialectical Biologist* (Cambridge, MA: Harvard University Press, 1985); Levins and Lewontin, *Biology Under the Influence.*
59. Levins and Lewontin, *The Dialectical Biologist*, v, 85, 89, 134–35, 286–88; Brett Clark and Richard York, "Dialectical Nature: Reflections in Honor of the Twentieth Anniversary of Levins and Lewontin's *The Dialectical Biologist*," *Monthly Review* 57/1 (May 2005): 13–22; John Bellamy Foster, *Marx's Ecology* (New York: Monthly Review Press, 2000), 251–52; John Bellamy Foster, Brett Clark, and Richard York, *Critique of Intelligent Design* (New York: Monthly Review Press, 2008), 178–79, 200.
60. Levins and Lewontin, *The Dialectical Biologist*, 279–80.
61. Richard C. Lewontin and Richard Levins, "What Does It Mean to Be a Radical?: Remembering Stephen Jay Gould," *Monthly Review* 54/6 (November 2002): 17.
62. Stephen Jay Gould, *The Structure of Evolutionary Theory* (Cambridge, MA: Harvard University Press, 2002), 1018. Gould described his father as "an idealist Marxist out of the 1930s, which was a common political attitude in this country and elsewhere, and I got pretty straight-line Marxist answers to most of my questions." Stephen Jay Gould, interviewed by Wim Kayzer, "Unanswerable Questions," in Kayzer, *A Glorious Accident* (New York: W. H. Freeman and Co., 1997), 104.
63. Lewontin and Levins, "Stephen Jay Gould," 22.
64. Stephen Jay Gould, *I Have Landed* (New York: Three Rivers Press, 2003), 113–29.
65. Lewontin and Levins, "Stephen Jay Gould," 17.
66. Gould, "Unanswerable Questions," 83, 99–100, 104, Stephen Jay Gould, *Eight Little Piggies* (New York: W. W. Norton, 1993), 49–51; Richard York and Brett Clark, *The Science and Humanism of Stephen Jay Gould* (New York: Monthly Review Press, 2011), 67–91.
67. "Ecology for the People," *Science for the People* 5/1 (January 1973): 34–37; Paul A. Baran and Paul M. Sweezy, *Monopoly Capital* (New York: Monthly Review Press, 1966), and Barbara and John Ehrenreich, *The American Health Empire* (New York: Random House, 1971).

68. Barry Weisberg, *Beyond Repair: The Ecology of Capitalism* (Boston: Beacon Press, 1971); Charles H. Anderson, *The Sociology of Survival: Social Problems of Growth* (Dorsey Press, 1976); Alan Schnaiberg, *The Environment: From Surplus to Scarcity* (Oxford: Oxford University Press, 1980).
69. Anderson, *The Sociology of Survival*, 54–61, 126.
70. Weisberg, *Beyond Repair*, 41–76.
71. Schnaiberg, *The Environment*, 227–30.
72. Herbert Marcuse, *Counterrevolution and Revolt* (Boston: Beacon Press, 1972); Murray Bookchin, *Post-Scarcity Anarchism* (Menlo Park, CA: Ramparts Press, 1971).
73. Paul M. Sweezy, "Cars and Cities," *Monthly Review* 24/11 (April 1973): 1-18.
74. Brodine, *Red Roots, Green Shoots*, vii, 12–22.
75. Christos Efstathiou, *E. P. Thompson: A Twentieth-Century Romantic* (London: Merlin Press, 2015), 27–28, 53–90: E. P. Thompson, *The Poverty of .Theory* (New York: Monthly Review Press, 1978), 245–301; Ellen Meiksins Wood, "A Chronology of the New Left and Its Successors, Or: Who's Old-Fashioned Now?," *Socialist Register 1995* (New York: Monthly Review Press, 1995), 22-49; Perry Anderson, *Arguments within English Marxism* (London: Verso, 1980), 59–99.
76. Efstathiou, *E .P. Thompson*, 116–30; Cal Winslow, "Introduction," in Winslow, ed., *E. P. Thompson and the Making of the New Left* (New York: Monthly Review Press, 2014), 26.
77. Winslow, "Introduction," 27–28; Brown, *J. D. Bernal*, 414–15.
78. Efstathiou, *E. P. Thompson*, 128–30; Winslow, "Introduction," 27–28.
79. E. P. Thompson, *The Making of the English Working Class* (New York: Vintage, 1963); *Whigs and Hunters* (New York: Pantheon, 1975); *Customs in Common* (New York: New Press, 1991).
80. Thompson, *The Poverty of Theory*, 50–57.
81. Ibid., 105; Giambattista Vico, *The New Science* (Ithaca, NY: Cornell University Press, 1984), 96; Marx, *Capital*, vol. 1, 493.
82. Thompson, *The Poverty of Theory*, 113–14. Thompson added: "The eviction of dialectics from the Althusserian system is deplorable, but it flows as a necessary consequence from the inner stasis of structuralism" (114); Vico, *The New Science*, 96.
83. Peter Linebaugh, *Stop, Thief!: The Commons, Enclosures and Resistance* (Oakland, CA: PM Press, 2014), 131.
84. E. P. Thompson, *Witness Against the Beast: William Blake and the Moral Law* (Cambridge: Cambridge University Press, 1994).
85. Thompson, *Customs in Common*, 107–8.
86. E. P. Thompson, "Ecology and History," *Trends in Ecology and Evolution* 8/4 (April 1993): 149–50; Maghav Gadgil and Ramachandra Guha, *This Fissured Land: An Ecological History of India* (Berkeley: University of California Press, 1992). Gadgil and Guha had referred in their work to Thompson's "moral economy of provision" still apparent in the eighteenth–century England that was completely displaced in the nineteenth century by the political economy of profit (175).
87. E.P. Thompson, "The Long Revolution," in Winslow, *E. P. Thompson*, 195.
88. Raymond Williams, *Culture and Society* (New York: Columbia University Press, 1983), 141-58. See also Raymond Williams, *Resources for Hope* (London: Verso, 1989), 210–26.
89. Raymond Williams, *Resources of Hope* (London: Verso, 1989), 210–26; Fred Inglis, *Raymond Williams* (New York: Routledge, 1995), 267; Robert Sayre and Michael Löwy, *Romantic Anti-Capitalism and Nature* (New York: Routledge, 2020), 106.
90. Perry Anderson, "Components of the National Culture," *New Left Review* 50 (1968):

11; Perry Anderson, *In the Tracks of Historical Materialism* (London: Verso, 1983), 83; Hilary and Steven Rose, "The Radicalisation of Science," in Rose and Rose, *The Radicalisation of Science* (London: Macmillan, 1976), 13.

91. On critical theory and the problem of the dialectics of ecology see John Bellamy Foster and Brett Clark, "Marx's Ecology and the Left," *Monthly Review* 68/2 (June 2016): 1–25.
92. Gary Werskey, *The Visible College* (London: Penguin Books, 1978), 325.
93. David King and Les Levidow, "Introduction: Contesting Science and Technology from the 1970s to the Present," *Science as Culture* 25/3 (2016): 367–72; Alice Bell, "Beneath the White Coat: The Radical Science Movement," *The Guardian*, July 18, 2013.
94. Hilary Rose and Steven Rose, *Science and Society* (London: Penguin, 1969); Hilary and Steven Rose, eds., *The Political Economy of Science* (London: Macmillan, 1976); Hilary Rose and Steven Rose, *The Radicalisation of Science* (London: Macmillan, 1976).
95. Rose and Rose, *The Political Economy of Science,* 13.
96. Efstathiou, *E. P. Thompson*, 131, 147–48; Bryan Palmer, *E. P. Thompson: Objections and Oppositions* (London: Verso, 1994), 128–29. Thompson, while the leading force behind END, did not separate himself from CND but was on its National Council and served as a vice president. Palmer, *E.P. Thompson*, 131, 136. Nonetheless, END represented a distinct strategy.
97. E. P. Thompson, *Double Exposure* (London: Merlin Press, 1985), 152.
98. Mary Kaldor, "Obituary: E.P. Thompson," *The Independent*, August 30, 1993; Palmer, *E. P. Thompson*, 132.
99. E. P. Thompson and Dan Smith, eds., *Protest and Survive* (New York: Monthly Review Press, 1981); E. P. Thompson, *Beyond the Cold War* (New York: Pantheon, 1982).
100. Palmer, *E. P. Thompson*, 126, 132.
101. See, for example, Thompson, *Beyond the Cold War*, 25–39; Thompson, ed., *Protest and Survive*, 11–39; Palmer, *E. P. Thompson*, 139.
102. Kaldor, "Obituary: E. P. Thompson."
103. In recent years, the famous Doomsday Clock of the Bulletin of the Atomic Scientists has been forced to consider both of these dangers.
104. Thompson, *Beyond the Cold War*, 64.
105. Karl Marx and Friedrich Engels, *The Communist Manifesto* (New York: Monthly Review Press, 1964); Rudolf Bahro, *Avoiding Social and Ecological Disaster* (Bath: Gateway Books, 1994), 19. See also John Bellamy Foster, *The Ecological Revolution* (New York: Monthly Review Press, 2009), 27–28; Ian Angus, *Facing the Anthropocene* (New York: Monthly Review Press, 2016) 179–80.
106. E. P. Thompson, "A Charm Against Evil," *Collected Poems* (Bloodaxe Books, 1999), 125; Efstathiou, *E. P. Thompson*, 165.
107. Karl Marx and Frederick Engels, *Collected Works* (New York: International Publishers, 1975), vol. 1, 413; A. Voden, "Talks with Engels," in *Reminiscences of Marx and Engels*, ed. Institute of Marxism-Leninism (Moscow: Foreign Languages Publishing House, n.d.), 332–33.
108. Lancelot Hogben, *Lancelot Hogben, Scientific Humanist* (London: Merlin Press, 1998), 105.
109. Benjamin Farrington, *The Faith of Epicurus* (London: (Weidenfeld and Nicolson, 1967), 76–87.

110. Farrington, *The Faith of Epicurus*, xi–xii, 134–49. On the political morality of later Epicureanism see Philodemus, *On the Good King According to Homer* (col.s 21–39), in Jeffrey Brian Fish, "Philodemus, De bono rege secundum Homerum: A Critical Text with Commentary (col.s 21–39)" (PhD diss., University of Texas at Austin, 1999), 39–50.
111. Benjamin Farrington, *Science and Politics in the Ancient World* (London: George Allen and Unwin, 1939), 125–26. On Epicurus's critique of religion see John Bellamy Foster, Brett Clark, and Richard York, *Critique of Intelligent Design* (New York: Monthly Review Press, 2008), 49–64.
112. Jean-Paul Sartre, *Literary and Philosophical Essays* (New York: Criterion Books, 1955), 207.
113. Cyril Bailey, "Karl Marx on Greek Atomism," *Classical Quarterly* 22/3–4 (July–October 1928): 205–6. Bailey emphasizes Marx's reference in his notebooks to the "immanent dialectics" in the Epicurean system. Marx and Engels, *Collected Works*, 1:413. See also Benjamin Farrington, "Karl Marx—Scholar and Revolutionary," *The Modern Quarterly* 7 (1951–52): 83–94; Farrington, *The Faith of Epicurus*, 8–9.
114. Farrington, *The Faith of Epicurus*, 149.
115. George Thomson, *The First Philosophers*, vol. 2 of *Studies in Ancient Greek Society* (London: Lawrence and Wishart, 1955), 313. Thomson adopted the usual view of the Epicureans as anti-political, retreating into the Garden. This was later refuted by Farrington.
116. Ernst Bloch, *On Karl Marx* (New York: Herder and Herder, 1971), 158.
117. E. P. Thompson to Lindsay, May 8, 1961, quoted in John T. Connor, "Jack Lindsay, Socialist Humanism and the Communist Historical Novel," *Review of English Studies* 66/274 (April 2015): 343.
118. Eric Hobsbawm, "The Historians' Group of the Communist Party," in *Rebels and Their Causes*, ed. Maurice Cornforth (Atlantic Highlands, NJ: Humanities Press, 1979), 25. On Lindsay see Paul Gillen, "Lindsay, John (Jack) (1900–1990)," *Australian Dictionary of Biography*, vol. 18 (Melbourne: Melbourne University Press, 2012), http://adb.anu.edu.au/biography/lindsay-john-jack-14177; David Movrin and Elżbieta Olechowska, ed., *Classics and Class* (Warsaw: Ljubljana, 2016), 20–31; Connor, "Jack Lindsay, Socialist Humanism," 342–62; Jack Lindsay, *Life Rarely Tells* (Harmondsworth, Middlesex: Penguin, 1982), 811–16.
119. Jack Lindsay, *Marxism and Contemporary Science* (London: Dennis Dobson, 1949), 77–78.
120. Lindsay, *Decay and Renewal: Critical Essays on Twentieth-Century Writing* (London: Lawrence and Wishart, 1976), 52. Lindsay's essay on Lukács in *Decay and Renewal* on Lukács's critical method and the historical novel was originally written at Lukács's own request for a festschrift in his honor. Lindsay had first met Lukács in 1949 and corresponded with him after that. In his essay on Lukács, Lindsay provided perhaps his strongest attacks on "the tyrannical pressures of the system under Stalin" and of the role of Zhdanov. Lindsay, *Decay and Renewal*, 41–43. In a personal letter to me on September 4, 2017, just weeks before his death, István Mészáros wrote: "Jack Lindsay was indeed a very fine comrade and scholar. Lukács had very high regard for him. As you know, Lindsay generously praised my books on Lukács and on *Marx's Theory of Alienation*. We corresponded for some time, but unfortunately, I never had the opportunity to meet him in person. He certainly deserves to be much better recognised than he is now even among the most serious Marxist scholars."

121. Jack Lindsay, *The Crisis in Marxism*, 123–27; Lindsay, *Life Rarely Tells*, 801–2.
122. Jack Lindsay: *Songs of a Falling World* (London: Andrew Dakers Limited, 1948); *The English Civil War: The Cromwellian Revolution* (London: Frederick Muller, 1954); *Thunder Underground* (London: Frederick Muller, 1965); *The Origins of Alchemy in the Graeco-Roman World* (New York: Barnes and Noble, 1970); *Blast Power and Ballistics: Concepts of Force and Energy in the Ancient World* (London: Frederick Muller, 1974); *William Morris* (London: Constable, 1974); *The Monster City: Defoe's London, 1688–1730* (New York: Harpers, 1978): *William Blake* (New York: George Braziller, 1978).
123. Lindsay, *Marxism and Contemporary Science*, 243.
124. This is Lindsay's translation of Marx. Lindsay, *The Crisis in Marxism*, 26; Connor, "Jack Lindsay, Socialist Humanism," 359; Karl Marx, *Capital*, vol. 1 (London: Penguin, 1976), 133.
125. Connor, "Jack Lindsay, Socialist Humanism," 345.
126. Jack Lindsay, "Discussion: Socialist Humanism," *The New Reasoner* (Winter 1957–58): 101–2; Jack Lindsay, *The Crisis in Marxism* (Totowa, NJ: Barnes and Noble Books, 1981), 24–29; Connor, "Jack Lindsay, Socialist Humanism," 359; Karl Marx, *Capital*, vol. 1 (London: Penguin, 1976), 133.
127. Lindsay, *Blast Power and Ballistics*, 430.
128. Marx and Engels, *Collected Works*, 5:141; Farrington, *Science and Politics*, 159.
129. Marx and Engels, *Collected Works*, 1:498.
130. Epicurus, *The Epicurus Reader*, 6.
131. Lindsay clearly relied heavily on H. S. Commager's pioneering analysis of Lucretius's passages here. See H. S. Commager, "Lucretius's Interpretation of the Plague," *Harvard Studies in Classical Philology* 62 (1957): 105–18; also William M. Green, "The Dying World of Lucretius," *American Journal of Philology* 63/1 (1942): 51–60; Lucretius, *On the Nature of the Universe* (Oxford: Oxford University Press, 1999), 179–217. The meaning and significance of Book 6 in closing Lucretius's poem, and whether the poem was simply unfinished, awaiting a more optimistic Epicurean ending, has long been in dispute. See Peta Fowler, "Lucretian Conclusions," in Deborah H. Roberts, Francis M. Dun, and Don Fowler, eds., *Classical Closure* (Princeton: Princeton University Press, 1997), 112–38. Lindsay's interpretation, building on Commager, offered a powerful rendition, in accord with Marx's view of the negative dialectics at the heart of Epicureanism.
132. Lindsay, *Blast Power and Ballistics*, 379.
133. Ibid., 379–81.
134. Carson, *Lost Woods*, 210.

Names Index

Subject Index